Writing and Reporting News:
A Coaching Method

From the Wadsworth Series in Mass Communication/Journalism

General Mass Communication

The Interplay of Influence, 3rd ed., by Kathleen Hall Jamieson & Karlyn Kohrs Campbell
Media/Impact, 2nd ed., by Shirley Biagi
Mediamerica, Mediaworld: Form, Content, and Consequence of Mass Communication, 5th ed., by Edward Jay Whetmore
Media/Reader: Perspectives on Mass Media Industries, Effects, and Issues, 2nd ed., by Shirley Biagi
Ethics in Media Communications: Cases and Controversies, by Louis A. Day
Communications Law: Liberties, Restraints, and the Modern Media, by John D. Zelezny
International Communications: History, Conflict, and Control of the Global Metropolis, by Robert S. Fortner

Journalism

Free-lancer and Staff Writer, 5th ed., by William Rivers
When Words Collide, 3rd ed., by Lauren Kessler & Duncan McDonald
The Search, by Lauren Kessler & Duncan McDonald
Writing and Reporting News: A Coaching Method, by Carole Rich
Creative Editing for Print Media, by Dorothy Bowles, Diane L. Borden, & William Rivers
Interviews That Work, 2nd ed., by Shirley Biagi
Mastering the Message: Media Writing with Substance and Style, by Lauren Kessler & Duncan McDonald
Newstalk I: State-of-the-Art Conversations with Today's Print Journalists, by Shirley Biagi
Newstalk II: State-of-the-Art Conversations with Today's Broadcast Journalists, by Shirley Biagi
Media Writing: Preparing Information for the Mass Media, 2nd ed., by Doug Newsom & Doug Wollert
Visual Editing: A Graphic Guide for Journalists, by Howard I. Finberg & Bruce D. Itule
Crafting News for the Electronic Media, by Carl Hausman

Photography

Introduction to Photography, 4th ed., by Marvin J. Rosen & David L. DeVries

Public Relations and Advertising

Creative Strategy in Advertising, 4th ed., by A. Jerome Jewler
Public Relations Cases, 2nd ed., by Jerry A. Hendrix
Public Relations Writing: Form and Style, 3rd ed., by Doug Newsom & Bob Carrell
This Is PR: The Realities of Public Relations, 5th ed., by Doug Newsom, Alan Scott, & Judy VanSlyke Turk
Computer Graphics Applications: An Introduction to Desktop Publishing and Design, Presentation Graphics, Animation, by
    E. Kenneth Hoffman & Jon A. Teeple

Research—Communications, Mass Media, Advertising

Mass Media Research: An Introduction, 3rd ed., by Roger D. Wimmer & Joseph R. Dominick
Fundamentals of Advertising Research, 4th ed., by Alan D. Fletcher & Thomas A. Bowers
Communication Research: Strategies and Sources, 3rd ed., by Rebecca B. Rubin, Alan M. Rubin, & Linda J. Piele
Contemporary Communication Research Methods, by Mary John Smith
The Practice of Social Research, 6th ed., by Earl Babbie

Writing

and

Reporting

News

A Coaching Method

Carole Rich

University of Kansas

Wadsworth Publishing Company
Belmont, California
A Division of Wadsworth, Inc.

Mass Communication Editor: Holly Allen
Editorial Assistant: SoEun Park
Production Editor: Deborah Cogan
Text and Cover Designer: Cloyce Wall
Print Buyer: Randy Hurst
Art Editor: Nancy Spellman
Permissions Editor: Peggy Meehan
Copy Editor: Rebecca Smith
Technical Illustrator: Teresa Leigh Roberts
Cover Illustrator: Barbara Melodia
Printer: R.R. Donnelley & Sons, Crawfordsville

1 2 3 4 5 6 7 8 9 10—98 97 96 95 94 93
Printed in the United States of America

Library of Congress Cataloging-in-Publication Data

Rich, Carole.
   Writing and reporting news: a coaching method / Carole Rich.
     p. cm.
   Includes index.
   ISBN 0-534-19074-X
   1. Journalism—Authorship.   2. Reporters and reporting.
I. Title.
PN4781.R42 1993
808'.06607—dc20   92-39680

Contents

11 Body Building   193

12 Story Structures   211

13 Storytelling Techniques   235

14 The Art of Brevity   263

15 Public Relations Writing   277

Preface

Writing news can be creative and exciting. This book aims to convince you of that.

The book uses the principles of the writing-coach movement among newspapers to bring coaching into the classroom. Good editors have always helped writers improve their stories. But during the 1980s many newspapers began hiring writing coaches to serve as mentors and to give writers more individual attention than they had been receiving. The concepts of coaching, which are now gaining widespread acceptance in the news media, were developed by Roy Peter Clark and Don Fry of the Poynter Institute for Media Studies in St. Petersburg, Florida, where they have trained hundreds of journalists to coach writers. But what is coaching?

Coaching is a way of helping writers help themselves. A coach doesn't emphasize how you have failed to write a good story. A coach emphasizes how you can succeed. A coach helps you discover your writing problems and suggests how you can find solutions. While an editor may concentrate on the end results of your writing, a coach concentrates on the process of writing. An editor helps you fix your story; a coach helps you improve your skills for writing many stories. A coach asks you what techniques worked well for you in your story and where you struggled. Then a coach helps you find ways to report and write more effectively by encouraging you to try new approaches and take risks.

This book aims to fill the role of a writing coach by anticipating problems writers have and offering solutions. It explains techniques writing coaches use at newspapers. Many other techniques in this book are an outgrowth of my experiences teaching journalism students at the University of Kansas and of my work as a visiting writing coach at several newspapers.

Each chapter begins with coaching tips so you can learn how to be your own writing coach and gain confidence as a writer. No book can substitute for your instructor. This book attempts to supplement what you learn in the classroom by providing you with hundreds of examples and tips from award-winning writers.

I have chosen the examples carefully in hopes of providing stories that not only illustrate the techniques in the chapter but also are fun to read. I have also included examples that reflect our multicultural society in subject matter as well as in the choice of writers.

The book also emphasizes current trends in news writing, such as the increasing emphasis on graphics. You will learn how visual and verbal elements work together and how to use graphics as a writing tool. Some of the other current and future-oriented topics in this book include:

- emphasis on multicultural sensitivity in reporting and writing
- tips from a Pulitzer Prize–winning writer for writing about AIDS
- how to write briefly
- how to use storytelling techniques

How the Book is Organized

The first three parts of this book are devoted to teaching you the techniques of reporting and writing, from generating story ideas to developing a writing process. Writers have many different ways of working. No one way works for everyone. This book offers you many tips so you can choose the ones that work best for you. It encourages you to take risks and find your own style. It urges you to consider revision as a crucial part of the writing process. If you learn the techniques of good writing, you can apply them to a variety of stories.

The fourth part of the book provides you with opportunities to apply those skills to many types of stories. It offers tips for solving problems you might encounter covering crime and court stories, government, or disasters, or writing features and various other kinds of stories.

The last part of the book includes information on how you can apply for a job. In the Appendix you will find a guide to using the Associated Press style.

Although the book is arranged sequentially to take you through the steps from conceiving the idea to constructing the story, you do not need to study the book in the order it is written. Each chapter is self-contained so that your instructor can design the course to fit the needs of the class, and so that you can use chapters of most interest to you.

Basic and Advanced Techniques

The book is geared to beginning and advanced journalism students. If you are a beginning journalism student, you will find detailed explanations of ways to develop your reporting and writing skills. If you are an advanced journalism student, you can study more complex writing techniques, such as those in the chapters on storytelling and features and specialty writing. You will also find many models of sophisticated writing styles by journalists who have won numerous awards.

Although the primary focus of this book is newspaper writing, the techniques of reporting and writing presented here will serve you well if you are planning a career in magazines, public relations or broadcasting.

I hope you enjoy using this book and that it helps you become a more confident reporter and writer. I welcome your suggestions for improvement. Most of all, I hope the coaching tips and writing examples entice you to try many techniques so your writing becomes a rewarding experience for you and your readers.

Acknowledgements

First I would like to thank my students for encouraging me to write this book. I also wish to thank many other people: my editor, Kristine M. Clerkin, for her vision and her guidance, production editor Deborah Cogan, designer Cloyce Wall, and other editors at Wadsworth Publishing Company; copyeditor Rebecca Smith; Don Fry, associate director of the Poynter Institute, for his inspiration and encouragement; Dick Thien, University of Nebraska journalism professor, for urging me to write about writing and for giving me my first job as a writing coach when he was a newspaper editor; Paul Comolli, for his constant support while I was writing this book; my colleagues Max Utsler, Adrienne Rivers, Tom Volek, Ted Frederickson, Chuck Marsh, John Broholm, Rick Musser, and Sam Adams; and my journalism students Katy Monk, Lara Gold, Patricia Rojas, David Silverman, Lee Hill and so many others who have given me the joy of teaching them and learning from them. I also want to thank the many journalists who shared their time and their expertise to provide tips for this book. Some of these journalists have changed jobs between the time they were interviewed and the publication of this book.

I also wish to thank the reviewers of this book whose comments and suggestions were invaluable: Charles Adair, State University of New York at Buffalo; Roy Atwood, University of Idaho; Retta Blaney, New York University; Ray Chavez, University of Colorado; Lynne Flocke, Syracuse University; Lee Jolliffe, University of Missouri; Linda L. Levin, University of Rhode Island; David C. Nelson, Southwest Texas State University; W. Robert Nowell III, Chico State University; Marshel Rossow, Mankato State University; Linda N. Scanlon, Norfolk State University; Norman Sims, University of Massachusetts; Martin D. Sommerness, Northern Arizona University; and Carl Stepp, University of Maryland, College Park.

Introduction

Tips From Award-Winning Journalists

Make the reader see. Make the reader care. Follow those two principles, and you will have the makings of an award-winning journalist.

Eugene Roberts, former executive editor of *The Philadelphia Inquirer,* tells this story about how his editor influenced him to make the reader see. Roberts was a reporter at the *Goldsboro News-Argus* in North Carolina. His editor, Henry Belk, was 6 feet 7 inches tall. Belk walked with an aluminum cane and wore a battered fedora. And he was blind. Many days Belk would call in Roberts to read his stories to him, and he would yell: "Make me see. You aren't making me see."

Advice from Roberts: "The best reporters, whatever their backgrounds or their personalities, share that consummate drive to get to the center of a story and then put the reader on the scene."

Roberts, who retired in 1990, should know. During the 18 years he was editor of *The Philadelphia Inquirer,* the newspaper won 17 Pulitzer prizes.

How do you become one of the best reporters? Observe. Gather details—more than you need. Ask questions. Be curious. Then write word pictures that make the reader see and experience the action.

Make the reader care. Make sure the story has a "so what" element. Write a compelling story that touches the reader's emotions. Use facts and quotes that make the reader angry, sad, happy, relieved or more informed about an issue that touches his or her life.

Ken Fuson, who has won several awards for outstanding writing at *The Des Moines* (Iowa) *Register,* has this advice: "Don't turn in a story you wouldn't read. If you tell a good story, people will want to read it. If you don't think many people will want to read it, make it short." Fuson is convinced that even stories about government meetings can be made readable with storytelling techniques. "Look for ways to show conflict; try to describe the mood," he says.

He worries that newspaper editors are too concerned about making stories shorter to appeal to impatient readers and to conserve space in the paper. "Some stories are better if they're long," Fuson says. "You could probably make *Moby Dick* a lot shorter, too. But I still think people will read a good tale."

For Fuson, the ending is even more important than the beginning of a story. "When I was a kid, the stories that would make me go back and read again were the ones that had the best endings," he says. "I know most newspaper readers don't read all the way to the endings. But I tell myself if I do it well enough, they'll read mine."

Julie Sullivan is more certain readers will get to the end of her stories. Her prize-winning stories run only 8 inches. Sullivan is a reporter for *The Spokesman-Review* (Wash.). She won the 1991 Best Newspaper Writing Award from the American Society of Newspaper Editors for a new category of writing: short news writing. She packs a wealth of descriptive detail into short sentences without resorting to adjectives. Like Fuson, she strives for strong endings, especially in short stories.

"You are trying to make a point with every paragraph," Sullivan says. "I think the last one is the one people remember." Her last paragraph in this story is just a simple statement that makes a powerful point about the daily dangers an 82-year-old man faces in a deteriorating, low-income apartment complex in Spokane. His watch had been stolen by a drug addict.

> "I'll get it back, you watch and see," he fumed later.
>
> He did. The $50 Seiko was returned without explanation Thursday morning.
>
> That night, they stole his food stamps.

Sullivan also thinks there is a place for longer stories, but she says the trend now is for brevity. Her advice: "Trust your instincts. Ask yourself what is important and what struck you during the interview. Then write what you remember. Then rewrite. Go back over the story and take out every word that is extraneous."

And some advice from that master storyteller, Edna Buchanan, Pulitzer Prize–winning former police reporter for *The Miami Herald*. Here is what she says in her book *The Corpse Had a Familiar Face:*

> What a reporter needs is detail, detail, detail.
>
> If a man is shot for playing the same song on the jukebox too many times, I've got to name that tune. Questions unimportant to police add the color and detail that makes a story human. What movie did they see? What color was their car? What did they have in their pockets? What were they doing the precise moment the bomb exploded or the tornado touched down?
>
> Miami Homicide Lieutenant Mike Gonzalez, who has spent some thirty years solving murders, tells me that he now asks those questions and suggests to rookies that they do the same. The answers may not be relevant to an investigation, but he tells them, "Edna Buchanan will ask you, and you'll feel stupid if you don't know."

A question I always ask is: What was everybody wearing? It has little to do with style. It has everything to do with the time I failed to ask. A man was shot and dumped into the street by a killer in a pickup truck. The case seemed somewhat routine—if one can ever call murder routine. But later, I learned that at the time the victim was shot, he was wearing a black taffeta cocktail dress and red high heels. I tracked down the detectives and asked, "Why didn't you tell me?"

"You didn't ask," they chorused. Now I always ask.

Writers like Edna Buchanan take risks. They try new approaches to make the reader want to read their stories.

This book is about risk-taking writing, the kind of writing that tells stories people want to read. It is about writing to make readers see and care. It is about the kind of reporting and writing that makes reluctant readers read.

Here are some general tips for good writing:

• Show people in action whenever possible. Show and tell.

• Use simple sentences. If you write long ones, follow them with short ones. Gene Miller, who won two Pulitzer Prizes at *The Miami Herald,* writes such short sentences that he once was described as a man who writes as though he got paid by the period.

• Use strong action verbs.

• Translate jargon into simple English that the reader will understand.

• Gather details. Then choose the ones that will help the reader see, smell, hear, taste, touch and experience the emotions and actions of the event.

• Take risks, Try new styles. The writer who takes no risks is taking the biggest risk of all—the risk of being mediocre.

ONE

Understanding News

COACHING

Ask yourself: What is the story about? Answer in one sentence.

Write the story as though you were telling it to a friend.

Write From the Start: 1
A Coaching Method

Lee Hill burst into her classroom to tell her professor about the dream she'd had the previous night.

"I dreamed I was on a basketball court, and you were coaching on the sideline," she said. "You were yelling, 'Focus, focus, focus.' I kept running around the court, and then I focused on the basket."

"Did you make the basket?" the professor asked.

"I can't remember," she said, laughing. "All I remember was you yelling, 'focus.' "

Hill, a graduate student at the University of Kansas, was taking a writing course taught by a coaching method. She had been learning how to construct her news stories around a main theme called the focus. Like a basketball coach who guides you from the sidelines, a writing coach doesn't fix the story for you; a coach helps you discover ways to fix it yourself. A coach asks questions and makes suggestions that help you understand how you can improve your writing. Hill likened the coaching process to cheerleading. It gives the reporter confidence to write, she said.

An outstanding reporter, Hill would gather reams of information. But like many professional writers, when she began to write her story, she would struggle to decide how to begin, what to include and in what order. The professor would coach her by asking her to describe the main point of her story—in one sentence. Once Hill established this focus, she could select the most important information related to that focus and discard unrelated material. Then the professor

Coaching skills are essentially reporting skills: asking good questions and listening to the answers.

Roy Peter Clark and Don Fry,

Coaching Writers: Editors and Reporters Working Together

would ask a few more questions, such as what struck Hill as most interesting or important, to help her determine the lead and the order for her story.

Those are the same techniques that writing coaches use at newspapers. Many of those techniques were developed by Roy Peter Clark and Don Fry, authors of *Coaching Writers: Editors and Reporters Working Together*. Clark, dean of faculty at the Poynter Institute for Media Studies in St. Petersburg, Fla., and Fry, director of Poynter's writing programs, have taught coaching methods to newspaper editors and professors throughout the country. The coaching concepts used in this book are based on their teaching.

Now imagine that you have your own writing coach to help you with all your news stories. Your coach would ask you some leading questions to help you discover the best way to write your story. If you learn to ask yourself those questions before you write, you can be your own writing coach. That is one of the goals of this book. Even if you have never written a news story, you can begin reporting and writing by following some simple coaching tips that are presented in this chapter.

The Reporting and Writing Process

The coaching method in this book has four phases:

1 Conceive: At this stage you develop the idea for the story. If you are covering an event, such as a meeting or an accident, you need to start with the idea—the main point of what occurred. If you are writing a news story about a problem in your community, you still start with a central idea, which is the focus of your story. Once you begin reporting, you may discover some information that is more important than your original focus. Thus you should be flexible and decide the focus for writing after you collect the material.

2 Collect: This is the reporting stage. You interview sources and gather as much information as you can about your topic. Contact enough sources to get balance in your story. Don't rely on one source; strive for several points of view. Ask more questions and take more notes than you plan to use. In addition to taking notes about what sources say, you should jot down your observations and gather as many details as possible.

3 Construct: This is the writing stage. You begin with a plan for your story developed around the focus. Then go through your notes and mark only the information related to that focus. Like a carpenter building a house, you need a blueprint. A good writer does not write a story without a plan. Jot down a few key words to indicate how you will organize your story. Then write a first draft of your story. You may revise your original draft in the next step.

4 Correct: This is the revision stage. After you have written your story, read it and make any changes you think are necessary. You may decide to add or delete information or to completely reorganize the story during this stage. You should also check the spelling of all names and the accuracy of facts, and you should correct grammar, style and typing errors.

These four steps are the basic process for all news stories. In the coming chapters you will learn many techniques for reporting and writing news. But how do you get started now?

How to Be Your Own Writing Coach

Many news-writing courses start by teaching leads (the beginning of the story) and the organization of news stories. But there are several ways to write a lead or to organize a story. Too many writers spend their time agonizing over the perfect lead without thinking about the whole structure of the story.

A news story is based on one main idea with supporting points. That's why it is important to establish that central focus. Once you get your focus, you should select only the information that supports the basic idea. It is the key to organizing your story. There are some exceptions, such as stories about meetings that involve several unrelated actions, but even those news stories should be organized around a primary focus.

Determining Your Focus

The coaching method for determining your focus involves two simple steps: deciding what the story is about and thinking about how you would tell the story to a friend. These steps will also help you find a lead and a structure for the story.

What's the story about? This is the first question to ask yourself. You should be able to write the answer in one sentence, preferably in fewer than 35 words. That is your focus statement. Put this sentence at the top of your story to remind you of the focus. This statement could be your lead if you decide you want the first sentence to get directly to the point of your story. If you prefer a more creative lead, this statement will become your focus paragraph—also called a "nut graph." Because readers are impatient to find out why they are reading a story, it is preferable to place this focus graph within the first five paragraphs of your story.

How would you tell the story to a friend? The tell-a-friend technique is a natural, conversational storytelling method. It also works for broadcast journalists, who must tell their stories anyway. In fact, the conversational method is a cornerstone of broadcast writing.

Imagine that your friend asks what the story is about and what happened. Chances are you might talk about the most interesting information first. Thinking in these terms will give you a clue for your lead and your organization.

If you mention something that isn't clear, a friend will probably ask you to explain. That's another clue for organizing your story. When you write one paragraph that raises a question in a reader's mind or has supporting material to explain it, follow it immediately with information that answers the question or substantiates the point, either with quotes or facts.

You also can use the tell-a-friend technique in the reporting stage. If you were trying to relate a story to a friend, what information would you need to know? What would *you* want to know? Let your natural curiosity be your guide when you are gathering information.

Almost all stories answer some basic questions: who, what, when, where, why and how. Add the question "so what" to make sure you have a story that will make a reader care.

Before you begin writing your story, don't forget to make a rough plan. Jot down some key words to remind you of the order you want to use. If you need more questions to determine how to start your story (the lead), try asking yourself these:

What struck you most about the story?

What do you think is the most important idea?

What do you think the reader wants to know?

What do you think might hook the reader?

Now write a first draft of your story. You'll revise it later, so don't struggle until you get the perfect words for the lead or for each paragraph. Write the story as quickly as you can. Then go over the story and change anything you don't like. In this revision stage, make sure you check the accuracy of all the names, facts and spelling.

Putting It All Together

Here is how Leslie Barewin, a University of Kansas journalism student, used the coaching method to write her first news story. Barewin got the idea for the story when she went to the university health center because she had been feeling ill. The nurse stuck a thermometer in her ear. Barewin was surprised. She had never seen a thermometer like that. She decided that other students might be unaware of that type of thermometer, and so it would make a good news story.

She started by asking herself what the story's about and wrote this focus statement at the top of her story:

> Temperature probes are being used to take patients' temperature through the ear at Watkins Memorial Health Center.

Then she used the tell-a-friend technique to write her story. Although you might tell your friend this story in a different order, the style is basically a conversational storytelling method.

Barewin's original lead on her first draft was as follows:

> You might not have to waste three minutes of your time at Watkins Memorial Health Center.

After she wrote her story, during the correcting/revision process, her professor asked her this coaching question to brighten the lead: What struck you as most interesting about this story? Barewin said it was the fact that the probes were used in the ear, the concept she had written in her focus statement.

That was what gave her the idea for her revised lead on the story. The focus statement on top of the page was not printed with the story. It was there only to help Barewin determine the main point and other information to include in her story.

Here is the revised version:

Focus statement: What's the story about?	*Temperature probes are being used to take patients' temperature through the ear at Watkins Memorial Health Center.*	"This thermometer tests the temperature of the skin in the ear canal, not the eardrum itself," said Jody Woods, director of nursing.	*Supporting material: How does it work? This paragraph raises a question answered in the next paragraph.*
Lead: What struck you as most interesting about these thermometers?	Don't be surprised if a nurse at Watkins Memorial Health Center tells you to stick it in your ear. It's the current method of taking your temperature at the center.	The temperature of the ear is close to brain tissue, Woods said. There is a concern in the medical profession that excessively high temperatures may cause brain damage. A fever is the body's way of trying to release heat, Woods said.	
Focus/nut graph: What's the story about? Note the similarity to the focus statement.	Watkins is using the latest in thermometer technology. For more than a year, temperature probes have been used to take a patient's temperature through the ear instead of through the mouth or rectum.	The electronic ear probe resembles an electric shaver. The smooth white base curves slightly upward and rests comfortably in the hand.	*Description of ear probe.*

Several buttons and a small digital screen that displays the temperature are on the front of the probe.

More elaboration about how the thermometer works

On the opposite side is the scanner. Covered by a plastic disposable cap, the scanner measures the body's temperature within 15 seconds.

The used cap is popped off, a new cap is installed, and the probe is ready for the next patient.

How does it compare to other thermometers?

Woods said that rectal thermometers were the most accurate but that most students preferred other methods.

Because the ear probes are relatively new to nurses, there is a tendency to question them a bit more, Woods said.

Each new probe costs about $450 and is issued by the state, Woods said.

Supporting material: cost

Lori Zito, a sophomore from Omaha, Neb., had her temperature taken with the ear probe recently.

Reaction from a student

"It's quicker," she said. "It only takes a few seconds. You don't have to sit there for two minutes with something in your mouth while trying not to cough."

Leslie Barewin, *The University Daily Kansan*

Visual Elements

Barewin's story was accompanied by a photograph. Visual elements such as photographs, charts and other graphic illustrations are crucial to news presentation. Research shows that 98 percent of readers are drawn first to a photograph on a newspaper page. Visual elements, then, are an essential factor to consider when you are planning a story.

Photographs and other graphic illustrations not only help make your story look good, they can also make it easier to read. Many of the visual elements—such as headlines, boxes of information and summary sentences—are written by copy editors, and decisions about display are made by these editors or by page designers. However, reporters are expected to plan picture possibilities for their stories and to provide information for some of the illustrations.

When a chart, a graphic or an information box will accompany your story, you need to consider whether the story needlessly duplicates information that could be presented visually. So in the writing process, don't just think about information to put into your story; think about information to pull out for visual devices.

The following sections describe the most common visual devices used with news stories.

Point of entry   The term "point of entry" indicates where the reader tends to look on the page, where a reader "enters" a story, or where the reader can be lured to look. Points of entry include headlines, photographs, illustrations, facts boxes, captions and subheads (small titles or captions within a story).

Summary blurb   A paragraph or sentence summarizing the story is called a "summary blurb." It is placed below the headline. When you ask yourself what the story is about, you are really writing a summary blurb. Even though copy editors write the summary blurb, you should use the concept to write your focus statement.

Here is an example of a summary blurb on a story about a term paper scandal at the University of South Florida:

Papers a lesson in criminology	*Headline*
A USF professor follows a paper trail to a former student, wanted on charges he sold term papers to criminology majors.	*Summary blurb*

If the story is topped by a summary blurb, the lead should not repeat the exact wording of the summary. As a result, the writer can be more creative in the lead. Here is the lead on the term paper story:

A. Engler Anderson's term papers weren't just bad. They were a crime, said one professor.

Anderson, 31, is wanted on charges that he sold term papers to two University of Florida students.

Their major?

Criminology.

The charge—selling a term paper or dissertation to another person—is only a second-degree misdemeanor, but if he is caught, Anderson will be held without bail because he failed to appear for a court hearing this week.

St. Petersburg (Fla). *Times*

The story then explains how William Blount, chairman of the USF Criminology Department, received two papers that he thought were "awful" and then discovered they were written by Anderson, a former student.

Facts box   Information from a story is sometimes set off in a facts box for reading at a glance. A facts box is also called a "highlights box," meaning that it highlights the key points in the story. For example, when basketball star Earvin "Magic" Johnson announced that he had the AIDS virus, many newspapers ran boxes containing highlights of his career. Others ran facts boxes containing information about AIDS, Acquired Immune Deficiency Syndrome.

A facts or highlights box can include key dates in a chronology, the main points of a new proposal or any other crucial information. It is especially useful for breaking statistics out of a story. Although some information from a facts box may be crucial to the story itself, the writer should guard against too much repetition.

This example illustrates why the writer, as well as the copy editor, should consider the facts box as part of the story content, not just a graphic illustration:

Nevada regents OK raises	*Headline*
Professors, administrators: Contracts force pay hikes despite budget crisis.	*Summary blurb*
While 23,000 other state workers sit and wait for their pay hike, professors and administrators in the University of Nevada System will get a 4 percent raise.	*Lead*

The Board of Regents' 6-2 vote Thursday for a pay increase beginning Oct. 15 came a week after a state board chaired by Gov. Bob Miller delayed all state pay raises until January to avert a budget crisis.

But regents, faced with signed contracts, are obligated to pay the raises, said Chairwoman Carolyn Sparks of Las Vegas.

"If we don't, we're up against thousands of lawsuits," she said.

Reno (Nev.) *Gazette-Journal*

Here are the two facts boxes that accompanied the story, the first on the front page and the second on the jump page (the page on which the story continued):

**UNR
salary ranges**

- **President:** $141,400 now; $147,056 with 4 percent raise
- **Dean:** $53,772 (minimum) now; $55,772 with 4 percent raise
- **9-month professor with Ph.D.:** $51,589 (minimum) now; $53,652 with a 4 percent raise

**University
pay raises**

Who gets them

About 2,000 professional employees on contract with the Nevada System, including

- 972 UNR professors and administrators
- 219 at Truckee Meadows Community College
- 88 at Western Nevada Community College

Who doesn't

- All university system classified employees, including secretaries, clerical and support personnel employed by the state

The statistics in these facts boxes were not repeated in the story.

Empowerment box An empowerment box contains information that lets readers know where they can call for help or whom they can contact for more information related to the story.

This is an example from another story in the *Reno Gazette-Journal* about an increase in nursing home complaints. The empowerment box contained this information:

Help for seniors
How to complain

To report a complaint about a nursing or group-care home, call these representatives of the Nevada Aging Services Division:

- **Northern Nevada:** Earl Yamashita at 688-2964
- **Southern Nevada:** Gilda Johnstone or Lisa Selthofner at 1-486-4545

Pull quote A good quote might be broken out of the story, placed in larger type and used as a point of entry to entice the reader. Although a copy editor will decide which quotes to pull for graphic display, when you write your story, consider which quotes could be used to entice readers. Then use your best quotes high in your story.

When Magic Johnson, announced that he was retiring from basketball because he had contracted the AIDS virus, *The Washington Post* pulled this quote for emphasis:

> *"This is not like my life is over*
> *because it's not."*
> *—Magic Johnson*

Infographic A chart, map, graph or other illustration meant to provide information, not just to make the story look good, is an infographic. *USA Today* provides daily infographics in the bottom left-hand corner of its sections to explain some interesting statistical information about American life (see Exhibit 1-1). Other examples of infographics are diagrams of plane crashes or major accidents and illustrations explaining how something works.

Exhibit 1-1

Infographic from USA Today

Courtesy of *USA Today*

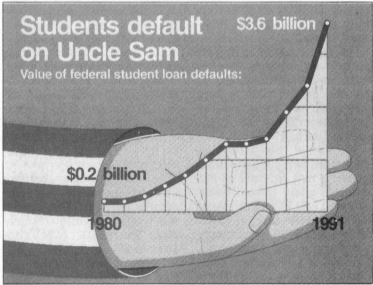

USA SNAPSHOTS®

A look at statistics that shape the nation

Students default on Uncle Sam
Value of federal student loan defaults:

$3.6 billion

$0.2 billion

1980   1991

Source: Department of Education   By Elys A. McLean, USA TODAY

The most common type of infographic, called a "location map," is a map that pinpoints the location of an accident, a crime or any other major news event. It is the reporter's responsibility to supply the information for those maps. So when you report a story that may need a map, make sure you gather information about the exact location of the event by noting the streets, the number of feet or yards from a spot where an explosion or major crime occurred, or any other crucial information that would help readers visualize the location.

Summary

Remember to ask yourself these simple coaching questions when you begin writing:

What's it about? Put the focus statement at the top of your story, like a summary blurb.

What struck you as most interesting? That could be your lead.

How would you tell the story to a friend? That is the key to your organization and may give you a clue for your lead as well.

What illustrations need to go with the story, and how will they affect the writing? Plan ahead for photos, graphics, boxes or maps that add information.

Activities

1   Basic news story: Read the following information, and write a focus statement summarizing the main point of the story. That focus statement might also work as your lead. Then write the story using the tell-a-friend technique. Future chapters will explain attribution, but for now, when you use a quote or information that is someone's opinion, attribute it to the person who said it. For this exercise, concentrate only on the writing, not on the visual possibilities. Here is the information, based on a story from *The Philadelphia Inquirer:*

Who: Inter-Fraternity Council of University of Pennsylvania

What: Voted to stop providing guests with alcohol at fraternity parties and to limit the amount guests can bring for themselves

When: Yesterday afternoon

Where: Council meeting at University of Pennsylvania

Why: To decrease fraternities' legal liability

How: In a decision made by a vote of 17 campus fraternities

Significance: Decision reflects a national trend

Attribution: All factual information about the vote comes from Bret Kinsella, IFC (Inter-Fraternity Council) president.

Backup information: Put the rest of the information in the order that you think makes sense and would be most readable:

Spokesmen for the council would not disclose the results of the vote. They only said a majority was needed to pass the measure.

The decision was made a week after a student at nearby Drexel University fell off a fraternity house roof and died. Police had said the student had been drinking.

There have been no lawsuits at Penn regarding liquor provided at fraternity houses. But lawsuits have been a problem at fraternities at other schools, said Kim Morrison, vice provost for university life.

Morrison said the policy grew out of concerns raised during a conference of national representatives and local alumni of fraternities on campus last week. At that conference there was an emphasis on requirements for accident insurance for college fraternities.

From Bret Kinsella, IFC president: "The action will help fraternity members provide a safe environment for our guests and our brothers."

Also from Kinsella: The new policy will allow guests who are of legal drinking age to bring two six-packs of beer or an equivalent amount of alcohol to parties. The fraternity chapter would be responsible for monitoring consumption through a ticketing system. The system would be enforced through an existing system of social monitors.

Kinsella said the decision was mostly to decrease the fraternities' legal liability, rather than to decrease student drinking.

2 Visual and verbal exercise: Write a story based on the following information. Before you write the story, place your focus statement at the top. For this story, your focus sentence should be the results of the study. If you want a lead that gets directly to the point, your focus sentence could also be your lead. Once you've written a focus sentence, add a suggestion for visual presentation—a photograph, chart, facts box or other graphic illustration. Decide what facts, if any, should be duplicated in the story and the graphic. Then use the tell-a-friend technique to relate what you thought was the most interesting information. The following material is based on a story from *The* (San Bernardino, Calif.) *Sun.*

Who/what: A study comparing the death and accident rates of left- and right-handed people

When: Study was conducted in 1989 and was reported in today's edition of the *New England Journal of Medicine.*

Where: Study was conducted by Diane Halpern, professor at California State University at San Bernardino, and Stanley Coren, researcher at the University of British Columbia.

Why: To determine why fewer left-handed people are among the elderly population

How: Researchers studied death certificates of 987 people in two Southern California counties. Relatives were queried by mail about the subjects' dominant hands.

Backup information: The following points are not necessarily in the order they should be used in your story:

The researchers found that the average age at death for right-handed people was 75, for left-handed people 66; left-handed people represent 10 percent of the U.S. population; right-handed females tend to live five years longer than left-handed females, and right-handed males live 10 years longer than left-handed males; left-handed people were four times more likely to die from injuries while driving than right-handers and six times more likely to die from accidents of all kinds.

Other researchers have shown that left-handers are more likely than right-handers to suffer from insomnia, schizophrenia and allergies.

Halpern said, "The results are striking in their magnitude."

Halpern is right-handed.

She said her study should be interpreted cautiously. "It should not, of course, be used to predict the life span of any one individual."

"We knew for years that there weren't as many old left-handers," Halpern said. "Researchers thought that was because in the early years of the century, most people born left-handed were forced to change to their right hands. So we thought we were looking at old people who used to be left-handed, but we weren't. The truth was, there simply weren't many left-handers left alive, compared to right-handers."

"Almost all engineering is geared to the right hand and right foot," Halpern said. "There are many more car and other accidents among left-handers because of their environment."

3 Visual and verbal exercise: This one is more challenging. Before you write the story, place your focus statement at the top. Add a suggestion for visual presentation, such as a chart, a photograph or a facts box. If you use a chart or fact box, don't forget to consider how much, if any, duplication you think is needed to make the story clear. Then use the tell-a-friend technique to relate what you thought was the most interesting information. Try to summarize the results in a conversational manner without flooding your story with statistics. This material is from a story that appeared in *The University Daily Kansan.*

Who/what: A survey of the health habits of freshmen at the University of Kansas

When: Findings were released yesterday by Robert Walker, assistant professor of health, physical education and recreation. Walker conducted the survey.

How: Survey was mailed to incoming freshmen and was included in a packet of health history forms. Participation in the survey was voluntary. About 10 percent of the freshman class—400 students—responded. Responses were confidential.

Why: Survey was intended to help health educators and officials at Watkins Memorial Health Center (the campus hospital) plan programs and services.

Backup information: The questions in the survey ranged from diet habits and exercise routines to sexual practices. Some general findings: 30 percent said they would not seek professional counseling if a serious problem developed; 41 percent are sexually active.

Here are the findings separated for men and women (but not in order of importance).

For men:

6 percent have considered suicide.

83 percent do not do monthly testicular self-examinations.

54 percent do not limit fat in their daily diet.

51 percent do not get aerobic exercise three or more times a week.

30 percent have ridden with a driver who had been drinking.

58 percent do not use seat belts.

17 percent describe themselves as highly stressed.

14 percent rarely or never eat breakfast.

8 percent have risked acquiring a sexually transmitted disease.

7 percent smoke cigarettes.

For women:

9 percent have risked acquiring a sexually transmitted disease.

77 percent do not use seat belts.

65 percent do not do monthly breast self-examinations.

40 percent have ridden with a driver who had been drinking.

58 percent do not get aerobic exercise three or more times a week.

42 percent describe themselves as highly stressed.

27 percent rarely or never eat breakfast.

11 percent have considered suicide in the last two years.

28 percent do not limit fat in their daily diet.

11 percent smoke cigarettes.

Walker said he was surprised by the number of students who reported they had considered suicide and the high percentage of students who did not use seat belts.

"The survey results can be used for planning and evaluative purposes," he said.

From Janine Demo, coordinator of Watkins health education department: "This shows us where we need to go with our programs and services." Demo said survey results indicated that more peer education training might be necessary to reach students who need help. "Every one of these are behaviors that they have direct control over."

Regarding the high percentage of men who did not practice testicular self-examination: "Men between the ages of 18 and 24 are at the highest risk of testicular cancer and especially should practice monthly self-examinations," Demo said.

Charles Yockey, chief of staff at Watkins Memorial Health Center, said he thought the percentages in the survey dealing with sexual activity were lower than the actual percentages.

COACHING

TIPS

Ask people in your community what they want to read in the newspaper.

Seek to include multicultural sources in your stories.

Consider whether your story needs a photograph or graphic.

Changing Concepts of News

2

"**G**ive everyone in the newsroom a gun. Shoot anyone who says, 'We've always done it this way.'"

A drastic solution. But the editor who issued this challenge recognized that it isn't easy to change the way journalists report and write news.

The big problem facing newspapers? People aren't reading them. Research shows a continuing decline in readership.

Many other editors have grappled with the same dilemma: how to make newspapers more appealing to readers. "I wish newspapers printed what you didn't see on TV last night," one editor said. "I wish newspapers had more utility for women," another editor said. "I wish we could figure out some new definitions for news," said a third editor. These comments were made at a series of programs conducted in 1989 by New Directions for News, a non-profit research and development institute based at the University of Missouri School of Journalism. And some newspaper editors are making these wishes come true, without shooting any journalists in the process.

If there were a wizard of change, it would be Jean Gaddy Wilson. She is executive director of New Directions for News, which conducts roundtable discussions with editors throughout the country to find solutions to problems facing the newspaper industry.

Wilson said newspapers must change the way they present news. "Readers are saying, 'Don't give me all this stuff that you have been throwing at me like a ball machine; give me stuff I can understand about a complex world.'"

Successful newspapers frequently will review their definitions of news, adjusting the mix of content to meet the requirements of the audience they wish to reach. This does not mean that bad news will be avoided or sugar-coated. This does mean that readers will receive a newspaper containing both what they need to know and what they want to know.

Burl Osborne, editor,

The Dallas Morning News

"I think the content will change," Wilson said. "I don't think it's a matter of shortening up the same old stuff. Local news will remain important, but it is not going to be the same ho-hum news. We can still report about city hall. We just haven't written about it compellingly to show how it affects people's lives. Journalists need to use investigative powers—not just to go get the damn rascals—but to investigate what a community is looking for, what people do, and how to serve their needs."

Sources of Change

Concepts of news are changing because people's needs are changing. For example, women now outnumber men in higher education, they purchase more than half of all the new cars, and they have made the catalog business and service industries grow, Wilson said. The content of newspapers needs to reflect these concerns of women.

The media also need to address the concerns of the growing minority population. Demographic experts predict that by the year 2010, one in three U.S. residents will be a member of a racial or ethnic minority.

Technology is another area that affects people's lives. Not only should journalists write about how people interact with machines, they ought to know how to use video, audio, and print, Wilson said.

In the future, the newspaper may not even be a paper. Several media companies are experimenting with "telecomputer" news delivered to subscribers by telephone lines hooked to computers or television sets via modems. Readers and viewers may call up the type of news they want or gain access to huge data bases of information, somewhat like pay-per-view television service. Roger Fidler, director of new media development for Knight-Ridder, has developed a prototype of the paperless newspaper: a flat, 9-by-12-inch portable computer with touch-sensitive displays that allow readers to select the news they want to read.

Although similar experiments conducted in the past were not popular, such as a computerized service called Viewtron from the Knight-Ridder Corporation, research in this area continues. However, despite the sophisticated delivery systems that are envisioned, few analysts predict the total demise of print newspapers in the near future.

Television news also is changing, because of a proliferation of cable channels and programming options for viewers. Competition for breaking news from cable news networks, such as CNN, and news magazine shows is forcing the major networks to reconsider the type of stories they present on the evening news broadcasts. Instead of recapping the events of the day, these shows may feature more in-depth reports and investigative stories or features about science, health and other issues relevant to viewers.

Attempts to Cope With Change

What constitutes news in this changing environment? News used to be defined as an event that happened. It still is. But now editors are asking reporters to add impact—what events mean to the reader or viewer.

And a new definition of news has emerged: news you can use. That can mean anything from news about transportation problems for commuters to news about leisure time.

In 1990, when *The Orange County* (Calif.) *Register* assigned a reporter to cover shopping malls on a regular basis because that was where readers spent much of their time, reactions in the newspaper industry ranged from scorn to accolades for innovation. Now many newspapers include such non-traditional assignments to grab readers' attention.

In the next decade the media will continue to seek ways to adapt to changing patterns of readers and viewers, and journalists need to be receptive to innovative concepts. But no matter how the content and delivery of broadcast and print news change, journalists will still need good basic skills to report and write the news.

The 25/43 Project

But what about people who have no time to read newspapers? The Knight-Ridder Corporation, which owns 34 newspapers, wanted to know how to reach the "baby boomers" from age 25 to 43, a group of endangered readers. The company gathered a team of experts to conduct focus groups, meetings with people in this age group, to discover their interests and needs. They called it the 25/43 project. They found that many of these people, particularly working women, were subscribing but were too busy to even take the paper out of its wrapper.

After a year of study, the experts redesigned and redefined news in one of the company's newspapers, the *Boca Raton News* in South Florida, and unveiled it in 1990 (see Exhibit 2-1). The major goal was to reach the 25-to-43 age group by presenting the news so readers could digest it quickly and easily. Some of the key changes in the *Boca Raton News*:

Exhibit 2-1

Boca Raton News front page

No stories that jump (continue) to another page

Maps and graphic devices throughout the paper

An emphasis on stories that interest readers—stories about parenting and education and news about women, whom the newspaper especially wants to reach

Wayne Ezell, editor of the *Boca Raton News,* said that despite the publicity about extensive use of graphics, the real change has been in content. Now the focus is on stories that affect readers. Ezell would argue that his newspaper achieves what the editors in the New Directions for News seminar wished for: stories you would not see on television and stories that follow a new definition of news. "Newspapers are terribly boring," Ezell said. "They tell you more about things you aren't interested in. One of the things we found in focus groups is that people's interests are different than you think they are." In the *News,* those interests translate to stories about the price of champagne and the best way to deal with children's temper tantrums as well as a "critter watch" column about bugs.

Most of the stories are short, less than 10 inches. "Nothing we have done is more popular than eliminating jumps," Ezell said. But he insisted that there is still a market for long stories if they are well written and about compelling subjects.

Ezell predicted that in the future, newspapers will provide more features, such as human interest stories and news about lifestyles. But they will still vie for the reader's time and attention now given to television. "I think newspapers of the future are going to demand far better writing than newspapers of the past," he said. "I think we're going to have great variety in the style and types of writing."

Reaction from the newspaper industry to the renovated *Boca Raton News* ranged from outrage over what some people called a TV newspaper filled with fluff to raves for its reader-friendly style. But its impact on the newspaper industry was negligible, unlike the major influence *USA Today* had on the industry, particularly in graphics, after it was created in 1982.

News 2000

In 1990, the Gannett Co., which owns *USA Today* and more than 80 other newspapers, undertook a major effort to revamp them. The company developed a project called News 2000 to explore ways of changing the content and presentation of news.

The News 2000 concept is like a pyramid of building blocks (see Exhibit 2-2). The most important block, community interest, forms the base. Other building blocks emphasize qualities that can be enhanced by using graphics and writing stories that make people care. But the primary emphasis is on making the news relevant to readers in local communities.

Editors at many of the Gannett newspapers conducted focus groups with readers to determine their needs and interests and then developed a plan for their papers to target those interest areas. For example, Ellen Leifeld, executive editor of the *Battle Creek* (Mich.) *Enquirer,* found that readers in her community want news about weather, local government and taxes, education, health, and fitness. So the *Enquirer* plays stories about those topics prominently.

The News 2000 program also urged newspapers to find ways to get readers involved—by polls, question-of-the-day features that

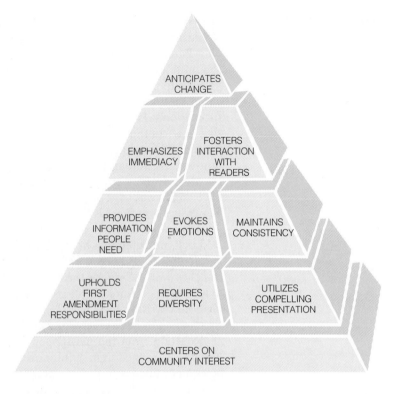

ANTICIPATES
CHANGE

EMPHASIZES
IMMEDIACY

FOSTERS
INTERACTION
WITH
READERS

PROVIDES
INFORMATION
PEOPLE
NEED

EVOKES
EMOTIONS

MAINTAINS
CONSISTENCY

UPHOLDS
FIRST
AMENDMENT
RESPONSIBILITIES

REQUIRES
DIVERSITY

UTILIZES
COMPELLING
PRESENTATION

CENTERS ON
COMMUNITY INTEREST

Exhibit 2-2

The News 2000 concept

Courtesy of The Gannett Co. Inc.

involve readers, or communication through town meetings and reader representatives.

Judy Pace, editor of the Gannett-owned *Jackson* (Tenn.) *Sun,* explained the changes this way: "The days of spinach journalism—read this, it's good for you—are gone."

The Influence of Graphics

Studies by the Poynter Institute for Media Studies in St. Petersburg, Fla., show an increased emphasis on graphic devices and color. In one study, called "Eyes on the News," researchers measured the movements of people's eyes as they read the newspaper. The results of this study, also known as the "Eye Trac" study, showed that readers are drawn to color photographs first, then headlines, cutlines (captions), briefs (stories abbreviated to one to three paragraphs) and a number of other graphic devices (points of entry).

The study also concluded that most people only scan the newspaper, looking at headlines and graphics, and that they read very few stories all the way through. The average reader skims about 25 percent of the stories in the newspaper but only reads half of those (about 12 percent) thoroughly, the study concluded.

To grab that reader's attention, news stories now are a mix of visual and verbal information. Graphics have become so important in news presentation that some newspapers, including *The Orange*

County Register and *The Dallas Morning News,* now have graphics reporters. When a major story such as an airplane crash occurs, these graphics reporters go to the scene with other reporters to gather information for the graphic. While the regular reporter gathers facts, quotes and other materials, the graphics reporter seeks such details as how many feet the plane skidded for scale drawings.

Since most newspapers do not have special reporters to gather information for graphics, those responsibilities will become part of the job for many regular reporters. And reporters will need to consider while they write what graphic devices will be part of their story.

That is precisely the emphasis at the *Reno* (Nev.) *Gazette-Journal,* a Gannett newspaper with extensive use of graphics. "We want reporters to visualize the information, not just as a story but as a total package," said Vikki Porter, managing editor of the *Gazette-Journal.* "Some stories, such as government coverage, may be told best just by a box or a graphic with a picture. We use summary graphs (on top of the story) to tell the reader what this story means to you. We don't try to do everything in cracker-size; we're still doing good writing and long stories. The challenge is to determine what is the best way to provide the information."

For example, a story about water rates explained the effect on readers in the lead and in this summary box above the story:

Water shock

What it means to you

- By 1994 a $15.41 monthly increase for the average residential customer
- By 1996 another $12.40 monthly hike

The story then began with this impact lead, which explains how the increased water rates will affect readers:

You may be paying almost 150 percent more for water in 1996 to cover costs caused by new federal drinking water standards and area growth.

    That's a $71.50 monthly bill for average residential customers and "the reality of what's facing the area," Phil Seges, Westpac Utilities president, said Friday.

Mike Norris, *Reno Gazette-Journal*

The graphs in Exhibit 2-3 were another piece of the total package.

    Mario R. Garcia, an associate director in charge of graphics and design programs at the Poynter Institute for Media Studies, said the majority of readers today do not remember life without television,

Exhibit 2-3

Infographic for story on water rates

Courtesy of the *Reno Gazette-Journal.*

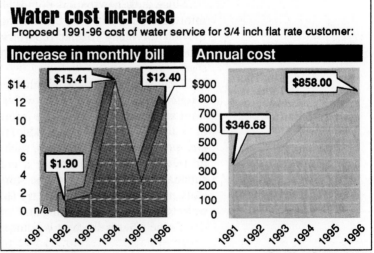

so visual elements are crucial in a newspaper. "The marriage of visual and words has to begin early—from the first time you learn reporting," he said.

Garcia, considered the leading authority on graphics, has redesigned more than 100 newspapers throughout the world. He said that redesigning a newspaper for appearance without considering the writing content is like cosmetic surgery. "It's like giving someone a new nose but you have the same old boring personality," he said.

There must be a renewed emphasis on good writing, Garcia said. "We have not lost the readers; what we have lost is good stories." His solution for the future is more of what he calls "invisible stories," the kinds of news stories a newspaper develops through investigative or enterprising reporting. "Visible news comes to you—police reports, meetings, etc. It's there, but television also hears the sirens and gets it sooner." He says newspapers must develop angles to stories and find unusual stories television doesn't have.

The Swinging Pendulum

All these efforts to give readers what they want worry some editors. Geneva Overholser, editor of *The Des Moines* (Iowa) *Register,* said newspapers are so afraid of offending anyone that they seem to have a new slogan: "All the News That Doesn't Displease Anyone."

"We have this notion that we must make sure that no one suffers," Overholser said in a speech at the University of California. "That is not the newspaper editor's role. . . . It is to make sure the truth is told, that word goes out, that the whole picture is presented. . . . Let us have confidence in what we know how to do: tell a story that brings tears or laughter. To explain a dilemma. To bring the unknown to light. Let us not care what one individual thinks of us on one given day. For truth-telling will have its victims."

She is not alone in her opinion. Many editors and experts predict that if newspapers are to survive, they must stop trying to mimic television and, instead, find their own unique identity.

Bill Kovach, a media expert who is curator of the Nieman Foundation at Harvard University, suggested this solution in an article in *Editor & Publisher* magazine: "Another way to address the competition is to do what none of the other media even try to do or can do: provide consistent, in-depth coverage of issues which matter to people." He said that many newspaper experiments are "full of flash but stripped of context, which trivializes content and usefulness to their readers."

But all the media experts agree that newspapers cannot survive by returning to their formats of the past and that graphics will continue to be a crucial part of news presentation in the future.

Hard News and Features

News falls into two basic categories: hard news and soft news. "Hard news" includes stories of a timely nature about events or conflicts that just happened or are about to happen, such as crimes, fires, meetings, protest rallies, speeches and testimony in court cases. The hard approach is basically an account of what happened, why it happened and how readers will be affected. These stories have immediacy.

"Soft news" is often characterized as news that entertains or informs, with an emphasis on human interest and novelty and less immediacy than hard news. For example, a profile about a man who designs model airplanes or a feature about the effectiveness of diets would be considered soft news. Soft news can also be feature stories that focus on people, places or issues that affect readers' lives. A story about the growing number of babies suffering from AIDS could be considered a soft news story. It isn't less important, but it isn't news that happened overnight.

If the action or event occurred the same day as or the day before publication of the newspaper, the event is called "breaking news." Here is an example of the lead of a breaking news story from a Saturday edition:

Tornadoes rapped Topeka and southeast Shawnee County Friday afternoon, damaging seven homes and sending residents scurrying for cover.

No one was injured by the short, severe storm that struck unexpectedly.

Steve Fry, *Topeka* (Kan.) *Capital-Journal*

Soft news includes many topics of interest to people but not necessarily based on breaking news events. These are called "feature stories." The line between hard news and features can be very fuzzy. A feature story, in its broadest sense, is one that focuses on a special angle of the news: human interest stories, profiles, issues, or general topics.

The preceding example of a hard news story told readers what happened. The newspaper also printed this feature story focusing on people affected by the storm:

Becky Clark of Topeka was told the tornado sirens that sounded Friday afternoon were a false alarm.

Then she got home from work and saw her back yard at 2411 S.E. Gemini Ave. in the Aquarian Acres neighborhood.

"I couldn't believe it," she said.

A tornado had lifted up the family pontoon boat, which was parked in the back yard, and tossed it into the family swimming pool, crushing part of the boat.

"It just wanted to get in the water," said Joe Clark, Becky's husband.

"I guess it was tired of being in dry dock. . . ."

Joe Taschler, *Topeka Capital-Journal*

The hard news story about the storm was the main story, called a "mainbar." Because the accompanying feature story was a different angle of the same topic, it was a "sidebar" packaged with the main story.

Many other features in a newspaper do not have a breaking-news peg. They are stories that focus on interesting people or topics. For example, the *Boca Raton News* printed a feature story on the growing popularity of waterbeds, a topic of interest to its readers.

The Wall Street Journal is famous for its features. Every day, the newspaper publishes a feature story on the front page about a news trend, like this example about the increasing number of homeless people in rural communities:

HUNTSVILLE, Mo.—The homeless, long a big-city phenomenon, are emerging as a rural crisis, too. Ask Lowell Rott. After his small, debt-ridden farm here was auctioned off on the courthouse steps in 1986, he slept for a time in his 1973 Dodge pickup. Now he's a squatter in an abandoned two-room house with no running water.

There isn't much demand for 50-year-old farmers like him. A high-school dropout, he works as a handyman for $10 a day and shower privileges. The faded old suit he wears for job interviews in town hasn't made him any more attractive. His face is streaked with cinders from a wood stove that generates so little heat he wears a parka to bed. He stubbornly keeps a hand in farming by raising castoff horses on the land of sympathetic neighbors. "The horses are homeless and so am I," he says. "We belong together."

A surprising—and growing—number of rural homeless like Mr. Rott are seeking shelter wherever they can find it: in caves near Glenwood Springs, Colo., under bridges in Des Moines, Iowa, and in junk cars close to Coventry, Vt. A scramble is on to build shelters in small towns from Boonville, Mo., to Wilmington, Ohio.

Scott Kilman and Robert Johnson, *The Wall Street Journal*

Qualities of News Stories

Definitions of news are changing. But these are some of these traditional qualities of both hard and soft news stories:

Timeliness: Some event that happened the day of or day before publication or an event that is due to happen in the immediate future is considered timely. Some events that happened in the past also may be considered timely if they are printed on an anniversary of the event, such as one, five or 10 years after the incident. Timeliness answers this reader's question: Why are you telling me this now? This story was timely because it was published the day after the accident:

> A bus loaded with elementary school children crashed head-on into a compact car in southwestern Jefferson County yesterday, injuring 24 students and the two drivers.
>
> The (Louisville, Ky.) *Courier-Journal*

Proximity: An event may be of interest to local readers because it happened in or close to the community. This story would be of particular interest to residents in the Oregon community where this man lived:

> A 71-year-old former psychologist received an eight-year prison sentence Monday for running the most sophisticated indoor marijuana-growing operation ever discovered in Clackamas County. Authorities said Arvord E. Belden of Estacada may be the oldest man ever sentenced to federal prison for a drug crime in Oregon.
>
> Dave Hogan, *The Oregonian*

Unusual nature: Out-of-the-ordinary events, a bizarre or rare occurrence, or an odd twist to the news are the focus of what *The Philadelphia Inquirer* calls "zig" stories: stories that zig instead of zag. They are stories that stress an unusual aspect of the news, and the *Inquirer* strives to put one on its front page frequently. The story can have a combination of news qualities, such as unusual, bizarre, entertaining or trendy. For example, the *Inquirer* ran a story about how single people were meeting each other by taking their dogs to the park. Another zig story featured a man who had marketed cricket dung as fertilizer, and another focused on why college students gain "the Freshmen 15" pounds.

Prominence of subject: People who are well-known for their accomplishments—primarily entertainers, athletes or people who have gained fame for achievements, good or bad—attract a lot of attention. This story ran on the front page because of the celebrity status of the entertainer:

Michael Jackson, whose inventive dancing and pop vocals have earned him worldwide fame and millions of dollars, did a new move Friday: He apologized.

Rocked by a barrage of viewer complaints about a sexual and violent segment of his "Black or White" music video, Jackson and Fox Broadcasting Co. said they were sorry and agreed to cut the offending segment from the video.

The video, which premiered Thursday night on Fox, will be rebroadcast Sunday night—minus a final sequence in which Jackson materializes into a panther and launches into a primal dance during which he grabs at his genitals, unzips his pants and smashes the windows of a car with a crowbar.

Ray Richmond and Anne Valdespino, *The Orange County Register*

Human interest: People like stories about people who have special problems, achievements or experiences. These stories can be profiles or unusual stories about people that make readers care about their plight. This example about a couple who spent $6,000 looking for their lost cat combines human interest and an unusual story:

Five-year-old Marble used to hide in the box springs of a spare bed in Bill and Carol Deckers' Denver home.

Now the Deckers' cat is hiding somewhere in the woods near Carthage, Mo.

Since Marble escaped from the couple's recreational vehicle Aug. 18, the Deckers have spent more than $6,000 trying to get her back.

"We taught her to live with us and we owe it to her," said Carol Decker, 41, a part-time accountant

who gave up her job to look for Marble. . . .

Since losing Marble, the Deckers have put up posters and placed newspaper ads in Colorado, Missouri and Oklahoma, and contacted a psychic to locate her, to no avail.

The Deckers have returned to the site, often sleeping outdoors in the hope that their presence would draw Marble to them.

Tillie Fong, *Rocky Mountain* (Denver) *News*

Conflict: Stories involving conflicts people have with government or other people are often newsworthy, especially when the conflict reflects local problems. This example affected people in Chicago:

Hundreds of protesters descended on the Chicago School Board's headquarters Tuesday to oppose school closings that they contend

will drive hundreds of students away from school and endanger the lives of others.

David C. Rudd and John Kass, *Chicago Tribune*

Impact: Reaction stories to news events or news angles that affect readers have impact. During the confirmation hearings for Supreme Court Justice Clarence Thomas, who was accused of sexual harassment by University of Oklahoma law professor Anita Hill, reaction stories abounded. Here is one example:

> Anita Hill is not alone. Working women around the country have joined her, crossing beyond confusion and fear about sexual harassment to share their experiences.
>
> "We've had a real outpouring of calls," said Barbara Otto of 9 to 5, the National Association of Working Women. "It's like they're coming out of the closet to tell their dirty secret. They're saying, 'Enough!'"
>
> The Associated Press

Some additional qualities of news to consider:

Helpfulness: Consumer, health and other how-to stories that help readers cope with their lives

Entertainment: Stories that make readers feel good or enjoy life

Special interest: Stories that appeal to people's interests in such subjects as science, business or religion or to such special groups as women, minorities, disabled people, veterans, college students or other groups with particular interests

Analysis: Stories that explain the meaning of events of interest to readers

Trends: Stories that indicate patterns or shifts in issues that influence readers' lives, such as increases in crime, social issues and other forces in society

All these kinds of stories have their place in the newspapers of today and of the future. And editors will continue to grapple with an old dilemma: Should they give people what they want or what they need? As Burl Osborne, editor of *The Dallas Morning News* said, a good newspaper contains both kinds of stories. Many will be short; others will be in-depth. Journalists will still need to learn how to present information to keep readers informed.

Activities

1 Try this classroom experiment to test your reading habits. Bring to class a copy of a newspaper you haven't read. Read the newspaper as you would for pleasure. Place a check on the first item you look at—a picture, graphic, headline or story. Mark the stories you read, and place an *X* at the point in the story where you decide to stop reading.

Where did your eye go first? Why are visual elements so important? Now analyze which stories you read and how much of them you read. Where did you stop on most stories? Why?

Because you are a journalism student, you may read more than the average reader. Guess how many seconds the average reader spends on a story before deciding to continue or switch to another story. (The answer is at the end of activity 4.)

2 Keep a journal of your reading habits for three days. Write a paragraph each day about the kinds of stories you read and didn't read, how many you read all the way through and how many you read just through the headline or the first few paragraphs. Clip some of the stories you liked and didn't like, and analyze your preferences. Record the amount of time you spend reading the newspaper for pleasure, not for an assignment. Then interview three other people—students, neighbors or strangers—and ask them what kinds of stories they do and don't read. Write a summary of your findings.

3 Using the concepts of News 2000, with special emphasis on community interests, analyze your local or campus newspaper for stories that fit some of the qualities in the pyramid. How would you improve your local or campus newspaper to meet these guidelines?

4 Analyze the role of graphics—maps, facts boxes, illustrations, photos—in your local or campus newspaper. Find stories that could benefit from more graphics.

(The answer to the question in activity 1 is three seconds. Now you can see why you must write compelling news stories that make the reader want to continue reading.)

COACHING

State the main idea of your story in one sentence.

Visualize your story with text and graphics or photographs.

The Basic News Story 3

T he basic news story is told upside down. It usually is called a
hard news story. That doesn't mean it should be hard to read.
Quite the contrary. It really should be called an easy news
story, because the facts are presented in a direct form that
makes it easy for the reader to get the most important
information quickly. A hard news story often presents the end
result of a news event first, so the key facts are in the first few
paragraphs. If a news story were a mystery story, you would
solve the mystery in the beginning and then devote the rest of
the story to telling the reader how and why it happened. Dan
Henderson, the late assistant managing editor of *The Commercial Appeal* in Memphis, Tenn., described it this way: "A
basic news story is similar to a formula for writing a novel
about the Old West: Shoot the sheriff in the first paragraph."

For example, if the state officials who regulate higher
education—often called the Board of Regents—met yesterday to discuss an increase in tuition at universities in your
state, you wouldn't write that the Board of Regents met to
consider a tuition increase. You would give the end results.
What did the regents decide? A direct approach would be
"The Board of Regents voted yesterday to raise undergraduate tuition next fall at state universities by $100 to $4,700."
Or you might say, "Tuition will increase next fall by $100 for
undergraduate students at the state's universities." Then you
could explain that the decision was made yesterday by the
Board of Regents and give details about the tuition increase

Too many stories fail to answer

the reader's most challenging

question: So what?

Roy Peter Clark, dean of Poynter

Institute for Media Studies

and its impact. Here is how one newspaper actually reported such a story:

> The cost of sending an undergraduate to Stanford University will climb in the fall to $21,262 for tuition, room and board, officials announced yesterday.
>   The 1991–92 tuition will go from $14,280 to $15,102, an increase of 5.75 percent, and room and board will increase 3.9 percent to $6,160.

San Francisco Chronicle

Not all basic news stories have to start with such a direct approach. There are many other ways of writing news stories and still delivering the information to readers in a quick, easy form. Several approaches will be presented in Chapters 10 and 12. But all news stories answer some basic questions: who, what, when, where, why and how? As newspaper readership declines, editors increasingly want the answer to another question: so what? What is the significance to readers? What information does the story contain that will make readers care?

Elements of the Basic News Story

Although a news story can contain a wealth of information, it should have one main idea. You should be able to identify the main idea in a sentence. All the other information should then support that central concept.

Various elements are used to support the main idea. Regardless of the topic, news stories contain conflict and resolution, headline, lead, backup for the lead, nut graph, impact, attribution, background, elaboration, ending and possibly graphics.

Like all stories, the basic news story has three parts: beginning, middle and end. Here's what they do:

Lead (beginning)

Sentence or paragraph that entices the reader to continue; explains some of the basic facts: who, what, when, where, why, how, so what

Body of story (middle)

Facts or quotes supporting the lead, including attribution to sources of information

Nut graph explaining the main point of the story (if it is not in the lead); the "so what" factor

Elaboration, or background of the situation and supporting points

Sources that provide balance by giving other points of view

Ending

Most commonly a quote from a key source summarizing the issue, an explanation of future action or an additional fact

Conflict and Resolution

Most hard news stories are about a conflict or a problem and the attempts to resolve it. Consider all the stories about crime, courts and government. The majority involve problems created or being resolved by the people who are involved.

The qualities discussed in Chapter 2—such as timeliness, unusual nature, prominence of subject and human interest—also help provide answers to the "so what" question. Here's one example of a conflict that is also unusual:

The family expected to mourn Anthony Romeo, who died of heart disease in September at his Seffner home. Instead, they found a stranger in his coffin. The Hillsborough Medical Examiner's Office had shipped the wrong body to the funeral home.	*Conflict*
The mix-up so upset Romeo's son Joseph that he filed suit Monday against Hillsborough County, the Brandon funeral home and the private courier that delivered the body.	*Resolution*

Rachel L. Swarns, *St. Petersburg* (Fla.) *Times*

Headline

The headline is the line on top of the story that tells the reader what the story is about. It usually is written by a copy editor or editor, not the reporter, except at very small newspapers where the editor also may be the reporter/writer. For a basic news story, the copy editor bases the headline on the main points of the story, which the reporter is expected to write in the first few paragraphs.

With the increased emphasis on graphics, more newspapers today are using secondary headlines, called "deck heads" or "summary lines," under the main headline. The two headlines together give the reader a quick overview of the story's content. Here is an example from a newspaper that uses summary lines on most of its major stories.

Salmon spawn a new crisis	*Headline*
Dwindling numbers and fading strength threaten to add the fish to the list of endangered species. But some question if the Northwest will pay the price to save the animals.	*Summary lines*

Los Angeles Times

Even though you won't write the headlines for your own stories, you can use the concept as a writing tool. If you are having trouble identifying the main point of a story, think of a headline for it.

Lead

The beginning of the story, the hook that tells the reader what the story is about, is the lead. A good lead entices the reader to continue reading. In a hard news story, the lead usually is written in one sentence—the first sentence of the story—and gives the most important information about the event. But even a basic story can have a creative lead, called a "soft lead."

The most common type of lead on a hard news story is called a "summary lead" because it summarizes the main points about what happened. It answers the questions of who, what, when, where, why and how. The rest of the story elaborates on what, why and how.

Hard news leads do not have to answer *all* those questions in the first sentence if doing so would make the lead too long and difficult to read. Shorter leads of fewer than 35 words are preferable, but that number is only a guideline. The writer has to decide which elements are most important to stress in the first sentence. This summary lead stresses who, what, when and where:

INDIANAPOLIS–Former heavyweight boxing champion Mike Tyson last night was convicted of sexually assaulting an 18-year-old beauty contestant in a predawn encounter at a posh hotel last July.

The Philadelphia Inquirer

Backup for the Lead

The lead should be backed up, or followed, with explanation that substantiates information in the lead. The backup should contain statements or quotes to explain your key point. Here is an example:

GAINESVILLE—A University of Florida law student suffering from amnesia after mysteriously disappearing in July has recalled her abduction under hypnosis, authorities said.	*Summary lead*
Elizabeth "Libby" Morris, 32, slowly has regained memory of her life before her disappearance from the Oaks Mall parking lot but has never consciously remembered what occurred during the five days she was missing, said Lt. Spencer Mann, a spokesman with the Alachua County Sheriff's Office.	*Backup*

The Associated Press

Nut Graph

The nut graph is a sentence or paragraph that states the focus—the main point—of the story. It should tell in a nutshell what the story is about and why it is newsworthy. (Some editors now call this the "gist graph," because it gives the gist of the story.) Although a news story may contain many comments and points, it should be developed around one major theme or concept, and all other information should relate to that focus.

In a hard news story with a direct summary lead, the nut graph and the lead often are the same. When the lead takes a softer, more creative approach that does not immediately explain the main point of the story, the nut graph is a separate paragraph. The nut graph is even more crucial when a story starts with a softer feature lead, because the reader has to wait for a few paragraphs to find out the reason for the story.

The nut graph should be placed high in the story, generally by the third to fifth paragraph. But if the lead is very compelling, the nut graph could come later. Rigid rules can ruin good writing.

Here's an example:

RAVENNA, Ohio—There's no room at the Portage County Jail for Matthew P. Dukes—and he's trying hard to get in.	*Lead*
The Newton Falls resident has tried six times in 15 months to serve a 30-day sentence for driving	

while intoxicated. But each time, deputies have turned him away.

The jail is full, they say. Come again.

But Dukes has gone to court, filing a federal suit against the county sheriff and alleging that he is suffering cruel and unusual punishment by being prevented from going to jail.

Several area lawyers say it may be one of the first cases of its kind—a test of civil liberties that may pave the way for others who are idling away the hours while they wait to serve sentences in filled-to-capacity facilities for crimes such as shoplifting, theft or drunken driving.

For Dukes, 26, the unserved sentence is a constant source of frustration and embarrassment, a situation that he said has helped to turn him away from a hard-drinking lifestyle.

He said that he had not had a drink in a year and that he wanted to put the sentence behind him.

Carol Biliczky, Knight Ridder Tribune News

Backup

Nut graph

Impact

Whenever possible, the writer should explain how the news affects readers. It is the impact sentence or paragraph that should answer the question: What is the significance of this story? What in the story makes the reader care? Sometimes the impact is explained in the lead or in the nut graph; sometimes it is lower in the story, in an explanatory paragraph.

In the story about the man who can't get into jail, the impact is the significance of his lawsuit. The significance is explained in the paragraph following the nut graph.

Not all stories can show direct impact on readers, but they should all have a clear paragraph explaining the reason for the story. In some stories, such as police stories, the impact is just that the news happened in the community and should be of interest to local residents.

When Oregon's mandatory auto-mobile seat belt law goes into effect Dec. 7, police won't have any trouble enforcing it—all they have to see is a shoulder harness or a lap belt dangling unused.	**Lead**
"Police officers routinely tell us that safety belt laws are easy to enforce," said Geri Parker, safety belt program coordinator for the Oregon Traffic Safety Commission.	**Backup**
Oregon voters approved a ballot measure Nov. 6 to extend mandatory seat belt use to people age 16 and older. Seat belts or safety seats already are required for everyone under 16.	
Beginning Dec. 7, everyone in the front and back seats of a car will need to buckle up—if belts are available—or face a fine of up to $50.	**Impact**

Phil Manzano, *The Oregonian*

In the following example, some of the impact is in the lead, and more is in the second paragraph:

President Bush's education budget includes more money for cash grants to college students, and new guidelines will push most of it to students from low-income families.	**Lead**
Losers in the already-difficult scramble for the Pell education grants could be students from middle-income families.	**Impact**

USA Today

Attribution

Where did you get the information? Who told you these facts? How can the reader be sure what you said is true? The attribution provides those answers. You need to attribute all quotes—exact wording of statements that people made—and much information that you did not witness. If the information is common knowledge or indisputable, you do not have to attribute it. (A more complete discussion of how to use quotes and attribution comes later in this chapter.)

The attribution should be in the lead for controversial or accusatory information, but in many other cases it can be delayed so it doesn't clutter the lead. Police stories often have attribution in the lead, especially if you get the information by telephone or if the information is accusatory:

ST. PETERSBURG—A 15-year-old boy was stabbed twice in the chest Thursday afternoon when he apparently tried to break up a fight in a crowded parking lot at Northeast High School, authorities said.	*Lead with attribution*
Police and school officials said the stabbing, believed to have occurred after one student took another's hat, was the first they could recall at Pinellas County schools.	*Backup*

St. Petersburg Times

In the next example, general attribution is in the lead, but the specific attribution is in the second paragraph. The names of the groups that did the study are too cumbersome to use in the lead.

U.S. college students, criticized as over-materialistic in the 1980s, are showing increased interest in social causes such as the environment and less interest in making money, a new study says.	*Lead with general attribution*
The 25th annual survey of college freshmen, conducted by the American Council on Education and the University of California, Los Angeles, shows steadily changing attitudes.	*Backup with specific attribution*

USA Today

Background

Is there any history or background the reader needs in order to understand how a problem or action occurred? Most stories need some background to explain the action, as in this example:

Lock your doors.	*Lead*
That's the advice of University of Iowa security chief Dan Hogan in light of recent reports of a prowler slipping into unlocked dormitory rooms at night.	*Nut graph*
"I can't stress that enough," he said. "It's a very serious situation."	*Backup*

> Since Aug. 24, there have been six reports of a man entering women's rooms between 3 a.m. and 5:30 a.m. Five incidents were in Burge Hall and one was in Currier Hall.
>
> Two times the man touched the sleeping women, Hogan said. But there was no force or violence. In each instance the man ran when the woman discovered him.
>
> More recently, a woman in Burge Hall heard someone at her door. She opened it and saw a man running down the hall, Hogan said.

Background

Valoree Armstrong, *Iowa City Press-Citizen*

Elaboration

Supporting points related to the main issue constitute elaboration. These can be statements, quotes or more detail to explain what happened, how and why the problem or action occurred, and reactions to the event. In this part of the story, seek other points of view to make sure you have balance and fairness. A story based on one source can be too biased.

The preceding story about the University of Iowa continued with more explanation:

> George Droll, director of residence services, said main doors to the halls were locked from midnight to 6 a.m. But each resident has a key. Some floors have 24-hour visitation.
>
> Often students feel more secure than they should because the buildings are large and are home to many of their friends, he said.

Elaboration

Ending

The most common type of ending includes one of these elements: future action, a statement or quote that summarizes but does not repeat the previous information, or more elaboration. If the future action is a key factor in the issue, it should be placed higher in the story. Avoid summary endings, which repeat what you have already said. In a basic news story, end when you have no more new information to reveal.

The ending on the Iowa story follows the residence director's comments about why students feel secure in large buildings where they have friends:

"That's a strength, but it can also be a weakness in terms of people securing their rooms," Droll said.	*Summary quote ending*

Here is the ending from the story about the prospective inmate who wants to go to jail to serve his sentence for drunken driving:

Although a new, 184-bed facility costing about $15 million is planned for 1993, that does nothing to stem the tide of today's inmates, who Howe said are coming in record numbers.	*Future action ending*

Graphics

Remember to consider a photograph, chart or other graphic device as a crucial part of your story. A copy editor may write the highlights box, an artist will design the graphic, and a photographer will shoot the picture. But the way the story is presented visually will affect the length of your text, and it will help you determine what information you can include or leave out.

Examples of Basic News Stories

The following examples will show you how elements of the basic news story fit together. The first example is a standard news story with a summary lead. The content involves conflict and a group's attempts to resolve it. The story is organized in inverted pyramid form, giving the most important information first and the rest in descending order of importance. (The form will be discussed in Chapter 12.) This story contains most of the basic news elements described in this chapter:

Thousands gather on Capitol steps for animal rights

By Joan Mower
The Associated Press

Summary lead: who, what, when, where, why

WASHINGTON—Thousands of animal rights activists rallied in the nation's capital yesterday, seeking to promote the humane treatment of animals in the wild, on farms and in research laboratories.

U.S. Capitol Police said an estimated 24,000 people attended a rally on the steps of the Capitol after a one-mile march down Pennsylvania Avenue under sunny skies. Organizers said more than 50,000 people from around the country showed up.

Backup for lead, with differing opinions about crowd size

Elaboration Marchers chanted, "Animal rights—now." Many carried banners and placards with pictures and slogans saying things such as "Fur Is Dead" and "Animals Have Rights, Too." Some brought their dogs.

Background Organizers said "March for Animals"—the first event of its kind—was a milestone in a movement they said was once viewed as outside the mainstream.

Among the groups participating were the American Society for the Prevention of Cruelty to Animals, People for Ethical Treatment of Animals, the U.S. Humane Society and the Doris Day Animal League.

Peter Linck, coordinator of the march, said the ultimate goal of the animal rights activists was to stop the use of animals in scientific research. However, he conceded it was unlikely the public would adopt that stance.

Impact "In the meantime," he said, "we want to improve the condition of animals and promote alternatives to reform society."

Elaboration The event attracted a wide variety of animal supporters, Linck said. They ranged from those who want protection of species, such as elephants, to those seeking to end medical testing on animals. Many were seeking changes in the way animals are raised for slaughter, as well as a ban on fur clothes.

Reaction: balance from different points of view Health officials are particularly sensitive about efforts to end animal testing, a move they say could be disastrous for science.

Health and Human Services Secretary Louis W. Sullivan has criticized the animal-rights advocates who use violence and intimidation to block testing of animals.

"They are on the wrong side of morality," he said last week.

Sullivan said some of the greatest advances in medicine, such as the cure for polio, never would have been achieved had animals not been used in tests.

Ending: future action Participants in yesterday's march planned to lobby Congress today in support of bills that deal with animal issues.

The second example is a basic news story with a softer lead that stresses the impact of the story. The nut graph gives the crucial information. It states the problem, the "so what" of this story. Attribution is limited in the beginning because the backup for the lead is factual: a law that has been enacted. Note, however, that quotes and opinions are attributed.

Throw the book at them

Deck headline *Law could lead to arrests for overdue library books*

Soft lead BOSTON—Drop the novel. Step away from the car. You're under arrest for having an overdue library book.

Nut graph: what, why, when, so what, impact and background Starting Thursday, overdue books could land you in police custody. A law signed by Gov. Michael S. Dukakis in June would allow the arrest of library scofflaws if they had received notice that their books were 30 days overdue.

The law also raises the maximum fine for an overdue book from $50 to $500.

Elaboration Although the law makes no provision for an overdue book, it allows for up to five years in prison and a fine of $25,000 for the theft of library property worth more than $250.

Reaction Gregor Trinkaus-Randall, a collection management consultant for the Massachusetts Board of Library Commissioners, said librarians needed tough enforcement tools.

Attribution for quote "Any library book that is not returned therefore has to be replaced by the library, and that is money out of the town's pocket that could be spent on other materials," he said.

More reaction David Linsky, a defense lawyer in Cambridge, criticized the measure.

"I think the police are having enough trouble chasing down murderers and rapists without having to keep up with people who have overdue library books," he said.

Linsky said that the law allowed the arrest of library scofflaws without a warrant, something that could not be done with an offense such as assault and battery. He said the measure was unenforceable.

Ending: reaction quote "If the police are told by an employee of the library that you have an overdue library book, then the police can arrest you in any public place and put the handcuffs on you," he said. "That's the real horror show of this thing."

The Associated Press

Quotes and Attribution

Coaching Tips Ask yourself: Is the quote memorable without referring to your notes? If so, it's probably a good quote.

Do your quotes repeat your transitions? Could the quote or the transition be eliminated?

A guide to attribution: If you don't attribute the statement to a source, are you sure it is a fact that can be substantiated by records or officials or that it is common knowledge?

Janet Malcolm called herself "a compulsively careful" writer. Jeffrey Masson called her a liar. And for seven years the two of them slugged it out in court.

Masson, a psychoanalyst who gained fame for his critical views of Sigmund Freud, said Malcolm fabricated quotes that she attributed to him in a profile she wrote about him in *The New Yorker* magazine. He sued her for libel. Malcolm insisted that she followed a common journalistic practice and only clarified his statements.

Although it is common practice to clean up quotes for grammar, major changes in wording are not acceptable. The case went to the U.S. Supreme Court, which ruled in 1991 that altering a quote for grammar and syntax is not grounds for libel unless the changes alter the meaning and make the statement false. Libel is defined as a false and defamatory written attack on a person's character. According to First Amendment precedents in libel cases, a public figure must show that the publication that injured his or her reputation was not only incorrect but also published with "actual malice," which is legally defined as publishing with knowledge of falsity or with reckless disregard for the truth.

By its ruling, the Supreme Court refused to create a separate libel category for quotations. But the court also refused to rule on the specific quotes in contention and, instead, sent the case back to a lower court for a decision on whether the disputed quotes were libelous.

Most editors insist that a direct quote contain only minor changes for grammar errors or deletions of extraneous words, such as "uh." The quotation marks are a signal to the reader that those are the source's words, not an interpreted version.

If a quote has to be substantially changed to correct it, paraphrase it and attribute it to the source without quotation marks.

When to Use Direct Quotes

Good quotes can back up your lead and substantiate information in your story. In addition, good quotes let the reader hear the speaker. They add drama and interest to your story. They can also bog down stories and make them boring. If they just repeat what you have already said, it's better to paraphrase or eliminate them altogether.

In the past, reporters were encouraged to use quotes liberally. Current trends are to limit quotes—unless they are really good—because it takes space to set them up, and they don't always convey as much information as paraphrased sentences can.

What is a good quote? One that is vivid and clear and that reveals strong feelings or reactions of the speaker. If the speaker's words are better than your words, the direct quote will add interest to your story. For example, Supreme Court Justice Clarence Thomas said at his confirmation hearing, "I'd rather die than withdraw." That's a statement worth remembering. When Magic Johnson announced that he had the AIDS virus, he said something worth quoting: "You don't have to feel sorry for me, because if I die tomorrow, I've had the greatest life."

In deciding whether to use a quote, the key is whether it is emotional or informational. It should be one or the other. Too many writers use quotes to prove that they legitimately received the information.

Susan Ager, writing coach for the *Detroit Free Press,* said reporters should consider quotes as the spice of the story, not the meat and potatoes. "Readers come to the newspaper the way they come to a party," she said. "They want to talk to interesting people. Long quotes usually are not very interesting."

Here are some guidelines for deciding when to use quotes:

• When the quote is interesting and informative (example from a story about a woman who drank too much water before a urine test)

> "As more people are subjected to urine drug testing, more people are going to accidentally drink too much water for their own good and become ill," said David Kloniff, a specialist in chemical and hormonal imbalance.
>
> Knight Ridder Tribune News

• To back up the lead, the nut graph or a supporting point in your story

> ATLANTA—The signs of dangerous cults are everywhere, including colleges, a cult expert told campus police officials.
>
> "You may not think it's a problem on your campus, but you have it," Marcia Rudin, director of the International Cult Education Program, said Friday at a meeting of the International Association of Law Enforcement Administrators.
>
> "We're concerned," Rudin said. "It's been 10½ years since Jonestown. People ask us, 'Haven't they gone away?' Unfortunately not."
>
> The Associated Press

• To reveal the source's opinions or feelings (quote by the president of a nudist club protesting laws that prohibit nude bathing in the St. Petersburg area)

> "I think the rules are silly. In most of Europe on the beaches you can go either nude or topless or clothed; it's entirely up to you."
>
> St. Petersburg (Fla.) Times

• If the quote is very descriptive or dramatic (example from a story about the aftermath of an earthquake in the Soviet Union)

> "This is what the end of the world must look like," said a factory worker.
>
> David Remnick, The Washington Post

- To express strong reactions from a source (quote from the mother of a 2-year-old shot by a 3-year-old playmate who found a gun under a pillow in the house)

> "My God, it was an accident. . . . I never in my life dreamed this could happen. I just wish it was me instead of my baby. I can't stand to think of him in pain."
>
> *The Seattle Times*

- To convey dramatic action

> A 24-year-old Wichita woman chased a burglar through her house Thursday morning before he managed to flee the house with less than $100 in cash.
>
> "I woke up to see someone peering through my bedroom door," said the woman, who did not want to be identified. "I rushed the door and smashed his arm between the door and the door frame."
>
> *The Wichita* (Kan.) *Eagle*

Good quotes enhance a story, but worthless ones just take up space. You don't need to quote someone just to prove you spoke to the source. Here are some types of quotes to avoid:

- Avoid direct quotes when the source is boring or the information is factual and indisputable. For example, a city official who says, "We are going to have our regular monthly meeting Tuesday night" is not worth quoting directly.

Consider the quotes in this story:

> President Bush took the first step toward his 1992 re-election effort yesterday, authorizing a fund-raising committee and designating Texas businessman Robert Holt as his campaign treasurer.
>
> "Although I am not yet formally declaring my candidacy for the Republican nomination . . . I am hereby authorizing this organization as my principal campaign committee," said Bush in a letter to FEC Chairman John Warren McGarry.
>
> "It is my hope that this committee will allow those people who have encouraged me to seek a second term as president a chance to express their support in a manner that fully complies with the federal election laws," Bush said.
>
> The Associated Press

The 78 words in the quotes devour space. If your purpose is to show that Bush can be boring, leave the quotes in. But if the purpose is to tell the news as quickly and clearly as possible, you could do it without those quotes.

• Avoid any direct quote that isn't clearly worded. If a government official says something in bureaucratic language that you don't fully understand, ask for clarification and paraphrase. Here's an example:

> The House on Wednesday over-whelmingly approved mandatory drug and alcohol testing for as many as 6.3 million transportation workers.
>
> "People have a right to know that those to whom they're consigned in the area of mass transportation are free of substance abuse and sober," said Rep. William Hughes, D-N.J.
>
> The Associated Press

• Avoid quotes that don't relate directly to the focus and supporting points in your story. Some of the best quotes a source utters may have nothing to do with your focus. It's better to lose them than to use them poorly.

• Avoid accusatory quotes from politicians or witnesses of a crime. If you intend to include any accusations, get a response from the person accused. A direct quote does not save you from libel. If police or other criminal justice officials make accusations in an official capacity, you may use direct or indirect quotes, providing you attribute them carefully.

Finally, here are some guidelines to determine if your material is quotable:

• Can you remember the quote or the essence of it without looking at your notes? If so, it might be memorable.

• Does the quote advance the story? If your transition repeats the quote, consider eliminating either the transition or the quote. A good quote should follow the previous paragraph naturally without requiring a long introduction.

• Is the quote emotional or controversial enough to add interest to the story? Consider whether you might want that quote highlighted as a pull quote. If you would, it will probably enhance the story.

• Can you state the information better in your words? If so, paraphrase.

• Are you including the quote for your source or for your readers? That is the most important question of all. The readers' interests always take priority.

How to Write Quotes

On the surface, writing quotes may seem easy: You just write down what somebody else has said. But in reality, you must observe the following guidelines if you want to use quotes correctly and effectively:

- Always put commas and periods inside the quotation marks:

> "There are no exceptions to that rule," the professor said.

- A question mark and other punctuation marks go within the quotation marks if the punctuation refers to the quoted material; otherwise, they go outside the quote marks:

> He asked, "When does the semester end?"

> Who said, "I hope it ends soon"?

- Each new speaker must be quoted in a separate paragraph.

> "Never place quotes from two speakers in the same paragraph," Professor Les Polk said.
> "Even if it's short?" Janet Rojas asked.
> "Yes," Polk answered.

- Don't attribute a single quote more than once. If you have two quoted sentences from the same speaker in the same paragraph, you need only one attribution:

> "You must study your Associated Press Stylebook," the professor said. "You will have a test Tuesday on material in the first 30 pages."

- Place the attribution after the first sentence in a quote:

> "When the quote is two or more sentences in the same paragraph, attribute it after the first sentence," Carol English said. "Don't make the reader wait until the end of the paragraph to discover who is speaking."

- Attribution in the middle of a quote is acceptable but not preferable if it interrupts the thought:

> "It isn't the best way," he said, "to use a direct quote. But it is all right if the quote is very long. However, it's better to put it at the end of a complete sentence."

• When you are continuing a quote from one speaker into another paragraph, don't close the quote (with closing quotation marks) after the first paragraph. Put quotation marks at the beginning of the next quote, and attribute the quote again in the second paragraph, as in this excerpt from a story about the Supreme Court ruling on quotes:

Justice Kennedy said, "We reject the idea that any alteration beyond correction of grammar or syntax by itself proves falsity in the sense relevant to determining actual malice under the First Amendment.

"A deliberate alteration of the words uttered by the plaintiff does not equate with knowledge of falsity," he added, "unless the alteration results in a material change in the meaning conveyed by the statement."

The New York Times

• Don't string together quotes from different people. Place the attribution at the end of the quote in most cases. But when you quote a new speaker immediately after the previous one, introduce the new speaker in a new paragraph with a transition.

In this example from a story about a bus accident in which 39 students were injured, the first paragraph of quotes is correct. But look how confusing it can be to change speakers without any introduction:

"I heard a big bang and then I hit the seat in front of me," said Felicia Slaughter, 17, an 11th-grader at Henry County Senior High School. "I saw a big flash of light as soon as I hit."

"Everybody hit something— either a window or the seat in front of them," said Peggy Brooks, 16, an 11th-grader, whose left arm was in a sling. "Everybody remained pretty calm, but we started complaining about where we were hurting."

Atlanta Constitution

It's easier for the reader if you introduce the new speaker in one of two ways:

Peggy Brooks, another 11th-grader, said, "Everybody remained pretty calm. . . ."

Peggy Brooks, an 11th-grader, also was injured in the crash. "Everybody remained pretty calm," she said.

• Quotes within quotes take a single quotation mark, followed by a double quotation mark:

> The woman testified, "He ordered me to lie on the floor, and then he said, 'I'm going to kill you if you go to the police.' "

• Don't tack on long explanations for the quote. If the quote isn't clear by itself, paraphrase. For example, avoid the following:

> When asked how he learned about the fire at his apartment complex, he said, "I heard the news on the television."

> "I heard the news on the television," he said when asked how he learned about the fire at his apartment complex.

Instead, introduce the quote with a transition:

> He was at a friend's house when the fire broke out at his apartment. "I heard the news on television," he said.

• Don't overuse transitions to set up quotes. If the quote follows your previous thought naturally, you don't need to introduce it with a transition:

> One in five people over 60 has had an adverse reaction to a prescription drug, causing serious problems for 43 percent of them, a new survey says.
> "This is clearly a big public health problem and could get worse as the population ages," says gerontologist Beverly Lowe, University of Southern California in Los Angeles.

• Limit the use of partial quotes. They are acceptable when the whole quote would be cumbersome, but too many partial quotes make a story choppy. And the reader wonders what was left out. If you follow a partial quote with a full one, you must close the partial quote.

> McDonald says he sees the government as "weak and inept" and fraught with "major-league problems."
> "There's a crisis in our leadership," McDonald said.

• Limit the use of ellipses, sets of dots that indicate part of the quote is missing. Use three dots for the middle of a sentence, four (one of which is the period) for an ellipsis at the end of the sentence. Use the ellipsis when you are condensing whole quotes or long passages from which you delete several sentences. It's useful for stories about speeches or excerpts from court rulings. Be careful not to leave out material that would change the meaning of the speaker.

> Four days before he was killed, the Rev. Martin Luther King Jr. stood before 4,000 people in the still unfinished Washington Cathedral and declared: "We must find an alternative to war and bloodshed. Anyone who feels . . . that war can solve the social problems facing mankind is sleeping through a revolution."
>
> *The Washington Post*

> "We must find an alternative to war and bloodshed. . . ."

Do not use an ellipsis at the end of a quotation that closes with attribution. This is improper:

> "We must find an end to war and bloodshed . . . ," King said.

Use this instead:

> "We must find an end to war and bloodshed," King said.

• Avoid stutter quotes, quotes that repeat the transition almost verbatim:

> Officials said some of the students selling drugs were the cause of violence at the school.
> "Some of the students involved in selling drugs have been responsible for the violent incidences on campus," said School Superintendent Howard Humes.

• Avoid quotation marks around words that you want to emphasize. Unless someone said it, don't enclose it in quotes.

> The school has had a "whopping" increase in enrollment.

When to Use Attribution

All quotes must be attributed to a speaker. In addition, you need to attribute information you paraphrase.

Plagiarism   Copying the words of other writers is plagiarism, a cardinal sin in journalism. In the 1990s, several cases of plagiarism in newspapers occurred, renewing concern about this issue. In one case a reporter copied a source's quote from another newspaper but failed to attribute it to that paper. Because electronic data bases now allow ready access to many newspapers, plagiarism is easier than ever. Even if you paraphrase information you receive from other publications, you are plagiarizing if you don't attribute it.

Plagiarism is grounds for dismissal at most newspapers. So if you take information from a written publication, make sure you attribute it to that source.

When all the information you gather is from your own sources, you still need to tell the reader where you got your material. However, you don't need to attribute everything. Here are some guidelines:

• You don't need to attribute facts that are on record or are general knowledge:

| The trial will resume tomorrow. |

| A suspect has been arrested in connection with the slaying of a 16-year-old girl in Hometown last week. |

• You don't need to attribute information that you observed directly:

| The protesters, carrying signs and chanting songs, gathered in the park. |

• You don't need to attribute background information established in previous stories about the same subject:

| The defendant is accused of killing the three Overland Park women whose bodies have never been found. |

• You do need to attribute information you receive from sources if it is accusatory, opinionated and not substantiated and if you did not witness it—especially in crime and accident stories. However, you don't always have to attribute everything in the lead.

The following statement is factual, so no attribution is needed:

> A 2-year-old girl escaped injury when a mattress she was sitting on caught fire and engulfed the studio apartment at Wheatshocker Apartments in flames.

Attribution is needed here, however, because the cause of fire is accusatory and the amount of damage is speculative:

> A 2-year-old girl playing with a lighter started the fire at the Wheatshocker Apartments near Wichita State University that caused about $400,000 in damages, fire authorities said Thursday.
>
> "She was just kind of flicking it, and she caught the bedding on fire," said fire Capt. Ed. Bricknell.

The Wichita Eagle

Wording of attributions For most hard news stories, the word *said* is preferable. Although there are many synonyms for *said*, they make the reader pause. *Said* does not. Don't worry about overusing the word.

• Strictly speaking, *said,* the past tense, should be used if someone said something once. If someone always says the same thing, use *says,* the present tense. However, that rule is very restrictive. You could also just use *said* for most hard news stories and use *says* for feature stories (if *says* seems appropriate to the context). In either case, keep the tense you choose throughout the story; if you start with *says,* continue using it for the rest of the story.

• Avoid substitutions for *said,* such as *giggled, laughed* or *choked.* It's almost impossible to giggle, laugh or choke at the same time you are speaking. If you want to convey the emotion, write it this way:

> "I'm going to try out for the circus," she said, laughing.

• Use *according to* when you are referring to inanimate objects: "*according to* a study." It is acceptable to say "*according to* police" but not preferable. People talk. Use *said* or *says* when you attribute to people; *according to* is vague.

• Normal speaking order is preferable. That is, you should place *said* after the name or pronoun. If the person has a long title, *said* can be placed before the name and title. The first example is awkward, the second preferable:

> "Normal speaking order is pre-
> ferred," said the professor.

> "Normal speaking order is pre-
> ferred," the professor said.

Overview attribution   A technique that allows you to attribute information to one speaker for a few paragraphs, without attributing each statement or each paragraph, is useful when you are giving a chronology of events, as in a police story. But if you change speakers, you need to use attribution for the new speaker. Overview attribution is a brief statement followed by a colon. Here are some ways of starting an overview attribution:

> Police described the incident this
> way:

> Witnesses said this is what
> happened:

> Police gave this account:

Second references   The second time you refer to a source in your story, use the last name only. If you have several sources—or two sources with the same last name, such as a man and wife—use the full name again or an identifying phrase.

> James Jones, the director of public
> safety, was injured in a three-car
> crash yesterday. Jones was taken
> to Memorial Hospital, where he
> was treated for bruises and
> released.

If you have mentioned several other people and want to get back to Jones later in the story, remind the reader who Jones is by using his title:

> Public Safety Director Jones said
> he would return to work Monday.

Titles   When a person's title is used before the name, capitalize it, as in the preceding example. When it is used after the name, use lowercase letters:

> Police Chief Ron Olin said the
> crime rate has gone down.

> Olin, police chief of Lawrence,
> said the crime rate has gone down.

Courtesy titles Most newspapers no longer use courtesy titles—Mr., Miss, Mrs. or Ms.—before the names. There are exceptions. *The New York Times* and *The Wall Street Journal* still use courtesy titles. Other newspapers use them in obituaries. For general purposes in this book, courtesy titles will be eliminated unless they are contained in examples from newspapers that still use them. The only way you can determine whether to use them is to check the style of the newspaper for which you are writing.

Activities

1 Here are some reminders about writing a basic news story:

Lead: Ask yourself what the story is about. Try stating that in one clear sentence of fewer than 30 words.

Statement of the problem or conflict: What caused the action in the lead?

Backup for lead: Provide details about how and why.

Impact: Was there any impact on the reader? What is the significance of the story?

Background: What background was relevant to current action?

Attribution: Make sure you tell the reader where or from whom you got the information.

Ending: Put whatever information you think is appropriate at the end—the least important, the final action or the next step.

Now try writing a basic news story based on the following information, which is from a story in *The Des Moines* (Iowa) *Register:*

Who: Iowa State University officials and leaders of the Heterosexual Society

What: Officials won't permit the Heterosexual Society to be a registered campus group; officers of the group object.

When: Use yesterday for the purposes of your story, but name which day of the week came yesterday.

Where: At the university

Why: University officials say the group discriminates against homosexuals, who can't be full members.

How: Lisa Norbury Kilian, assistant dean of students, said the university turned the group down because it refuses to admit homosexuals as full members. No registered campus group can discriminate on the basis of age, color, handicap, nationality, race, religion, marital status or sexual orientation, she said.

Significance: Group officers say the decision violates their rights of free speech and freedom of association.

Attribution: Most of the comments come from De Backes, a member of the group, and from Lisa Norbury Kilian.

Backup information: Put this information in the order that you think makes sense and would be most readable:

De Backes, a senior from Decorah and a member of the Heterosexual Society, said she suspects the group already has a gay member, but she thinks he is a plant from one of the two gay campus groups. She said homosexuals can join the group's two lower levels of membership, but to be promoted to the top two levels, members must sign forms promising that they are straight.

Backes said the Heterosexual Society would bring in speakers, sponsor a heterosexual pride week and have other activities "to fight the misinformation on homosexuals and AIDS." She insisted that the university decision violates her rights of free speech and freedom of association. "We want to be a registered group because we have the right to be a registered group."

Lisa Norbury Kilian, assistant dean of students, said that giving special membership privileges and rank to only particular members of a group because of sexual orientation is against ISU policy. Except for fraternities and sororities, which are allowed to discriminate by gender, no other group can exclude a particular group from its ranks.

2 Finding questions exercise: Choose a news story that you enjoyed reading. Write a list of questions you would have asked to get the information in the story. In addition to the basic questions of who, what, when, where, why and how, devise questions that would have resulted in elaboration. Now write a rough outline for the order in which the story was written. This exercise will give you some idea of how to get information for the basic elements and how to structure the story.

3 Quotes and attribution exercise: In the first part of this exercise, check the appropriate column if you think attribution is or is not needed:

Needed	Not needed		
_____	_____	**a**	Two leading figures in the growing national debate about political correctness on American college campuses will be at the University of South Florida in Tampa tonight.
_____	_____	**b**	Dieting doesn't work for the vast majority of people.
_____	_____	**c**	A 40-year-old woman went berserk in her ex-boyfriend's apartment early Monday, shooting him to death with seven shots from two guns.

	Not	
Needed	**needed**	
_____	_____	**d** Members of a local gay rights group protested Thursday in support of a gay University of Tampa student's efforts to take an Army ROTC class.
_____	_____	**e** City council members voted unanimously Thursday to increase city fines for prostitution.
_____	_____	**f** A York College sophomore died early yesterday after drinking at a dormitory party.
_____	_____	**g** Alumni members of Skull and Bones, an all-male secret society at Yale University, have voted to admit women.

The next three statements are from the same story. You may want to read all three before making your decision.

_____	_____	**h** A Temple University student was gang raped during an off-campus party early Thursday at a fraternity house.
_____	_____	**i** Philadelphia police have arrested a fraternity member and a former student on charges that they raped the woman, 19, on a pool table in a first-floor common area.
_____	_____	**j** The university and the fraternity's national organization immediately suspended the local chapter.

In the second part of the exercise, punctuate the quotations, which are from a story by Lee Siegel of The Associated Press:

Not a direct quote: One of life's simple pleasures—a frothy glass of beer—contains incredibly complicated physical phenomena, according to scientists who studied how bubbles form and rise in the malt beverage.

Direct quote: You might think that in the several millennia that beer has been with us we would already have learned all there was to know about this curious brew Stanford University chemists Neil Shafer and Richard Zare wrote in the October issue of *Physics Today* magazine.

Direct quotes: A glass of beer reveals a remarkable interplay among gases, liquids and solids, temperature, pressure, and gravity—an interplay that is still not completely understood they wrote. Once you begin to learn about the nature of beer bubbles, you will never again look at a glass of beer quite the same way.

Partial quote (beginning with *I*): Zare said Friday that his curiosity was inspired by a friend who asked how beer bubbles work, and I couldn't stop thinking about it every time I drank a glass of beer.

Partial quote (beginning with *but*): The chemists also conducted a limited study of champagne bubbles, but it's a more expensive form of research Zare said.

Full quote: The formation of beer bubbles is very similar to the formation of rain clouds, they said, in which rain droplets grow on dust particles.

Quote continued: That's why you can make your beer bubble even more by tossing in a few grains of sugar or salt.

No quote: Why do beer bubbles rise? The answer is that the density of a carbon dioxide bubble is less than the density of the surrounding beer the scientists said.

Two full quotes (the quotes begin following the question; insert the attribution "Shafer said" where appropriate): Why do bubbles speed up as they rise? As a bubble rises, it encounters resistance or drag. But as a bubble grows, the drag force increases slower than the buoyancy force, which increases in proportion to the bubble's volume.

No quote (but insert attribution from Zare): Why does a head of foam form? Beer contains natural and added substances called surfactants. Similar organic matter on the ocean's surface helps create whitecaps on the top of waves.

No direct quote (but insert attribution from Zare): Why does beer go flat? The bubbles escape into the air if beer is left in an opened container.

Not a direct quote (but punctuate attribution from Zare): No federal government money was spent on beer research Zare said. Stanford has been the target of federal investigators recently because of misuse of government research funds.

4   Write your own story: Attend an event on your campus, and write a basic news story about it. (Look in your campus newspaper for a list of activities that will take place during the week, or check bulletin boards for notices of activities.)

COACHING
TIPS

Does your idea have a strong news element, so you can answer the question "What's new?"

Ask yourself if the story passes the "so what" test. Would the reader care?

Can you state the idea in a sentence that is focused on one central concept?

Have you considered a photograph, map, chart or other graphic illustration that would enhance your story?

Story Ideas

4

It was called "Operation Shoeleather." It wasn't an investigative project of the traditional sort. It was the Rome (Ga.) *News-Tribune's* way of investigating what the newspaper's readers wanted to read. Everyone in the newsroom, from the copy clerk to the editor, was assigned to walk around a different area of the Georgia community. They were told to chat with the mail carriers, folks on the front porch, shopkeepers and anyone else they came across to discover the concerns people had in their daily lives. The reporters and editors returned with dozens of story ideas geared to readers' interests, ranging from health to religion.

That's one way of finding story ideas. When you are in a supermarket, a shopping mall, a self-service laundry or any other gathering place, ask people what they are concerned about and what they want to read in newspapers.

Throughout the country, editors are doing just that. They are conducting focus groups, surveys and town meetings with readers and installing special telephone numbers so readers can call about their concerns. And they are tailoring the content of the news to meet those needs.

If you can't write your idea on the back of my calling card, you don't have a clear idea.

David Belasco, theater producer

Ways to Find Story Ideas

Some of the traditional ways of finding news are still important. The basic concepts for news—local interest, human interest, timeliness, unusual events, conflicts, celebrities, impact of news events—can generate story ideas. A major national or local news event might be worth a local reaction story. If you are on a college campus, you are surrounded by experts in many fields. Professors can be good sources for national stories that need a local angle or interpretation.

The primary way to get story ideas once you become a reporter, especially if you are assigned to a beat, is to contact your sources regularly and ask them what is going on in their workplace. Another way of getting story ideas is to examine records related to your beat, such as documents generated by government agencies. (Chapter 6 will provide more information about getting story ideas from sources.)

Many good stories result from observation. Do you notice anything unusual or different on campus? Photojournalists usually excel at observing people and places for good pictures. An idea for a good photograph might also be an idea for a good story.

The visual concepts are as much a part of the story idea as the verbal concept. So when reporters and editors conceive story ideas, they also need to consider presentation. Does the story need a photograph, graphic illustration (such as a chart or map) or highlights box? Think about those elements when you devise your story idea.

Here are some other suggestions for ways to find stories:

Brainstorm. Discuss ideas for stories with other students and with people in your community. What topics on campus or in your community are of interest to people? Does anyone have an unusual course, a professor worth a profile or interest in an organization that is newsworthy? What about consumer stories—how to get the best buys on books or how to get scholarships and loans?

Map the topic. Mapping is a form of brainstorming suggested by researchers who have studied the functions of the left side of the brain (the logical reasoning part) and the right side (the creative part). It is a creative process of word association.

Mapping is basically exploring different facets of a topic of interest to your readers. Draw a circle or a trunk of a tree for the main topic, and list the related ideas as spokes or branches. For example, you might want to explore whether tuition is increasing. Tuition is the topic in the center of the circle or on the trunk of the tree. The related topics might be effects on out-of-state students, where the money goes, a comparison to other colleges and so on. Once you have generated all the ideas you can that are related to the main focus, you can eliminate the ideas that don't seem worthy of a separate news story.

Another topic for possible mapping is a holiday. How many ideas can you devise for stories related to Thanksgiving, spring break or Valentine's Day?

Try this technique with the weather. If your area has had floods or an extended drought, you could try to think of all the people, businesses and other groups affected by the weather. Exhibit 4-1 shows how the topic of floods could be mapped.

Assume other points of view. This technique is similar to mapping. Take an issue and role-play to discover how others might think about it. Does that process give you an idea for a feature or a profile about someone who is affected by the issue? If the state cuts its funding to your university, how are students, programs, departments and related campus activities affected?

Another potential source of ideas is special interest groups. What groups of people don't get much coverage in your newspaper? Do minorities on your campus have concerns that could generate news stories? What problems do the elderly residents in your city have? Do women's groups in your school or town have special problems

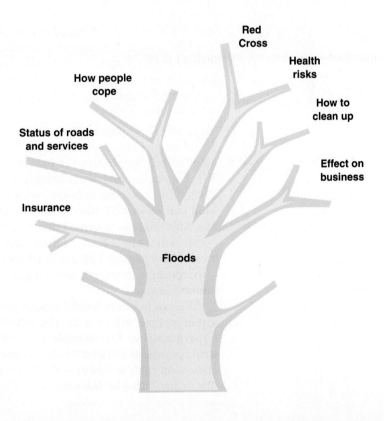

Exhibit 4-1

Story ideas generated by mapping

and interests that would make good ideas for news? What are the needs of people with disabilities? Do veterans in your community have special needs that are newsworthy? Do you have an active gay rights group on campus? Contacts with members of these groups can generate scores of story ideas.

Observe. Look at bulletin boards on campus. Look around your city. Are there new stores or buildings that are worth telling the reader about? Are there old buildings, landmarks or stores that are closing, such as a famous hangout? Does anything make you curious? Do you notice something new? Is there a program or event that might be newsworthy?

Talk to people. Ask your friends what interests them. Eavesdrop at lunch to find out what people are talking about. When you are out in the community, ask people what they read in newspapers and what they would like to read.

Check directories. Universities and many government agencies have directories listing departments and personnel. Do any people, places or programs seem newsworthy? Does your school directory list organizations or departments that sound unusual or worthy of a feature?

You could also check the yellow pages of your telephone book for ideas about interesting services and places. For example, how many escort services are advertised in your city? In Fort Lauderdale, Fla., the yellow pages listed more than 20 escort services. Dan Lovely, a former reporter at the now-defunct *Fort Lauderdale News,* began by checking out the escort services and ended up writing an investigative story about some of the escort services that were a front for a prostitution ring.

Read local newspapers. Does a news story suggest angles that could be developed into a separate story? Does it name people who could be profiled? Sometimes the best feature stories are offshoots of a breaking news story. Tom French, a reporter for the *St. Petersburg* (Fla.) *Times,* became so fascinated with a news story about a murder trial that he wrote a 10-part feature series about it called "A Cry in the Night." He even turned the story into a book, *Unanswered Cries.*

Alternatively, is there a larger story to be developed from a news event? If a nursing home in your community is cited for improper procedures, is there a larger story about problems and licensing in nursing homes?

When a big story breaks in your community, are there experts or other people affected by the problem who would be worth a separate story? For example, if the teachers in your town are on strike, consider all the different people who are affected. Is there an expert on campus or in your city who is worth a feature because of his or her views on the issue?

Almost all major stories affecting your community—such as disasters, strikes, crimes and court rulings—need follow-up stories to explain the next step or action resulting from the issue.

Read classified advertisements. Look for unusual items. Lara Gold, a reporter for the *Fort Myers* (Fla.) *News-Press,* was curious about an ad for nannies that she found in the campus newspaper when she was a student at the University of Kansas. She checked it out and discovered that the nanny agency was a thriving new business started by a local woman who was hiring college students for child-care jobs. The result: Gold wrote a business story that was published in the local newspaper's business section.

Look in the lost and found column. Is there a human interest story behind a lost pet or other item? Patricia Rojas, a reporter for *The Des Moines* (Iowa) *Register,* was scanning the classified section of her newspaper when this ad caught her attention:

> LOST WARRIOR, blue tick Coonhound, male, stupid but friendly.

"When I saw 'stupid but friendly,' I had a feeling there was a good story behind this ad," Rojas said.

There was. The dog had wandered two blocks from home and couldn't find his way back. It turned out that the dog had led a difficult life. One time he was stolen from his owner, Lisa Volrath of Des Moines, and he nearly starved after his captor abandoned him. This time he was luckier. Someone found him and took him to an animal shelter.

Rojas ended her story with this quote from Volrath after she had recovered her dog:

> "I could tell from his stupid expression that he was my dog," Volrath said.

It was just a little story, but people enjoy reading about dogs. And Rojas said her editors enjoyed her initiative in finding the story.

An advertisement for a lost pet cobra turned into a fun story for another reporter. This story could be broadened into a feature about unusual pets.

Localize national news. Is there a national story that you can apply to your area? What are the local angles? What are the reactions of people in your community? In 1990, the U.S. Department of Education ruled that colleges and universities receiving federal funds could not offer scholarships specifically designated for minority students. Several newspapers localized the story by getting reactions from officials and students in their communities.

The (Cleveland) *Plain Dealer* rated the accuracy of forecasts from weather bureaus around the country. The Associated Press distributed the story on the wires. *The Kansas City* (Mo.) *Star* then localized the story idea by checking the accuracy of weather reports in Kansas City and getting reactions from local weather forecasters.

Think about people. Is there a person who is in the news or someone who should be in the news because of his or her accomplishments? Is someone mentioned in a story as an expert worthy of a separate profile?

Can you find stories about people who have accomplished something special, triumphed over adversity or experienced pain or joy in relation to a news event or people who represent a particular aspect of a news event? Such stories often make good human interest features.

Track programs and events. Is there a campus or government program that would be of interest to your readers? Is it a new program? Is an old program approaching an anniversary? Is it one that has been particularly effective or ineffective? Is there a program that a private citizen or group is trying to establish? Is the program somehow related to the season or an event in the news? For example, is there a program that is affected by budget cuts at your university?

Holidays, news events and anniversaries of major news events also make good features. Plan ahead and think of stories related to these topics. Check your newspaper's files or microfilm of newspapers from a year ago or longer. What were some of the major stories? Do they merit follow-up stories? Good newspaper editors and reporters keep tickler files, which are organized by weeks or months to remind them about stories that should be followed. When you are reporting, especially on a beat, you should start your own tickler file so you can remind yourself about stories you should follow.

Rewrite press releases. Government agencies, organizations in your community and campus organizations issue press releases about news events. These press releases often contain ideas for features. If you are assigned to cover a specific beat, ask the key sources to send you any press releases they issue. (More about using press releases follows in this chapter.)

Follow issues and trends. Are there problems on campus or in your community that reflect national problems? Have there been a few news events recently that reflect a larger problem? For example, if four women have been attacked on campus in separate incidents, is there a larger story about rape on campus or lack of security?

When you do issue stories, make sure you have a narrow focus. Topics such as AIDS or homeless people are too broad. Focus the story on one aspect of the problem. You might do a story about the growing number of AIDS cases on your campus or a story about how your city is or isn't handling the problem of caring for AIDS patients. Or you might do a story about an aspect of the homeless problem in your city, such as an increase in the number of homeless women with children.

Be curious and concerned. These qualities, above all, will lead you to good stories.

Idea Budgets

Some story ideas are assigned by editors, but most editors expect reporters to provide their own story ideas, especially if the reporter covers a beat. Reporters need to notify their editors about stories they want to write so that editors can plan the daily and weekend newspapers.

Most newspapers use a daily "story budget," which contains a brief description of each story planned for the next day's newspaper. Each budget item begins with a "slug" (a one-word title) and is followed by a few sentences describing the story. Many newspapers also use a planning story budget, describing story ideas for the week and long-range stories.

Of course, reporters can't plan for unexpected, breaking news. Newspapers expect to respond to those stories.

The story budget also is a tool to help you focus your ideas. As you write your budget, you should be keeping the focus—the "so what" factor—in mind. Your budget is your way of selling the story idea to your editor, so you need to make it sound like an essential news story or a compelling idea.

To write a story budget, give your story a slug, and describe the idea in a paragraph or two. Include potential sources and possibilities for photos or graphics. Here's an example of a budget line by Buddy Nevins, a reporter who covered the transportation beat for the *Sun-Sentinel* in Fort Lauderdale, Fla.:

> **Pedestrians:** Broward has one of the highest rates of pedestrian deaths in the nation. One problem is that the roads haven't been designed for pedestrians, and many don't have sidewalks or crosswalks because of a lack of money. What is being done to solve the problem?
>
> Graphics: Charts, maps of worst roads

Here is an example of a budget line written by a student for the story in Chapter 1 about a new type of thermometer:

> **Thermometers:** Watkins Memorial Health Center is using a new type of thermometer, called a probe, to take patients' temperature through the ear instead of the mouth.
>
> Sources: Watkins nursing director Jody Woods and students who have had their temperature taken by the probe
>
> Graphics: Photo of a student having his or her temperature taken with the probe

Press Releases

Coaching Tips

Remember that a press release is written by an advocate for the organization. It is not a balanced news story.

Check the information with sources listed in the press release.

Seek other sources to confirm, deny or give other points of view.

A press release is an announcement or a story written by a public relations officer or employee of some organization. The organization that sends it hopes a newspaper, magazine, radio or television station will use it—either as an idea for a story or just as it is written. Videotaped press releases are also becoming popular as a way for corporations to promote their views, and some television stations have been using these prepackaged news stories.

Even though you may copy information in the release without fear of plagiarizing, you should always check the information. Good reporters use a press release only as a starting point for a story. Then they seek additional information.

Remember that a press release is not a balanced news story. It is a story to promote the organization or person in the release. Any critical or controversial information is likely to be missing.

It is not illegal to use press releases as written, but it is unethical to use them without stating that the information was from a release. Readers and viewers should not get the impression that the news was gathered by unbiased reporters. By not informing the audience that the news was produced by a promotional source, the station or newspaper jeopardizes its credibility.

In many cases, the press release contains quotes from an official or source within the organization. If you can't reach the source to get comments yourself, you may use the quotes. But you should attribute them to the press release. For example, write "the chancellor said in a press statement" or "according to a press release."

Here is an example of a press release issued by the University of Kansas public relations office and a local newspaper story that was based on it. Compare the story to the press release. What information came directly from the release, and what came from interviews? Note that the newspaper story contains more sources than the press release, including an interview with a campus police official.

Press release

A survey to measure the extent and impact of sexual violence on the University of Kansas Lawrence campus will be mailed to a random sample of students during the week of April 8.

The survey is intended to gather data about attitudes and assumptions about sexual violence at KU as well as numbers of incidents known by the responding students.

The Office of Student Affairs Research Committee is conducting the survey, developed specifically for KU, according to David Ambler, vice chancellor for student affairs. Stanford University conducted one of the first surveys on sexual violence on campuses.

KU's survey seeks to answer some of the most-asked questions about sexual violence, rape, and sexism.

KU officials expect that the facts and data from the survey will become the basis for future educational activities and programs designed to change attitudes that allow sexual violence to persist on campus and in society.

Students receiving the survey in the mail are asked to complete it anonymously and return the answer sheet in the envelope provided.

No individual, group or population has been chosen for the survey. It is a representative sample of the student body, making participation by every individual important.

Results will be released publicly during the fall 1991 semester after all data have been analyzed.

Contact:

Caryl K. Smith, associate vice chancellor for student affairs (913) 864–4060

or Jeff Weinberg, assistant vice chancellor for student affairs (913) 864-4381

Newspaper story

Comprehensive surveys about sexual violence were sent to 1,500 Kansas University students on Monday, and an official with the student affairs office today said he hoped students would take the surveys seriously.

The Office of Student Affairs Research Committee is conducting the survey. Jeff Weinberg, assistant vice chancellor for student affairs, said the survey was sent to a random sampling of students.

No individual, group or population was targeted in the survey, which is intended to gather data about attitudes and assumptions about sexual violence at KU as well as incidents known by the responding students.

Students were asked to complete the survey anonymously, and Weinberg said the mailing list already has been destroyed.

He said the Office of Institutional Research and Planning assisted student affairs with the survey, which he hopes will help KU officials determine how to confront sexual violence on campus.

"Certainly, we have been concerned about the problems of sexual violence," Weinberg said. "There's been an awful lot of time and money spent on lighting, transportation and escort services on campuses. But there's never enough money. Throwing money at the problem doesn't get to the root of the problem, which is attitude."

Students targeted in the survey will be asked about their attitudes on sexual violence, rape and sexism. Weinberg said the survey also will allow students to make any comments they wish to about sexual violence.

Weinberg said the survey is patterned after a 1988 survey at Stanford University, the final report of which he said was re-leased about eight weeks ago. However, he said KU's survey was developed specifically for the Lawrence campus.

The student affairs research committee was restructured in the summer and began reviewing literature on sexual violence in September, Weinberg said. He added that the office hopes to be able to release survey results during the fall semester.

"The most important thing is to use the facts to identify on our campus those changes that we have to make in our educational programs here," Weinberg said. "We are hoping students will take the survey as seriously as it certainly is."

Students have been asked to return the surveys by April 22.

Lt. John Mullens of the KU police department said that because the surveys are confidential, police would not be able to respond to any incidents reported in the surveys.

"The individuals would have to come to us with incidents," he said.

No rapes were reported on the KU campus during 1990. Two rapes have been reported to KU police this semester. One occurred in March, and the other occurred in mid-January and was reported later that month.

Deb Gruver, *Lawrence* (Kan.) *Journal-World*

Activities

1 Conduct an "Operation Shoeleather" survey. Talk to people on your campus and in your community about what they read or don't read in the campus or local newspaper and what kinds of stories they would like to see in their newspaper.

2 Analyze your local or campus newspaper. Try to determine its primary audience from the kinds of stories it runs. Discuss whether the newspaper includes stories targeted for certain audiences, such as college students, minorities, women and other special groups. Perhaps one student or a group could interview the editor about his or her vision of the community.

3 Identify stories in your local paper that fit the description "news you can use." List five topics of news you can use that your paper does not cover.

4 Look in your local newspaper for ideas for profiles. People used as sources might be interesting subjects for a separate story.

5 Read the classified advertising section of your newspaper and look for items that could generate stories of human interest, new businesses, trends or unusual news.

6 Write a story budget with three ideas for stories you would like to cover. Identify some sources you would interview, and consider photo or graphic possibilities. Use the story budget format in this chapter, or modify it as you or your instructor wishes.

7 Take a walking tour of your campus or your community (individually, in small groups or as a class). Write as many story ideas as you can based on your observations.

TWO

Collecting Information

Curiosity and Observation

Sources

Listening and Note-taking Skills

Interviewing Techniques

COACHING

Imagine yourself as an eyewitness at the scene of the story you are covering. How would you describe the situation if you were being interviewed?

Using all your senses, record the sights, sounds, smells and other details you can observe when you are reporting. Use concrete nouns; avoid adjectives.

When you are gathering information, ask yourself what vivid, action verbs could describe your observations.

Curiosity and
Observation

5

The blood spots made the difference.

A woman shot her boyfriend. He fled to a nearby store to seek help, and he died two hours later in a hospital.

It was just a basic news story for Martha Miller, then a police reporter. But when she went to the scene, she saw the blood spots. First Miller measured the spots with a dime. But they were larger than that. So she tried a nickel. That fit. Then she counted the spots. She wrote a hard news lead stating that the woman had shot and killed her boyfriend, and in the middle of the story she wrote this:

> Brown, who was shot several times, staggered out of the apartment and down two houses to the Waystation convenience store on Virginia Street—his path, easily traceable by 41 nickel-size blood splotches that dotted the sidewalk.

Martha Miller, *Reno* (Nev.) *Gazette-Journal*

Why bother measuring and counting the blood spots? "I was curious," said Miller, now a reporter for *The Orlando* (Fla.) *Sentinel.* "I saw them and I wanted to follow where they led. I wanted to show how he fled and that he was dripping blood. I wanted the reader to picture that."

The technique is one you learned in kindergarten: Show and tell.

You tell your readers a story by not telling them. You show it. You write it so they feel it. Use all of your senses to put the reader there. Get in the smells and the sounds.

Martha Miller, reporter,

The Orlando (Fla.) *Sentinel*

Curiosity

Martha Miller, reporter

A good reporter also possesses a trait you had in kinder-garten—curiosity. You probably badgered your parents with questions. What's that? Why? Those are still good questions for gathering news. Just add a few more: who, when, where, how and so what?

Most writing teachers tell you, "Show, don't tell." But you need to do both. To show, you need to observe. To show and tell, you need to be curious. You need to ask questions the reader will want answered in the story.

How do you know what questions to ask, what to observe and report? Start with the basics:

Who: Get the full names of people involved, complete with middle initials, and always check the spelling.

What: Get an account of what happened. In some stories, especially police stories, you may want to recount the sequence of events. You don't have to write the story chronologically, but you need to understand the sequence.

When: Note the day and time of the event.

Where: Get the location. Describe the scene.

Why: Understand what caused the event. What was the conflict and the resolution, if any?

How: Seek more information about what happened. How did it occur? In what order did events unfold?

So what: What impact did this event have on the participants? What impact could it have on readers?

Now for the harder questions. What does the reader need to know to understand and care about your story? You can't explain the event unless you understand it yourself, and you can't understand it unless you dig for answers. The key is to unleash your curiosity. Here are some techniques for developing your curiosity.

Role playing: Put yourself in the role of the reader. What makes the story important and interesting? If you were affected by this story, what would you want and need to know?

Imagine that you are a reporter for your campus newspaper. The phone rings. The caller tells you there is a fire and then hangs up. You call the fire department. A dispatcher gives you the address of the fire. It's your address. What are the first questions that come to your mind? If you have a roommate, chances are you would want to know if he or she was injured. Was anyone else in the building killed or injured? Is your cat OK? Was your apartment or room destroyed? What was the extent of the damage? What caused the fire? When did it start? How long did the building burn? Where will residents of the building live if their apartments were destroyed or heavily damaged? Then you might be concerned about other questions. How long did it take to put the fire out? Were there eyewitnesses? Who called the fire department? How quickly did the department respond? Is this the first time this building has been struck by a fire? Did the building have sprinklers? If so, did they work?

The list could go on. That's the basic concept of role playing, and it can generate scores of questions for you in many stories.

Using time lines: Another method of using curiosity to generate questions is pinning down the sequence of events. Start with the present, then go to the past and then to the future. What is happening now? How did this action develop? In what order did the event evolve? What is the next step?

Questions involving time sequence will give you answers for background and chronology in your stories.

Being a detective: Imagine that you are a detective at the scene of a crime, a protest rally, or any other event that involves a mystery or conflict. What questions would you ask to solve the crime or the problem? These questions will center on what happened, the motives, consequences and clues to uncovering the truth.

Brainstorming and mapping: These are the same techniques discussed in Chapter 4, but you can use them to generate reporting questions as well. Make a list of all the questions that come to your mind about your story idea. Using all of the techniques above, just start thinking of key points you want to cover in the story.

Observation

Nothing prepared David Remnick for what he saw when he went to the little town of Spitak in Armenia five days after a massive earthquake in 1988. In fact, that's exactly what he wrote in this story, which is based largely on his observations:

In Spitak, the living are searching for the dead.

One young man in his 20s walked up and down the rows of coffins today, opening their lids, looking for his brother. Finally, he found what he did not want to see, and at the sight of his brother, he climbed into the coffin with him, ready to join the dead.

Nothing prepares you for Spitak. Nothing prepares you for a small town stadium filled with coffins and bodies left out in the cold. A town of 20,000, surrounded by the Armenian Caucasus Mountains, Spitak was a beautiful place to live a week ago, people here say. But then the earth moved beneath it, and in minutes Spitak was destroyed. At least half its people are dead. Eight kindergartens, eight schools, factories for soap, sugar, and elevators—all of them are rubble.

On every street, the curbs are lined with coffins and the detritus of ordinary life: a stack of Armenian novels, a pile of cabbages, a boot, a half-eaten loaf of bread, a torn reproduction of a portrait. And everywhere the smell is of smoke and snow and the dead, rotting in their makeshift coffins of rough pine.

David Remnick, *The Washington Post*

Nothing prepares the reader to see, think and care about a story as well as such details. They help a writer show and tell.

Good writers must be good reporters first. And good reporters show and tell by observing and gathering details with all their senses: sight, sound, smell, and less often, taste and touch.

That's what Ron Davis did to reveal conditions in the Laclede County Jail:

"Hey! Turn up the damn heat!"

The voice ricochets down the concrete and steel halls of the Laclede County Jail and is immediately followed by a series of violent booms, as an inmate pounds on the walls. Something is wrong with the heating system at the Laclede County Jail. But what's new? The inmates say this happens every night.

It's 38 degrees outside on this March night, and the men in the upstairs security cellblock are too cold. They always are; no matter how high the guard at the main level dispatch desk cranks the thermostat, the heat never makes it to the security wing. . . .

In the basement is the drunk tank, a cavernous bunker that reeks of urine and vomit. A hole in the floor serves as toilet and trash can.

The tank is empty tonight, but its stench overpowers the smell of food from the adjoining pantry. . . .

Ron Davis, *The* (Springfield, Mo.) *News-Leader*

Observation does not have to be limited to tragedies and the grim side of life. You can use your observation powers in any story—from a fire scene to a county fair.

Mary Ann Lickteig turned an ordinary story about the Iowa state fair into a fun one by observing these details:

Off in an exhibit room, Nancy Pelley, a home economist from Tone Brothers spice company, looked over five cakes. One of them looked back. It had teeth and a tongue hanging out between the layers. "Isn't that something," Pelley mused. "What category is that?"

It was the Ugliest Cake category. A green one with gummy worms on top won first place. Eight-year-old Jonathan Eddy of Des Moines named his entry "Green Mean Wormy Machine."

To satisfy the requirement to include his recipe, Jonathan penciled on an attached card: "I made a cake. I frosted my cake. I made it ugly."

Mary Ann Lickteig, *The Des Moines* (Iowa) *Register*

The Show-in-Action Technique

If you want the reader to visualize your source or the scene, one of the best techniques is to show the person in action. This technique is more commonly used in feature stories with descriptive writing. But it also can be used in hard news stories or for a soft lead on a news story. Regardless of the type of story, you need good observation skills. Here is an example of the show-in-action technique:

The softball lands with a disappointing thud on the gym floor.

"Come on, Dan. You can do better."

This is an important practice for Dan Piper. In one week the eighth-grader will represent his Ankeny school at a track meet. If he is to win a blue ribbon, he must improve.

Jim Mollison knows this. He is coaching Piper in the long jump and the softball throw. He urges Piper to throw the ball from one end of the gym into a net halfway across it.

"Try it again," he said.

By now a crowd has gathered, about two dozen junior high school students on their way to gym class. They are healthy, robust students, for whom throwing a softball is about as hard as chewing gum, but they care about this throw because they know how much effort it requires.

Dan Piper, 16, is not like other students. He is mentally retarded, born with Down's syndrome.

Jim Mollison, 13, is not like other coaches. He's an eighth-grader, a bright student, a talented athlete and Dan Piper's best friend. He is helping Piper prepare for the Special Olympics.

The students root along the sidelines.

"Go, Dan!"

"You can do it, buddy!"

"All the way, Danny boy!"

Piper grimaces, reaches back and fires. Like most youngsters born with Down's syndrome, a genetic defect caused by an additional chromosome, his features are slightly out of proportion—the eyes set a little too close together, the ears a little too small, the tongue a little too large. He does not simply set forward and fling a softball. He heaves his entire body into the motion.

Higher and higher the ball soars, not just into the net but over it, landing a mere two linoleum tiles short of the far wall. Piper raises his arms in triumph, then slaps hands with Jim Mollison.

Ken Fuson, *The Des Moines Register*

Hard Versus Soft News

You need good observation for both hard news and feature stories. Although descriptive detail based on observation is more common in feature stories, such as the stories about the county fair and the Special Olympics, you can use the same observation techniques in gathering information for hard news stories. Stories about weather disasters, fires and other events where the scene is crucial especially lend themselves to descriptive detail based on observation. At a protest, use observation to report what signs the protesters carried and what they were chanting. At a trial, use observation to help the reader see how the defendant and other people in the courtroom reacted.

Here is an example of descriptive detail based on observation of eyewitnesses and reporters in a hard news story about a train wreck. SEPTA stands for Southeastern Pennsylvania Transportation

Authority, well-known to Philadelphians, so this acronym is not defined in this story.

A SEPTA train crowded with morning rush-hour passengers derailed beneath Market Street yesterday, killing three people and injuring more than 100 others in the underground wreckage.

In what sounded like scenes from a mine disaster, witnesses described flashlights playing in the darkness over knots of terrified victims, a rail car disemboweled by tunnel girders and passengers' cries for help in the damp cold just on the west side of the Schuylkill River.

Amid the subterranean chaos of the deadliest SEPTA disaster ever, doctors wearing green scrubs and firefighters in yellow helmets used knives and power tools to cut flesh and metal in order to free trapped victims, while a policeman asked surviving passengers to pray. . . .

Physicians and paramedics wriggled through the jagged wreckage to inject victims they could barely reach with pain-killing morphine and saline solutions.

Michael E. Ruane, *The Philadelphia Inquirer*

Fact Versus Opinion

Observing action and the details that you will include in your story is not the same as voicing your opinion. You need to use your senses to gather the information, but you should not express your opinions about what you saw. In news stories, all opinions, judgments and accusations must be attributed to a source. Reporters should keep their views out of the story. The only places for reporters' opinions or interpretations are in columns, stories labeled "analysis" or first-person stories, which are usually labeled or preceded by an editor's note.

A few newspapers have been allowing reporters to insert first-person references (*I* or *me*) in feature stories, but that is a technique usually reserved for magazines. Most newspaper editors insist that the reporter stay out of the story.

In the previous examples, the writers reported the sights, sounds and smells they observed. Those observations were factual— evidence of conditions that anyone on the scene could have observed. The writers let the readers form their own opinions.

The left-hand column that follows is an example of description from a story about a plane crash. Most of this story is detail based on observation. The second paragraph contains a vivid description of the crash site. Note that an opinion is expressed in the last paragraph, although it is attributed to someone on the scene, not to the reporter. In contrast, the right-hand column shows how not to write the story. Note the improper use of the first person (inserting the reporter in the story). Opinion that is not attributed to someone else is printed in italics.

Appropriate	Inappropriate
A US Air jetliner landing at Los Angeles International Airport collided on the ground with a Sky-West commuter plane Friday night, creating a fiery tangle of wreckage. At least 12 people were killed, 24 were injured and 21 were missing, officials said.	A US Air jetliner landing at Los Angeles International Airport collided on the ground with a Sky-West commuter plane Friday night, creating a fiery tangle of wreckage *that was horrifying to behold.*
Orange flames boiled up from the fuselage, and a huge column of smoke towered over the airport. Spotlights and the lights from police, fire and other rescue vehicles silhouetted the smoldering wreckage against the darkened sky.	*I saw* orange flames that boiled up from the fuselage, and a huge column of smoke towered over the airport. *It was eery to see* the spotlights from police and other rescue vehicles silhouetting the smoldering wreckage against the darkened sky.
"It was a sight beyond belief," said Brett Lyles, 23, of San Francisco. . . .	*It was a frightening sight.*

Los Angeles Times

Observation to Find Questions

Use observation as a reporting tool, not just as a writing tool. When you observe action or details at a scene, what questions occur to you? Imagine that you are walking through your state capitol and notice something as simple as two men changing the light bulbs. What questions would your observation raise? Is that a story? It is if the story shows how taxpayers' money is spent. It is if you are as curious and observant as Robert Zausner, who wrote this story:

HARRISBURG, Pa. — How many state employees does it take to change a light bulb?

Only two.

But they also need a $9,447 machine to reach the socket, at least in part of the East Wing of the Capitol complex.

Although the massive building has been opened for more than two years, there was not until recently any way to reach some of the light fixtures, particularly those situated in the middle of the expansive glass ceilings and far away from any walls.

"With the new wing, there isn't anything to lean a ladder against," explained Pamela DiSalvo, press secretary for the Department of General Services.

To help shed light, the department bought a "hijacker," a device that is able to straddle obstacles on the ground—like the Senate's granite-encased fountains—and hoist a bulb changer to heights up to 40 feet.

How did the state change those bulbs before it got the machine? It didn't.

It takes two workers to change a light bulb using the hijacker, one to screw in the bulb and the other to watch.

Robert Zausner, *The Philadelphia Inquirer*

Observation for Visual Presentation

When you are at the scene of an accident or look at a photograph, many of the basic reporting questions are likely to come to mind. What may be less likely to occur to you are ideas for a good photograph or graphic illustration. Does the story need a diagram to explain how something works? Would a photo or graphic eliminate the need for lengthy explanation in your story? What do you see that you would want the reader to see as well? Don't forget to observe locations, and pinpoint them by proximity to major streets or specific distances from a site that the artist can interpret and the reader can understand. You need to see your story as well as hear it when you collect information.

Activities

1 Discover the questions (a reporting exercise): Read the following story to discover how other reporters gather information. Make a list of questions you think the reporters asked. Note which information came from sources and which from observation. List the sources. How would you have gotten the same information? Does the story answer the basic five W's, how and so what questions? Would you have asked other questions?

Explosion levels home; five are hurt

An apparent gas leak is blamed for the blast, which damages houses in two square blocks

ST. PETERSBURG, Fla.—A spectacular explosion triggered by an apparent propane gas leak reduced a north St. Petersburg house to "toothpicks" Thursday, rattling windows several miles away and injuring five people.

The blast leveled the house, sent debris flying hundreds of feet in the air and damaged at least 12 other houses in two square blocks. Damage to four homes was so severe that resi-

dents were evacuated, authorities said.

"I ran out there and saw the house in the street blown apart and in flames," said Gail Logsdon, who lives a few houses north of the explosion. "It was louder than some chemical plants that I've heard blown up in Niagara Falls."

A woman inside the house told authorities the explosion occurred after she tried to light the stove.

"She remembers lighting the oven or lighting the stove," said St. Petersburg District Fire Chief Skip Hawkins. "All indications are there was some kind of gas leak."

Neighbors and rescuers pulled the woman and a man from inside the house in the 4300 block of 20th Street N shortly after the explosion about 6:30 p.m., authorities said. The two were taken to Bayfront Medical Center.

"If they don't go to church on Sunday, they ought to," Hawkins said. "They were extremely fortunate."

At least three other people were injured by the shattered glass and flying debris, Hawkins said.

The sound of the explosion jarred people several miles away. Immediately afterward, hundreds of frightened residents in the neighborhood ran out of their homes toward the shattered house.

"It looked like toothpicks," said Gail Logsdon's husband, Lyndell.

Residents began digging through the debris, trying to rescue the man and woman, who had bought the house only a couple of days before, neighbors said.

"I was holding the flashlight, and we were digging the rubble out around them," said Darrel Flint. "There were five or six people around digging them out. . . . We asked them (the couple) if there was anyone else in there, and they said there wasn't. I hope to God there wasn't anyone else in there."

Authorities could not identify the couple late Thursday night.

Hawkins said the woman suffered second-degree burns over a third of her body. She was being flown late Thursday from Bayfront Medical Center to the burn unit at Tampa General Hospital, he said. She was in very critical condition, a spokesman at Bayfront said.

The man, who suffered second-degree burns over 10 percent of his body, was expected to remain at Bayfront, Hawkins said. He was in critical but stable condition.

A man who lived just north of the couple was taken to Bayfront with wounds from flying glass. Flint said the man was talking on the telephone in front of the window when the explosion occurred.

Two other people were treated at the scene for injuries caused by flying debris. Chunks of the house were blown at least 200 yards away.

"I heard it before I saw it," said Janice Zimmerman, who was sitting on her steps across the street from the explosion. "I was getting out of the way of the stuff coming at me. My whole house is damaged. Nails are actually coming out of my bedroom walls."

Gail Evans, who lives a couple of doors south of the demolished house, said her home also was seriously damaged.

"It blew my door and windows out," she said. "It scared the hell out of me."

Although four homes were evacuated, officials were uncertain how many people had to be moved. The American Red Cross said late Thursday that evacuees would be taken to a nearby motel.

The damaged windows were covered with plastic sheets, and a bulldozer and a city road sweeper were brought to clear the road. Fire officials also had to remove boards dangling from trees.

Mark Journey and Karen Datko
St. Petersburg (Fla.) *Times*

2 Role playing for curiosity training: You have lent your car to a friend. You find out that your friend has had an accident with your car. Write a list of questions that come to your mind. Now add any questions you might need to make the incident a news story. Write a list of the sources you would contact as a reporter.

3 Observation for curiosity training: You are gathering information for a graphic about a fire at your apartment, home or residence hall. What information do you need so the artist can draw a map pinpointing the location of the fire? Try to draw a location map.

4 Sequence for curiosity training: Write directions for a recipe for any food you know how to prepare. Be specific. First give the ingredients. Then give the directions for preparation in the proper sequence.

5 Detective role for curiosity training: Interview a detective, or invite a member of the police force to class. Ask how the officer investigates a crime, what kinds of questions he or she asks, what reports must be filled out and what information they contain. What information must police release to the public, and what can they withhold?

A group of people at the University of Kansas who are advocating choice in the abortion controversy
Courtesy of Philip Meiring

6   Brainstorming for curiosity training: Imagine that you are a reporter and your editor gives you the following assignments with only this limited information. What questions can you brainstorm for each incident?

a   A man has been shot in a local bar that is a popular student hangout.

b   Two people have been injured in a three-car crash on a main street in your community.

c   Minority students on your campus are staging a protest.

7   Description for observation training: Describe in detail some statue, painting or special landmark at your school. Or describe the scene in the photo above showing an abortion-rights demonstration.

8 More description for observation training: Without looking at the person next to you, write a brief paragraph describing what he or she is wearing and everything else you can remember about the person's appearance.

9 Show-in-action technique for observation training: Write a descriptive paragraph about a professor you have had. Use the show-in-action technique to describe the professor's mannerisms, characteristic expressions and other details about the professor's appearance.

10 Observation: Describe the office of a source you have interviewed or of a professor you confer with frequently. List at least 10 items that are memorable. Do not include such standard items as desk and bookcase.

11 More observation: Write a few paragraphs based on this premise: You have been missing for a week, and a reporter has come to your apartment, home or room to write about your disappearance. The story might start as follows: "The room was just as she (or he) left it." Include only those details that reveal your personality or habits.

12 Blindfold experiment for observation training: This exercise is designed to help you increase your awareness through your senses of hearing, smell and touch. Pair up with a classmate, and cover your eyes with a blindfold. Your partner will be your guide. As you walk around your campus together, tell your partner what you hear, smell and feel. Try to be as specific as possible. Your partner should take notes on your observations. Then let your partner put on the blindfold and describe his or her observations to you. When you return to class, write a descriptive paragraph about your experience.

13 Graphic exercise for observation training: Imagine that a rare painting was stolen from a museum on your campus or in your city but was discovered the next day in a recycling bin or large trash receptacle on your campus. Go to that site (choose any area containing a large bin), and collect all the information you can for a location map or graphic illustration describing exactly where the painting was found. Write a list of information that you would give to an artist so he or she could draw a location map. Make sure you include nearby streets, the number of feet or yards from a recognizable spot, dimensions of the garbage bin, and other details you think would be helpful to the artist. Then using your own directions, draw a location map to test whether you have gathered good information.

COACHING

TIPS

Use the matchmaking technique: Ask one source to recommend another one who is knowledgeable about the subject you are researching.

Check newspaper clips or data bases before you begin your reporting.

Check any records or documents related to your story.

Sources

6

Mark Potter calls it his "bible." He takes it with him everywhere. It is his source book, a 7-by-9-inch address book, so worn that it is held together by sturdy strips of packing tape. Potter, an investigative reporter for the ABC television network, says he couldn't function without his source book. It is so crucial to his job that he keeps a duplicate in his home.

Potter cross-indexes his source book three ways: by name of the source, occupation and location. If he wants to contact an FBI agent he once interviewed in Detroit but whose name he may have forgotten, Potter looks it up under FBI or Detroit. Under each listing, Potter records the source's address and telephone numbers for work and home.

But getting the home phone numbers is not always easy, especially for police officers who keep their numbers unlisted. So Potter asks for the information this way: "How can I reach you in the off-hours?" That way, if the source does not want to reveal a home number, he or she can give you an option of another way to be contacted, Potter said. It avoids placing a negative tone on the interview.

Potter and many other reporters also note in their source books some personal information, such as sources' birthdays, favorite pastimes or anything else that would be helpful to remember.

It's not too early in your career for you to start a source book. The people you interview in college, such as professors who are experts in foreign policy or the economy, may be good sources for stories later in your career.

But how do you get sources, and how do you know which ones to use for a given story?

If you are looking for authoritative sources on anything, there are people of all nationalities. . . . The feedback from readers—whites and minorities—about the use of multicultural sources has been good. It's not only the right thing from a standpoint of fairness and equality, it's smart. The opportunities are there, and anyone who fails to exploit them is stupid.

Taylor Buckley, senior editor, *USA Today*

Where to Find Sources

A good reporter needs human sources, people to interview, and written sources, such as records and library materials. Scott Thurm used both types of sources to write a story that won the Pulitzer Prize in 1989 when he was part of a *Courier-Journal* team in Louisville, Ky., investigating a school bus crash caused by a drunken driver. Thurm's editor asked him to investigate whether the structure of the bus had contributed to the deaths of the 27 people on the bus.

Thurm said that within a few hours he and his partner, Hunt Helm, had more sources than he could imagine. At a conference of the Investigative Reporters and Editors, he described how he developed them. "We began with nothing," he said. "We drew up a list of possible factors: Was the bus too crowded? We looked at seat belts, regulation of school buses and maintenance. Then we got lucky. A former school superintendent called and said, 'You ought to look at the seats.' They were highly flammable."

That tip led to many others. "For every issue, I'm convinced there is a group of people crying in the wilderness about the issue," Thurm said. "You've got to find them. In this case the people were school transportation directors."

One way he acquired those sources was through computerized collections of articles from newspapers, magazines and trade journals. He asked the newspaper librarian to find articles in the data base about school buses. He called up the author of one article, interviewed him and then asked the author to recommend other people who knew about school bus safety. "One guy had a bad bus fire so he was working on research about seats," Thurm said. "Another was worrying about exits. Another was worrying about gas tanks. By the end of the first morning, I had more avenues than I could pursue in a month just by going from one person to another."

Other sources were survivors of the bus crash, whom he was reluctant to interview at first. "I can hardly explain how traumatized they were. A lot of them had lost siblings, best friends. I would say, 'Look, I understand what you've been through. We're trying to do some stories that can prevent this from happening to other people.' I was shocked by the amount of cooperation we got. We did a detailed reconstruction of the accident based on survivors."

He also relied heavily on records of the National Transportation Safety Board. As a result of his investigation and other stories in the *Courier-Journal* series, the state of Kentucky changed regulations for school buses.

Human Sources

Very often, what separates news writing from other types of writing is the reliance on human sources. Information from eyewitnesses and participants lends immediacy to a story, and direct quotes make a story interesting. Here are some ways to find human sources:

Newspaper files: All newspapers have reference libraries, which used to be called "morgues," where clips of stories that have been published in the paper are stored. At many newspapers, these clips are now filed in a computer data base. Before you begin reporting for any assignment, your first step is to check the clips. There you can find the names of people cited in previous stories about the subject. If you are writing a story about a topic but have no idea whom to contact, check magazine articles as well as other clips on the subject.

When you are assigned to a breaking news event, such as a fire or accident, you may not have time to check the clips before you leave the office. But you should check them before you begin writing. The building that burned may have had problems with sprinkler systems or previous fires in the past.

The same recommendation applies to crime stories. A suspect arrested on charges may have been arrested previously for the same or other charges. Caution: Newspaper library files may not be up-to-date, and follow-up stories may not have been written about crime suspects. If you find a clip about a suspect's previous arrest, make sure you find out if the charges were dropped or what happened in the case.

Plagiarism, using information from published or broadcast material and passing it off as your own work, was mentioned in Chapter 3 but is worth mentioning again here because it is such a serious offense. If you are using information from other newspapers, magazines, broadcasts or other published sources, you must attribute the publication where the material appeared.

Sponsorship: Suppose you find a source who is reluctant to talk to you, such as a police official. You can use a technique that Mark Potter calls "sponsorship," getting someone who knows and trusts you to recommend you to the new source.

For example, when Potter was working on a story about the problems of Haitians in Miami, the Haitian refugees were reluctant to talk to him. Many of them were illegal aliens. Potter said they thought he was an immigration official who was seeking to deport them. So he asked a community social worker who had gained the trust of several Haitians to recommend him to one of the Haitians. The social worker introduced him to a Haitian named Pierre, but he

didn't have the information Potter wanted. However, Pierre said his brother-in-law might help, and Pierre introduced Potter to him. After establishing trust with the brother-in-law, Potter asked him to get other Haitians to talk to him. And that's how he got the people he needed for his story.

You also can use sponsorship as a self-introduction technique when you set up an interview. Give your name and say, "Chief Joe Smith suggested I call you" or "Chief Joe Smith gave me your name." Then explain the purpose for your call.

Self-sponsorship: Nancy Tracy, a former reporter for *The Hartford* (Conn.) *Courant,* was in trouble. She was working on a follow-up story about three people who survived when the Mianus River Bridge collapsed and their vehicles plunged into the river. But a key source, Eileen Weldon, wouldn't talk to her or anyone else in the media. Weldon had severe injuries and was tired of press coverage.

So Tracy tried self-sponsorship, a way of recommending herself. "I'm going to send you some clips of other stories I have done to show you that I am a very sensitive reporter," she told Weldon. "Please read them. I'll call you in a few days. If you don't think I can be fair, I won't ever bother you again."

Tracy got the interview. Her clips "sponsored" her.

Matchmaking: You have found a source, and you are interviewing her or him. But you want the names of other sources for the story. Try matchmaking, a form of sponsorship. Ask the source who else might know something about the subject or have an opposing point of view. Who else is involved in the issue? Ask how you can reach those people. Your source may even provide telephone numbers of others who are close to the subject.

Primary and secondary sources: When you are conducting an interview, if your source says something about another person, particularly if it is derogatory or controversial, make sure you check with that second person. The first source's statements not only could be wrong, they could also be libelous. You should even check out written information about sources to make sure it is accurate. In most cases, except when your secondary sources are famous people, such as the president or celebrities who cannot be contacted, do not use someone's name in a story without making an attempt to check with that person.

Up/down principle: If you want to learn how to sweep floors, talk to a janitor, not to the corporation president. The same principle is involved in reporting a story. If you want to get the most accurate and vivid information about a story, talk to the people who were directly involved. Go *down* the organizational ladder. Contact the police officer who wrote the report (the name is listed on a police report), the researcher who conducted the study or the source closest to an incident.

Another version of the down-the-ladder principle is to be kind to secretaries. Remember their names, and be genuinely friendly. A good secretary can be like a pit bull guarding the boss. If you want to reach an official as a source, your first source is the person who schedules that official's time.

After you have interviewed people down the ladder, go up the ladder of the organization. Who is the next supervisor with responsibility? Who is the official with ultimate responsibility for the department or organization?

You can proceed either way. You can start with a top official and then go to the primary people or the reverse. In many cases, police officers and people in corporations, government and other bureaucratic organizations will refuse to talk to you until you have been cleared by higher authorities. As a result, you may often have no choice but to start with the top officials.

Anonymous Sources

Many people will be willing to talk to you if you promise not to use their names. An anonymous source is one who remains unnamed. But should you make this promise? Most editors today would say no, unless there is no other way to get the information. And even then, many editors would refuse to grant that immunity from identification. The more you rely on unnamed sources, the less credibility your story has.

If you must use anonymous sources because you have no other alternative, you should check the information with other sources, preferably ones who will allow use of their names, and check documents.

When using unnamed sources, you may identify the person with a vague reference, such as "according to one official." Or you might give the person a pseudonym, a false name. Although most editors discourage pseudonyms, they are sometimes allowed in feature stories about sensitive subjects such as rape. But they are rarely used in hard news stories. It is preferable to use no name or a first name only. If you use a full-name pseudonym, which is not preferred, you should check your local telephone directories to make sure you aren't using the name of someone in your community. And in all cases, you must tell the reader that this is a false name to protect the identity of the source.

Janet Cooke didn't do that. And she touched off a furor in the newspaper industry that persists, years after the incident. Cooke, then a reporter for *The Washington Post,* won the Pulitzer Prize in 1981 for a story called "Jimmy's World," about an 8-year-old heroin addict. There was only one problem. Jimmy didn't exist. When she first discussed the story with her editors, she said she had located the child's mother, who was reluctant to talk. Her editors said she could grant the mother anonymity. Cooke turned in a compelling story about the child and his mother. But when Cooke won the Pulitzer and was profiled in newspapers, some discrepancies in her resume were discovered. That led to questions about her story. She ultimately admitted that she had made up the story about Jimmy and his mother. The *Post* returned the Pulitzer, and Cooke resigned in disgrace.

Cooke's story wasn't based on an anonymous source; it was a false source. But the impact was a crisis of credibility for the press. Newspapers throughout the country began developing policies against using pseudonyms, and many editors banned the use of anonymous sources altogether. But the policy is difficult to enforce, especially since many people, such as officials in Washington, refuse to be quoted by name for fear of revealing information their supervisors might not like. *The Washington Post* relied heavily on anonymous sources for its investigative stories in the early 1970s about the Watergate scandal, which led to the resignation of President Nixon. The *Post* still uses many unnamed sources. But most reporters, especially investigative reporters, use anonymous sources primarily for tips that can be confirmed with documents and other on-the-record sources.

Many sources, named or unnamed, have their own agenda and want to manipulate reporters so the sources can promote their cause. For fairness and balance, it is crucial for reporters to check with other sources to confirm, deny or provide other points of view.

Promises   Dan Cohen had an agenda, and he made the issue of anonymous sources even more complicated. He was a public relations executive. In 1982 he gave reporters from the Minneapolis *Star Tribune* and the *St. Paul* (Minn.) *Pioneer Press* damaging information about a candidate for lieutenant governor in Minnesota on the condition that they would not reveal him as the source. The information was a record of the candidate's shoplifting conviction that was no longer available in court records because it had been expunged (erased by court order). Reporters agreed to grant Cohen anonymity. But editors of the two newspapers overruled the reporters and insisted on printing Cohen's name in the story. The editors decided that since Cohen was working for the opposing political party, the readers had a right to know the source of the information.

Cohen sued. He claimed that the newspapers had violated an oral contract of confidentiality and that, as a result, he had suffered harm by losing his job. A jury at the first trial level agreed that a reporter's promise of confidentiality is as legally binding as an oral contract. The newspaper appealed and lost. The case went all the way to the U.S. Supreme Court, which ruled in 1991 that the First Amendment does not protect journalists from being sued if they break promises of confidentiality. The high court sent the case back to the Minnesota Supreme Court for a ruling on damages, and Cohen was awarded $200,000.

If you promise a source anonymity, you are bound by your promise. Before you agree to anything, however, you should check with your editors to determine the policies of your organization.

The *Star Tribune* established policies regarding anonymity and other relationships with sources as a result of Dan Cohen's lawsuit. In the policy, the newspaper says: "Always review the ground rules of a promise with the source before you receive the information, so that both persons completely understand the conditions. Do not make vague statements, such as 'I probably won't use your name,' and don't rely on a term such as 'off the record,' which means different things to different people."

The terms "anonymous source" and "confidential source" are used interchangeably by most people. *The Wall Street Journal,* however, makes a distinction. The newspaper considers an anonymous source a person whose name is not used in the story "but whose identity we may later need to disclose—in the event of a libel suit, for example." The newspaper defines a confidential source as one whose name will not be published and whose identity will not be revealed in court, even if the reporter has to go to jail to protect the source. Sources, however, may not recognize such distinctions.

Even when sources agree to be identified, they often ask for anonymity for portions of the interview. They'll say, "This is off the record." Sometimes they aren't even aware of what the term means.

On and off the record Here are some definitions of the terms used most often to establish ground rules in an interview:

On the record: The source agrees that all information can be used in a news story and that he or she can be identified as the source of it. The easiest way to establish this understanding is to identify yourself as a reporter and immediately state your purpose for the interview. For example, "I am a reporter for *The Campus Review,* and I'm calling to interview you about . . ." If you are interviewing people who are not accustomed to dealing with the media, you may need to remind the source during the interview that you are quoting him or her about the material, especially if you are writing about controversial issues. Such a reminder may jeopardize your chances of using some of the material, but it is better to take that chance during the interview than later in a courtroom after you have been sued.

Off the record: The information from this source may not be used at all. If you can get the same information from another source, you may use it, but you may not attribute it to the source who told it to you off the record.

Not for attribution: You may use the information as background, but you may not identify the source.

Background: This is similar to the term "not for attribution." Generally, it means that you may use the information but can't attribute it. Some reporters define background as the ability to use the information with a general attribution, such as "a city official said." If you are in doubt during the interview, ask the source how you can identify her or him, and give the specific wording you intend to use.

Deep background: This term is rarely used or understood by most sources except for officials in Washington, D.C. It means you may use the material for your information only but may not attribute it at all, not even with a general term, such as "government official."

Multicultural Sources

How you deal with sources is one problem. Which sources you choose is another important factor in gathering news. For example, can you imagine a modern newsroom without women? Today, when 60 percent of the journalism students are female, it may be difficult for you to conceive of a newspaper without the opinions of women. But in many newsrooms, women don't have key managerial positions, and several studies show that women are not quoted or featured as often as men in news stories. Do women have different views from men about how news should be covered? Perhaps not, in some cases. But you and your readers will never know if you don't seek their views.

The same is true for minority groups. The overwhelming amount of news about minorities is negative and promotes stereotypes, according to a series of articles on the subject by David Shaw, media critic for the *Los Angeles Times*. "If all one knew about real-life blacks and Latinos in particular was what one read in the newspaper or saw on television news . . . one would scarcely be aware that there is a large and growing middle class in both cultures, going to work, getting married, having children, paying taxes, going on vacation, and buying books and VCRs and microwave ovens," Shaw wrote.

And that's the problem. If a racial disturbance occurs in your community, you would seek opinions of community leaders representing the groups involved. But would you seek opinions of African-Americans (the term preferred by many blacks), Latinos and Asian-Americans who are experts in various fields for other stories?

Reporters from *USA Today* do. The newspaper's editorial page features a standing quote by the founder, Allen H. Neuharth, which says, "*USA Today* hopes to serve as a forum for better understanding and unity to help make the USA truly one nation." To do that, the newspaper urges reporters to make an effort to get views in all news stories from people of both sexes and various ethnic and racial groups.

"It comes up in every story conference or in every photo/graphic assignment," said J. Taylor Buckley Jr., senior editor at *USA Today.* "If you are doing a story on the new techniques of orthodonture, it's just as easy to find a black kid with braces as a white kid. The feedback from readers—whites and minorities—about the use of multicultural sources has been good. It's not only the right thing from a standpoint of fairness and equality, it's smart. The opportunities are there, and anyone who fails to exploit them is stupid.

"In the early days of the newspaper in our effort to just get gender diversity, the editor would tear up pages if they didn't feature women," Buckley said. "If you are looking for authoritative sources on anything, there are people of all nationalities. Over the years we have accumulated those kinds of sources. We have a committee on diversity that is consolidating a source book."

Like reporters from *USA Today,* if you start your source book now and accumulate multicultural sources, you will have them when you need them for future stories.

A related issue is the identification of people in newspaper stories as black or some other ethnicity. Almost all newspapers have policies against mentioning a person's race or ethnic background unless it is relevant to the story. To show that it uses multicultural sources, *USA Today* prints pictures, especially in columns containing readers' points of view.

Written Sources

As mentioned earlier, the search for human sources starts in the newspaper library. You can find many additional clues for human sources and other information from a variety of written sources.

Telephone Directories

The white and yellow pages of telephone books are primary places to locate sources. Most local telephone books also contain information about city and county government agencies, utilities, and other frequently used services.

Cross-directories

These directories list residents of a community three ways: by name, address and telephone number. Imagine that you are on deadline and have the address of a woman whose house is on fire and that you want to reach her neighbors for comments. How can you do this if you don't know the neighbors' names? You can look in the cross-directory under the address you have. The adjacent homes will be listed first by address, with names and telephone numbers of the occupants beside the address (unless they have unlisted telephone numbers). If you have a phone number but not the name, check the section for phone numbers.

The cross-directory is one of the most useful ways of locating people for comment when you can't go to the scene. These directories are published by realtors in most major communities and are kept in most newsrooms. If you don't have access to one, your local library should; you can ask the reference librarian to look up the information you need.

Libraries

Your local public library and your college library contain a wealth of source material to help you find background about a story. Some of the most useful reference works are *The Reader's Guide to Periodical Literature,* encyclopedias, almanacs, and other books of facts, population data and financial records of major corporations. Most college and university libraries also have a section devoted to federal and state documents and publications. In this section you can find transcripts of congressional hearings, publications from federal and state agencies, and reports from all sorts of government offices.

Data Bases

A data base is a collection of information. The term now generally refers to massive collections of information stored in computers. Many newspapers subscribe to data bases containing newspaper and magazine stories compiled by a commercial company. Many public records are also stored in data bases. (Both types are discussed later in more detail.)

For daily news stories such as meetings, local events and other breaking news, checking a data base is too time-consuming. But when you are seeking background for an in-depth story or feature, it is worth checking one. For instance, if you are working on an in-depth story about date rape on college campuses, a data base check would be helpful. By reading other stories, you can get ideas for an angle on your story or find expert sources to contact.

An increasingly popular type of reporting, called "computer-assisted journalism," involves the use of huge data banks of statistics and other information. Instead of sifting through paper records to find information, many reporters are now using their computers, with special software, to do complicated searches and analyses of records that are available in computerized form.

For example, if you want to find out who earns the highest salaries in each department at your university or college, you could spend days sifting through a printed version of the budget and trying to compare salaries. But if the budget is available on a data base, you can use a computer program to analyze this information for you in minutes.

The best way to learn how to use a data base is to go to the library and ask for assistance. Each data base has a different set of instructions; many include charges for use.

Some of the data bases most frequently used by newspapers and most often found in libraries are these:

NEXIS: Provided by Mead Data Central of Dayton, Ohio. This collection of newspaper, business and trade sources contains the full text of about 25 newspapers, including *The New York Times,* and 100 magazines.

LEXIS: Also provided by Mead Data Central. The legal version of NEXIS contains the text of federal court cases and information about case law.

VU/TEXT: Provided by a company of the same name in Philadelphia, Pa. The largest newspaper data bank in the United States has the full text of more than 70 newspapers and 160 regional business journals. It also provides stories from news wire services.

Data Times: Operated by Dow Jones (the company that owns *The Wall Street Journal*) and based in Oklahoma City, Okla. This data base provides the full text of many regional, national and international news stories as well as news wire, magazine and financial data bases. It includes the text of more than 50 major metropolitan newspapers, such as *The Washington Post, Newsday, St. Petersburg* (Fla.) *Times, Seattle Times* and *USA Today.* It also provides information from industry trade magazines, such as publications about trucking, beverages and mining.

The possibilities for investigative journalism and thorough reporting are enormous with computer-assisted journalism, and this type of reporting is expected to grow as more journalists gain the expertise and equipment to analyze the data.

Public Records

Many government records, such as data from the U.S. Census Bureau and documents from state and local agencies, may be obtained from data bases consisting of public records. Often they are available only on nine-track tape, which requires a special drive and storage capacity in a personal computer. The hardest part of using such data bases may be convincing public officials to release the computer-taped records. You may have to file a request under the Freedom of Information Act (which is explained later in the chapter).

That is what Mike McGraw and Jeff Taylor did to receive 8.2 million records about farm programs from the U.S. Department of Agriculture. With the help of their newspaper's data base expert, Gregory Reeves, they spent 16 months analyzing those records and

Jeff Taylor (left) and Mike McGraw (center) on the day The Kansas City *(Mo.)* Star *won the Pulitzer Prize for national reporting, for a series about the U.S. Department of Agriculture.*

Courtesy of Tim Janicke/
The Kansas City Star

conducting hundreds of interviews, which resulted in a seven-part series about abuses in the USDA. They won the Pulitzer Prize in 1992 for their efforts.

For example, they analyzed all records of USDA meat inspection sites, which are responsible for the nation's 7,000 meat-packing plants:

Poor sanitation and failure to control rodents and insects remain major problems in the meat-packing industry nationwide, a computer survey by the Kansas City Star shows. . . . Of the 137 problem plants chosen for government review, 133—or 97 percent—were cited for sanitation problems.

Mike McGraw and Jeff Taylor,
The Kansas City (Mo.) *Star*

They also analyzed the data base of taxpayer-assisted subsidies to farmers, which are supposed to be limited to $50,000 per farmer:

The Kansas City Star reviewed all farm payments and refunds last year (1990) in all 50 states and U.S. territories. But the newspaper's study found that nearly 8,000 farms last year exceeded the $50,000 in payments. Of those, nearly 1,300 collected $100,000 or more; some collected more than half a million dollars. . . .

Stevens County, Kan., has exactly 300 farms, at least according to the U.S. farm census. But last year the Agriculture Department sent checks to 1,342 "farmers" there.

That's four times as many farmers as farms. It appears that phantom farmers must be working the prairie.

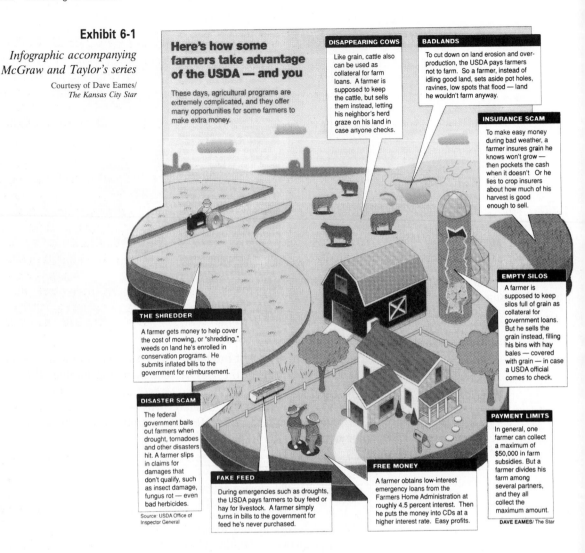

Here's how some farmers take advantage of the USDA — and you

These days, agricultural programs are extremely complicated, and they offer many opportunities for some farmers to make extra money.

DISAPPEARING COWS

Like grain, cattle also can be used as collateral for farm loans. A farmer is supposed to keep the cattle, but sells them instead, letting his neighbor's herd graze on his land in case anyone checks.

BADLANDS

To cut down on land erosion and over-production, the USDA pays farmers not to farm. So a farmer, instead of idling good land, sets aside pot holes, ravines, low spots that flood — land he wouldn't farm anyway.

INSURANCE SCAM

To make easy money during bad weather, a farmer insures grain he knows won't grow — then pockets the cash when it doesn't Or he lies to crop insurers about how much of his harvest is good enough to sell.

EMPTY SILOS

A farmer is supposed to keep silos full of grain as collateral for government loans. But he sells the grain instead, filling his bins with hay bales — covered with grain — in case a USDA official comes to check.

THE SHREDDER

A farmer gets money to help cover the cost of mowing, or "shredding," weeds on land he's enrolled in conservation programs. He submits inflated bills to the government for reimbursement.

DISASTER SCAM

The federal government bails out farmers when drought, tornadoes and other disasters hit. A farmer slips in claims for damages that don't qualify, such as insect damage, fungus rot — even bad herbicides.

Source: USDA Office of Inspector General

FAKE FEED

During emergencies such as droughts, the USDA pays farmers to buy feed or hay for livestock. A farmer simply turns in bills to the government for feed he's never purchased.

FREE MONEY

A farmer obtains low-interest emergency loans from the Farmers Home Administration at roughly 4.5 percent interest. Then he puts the money into CDs at a higher interest rate. Easy profits.

PAYMENT LIMITS

In general, one farmer can collect a maximum of $50,000 in farm subsidies. But a farmer divides his farm among several partners, and they all collect the maximum amount.

DAVE EAMES/ The Star

Exhibit 6-1 is an infographic illustrating some of the abuses McGraw and Taylor described in their series.

Fire officials' inspection reports, city building records, police reports and other records are crucial sources. Not only do they provide detail about investigations, but they also give names of people to contact. When police investigate an accident or a crime, they fill out reports with details of the scene and crucial information about the people involved, including names, addresses, birth dates, physical descriptions and other material. Most records are public.

The most complete listing of where and how to find records is *The Reporter's Handbook: An Investigator's Guide to Documents and Techniques,* edited by John Ullmann and Jan Colbert and written by members of Investigative Reporters and Editors, Inc.

The following list mentions just a few of the public records that should be available to you locally. In addition, government offices in your state capital contain records from all state agencies, including your university if it is state-owned. Federal offices in a state capital contain many records of federal agencies and of federally funded programs in your locale. The location of these records may vary from city to city, and access may also vary.

Real estate records: Mortgages, deeds (which record the property owners, purchase date and sale price in some states), the legal property description, indexes listing previous property owners, and commercial property inventories (lists of everything the commercial property owner has, such as trucks, supplies, equipment, etc.) are available in the Register of Deeds office. This office also has maps showing all the property in the county and individual maps called "plats," which show the zoning of each piece of property. Records for tax rates and assessed value of the property are located in the county assessor's office. If you don't have a property description or know what property your subject owns, the county clerk's office has a listing of who owns what.

Voter registration records: These records, located in the county clerk's office, list the person's political party if he or she is a registered voter, as well as the person's address and date of birth. They also list telephone numbers. In some cases, people who have unlisted telephone numbers may have listed their numbers on these records.

Fish and game licenses: These are also recorded in the county clerk's office.

Salaries of county employees: The salaries are listed by position only (not by employees' names) in the county clerk's office. In some counties or cities, names may be included.

County government expenses: These can also be found in the county clerk's office.

Corporate records: Articles of incorporation, which list the officers of the corporation and the date the company registered with the state, are very useful if you are trying to find out who the company officers are. Articles of incorporation are located in the Register of Deeds office or in the state office that regulates corporations.

Court records: Filings in all civil and criminal court cases except juvenile cases are open to the public. They are located in your county courthouse.

Military records: You can find out the details of individuals' military service in the Register of Deeds office in some municipalities, but only for people who registered for the service in that county.

Otherwise, you have to file a request under the Freedom of Information Act to the individual branch of the service.

Personal property loans: If a person has taken out a loan over $1,000 or bought something on time, such as a stereo, worth more than $1,000, the information could be on file under the Uniform Commercial Code listings kept in your county courthouse.

Tax payments or delinquent tax records: These records are kept in the county treasurer's office.

Motor vehicle registrations: These records and the personal property tax are on file in the county treasurer's office.

Building inspection records and housing permits: These are available in the city's building inspection and housing department. Also available there are all the complaints that have been filed against a property owner, which are useful for stories on substandard housing. This office also has records on all permits issued for construction or building improvements.

City commission meeting records, local ordinances and resolutions: The city clerk's office keeps these records.

City expenses: Information about purchase orders, accounts payable, the inventory of city agencies, budgets, expenditures and the like are available in the city's finance department. Records of purchase orders and accounts payable are extremely useful if you are investigating the expenditures of any city department or the actions involving any contract the city has with a vendor or builder.

Public works records: Plans for public works projects—such as sewers, traffic signals and traffic counts—should be available in the public works department of your municipality.

Fire department records: These include records of all fire alarms, calls (including response times), fire inspections, and firearms owners and registration (which may be in a different location in some cities). Also on file, but not available to the public, are personnel records, including pension records and other items of a personal nature. Salaries, however, are public record. These are in the fire department or in your city or county clerk's office.

Police records: Criminal offense reports, statistics of crime, accident reports and driving records are in the local police department and the sheriff's department. Records of ongoing investigations generally are not available to the public.

Utility records: Water records—such as bacterial counts, water production, chemical usage, and other items pertaining to the city's water and sewage operations—are available in the city utilities department.

School district records: Almost all information pertaining to the expenditure of public school funds—including purchase orders, payroll records, audits, bids and contracts—is available from the school district. Personnel records of employees are also available in limited form. Names, addresses, home phone numbers, locations of employment, social security numbers, birth dates, dates hired and work records are available, but information about the employee work performance and other personal information is not public. Information about students, other than confirmation that they are enrolled, is not public.

An example of a records search   The assignment for this records search was to compile as much information as possible about a person without talking to sources. All information had to be from records, but the reporter was allowed to drive by the person's house and use observation. The information is not written in story form; it is simply a report of the information gained from records.

Bonnie Short, the writer who conducted this search, chose to investigate a state senator. She visited the house to get the description of the outside, but the description of the inside comes from land records. For elected officials, information on campaign contributions is usually on file in the state or county office. Short called the senator's office and asked for a copy of the records. In addition, she found biographical information about the senator in the Kansas Legislative Handbook in the library. Almost all states have legislative directories containing basic biographical data about state officials.

Here is Short's report:

The quiet tree-lined residential street in historical old Lawrence echoes thoughts of days gone by. The large two-and-a-half story masonry and frame house at 737 Indiana Street was built in 1906 and belongs to Winton Allen Winter Jr. and Mary Boyd Winter.

The dark brown shingled house with white trim sits across three lots in the middle of the block. The stone foundation and plaster walls are reminiscent of homes built around the turn of the century. Large oaks provide shade from the Kansas sun, and a massive porch stretches across the front of the house. Red and yellow tulips border the front flower bed, and a white flowering tree adds a touch of spring to the side yard. A swing set and fenced play area in the back yard make a perfect place for their three daughters—Katie, Molly and Elizabeth—to play. A drive off the rear alley leads to a detached garage. Two speed boats sit behind the garage, covered for protection from the winter months and awaiting the family's summer fun.

The house has nine rooms, including five bedrooms, a family room, and two and one-half baths as well as an attic and full basement. Carpet covers the majority of the house, which is cooled in the summer by central air and heated in the winter with gas.

A large oak front door with leaded glass makes an inviting entrance. Two stone hitching posts flank the front sidewalk and signal the way to welcome guests.

Winton and Mary Winter are the third owners since 1934 of the Indiana property in the Lane's First Addition. They bought the property from Richard A. Barber, an agent and power of attorney for Jane Barber, et al. The deed was recorded on Jan. 23, 1986.

They have two outstanding mortgages on the property, totaling $100,000. The first, for $75,000, is with Standard Mutual Life Insurance Company and was taken out on Dec. 3, 1986. The second, for $25,000, is with People's National Bank and was taken out June 1, 1988. They pay

$62.50 per year to the state for mortgage registration.

Reappraisal in 1990 increased the assessed value of the home $18,300, from $142,600 to $160,900. The land is valued at $15,900. With the tax rate in Lawrence at 125.80 mills (a mill equals $1 per every $1,000 of assessed property value), in 1990 Winter will pay $2,669.48 in taxes, based on 12 percent of the market value—$21,220.

Winter and his wife jointly own a 1988 Dodge and paid $555.46 in Douglas County property tax in 1989. A 1979 Chevrolet is registered in Winton's name, and he paid $37.86 in property tax last year. Their insurance company is West America Insurance Company.

Winton was born April 19, 1953. His father was Winton Allen Winter Sr., also of Lawrence. The elder Winton was born Aug. 20, 1930, and served in the Korean War and received the Korean Service medal. The younger Winton is married to Mary Boyd Winter, who was born Nov. 24, 1953. Both are registered Republicans and belong to Alvamar Country Club.

In 1984 Jerome A. Smith and Beverly Smith deeded to the Winter School Preservation, Inc., a not-for-profit corporation, 1.75 acres of land near Ottawa as a gift. Wint Winter is listed as the second owner of the property.

The property is on a secondary artery with access off a paved road. A small frame utility building is the only structure on the property, which has no utility hookups. The market value of the property totals $2,700, including $2,100 in land value and $600 in value on the shed.

Winter received his B.S. degree from the University of Kansas in 1975 and his J.D. in 1978. He is an officer, director and stockholder in the Lawrence law firm of Stevens, Brand, Lungstrum, Golden and Winter, located in the First National Bank Building on Massachusetts. He is a director and stockholder of Winter Land and Cattle, Ltd., Ottawa.

First appointed to the Kansas Senate in 1982, he was elected in 1984. In the 1988 general election he defeated Democrat Michael C. DuPree with 67 percent of the vote. Winter received

campaign contributions in 1988 totaling $23,909 and had expenditures of $20,748. The total political committee, business and union campaign contributions were $12,225.

Since becoming a state senator, Winter has served as chairperson of the Economic Development and Special Claims Against the State committees. He has been vice chairperson of the Governmental Organizations committee and a member of the Judiciary, Local Government, State Building Construction, and Ways and Means committees.

In addition to being a member of the American Bar Association, Winter is on the board of directors of the Boys Club of Lawrence, Lawrence United Fund and The Shelter, Inc. He is a member of the Chamber of Commerce, Kansas Bar Association, Kansas University Alumni Association and Rotary Club.

Bonnie Short

The Freedom of Information Act   The Freedom of Information Act was established by Congress in 1966 to make federal records available to the public. It applies only to federal documents. In addition, the act allows for several exemptions that prohibit the release of documents. Records classified by the government because their release would endanger national defense or foreign policy are exempted. So are certain internal policies and personnel matters in federal agencies, as well as a number of records involving law enforcement investigations.

In many cases, the document you request comes with information blacked out or cut out. Some documents look like paper doll cutouts by the time they are released. If an agency refuses to release documents you have requested through the FOIA, you may appeal the decision.

Another drawback to using the FOIA is that it is time-consuming. Although an agency is required by law to respond to your request within 10 working days, delays are common. However, many reporters have found the FOIA invaluable, and the documents they have received have led to major investigative stories.

Tom Shields is one of those reporters. In 1990 he wrote a four-part series about the dangers of flying over the Grand Canyon. More than 260 people have died in at least 106 aircraft crashes in the canyon area since the mid-1950s, many in sightseeing planes. The series, which won the prestigious Roy W. Howard Award for Public Service, was based primarily on documents Shields received by using the FOIA.

Shields, a reporter for the *Tucson* (Ariz.) *Citizen,* said that at one point the Federal Aviation Administration sent him a box containing 26 pounds of documents that included records of all plane crashes in the Grand Canyon. The documents also included memos and letters from various agencies detailing causes of the crashes, disciplinary action that was taken, names of pilots and other information that proved invaluable.

Shields said he had been dealing with the FAA about this series for a while before he filed the request. "I'm great at bugging people," he said. "I'll call every day if I have to. But I wasn't getting anywhere. Finally, this guy in a Los Angeles regional office said you won't get anything unless you file a request, so I did. They want you to be as specific as possible. The FAA covers all air safety in the country, so that's a broad field. I narrowed it down to air safety in the Grand Canyon area. They sent me everything they had, including all these letters they had answered, memos from congressmen who had complained and records of all crashes.

"It was fun going through it," Shields said. "A lot of the documents were on technical things that didn't mean a lot. It's easy to get rid of the stuff you can't use. But mixed in with that was a lot of good stuff."

Here's an example of how Shields incorporated public records into his stories:

On Oct. 15, 1987, a Boeing 727 jet owned by the late millionaire publisher Malcolm Forbes flew low in canyon airspace.

Forbes' plane was carrying Chinese VIPs and U.S. State Department officers from the Kennedy Space Center at Cape Canaveral, Fla., to Burbank, Calif. One of the passengers, the son of a Chinese leader, asked to see the Grand Canyon, according to a report Wimmer L. Coder, chief pilot for Forbes, made to the National Park Service.

Coder, who said his airplane was on a "diplomatic mission," rerouted the flight to accommodate the request.

FAA investigators later told the park service they could not prove Forbes' pilot violated any regulations. Consequently no legal action was taken, park service records showed.

Tom Shields, *Tucson Citizen*

Shields said he tried to contact people named in the records. "If you have a document, you can call people and get better information from them." In the Forbes' case, he said he tracked down the pilot but learned that he had died. So he went with the material he had from the records.

Shields also received scores of documents from the National Transportation Safety Board, but he did not need to file an FOIA request for that agency. Sometimes it's best to first ask for something directly, he said.

It is also a good idea to check first and make sure you are contacting the appropriate agency for your request. For questions or more advice, you can call the libel and FOI hotline, 24 hours a day, seven days a week: 800-F-FOI-AID.

To file your request, you must write to the agency. Be sure to write "Freedom of Information Request" on the envelope and on the letter. You do not have to explain your reason for the request. The agency may charge for copying and processing fees, but if you are not using the material for commercial purposes and the material is likely to contribute to an understanding of government operations, you may be entitled to a fee waiver.

You can use a form letter for your request. The following sample is recommended by the Society of Professional Journalists:

[Date]

[Agency head or Freedom of Information Officer]
[Agency]
[City, state, Zip Code]

Freedom of Information Act Request

Dear [FOI Officer]:

This is a request under the federal Freedom of Information Act.

I request that a copy of the following documents [or documents containing the following information] be provided to me. [Identify the documents or information as specifically as possible.]

In order to help determine my status to assess fees, you should know that I am [insert a suitable description of the requester and the purpose of the request, such as

a representative of the news media affiliated with the newspaper (magazine, television station, etc.), and this request is made as part of news gathering and not for a commercial use.

affiliated with an educational or noncommercial scientific institution, and this request is made for a scholarly or scientific purpose and not for a commercial use.

an individual seeking information for personal use and not for a commercial use.

affiliated with a private corporation and seeking information for use in the company's business.]

[Optional] I am willing to pay fees for this request up to a maximum of [dollar amount]. If you estimate that the fees will exceed this limit, please inform me first.

[Optional] I request a waiver of all fees for this request. Disclosure of the requested information is in the public interest because it is likely to contribute significantly to public understanding of the operations or activities of government and is not primarily in my commercial interest. [Include a specific explanation.]

Thank you for your consideration of this request.

Sincerely,

[Your name]
[Address]
[Optional telephone number]

If you prefer to be contacted by mail, omit your telephone number.

Sources for Beat Reporting

A beat is a specific area of coverage; it can be the entire municipality or parts of the government, such as the police department, the school board or the city officials. It can be a topical beat, such as environment, business, minorities or social services. However it is defined, if it is your beat, you are expected to know what is happening, what has happened, and what will happen in that department or about that topic.

If you are a good beat reporter, your sources eventually will call you to let you know what news might be of interest. But first you need to cultivate those sources. The easiest way is to meet them and tell them that you want to check with them regularly for news about their work. Then check with them every day or every week. Some of the techniques for developing sources and ideas, mentioned earlier in this chapter and in Chapter 4, are the same for developing a beat.

Imagine that you are just starting as a reporter at a newspaper and your beat is to cover a municipality that is unfamiliar to you. Here are some tips for starting a municipal beat; if you have a more specific beat, you can apply these techniques to your area of coverage.

Use shoe leather. Get to know your community or the people in the agency you cover. Take a walking tour of the community. Talk to people. Eat where the politicians and the city employees eat or socialize after work. Get your hair cut by the barber or beautician who has been in town a long time. Ask people what they are interested in and what they want to read in their newspaper. Get a map. Cruise the streets. See where the rich and poor, famous and infamous people live.

If you have a campus beat, introduce yourself to the officials, department heads, or leaders of a department or an organization. Tell them that you are interested in what they do and are seeking story ideas on a regular basis. In many cases, the people on your beat will want the coverage.

Let your fingers do the walking. Read the classified pages of your telephone book. How many churches are there of each denomination? Are massage parlors, astrologers or other unusual services advertised? Check the municipal services, sometimes listed in a separate section. Is there a poison control center or a government agency that sounds interesting? A quick scan of the classified section of your telephone book can give you some idea about your community.

Study the classifieds. Check newspaper classified sections, such as the real estate section. What is for sale? What prices are the houses? This information will give you some idea of the economic climate of the community. Maybe there is a story about an area of town where many homes are for sale. If so, why? Check the personal ads. Sometimes you'll find a touching story. Check the rewards for lost dogs, cats, birds, and snakes or unusual pets. And check the legal notices. They'll tell you what the city must advertise, such as notices for meetings or items the city wants to buy.

Plan for the future. Read the news. Are interesting people mentioned in news stories who are worth profiles? Are there briefs in the newspaper that are worth features? Are ideas tucked into a news story that need exploring or follow-up stories? Start your own idea file.

Visit the library. You may not have time to check out books for recreational reading, but the local librarian is often a good source for information.

Check bulletin boards. Visit the offices or agencies you cover, and read the notices on bulletin boards. You will find notices for job openings and other interesting information that could lead to news and feature stories.

Check with your predecessor. If the person who previously covered your beat is still at the newspaper, ask for a briefing about the beat and for key sources.

Visit the morgue. The newspaper morgue, now called a library or resource room, is a starting place for your beat and for every story you write. Check clips on topics related to your beat. When you find clips about unsolved murders or other issues, consider an update story.

Visit the real morgue. Get to know the county or city coroner or medical examiner. She or he is an invaluable source, especially if you are doing police reporting. The coroner does the autopsy reports, which provide crucial information. The coroner may also be a good source for features about how crimes are solved.

Be a tourist. Visit the historical society, the chamber of commerce and other community agencies. Find the places of interest, and investigate what they were years ago. You might develop angles for features. At the very least, you will gain some understanding of your community.

Press for press releases. Get on mailing lists. Call the city or town clerk, and get the releases from your city and county government or from the agency you cover. Call the public relations officers of agencies and businesses in your community. Introduce yourself. Tell them you are interested in ideas for stories. It's their job to provide them. You don't have to use their handouts, but having them will give you ideas about what is happening in your community. Call agencies like senior citizen organizations, the Red Cross, churches and social service organizations, and make sure you are on their mailing lists for announcements, reports and news.

Find out who's in charge. Be kind to the folks who prepare the memos for officials. Get to know them, and use their names when you see them or call their offices. Talk to the janitors, the security guards, the people behind the scenes. They know what is going on, and they can be sources for tips. Meet the officials, of course, and then find out who heads the unions and professional organizations in the schools and government. The leaders of these organizations know what is going on behind the scenes. They also have stories from the workers' point of view. Use the up/down reporting principle: Go up and down the organizational ladder.

Hit records. Know how and where to find records. Start with the city or county clerk, who will direct you to municipal offices where records are available. Visit the courthouse, and familiarize yourself with the filing system there by asking the clerks for help. These are public records, and it's the clerks' job to serve the public.

Write a source book. Write names and telephone numbers for everyone you interview, call or meet on your beat. Develop a filing system and a cross-listing system. Put a memo after each name. If a source tells you something personal about a child or a family member who is ill, make a note and call in a few weeks to find out how the person is doing. Or mention the person the next time you talk to your source. Be thoughtful. Your source will appreciate your interest and be more receptive when dealing with you.

Activities

1 Cross-directory: Imagine that the mayor of your town, another city official or a university official has disappeared. You want to talk to members of his or her family and to the neighbors. Find the missing person's telephone number in the cross-directory. Now find three neighbors you could interview.

2 Data bases: Select a topic for a feature story about an issue on your campus, such as date rape, racial tensions on college campuses, alcohol bans, political activism or such health issues as sexually transmitted diseases among college students. Now go to your library and use a data base to find stories about your topic. Make note of any national experts on the subject and any statistical material or reports you would find helpful in your story.

3 Get copies of a police report, a university study, or any other report that has been released at your school or in your community. Make note of the primary sources (officers, investigators or researchers) you would contact.

4 Make a list of multicultural sources at your college or university who are experts in a field such as foreign policy, Mideast relations, the environment or any other subject.

5 Sponsorship: Select a topic that would require you to interview sources in your community who might be reluctant to talk to you. Or just choose a topic for any story that would require several sources. Whom would you contact as a primary source to sponsor you to other people you need to interview? Where would you start your reporting? Make a list of sources who would help introduce you to others related to your topic.

6 Beat reporting:

a Select a beat you would like to cover for your campus newspaper. List at least five sources you would contact for story ideas.

b Read clips or consider some recent stories that have been written about this beat. Write ideas for three follow-up stories you might do.

7 Conduct a record search of a person, preferably a politician or other person in your community who owns property. Your task is to construct a paper-trail profile. Try to find out all you can about the person without ever talking to him or her. However, you could drive by the person's home to observe the property and include that information in your report. Write the profile based only on records and observation. You may be surprised how much you can write. Here are some suggestions for records that should be available to you.

Land records, which should include a complete description of the person's house

Court records of criminal and civil suits, possible marriage or divorce, or even birth records

Delinquent tax records

Corporation records for ownership of personal property or corporation papers (if applicable)

Records of voter registration, auto registration and tax liens

Educational background, including curriculum vitae for university employees

Financial disclosure (for politicians)

8 Write an FOIA request for some information from a federal agency that funds a program in your school or community.

COACHING

Write your observations in your notes; include specific details.

Write questions in notebook margins or on notebook covers as they occur to you during the interview.

Mark the information in your notes, such as quotes and facts, that you plan to use when you write the story.

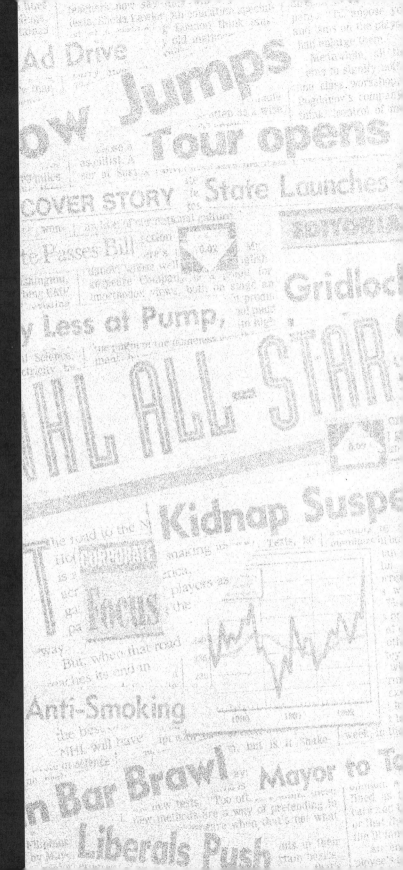

7

Listening and Note-taking Skills

Truman Capote knew how to be a good listener. He didn't take notes during his interviews for his book *In Cold Blood*. Nor did he use a tape recorder. He was convinced that a notebook or a tape recorder would inhibit his sources. "People would reveal themselves, he maintained, only in seemingly casual conversations," wrote his biographer, Gerald Clark.

With his childhood friend, Nelle Harper Lee, Capote conducted scores of in-depth interviews for the book, a nonfiction story recounting how two men murdered a family in rural Kansas. Each night Capote and Lee would return to their hotel and write notes about the interviews they had conducted that day. "Each wrote a separate version of the day's interviews; then they compared notes over drinks and dinner. . . . When their combined memory failed, as it sometimes did, they went back and asked their questions in a slightly different way. On occasion they talked to the same person three times in one day," Clark wrote in his book *Capote: A Biography*.

That technique is impractical for a reporter on a daily newspaper. And in these days, when the credibility of newspapers is under attack, trying to reconstruct interviews and direct quotes from memory is downright dangerous.

But Capote said he trained himself to be a good listener. "I have a fantastic memory to begin with," he said in an interview with Charles Ruas, author of *Conversations with*

It is the disease of not listening, the malady of not marking, that I am troubled withal.

William Shakespeare,

King Henry IV

American Writers. "I can repeat almost verbatim any conversation up to as long as eight hours. I could never have written *In Cold Blood* if I had ever produced a pencil, much less a tape recorder."

The Pros and Cons of Tape Recorders

Capote's objections to using tape recorders are well-founded. A tape recorder is not a substitute for good notes. Tapes can break, and machines can fail you when you need them most. They can inhibit a source. They can also prevent you from taking good notes if you rely on them too much. And tape recorders can't pick up observations—a smile, a nervous tic, a source's appearance or mannerisms. But they can be useful.

If you want to get the exact wording of quotes, or if you are interviewing a source about a controversial subject, a tape recorder is beneficial. But you shouldn't play back the entire tape and transcribe it before you write your story. That is too time-consuming. If you use a tape recorder, scan the tape until you get to the quotes you need.

Before you begin taping your interview, follow some etiquette. Start your interview with basic introductions—who you are and why you are there—and some opening conversation. To put the source at ease, you might even ask a question or two before you ask the source if he or she would object to the recorder. Then, if the source agrees to allow the recorder, don't place the machine directly in her or his face. Put it off to the side of the desk or table, where it is not so intrusive.

If you want to record a telephone interview, be aware of the laws in your state. Eleven states prohibit tape-recorded conversations without the consent of the person being taped: California, Florida, Georgia, Illinois, Maryland, Massachusetts, Montana, New Hampshire, Oregon, Pennsylvania and Washington. Other states mandate that only one person must be aware of the taping, either the reporter or the person being interviewed.

But you can't secretly tape any conversation between two other people when you are not a part of the discourse. For example, if you are on an extension phone and neither party knows you are taping the conversation, you are violating a federal law against wiretapping. The Federal Wiretap Statute provides for penalties of up to $10,000 in fines and up to five years in prison.

The most ethical approach is to let your source know you are taping the interview, except in a very few situations. For example, if you are conducting an undercover investigation in a state where the one-party rule applies, you could tape a conversation without knowledge of the source. However, most editors consider the use of deception or other undercover techniques a last resort.

Listening Tips

Before you write notes or record conversations, you should follow Capote's example and develop good listening skills. Here are some tips:

Focus on the "hear" and now. Concentrate on what the source is saying now, not on what you will ask next. One of the major obstacles to good listening is poor concentration caused by worrying about what you will say instead of focusing on what the source is saying. Your next question will be better if you have heard the answer to your last one.

Practice conversational listening. Base your next question on the last sentence or thought the source expressed, as though you were having a conversation with your friend. If you want to move to another topic, you can do so either with a transition—"on another subject"—or by just asking the question. But if you are really paying attention, the order of your questions will be more compatible with the source's trend of thought.

Practice critical listening. Evaluate what the source is saying as you hear it. Listen on one level for facts, on another for good quotes and on a third level for elaboration and substantiation. Is the source making a point clearly and supporting it? Do you understand the point? If not, ask the source to repeat, elaborate or define the meaning. If you listen for meaning, you can direct the interview instead of letting the source control it.

Be quiet. Whose interview is this anyway? Do not try to impress the source with what you know. You can't quote yourself. Let the source explain a point, even if you understand it, so you can get information in the source's words.

Be responsive. Make eye contact frequently so your source knows you are listening. Nod, smile, say yes, mumble "uh-huh," or look confused. Just let the source know you are paying attention. If you don't understand something, say so. "Why? How? I don't understand" and "Please explain" are good follow-up reporting questions based on good listening. Conversely, if the source makes a strong point or gives you a great quote, you might smile or nod affirmatively, encouraging the source to continue.

Listen for what isn't said. Is the source avoiding a topic? Who or what isn't the source talking about—a family member (in a personal profile), a close official, a crucial part of his or her background? Sometimes what is omitted from a conversation is more revealing than what is included.

Listen with your eyes. What kind of body language is the source displaying? Is the source fidgeting or showing signs of nervousness at some point in the interview? Is the source smiling, frowning or exhibiting discomfort when you ask certain questions? Does his or her mood change during the interview? Are these telltale signs that the source may be lying or withholding information? Observation can be a good listening tool.

Be polite. If the source starts to ramble or give you irrelevant information, don't interrupt. Wait for the source to pause briefly, and then you can change the subject.

Block out personal intrusions. You've had a bad day, your car broke down, you failed a test, or you have some emotional concerns. Make a willful effort to block out these personal thoughts. They intrude on your concentration while you are trying to listen. Your problems will still be there when the interview is over. The source will not.

Note-taking Tips

When Foster Davis was a writing coach at *The Charlotte* (N.C.) *Observer,* he checked reporters' notes to determine if problems in the stories originated in the reporting process. "The quality of stories has something to do with the quality of notes," said Davis, now managing editor of the *St. Louis* (Mo.) *Post-Dispatch*. "Writing is the least important part of it; everything that leads up to it is what matters."

Davis said he looked at notes to see if they were legible and if they included names and dates as well as reporters' observations. "When the notes said 'trees,' were they specific trees? Were the notebooks dated? Were exact titles spelled out? Detail is what makes the difference between good and bad notes," he said.

Davis learned from personal experience. He used to take very brief notes, but one day he noticed another reporter taking voluminous notes. Davis started doing the same thing, mostly out of embarrassment, he said. Then he noticed that his stories had become much more vivid.

Detailed notes give you this advantage: When you begin writing your story, you may need more information than you anticipated during the reporting process.

When you take notes can be as important as how you take them. Note taking can make some sources nervous. If you are dealing with people who are not accustomed to being interviewed, start your interview slowly by asking a few non-threatening questions. After you have established some rapport with the source, take out your notebook.

Here are some tips to help you take good notes:

Concentrate. When you hear a good quote or the start of one, write rapidly. Then concentrate on what you have just heard and block out everything else until you have written the quote. Even if you are concentrating on a previous thought, you will still hear what is being said. So if the person says something better than the last quote, you can switch your concentration to the new information. Thinking of your next question while you are trying to write down a complete quote will interfere with your concentration.

Use key words. Jot down key words to remind you of facts and statements when you are not trying to get a direct quote. The better your memory, the fewer full sentences you will need in your notes.

Develop a shorthand. Abbreviate as many words as possible. Don't waste time writing unimportant words, such as conjunctions. The word *government* might become *gov,* and *you* could be abbreviated as *u.* Some type of shorthand is especially important when you are trying to write complete quotes.

Slow the pace. When you are taking notes for a quote, slow the pace of the interview by pausing before your next question until you write the quote. If you think you are pausing too long, ask a question that will not require a crucial answer. You could ask the source to elaborate about the last statement. If your source is speaking too fast, politely ask him or her to slow down.

Request repetition. Don't be afraid to ask your source to repeat a quote or fact you missed. Although the quote may not be worded exactly as before, it will be close enough. In fact, the repeated statement may be even better. When people have had a chance to think, they often state things more clearly.

Make eye contact. Don't glue your eyes to your notes. Make sure you look at your source during the questioning and while you are taking notes. Practice taking notes without looking at your notebook.

Give praise. If your source gets nervous as you take notes, you can ease his or her concern with sincere praise. You can say, "That was interesting" or ask the source to tell you more about the point. That's one way of gaining some time as you take your notes.

Mark your margins or notebook covers. When you hear something that prompts another question in your mind—a fact you want to check or the name of another source you want to contact—jot it in the margin as soon as you think of it. Don't depend on your memory to think of it later. Some reporters use the covers of their notebooks to write questions that come to mind during the interview so they can find them easily without flipping through notebook pages. And don't forget to take notes on your observations, either in the margins or elsewhere.

Verify vital information. Make sure you get the exact spelling of your source's name and his or her title during or at the end of the interview. Don't go by a nameplate on a door or desk. That could be a nickname. Ask the source the name he or she prefers to use, and ask for the spelling even if you are sure of it. A simple name like John Smith could be spelled *Jon Smythe.* If you get this information at the end of your interview, you also could ask for a home telephone number at this time.

Double-check. If your source says he or she has three main points or reasons for running for office, make sure you get all three. Write *3 reasons* in the margin, number them as you hear them, and check before you conclude the interview.

Be open-minded. You may have one idea for the story when you begin taking notes. But don't limit your notes to one concept. Your story angle could change any time during the interview. You can't always envision how you will write the story. When you do, you may be sorry you didn't take better notes, especially if you decide to change the focus during the writing process.

Use a symbol system. To save time writing your story, put a star or some symbol next to the information or quotes you think will be important while you are taking notes. Develop your own system. Some reporters put one or two stars next to quotes they want or a note next to information that will work for a lead. Other reporters use highlight pens to mark the notes they will use in their stories; most do this after the interview, while they are planning to write the story.

Stand and deliver. Practice taking notes while you are standing. You will not have the luxury of sit-down reporting, especially at the scene of fires, accidents, disasters and most other breaking news stories. And practice taking notes and getting full quotes everywhere else you get the chance—in your lecture classes, when you are watching television news and in any meetings you attend. The best way to become a fast note taker is to gain experience.

Save your notes. You should save your notes before and after the story is published. How long you should save them is debatable. Lawyers disagree whether notes are helpful or harmful in court cases if you are sued for libel or any other reasons. But most editors advise saving the notes at least for a few weeks after the story in case any questions about it arise. For this reason it is helpful to date your notebooks.

Activities

1 Listening: This exercise is designed to test your ability to listen and follow up with related conversation or questions. The technique is to concentrate on a key word or thought that was expressed by the person who precedes you and follow with a related thought.

To do this exercise, one person should begin a conversation. It can be based on a controversy on campus, or it can be a fictional story. The instructor will call on students at random, stopping the speaker at any point. When you are called on, you should pick up one word from the last thought that was spoken and develop the story from that point. For example, if the person before you starts a story with "Jack and Jill went up the hill to fetch a pail of water," you might pick up on the key word *water* and elaborate: "And when they got the water, they discovered it was polluted." The point is to test your conversational listening ability, which will lead to better follow-up questions during interviews.

2 Note taking: The object of this exercise is to see how accurately you can quote sources. Tape an interview from any television news show. Use a VCR or regular tape recorder. As you are watching the show, write down some direct quotes. If you use videotape, watch the screen periodically as though you were making eye contact with a source. Then play the tape and test your accuracy. If you do this in a classroom, you can compare your notes with classmates' notes. Analyze what caused you to be inaccurate—if you were—and how you can improve your note taking.

3 Notes: Submit your notes for the last story you wrote. Share your notes with another student, and critique each other's notes for the points Foster Davis recommends. Are your notes legible? Do they have names, dates, titles and details? Compare your rating of your notes with another student's evaluation of them. Discuss improvements in your note taking that might have helped your story.

COACHING

TIPS

Brainstorm: Ask a friend to listen to your story idea. Discuss questions and points of interest to pursue.

When interviewing athletes or people who have been interviewed frequently, try to find a new angle or a question they haven't been asked.

Always check spelling of the source's name and wording of job titles.

Ask the follow-up questions "Why" and "How," and ask sources to give you an example.

Gather details for graphics; ask questions as though you had to describe the scene to a blind person. Get information an artist would need to draw a map or other illustration. Details will make your writing more vivid as well.

Interviewing Techniques

8

Barbara Walsh had tried for months to get an interview with convicted murderer William R. Horton Jr. Finally his lawyer gave her permission. She walked into the jail, met Horton and learned a painful lesson.

"Willie" Horton was serving two life sentences plus 85 years in a Massachusetts prison for the murder of a gas station attendant and a subsequent crime he committed while out of prison on a furlough (a brief stay in the community). He broke into the home of a Maryland man, slashed him repeatedly and raped his fiancee twice. That crime made him infamous in advertisements that the Republican Party used in 1987 to criticize former Massachusetts Gov. Michael Dukakis, the unsuccessful Democratic presidential candidate. Republicans blamed Dukakis for operating a system in Massachusetts that allowed murderers to leave jail on furloughs.

Walsh, then a reporter for the *Lawrence* (Mass.) *Eagle-Tribune,* faced Horton through the window that separated them. "The first question I asked was 'How the heck did you get out on furlough?' It was the stupidest thing I've ever done," she said.

Horton wanted to terminate the interview. Walsh salvaged the interview with Horton by switching to something he wanted to discuss. "I asked him, 'What do you want to tell me?' And he said, 'I'm not a monster. You people (the press) have made me out to be a monster,' " Walsh said.

The interview then went on for two hours, and eventually Walsh returned to the tough questions she wanted to ask Horton.

Being a reporter is great because you can ask people questions no one in their right mind would ask a complete stranger.

Diana Griego Erwin, columnist,

The Orange County (Calif.) *Register*

Barbara Walsh, reporter

The story was one of a series about the Massachusetts furlough program that earned Walsh the Pulitzer Prize in 1988. Walsh, who later became a reporter for the *Sun-Sentinel* in Fort Lauderdale, Fla., said she was lucky that Horton talked to her, but she learned a valuable lesson about interviewing techniques: "Save your tough questions for last."

She still covers prisons, and she still asks tough questions—but at the end of the interview. "I've learned to be real slow and real patient," she said. "I'm more inclined to let people talk longer. You may not use all the information, but you can offend them if you rush."

Walsh said the key to good interviewing is good listening. "In interviewing, if you are sincere and the sources know that you have compassion, they're going to talk. A lot of the skill is just being open to what they have to say."

But when sources are reluctant to answer her questions, she rephrases them and asks them again—sometimes three or four times—as in the following story about women in a Florida prison. "I asked one of the female inmates on death row, 'What's it like to sit there and know the state wants to electrocute you?' She skirted the question the first time. I asked it three times during the interview." Eventually Walsh got the answer. "If you ask—not in a cold way, but sincerely ask what was it like for you—they'll answer." The result was this revealing portrait (also notice how Walsh weaves in her own observations):

Kaysie Dudley spent two years on Death Row meditating and learning more about how the state was going to kill her.

"I did a lot of research on what they were going to do to me," Dudley says. "It was very morbid, but I wanted to know."

Dudley, 28, was sent to Death Row at Broward Correctional Institution in 1987 after she was convicted with her boyfriend of strangling and slicing the throat of an elderly Clearwater woman.

"My boyfriend killed her," Dudley says. "I held the woman in my arms as she took her last breath. It was a terrible experience."

As she talks, Dudley sits in the cafeteria of the woman's prison, nervously rubbing her fingers together, her nails raw and bitten to the quick. From her neck hangs a small silver cross.

It is cool, and Dudley wears a black sweater over her state-issued aqua dress.

"I wasn't afraid of dying," Dudley says. "But I didn't like to think about electricity running through my body. . . ."

After spending two years on Death Row, Dudley says, she feels she has suffered more than enough.

"I was 22 when they locked me up in there," she says. "I feel like in a way they've already killed me. It took me almost a year to get my facial expressions back, my emotions, my ability to laugh.

"I was a zombie when I came out of there," she says, absently twisting her hair with her constantly moving fingers.

Barbara Walsh, *Sun-Sentinel*

Walsh is a master interviewer once she meets her sources, but getting the interview is sometimes the major hurdle. Walsh recounts an experience she had when she went to interview the parents of a child who allegedly had been molested by a teacher. The parents refused to be interviewed. So Walsh tried this technique: "I said,

'Let's just talk about doing an interview. Here is the kind of story I want to do and these are some of my questions.' I ended up spending three hours with the parents, and I never wrote down a word. Then they said I could use what they said."

She wrote the story from memory. "It was easy," she said. "I would never forget some of the mother's quotes. I did call back and check quotes, however."

Although Walsh usually takes notes, she said a notebook can be threatening. She waits until she has established rapport with her source before she opens her notebook. And she rarely uses a tape recorder—too unreliable and threatening, she said.

Her advice to student reporters? Don't overlook anyone as a source. "When I go to the courthouse, I consider anybody who talks as a source—from the janitor to the people who sell coffee. These are real people who may not be high-priced attorneys, but they know what is going on. Reporters narrow their sources too much."

Manipulation

The way you deal with sources can differ, depending on whether they are public or private individuals. Because public officials are accustomed to dealing with the media, you have a right to expect them to talk to you. Private individuals do not have to deal with the media, and you need to exert even more sensitivity when interviewing them. If a public official utters an outrageous quote, it's fair game. When a private individual does, you could remind the person that it will be published and make sure the source will stand by the comment. Although many reporters believe that once they have identified themselves as members of the media, anything in an interview is fair game, reporters who display extra sensitivity usually end up with more information.

All sources, public and private, want to be portrayed well in the media. Many sources, especially public officials, will manipulate reporters by revealing only information that furthers their cause. As a result, reporters need to be aware of the source's bias and ask probing questions that go beyond what the source wants to reveal. It is also crucial to check the information and seek alternative points of view.

Tips for Interviewers

The following sections present some other tips to help you become a good interviewer. But before you even start, consider your mission. You are a reporter, not a stenographer who just receives information and transcribes it. A reporter evaluates information for its accuracy, fairness, newsworthiness and potential to make a readable story. During the reporting process, you will look for facts, good quotes, substantiation and answers to the five W's—who, what, when, where, why—and also "How" and "So what." One question should lead to another until you have the information you need.

An interview with one source is just the beginning of reporting for most stories. For credibility and fairness, you need other sources—human and written—for differing points of view and accuracy checks.

Planning the Interview

If you are sent to cover a breaking news story, you should get to the scene quickly and find sources there or start calling sources on the telephone. The planning stages described here apply only to interviews that you need to set up in advance. Most of the other reporting techniques apply to both kinds of stories.

Research the background. Check news clippings and available documents—court records, campaign records or other relevant written sources—to familiarize yourself with the topic and the source. Check with secondary sources—friends and opponents—before or after you interview the subject of a story. Ask the source's friends, secretaries or co-workers to give you anecdotes and tell you about the person's idiosyncracies.

Plan an interesting question to start your interview. Try to find a question or approach that would interest the source, especially if the person is a celebrity, an athlete or an official who has been interviewed often. These people often give standard answers to questions they consider boring because they have been asked the same questions so many times. If you use your research well, you will find some tidbit or angle to a story that might lead to an unusual question—and an interesting answer.

Identify your goals. What kind of information are you hoping to get from this source? Is it primarily factual, as in an interview with a police officer for a story about an accident? Do you want reaction from the source to an issue or to something someone else said? Or, for a profile or a story about a program, do you want to center the story around your source? Get a general idea of why you need this source so you can explain briefly when you call for an interview.

Plan your questions. This step may seem premature, considering that you haven't even been granted an interview. However, if the person refuses to see you when you call for an interview, you might be able to ask a few questions while you have the source on the phone. If you are a good interviewer, you can prolong the conversation and wind up with a good interview.

To plan your questions, try the mapping technique: Draw a circle or tree, with the main topic in the center or on the tree trunk, and jot down related issues. Then narrow the list to important questions.

Prepare your list of questions by first jotting down all the questions you want to ask, preferably in an abbreviated form. Then mark the questions you *must* ask to get the most crucial information for your story. If your source refuses to grant you the time you need, you can switch to the crucial list during your interview.

Request the interview. Now you are ready to call for an appointment. The most important point is to plan ahead. Officials, educators and many other sources are busy people. They may not be able to see you on brief notice.

When you make the call, first state your name and purpose. If you are a reporter for your campus newspaper, make that part of your identification: "I'm Joe Smith, and I'm a reporter for the *University Daily Tribune.* I'd like to interview you for a story I'm writing about the increase in tuition." Or better yet, try the sponsorship technique: "I'm working on a story about date rape on campus, and Officer John Brown suggested that I call you. I understand that you have some information about a survey the university conducted on this subject." Try to convince the source that her or his opinions are important to you.

Then ask what time would be convenient. Negotiate the length of time you need. If you want an hour but the source can't spare the time, settle for a half hour.

If you are calling an official, you probably will have to negotiate through a secretary. Be courteous and persuasive. First ask to speak to the source. If that's not possible, tell the secretary that you would like to interview her or his boss about a story you are writing. You don't need to elaborate unless you are asked to do so.

Dress appropriately. If you are interviewing a source on a farm, don't wear a three-piece suit. On the other hand, show your source respect by dressing neatly. Avoid wearing tattered jeans and sloppy shirts. However, if you are interviewing corporate officials or people in more formal business settings, you should dress as though you worked there—tie and jacket for men, a dress for women.

Arrive on time. You could arrive 10 to 15 minutes early, but don't arrive too early, because you could inconvenience people who are busy. And never come late.

Conducting the Interview

Interview questions can be classified as two types: closed-ended and open-ended. You need both types.

Closed-ended questions are designed to elicit brief, specific answers that are factual. They are good for getting basic information, such as name and title, yes or no answers, and answers to some of the who, where, when questions. For example, these are closed-ended questions: "How long have you worked here? Who was at the meeting? How many people were at the rally? When did the accident occur?"

Open-ended questions are designed to elicit quotes, elaboration or longer responses. Follow up your closed-ended questions with open-ended ones, such as why and how. Some others: "What is the purpose of your program? What are your goals in starting this organization? What is your reaction to . . . ?" When you want anecdotes, ask, "Could you give me an example?" or "Can you recall a specific incident when this happened to you?" To clarify anything you don't understand, just ask the source to explain further.

Keep your questions brief. A long lead-in to a question can confuse the source. Slow the pace between questions so you can take notes. Ask unimportant questions or ask for elaboration while you are writing down quotes.

Remember to be responsive—smile, nod or react appropriately—and make eye contact frequently during the interview.

Beginning reporters often worry that they will appear dumb to sources. Don't worry about what you don't know. You are there to listen and learn, not to be the expert. The whole point is to get information from the source. In fact, acting dumb can give you an advantage. Even if you know the answer to a question, you should ask it anyway, so you can get the information in the source's words. If you think a question is too simple, you might apologize for not knowing more about the subject. You might say, "I'm sorry I don't understand this. Could you explain so I can write it clearly for my readers?" Most sources enjoy the teaching role or showing off what they know.

Acting dumb does not mean forgetting about preliminary background work. It is dumb if you can't tell your readers something because you were afraid to ask. It's better to feel dumb during the interview than afterward, when you turn your story in to an editor or when you read it in the newspaper.

Here are some ways to conduct the interview and some types of questions to ask. Not all of these techniques and questions apply to every story.

Start out by using icebreakers. Introduce yourself and briefly state your purpose. Be friendly. Establish rapport with some general conversation. Don't pull out your notebook immediately. Try to sit at an angle to your source so you are not staring directly at her or him in a confrontational manner. A desk might serve as a barrier and provide enough distance so you don't appear threatening.

Observe the surroundings. Do you notice something you can mention as an icebreaker, a way to establish rapport? Barbara Walsh said that during one interview she noticed a map of Ireland on the wall and commented that she had lived in Ireland. That comment broke the ice. Don't be artificial. If an official has a picture on his desk of his family, don't get overly familiar. Use good judgment. Then explain a little more about what you are seeking in your story.

Put your questions in non-threatening order. In most cases you will want to follow Walsh's advice and start with non-threatening questions. However, if you have only five minutes with a source, you may have to ask your toughest question first or whichever one will yield you the most crucial information for your story.

Ask the basic questions. Who, what, when, where, why and how are the most basic. Then add the *"so what"* factor: Ask the significance. Who will be affected and how? This question will give you information for your impact and scope paragraphs.

Ask follow-up questions. These are the questions that will give you quotes and anecdotes. Use a conversational technique. Let the interview flow naturally. When a source answers one question, follow the trend of thought by asking why and how and asking the source to explain or give examples. Frame your next question on the information you have just heard by focusing on key words in the last answer. When you want to change the subject, ask an unrelated question or use a transition: "On another topic . . ." or "I'd like to go back to something you said earlier. Could you explain why you were at the scene where the murder occurred?" Use follow-up questions to go from the general to the specific. If the source makes a vague statement, ask for specific examples.

You may have a long list of questions, but don't let your source see them. A long list can make the source watch the clock. Write your questions on the front or back of your notebook so you can refer to them easily without turning pages frequently. One student reporter took out a press release during the interview. When the source saw it, he told the student to use the comments in the release and terminated the interview.

Control the interview. If your source rambles or prolongs an answer and you want to move the interview in another direction, don't interrupt. Wait for a natural pause and ask your next question, using follow-up question techniques.

Repeat questions. You've asked an important or sensitive question, and the source has given you an evasive or incomplete answer. Even a request to elaborate does not produce a satisfactory response. What should you do? The best tactic is to drop the question and continue the interview. After you have discussed a few other points, repeat the question you want answered, but state it in a slightly different way. Sometimes a source will recall more the second time the question is raised.

Ask background questions. Get the history of the issue, if applicable. How and when did the problem or program start? Why?

Ask about developments. Go from the present to the past and to the future. What are the current concerns and developments? How did the issue evolve? What is likely to happen in the future? The answer to the future developments question may provide you with a good ending for your story. In some cases, it may give you a lead and a new focus for your story. The next step is often the most newsworthy angle. Many newspapers prefer this approach, which is called "advancing the story."

Construct a chronology. This tip is somewhat related to the previous point. When appropriate, ask questions to establish a sequence of events. You don't need to write the story in chronological order, but you need to understand the order in which events occurred.

Role play. If you were in the reader's place, how would you use the information? For example, if you needed to apply for a loan, what steps would you have to take, and where would you go? What does the reader need and want to know? Ask the source questions that will meet the reader's needs.

Ask about pros and cons. Ask your source to discuss both sides of an issue, when relevant. Who agrees and disagrees with her or his point of view? What are her or his responses to the opposition?

Ask for definition. Your job is to translate jargon for readers. So always get your source to define any bureaucratic or technical terms in language that you and your readers will understand. Don't accept any information—or write it in your story—that you can't explain. To clarify, you might restate the information in your own words and ask the source if you have the correct interpretation. For example, you might ask "Do you mean that . . . ?" or "Are you saying that . . . ?"

Verify. Ask questions even if you know the answers. You need to quote or attribute information to your source, not yourself.

Always check the spelling of your source's name—first and last names and middle initial. Check the person's title and the dates of crucial events. Check the accuracy of information on a resume or press release. You don't have to repeat everything, but you should ask the source if the information released is correct. Then ask some questions that expand on the basic information. For example, if you are interviewing the president of MADD (Mothers Against Drunk Driving), you might ask, "Have you ever been involved in an accident involving a drunken driver or were you ever arrested for drunken driving?" Such a question may not be as insensitive as it seems, because many people get involved with causes after they have had a personal experience with the problem.

Also, remember that if the source tells you something about another person, you must check it out with that person.

Use the "lie detector test." Bill Marimow, assistant to the publisher of *The Philadelphia Inquirer* and two-time winner of the Pulitzer

Prize, assumes that his sources might lie to him. When he interviewed sources for his prize-winning series about police brutality, he warned sources who were accusing police that if he found out they were not telling him the *whole* truth, he wouldn't print a word they said. He got their police records before he interviewed them. In one case, he asked a source if he had ever been arrested, and the source said no. "I took out the file and said, 'What about this attempted rape?' I knew then that I wouldn't write anything about that source," he said at a conference of investigative reporters. "I believe in laying 51 of 52 cards on the table. But I want to keep one card. The arrest report was that one card."

Use the silent treatment. Pause for a few seconds between questions to let the source elaborate. If the pause seems uncomfortable, the source may break the silence first. One reporter was writing a profile of a nun. He asked her if she missed having a sex life and how she coped without one. She gave a brief, expected answer that she had made a conscious choice of abstinence when she took vows of celibacy. The reporter was disappointed with the answer. He said nothing. She said nothing. For several seconds they just sat in silence. Both were slightly uncomfortable. Then she broke the silence and began elaborating about how difficult celibacy was for her at times. Sometimes the best follow-up question is no question.

Use the "not-my-fault" technique. When you have to ask tough questions, blame someone else: "Your opponent says you cheated on your income taxes. How would you respond to that?"

Reporters and editors have mixed feelings about warning the source that a tough question is coming. Don't do it, they say, in confrontational interviews when you are trying to get a source to reveal information that could be damaging. It puts the source on notice and gives him or her a few seconds to become defensive and evasive. But do warn the source or apologize if it's going to be a tough, emotional question, especially if you are interviewing grieving people, said Jacqui Banaszynski, a *St. Paul* (Minn.) *Pioneer Press* reporter who won a Pulitzer Prize for a series about a man with AIDS. She tells sources that she will ask tough questions but they don't have to answer them. "But I'll try to convince them to do so," she said.

Handle emotional questions with tact. Emotional questions can be difficult. Ask your source to recall how he or she was thinking or feeling at the time of an incident. "Were you frightened when the train lost power? What were you thinking at the time?"

Avoid insensitive questions. There's a saying in journalism that there are no stupid questions, only stupid answers. That's not exactly true. "How do you feel about the death of your three children?" is not only a stupid question, it's insensitive. Instead of asking such an emotionally loaded question, ask the person to recall specific memories about his or her children, or ask how the source is coping with the tragedy.

Ask summary questions. Restate information, or ask the source to clarify the key points he or she is making. For example: "Of all the goals you have expressed, which would you say are the most important to you? What do you think are the three major issues you face?"

Use the "matchmaker" technique. Ask your source to suggest other sources for your story. Ask if anyone else is involved in the issue, anyone who is an expert on the subject or other people the source would suggest you contact. Remember that you will want more than one source for your story so you can strive for fairness and balance.

Ask free-choice questions. Ask the source if there is anything he or she would like to add.

When you have finished the interview, thank your source. Ask if you can call back if you have any further questions. At this point, you also could ask for a home telephone number or another way to reach the source.

Reporting for Graphics

If you had to draw your story instead of write it, how would it look? You may have gathered enough information through an interview for a verbal presentation. But you still have to think about visual presentation.

Whenever you go on an assignment—especially a breaking news story involving an accident, a disaster such as a flood or explosion, or a crime—gather information for the graphic artist. Even if you don't use all these details for a graphic, you can use many of them to make your writing more vivid. Get maps, brochures or any other written materials that might be available to help the graphics department pinpoint the location of the crime or disaster scene.

And ask questions as though you had to describe the scene to a blind person. How many feet or yards away from the landfill is the nearest house? What buildings are in the area? When the gas pipe exploded, how many feet from the gas line was the nearest building? What are the names and exact locations of the businesses in the area? Detail, detail, detail!

Here are some types of information to gather for a graphic that could accompany your story:

Locations: Get the names of streets and major intersections nearest to the site of the incident. Ask details about specific measurements: yards, feet, number of city blocks or whatever else would help pinpoint locations.

Chronology of events: Get specific times or dates and other information to recount the sequence of events. For example, suppose a terrorist takes a hostage. When did the incident occur? At what time did each development occur before the hostage was released or killed?

Weather data: Suppose that your community has had a drought. How many days or months have gone by since the last rainfall? What were the temperatures in the last 30 days of a heat wave or cold spell? How many inches of rain fell during each day or week in a period of flooding?

Statistics: Think of charts. If your city council has raised taxes, what have taxes been during the past five years? How much has tuition increased during the past several years? How many students have dropped out of college? How does this year's enrollment compare with enrollments in previous years? Statistics like these can be boring to read. But they are easy to understand in chart form.

Highlights: Gather information for a facts box, such as important dates or highlights of someone's career. Suppose you are doing a profile. Instead of listing key dates and incidents in your story, could you place them more effectively in a box? Ask about interesting hobbies, favorite books, favorite movies, marital status or other personal information that might help the graphic artist—and the reader.

Think of yourself as part of a team and the graphic artist as one of the key players. The better your story looks, the better chance you have of attracting the reader to those words you have worked so hard to report and write. In the past, when a reporter turned in a story that was reported and written well, editors used to say, "Your story looks good." It's up to you to make sure it does—verbally and visually.

The GOAL Method of Interviewing

The "GOAL method" is a concept to help you frame questions for a variety of stories, especially profiles, features, and stories about programs and issues. It is a variation of a technique called the GOSS formula, which was devised by LaRue W. Gilleland, a former professor at the University of Nevada. *GOSS* stands for asking questions about goals, obstacles, solutions and start (background). The GOAL method is essentially the same formula but with different words to jog your memory:

G = goals

O = obstacles

A = achievements

L = logistics

Many interviews can be designed around this GOAL concept. Your questions should not be restricted to these four concepts, but if you structure your questions around these ideas, you will get answers to the questions of why, how and what. Here are some ideas for specific questions using this method:

Goals: What are or were some of your goals in this program (or in your career)? What are you trying to accomplish? Why do you want to do this? Try to discern the person's motivation for his or her actions.

Obstacles: What were some of the obstacles you faced (or are facing)? Get specific examples or anecdotes. What is one example of a difficult problem you experienced? Try not to qualify your question by asking for the most difficult problem or the funniest or happiest moment. People have difficulty deciding what is best, worst, hardest, easiest, happiest or saddest. They need clues, such as a specific period during their life.

Achievements: How did you overcome these obstacles? How did you achieve your goal (or how do you plan to achieve it)? Again, get specifics.

Logistics: How did the source or the program get to this point? This is the background, past, present and future. How did the source's background affect his or her goals, obstacles and achievements? What factors in the person's background relate to the focus of your story? Is there a chronology of events you need to get so the reader can understand the story? Weave in the background where it will be interesting and relevant.

Telephone Interviewing

Edna Buchanan was persistent. The former *Miami Herald* police reporter spent much of her life making difficult phone calls to people who were grieving. If a source hung up on her, Buchanan waited a minute or two. Then she called back. The second time she identified herself again and said, "We were cut off." Sometimes her sources changed their minds, or someone else who was willing to talk answered the phone. But if they hung up again, she didn't call a third time.

More often than not, people are willing to talk to reporters, especially on the telephone. For many sources, talking about a loved one who died is cathartic.

Not all telephone interviews involve difficult situations. Reporters on a daily newspaper get many of their stories by telephone—from daily checks with police about crime stories to interviews with politicians, government officials and community leaders for reaction stories, issue stories and a wide range of features.

Nancy Tracy, a *Hartford* (Conn.) *Courant* reporter who died in 1988, had a way of almost seeing through the telephone. She would ask her sources for details. She asked what they were wearing, what they were doing, what they were thinking, how they were coping and reacting. She was always empathetic. Sometimes she would apologize for asking difficult questions; sometimes she would sympathize. Then she would ask more questions. And rarely did anyone refuse to answer her.

Here is an excerpt from a story Tracy did about a Georgia couple who survived when their truck plunged into the Mianus River in Connecticut when the bridge collapsed. In her telephone interview with David Pace, Tracy asked such questions as "Where are you sitting now?" "What is your daily routine?" "What do you think about and dream about?" and even "What is the weather today?"

Some days when the pain isn't too bad, he stands by the front door, watching trucks roll by on Highway 41 on their way to Macon. Then the memories come flooding back, the crash, the pain.

Inside the small mobile home, his wife also remembers the day their world fell apart, when a metal and concrete span that was the Mianus Bridge split, sending them and four others tumbling 70 feet to the Mianus River in Greenwich.

It is a year today since the bridge collapsed, but for David and Helen Pace of Perry, Ga., it's as if it happened yesterday. It still figures in their nightmares, still limits their days.

A living hell, 27-year-old David Pace calls the past year.

It is raining. Helen Pace has taken to her bed. On damp or rainy days, her back hurts more than usual. On the days she is up, she wears dark stockings to cover the scars on her legs. She used to be proud of those legs, her husband says.

They had been married six months, and he'd gotten into the habit of bringing her with him on the long-distance runs. The night the bridge fell down, they were on their way to New Hampshire with 26,000 pounds of empty beer bottles in their semi-trailer.

He loved trucking—the good money it brought, the chance to see the country. Now, David Pace says, his and his wife's injuries are so severe that his parents are afraid to leave them alone.

"I've had to turn to my mother-in-law, my father-in-law, my mom and dad," he says. "It kind of takes a part of my manhood away from me. It hurts. It hurts bad."

Nancy Tracy, *The Hartford Courant*

Tracy got all that information by telephone.

Although interviewing people in person is preferable, it is often not practical, especially if you are on deadline. You won't be able to observe facial reactions, gestures and surroundings when you conduct telephone interviews, but you still can gather information accurately and thoroughly.

The techniques of telephone interviewing are very similar to methods of interviewing in person. The major difference is that you need to work harder at keeping the source's attention and focusing your questions. Researchers suggest that the average telephone interview should be limited to 20 minutes. After that, the attention span of the person responding wanes. If you call a source at home, he or she may be further distracted by children or other family concerns.

Here are some guidelines for telephone interviewing:

Identification: Immediately state your name and affiliation and the purpose for the call.

Icebreakers: These may not be necessary. Get to the point quickly. If you use any icebreaker to establish rapport, keep it very brief.

Length of questions: Keep them very short. Phrase each question clearly and simply. Limit questions to no more than two sentences; one is better.

Clarification: Make sure you understand the information you receive. It may be harder to understand information in a telephone interview, so clarify anything that is confusing. Repeat any confusing terms or information in your own words, and ask your source to verify your interpretation.

Specifics: Ask for details and examples. If you need to describe anything that you might see if you were on the scene, ask your source to give you the descriptive details.

Chronology: A chronology is especially important in police and fire stories you receive by telephone. Make sure you understand the sequence of events so you can write the story clearly. If you do not understand how an event occurred, try restating the chronology: "Let me understand, is this how it happened?" Or after a source tells you the high points of what happened, you could ask him or her to explain the order in which events unfolded.

Limits: Because your time may be limited by many events beyond your control, limit the number of questions in a telephone interview. Plan two lists: all the questions you want to ask and crucial questions. If you have time for only a few questions, switch to the crucial list. You may also want to ask your questions in a different order. Don't wait too long to ask the crucial ones. You never can tell when the source will be interrupted and will terminate the interview.

Control: Changing the subject to get to the questions you need to have answered is even more crucial in a telephone interview than in person. You can't spare too much time establishing rapport or engaging in non-productive conversation. Be mindful of the information you must get for your story.

Verification: Double-check the spelling of the name, title and other basic information. If you haven't heard it clearly, spell it back to the source. This basic information is crucial when dealing with police officers. They usually do not identify themselves by their full names when they answer the phone on duty, so make sure you get first and last names and the proper rank, such as lieutenant, sergeant or captain.

At the end of the interview, thank the source and ask if you may call back if you have more questions. Use judgment here. Don't ask this of police or reluctant sources; just call back if you must have more information.

Activities

1   Interview a reporter from your local newspaper about his or her reporting techniques. Or choose a reporter whose stories you like, and interview him or her about techniques.

2   Make a list of questions you would use as icebreakers to interview a professor or a source whose office you have visited.

3   Write a reaction story based on interviews with students or local residents about any controversial topic that is in the news, preferably an issue of concern in your university or community. Try to get good quotes. Analyze which questions bring the best responses.

4   Attend a demonstration, rally, meeting, speech or other public event on your campus or in your community, and write a basic news story about it.

5   Interview a local police officer about a crime or accident. In addition to getting basic information, ask questions to establish the chronology of events. If possible, get a copy of the police report. If the class is not doing this exercise as a group, check to make sure several people will not be bombarding the same officer at different times.

6   **Technical clarity:** This exercise was suggested by *St. Paul Pioneer Press* reporter Jacqui Banaszynski. Interview a source about some technical information you don't understand. The source could be anyone from an auto mechanic to a scientist. Work on clarifying jargon and other information you don't understand. Then write the results of your interview in a brief story or several paragraphs explaining the technical information clearly.

7   Plan 10 questions to ask a community leader, college official or other person you might interview about an issue in your community. Or, if you prefer, take any issue in the news and imagine that you are a reporter covering that story. Plan 10 questions you would ask.

8   **Telephone interviewing:** This exercise comes from Tina Lesher, a journalism professor at William Paterson College of New Jersey. To do it, you need a speaker telephone system in the classroom. Lesher arranges a time for an interview with a media professional—an editor, writing coach, reporter or writer. During class, her students take turns questioning the person on the phone, and the class takes notes. Students must write a story based on the telephone interview.

9   **Graphics:** Check your local newspaper or another newspaper that uses graphic illustrations. Study a graphic, and write a list of questions you would have asked to gather the information that the artist used to design it.

THREE

Constructing Stories

COACHING

TIPS

Find your focus by writing one sentence explaining what the story is about.

Plan an order for your story using key words for the ideas and quotes from your notes. If graphics will accompany your story, consider what you should leave out of the text.

Write a highlights box to find key points; use the box as a guide for your organization.

Write a first draft quickly; then revise it.

The Writing Process

9

When Bill Ryan begins writing his stories for *The Hartford* (Conn.) *Courant,* he doesn't use a pencil, a tape recorder or a computer. He uses his mind. He thinks about the story before he begins writing.

"If you start writing right away, you're wasting a lot of time because you'll have to keep backtracking through your notes," says Ryan, who has been a writer for more than 40 years at newspapers and magazines. "If you do nothing for five minutes except think about it, you'll have a better story."

Ryan says he starts thinking about his story in the car when he is returning to his office from an interview. "I almost never do formal outlines," he says. "I'm not a super-organized person. Occasionally I'll sketch some notes to tell myself, 'This will go here and this should go there.' I take what interests me first and put that in a primary spot in my mind. Then I think about all the other stuff you have to know. I think you should write a story in the order in which it interests you."

Writers work in many different ways. Some writers pace around the newsroom before they write. Others outline their stories or write a rough draft first. And many writers just stare at their computer waiting for a muse to inspire them to create the perfect lead. They insist that they can't write the rest of the story until they find their lead. Deadline approaches, and the rest of the story gets short shrift because the writer is almost out of time. But the writing process doesn't have to be that painful; you can use several techniques to develop a writing process that works for you.

There's nothing to writing.

All you do is sit down at the

typewriter and open a vein.

Red Smith, sportswriter,

The New York Times

Ways to Approach the Writing Process

Don Fry, associate director of writing programs, Poynter Institute for Media Studies

Courtesy of Don Fry

Don Fry almost never worries about what he is going to say first. He writes his leads last. Fry, one of the foremost writing experts in the country, takes less time to write an entire story than most writers spend on their leads.

Fry says he begins the writing process long before he sits down at his computer. "I'm imagining the story while I'm reporting it," he says.

After Fry gathers his information, he thinks about his story, "rehearsing" it in his head. Then he plans an order for his story. He codes his notes, marking just the material he intends to use—usually only 5 percent of the notes he took.

Then he puts his notes aside and writes a plan for his story, a rough order with just a few words for each point he wants to make. "I ask myself what are the parts and in what order do I want to put them," he says. Other questions he asks in the planning stage: What questions does the reader need answered and in what order?

Fry concentrates on what he calls the "point statement," also known as a focus graph or nut graph. He asks himself what the story is about and what the point of the story is. Any information that doesn't relate to the point statement isn't included in the story.

And then he starts writing. Not at the beginning, but at the paragraph containing the point statement. He continues writing until he gets to his ending, which he calls the "kicker." Then he writes his lead. After that he revises.

Fry has a five-step writing system: Conceive the idea, report, organize (plan an order), draft and revise. The four-step coaching process used in this book (see Chapter 1)—conceive, collect, construct (which includes planning) and correct—is adapted from Fry.

Although revision or correction is the last step in the writing process, it is a good check on the other steps. Revising your story doesn't mean just going back and cleaning up the grammar and style. Do what a writing coach does when working with a reporter to discover the problems in a story: Ask questions to reveal where the problems originated. They could be at any point in the process, from conception to collection to construction. A coach would ask questions like these: What did you like about the story? Where did you struggle? What were you trying to say?

When you revise your story, ask yourself some of these coaching questions as well:

Conceive: Is the idea well focused? Should the story be developed around another angle?

Collect: Does the story need more information?

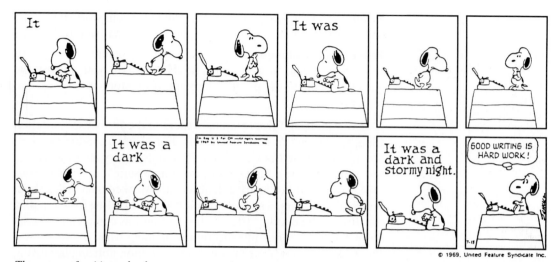

© 1969. United Feature Syndicate Inc.

The agony of writing a lead

Reprinted by permission of United
Features Syndicate, Inc.

Construct: Does the order work? Is it logical and interesting? Is the focus clear?

Correct: Did any problems occur in the earlier steps? Are any minor corrections necessary to improve grammar or spelling or to tighten sentences?

No single writing process will work for everyone. Good writers develop their own methods.

The FORK Method

In the coming chapters, you will study many ways of writing leads and organizing stories. But before you get to those specific methods, try the following writing process to help you organize stories before and while you write:

The FORK method of organization

F = focus

O = order

R = repetition of key words

K = "kiss off"

Focus   This is the main point of your story. In a hard-news story, the focal point could be in your lead. In a soft-news story, it is your nut graph. But it is also a crucial organizing tool; once you find it you have to keep it. Your lead should lead to the focal point, and all other information should relate to it. Information in your notes that does not relate to this focus should not go in the story. If you don't know the focus of your story, your story will ramble.

Here are some tips for finding your focus:

Headline technique: Try writing a headline for your story. If you had only a few words to express the main point, what would they be?

Tell-a-friend technique: If you were telling someone about your story, how would you describe it? How would you answer the question "What's it about?" Explain your story in one or two sentences.

Even Pulitzer Prize–winning writers and editors use the tell-a-friend technique to find their focus. For example, Laura Sessions Stepp, a writer at *The Washington Post,* tells a story about when she was the editor of a Pulitzer Prize–winning series at *The Charlotte* (N.C.) *Observer.* For nearly a year, she had worked on a series about brown lung disease, which cotton pickers were getting from inhaling the dust of the cotton. After all the editing was completed, she sat down to write a brief introduction explaining what the series was about. And she sat. And she sat. The city editor, noticing her agony, came over and asked what the problem was. "I'm stuck. I can't write a lead for this," she said.

"What's it about?" he said.

"Cotton dust is killing people, and farmers are . . ."

"Stop!" he said, as she was about to drone on.

Cotton dust is killing people. That was the lead. And the focus of the series.

Steve Lovelady, an associate executive editor at *The Philadelphia Inquirer,* uses a slightly different version of the tell-a-friend technique, the "challenge technique," which forces the writer to justify the "so what" "who cares" aspect of the story. Lovelady, who edited many of the *Inquirer's* Pulitzer Prize–winning stories, uses the following scenario to bait writers into finding their focus. He envisions himself at a party, where he meets a reporter who works for another editor at his newspaper. "Hi, Charlie, what are you working on?" he says.

"I'm working on a story about how toxic waste is seeping into the underground water supply in the suburbs," Charlie says.

"Sounds boring," Steve replies.

"Boring! Are you kidding? Kids are deformed for life, the trees have died, houses are worth nothing . . ."

"Thanks, Charlie."

Jacqui Banaszynski, a reporter at the *St. Paul* (Minn.) *Pioneer Press* and winner of the 1988 Pulitzer Prize for feature writing, uses the "stoplight technique." Imagine that you are at a stoplight and have 30 seconds to tell your story before the light changes. Chances are in 30 seconds you'll express the focus—or the lead. This technique is the supercharged version of "What's it about?"

Order Look through your notes, and mark information you want to use. On a separate piece of paper or in your computer, write key words or phrases to remind you of the items you want to use. Then put them in the order you will use them in your story. You can change the order when you start writing if you don't like your initial plan.

Some writers need a very complete outline; others need only a few words to plan their stories. Decide what works for you.

Susan Ager, writing coach for the *Detroit Free Press,* calls the "order" step a road map. Envision a story as though you were planning a trip. You need a map to tell you where you are going, she says.

Graphics also affect your story content and order. Consider whether some statistics or other material to be presented in a graphic would be redundant in the text. However, if the information is crucial to understanding the story, leave it in both places.

Here are some suggestions to help you decide an order:

Topics: List all the main points you want to cover. Decide which are the most important and which point naturally follows another. Then put them in that order. Arrange information from the most important to the least important. Then group together all the information—quotes, supporting facts—related to a specific point or topic.

Graphics: If you were writing a highlights box, what would your main points be? Use the highlights as a guide for organization, giving clues about what to include and in what order.

A test: If you had to test the reader on the most important points of your story, what questions would you write? Put the questions in natural order, with answers for one question leading to another question.

Question/answer: Jot down an idea for your lead (you don't need the exact wording at this point). What questions does it raise that need to be answered and backed up in the story? After you answer those questions, continue asking what additional questions need to be answered and in what order of importance or interest.

Ending: Decide how you want to end the story. Do you have a quote that summarizes the main point or refers back to the lead? Is there a future angle? After you have a lead and an ending, figure out what kind of information you need to get from the beginning to the end. Many writers consider the ending just as important as the lead, and they want to know where they are going when they organize their stories.

Time sequences: Does the story have distinct time elements? Consider arranging the story in some chronology. You could start with what is happening now, go to background (the past action), then return to the present and end with the future. You may decide that only a part of your story should be in a chronological order.

a   Quotes: Mark the quotes that are most important, and design your story by sources, starting with the ones who have the most important points to make and proceeding to the lesser quotes. Vary the pace. Mix quotations with paraphrased information, facts and anecdotes. If you have a very good quote, you might base your lead on the concept and use the quote for backup to the lead.

b   Free-writing: If you are stuck, put away your notes and just write what you remember. Then review what you have written, and arrange it in an order that seems logical. Plug in quotes and facts later.

c   Tell-a-friend technique: The method of telling a friend may also give you an order.

Repetition of key words   This is a technique that provides smooth transitions during the writing process or serves as a thought bridge to get you from one concept to the next. The technique also is known as "stitching," because it helps stitch one paragraph to the other.

As you write, look at the last sentence in each paragraph and find a key word that will lead you to the next paragraph. That key word can trigger a question you can answer in the next paragraph or can serve as a bridge for the next thought. You may either repeat the word in the next sentence as a transitional device or just use the concept of the word as a bridge to the idea in your next paragraph. Don't overuse the exact repetition of key words for transitions, because your writing may become boring.

In the following example, the underlined key words serve as transitions to the next thought. In some cases the writer repeats the key word, and in others he uses it as a thought bridge.

Key word **drugs** *serves as a bridge to the next thought.*

What we need are some mandatory classes that you would attend before you attempted to move your household. These would be much more useful than those classes you go to before you have a baby.

When you have a baby, you are surrounded by skilled professionals, who, if things get really bad, give you drugs, whereas nobody performs any such service when you move. This is wrong.

The first thing the burly men should do when they get off the moving van is seize you and forcibly inject you with a two-week supply of sedatives, because mov-ing, to judge from its effect on my wife, is far more stressful than childbirth.

Even in the worst throes of labor, even when she had become totally irrational and was making voices like the ones Linda Blair made in "The Exorcist," only without the aid of special effects, my wife never once suggested that we should put wet, filthy scum-encrusted rags, which I had been cleaning toilets with, into a box and have paid professionals to transport them 1,200 miles so we could have them in our new home.

Dave Barry, syndicated columnist

Key word **child-birth** *serves as a bridge to elaborate the idea.*

The kiss off This technique is a way of organizing information in blocks to avoid confusing the reader about the speaker, especially in stories with several sources. Newspaper style calls for using only the last name of a source after the first full-name reference. The kiss-off technique eliminates confusion when you mention a source by last name later in a story, especially in a long story or on a jump page. The writer is familiar with the sources; the reader is not. And the reader has a short memory for names in a complex story.

The general rule is this: When you have three or more sources in a story, use each source once, blocking all his or her comments in one place, and then kiss off that source. Do not weave back and forth with sources, unless you have fewer than three. If you must use a source again in another part of the story, reintroduce the person by title or some reference to remind the reader of the person's identity. The exception is a well-known source, such as the mayor, the governor, the president, a celebrity or the central character in a story. The name of such a source may be placed anywhere in the story without confusing the reader.

The kiss-off concept also may be used for a story that has several different supporting concepts. After you have determined your main focus, plan an order for each supporting point. Block all the backup material related to that point, and then kiss it off. If you have several people discussing several ideas, as in a meeting, you will have to be selective about which comments to include. Even in a story arranged by topics, you still should try to block information from each source—if you have more than three—in one place, so you don't confuse the reader by weaving too many people throughout the story.

In this example of the kiss-off technique, notice how the sources are organized in blocks:

Focus

Beginning next spring, smokers at Lansing Community College will have to take their habit outside.

The LCC Board of Trustees has approved a smoke-free campus at the end of the next spring term. It is expected to make LCC the first campus with totally smoke-free facilities in the state.

1 (first speaker)

"It gives a year for the thing to settle in and for people to accept it and adjust to it," said Erik Furseth, chairman of the board.

Under its current policy, smoking is permitted only in designated areas, such as portions of cafeterias. When the new policy takes effect, smoking will be banned in all parts of all buildings.

"We do have a smoking area. It's outside the building," said Trustee Judith Hollister.

Karen Krzanowski, assistant executive director of the American Lung Association of Michigan, said she believes that LCC is the first community college in the state to adopt a smoke-free policy.

"We're delighted," she said. "I think they are taking the lead and others will follow."

A growing number of employers statewide are banning smoking, Krzanowski said. Those in-

Key word **buildings** *leads to next thought.*

2 (second speaker)
3 (third speaker)

3
Key word **others** *leads to next thought.*

3

clude Michigan Bell, Comerica and the state Public Health Department.

LCC trustees adopted the policy after holding hearings and developing a comprehensive report on smoking. The one-year delay in implementation is designed to give employees and students a chance to prepare.

The college will offer assistance to people trying to quit, perhaps by offering smoking cessation sessions, said Jacqueline Taylor, vice president for college and community relations. **4 (fourth speaker)**

LCC also will develop an education program to explain the policy and encourage people not to smoke.

"I think it's great," said Elizabeth Saettler, a non-smoker from Owosso. "I certainly think it benefits the majority of people." **5 (fifth speaker)**

Sherry Brettin of East Lansing said she could accept the new policy. "I smoke, but I'll go outside. It doesn't bother me," she said. **6 (sixth speaker)**

"I plan to stop smoking anyway," said Geoff Waun of East Lansing. "I still think there should be a place for people to smoke." **7 (seventh speaker)**

Chris Andrews, *Lansing* (Mich.) *State Journal*

Writing Process Tips

Here are some other tips to help you during the writing process:

Remember your focus. While you're writing, put your focus graph (the "so what" paragraph) at the top of your story as a reminder. It still needs to be placed within your story. Then choose only material that is related to the focus. A news story should have one main idea, and all other points, facts and quotes should substantiate, elaborate or somehow relate to that focus graph.

Write many leads. Instead of struggling to get the perfect lead, try writing several leads. Then write the rest of the story. Choose one lead when you've finished.

Fix later. As you are writing, when you get to a sentence or paragraph that doesn't sound right, write *fix* next to it or follow it with question marks to indicate that you want to return and polish it. Don't get slowed down by perfectionism as you draft your story.

Use the question/answer technique. As you are writing, does one paragraph raise a question or point that should be answered or explained in the next? Try to anticipate the reader's questions and answer them.

Read aloud. If you are struggling with a sentence that doesn't sound right, read it aloud. Also read your story aloud after you finish writing it. You'll hear the cumbersome parts that your eye didn't catch. Find them and fix them. This technique is especially helpful for broadcast journalists.

Check accuracy. Go back and check names, titles and quotes. Make sure you have the right person's name attached to the quote you have used. Check for typos and spelling.

Try pillow therapy. Go to sleep and return to the story the next day if you are not meeting a breaking-news deadline. Or at least take a break from the story. Then come back to it, reread it, and revise.

Writing Style

Newspapers reach a diverse audience. The general guideline is to write for an audience with an eighth-grade reading ability. That doesn't mean you should talk down to your reader. It means you should write clearly. The television audience is even more diverse. And clarity is equally crucial.

Here is some advice from some of the great writers who have appealed to people through the ages:

Mark Twain: "The difference between the right word and the nearly right word is the same as that between lightning and the lightning bug."

Robert Southey, English poet: "If you would be pungent, be brief; for it is with words as with sunbeams—the more they are condensed, the deeper they burn."

William Strunk Jr.: "Vigorous writing is concise. A sentence should contain no unnecessary words, a paragraph no unnecessary sentences, for the same reason that a drawing should have no unnecessary lines and a machine no unnecessary parts. This requires not that the writer make all his sentences short, or that he avoid all detail and treat his subjects only in outline, but that every word tell."

This quote is from a book that has become a classic for journalists and other writers. It was originally published in 1959 and has been reissued many times. *The Elements of Style,* first printed privately in 1918 by the late Professor William Strunk Jr. of Cornell University, was compiled by one of his students, writer E.B. White. Originally known as "the little book," it still is just 71 pages. But the rules and style tips have made a huge impact on writers for years. One of the most famous is "Omit needless words." For example, "the question as to whether" becomes "whether." The message is so simple. Perhaps that is why the book is so enduring.

William Zinsser: "Clutter is the disease of American writing. We are a society strangling in unnecessary words. . . . Fighting clutter is like fighting weeds—the writer is always slightly behind." This quote is from *On Writing Well,* which also offers many good writing tips for journalists.

Here are some additional writing tips that are generally recommended by and for journalists:

Use active voice whenever possible. Here's an example of passive voice:

Her first story always will be remembered by her.

The active voice has more impact:

She always will remember her first story.

Write short sentences—fewer than 25 words on average. David Finkel writes short sentences. And he wins writing awards. He mixes short sentences with long ones but stresses the short ones. Finkel, who now writes for *The Washington Post,* wrote this for the *St. Petersburg* (Fla.) *Times:*

Her weight's gone up. Gray hairs have sprouted. She's gotten used to flat shoes instead of heels and eggplant-shaped dresses instead of the gowns and furs she used to wear. But after a decade in prison for having her husband killed, Betty Lou Haber, closing in on 50, is still as polite and sweet-sounding as ever.

"There's never a night that I go to bed and don't say my prayers," she said last week. "I just do the best I can."

And that's why Albert Haber's surviving children are worried.

Ten years ago, after a sensational trial in Tampa, Mrs. Haber was convicted of planning the murder of her fourth husband, a well-known department store owner in Tampa and St. Petersburg. Her motive was to seize control of his estate. Her sentence was life in prison with a 25-year minimum before any chance of parole.

Sickened by the murder, Haber's four children took consolation in the thought that their stepmother would be locked up and gone from their lives at least until the year 2000.

But now, because of a little-known Florida law, she could be freed much sooner.

David Finkel, *St. Petersburg Times*

Write simple sentences. Keep the subject and verb close together. This example shows what happens when you don't. It is from a story about school board approval of remodeling and construction projects at the city's two schools.

Those two projects—calling for construction of classrooms, office area and media center at Wakefield and construction of a new district-wide kitchen and computer lab plus remodeling projects at the high school—will be paid for by using approximately $800,000 of the district's special capital outlay fund.

Whew! That's a long sentence. The subject is *projects,* and the verb is *will be paid.* They are separated by too many words. Split it into two sentences:

The two projects call for construction of classrooms, office area and media center at Wakefield and construction of a new district-wide kitchen, a computer lab and remodeling projects at the high school. The $800,000 approximate cost of the projects will be paid from the district's special capital outlay fund.

Vary the pace. Follow long sentences with short ones. If you use complex sentences, follow them with short, punchy ones:

Pamela Lewiston thought she was leading a normal life as the daughter of Dr. Normal Lewiston, a respected Stanford University physician, and his wife, Diana.
  She thought wrong.
  Her father had been married to—and lived with—two women besides her mother, all at the same time. His carefully managed deception ended in a cascading series of revelations after his death from a heart attack in August.

S.L. Wykes, *San Jose* (Calif.) *Mercury News*

Avoid jargon. Translate bureaucratic terms into simple ones; define technical terms. Here's advice from writer George Orwell:

> Never use a metaphor, simile or other figure of speech which you are used to seeing in print. Never use a long word when a short one will do. If it is possible to cut a word out, always cut it out. Never use the passive when you can use the active. Never use a foreign phrase, a scientific word, or a jargon word if you can think of an everyday English equivalent. Break any of these rules sooner than say anything outright barbarous.

And here's an example of garble purposely written by Orwell to demonstrate how not to write:

> Objective consideration of contemporary phenomena compels the conclusion that success or failure in competitive activities exhibits no tendency to be commensurate with innate capacity, but that a considerable element of the unpredictable must invariably be taken into account.

The translation is a passage from Ecclesiastes:

> I returned and saw under the sun, that the race is not to the swift, nor the battle to the strong, neither yet bread to the wise, nor yet riches to men of understanding nor yet favor to men of skill, but time and chance happeneth to them all.

And here's an example of garbled writing from the U.S. federal budget:

> Funds obligated for military assistance as of September 30, 1979, may, if deobligated, be reobligated.

Write the way you speak. Unless you speak like the bureaucrat who wrote that budget item.

Activities

1 Using information for any story you have gathered, write a plan for organizing it. Then write a draft and revise.

2 Try free-writing a story you have reported. Then write your first and final versions.

3 Take a newspaper story that you think is hard to understand or filled with jargon and rewrite it clearly, cutting unnecessary words and translating jargon.

4 FORK exercises: Write the following stories using the FORK method.

a Organize this story using a feature lead and the kiss-off technique. Consider repeating key words to make transitions. Make sure you have a clear nut graph (focus paragraph). Put it at the top of your story to guide you and in the body of your story where you think it is appropriate.

This story is about the resurgence of blind dating in New York City. You have interviewed several authorities, as well as people who have had blind dates. Feel free to paraphrase when appropriate; you do not have to use all these quotes or even all these sources. Do not just string quotes together. This information and these quotes, based on a story from The New York Times News Service, are not in good order:

Nathaniel Branden, a Los Angeles psychologist and author of _The Psychology of Romantic Love_ and _How to Raise Your Self-Esteem_: "Today, when people find it so hard to meet other people and when there is so much fear of different diseases, it's predictable and inevitable that we would see a resurgence of blind dating."

Amy Jaffee, 29, a journalist from New York who considers herself a matchmaker: "There's a Jewish legend that if you fix up two people and they get married and have children, you're guaranteed a place in heaven. I have three marriages under my belt, so I guess I'm in good shape." She says most romances that are arranged fizzle after the second or third date. "Usually, people try to fix others up on the basis that they both like to ski or they both like Islamic art. But I find those things don't make any difference. Instead, I ask friends to describe the last person they were in love with."

Herbert J. Freudenberger, a New York City psychologist: "Not long ago, a person willing to go on a blind date was perceived as a poor nebbish who had to rely on someone else to meet people. There's a complete shift in attitude now. It's a subtle swing back to a more conservative time."

Steven Veer, 28, a Manhattan attorney who has been on dozens of blind dates: "Personals are a last resort. A blind date is much better. It's a screen. You know the person hasn't 'overcirculated' in this time of caution" (referring to AIDS).

Melissa Mack, 24, a public relations writer: "New York can be a really lonely place. Everyone acquires an anonymous character. On the subway, the same people kicking and shoving and ignoring you might be loving and caring in a relationship." She is discouraged by the club scene. "What's so disenchanting about the club scene is that being cool and detached is the order of the day."

Morris Panner, 25, in his last semester at Harvard Law School: "In law school, my friends and I live on blind dates. Five years ago I would have thought it was really crass."

Barbara Wasserman, a New Yorker who met her husband, Bob Goldman, on a blind date: They had arranged to meet for their blind date by the Dumpster in front of Jeremy's Ale House, a popular hangout at Manhattan's South Street Seaport. They had low expectations that it would work out. Goldman had already had five unsuccessful blind dates.

Wasserman said that she was turned off when her date said on the telephone that he would be the good-looking guy in the blue suit. "I found the Dumpster, put down my briefcase and saw a sea of blue suits. All of a sudden, a truly good-looking guy in a blue suit came out of the crowd, smiling, and kissed me on the cheek."

They walked to Chinatown, ate dinner and shared a pitcher of beer. They spoke in French and discussed work, politics, travel, mutual friends and college experiences.

Goldman proposed 14 months later by tucking a diamond ring inside a fortune cookie.

Part of the reason for the popularity of the blind date is the AIDS epidemic. Another reason is dissatisfaction with the club scene and the overall loneliness of living in a big city like New York.

Pamela Harris, 26, a New York associate art director: "Someone you trust says there's this guy who's really great. There's a sense of safety. You feel like you're not being thrown to the wolves. A friend has insight into me and knows the kind of men I like, so basically, she's just cropped out 80 percent of the male population."

Sharon Lependorf, a consultant at People Resources, a New York singles club: "I've had at least three friends who got married in the last year and a half who met on blind dates."

b   This is a more challenging exercise. The notes are based on a feature story about college freshmen who gain the "Freshman 15" pounds. The story is by Tanya Barrientos from *The Philadelphia Inquirer.* Organize this story by using the basic FORK method. First read all the notes, find your focus, and write that at the top of your story. Then jot down a basic order for the story, blocking all the material from each source. Because this is a feature story, there is no single correct way to organize the information. Try to put it in an order that makes sense and avoids unnatural transitions. Also try to avoid stringing many quotes together. After you have found your focus, try to find an anecdotal lead based on a person or a creative lead based on the topic. If the information is not enclosed in quotation marks, the comments are not direct quotes.

General notes: Nutritionists agree it's understandable that students who stay up late to study need to eat to keep going. The nutritionists' newsletters suggest that fruit or even pretzels would be healthier snacks than candy or pizza.

The fabled Freshman 15 affects men and women, according to students.

Many schools send new students another helpful message during orientation: Find time between study and socializing to exercise every day, be it through sports, aerobics classes or a simple walk.

Some schools, such as the University of Pennsylvania and Rutgers University, offer special workshops to freshmen students to help them avoid the weight gain.

Those nasty 10 to 15 pounds that students tend to gain in the first few months of college have become as much a part of higher education as reading lists and blue-book exams.

Gene Lamm, a junior at Beaver College in Glenside: "I've gained 20 pounds since I left home." He made the comment as he shared an entire chocolate cake with two friends. "I used to have abs (abdominal muscles); I don't know what happened to them," Lamm said, chuckling, as he lifted his gray T-shirt.

Peg Abell, a nutritionist at Widener University: Often students eat out of stress and even more often in an effort to socialize and fit in. "Some people eat to feel better since eating can have a soothing effect, and some use eating as a way of maintaining control of at least one portion of their life."

Joe Leung, a junior at Villanova: "I went up for second portions every day. I weighed 115 when I came, and I got up to 140."

Missy Palko, a sophomore at Beaver College: "I gained 30 pounds last year. If you look in the closets around here, they're all packed with food."

An informal survey of dorm residents proved her right. Room after room held stashes of cheese crackers, doughnuts, popcorn, frosted breakfast cereals, chocolate and sodas.

Vanessa Varvarezis, a freshman who had been at Villanova only three weeks at the time of this interview: "I think I've already gained it. My parents sent me away with four bags of junk food, and it's almost half gone already."

Eating at Donahue Hall one recent evening, Varvarezis had spaghetti, garlic bread, vegetables, about eight cookies and a fudge ice cream pop. "It was Weight Watchers, though" (she said about the dessert).

According to a calorie chart given out by the Villanova food services staff, Varvarezis had eaten more than 900 calories for dinner. And that was before the late-night pizza run.

"I order out a lot," Varvarezis said. "Grease, grease, lots of grease."

Jim Martin, manager of California Style Pizza, near Villanova University: "We call them the pie hours." From 9 p.m. to 2 a.m., he said, his six employees deliver up to 50 pizzas per hour to the nearby campus. He routinely makes four extra pizzas for them to take along and sell on the spot. He said his delivery people have no trouble "hawking pizzas."

Craig Zabransky, a Villanova freshman: He was at Donahue Hall, eating dinner. "Well, I'm not having nightmares about it," he said, as he dug into a generous spaghetti dinner and his fourth piece of buttery garlic bread. "I'm just going to exercise more. I'm going to start tomorrow."

Stephen Bailey, a sociology professor who conducted a weight-gain study for Tufts University in Massachusetts with Tufts nutrition professor Jeanne Goldberg: They tracked 120 women through their first year of college. He said the Freshman 15 is "a myth." "Basically we came up with some results that surprised us. On average, the women gained a little bit less than a pound. They gained a bit between the fall and spring and lost all of that over the course of the summer." The participants were volunteers.

COACHING

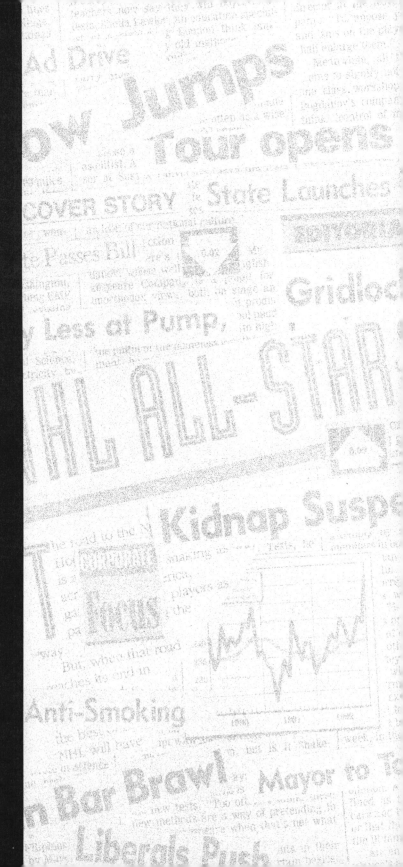

TIPS

Keep leads short—preferably fewer than 35 words.

Points of emphasis: Place the key words at the beginning or the end of the sentence for emphasis.

Tell it to a friend: In one sentence, explain what the story is about as if you were telling it to a friend.

Write a focus sentence at the top of your story.

Write a "so what" (impact) line at the top of your story.

Leads and Nut Graphs 10

The lead is crucial. It's the beginning of your story, a promise to the reader of what is to come. "Three seconds and the reader decides to read or turn to the next story. That's all the time you have to catch a reader's glance and hold it; all the time you have to entice and inform," says Donald Murray in his book *Writing for Your Readers.* No wonder writers are paranoid about their leads.

Research such as the Eye Trac study has revealed that readers scan headlines. Many of them don't even read the story. And if they start reading, many of them don't finish it. The study also revealed some startling news about how readers view a story: They often skip the lead and go to the third or fourth paragraph to find the nut graph, an interesting quote or an impact statement, because they are so conditioned to reading summary leads that reiterate headlines.

It's up to you to write leads that are enticing enough to make readers continue. There are many ways to do that.

The best day is the one when I can write a lead that will cause the reader at his breakfast the next morning to spit up his coffee, clutch at his heart and shout, "My God! Martha, did you read this?"

Edna Buchanan, former police reporter, *The Miami Herald*

Hard-News Leads, Soft Leads and Nut Graphs

The lead (originally spelled *lede* to differentiate it from "lead" type) tells the reader what the story is about. Think of the lead as a teaser or foreshadowing of what will come in the story. No matter what type of lead you write, you must back it up with information that substantiates it. If you haven't got material to support your lead, you have the wrong lead.

If you have been writing focus statements above your stories, you have a head start on writing leads. To write a focus statement, you asked yourself: What is the story about? What is the most important information? What is the point of this story? Those are the same questions you need to ask yourself to write a lead or a nut graph.

Sometimes nut graphs and leads are the same; sometimes they aren't. Here's how to tell the difference:

Hard-news leads: Also called a "direct lead" or a "summary lead." A hard-news lead summarizes in the first sentence what the story is about. A hard-news lead usually is only one sentence or two at most. It gets directly to the point. In this example, the first sentence is a summary lead. It tells who, what, when, where and why.

> HUDSON—A 13-year-old girl shot and slightly wounded her stepfather with a BB gun after he hit her mother on the head with a frying pan Saturday afternoon, according to the Pasco County Sheriff's Office.

Larry Dougherty, *St. Petersburg* (Fla.) *Times*

Nut graphs: Also called the "focus graph." The nut graph is a paragraph that explains the point of the story—what the story is about. A summary lead often tells that information and takes the place of a nut graph.

Soft leads: Also called a "feature lead" or a "delayed lead." A soft lead takes a little longer to get to the "what's it about" point of the story. It delays the answer to that question by teasing the reader with description, an anecdote or a storytelling approach called a "narrative lead." With a soft lead, you must tell the reader the point of the story in the nut graph. A soft lead may be several paragraphs. But in these days of impatient readers, the nut graph should be early in the story—usually by the third to fifth paragraph. Here is an example of a soft lead (a narrative one) and the nut graph:

SAN JOSE, Calif.—A nervous flight attendant was having trouble taking a urine drug test. So she drank a glass of water—and another—and another.

Soft lead: who, what

After guzzling three liters in three hours, she still couldn't urinate. But hours later, the 40-year-old woman staggered into a Burlingame, Calif., hospital, her speech slurred, her thinking fuzzy.

More what

Where

The diagnosis: She was drunk—on water.

The unidentified San Mateo County resident is the first drug-test taker known to suffer from "water intoxication," doctors reported yesterday in the *Journal of the American Medical Association.* There have been only seven other reported cases of healthy people with the dangerous condition, which causes water-logged brain cells and a dilution of body minerals. One died.

Nut graph: The focus tells "so what." The story is about the dangers of water intoxication in connection with drug testing.

Knight Ridder Tribune News

Many editors object to soft leads because they take too long to get to the point of the story. In a 1982 article in *Washington Journalism Review,* New York University journalism professors Gerald Lanson and Mitchell Stephens fueled that concern, blasting the soft lead as "Jell-O journalism." The professors provided alarming examples of ineffective soft leads. Consider this one:

Emma and Alfred Mitchell are surrounded by broken beer bottles, crumbling cigarette packages and other rubbish. But even when trespassers start grass fires, the couple never complains.

They can't. They're dead. The story was about deterioration in local cemeteries. That lead isn't just soft; it's deceptive.

But there is a middle ground between a hard, summary lead and a soft one that misses the point. It's a creative lead that gets to the point quickly without summarizing all the information in the first sentence. One version is an "impact lead"—telling the readers quickly how the story will affect them. In this example, the summary is in the second paragraph:

If the state commission says OK, you might never have to talk to an obnoxious salesman, harassing caller—or for that matter your whiny brother-in-law—over the phone again.

Pacific Bell, GTE California and Contel are seeking approval of a controversial service that allows subscribers to see the phone numbers of an incoming call before answering.

Michelle Vranizan,
The Orange County (Calif.) *Register*

How do you decide whether to use a hard or soft lead? The choice depends on several factors: the significance of the news, the timing, proximity (interest to your local readers), subject matter and, in many cases, your editor's preference. If the subject is serious—death, disasters, a major change in the law—consider a hard-news approach. Breaking news that happened yesterday or today also lends itself to a hard lead.

The next two examples are about the same subject. Consider why one was written with a soft lead and the other with a hard lead. (Note that these examples begin with a location in capital letters, called a "dateline." It indicates that the news occurred in a location outside the newspaper's circulation area. Newspapers have their own guidelines about when to use datelines.)

Soft lead

SAN MATEO, Calif.—The dog in her arms was shaking, its rheumy eyes wide with fear.

"Just relax, sweetheart, it's OK," crooned Chris Powell, the manager of the Peninsula Humane Society animal shelter, where 10,000 unwanted pets are put to death each year.

The dog settled into Ms. Powell's embrace, making it easier for a veterinarian to inject a lethal dose of sodium pentobarbital.

In seconds, the dog was dead, carried to a can, atop a mound of puppies and kittens, all awaiting pickup by a rendering company that would turn the animals into fertilizer.

"There's not a day when you don't think about walking away from this misery," Ms. Powell said.

Tired of carrying out the daily killings, officials at the Humane Society in San Mateo, on San Francisco Bay, have proposed a novel solution to the pet overpopulation problem: a moratorium on breeding cats and dogs that will be considered by the San Mateo County Board of Supervisors on Nov. 13.

The ordinance, thought to be the first of its kind in the nation and opposed by professional breeders, would fine animal owners to allow their pets to reproduce and would prohibit transporting cats and dogs outside the county for that purpose.

Jane Gross, *The New York Times*, Oct. 31, 1990

Nut graph

*Hard-news lead
and nut graph*

REDWOOD CITY (Calif.)—In an effort to reduce the number of unwanted pets put to death each year, the San Mateo County Board of Supervisors on Tuesday passed the nation's first law requiring owners of dogs and cats to buy a breeding license or get their pets sterilized.

The action, which affects pet owners in the unincorporated area of San Mateo County, culminates a heated and emotional two-month effort by local humane society officials to educate the public about the problems of pet over-population.

Fed up with putting more than 10,000 unwanted cats and dogs to death each year, the Peninsula Humane Society launched a grisly campaign to generate support for the ordinance. First, the group bought advertising inserts in local newspapers and subjected readers throughout the Bay Area to pictures of trash barrels full of dead cats.

Then the society held a public pet execution at a press conference, injecting five cats and three dogs with poison from a bottle marked "Fatal Plus" as cameras whirred and reporters jotted notes.

Miles Corwin, *Los Angeles Times,* Dec. 19, 1990

Timing and proximity were factors in the choice of lead. The story in *The New York Times* was written in October 1990, before the law passed and for a national audience not directly affected by the law. The hard-news version in the *Los Angeles Times* was written immediately after the law passed, and it affected people in the newspaper's circulation area.

There is no set rule to determine whether you should use a hard-news lead or a soft lead. The choice is really a matter of judgment. And graphics may affect your judgment.

The Impact of Graphics on Leads

It's a catch-22 situation. The reporter writes a summary lead. The copy editor writes a headline and a deck headline (the secondary headline) to hook the reader. The reporter doesn't know what the copy editor will write. And the copy editor needs to summarize the story in the headline. By the time readers get to the lead, they have read the same information three times. Consider this example:

Headline

MU fraternity punished for hazing

Deck headline

Hitting was alleged

Second deck headline

This was the 2nd group suspended this year

Summary lead

A University of Missouri fraternity has been suspended after a pledge complained he was hit so hard during initiation rites it made his head ring.

The fraternity, Phi Beta Sigma, became the second MU fraternity suspended this year for hazing. Earlier Phi Kappa Theta was suspended.

The Associated Press

The increasing use of graphics compounds the dilemma for the reporter. Studies show that readers are drawn first to pictures, then to headlines, briefs and other graphic devices. Highlights boxes, pull quotes and subheads (miniheadlines within the story to break up paragraphs) all vie for readers' attention.

Copy editors strive to avoid repetition, but they still need to summarize the story. Much of the burden is on the reporter to devise more creative leads that still get to the point quickly. To be a good writer, you need to know how to do many types of leads.

Hard-News Leads

Sometimes the lead on a hard-news story doesn't get right to the point in the first sentence. But most breaking stories use hard-news leads, also known as summary leads.

Summary Leads

A summary lead should answer several, but not all, of the basic questions: who, what, when, where and why, plus how and so what. If you cram all of them into the lead, it could be cumbersome.

Choose the most important factors for the lead. Save the others for the second or third paragraph. Here are some examples:

The Supreme Court yesterday forced the last remaining all-male eating club at Princeton University to admit women as members, letting stand a ruling that fraternities said presents "a grave threat" to their existence.	***Who, what, when***
The court declined to hear arguments by Tiger Inn, an exclusive century-old undergraduate club, that a New Jersey Supreme Court ruling requiring it to admit women interfered with its constitutional right of freedom of association. The club, a social organization and dining hall, will now have to admit women when it accepts new members this spring in the annual Princeton ritual known as "bicker."	***Why*** ***So what (impact)***

The Washington Post

The next example stresses "why":

| Brown University has expelled a student for shouting racial epithets, violating an anti-harassment rule enacted in 1989 as part of an effort by the university to combat racism on campus. | *Who, what, why* |
| It is the first time that a Brown student has been expelled for such a violation and is thought to be the first such expulsion in the country. | *So what (impact)* |

The New York Times

In the next example, "what happened" is stressed. It is also an example of cramming; the lead has 68 words! Try reading this aloud:

| NEW YORK—Police scuba divers inspecting the hull of an oil tanker in New York Harbor made an unusual discovery Thursday, and it was not only 366 pounds of cocaine hidden under water in the rudder compartments, but also the people who were guarding it: two shivering and louse-infested Colombians who had survived five stormy days in a 10-foot square compartment, virtual prisoners of the sea, authorities said. | *Who, what, when, where* |

The New York Times

Order of information   When you write a summary lead, how do you decide which basics to include and in what order? The points of emphasis should be the first or last words in the lead. Decide which elements are the most important—who, what, where, when, why, how or so what. Usually it is safe to use a subject-verb-object format: who did the action, what happened, to whom. But sometimes the how or why is most important.

Here are some facts presented in a story:

Who: three boaters

What happened: two killed, the third injured when the boat capsized

When: Sunday

Where: Lake Harney near the Volusia-Seminole county line in Florida

Why: high winds and waves

How: explained later in the story

The lead that appeared in the newspaper stresses "who" first, followed by "what":

> Two boaters were killed and a third was injured Sunday when their small boat capsized in high winds and waves on Lake Harney near the Volusia-Seminole county line.
>
> *The Orlando* (Fla.) *Sentinel*

Now look at the way the lead would read with different elements placed first:

What | A small boat that capsized in high winds and waves on Lake Harney near the Volusia-Seminole county line caused the death of two boaters and injuries to a third Sunday.

Where | On Lake Harney near the Volusia-Seminole county line, a small boat capsized Sunday in high winds and waves, causing the death of two boaters and injuries to a third.

When | On Sunday two boaters were killed and a third was injured when their small boat capsized in high winds and waves on Lake Harney near the Volusia-Seminole county line.

Why | High winds and waves on Lake Harney near the Volusia-Seminole county line caused a small boat to capsize Sunday, killing two boaters and injuring a third.

The actual lead from the newspaper seems the most logical because the point of emphasis—the important news (boaters died)—is first. The last lead, focusing on why, is the next best option; the point of emphasis (boaters died) is at the end.

Most of the time when you write a hard-news lead, you will put the most important information first. Or you might want the point of emphasis at the end of the sentence, as in this example:

> A consumer group said Thursday that some sunscreens and cosmetics contain an ingredient that can promote cancerous skin tumors and it called on the government to halt their sale.
>
> The Associated Press

Active versus passive voice   Active voice is generally preferable to passive. Active voice stresses who is doing the action; passive voice stresses those to whom the action is done. But you may need to use passive voice when the emphasis is on what happened instead of who caused it to happen, especially in police or court stories.

Here is an example of a lead written in the active voice:

> WEST PALM BEACH (Fla.)— Three students on spring break from Massachusetts remained in critical condition Sunday from the near-fatal effects of a carbon monoxide leak in a hotel.
>
> The Associated Press

Here is an example of a lead written in the passive voice:

> A former employee of the University of Pennsylvania's Van Pelt Library was sentenced to seven years of psychiatric probation yesterday for the theft of $1,798,310 worth of rare books and documents.
>
> The Philadelphia Inquirer

The sentence was imposed by Philadelphia Common Pleas Court Judge Russell M. Nigro, as the story later explains. The emphasis in the lead is on the employee who was sentenced. Here is how the lead would sound in active voice:

> Philadelphia Common Pleas Court Judge Russell M. Nigro yesterday sentenced a former employee of the University of Pennsylvania's Van Pelt Library to seven years of psychiatric probation for the theft of $1,798,310 worth of rare books and documents.

In this version, it takes longer to get to the point of the story, and the emphasis is on the judge, not the employee.

Where to say when   The time element can be confusing in a lead. In breaking news, when something happened yesterday, the time element usually does not come first in the sentence. You need to place it where it is accurate, even if it sounds awkward.

Here is an example of confusing time elements:

> University officials agreed to raise tuition by $100 Monday.

As written, the lead indicates the tuition will increase on Monday. Wrong. Tuition won't go up until next fall. Here's what really happened:

| University officials agreed <u>Monday</u> to raise tuition by $100. |

Delayed identification When the "who" in your lead is not a well-known person in your community or in the nation, you can identify the person by age, location, occupation or another modifier in the first paragraph. Then identify the person by name in the second paragraph. When you use delayed identification, even if your story involves several people, the first name you use should be the one you referred to in your lead.

All states have laws restricting the release of juvenile offenders' names, and several states prohibit the release of names of rape victims. In addition, many newspapers have policies to withhold the names of criminal suspects until they are formally charged with crimes. Therefore, you need to use alternative forms of identification in these situations as well.

The following examples show how to say "who" in the lead and delay identification:

Age

An 18-year-old Tampa man was shot and killed Wednesday after he and two friends confronted a gunman who had beaten a friend of theirs, Tampa police said.

Warren Smith III, of 3524 E. 26th Ave., was shot behind his right ear at 6:40 p.m. and was pronounced dead shortly after arriving at Tampa General Hospital, police said.

St. Petersburg Times

Occupation

Two Minneapolis meter monitors have been charged with stealing an estimated $35,000 worth of nickels, dimes and quarters from parking meters.

Dale Timinskis, 42, and Leroy Siner, 40, both of Minneapolis, were arrested Tuesday after police watched their activities.

Star Tribune (Minneapolis)

Location

A Joliet man who got up to change the channel on a TV set was hit in the forehead by a stray bullet and critically wounded, Joliet police said Monday.

Jimmie Anderson, 28, of 211 S. Chicago St., was being kept alive Monday by life-support machines in St. Joseph's Medical Center, said Detective Thomas Stein of the Joliet Police Department.

Chicago Tribune

Other identifier

A former Duke University student who posed as a wealthy French baron was a con artist with lavish desires, said a judge who sentenced the imposter to three years in prison for fraud.

Maurice Jeffrey Locke Rothschild, 38, who changed his name from Mauro Cortex Jr., was sentenced in Greensboro, N.C. for bilking two banks by posing as a nobleman from France's wealthy Rothschild family. The charges involved $12,000 Rothschild received after submitting false information on credit and credit card applications.

Newsday (New York)

If you are writing a story about a person who has been in the news frequently, such as a suspect in a trial, you may use the name, but add a phrase or clause to identify the person, as in this example:

Lisa Fox, the Ames (Ia.) woman convicted of shooting an Iowa State University professor, has asked for a new trial, saying her daughter, who wasn't allowed to testify, can prove she is innocent.

Fox, 34, was found guilty March 15 of attempted murder for shooting poultry science professor Robert Hasiak a year ago in the home they shared. Her daughter, Sonya, 17, also charged with the shooting, pleaded guilty the week before.

The Des Moines (Iowa) *Register*

Attribution in Leads

Attribution tells the reader where you got your information. Too much attribution can clutter a lead. Too little can get you in trouble. So when should you use it?

• If you know the information is factual and you witnessed it or have firsthand knowledge that it is true, you may eliminate the attribution. If you received the information by telephone, as in police or fire stories, attribute it to your source.

• Whenever you are saying anything accusatory, as in police or political stories, you must attribute the information.

• You also must attribute the quotes or partial quotes you use in a lead.

To keep attribution clutter to a minimum, you may give a general reference to some sources—such as "police said" or "experts say"—if their titles are long. Then, as in delayed identification, give the specific name and title in the second reference.

Fact versus opinion Here are some examples that demonstrate when to use attribution:

An 88-year-old man died Monday afternoon when fire spread through his second-floor apartment at the Wellington Arms Apartments in north St. Louis County.	*Fact: No attribution is needed.*
An 88-year-old man died in north St. Louis County Monday afternoon, apparently after he started a fire while smoking in bed, authorities said.	*Opinion: Speculation about the cause needs to be attributed.*
The body of a man who had been fatally stabbed was discovered Monday morning in a city trash bin in the Lewis Place neighborhood, police said.	*Attributed fact: Attribution for fact is needed because the reporter got the information secondhand (by telephone).*

St. Louis Post-Dispatch

Accusations   A person is innocent until proven guilty in court. In crime stories, attribute any accusatory statements to police or other authorities, especially when you are using a suspect's name. If the person has been charged with a crime, you may state that without attribution. The word *allegedly* can be used when the charges have not been proved, but direct attribution to the police is preferable. Here are some examples:

| A University of North Florida chemistry major has been charged with building a 35-pound "mega-bomb" powerful enough to destroy everything within a radius of 150 yards. | *No attribution is needed.* |

The Associated Press

| David Roger Flint killed 16-month-old Brittany K. Boyer on Monday by dangling her by the arms, swinging her side to side and beating her head against the floor and wooden furniture, police say. The 23-year-old Flint was arrested about 10:30 p.m. Tuesday and accused of murder. | *An attribution is needed for an accusatory statement.* |

Jane Meinhardt, *St. Petersburg Times*

| A 38-year-old paroled murderer has been arrested in St. Croix County, Wis., for allegedly kidnapping and raping two 16-year-old girls in Minneapolis last month. . . . | *The word allegedly is used because it has not yet been proved that the kidnap and rape occurred.* |

He was charged with two counts of first-degree criminal sexual conduct and two counts of kidnapping.

St. Paul (Minn.) *Pioneer Press*

Later, the lead is backed up this way.

A 38-year-old paroled murderer has been charged with kidnapping and raping two 16-year-old girls in Minneapolis last month.

This lead would be a safer alternative.

Quotes Whenever you quote someone directly, indirectly or partially, you need to attribute the statement. Full quotes are difficult in leads and can be awkward. They are more common in feature stories than hard news but may be effective in some hard-news stories like speeches or court cases. A more effective technique is the use of partial quotes, especially when the speaker says something controversial or dramatic. Leads also may contain reference quotes, just a few words referring to something controversial. These do not need immediate attribution. Both partial and reference quotes should be backed up later in the story with the full quote or with the context in which the statement was made. Here are some examples of how quotes are used and attributed in leads:

Clarence Thomas, defiant in the face of allegations of sexual harassment, told senators Saturday that he would not give up his nomination to the Supreme Court, saying, "I'd rather die than withdraw."

Knight Ridder Tribune News

A full quote is used in the lead.

"I've done everything out there," 31-year-old Gilbert Franco told his wife Thursday. "All that's left to do is learn the Bible and to die."

The next day, San Jose police say, Franco entered the C&S Market at East Julian and 26th streets and shot to death Katherine Young Suk Choe, 40, whose family owns the store.

Seconds later, 50 yards away, Franco fatally shot himself in the head.

San Jose (Calif.) *Mercury News*

A full quote is used in this lead because it is dramatic.

Although there have been important changes in the lives of women around the world over the last two decades, with some significant regional gains, "the majority still lags far behind men in power, wealth and opportunity," Secretary General Javier Perez de Cuellar concludes in a new United Nations report on women.

The New York Times

Because the partial quote used in the lead is rather complete, it is not repeated in the story.

The University of Pennsylvania announced yesterday that it was penalizing a senior scientist for "lapses of judgment" in an experiment last April in which more than 120 people may have been exposed to a virus that can cause a fatal form of leukemia. . . .

The committee concluded that the professor was not guilty of research misconduct as defined in a school policy. However, the committee concluded that there were "lapses of judgment and failures of communication" in the experiment.

The Philadelphia Inquirer

A reference quote is used in the lead.

The backup puts the partial quote in context.

Amid charges of "smelly politics," Gov. Terry Branstad and key legislators sparred Monday over the state's obligation to finance a pay raise for state employees. . . .

"Smelly politics is what it amounts to, and we're not going to stand for it," said Sen. Mike Connolly.

The Des Moines Register

A reference quote is used in the lead.

The backup uses the full quote.

Attribution first or last   The rule of thumb in the lead is to put the most important information first. If the attribution is cumbersome and will slow the lead, put it at the end. If it is brief, you can put it first.

Casual drug use has dropped sharply during the last five years, but the number of addicts using cocaine daily has not changed significantly, the federal government reported yesterday.

The Philadelphia Inquirer

Attribution last

The federal government reported yesterday that casual drug use has dropped sharply during the last five years, but the number of addicts using cocaine daily has not changed significantly.

Attribution first (acceptable but not as strong)

Women who work full time earn about two-thirds the annual income of men, according to a report on the status of American women.

The report by the nonprofit Women's Research and Education Institute also said female college graduates normally make less than males who have finished only high school—$25,444 in 1987, compared with $27,293 for the men.

The Washington Post

Attribution last (because name is cumbersome and not as important as conclusions)

Cluttered attribution In the first example, note how a long attribution at the start of the sentence clutters the lead:

Karen Davisson, child protection worker with the Kansas Department of Social Rehabilitation Services district office in Emporia, said Tuesday that only rarely are neglected or abused children removed from their parents' care and placed in foster homes or put up for adoption.

Cluttered

Neglected or abused children are rarely removed from their parents' care and placed in foster homes or put up for adoption, a state social worker said Tuesday.

Uncluttered (identification in second paragraph)

One of the most common causes of clutter in leads is too much information about where and when something was said. Put some of this material in the second paragraph. Put the location of the meeting much further down in the story, or eliminate it altogether unless it is important to the reader.

Fort Riley is being considered as a possible host for the proposed joint landfill for Geary and Riley counties, Riley County Director of Public Works Dan Harden said during an informational meeting Tuesday night at the Geary County 4-H Senior Citizens Center.	*Cluttered*

Fort Riley is being considered as a possible site for a landfill, a Riley County official said Tuesday. Dan Harden, director of public works, said. . .	*Uncluttered*

Impact Leads

The summary lead usually stresses basic facts about the news in the immediate past, and it is usually written in past tense. This type of breaking-news lead often is referred to as a "first-day" lead, as if readers were hearing the news for the first time.

Because television provides more immediate news, newspapers often focus on the impact of the story or the next step. A "second-day" lead is used to advance the story. It answers these questions: So what? What does this news mean to a reader? How will a reader be affected? What is the next development in this news story? This type of lead is called an "impact lead."

In the past, editors favored first-day leads for newspapers delivered in the morning, because they presumed readers were getting the news for the first time. Editors of afternoon newspapers usually stressed advancing the story. Although that distinction still holds for many editors, a more popular trend at all newspapers is to provide something new—the impact or a different approach from the news that readers might have heard on television.

Heath Meriwether, executive editor of the *Detroit Free Press,* is committed to making sure that stories at his paper contain the impact—within the story if not in the lead. He insists that writers place an impact statement explaining "so what" at the top of their story, as a guide to editors. That's a good idea you can use: Add an impact statement after your summary line at the top of your story.

Impact leads can be written in a summary form or in a more creative form, like a soft lead. However, the story is still hard news, not a feature. The information you give must be factual, not your interpretation. And if you use an indirect lead, you must write a clear nut graph early in the story.

In this example, the writer is showing the impact of the Rhode Island governor's attempts to cut state spending:

Nut graph— main point of story

PROVIDENCE, R.I.—No welfare checks were written Friday in Rhode Island. No criminals were prosecuted, no driver's licenses were issued or renewed, no legislation was passed and not a single lawyer filed a new case in state court.

State government, the largest employer in Rhode Island, simply did not open. And it will do that nine more times before the end of the fiscal year on June 30 in an effort not to go broke.

From state parks to the Statehouse, doors were locked and most workers were told to stay home.

"It's a total hardship," said Norman Miller, who led a small band of Transportation Department workers picketing in front of the Statehouse and the Registry of Motor Vehicles in downtown Providence.

They were among the roughly 19,000 state workers furloughed Friday.

The workers face the prospect of losing 10 percent of their annual pay as Gov. Bruce G. Sundlun tries to rein in what he describes as the worst state budget deficit in the nation, when measured as a percentage of total spending.

Ross Sneyd, The Associated Press

Secondary nut graph— more impact

Here is a summary lead with an impact approach:

Summary lead with impact

Southwest Missouri State University must release its campus crime reports to the public, a federal judge ruled Wednesday in a case that could affect colleges across the nation.

U.S. District Judge Russell G. Clark called the withholding of those reports unconstitutional and ordered university officials to provide the public and media access to them.

The ruling, thought to be the first of its kind in the nation, has prompted the U.S. Department of Education to begin re-evaluating its stand on the release of campus reports.

Backup with more impact

The Kansas City (Mo.) *Star*

Soft Leads

Coaching Tips Try writing many different leads instead of struggling to find the perfect one. Don't wait for a creative muse.

Make sure your lead is related to your focus and can be backed up in your story.

Do not strain to "create" a lead from your head. Pull from the story, not from your head, for inspiration.

Soft leads can be fun to write and fun to read. They can also be painful. If you don't get to the point quickly, they can be tedious.

Although soft leads are also called delayed leads, the lead is still first. Only the nut graph is delayed. Remember that all leads, especially soft leads, must be backed up in the story and must lead to a nut graph. In some cases, if the lead is very compelling, you may delay the nut graph until the 10th paragraph or more. But it is still better to place the nut graph higher in the story, preferably by the third to fifth paragraph.

The graphic device of a "so what" summary line is one way of compromising between the soft lead and the immediate need for the point of the story. The *Reno* (Nev.) *Gazette-Journal* uses that device as its way of reaching readers quickly. "A good summary allows you to still have an anecdotal lead, but you're not delaying the information," says Vikki Porter, managing editor. She wants reporters to think "what does this story mean to you" before they write their leads. Here is an example of a soft lead with a summary line:

Headline	**Doctor seeks vending machine ban**
Summary line	*In unincorporated Washoe: A deputy district attorney is compiling information on California ordinances*
Anecdotal lead	One of cardiologist Richard Seher's patients started smoking before puberty. He was up to two packs a day when he had a heart attack—at 19.

The teen was diagnosed with coronary heart disease and cholesterol blockage of the arteries, the doctor recalls.

Because of young patients such as that teen-ager, Seher has proposed Washoe County Commissioners ban cigarette vending machines outside of Reno and Sparks. — **Nut graph**

Darcy DeLeon, *Reno Gazette-Journal*

There are many types of soft leads. They can be used on news or feature stories. Most of them follow a simple concept: Use a specific example to illustrate the main point of the story.

Many soft leads start with a person who is one of many people sharing the same problem. The idea behind these soft leads—called "anecdotal leads"—is that readers like to read about people. Readers can relate better to one person's problems than to a general statement of a problem.

Other common types of soft leads are descriptive and narrative. "Descriptive leads" describe a person or a scene. "Narrative leads" are storytelling leads that recount the event in a dramatic way, like the plot in a novel, to put the reader on the scene as the action occurred.

And then there are leads that are just clever or catchy and don't fall into any distinct category.

It's not what you call them that matters. It's how you write them. The important point is to tell a good story. When writers struggle with soft leads, it is often because they think they must create something clever. All too often, the result is a cliche. It is best to look at your notes and build a lead based on something interesting in the story, instead of waiting for the creative muse.

The sections that follow show a variety of ways to structure a soft lead. The basic techniques are descriptive, anecdotal and narrative. The others are applications of these three.

Descriptive Leads

This type of lead describes a person, place or event. It is like the descriptive focus-on-a-person lead, but it doesn't have to focus on a person who is one of many. It can be used for news or feature stories.

In this example, the story focuses on the man who is causing the problem:

Skippack farmer John W. Hasson stood ankle-deep in mud, pumping milk into a wooden trough as his pigs, squealing and grunting, snouts quivering, climbed over each other to get to their feed.

Hasson inhaled deeply.

"Does that smell sour to you? That's what they call noxious fumes," he said with a sniff toward his new neighbors, Ironbridge Estates, a subdivision of two-story colonial houses costing $200,000 plus.

Ironbridge's developers say Hasson's farm smells.

And his 250 pigs squeal too much.

So they have filed suit in Montgomery County to force him to clean up his act. The case is scheduled to be heard May 8.   ***Nut graph***

Erin Kennedy, *The Philadelphia Inquirer*

Anecdotal Leads

This type of lead starts with a story about a person or an event. In a sense, all soft leads are anecdotal, because they are all storytelling approaches. Many combine descriptive and anecdotal techniques.

This lead is an anecdote—the story behind a woman's court case:

Late one spring night in 1981, after drinks at a bar and a bit of protest, Elaine Hollis agreed to her boyfriend's desire to capture their passion on videotape.

Inside Edward Bayliss' apartment, the video camera rolled at the foot of his bed.

He promised to erase the tape.

Seven years later, Hollis, who has a son with Bayliss, was in Delaware County Court accusing him of contriving to bring her into disrepute by exhibiting the tape.

Bayliss, president of Philadelphia Suburban Electrical Service in Upper Darby, admitted showing the tape to one of his friends.

Hollis contended he showed and distributed the tape in Delaware County and surrounding areas, as well as gave copies of it to two bar owners in Darby, who played it for customers.

Last week, after three years of litigation, a county judge upheld an Oct. 15 Common Pleas Court order that mandated Bayliss pay Hollis $125,000 to settle her lawsuit.

Patrick Scott, The Philadelphia Inquirer

Nut graph

This lead uses both anecdotal and descriptive techniques:

Dawn Clark's cat walked carefully across the lawn, then stopped suddenly, looking bewildered.

The cat sniffed tentatively, then bolted off the grass and spent the next few minutes licking its paws—trying to clean the paint flecks from them.

The lawn had recently been mowed and was green as a billiard table, because it had just been painted with a vegetable dye.

Nut graph Santa Barbara residents have devised innovative ways to keep their yards green since the city, faced with an expected water shortfall of nearly 50 percent for the year, declared a "drought emergency" in late February and banned lawn watering.

Clark's cat had just experienced one: Several landscape companies now offer painting and local nurseries are stocking their shelves with green paint and pump sprayers.

Miles Corwin, Los Angeles Times

Extension of nut graph

Narrative Leads

Like an anecdotal lead, a narrative lead tells a story. It relates the story or reconstructs the incident so readers can feel as if they are witnessing it. Narrative writing uses all the techniques of fiction, including dialogue, scene setting and foreshadowing—giving the reader clues to what will happen. It takes longer to set up the nut graph for this kind of lead, but if the story is dramatic enough, the narrative approach may work.

Here is an example. (Note: Although this lead is accusatory, it is OK because the man has been convicted.)

Foreshadowing

DADE CITY (Fla.)—It was a little past 2:30 a.m. at the Circle K and the 35-year-old woman on duty as clerk was alone. Her terror was about to begin.

The door swung open and in walked a customer. She greeted him and he smiled. But in an instant, he held a large knife against her neck, dragged her to a back room of the store and raped her.

"I kept thinking, 'I know this guy,' even while it was happening," she recalled on Monday, still shaken three years after the ordeal. She was convinced he would kill her.

But she lived.

"For five or six days after, I would lie awake thinking about where I had seen him," she recalled. "It came to me in the middle of the night."

The single mother, who had been working at the remote convenience store to support two sons, believed she had seen her assailant hanging out with high school kids at a different convenience store in Dade City where she had previously worked. She obtained old yearbooks from Pasco Comprehensive High School and began thumbing through the pictures.

"I found his picture in the third one I looked at. I instantly recognized him," she said.

Douglas Collier Wilson. Class of 1986.

She went to the Pasco County sheriff's detective handling the case and showed him Wilson's picture. Five days later the detective went to Wilson's apartment two and a half blocks from the store where she was attacked and arrested him for rape.

Nut graph

On Monday Wilson, 22, pleaded no contest before Circuit Judge Maynard Swanson and was found guilty. He was sentenced to nine years in state prison.

Nancy Weil, *St. Petersburg Times*

Focus-on-a-Person Leads

You can focus on a person in two ways: use an anecdotal approach, telling a little story about the person, or use a descriptive approach that describes the person or shows the person in action. This type of lead can be used in profile stories about the person or in news stories about issues, where the person is one of many affected by the point of your story.

This example uses the descriptive approach:

Nita walked slowly down the narrow hall, deftly guiding her tottering 11-month-old son around the abandoned baby walkers, strollers and toys.

Inside her tiny bedroom, the 17-year-old mother pointed to photographs of her son's father and some of her friends. Cards congratulating her on her recent high school graduation were nearby. The baby's crib was crammed into an area near the door.

Nut graph— points out that person is one of many

Nita, one of 85 residents at Florence Crittenton Services in Fullerton, is one of a growing number of teen-agers having babies in Orange County—a figure that has increased 36 percent in five years.

Janine Anderson, *The Orange County Register*

This example uses an anecdotal approach to focus on a person for a story about a larger issue. The concept is to use a specific example of the general problem.

The state of Kansas took Mary Jaramillo's daughters. Now it wants her money.

Jaramillo, a 38-year-old single mother, didn't object when social workers took custody of two unruly daughters even Jaramillo admits she couldn't control.

But she never knew she would get stuck with the bill for the year her 18-year-old spent and the seven months her 13-year-old spent in foster homes.

In her case, the bill, which totals $19,600, came without warning when it popped up one day in her mailbox. Jaramillo, a hospital secretary, earns $11,000 a year. She already teeters on the brink of poverty.

"I couldn't believe it," Jaramillo said about the day she learned of the debt. "I thought, 'What in the world am I going to do?' I can't come up with money I don't have."

Jaramillo is not alone. Each year, the Department of Social and Rehabilitation Services files hundreds of lawsuits seeking to recoup from parents at least part of the cost of foster care, juvenile detention, drug programs and other youth services the agency provides. Currently there are several thousand children in the state under foster care.

SRS officials maintain their policy stems from a legitimate premise: Taxpayers shouldn't pay for services that parents ought to provide. No matter how poor, parents are financially responsible for their children, a philosophy entrenched in common law, agency officials said.

Critics contend that SRS is mishandling the operation and violating parents' rights.

Steve Kraske, *The Kansas City Star*

Nut graph— points out that person is one of many

Extension of nut graph

Contrast Leads

This type of lead can be used to set up stories about conflicts or unusual circumstances. The two most common ways to write contrast leads revolve around circumstances and time.

But-guess-what contrast Contrast leads that revolve around circumstances can be used to explain something unusual:

William Pearce, known to his patients as Dr. William J. Rick, was charming and slick, say his former associates and police detectives.

He came to town with medical degrees, numerous national board certificates and myriad other qualifications.

But the real Dr. Rick died in 1986, police say.

And now William John Pearce, 57, is in jail on charges of impersonating a doctor.

Sharon McBreen, *The Orlando* (Fla.) *Sentinel*

Nut graph

Here is a descriptive lead setting up contrast without the "but":

DENVER—Above a pond labeled "Industrial Waste," two bald eagles perch on a tree limb. Down the road from workers in white protective suits, scores of prairie dogs scurry across a field. Around the corner from hundreds of barrels containing remnants of mustard gas, a dozen mule deer stand in a thicket.

It's a paradox that some view as almost poetic: The Army's Rocky Mountain Arsenal—a shut-down war factory, a boarded-up lesson in how not to treat the environment, one of the most poisoned pieces of land in the United States—has become a haven for wildlife.

Nut graph

John Woestendiek, *The Philadelphia Inquirer*

Then-and-now contrast   Time contrasts—then and now—are useful ways to show change. This type of lead also can be used when the background is interesting or important and is relevant to the focus.

It was March 1964 when Lewis "Hackie" Wilson, the 7-year-old son of a St. Petersburg firefighter, disappeared after stopping to pick up flowers on his way home from school.

His case received national attention a month later when a sheriff's posse on horseback, flushing out rattlesnakes ahead of a line of 80 searchers, found the child's bones in a field south of Venice.

Now, nearly 27 years later, the case may be revived. Prosecutors in Sarasota County have realized that Joseph Francis Bryan, a convicted child kidnapper indicted for Hackie's murder in 1965, has never been brought to trial.

Nut graph

Karen Datko, *St. Petersburg Times*

Teaser Leads   These leads use the element of surprise to tease the reader into the story. The nut graph may also be a contrast, but the first sentence sets it up as a tease into something unusual.

BURLINGTON, Vt.—This is no ordinary public library.

For one thing, there are only four books on the shelves. For another, you won't find any of these works, or the many that are expected to join them soon, at other libraries or bookstores.

You probably never will.

That's because the Brautigan Library, which opened here last weekend, has a unique policy—it only accepts books that have never been published.

Nut graph

Steve Stecklow, *The Philadelphia Inquirer*

Motorists heading north on U.S. 101 customarily slow down when they see Officer Gregory—with his radar gun—sitting in his patrol car.

But he's never pulled anyone over and never will.

Officer Gregory is a dummy.

The mannequin is not meant to be a trick, but Police Chief A.C. "Andy" Anderson just wants people traveling through Fold Beach to wonder: Is it live or is it Gregory?

The department obtained Gregory three weeks ago on the premise that drivers invariably slow down when they see a policeman with a radar gun. **Nut graph**

The Associated Press

Mystery Leads

Like teasers, these leads promise the reader a surprise or a treat for reading on. They set up the story like a mystery novel. They're fun to write and fun to read, but they won't work unless the subject matter lends itself to this approach.

They know who you are, what you eat, how you procreate—and where to find you.

Do you like ice cream? The U.S. government has used that information to track down draft-dodging 18-year-olds who signed up for ice cream parlor "birthday clubs."

Can't have kids? Georgetown University Medical Center last year got a mailing list of upscale, childless couples and sent them a letter reading: "...with proper treatment, nearly 75 percent of infertile couples can go on to conceive and successfully deliver a child."

Been turned down for a MasterCard or Visa? List Brokerage and Management, a New York list marketer, may have your name. It rents a list of 1.6 million people rejected for bank cards—obtained, the company says, from the very banks that turned you down. "All kinds of businesses" use the mailing list, "because someone turned down for credit is looking for opportunity," says Phil Hurowitz, a broker at List Brokerage.

No fact, it seems, is too private to market. From your belt size to your Playboy subscription, details about your life are routinely traded, rented or sold. And thanks to modern technology, it's only going to get worse—or better, if you like getting lots of direct mail that's sent to you specifically because of those personal details.

For the first time, computer companies are hooking up with credit bureaus and massive data banks to allow people with only a desktop computer to single you out by income, age, neighborhood, car model or waist size. **Nut graph**

Stephen Koff, *St. Petersburg Times*

This lead uses not only the mystery approach, but also the format of the novel as part of the lead:

The case has all the elements of a 1950s film noir mystery.

The characters: the scheming husband, the trusting wife, the other woman.

The story: The husband, Ray Valois, buys a lottery ticket, scratches it and finds three "Spin, Spin, Spin" symbols. That makes him eligible to win up to $2 million in the California "Big Spin" lottery, but he does not want to tell his wife, Monica, according to his statement in San Luis Obispo County Superior Court records. So he gives the ticket to another woman, waitress Stephanie Martin. She agrees to cash in the ticket, according to court records, and secretly give him half.

The inevitable plot twist: Valois and Martin turn on each other. He claims that he owns the ticket. She claims that she owns the ticket.

The conclusion: Martin spins and wins $100,000. But the wife finds out and sues both of them for fraud.

Now neither Martin nor Valois has the $100,000. His wife's attorney, Gary Dunlap, obtained a temporary restraining order, restricting lottery officials from awarding the winnings until a court hearing today.

Nut graph

Miles Corwin, *Los Angeles Times*

Build-on-a-Quote Leads

If you have a great quote, build your lead around the quote that will back up your first sentence. But be careful not to repeat too much of the quote in your lead; that's boring and repetitious. Building on quotes is an easy and effective way to find a lead, providing the quote is related to the focus of the story. This technique works equally well for hard-news leads.

ANDOVER, Kan.—Melinda Easterbrook knows exactly how long it took for a tornado to blast apart her comfortable home while she and her husband huddled in the basement.

"It lasted five Hail Marys and two Our Fathers, but you have to say them quickly," she said yesterday.

While she was praying, the concrete basement rumbled and shook. When she and her husband, Bryan, came upstairs, they were hardly prepared for the scope of the destruction that had swept through this small town about five miles east of Wichita.

Nut graph

Larry Fish, *The Philadelphia Inquirer*

The next example is the kind of build-on-a-quote lead to avoid. The backup quote says the same thing as the lead, and it's right after the lead, so it's boring.

Cesar Chavez is calling for a boycott of California grapes because he says farmworkers are exposed to pesticides that are natural poisons.

"Pesticides by nature are poison," said Chavez, president of the United Farm Workers of America. "The pesticides are absorbed from the grape leaves into the skin of farm workers and are causing cancer at alarming rates."

Chavez spoke last night to about 700 people at the University Forum in a speech sponsored by the Hispanic-American Alliance.

Nut graph

List Leads

If you have a few brief examples to lead into your focus, you may list them in parallel sentences—making sure your sentences have the same construction, such as subject-verb-object order. Or if you start with clauses, make sure all the sentences start that way. Three seems to be a magic number; more than three can be awkward and tedious.

Boston College has an assistant dean for alcohol and drug education. Rutgers University sets aside dorm rooms for recovering student alcoholics. The University of Nevada bars students from leaving school sports events to make alcohol runs. Increasingly, colleges are confronting problem drinking by providing education and rehabilitation programs, alternatives to the campus bar scene and stricter regulation of on-campus parties.

The Associated Press

Nut graph

Question Leads

These can be effective if the reader is interested in finding the answer to the question you pose. If not, you could lose the reader. One way to test question leads is to determine if the answer would be yes or no. Those are the dangerous ones. A question that raises a more thoughtful, and more interesting, answer is preferable.

What are the odds of finding your true love by placing an ad with a telephone dating service?

About one in 40, according to Terry Ehlbert.

On April 13, Ehlbert is planning to marry Scott Anderson, who was the last of 40 guys she agreed to meet after placing a voice-mail ad with the 1-976-DATE service she saw advertised on TV....

The phone services work in much the same way published personal ads do.

Rich Shefchik, *St. Paul Pioneer Press*

Nut graph

The next example is a little dangerous. What if you don't want to buy cigarettes at all? Will you read on?

Want to buy cigarettes while at the gas station? Or while sipping a cocktail at your favorite bar?

Not in Lower Merion, if township officials have their way.

Nut graph   Officials there, concerned about the availability of cigarettes to minors, have proposed a municipal law prohibiting cigarette vending machines in the township. The law would be the first of its kind in Pennsylvania.

The Philadelphia Inquirer

Cliche Leads

In general, avoid them. But occasionally, a play on words will work as a clever lead. Consider this:

Nick Agid's workshop is just a stone's throw from the Torrance post office. Good thing, too. When Agid drops a postcard into the mail, it lands with a five-pound thud.

Nut graph   Agid is a sculptor who carves messages on leftover chunks of marble and granite. They become postcards when he adds scratched-on addresses and slaps stamps on the slabs.

Bob Pool, *Los Angeles Times*

Leads to Avoid

The leads in this section are strained, obtuse, rambling or just plain awful. They don't work for a variety of reasons.

Good news/bad news leads   The bad news is this type of lead. They're cliches, and they're used so often that they're boring. They're also judgmental.

Some good news for city workers: The Dinkins administration has been giving signals that it might not have to give out any pink slips, at least for now.

Some bad news for city taxpayers: The Dinkins administration has shown no signs of scaling back its proposal to raise taxes for the next several years.

Newsday (New York)

Crystal ball leads   These are dream-sequence leads that foretell the future. If you were writing about psychics, perhaps you could write this kind of lead. But most people can't predict the future. "John Jones never imagined when he boarded the plane that it was going to crash." Would he have been stupid enough to board it if he had known? Leads that emphasize "if only they had known" are farfetched. Consider the following. It's unlikely that a child who is choking is thinking about the future—much less about what he can do for someone else.

When 10-year-old Jason Finser of Clermont was saved from choking to death at a family dinner two years ago, he never dreamed he would be able to return the favor.

But luckily for his classmate, 9-year-old Abby Muick, Jason knew exactly what to do when she choked on a chocolate-and-Rice Krispies treat in the lunchroom at Minneola Elementary School.

Nut graph

The Orlando Sentinel

Nightmare leads   These are also dream leads, usually relating to a past experience. The nightmare analogy is overused. "The past three days were like a nightmare for John Jones." For the reader, too. Every bad experience someone has does not have to be compared to a nightmare. Nightmare leads appear in both hard and soft leads.

The laughter and frivolity of lunchtime recess turned into a horrifying nightmare of terror and death Tuesday when a heavily armed gunman shot and killed five children and wounded 30 others at Stockton's Cleveland Elementary School.

The Stockton (Calif.) *Record*

The nightmare became reality for local police on Dec. 5, 1985 when a Niagara Falls drug dealer was arrested at the Greater Buffalo International Airport. Hidden in his baggage were $50,000 worth of heroin, some PCP, and a sampling of a new drug he referred to as "smokable cocaine."

Niagara (New York) *Gazette*

Chair-sitter leads   This type of lead is a pet peeve of Jane Harrigan, a journalism professor at the University of New Hampshire, who coined the term. Setting the scene is fine, she says, but if sitting in a chair is the most unusual thing that the subject of the story does, can you blame a reader for turning the page? Harrigan makes a good point.

Consider this lead from a story about a very famous author. Is sitting in a chair the most interesting thing the writer could find about this world-renowned man? This example is a poor use of the but-guess-what lead because the reader may be too bored to get to the twist.

ST. PETERSBURG—He sits behind his desk in a yellow nylon jacket, blue shirt and khaki pants. With his thin face, glasses and fringe of white hair, he could be any winter visitor.

But he is not. He's author James Michener, who is about to end his first winter in St. Petersburg.

Nut graph

St. Petersburg Times

Plop-a-person leads   This type of lead is a misuse of the focus-on-a-person lead. When the writer just tops the story with a sketch of a person and does not back it up in the text, that's plopping. It's also misleading. The reader starts the story thinking the person has something to say or do in the story. But after the lead, the person disappears.

Tuesday was a good day for psychology professor Carnot Nelson.

He spent most of it helping an honors student work on her thesis. He read another student's doctoral dissertation and two master's thesis proposals. Then he went to a meeting, which he left after an hour and a half so he could do some reading of his own.

This is the last time we hear about Nelson, despite his being a good example.

Nelson, a senior professor at the University of South Florida, who also teaches large undergraduate classes and small graduate seminars, is a good example of the range of activity involved in teaching Florida university students.

"Education is a one-at-a-time, hand-made business," said state university spokesman Pat Riordan. "You can't mechanize it, you can't computerize it and you can't put it on an assembly line.

But college professors in Florida are under increasing pressure to do exactly that. Recurring state budget cuts have made some classes larger and eliminated many others. And a political climate that says there can be no new taxes until a state government becomes "more productive" has fueled a drive to force professors to spend more time in the classroom.

Nut graph

St. Petersburg Times

Strained leads   The lead must relate clearly to the nut graph. When you try too hard to be clever, you may miss the point.

This story is about a farm show featuring sheep and other animals. Although the lead is backed up, it doesn't really relate to the focus of the story:

Men with discriminating taste read GQ and women in the know read Cosmo.

For sheep, there's just one place to learn what's cool in wool—the Pennsylvania Farm Show, the yearly agricultural exhibition that opens for the 75th time today.

Unless you were raised by shepherds, you may not realize that the way sheep are sheared for shows changes year after year, just as, well, haircuts and clothing styles for people.

Nut graph

The Philadelphia Inquirer

Suitcase leads   These are leads written as though you were packing for a trip, squeezing everything you can in your suitcase and then sitting on the lid to close it. They're cluttered.

Tens of thousands of children with no identifiable physical or neurological defects are being shunted into expensive programs for the handicapped, programs established with the best of intentions for children with specific disabilities but now often used for children who simply need counseling and smaller classes.

The New York Times

Stereotype leads   These are most common in features about older people, women and groups with special interests. The writer tries hard to be complimentary but instead only reinforces stereotypes.

This is the lead for a story about senior olympics, games for people over age 60:

At the age when most of their contemporaries are in rocking chairs, these athletes will be competing in swimming, archery, badminton, bicycle racing—just about every imaginable sport, through the long jump and shot put.

The Baltimore Sun

If you look around your college campus, you're likely to see many professors in their 60s, and most of them don't spend much time in rocking chairs.

Unsolved mysteries   The lead teases the reader, but the mystery is that the story is about something else. These leads must relate to the focus and be backed up with the answer to the mystery. If they don't, they're misleading.

> The man couldn't believe what he was hearing.
>
> "You mean I could go to jail for this?" he asked Detective Bob Ankenbauer.
>
> Only minutes before, the man had been arguing vigorously with officials from the state Department of Environmental Regulation (DER), claiming that what he had done wasn't that bad.
>
> Then Ankenbauer explained he was doing a criminal investiga- tion for the Pinellas County Sheriff's Department and the man's mouth dropped open. Ankenbauer has become accustomed to that kind of reaction in the past 10 months. As the Sheriff's Department's first full-time investigator of environmental crimes, Ankenbauer is treading unexplored ground.
>
> *St. Petersburg Times*

So is the reader. What was the man's crime? The reader never finds out. The rest of the story is about Ankenbauer's new job. Remember to back up your leads.

This next example is a deceptive mystery lead because it is not about the "dragons" in the lead; it's about a woman who gets to hunt them. By the time readers find out what these mysterious creatures are, they may quit anyway. This example also contains negative stereotypes—little old ladies from Des Moines.

> They do, from time to time, eat people.
>
> They have teeth like a divorce court lawyer. They can be longer than a Sunday sermon in South Georgia and wider than a Japanese pickup.
>
> They rip chunks out of boats and scare the mortal hell out of everyone from commercial fishermen who catch them in nets to little old ladies from Des Moines who see their pet poodles disappear into their cavernous maw on the banks of the condominium pond.
>
> **It still isn't quite clear what "they" are.** They are the dragons of the New World, actually peaceful creatures unless aroused or hungry, but so wrapped up in lore and mystique that it is never quite clear where myth ends and reality begins.
>
> But where there is a dragon there must be a dragon-slayer. That's just the way it is.
>
> Her name is Sharen.
>
> **Nut graph** Her full name is Sharen Thomas Groene, of the Polk County Thomases, which explains a lot. Sharen was one of the 177 people whose name was picked at random in this year's lottery in the state-sponsored commercial alligator harvest. But the Thomas family has been hunting gator, legally for the most part, though not exclusively, for generations.
>
> *St. Petersburg Times*

Soft leads can be enticing and creative, but they must be accurate. Remember that the lead must lead to the focus. If it doesn't, the reader may never wade through it.

How to Find Your Lead

To find a lead that will work for you in your story, first find your nut graph. Ask yourself what the main point of the story is. Then ask some of these questions to find your lead:

Reader interest: What did you or would the reader find most interesting about this subject?

Memorable item: What was the most memorable impression or fact?

Focus on a person: Is there someone who exemplifies the problem or issue? If you tell a story about this person or show the person in action, will it lead to the point in the nut graph?

Descriptive approach: Will a description of the scene relate to the focus?

Mystery approach: Can you tease the reader with a surprise that leads to the nut graph?

Build on a quote: Is there a great quote to back up the lead? If so, write the lead so it refers to the quote without repeating it.

Contrast: Would a then-and-now approach work?

Problem/solution: Can you set up a problem so the reader wants to discover the solution?

Narrative storytelling: If you were just telling a good story, how would you start? Can you reconstruct the events to put the reader on the scene?

Activities

1 Leads analysis: Read at least three different newspapers to locate the types of leads listed below. Analyze the good and bad leads, and attach a copy of the leads to your analysis.

a Find an example of a cluttered hard-news lead. Rewrite it.

b Find examples of a descriptive, an anecdotal and a narrative lead. Label each type. Analyze whether your examples are effective and why or why not.

c Find five feature news leads that you like. Explain what techniques the writers used and why you liked them.

d Find five feature leads you did not like, and analyze the techniques.

e Rewrite two hard-news leads into impact leads.

2 Impact lead activity: Look in your newspaper for three hard-news stories that could lend themselves to impact leads; then rewrite the leads with the impact approach.

3 Rewrite activity: Here are some stories with very dull leads. Rewrite the leads as suggested.

a Try a focus-on-a-person lead for this story, going from the specific to the general. Make sure you write a nut graph to follow the lead.

Students from Gay and Lesbian Services of Kansas spoke yesterday to a psychology class about their lives and experiences.

Two gay men and two lesbian women spoke to a Psychology 104 class of about 200 students as part of GLSOK's Speakers' Bureau, a program designed to educate students about the gay and lesbian experience.

Scott Manning, a graduate teaching assistant in French and Italian who spoke to the class, said the Speakers' Bureau often was the introduction for many students to gay and lesbian people.

The organization speaks to between 20 and 30 classes a semester, but this was one of the largest classes it ever had addressed.

Manning told the students in the class they could ask questions about any subject but religion or AIDS.

He said that discussions about religion often degenerated into dogmatic battles and that AIDS was a disease that affected everyone, not just homosexuals.

The first question students asked was whether speakers thought gays and lesbians should have children.

Jamie Howard, co-director of GLSOK, said the belief that gay and lesbian people could not be good parents was a myth.

People often think that because the parents are homosexual, their children also will be, she said.

"My parents are very heterosexual," Howard said. "And I am not."

She said homosexual couples had to think a lot about having children, and as a result, they might be better parents.

Homosexuals also are more accepting of differences in other people, she said.

One of the speakers, Jennifer Ansley, a Lawrence senior, said her girlfriend had lost her job because she was a lesbian.

"We hardly ever go out in public in her hometown," she said.

Ansley said she had been harassed and threatened.

"It gives me the determination to do something about it," she said.

b Try an impact lead for this story. Write from the lead to the nut graph. Here is some basic information:

The Board of Regents has approved an increase in rates for campus housing at your university.

The biggest increase will be in residence halls, where rates will increase 14.8 percent for double-room occupancy. The current rate is $2,684 and will increase to $3,080 next fall.

The cost of other campus housing facilities will increase about 6 percent. For example, rates at scholarship halls will increase to $2,216 from this year's rate of $2,090.

4 Summary and impact leads:

a Write a summary lead based on the following information:

The Centers for Disease Control released the results of a survey today. Nutritional supplements include vitamins, protein supplements and products promising muscle growth. Only supplements in powder, capsule or tablet form were surveyed. "It turned out that at least half of the ingredients have no documented medical effect," said Rossanne Philen, a medical epidemiologist at the National Center for Environmental Health and Injury Control. She was part of the surveying team. The survey said many nutritional supplements have no medical support for their advertised claims.

b Write a summary lead based on the following information from the *Rocky Mountain* (Denver) *News:*

A study was released Monday by the University of Colorado. The study was funded by the Alfred P. Sloan Foundation. The study said that 60 percent of college students who begin studying science, mathematics or engineering switch to another major. The study said that 75 percent of the students who switched majors cited poor teaching and an aloof faculty as the cause. The study said that professors who motivated students and made difficult material comprehensible were the exception.

c Write a delayed identification lead based on the following information, adapted from the *Topeka* (Kan.) *Capital-Journal:*

Janice Jones, 28, of southeast Topeka was arrested Saturday. She was charged with burglary and criminal damage to property. She was arrested at 2:15 a.m. after a police dog found her inside a house at 509 S.E. 35th St., said Detective Sgt. Eldon Wilson. Police said that the house had been burglarized. Wilson said a neighbor called police at 2:02 a.m. and reported hearing glass breaking and seeing someone climb into the house. Police arrived two minutes later. Officer Mike Perry and his dog arrived and began searching the house. King found Jones hiding in a closet, and she was arrested. A VCR was outside the closet door where Jones was hiding, Wilson said. The residents of the house were away on a camping trip.

d Write a delayed identification hard-news lead based on the following information:

Lt. Jason Kane of the Rockville Police Department said two officers were trying to arrest Thomas A. Finicky, 26, because of reports that he was trespassing at 725 Maple Street. A Rockville police officer, Bill Glauber, suffered a broken ankle in an altercation with Finicky when Glauber was kicked in the leg. Finicky is expected to be charged with aggravated battery on a law enforcement officer, trespassing and resisting arrest.

e Write a summary lead based on this information:

The Rockville City Council will meet at 7 p.m. Tuesday. The council will consider adopting an ordinance. The ordinance would impose penalties for false alarms that are sent to the police department from faulty or improperly operated electronic security systems. Under the proposed ordinance, an alarm system owner would be allowed six free false alarms. The owner would have to pay a $30 penalty for each additional false alarm.

f Now use the information from activity *e* to write an impact lead.

COACHING

Write a first draft; mark "fix later" if you get stuck. Don't perfect every line during the drafting process.

Read your story aloud when you finish. You will hear the pacing and catch errors.

Use lists to move the reader quickly through the story.

Use parallel structure: a few sentences (three is the magic number) in identical structure with some repetitive beginnings.

Test your endings to see if you have overwritten or strained your last paragraph. Put your hand over your last paragraph and see if the previous paragraph or the one before that is a better ending.

Lead reversal: Would your ending work as well as a lead? Sometimes the lead and ending could be reversed.

Body Building

11

When Ken Fuson was in high school, he played the drums. He still hears the beat of the drums when he writes his stories for *The Des Moines Register.* "I think a lot about rhythm," he says. "I work at getting the tap, tap, tap. I want to make sure every paragraph doesn't sound the same." To achieve that musical quality, Fuson reads all his stories out loud.

Rhythm helps readers move through the middle of a story. And Fuson wants to make sure they read to the end. "I probably spend as much time on the ending as I do on the beginning," he says. He thinks a good ending makes a story memorable. "If readers remember a story I wrote, that's better than money." One time, after he won a prestigious award from the Gannett Company, which owns *The Des Moines Register,* he told company executives that editors who cut the ending of a story should be executed.

Getting from the beginning to the end of a story isn't a haphazard process for Fuson. He carefully plans the parts of his stories. First he thinks. "I look for ways to show conflict and to describe the mood. I think a lot about what is the right tone and the personality of the story." Then he starts organizing his material. "I type up all my notes. I select what I want to use. Then I put that information in an order. I need to know where I'm going and what the ending will be. Once you know what you're going to say and the way you're going to say it, then you can worry about what goes first."

And worry he does. "The first paragraph has to be perfect," he says. "And the second paragraph has to be

I know most newspaper readers don't read all the way to the endings. But I tell myself if I do it well enough, they'll read mine.

Ken Fuson, reporter, *The Des Moines* (Iowa) *Register*

perfect. I wish I had learned a better way of writing instead of worrying about what I'm going to say first."

It may not be the best writing process, but it works well for Fuson, who consistently wins awards. This chapter explains some other ways you can construct the body of your story.

Middles of Stories

Journalists need to be optimists. They have to believe people will read stories all the way through, even though research says otherwise. The trick is to keep the middle moving.

If you have followed the advice presented in Chapter 9, you are planning an order for your stories before you write. In most cases, you map that order by topics that support your focus or by chronological order for all or a part of your story. However, good organization is only part of what makes a story readable. You can use other writing techniques as well.

Transition Techniques

Getting from one paragraph to the next smoothly may require a transition. But the best transition is no transition—a story so well organized that one thought flows naturally into the other. The information in one paragraph should raise a question that needs to be answered in the next. Or it can present information that can be backed up with a supporting quote or facts in the next. If it does that, you don't need any special transitions. But when you do, you can try some of these techniques to pave the way for the next paragraph:

• Use cause and effect. If one paragraph raises a question, answer it in the next paragraph or elaborate with an example or quote. Try to anticipate questions the reader might have.

• To introduce a new speaker after a previous speaker, use a statement about or from that person. Then lead into the quote or paraphrased material. For example:

A controversial proposal that would require all Temple University undergraduates to take a course related to racism drew strong support yesterday from a racially mixed group of students and faculty members who testified at a campus hearing.

Anika Trahan, a junior, said the proposed requirement would encourage more dialogue among students who come to the university from largely segregated neighborhoods. "They (white students) come from communities where they are never able to interact with black people," she said.

But opinion was sharply divided on whether the course should focus on black-white relations in America or include racism against Asian Americans and other groups.

Molefi K. Asante, chairman of Temple's African American studies department, contended that

Transition to new speaker

the requirement should focus on the white racism toward African Americans because that has been "the fundamental pattern of racism" in the United States.

A white student, sophomore Amy Dixon, agreed. "Our predominant problem on campus is black-white relations," she said.

Huntly Collins, *The Philadelphia Inquirer*

Transition to new speaker

• To insert background, you can use words and phrases, such as *Previously* or *In the past,* or specific time elements, such as *Two months ago.* If you are going to recount part of the story chronologically, you can set it up with a phrase like *The incident began this way.*

• To get from one point to another, especially in stories about meetings where several issues are discussed, you can use transitional phrases: *In another matter, On a related issue, Other items discussed included.*

• A word or phrase from one paragraph can be repeated in the next. Here is an example that uses repetition of key words:

With a relentless sun beating on him as he cut through fields, swamps and shaggy forests, Earl Davis always looked ahead to the next leg of the project.

The legs were long and stretched interminably. The crews made slow progress. Mosquitoes whined about their heads, and snakes thrashed away when the right-of-way crews stumbled across them. . . .

Davis, who had lived in Pinellas County for almost 50 years, sympathized and suffered with them (the road builders).

The suffering wouldn't be over for a long time.

Mark Davis, *Tampa* (Fla.) *Tribune*

Repetition can also be achieved with parallel structure:

Nurses on the late shift called the twins miracle babies, but there never seem to be enough miracles to go around.

Most babies in the neonatal intensive care unit at All Children's Hospital are born too soon, incomplete. Some last for a while and then slip away, like beads off a broken string.

The nurses are used to cases that mock the joy that birth is supposed to be. The two babies that came to them Feb. 28 showed that it can be even meaner.

Jakob and James Watkins were Siamese twins, two apparently whole infants joined at the chest and abdomen. The boys lay face to face, wrapped in each other's arms.

Somewhere in conception, the cell that should have divided cleanly to form two normal, identical babies did not completely separate.

It left nurses and doctors with a medical phenomenon, one that would peel away their professional detachment.

It left the Tampa Bay area

with a cause, something important but uncomplicated, without sides.

It left a young couple from St. Petersburg with choices no parent should have to make, including the decision to separate the infants even though it might doom the weaker child.

It left, when it was over, a two-grave plot in St. Petersburg's Memorial Park.

Rick Bragg, *St. Petersburg Times*

Techniques for Maintaining Interest

There are many other ways a writer can keep the middle moving. Here are some of them.

Parallelism Parallel sentences help the reader move quickly through the story. Parallel construction means the sentences are worded in the same grammatical order. Some of the words can be repeated for effect, especially those at the beginning of sentences. In this example, the writer uses parallelism at the beginning of the story, but you can use it anywhere:

Rudolph Almaraz kept his battle with AIDS his personal business, even though his professional business was surgery.

He didn't tell his patients. He didn't tell officials at Baltimore Johns Hopkins Hospital, where he was a cancer surgeon. He didn't tell the doctor who bought his medical practice earlier this year.

But now the case of Dr. Almaraz, who died of AIDS on Nov. 16 at the age of 41, has frightened his patients.

Matthew Purdy, *The Philadelphia Inquirer*

Pacing Vary the length of sentences. Follow long ones with short, punchy ones. This excerpt is from the middle of a story about the Bill of Rights:

Today, few would question the trial system, but one aspect of the American judicial system still triggers considerable debate. It is the last part of the Eighth Amendment, the part that prohibits inflicting "cruel and unusual punishment."

In general, the amendment has been interpreted to mean punishment that is inappropriate, such as torture, or considered too harsh for the crime.

But for others, it is simple: the death penalty.

Gary C. Rummler, *The Milwaukee Journal*

This example is from a long story about a mother infected with AIDS:

On New Years Eve Lisa Botzum visited the emergency room of the Hospital of the University of Pennsylvania, complaining of nausea and vomiting. She was given a pregnancy test. She was elated by the result.

Few others were.

Loretta Tofani, *The Philadelphia Inquirer*

Anecdotes You often use anecdotes in your leads; consider them for the middle of your story as well. An interesting little story or experience can brighten a long story or a bureaucratic one.

This example is from a story about a law that allows federal agents to confiscate the property of suspected drug dealers. But many of the people mentioned in the story were not drug dealers. Throughout the story, anecdotes help keep the reader's interest. Here is one:

Ethel Hylton of New York City has yet to regain her financial independence after losing $39,110 in a search nearly three years ago in Hobby Airport in Houston.

Shortly after she arrived from New York, a Houston officer and Drug Enforcement Administration agent stopped the 46-year-old woman in the baggage area and told her she was under arrest because a drug dog had scratched at her luggage. The dog wasn't with them, and when Miss Hylton asked to see it, the officers refused to bring it out.

The agents searched her bags, and ordered a strip search of Miss Hylton, but found no contraband.

In her purse, they found the cash Miss Hylton carried because she planned to buy a house to escape the New York winters which exacerbated her diabetes. It was the settlement from an insurance claim and her life's savings, gathered through more than 20 years of work as a hotel housekeeper and hospital night janitor.

The police seized all but $10 of the cash and sent Miss Hylton on her way, keeping the money because of its alleged drug connection. But they never charged her with a crime.

Andrew Schneider and Mary Pat Flaherty, *The Pittsburgh Press*

Dialogue   When possible and appropriate, use dialogue in your story. It works well in feature stories, news stories about council meetings and especially stories about court cases. Note that in this example the attribution is not given every time the speaker changes, because in dialogue the speakers sometimes are understood. This excerpt is from a story about a child-abuse murder trial:

"This is a photo of the belt you used to strike Keith, isn't it?" asks Assistant State's Attorney Tom Gibbons, who is cross-examining defendant Edward Thirston.

"Looks like it," answers Thirston, who is on trial for murdering 22-month-old Keith Jones.

"Is that where you struck the baby with the belt?"

"No," the defendant says.

Linnet Myers, *Chicago Tribune*

BBI: Boring but important stuff   Many stories, especially government stories, need explanation or background that could be boring. Don't put all the boring information in a long block. Break it up into small paragraphs and place it where it will fit, but not in one long, continuous section. Also consider graphics as a way to present statistics and other information that could clog a story.

In their Pulitzer Prize–winning series about the U.S. Department of Agriculture, reporters Mike McGraw and Jeff Taylor used charts for many of their statistics (see Exhibit 11-1). But in the body of this story, called "Deadly Meat," they broke up much of the potentially boring but important factual material with quotes, anecdotes and lists. (They also used shorter sentences for complex material, as suggested in the next section.)

Exhibit 11-1

Graphic illustration from McGraw and Taylor's "Deadly Meat" series

Dave Eames, *The Kansas City* (Mo.) *Star*, December 10, 1991.

DIRTY MEAT

The USDA groups the country's 7,000 meatpacking plants into 190 "circuits" and inspects each circuit for sanitation, processing and labeling. Below are the 10 worst circuits, according to the most recent USDA reviews available.

Rank	Area/% of plants with major problems		Problems include
1	Fresno, Calif.	75%	Flaking paint and rusty equipment touching meat; water not hot enough for sanitation; doors allow rodent entry; mold on sausage.
2	Dallas*	45%	Hand soap not available; flaking paint; employees with soiled hands touching meat; water not hot enough for sanitation; sausage dropped on floor; insect traps not emptied.
3	North Philadelphia	33%	Unsanitary plants; hand tools dirty; insects and rodent droppings; ground beef contaminated with black residue.
4	Rochester, N.Y.	29%	Rusty, dirty equipment; water not hot enough for sanitation; flies; rodent droppings.
5	San Francisco	27%	Mold in coolers; rodent droppings; insects; flaking paint; dirty tools.
6	Petaluma, Calif.	26%	Dirty tools; rust and flaking paint; carcasses not protected from contamination; rodents; insects.
7	Peoria, Ill.	25%	No hand soap; flaking paint and rust; rodents and rodent nests in plant.
8	Tampa, Fla.	22%	Tarlike residue on bacon; pork bellies in contact with grease; water not hot enough; waste water on carcasses.
9	Baltimore*	22%	Contaminated hand tools; bad lighting; flaking paint; water not hot enough.
10	Lemoyne, Pa.	21%	Unsanitary knives; insecticide mist on exposed product; rat droppings; carcasses contaminated.
76	Kansas City	0%	No major problems found in April 1989 after a highly critical report identifying it as a "weak" circuit in June 1988.

* One of two circuits in the area.

Each year tainted food kills up to 9,000 Americans. And it makes anywhere from 24 million to 81 million people sick, according to estimates gathered by the Centers for Disease Control. At least a third of the cases, according to congressional research, can be traced to meat and poultry.

Why is this happening? Agriculture Department officials typically blame consumers for the outbreaks. Families undercook their dinner, they say, or food service workers don't wash their hands. . . .

For consumers, one of the most crucial breakdowns may be in the warning system designed to keep those problems from ending up in the meat drawers of their refrigerators.

In its simplest form, it's supposed to work this way: In about 7,000 federally checked meat plants across the country, 7,000 USDA meat inspectors ensure that only wholesome meat comes off the assembly line. Slaughter plants must always have an inspector on duty, but processing plants operate under a system in which one inspector can check several plants each day.

If those inspections fail, and hazardous meat gets to consumers, the Washington-based "emergency programs staff" is supposed to recall it and issue a public warning.

Sometimes both systems fail. Indeed, sometimes even the watchdogs don't feel safe.

Earlier this year, after a day of classes at the USDA's training center in College Station, Texas, six veterinarians told a reporter they don't order rare beef for dinner. Too big a chance of getting sick, they say.

Halfway across the country in suburban Virginia, Carl Telleen serves reporters a vegetarian dinner. After working 30 years for the inspection service—including several years on an inspection review team—the retired veterinarian won't eat poultry and eats little red meat. He doesn't trust the process.

Mike McGraw and Jeff Taylor,
The Kansas City (Mo.) *Star*

Simple sentences for complex information The more difficult the information is, the simpler your sentences should be. Use short sentences with simple construction especially for bureaucratic information that would be hard for the reader to comprehend.

This excerpt is from a story explaining how the judiciary committee of the Connecticut legislature works:

The judiciary is one of the legislature's busiest. By the end of the five-month session in June, the committee will have drafted, amended, approved, or killed about 500 bills—about 14 percent of the 3,649 bills filed with the Senate and House clerks.

Judiciary's 14 percent will touch nearly everyone. The committee considers matters of life and death, marriage and divorce, freedom and imprisonment.

This year's issues include surrogate parenting, birth certificates, and adoption. The death penalty and letting the terminally ill die. Longer prison sentences and home release. Committing the mentally ill to hospitals.

Mark Pazniokas, *The Hartford* (Conn.) *Courant*

Lists Itemizing information, especially results of studies or the main points in governmental actions, is an excellent way to keep the flow going through the middle of your story. You may use lists in a variety of ways:

• To itemize a group of statistics or any other cumbersome information

• To highlight key points within a story

Lists are usually preceded by a dot called a "bullet" or by some other graphic device.

This example from a story about budget cuts at California State University is a very common way to use lists:

> Despite an outcry from students, California State University on Wednesday increased academic fees 20 percent to $936 a year. . . .
>
> Meeting at Cal State Long Beach, the trustees reduced the budget from $2.1 million to $1.65 billion and called for:
>
> - Eliminating 420 faculty positions and leaving vacant an additional 330.
> - Not replacing 229 professors when they go on sabbatical.
> - Reducing other staff by 856 positions.
>
> "None of these is a happy solution." . . .
>
> Steven Silberman, *The Orange County* (Calif.) *Register*

Exhibit 11-2

*Cliffhanger,
or suspense ending*

Cliffhangers: Mystery middles In 1990 a nighttime television soap opera called "Twin Peaks" captured the attention of American viewers. Every Saturday night, millions of "Peakies" stayed home to find out who killed Laura Palmer. Once they did, after a season and a half of suspense, the show lost its appeal. But the phenomenon of soap operas remains. They are so popular that the *Iowa City Press-Citizen* and other newspapers even print weekly summaries of the shows for viewers who missed some episodes.

The concept is a simple one: Give readers or viewers a mystery and make them want to find out what happens next. In writing, this kind of suspense ending is called a "cliffhanger" (see Exhibit 11-2). It is usually reserved for the endings of stories arranged in sections or in series, when another part appears the next day.

But why wait for the ending? Why not use the same technique to make readers continue reading? Edgar Allan Poe used cliffhangers throughout his stories. In "The Pit and the Pendulum," he described a prisoner of the Inquisition in Paris. The story, told in first person, described the prisoner in a dungeon with a pit. One more step and he would have fallen into the chasm. But then he looks up and sees a glittering steel pendulum, "the under edge evidently as keen as that of a razor." It is descending slowly. Will he be sliced by the sharp crescent blade?

Down—certainly, relentless down! It vibrated within three inches of my bosom.... I gasped and struggled at each vibration. I shrunk convulsively at its every sweep. My eyes followed its outward or upward whirls with the eagerness of the most unmeaning despair; they closed themselves spasmodically at every descent, although death would have been a relief.

Can the reader dare stop now before finding out if the prisoner will live or die? The prisoner is spared in the last four sentences:

An out-stretched arm caught my own as I fell, fainting, into the abyss. It was that of General LaSalle. The French army had entered Toledo. The Inquisition was in the hands of its enemies.

Not all newspaper stories lend themselves to cliffhangers. But many could be structured that way by putting the key points of the story on the front page and stopping before the jump page with a question or suspenseful point that makes the reader want to find out more. Of course, reporters, editors and the copy desk, which lays out the pages, would have to cooperate. However, even without placing the cliffhanger at a jump point, the technique works to keep the reader moving through the story.

This method is much more conducive to narrative storytelling, especially in a long feature, but it can be applied to hard news if the story stops at a crucial point. The headline also is crucial. It can give a clue to the story, but it shouldn't give away the punch line.

This is only the beginning of a story that uses cliffhangers. Would you want to turn the page to continue reading?

Cliffhanger

In Fort Myers: Money, mercy and murder

Patricia Rosier's death was supposed to be peaceful and dignified.

She had made all the arrangements. Ordered food for the wake. Said a final goodbye to friends and family. Put the children to sleep.

On the nightstand rested a bottle of Seconals, powerful sedatives prescribed by her husband, Dr. Peter Rosier. Suicide would finally free Pat, 43, from the pain of invading cancer.

When the time came, she downed Seconals like "jellybeans," one witness recalled.

But something went wrong in the Rosier's stylish Fort Myers home that January night in 1985.

Pat wouldn't die.

Peter frantically began injecting doses of morphine to finish the job. Pat's breathing slowed to a rasp.

But after 12 hours of the grim ritual, Pat would not die.

Finally, Pat's stepfather, Vincent Delman, decided something had to be done. Pat, he would later tell prosecutors, was suffering too much.

He took Pat's two half brothers into the bedroom and closed the door.

Twenty minutes later, the door opened. The Delmans walked out, their faces sullen. Peter was waiting in the living room, calming his ravaged nerves with a beer.

"Patty is dead," Vincent said.

Another cliffhanger

After the funeral, the Delmans left Fort Myers. They carried with them the dark secret of what happened behind the bedroom door.

On Monday, Peter Rosier, 47, is scheduled to go on trial for the first-degree murder of his wife of 22 years.

The Rosier story has it all—sex, love, wealth, murder and a major mystery: Who really killed Pat Rosier?

Mark Stephens and William Sabo, Fort Myers (Fla.) *News-Press*

And another cliffhanger

On the jump page you would find out why Peter is on trial and what kind of evidence exists to try him. You also would find out why this is an unusual case: There's no body and no autopsy report. Pat's body was cremated. There are no morphine syringes; they were thrown away when she died. And there is one other unusual twist: Peter wasn't even in the room when Pat was killed.

Court stories lend themselves to this kind of dramatic structure. But so do many others.

Endings

Call them lasting impressions. To many writers, the ending is as important as the beginning of the story. Unfortunately, many readers don't get that far. But if they do, you should reward them with a memorable ending.

The ending also is called the "kicker." Think of it as a clincher. It should give a summary feeling to your story without repeating any information you have stated previously.

For columnists, the ending is more important than the beginning. The twist or main point the writer is trying to make is at the end of the column. Roger Simon, an award-winning columnist for *The Baltimore Sun,* once said he sometimes switches his leads and endings. He uses whichever is strongest. In many cases the lead could be an ending. And returning to your lead as a way to find your endings is an excellent technique.

The following sections describe some ways to form your endings.

Circle Kickers

When you return to your lead for an idea to end your story in a full circle, you are using a circle kicker (see Exhibit 11-3).

Ken Fuson frequently uses this technique to devise his endings. Here are some examples:

Exhibit 11-3

Circle kicker, which ties together the lead and the ending

WARSAW, POLAND—How long, old man?

"I don't know," Joseph Golaszewski replies. "It's very hard. Just look at what the prices are."

The old man has come to the outdoor market in the middle of Warsaw. In the cold mist of a gray morning, Golaszewski stands in line to buy eggs, butter and other food staples that are sold from the trunks of cars or the backs of trucks.

He is 69. The old men and old women next to him look as tired and desperate as he does. They wear ratty winter coats and matted fur hats and clutch wrinkled bills that they hope will buy today's meal.

This is the human laboratory in Poland's grand experiment to do what has never been tried before: Transform a Communist-dominated, centrally planned economy to one driven by market forces.

The story continues with explanation about life in Poland and interviews with many different people. Fuson returns to the beginning for the same concept in the ending, but with a different person.

How long, Poland?

"Until I die," Zofia Drzewiec says.

The old woman stands in the middle of the outdoor market. Her basket is empty of food. Her voice is full of steel.

Ken Fuson, *The Des Moines Register*

In this example from a story about how families cope with Alzheimer's disease, Fuson repeats phrases from the lead—but ends with a twist:

"Mother, mother, mother, other, other, other. . . ."

The sound comes in short, grating bursts, like a children's record played at too high a speed.

Every day, relentlessly, another small slice of the person that once was Betty Jennings disappears. The brand of hell called Alzheimer's disease has reduced the 58-year-old woman to a stoop-shouldered, hand-wringing blabber of meaningless words and phrases.

She must be fed, bathed and diapered. Some mornings, after a particularly brutal night, Gordon Hanchett will look in the living room and see that his sister has attacked her plastic diaper, ripping it apart with her fingers and leaving small pieces littering the floor.

"It looks like a miniature snowstorm," he says.

The limits of devotion are stretched thinnest in the homes of Alzheimer's victims. Often operating on little or no sleep and frequently ruining their own physical health, family members witness the disintegration of a loved one's mind with the understanding that no matter what they do today, tomorrow will be worse.

The story continues with more about the family in particular and the disease in general. Here's how it ends:

"Mother, this mother, this other . . . Daddy, daddy, daddy."

The chatter is loud, constant and haunting. His sister's voice fills the house.

"Oh that," says Hanchett, waving his hand. "I don't even hear that anymore."

Ken Fuson, *The Des Moines Register*

Quote Kickers

The most common type of ending for features and hard-news stories is the quote kicker. Look for a quote that sums up the mood or main idea of the story. When you end with a quote, put the attribution before the quote or, in a two-quote ending, after the first sentence. Do not let the last words the reader remembers be "he said."

Employment counselors often advise job seekers to treat the interviewing process as a time for personal enrichment. But Eugene Roscoe may have gotten a bit carried away.

According to Houston Police Sgt. Roy House, Mr. Roscoe was pulling in $100,000 to $150,000 a year—not from jobs, just from interviews. In an indictment returned last month by a state grand jury in Houston, Mr. Roscoe is accused of bamboozling interviewers into reimbursing him for travel expenses that were never incurred or that had already been covered by another interviewer, if not three or four.

"He was making very good money doing job interviews as a career," says Sgt. House.

The story continues with details and ends with this kicker quote:

Mr. Roscoe was arrested earlier this week when he showed up for his last interview—the interviewer was Sgt. House. "We let him fill out a voucher for his travel expenses," the sergeant says. "Then we told him we had just the position for him. It was down at the county jail."

Christi Harlan, *The Wall Street Journal*

Future Action Kickers

Many stories end with the next step in the development of an issue. But this technique works only if the story lends itself to a future element. If the next step is crucial to the story, it should be higher in the body. But if it works as a natural conclusion, then it can be the ending. It can be in the form of a statement or a quote.

> HERRING BAY, Alaska— World attention focused Friday on the attempt to rescue birds and animals from the oil spilled in Prince William Sound. Cameras in Valdez focused on the few animals saved—fewer than 20 birds and four sea otters by evening Friday. The birds on the evening news were expensive symbols for Exxon, costing more than $1,000 apiece to rescue.
>
> But on the water, the rescue efforts getting all the attention stumbled along with the air of a Sunday outing. In this bay at the north end of Knight Island, a diverse and committed group of people tried to learn to perform a futile task.

The story continues with detail about the rescue operation. Here is the ending:

> By Friday afternoon, about two miles of the shore of Herring Bay had been thoroughly searched.
> Only a few thousand left to go.

Charles Wohlforth, *Anchorage* (Alaska) *Daily News*

Climaxes

This type of ending works on stories written like fiction where the reader is kept in suspense until the end. It is more suited to features in narrative style or short news stories that tease the reader in the beginning and compel the reader to find out what happens. It can be used on stories structured in the pyramid style (described in Chapter 12).

Here is an example:

> Scott T. Grabowski sat Tuesday in the courtroom where a federal judge would determine his future, hoping that when the words were pronounced he would hear probation and not prison.
> But Grabowski, 27, of Greenfield, is an admitted drug dealer.
>
> Early last summer, he pleaded guilty to a charge of possessing 3 ounces of cocaine on June 5, 1988, that he intended to sell on behalf of an international drug network.

The story continues with the arguments from Grabowski's defense lawyer and the prosecutor. But what sentence did he receive? The reader doesn't find out until the end.

Finally, after a 2½-hour hearing, Curran (the judge) sentenced Grabowski to 30 months in prison, to be followed by three years of parole.

And with a nod to the parents, Curran told Grabowski: "I'm sure their hearts are aching as they sit here today."

Jill Zuckman, *The Milwaukee Journal*

Cliffhangers

Cliffhangers were described earlier in regard to mystery middles. But cliffhangers are more commonly used as an ending, particularly in series that will continue to another day. This technique can also be used in stories written in sections, with the cliffhanger at the end of a section so the reader is compelled to continue. The concept is "What will happen next?"

This example is an excerpt from a series about an FBI undercover operation to catch Colombian drug dealers. In this segment, the FBI undercover agent Robert Paquette has convinced the Colombians that he is a Wall Street financier who can launder money for them. But will the drug dealers believe him? The section ends on a suspenseful note.

One day Paquette scored big. Juan Restrepo, who ranked at the top of the laundering operation (of the Colombian drug dealers) made a rare visit from Medellin and decided to deliver some cash in person.

"You know," Paquette remembers saying, "I've got this special solution in this bottle. You know dogs can be trained to smell money that comes from an area where there are narcotics."

Dropping to his hands and knees, Paquette clambered over the scattered bills, blasting them with his blue pepper spray.

"This throws the dogs' scent off," he said.

Restrepo's expression became earnest. He, too, dropped to the pile and meticulously shifted the cash to ensure Paquette's miracle spray was liberally and thoroughly applied.

He also tasted it. But he didn't say anything about its distinctly unpeppery flavor. He just looked at Paquette, quizzically.

In another section, the ending also is a cliffhanger:

There was an odd kind of trust between Paquette and the Colombians. . . .

By following the dealer and money couriers, the agents believed they had enough evidence to crack the ring. On Sept. 4, 1986, they struck in a series of coordinated raids.

Paquette spent Sept. 4 in his Greenwich office, wondering whether the Colombians would realize he had set them up. Was his cover blown?

Edmund Mahony, *The Hartford Courant*

Factual Kickers   These are strong factual statements that could sometimes substitute
as leads. They are statements that summarize the mood, tone or
general character of the story. They are harder to write than quote
kickers, but if done well, they give the reader a powerful punch.
They are truly kickers. Strive for a very short, simple sentence that
states a fact. But choose a meaningful fact that will leave a lasting
impression. Fuson's story about Poland and Wohlforth's story about
the Alaska oil spill also have factual kicker endings.

   Julie Sullivan is a master of the factual kicker. One of hers
appears in the introduction to this book. In the following example,
she is writing about a man who lives in a run-down hotel in Spokane.
(The full story will appear in Chapter 25.) This ending is a simple
statement that is circular in its reference to the lead.

   Here is the lead:

Joe Peak's smile has no teeth.

   His dentures were stolen at
the Norman Hotel, the last place
he lived in downtown Spokane
before moving to the Merlin two
years ago.

   Gumming food and fighting
diabetes have shrunk the 54-year-
old man's frame by 80 pounds. He
is thin and weak and his mouth is
sore.

   But that doesn't stop him from
frying hamburgers and onions for
a friend at midnight or keeping an
extra bed made up permanently in
his two-room place.

   "I try to make a little nest here
for myself," he says.

The story continues with detail about the difficulties Peak encounters living in the Merlin. It ends with factual statements. Here are
the last few paragraphs:

When conditions at the Merlin
began worsening three months
ago, junkies and gray mice the size
of baby rats moved in next door.
He hated to see it, but he isn't
worried about being homeless.

   He's worried about his diabetes. He's frightened by blood in his
stool and sores on his gums. He
wonders whether the white-
staffed hospitals on the hill above
him will treat a poor black man
with no teeth.

Julie Sullivan, *The Spokesman-Review*
(Spokane, Wash.)

Out-of-Gas Endings

Just end when you have no more to say. This method is appropriate for hard-news stories, particularly those structured with a summary lead and arranged with supporting points in descending order of importance. You can end on a quote, future action or another fact in the story.

Here is a factual out-of-gas ending:

> TAMPA (Fla.)—For the first time, a shrimper has been imprisoned for failing to use a federally mandated turtle protection device on his boat, the National Marine Fisheries Service said.

The story continues with the basic who, what, why, when, where and ends with this fact:

> The government estimates more than 11,000 sea turtles drown in shrimp nets in U.S. waters each year.
>
> The Associated Press

Body-Building Checklist

For middles:

• Read aloud to check your pacing. Do short sentences follow long ones? Do your paragraphs start different ways? Do you have too many sentences with clauses?

• Would lists of short sentences itemizing findings or material substitute for lengthy paragraphs?

• Could you eliminate any transitions? Would some quotes naturally follow the previous point without needing a transition?

For endings:

• Have you overwritten or strained the ending? Try the hand test. Put your hand over the last paragraph and see if the previous one or two paragraphs would make a better ending. Is your ending repetitious of previous points?

• Have you avoided ending with the attribution?

• Is your ending memorable? Could it even be a lead?

• Is your ending too repetitious? Does it summarize the story like a term paper? If you are repeating information, cut it to the last important point or last good quote.

Activities

1   This is an exercise for awareness of pacing. Listen to classical music or other music of your choice. With your eyes closed, draw lines on a piece of paper to express the rhythm or movements of the music. Then find a story that you think has good pacing and compare it to the rhythm of music.

2   Watch a mystery television show, a movie or even a soap opera and note the foreshadowing elements and the cliffhangers. Analyze whether these elements keep you interested, and consider how you can apply the concepts to writing.

3   Read aloud a story you have written. Note where you can improve the pacing or how you can make the middle flow better.

4   Take any story you have already written and try a different ending, using a circle kicker, quote kicker or factual kicker.

5   Take any news story from your local or campus newspaper and rewrite it to improve the middle and ending.

COACHING

TIPS

Envision your story order as a blueprint for designing a building. What shape will the story take?

Consider a model for your story during and after the reporting process. Some forms require more anecdotal material. Always gather more information than you need so you can be flexible during the design process.

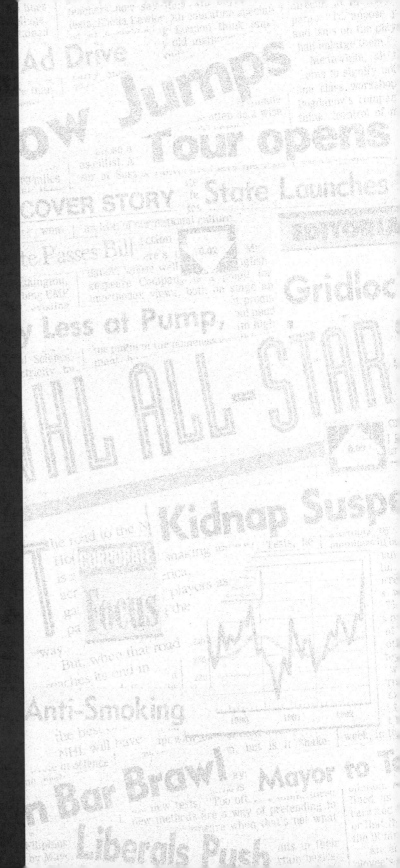

Story Structures

12

J ack Hart tells writers to think logically when they organize their stories. He calls the process "sequencing." Hart, writing coach at *The Oregonian,* says writers should organize the information in a sequence that helps readers understand how one item leads to another.

Hart also says sequencing helps writers visualize a shape for their story. When he coaches writers, he uses models of organization and gives them names so writers will remember them.

"I think we are lexicon impoverished," Hart says. "We haven't had many names for story structures. I am a firm believer that if you walk through the woods and you know the names of all the plants, you'll see a lot more. A lot of writers get halfway through a story and don't realize that they are writing in a particular structure."

Although many other writing coaches don't stress names and shapes of stories as much as Hart does, almost all coaches talk about order and logic and storytelling. They ask writers to envision what the reader needs to know and in what order. And they often tell writers to let the story flow naturally, as though they were telling it to a friend.

All stories should help readers understand the focus, the conflict, the background and solutions to the central topic. Most stories can be arranged by a topical order, points of view or chronological order for all or part of the story. Models of story structures can help you plan the organization. Your choice of structure depends on the type of material you have.

An effective story has a shape that both contains and expresses the story. . . . The writer must find a form that gives the reader a satisfying sense of completion, a feeling that everything in the story flows toward an inevitable conclusion.

Donald Murray,

Writing for Your Readers

Although there are many structures—Hart has designed at least 20—the following six structures are the most common:

Inverted pyramid: This is one of the most basic story forms. It is used most often for hard-news stories. The structure is a summary lead that gives the focus, followed by supporting points in descending order of importance.

***Wall Street Journal* formula:** This structure is based on the principle of specific to general. The formula is to start with an anecdotal lead, usually focusing on a person or event that exemplifies the main issue, which is expressed in a nut graph. Then the organization of the story is backup for the nut graph, explanation, and more supporting points and elaboration until the ending. The ending usually comes full circle, referring back to the lead. This structure is useful for stories about trends, major issues, features, news sidebars and news events that lend themselves to a feature approach. Although it is used in newspapers throughout the country for many news and feature stories, it is named after *The Wall Street Journal* because that newspaper became famous for using it in its front-page trend stories every day.

Hourglass: The hourglass form starts with the hard news and then proceeds in a chronological order for part or the rest of the story. It ends with comments or the outcome of the news. It is useful for police and court stories and other stories that lend themselves to some storytelling. It also is a good technique for avoiding attribution in every sentence, because the writer can use an overview attribution before the chronological portion—for example: "Police gave this account" or "Neighbors describe the incident this way."

List technique: This structure, used most often by *USA Today,* starts with a lead and a few paragraphs of backup information and then includes lists of supporting points. The list items are usually presented in brief form with a large dot, square, check or other graphic item to set them off. This technique is useful when you want to give many facts in short form. Lists can be used anywhere in the story.

Pyramid: This structure is chronological storytelling from beginning to end. It works best on shorter stories or those with enough suspenseful action to carry the reader to the end. Although you still need a nut graph high in the story and some foreshadowing, this structure works best if the story is very compelling and is written in narrative style.

Sections technique: This is a technique of dividing a story into sections, like book chapters, and separating them by a graphic device such as a large dot or a large capital letter. Each section can present a different point of view or a different time element (present, past and future). It works best for in-depth stories such as investigations or long features. The most effective section stories have good leads and good endings for each section. This form lends itself to cliffhanger endings for each section or for each day's installment if the story is presented as a series. Think of the sections as separate stories, complete in themselves but tied together by the overall focus.

Understanding these basic structures will help you plan the lead and the order of your story. Regardless of the structure you use, you still can organize your information by topics, points of view or chronology.

Inverted Pyramid

Summary lead

Backup (quotes or facts)

Supporting points

Ending

Exhibit 12-1
Inverted pyramid structure

This structure organizes the story from the most important information to the least important (see Exhibit 12-1). It usually starts with a summary lead that gives some of the basics: who, what, when, where, why. The elements that can't fit in the lead are in the backup. This is one of the most common forms for hard-news stories.

How do you decide what is most important and what should follow in descending order of importance? Use your judgment. Some questions to ask: What will affect the reader most? What questions does the lead raise that need to be answered immediately? What supporting quotes are strongest?

The advantage of this form is that the reader gets the crucial information quickly. The disadvantage: The reader may not read past the crucial information.

Headline

Teen sentenced to read book about Holocaust

Summary headline

He must write report on 'Diary of Anne Frank' for his role in cross burning on black family's lawn

Summary lead: who (delayed identification), what, why

SEATTLE—Instead of being sent to jail, a teen-ager was sent to the library to read the grim Holocaust tale, *The Diary of Anne Frank,* for his part in a cross burning on a black family's lawn.

Matthew Ryan Tole, 18, was sentenced Friday to read the famous story by a young Jewish girl of her family's failed attempt to escape Nazi persecution during World War II.

King County Superior Court Judge Anthony Wartnik said Tole received a light sentence because he was not one of the leaders in the April 16 cross burning in Bothell, a suburb north of Seattle.

"The Anne Frank book is great for someone to get a picture of the most extreme thing that can hap-

Backup: who, when

Supporting facts: why

Supporting quote

More explanation

pen if people aren't willing to step forward and say this is wrong," Wartnik said. "I'm hoping it will make him more sensitive."

Wartnik told him to write a book report on *The Diary of Anne Frank* within three months.

Background

Tole pleaded guilty to rendering criminal assistance in the cross

burning, which involved at least a dozen Bothell High School students. The cross was built during a party at Tole's home.

Tole did not help build or light the cross, but some of the materials belonged to him.

Factual ending

The Associated Press

As newspapers experiment with ways to gain readers, many editors are viewing the traditional inverted pyramid with disfavor, because it does not entice readers to read much beyond the top of the story. In addition, it is often difficult for the writer to decide what is most important in descending order.

High Fives Formula

Lionel Linder, the late editor of *The Commercial Appeal* in Memphis, Tenn., devised an alternative to the inverted pyramid that still puts the crucial news high in the story. Because it contains five key elements in the first four paragraphs, it is called the "High Fives" formula. This structure gives readers the important information quickly but also lets them know how the news affects them. The five elements:

News: What happened or is happening? That element usually goes in the lead.

Context: What is the background for the event or trend? You don't need to tell the entire history of the event, but a brief paragraph can help the reader understand the setting for this story and how past or related events provide the current context.

Scope: Is this local event part of a larger, national set of events or a trend?

Edge: Where is this news leading, and what happens next? Is this event or trend unique? Is it a first, an ending or a transition to the next development?

Impact: So what? How does the news affect anything? Why should anyone care? Does the news have any meaning?

The order of these elements is flexible. Sometimes impact is in the lead, and other times it is in the fourth paragraph. After the first four paragraphs, which contain all five elements, the rest of the story should contain supporting information: specifics, description, quotes and explanation.

Dan Henderson, the late assistant managing editor of *The Commercial Appeal,* said the High Fives method helps make writing more powerful: "The old inverted pyramid has been interpreted narrowly. You might not get the explanation about scope until paragraph 23. This new interpretation gives the significance immediately. Overall the reaction from readers has been tremendous."

Here is an example of how the High Fives method works:

News: what is happening	The District Attorney General's Office won't investigate whether state law was followed in the inquiry into Elvis Presley's death.	Smith led the call for the investigation to scrutinize Dr. Francisco's performance, not to impugn Presley's reputation, he said.
Backup for lead: why	Dist. Atty. Gen. John Pierotti told the Shelby County Commission on Monday that his office could investigate the matter only if there were reason to think the death was a homicide, which isn't the case.	Smith has criticized Dr. Francisco's handling of cases involving blacks who died under controversial circumstances during the past 17 years. — ***More supporting context (previous background)***
Context: background	His comments came two weeks after the commission passed a resolution asking for the investigation because of recent claims by pathologists and authorities that Presley died of drug interaction on Aug. 16, 1977. The singer's death certificate lists cardiac arrhythmia (heart attack) as the cause.	Initially, Pierotti was going to seek an opinion from the state attorney general on the matter. However, after reading the resolution, he decided it was clear that his office could not get involved, Pierotti said after speaking to commissioners. — ***Support for lead***
Scope (limited in this story to the local issue) Impact: so what, how does the news affect anything Edge (in this case, in the fifth paragraph): what happens next Backup quote	Pierotti's decision will leave unresolved a longstanding dispute between Commissioner Vasco Smith and Dr. Jerry Francisco, Memphis and Shelby County medical examiner. Smith said he would not drop the issue. He charged there was a coverup by Dr. Francisco. "That's not true," Dr. Francisco said when reached by telephone Monday night. "I followed the law under advisement by the county attorney and the state attorney general."	The Tennessee Supreme Court ruled about a decade ago that Presley's autopsy was a private matter, Pierotti said. — ***Elaboration*** "In this situation I have no authority to get involved with it since it was not a homicide," Pierotti said after speaking to commissioners. — ***Supporting quote*** Smith charged Dr. Francisco with failing to follow state law. Photographs and lab reports were not placed in an official file, Smith charged. — ***Supporting facts***
More background	Smith spent more than 30 minutes Monday questioning Pierotti about his decision and criticizing Dr. Francisco's actions.	"I assure you, the pursuit of this noble agenda has not ended," Smith said after the exchange with Pierotti. — ***Future ending (next step)*** Anthony Hebron, *The Commercial Appeal*

Wall Street Journal *Formula*

This structure starts with a soft lead, focusing on a person, scene or event (see Exhibit 12-2). The idea is to go from the specific to the general, starting with a person, place or event that illustrates the main point of the story. The concept, whether stated or implied, is that this person or scene is one of many affected by the issue in the nut graph. The lead can be anecdotal, descriptive or narrative.

It is followed by a focus graph—nut graph—which gives the main point of the story. This paragraph should explain what the story is about and why it is important (so what).

The story then presents backup for the lead and supporting points. The body of the story may be organized by different points of view or developments related to the focus.

The ending is often a circle kicker, using a quote or anecdote from the person in the lead or a future development of something mentioned in the beginning of the story.

This is a very versatile formula that can be applied to many news and feature stories. It is very useful for brightening bureaucratic stories. While you are reporting, consider this writing form and seek out a person who is one of many exemplifying your point or try to find an anecdote that illustrates the main point of your story.

If you had written a news story about a government hearing in inverted pyramid style, the lead might sound like this:

> About 350 people attended a federal hearing yesterday by the bipartisan Commission on Comprehensive Health Care to discuss problems of long-term health care.

Exhibit 12-2
Wall Street Journal *formula*

Soft lead

Nut Graph

Backup for lead and nut graph

Supporting points: quotes, facts, anecdotes

Developments: cause/effect, explanations, points of view

Circle kicker: anecdote, description, future action related to lead

This is how the lead sounded using the *Wall Street Journal* formula:

> Terry Idleson of South Philadelphia never sleeps more than three hours at a stretch a night. It's the only way she can tend to her brain-damaged 2-year-old daughter, Stephanie, who needs round-the-clock attention.
>
> Miriam Burnett of West Philadelphia used to be a school-teacher. But she quit her job to care for her 76-year-old mother, who has Alzheimer's disease.
>
> Joyce Singer of York, Pa., could think of only one thing to do when her husband, Michael, had a stroke at age 38, incurring medical expenses that threatened to bankrupt her family. She divorced him.

Nut graph | These three caregivers— mother, daughter, wife—were among a dozen witnesses who testified yesterday at a federal hearing on long-term care and its often devastating impact on the family.

The hearing before the bipartisan Commission on Comprehensive Health Care—called the Pepper Commission for its original chairman, the late U.S. Rep. Claude Pepper (D.-Fla.,)—drew an overflow crowd of about 350 to the ceremonial courtroom in the U.S. Courthouse at 601 Market Street.

Beth Gillin, *The Philadelphia Inquirer*

In this example, the formula is used in a feature story about a program:

Nearly a year ago, Rebecca Antholz was in despair.

She had a stack of medical bills she could not pay, no health insurance and nowhere to turn if her children became sick.

"I was between a rock and a hard place," she said.

Nut graph | Then she heard about the Caring Program for Children, which raises money to provide free health care to families who can't afford health insurance for their children.

"I was just frantic trying to figure out how to get coverage for my kids," Antholz, 313 W. Sixth, said. "It was a tremendous blessing."

Her family was one of the first in Ellis County to join the program, which began last March in Ellis and Shawnee counties and will begin in Sedgwick County in February.

Secondary nut graph

Merry Hayes, *The Hays* (Kan.) *Daily News*

The next example is a complete version of the *Wall Street Journal* formula, from the paper for which it is named. This is a trend story about the dangers of farming. Note that it also illustrates how the FORK method works:

Focus: Farming is the most dangerous occupation.

Order: The story is arranged by topics that substantiate the focus: (1) extent of the problem, (2) government role, (3) effect on children, (4) illnesses of farmers.

Repetition of key words: In the last sentence of several paragraphs are key words that serve as thought bridges to the next paragraph. In some cases, the key words are repeated to make a smooth transition.

Kiss off: Each new source is blocked; the source's comments are in one place, and then the source is not mentioned again, except for the central character introduced in the lead. He is used in the circular ending.

Farming Is Dangerous, but Fatalistic Farmers Oppose Safety Laws

By Bruce Ingersoll
The Wall Street Journal

Soft lead: focus on a person who illustrates main point of story

BATAVIA, N.Y.—Behind the barn, in a swale of sweet clover, Leo Bolas lost part of his right leg. The 69-year-old farmer had been funneling fodder into a silo when his tattered overalls caught in a spinning power-attachment on his tractor. In an instant he was yanked into the whirring drive shaft, and in a bloody blur his leg was nearly severed below the knee. To free himself he finished the amputation with a jackknife. Otherwise, he says, "it could have dragged me in further and finished me off."

First person quoted

Farm life belies its tranquil image. Farming is America's most dangerous line of work.

Nut graph

Agriculture has eclipsed mining as the occupation with the highest death rate. More precisely, while mining has reduced the number of fatalities substantially over the past decade, farming hazards continue for the most part unabated. Agriculture's accidental-death rate—48 per 100,000 workers—is five times higher than the national average for all industries.

Backup: elaboration for nut graph

About 1,500 farmers and farm-hands are killed each year, according to the National Safety Council. Many die in tractor accidents, are electrocuted, suffocate under tons of grain or are killed by bulls and cows and sows. Some 160,000 people suffer serious injuries. Still others fall victim to farm-related illnesses.

Foreshadowing: gives clues of information later in story

Hardly a farming community is

More specifics

untouched. An Iowa farmer, over morning coffee, counts 20 neighbors he knows by name who have been killed or crippled in farm accidents since 1980. Three of them were children. Each year, 300 youngsters under the age of 16 die in farm-related accidents, and 23,500 more are hurt.

Farming is inevitably hazardous. But accidents also reflect economic pressures that have farmers taking dangerous shortcuts, and they reflect meager safety initiatives at all levels of government.

For the most part, agriculture is exempt from federal regulation by the Occupational Safety and Health Administration. Unlike nations such as West Germany and Britain, "We (the U.S.) really have no policy whatsoever," says Kelley Donham, a University of Iowa associate professor of agricultural medicine.

Supporting topic: government role (government is key word to next thought)

Regulation is fiercely resisted, notably by farmers themselves, who fear the loss of independence and aren't sanguine about the possibilities.

Second source quoted, then kissed off

Nor do farm policy makers or Farm Belt politicians seem prepared to confront a problem that costs the U.S. economy more than $3 billion a year. "You start talking farm safety, and you're unpopular," says Rep. David Nagle, an Iowa Democrat. "But we can't continue to lose 300 kids a year; we can't continue to have farmers maimed and killed. These injuries are predictable and preventable."

Third source blocked

Marilyn Adams of Earlham, Iowa, agrees that more needs to be done. Her 11-year-old son Keith was helping his stepfather in 1986 when the boy fell into a wagonload of corn and suffocated. "They

Second supporting topic: children injured

Fourth source blocked

call it drowning in grain," says Mrs. Adams. "It works like quicksand. Within 8 to 10 seconds an adult can be completely submerged in grain. It takes less time for kids."

Key word (kids) repeated for transition

The risk is especially acute if grain is being unloaded through a chute at the bottom, creating a current that can suck a person in. In her grief, Mrs. Adams organized a group called Farm Safety for Just Kids. She is urging rural women to curb child labor on the farm. "Dads are building up tractor pedals so eight-year-olds can drive," she says. "Moms and kids have to learn to say no to dads."

Fifth source blocked

Unless agriculture solves its "kids problem," lawmakers may ban child labor, predicts John Pollack, a Cornell University farm-safety specialist. "They could call it a form of child abuse." He favors setting a minimum age of 12 for driving tractors. Tractor rollovers are the No. 1 killer on farms. Some groups seek federal requirements for roll bars on new tractors.

Third supporting topic: farmers' illnesses

Farmers also have the highest hospitalization rate and, oddly, the lowest rate of doctor visits of any occupation. Farmers have more serious illness but tend not to seek medical attention for the little things. The good life of the farm—the sunshine and the fresh air—is something of a bill of goods. Of all occupational groups, farmers have the highest rate of skin disorders, including skin cancer resulting from too much sun, and eczema from handling detergents and chemicals. Farmers, sometimes insouciant about wearing face masks, inhale clouds of dust, animal dander, even deadly fumes. Many suffer hearing loss from the clatter of machinery.

Ending: back to beginning source

The contradictions of rural life strike home here on Leo Bolas's farm in the dairy belt of upstate New York. As cows graze on a lush hillside, lowing in the twilight, Mr. Bolas re-enacts how he became entangled in the power-takeoff attachment to his tractor three years ago. Scattering chickens with his cane, he retraces the path he crawled—through standing corn across the barnyard into a machine shed—to reach a telephone and call for help. "It took four phone calls," he says. "I never thought of 911."

Circular wrap-up

But like many farm-accident victims, he blames himself. He should have replaced the broken shield on his tractor; he ought to have discarded the torn overalls before they could get caught in the works. "You get careless," he says, hobbling along on his artificial leg. "I ain't the only one. Farmers are the most dangerous people there is."

Quote ending

Hourglass

The hourglass form can start like the inverted pyramid, giving the most important hard-news information in the top of the story (see Exhibit 12-3). Then it contains chronological storytelling for a part or for the rest of the story.

Use the hourglass structure when the story has dramatic action that lends itself to chronological order for part of the story. The technique is useful in crime or disaster stories to recount how the event happened.

To set up the chronological narrative, an overview attribution often is used, such as "Police gave the following account" or "Witnesses described the accident this way." However, this type of attribution should be used only for a few paragraphs so the reader does not forget who is speaking. All quotes still need attribution. If the speaker changes, the new source also must be attributed.

Advantage: The narrative storytelling in the chronological portion adds drama to the story. Disadvantage: The chronological portion of the story may repeat some of the key information in the top of the story, making it longer than a basic inverted pyramid.

Summary lead

Backup

Overview attribution

Chronological storytelling

Exhibit 12-3
Hourglass structure

Boy, 3, shoots 16-month-old

TAMPA (Fla.)—A 3-year-old boy shot and seriously wounded his 16-month-old half brother Thursday after he found a .32-caliber pistol under a chair cushion in the family's apartment, Hillsborough sheriff's deputies said.

Melvin Hamilton, shot once in the chest about 9:30 a.m., was flown by helicopter to Tampa General Hospital, where he was in serious but stable condition late Thursday after surgery, hospital officials said.

Otis Neal, who pulled the trigger, did it accidentally, authorities said.

Sheriff's officials said they did not know who owned the handgun but were still investigating. Under state law, the gun's owner could be criminally liable for leaving the gun in a place where a child could get it.

The state Department of Health and Rehabilitative Services (HRS) was contacted by authorities, and it too is investigating the incident. HRS spokesman Tom Jones said the agency has no prior involvement with the family but gave no further details.

Summary lead

Attribution
Backup for lead

Attribution
Basic inverted pyramid structure with attribution for each point

Observation: no attribution needed

Hours after the accident, Otis sat bewildered on a curb outside his family's apartment as television camera crews and reporters jockeyed around him.

"He is saying very little. I don't think he really knows what is going on," sheriff's spokeswoman Debbie Carter said.

Facts

Otis and Melvin live with their mother, Dina Varnes, in the Terrace Oaks Apartment complex at 6611 50th St.

Overview attribution: chronological narrative begins and continues to the end

Relatives and sheriff's officials gave this account:

The two youngsters were downstairs in the living room playing Thursday morning, while a 15-year-old friend of the family slept on the couch. Ms. Varnes was upstairs.

Melvin was walking around the living room when Otis found the gun under the seat cushion. He pulled the gun out and fired one shot.

Arabell Ricks, Ms. Varnes' aunt and neighbor, said she was walking to the store when her niece ran out of the apartment screaming.

"She said, 'Melvin is shot.' She said the oldest shot Melvin," Ms. Ricks said. "I went in and looked at him, and then I just ran out of the house and started praying."

She said she flagged down a sheriff's deputy who was patrolling the area.

Ending reaction quote

"I said, 'Lord, please don't let him die,' " Ms. Ricks said.

Heddy Murphy, *St. Petersburg* (Fla.) *Times*

List Technique

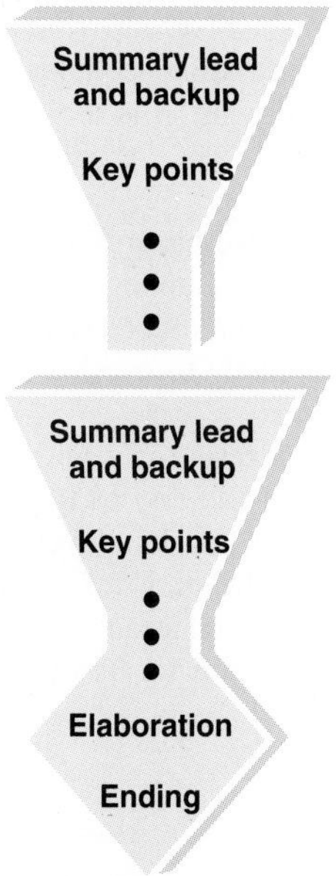

Exhibit 12-4
List technique

Lists can be useful in stories when you have several important points to stress. Think of a list as a highlights box within the story or at the end of the story. This technique works well for stories about studies, government stories such as meetings, and even features about people or programs if there are several key points to list. *USA Today* uses this structure in most of its stories.

When you use a list for the body and ending of your story, you can start with a summary lead or a soft lead followed by a nut graph (see Exhibit 12-4). Then give some backup for the lead in quotes or facts or both. Then itemize the main points until the ending.

If you use a list in the middle of your story, you can start with a hard or soft lead. Put the list where it is most appropriate for the content. Investigative reporters often use the list high in the story to itemize the findings of their investigation. Then add elaboration and an ending.

Limit lists in the beginnings and middles of stories to five items or fewer; lists at the end can be longer. Parallel sentence structure is most effective, but not essential, for lists. Each item should be in a separate paragraph. Lists often are used in stories about meetings to itemize actions not related to the lead. The list is preceded by "In other business" or a similar transition.

This example uses two sets of lists:

Summary lead

Campus crime records must be open to the public, a judge in Springfield, Mo., ruled Wednesday in a case with far-reaching implications.

Backup: reaction quote

"The gentlemen who wrote the Constitution would be proud," says Traci Bauer, 22, editor of the Southwest Missouri State University newspaper.

Background

Bauer sued the school, saying it concealed crime reports to protect its image. Federal Judge Russell Clark ruled:

- Withholding crime investigation and incident reports is unconstitutional.
- Campus crime records aren't exempt from Missouri's open-records law or protected as educational records.

Media-law experts say the ruling could set a precedent.

Testimony showed:

- A rape allegedly committed by a star athlete was not disclosed and no charges were filed.
- Springfield police were not told of several crimes.
- Drugs were seized and destroyed without disclosure.

University spokesman Paul Kincaid says regents will meet Friday to consider an appeal.

Future action kicker

Claude Burgett, *USA Today*

Here is an example of how the list technique can be used in the middle of a story:

Finally, some facts to justify cursing at people with car phones.

A recent study of car phoning showed that drivers involved in car-phone conversations were 30 percent more likely to overlook potential hazards, such as your rear bumper.

"They were so engrossed in the phone call that they were oblivious to what was going on," said James McKnight, whose experiments with 51 drivers were the basis for the findings.

What McKnight found through controlled tests on driving simulators was this:

- Even casual chitchat or just dialing a car phone distracted drivers enough so that they failed to respond to hazards nearly 7 percent more often.
- When talk turned to solving simple math problems—designed to simulate business conversations—drivers failed to respond to hazards nearly 30 percent more often.
- When engaged in casual or businesslike conversations, drivers 50 or older failed to respond to hazards 38 percent more often than younger drivers.
- Drivers who had experience with car phones were as easily distracted as drivers who were using the phones for the first time.

And his No. 1 finding:

"If there is any group that should not be using cellular phones while driving, it is those in the older age group," McKnight reported.

Failing to notice hazards was even more common among drivers 50 years old or older. They were twice as likely to overlook your bumper.

McKnight, a researcher with the National Public Services Research Institute in Landover, Md., conducted the study for the Automobile Association of America Foundation for Traffic Safety.

Mark Vosburgh, *The Orlando* (Fla.) *Sentinel*

Pyramid

Exhibit 12-5
Pyramid structure

Once upon a time, storytellers began at the beginning and continued to the end, saving the climax for last. Chronological storytelling is still the form used by fiction writers. It can be used in some news stories as well—with one difference. You still need to give the reader a clue to what the story is about high in the story. That is called foreshadowing.

This structure is similar to the hourglass, but with the pyramid, the chronology begins almost immediately and continues until the end (see Exhibit 12-5).

This structure works best in brief stories so the reader doesn't have to wait too long to find out what happened. It also can be used in longer stories with a dramatic plot, providing you have a nut graph and some foreshadowing—clues of what will come later in the story.

Advantage: The suspense of what happened can compel the reader to finish the story. Disadvantage: An impatient reader won't bother waiting to find out what happens.

In the following example about a fire, the last three paragraphs would be the top of the story in inverted pyramid form. In this story, the lead tells the reader what the story is about. From that point on, the story is told in chronological order. In more dramatic, suspenseful stories, the climax of the chronology would be at the end.

Hard-news lead

NEW PORT RICHEY (Fla.)—Help came to the Knight family in the form of a stranger and a cat named Gizmo when their house caught on fire early Sunday.

Chronological storytelling begins

Family members were sleeping in their rented home at 4633 Gazania St. when fire broke out shortly after midnight. Susan Knight awoke when Gizmo, a 6-month-old white cat, ran across her face.

Mrs. Knight sat up and saw smoke and flames. She woke her husband, Thomas, and got their three children out of the house.

"The smoke was so bad we just had to get out," Mrs. Knight, 30, said Sunday afternoon. "He tried to call 911, but the smoke was so bad he couldn't give the address."

Outside, Thomas Knight, 33, dragged a hose toward the front door. But it wasn't long enough to reach the flames.

That's when the "mystery guy," as Mrs. Knight called him, appeared. The man took the hose from her husband and told him to call for help. The stranger carried the hose around the house and sprayed water through a window into a bedroom where the fire had started.

The man helped slow the flames until Pasco County firefighters arrived, Fire Rescue Chief Mike Morgan said. Ten minutes later, the fire was out.

The stranger spoke to Mrs. Knight before he left.

"I hope I've helped you in some way. I've done everything I could," Mrs. Knight recalls him saying. She had never seen him before and with the confusion, couldn't remember what he looked like.

The fire began with a short circuit in a cord leading to a lamp and a fan, Morgan said. The house

*Chronology ends
Basic news summary information*

received more than $15,000 in damage.

Smoke and heat damaged all the family's belongings, Mrs. Knight said. "The little girls lost everything they had."

(In more dramatic stories with suspense, the climax is at the end)

None of the children— 11-year-old Michael, 6-year-old Ashley and 3-year-old Jenna— was injured. Their father was treated for smoke inhalation.

Larry Dougherty, *St. Petersburg Times*

Sections Technique

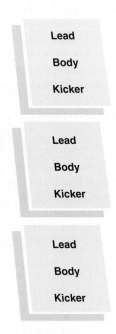

Exhibit 12-6
Sections technique

The technique of separating the story into sections is very useful for in-depth stories. It can be used with many kinds of feature and news stories. The key to the section technique is to treat each section like a separate news story with a lead and an ending that will compel readers to continue (see Exhibit 12-6). Think of each section as a chapter in a book.

One common way to organize section stories is by points of view. For example, in a story about a controversial government issue, such as a new landfill, you could arrange the story by different points of view—a section for each group affected by the proposal.

The other way frequently used to organize section stories is by time frames—starting with the present, then to the past for background, back to present developments and ending with the future. Although the order can be flexible, the opening section must contain a nut graph explaining why you are telling the reader this story now.

This technique is very effective for stories written in narrative style. To determine whether your story is suitable for sections, envision subheads for it. Then decide if you have enough information in each subheaded group to warrant a separate section.

The following story weaves back and forth between two people, each one's experience in a separate section. The short ending ties their lives together. Here are some excerpts:

They got out alive, but no one was spared

BOULDER, Colo.—For weeks after the crash, David Hooker found the love notes his fiancee had hidden around the house.

In the medicine cabinet: "David, I love you this much."

In the sock drawer: "Poo— Here's a hug for you! Susan."

In the silverware tray: "I'll miss you! Take care."

Five months have passed since Susan Fyler boarded United Airlines Flight 282. Hooker carefully stacks the yellow slips of paper into a neat pile on the corner of his dresser, next to the framed photo-

This paragraph tells why you are reading this story now.

graphs of Fyler and the mahogany box that holds her ashes.

■

Less than a half-hour away in Denver, Garry Priest can't sleep.

He watched a movie—he doesn't even remember what it was about—and one scene stuck. A woman is thrown from a car and the pavement scrapes her skin raw.

Suddenly it was July 19 again and Priest was back in Sioux City, Ia., escaping from the plane, racing along the runway, seeing the debris, the charred metal, the boy's body.

Then he thinks of Christmas. And his eyes will not close.

■

<!--margin note-->
This section gives the crucial information that ties the story together.

Five months ago, they were strangers, bound only by an airplane flight.

Susan Fyler was headed to Ohio to surprise her parents with news of her engagement. Garry Priest was going to Chicago on business.

Both boarded Flight 232 in Denver. She sat in seat 31K, he in seat 15G.

Fyler was one of 112 people killed in the crash. She was 32. Priest was one of 184 survivors. He is 23.

For those most directly affected—the family and friends of the victims, the survivors and their families—the holidays are proving that time has not healed all wounds. . . .

Five months later, they are strangers, but David Hooker and Garry Priest share a common grief.

■

This section is about David Hooker and how he is dealing with the loss of his fiancee.

Every night, David Hooker walks into his bedroom, lights a candle and shares his day with Susan Fyler.

Shortly after the crash, a friend admonished Hooker to stop feel-

ing sorry for himself and to ask Fyler for guidance.

"I asked Susan to come live with me inside my body and to stay alive inside my body," he says, "and right after I did that, I felt a very dramatic change going on in me. I just felt all this energy coming over me."

After he lights the candle, Hooker may read the Lord's Prayer or flip through the love notes Fyler left him or look at the five photographs on his dresser. . . .

Weeks later, when Fyler's belongings were returned, he opened the suitcase. Bear looked up at him.

■

It didn't make sense.

Why, Garry Priest wondered, were people acting this way? He had survived one of the worst airplane disasters in U.S. history. He had seen horrible things, scenes that made his legs shake, pictures he will remember the rest of his life.

So why was everyone calling him lucky?

"People want to pinch you," he says. "They say, 'Let's play bingo,' or 'Let's buy a lottery ticket.' They pat your head.

"I don't feel lucky at all. If I was lucky, I wouldn't have been on that plane. Nobody would have been on the plane."

■

They are strangers, but Garry Priest would like David Hooker to know that he, too, mourns Susan Fyler.

"Could you do me a favor?" Priest asks. "Could you tell all the people who lost loved ones and all the people who survived that I wish them a merry Christmas and that my thoughts and prayers and love are with them?"

Ken Fuson, *The Des Moines* (Iowa) *Register*

This section discusses how Hooker had sent Susan a teddy bear that she loved—she named it Bear—and always took with her. It ends with this kicker.

This section gives Garry Priest's point of view.

The story continues with another section devoted to Hooker. Then another section gives more of Priest's point of view. And it ends with this section.

The next example is a long story about a convicted murderer who was sentenced to be executed. It is arranged by time sequences.

Inmate reaffirms desire to die

Present time frame: sets up the reason for the story and foreshadows what will come

JEFFERSON CITY (Mo.)—"I think I been heading here since I was 8 years old," Gerald Smith once said, looking around the Missouri State Penitentiary. "The only way I'll ever leave here is in a box."

He made that comment in 1982, and he said then he wanted the state to carry out the death sentence imposed for the murder of a former girlfriend. He's changed his mind often, at times asking for death and at other times allowing appeals on his behalf.

Now Smith again wants to die, and if he continues with that death wish, he will become the first prisoner executed in Missouri since 1965, the first to die by lethal injection in the state and the first executed since the death penalty was reinstated in 1977.

At 12:01 a.m. Tuesday, Corrections Director Dick Moore is to read a death warrant to the 29-year-old, who will be strapped to a hospital cart. An instant after the warrant is read, a series of three deadly chemicals will be injected into a vein in Smith's arm and he will die.

Smith granted interviews to two reporters Friday because he said he wanted people to know that he is prepared to die and does not want third parties to interfere on his behalf.

"About the only time I'm uncalm and unrelaxed is when they (third parties) are out there interfering the way they are," Smith said.

Prison officials say he has held that position for some time now, and they're moving ahead with execution plans, lining up witnesses, testing out the never-before-used lethal injection machine and setting up plans to control other prisoners and any protesters who might be outside the prison.

Since he has been on death row in the old prison in Jefferson City, Smith has killed another death-row inmate, gone on hunger strikes demanding that he be executed, written threatening and profane letters to newspapers and judges, and threatened to "wring the neck" of his lawyers.

He also has gotten married, allowed his family to file appeals on his behalf and joined a class-action lawsuit contending that living conditions on death row were not acceptable.

His life behind bars has been just one more confused chapter in a twisted and troubled life.

■

In the hard-luck south St. Louis neighborhood where Smith grew up, hassling the cops, having several girlfriends at a time, drinking and taking drugs were common.

The Smith home on Delaware Street has been torn down. But the area where Gerald Smith beat a former girlfriend to death hasn't changed much since that September 1980 evening.

In a 1982 interview, and in court records, Smith has often recounted the crime, in his usual, monotone delivery.

It was Sept. 8 and Smith and another girlfriend, Dana Osia, were in Osia's car, driving around,

Past time frame: background of the issue

drinking. He told Dana that he was going to visit someone, a girl who had given him a venereal disease.

Smith was referring to Karen Roberts, a neighbor. Smith found Roberts, 20, and the two of them started walking along a side street, near a railroad track.

Smith said he and Roberts argued, and she cussed at him when he accused her of giving him gonorrhea. She ran from him after he shoved her down, and the chase was on.

Smith picked up an 8-pound iron bar, and when he caught her, bashed her head repeatedly with the weapon. Medical examiners later said that any one of the blows would have been enough to kill her.

"I caught up to her and beat her lousy head in," Smith said. "I had a gun with me, but I wanted her to hurt before she died."

"She did," he said, a slight smile crossing his face.

Roberts' body was found the next morning, clad in blue jeans and a black T-shirt with a Harley-Davidson logo across the back. She had been hit so many times the fractures and wounds could not be counted.

After his arrest, Smith showed his first impatience with the judicial system. Before his trial, he wrote a letter to a St. Louis newspaper, which read, in part:

"I Gerald Smith killed Karen Roberts. I have been looking for her for 4 months so I could kill her. On September the 8, 1980 I finally got my chance to kill her and I done just that. . . . Now that I have had a taste of killing I like it. If these people in court don't sentence me to the death penalty I will get out of jail some day and kill every last one of them including the judge and the prosecutor."

He signed the letter, "Gerald Smith the cold blooded killer." A jury in the summer of 1981 took little time to find Smith guilty and sentence him to death.

■

An admitted brawler, thief and heavy drinker and drug user, Smith's been in trouble since he was 10.

He started out stealing, often accompanied by other family members. His father and three of his brothers are currently in prison in the state.

"I was always getting arrested for raising hell, peace disturbance, resisting arrest, stealing, something," Smith has said.

A policeman in the neighborhood at the time remembers arresting Smith more than 30 times as a teen-ager.

"He was just typical," Tom McEntee said. "He was just one of the neighborhood criminals."

■

Not long after his arrival in Jefferson City, Gerald Smith started demanding that he be put to death.

He stuck to that position through the summer of 1983. At one point he overdosed on prescription medication, but he later said he wasn't trying to commit suicide but just wanted to "get high."

After the overdose, Smith had a change of heart and decided he wanted to pursue the stalled appeals. He helped family members in efforts to stay the execution though higher courts later rejected those appeals.

Since then he has gone back and forth, seeking execution for a few months and then fighting the

More past time frame: background of the character

Return to present

process for a time. He has gone through repeated tests of his competency. Most recently a federal judge in Kansas City found him able to decide his own fate. That ruling came in 1986.

In February 1987, Smith married a California woman, Lyn Short, whom he became acquainted with through letters. And in July 1987 he was found guilty of murdering another death-row inmate, Robert Baker, in 1985. He was sentenced to die for that crime, also.

This August, Smith again decided he wanted to be executed and started efforts to block all appeals on his behalf, dismissing attorneys and writing to courts and judges indicating he was ready to die.

A federal judge on Friday rejected a suit filed by two inmates seeking to stop Smith's execution on the grounds the death penalty had become a political issue in an election year. Also, the Missouri Public Defender Commission filed a petition Friday for a rehearing before the entire 9th U.S. Circuit Court of Appeals in St. Louis. On Thursday, a three-judge panel of the appellate court rejected the commission's first request for a rehearing on Smith's competency.

And an emergency request was filed by the commission with U.S. Supreme Court Justice John Paul Stevens to stay Smith's execution.

Gov. John Ashcroft, a death penalty proponent, said this week that he did not plan to block the scheduled execution.

■

If Smith dies early Tuesday, his execution will be the first in Missouri since 1965 when Lloyd Lee Anderson was placed in the gas chamber and executed for killing a 15-year-old delivery boy during a robbery.

For Smith, the final days before his latest date with death have been filled by "watching TV, drinking Pepsi-Cola and smoking Camel cigarettes," according to Dale Riley, the assistant director for adult institutions in the Department of Corrections.

Smith has been described as calm and has been visited by his wife of several months almost daily in the final week. A 9-year-old daughter of a south St. Louis friend also apparently has visited him. He's shown no indications of changing his mind.

His family has made arrangements to claim his body after the execution.

Tom Miller, *The Kansas City* (Mo.) *Star*

Future time frame for ending

Smith was executed in 1989, a year after this story was written.

Activities

1 Inverted pyramid exercise: Organize the information for this story in the inverted pyramid order. Here are your notes, based on a story from The Associated Press:

Who: Connecticut State Police

What: Ordered ban of hand-held radar guns

When: Yesterday

Where: Meriden, Conn.

Why: Because of concerns that troopers could develop cancer from long-term exposure to the radiation waves emitted by the devices. The ban was ordered as a precaution while studies are conducted into the possible links between cancer and use of the devices.

How: The ban affects 70 radar guns that will be withdrawn from service. State troopers will continue to use radar units with transmitters mounted on the outside of their cruisers.

Source: Adam Berluti, a state police spokesman

Backup information: "The feeling here is to err on the side of caution until more is known about the issue," Berluti said. "The whole situation is under review."

The move is considered to be the first of its kind by a state police agency. It comes two months after three municipal police officers in Connecticut filed workers' compensation claims, saying they developed cancer from using hand-held radar guns.

2 *Wall Street Journal* **formula:** Organize this story according to the *Wall Street Journal* formula. The information is taken from a *Los Angeles Times* story by Barry M. Horstman and Jennifer Toth. Use an anecdotal lead, and label your nut graph. There is no one right order. Write the story so it reads smoothly. To give you a clue, here are the headline and summary lines that appeared above the story:

Answer to Idealism or Joblessness

Volunteer agencies are seeing a surge of interest from college seniors. For some students it's a shift away from the Me Decade. For others, it's mostly the path to a paycheck.

The flood of young applicants eager for public service contradicts common assumptions about the supposed apathy of the twenty-something generation.

Volunteerism, seen at best in recent years as a well-intentioned diversion from the fast track, is being increasingly viewed by college students as a logical entry point into the workplace instead of postponement of a career.

College students already account for a growing share of the 3,300-member volunteer force of VISTA (Volunteers in Service to America)—about 240 of whom work in California. People 55 and older make up another 20 percent, as do people without college degrees between 18 and 27. The remainder of the volunteers are widely distributed among other age groups.

"I'm, basically very, very conservative, so I'm skeptical about a lot of government programs," said Douglas May, a VISTA volunteer working in Los Angeles' Chrysalis project in a job-development program for the unemployed. "But I like the idea of putting a federally paid volunteer in the hands of a private nonprofit organization. That's much more effective."

During its 2½-year history, Teach for America also has struck a responsive chord on college campuses. When news of its establishment hit campuses in 1990, the organization received 2,500 applications for 500 positions. Last year it had 3,100 applications and accepted 700 people, about 90 percent of them recent college graduates.

A stagnant economy, changing attitudes toward volunteer work and heightened interest in world affairs have given organizations such as the Peace Corps, VISTA and Teach for America a higher profile on college campuses, generating applications at an unparalleled rate.

In the first week of January, for example, the Peace Corps' Washington telephone lines were jammed with so many calls—nearly 900 a day at one point—that the system broke down, according to Mike Berning, the agency's director of recruitment. At the same time last year, the Peace Corps' information hot line drew 150 to 200 calls a day, he added.

Recent visits to campuses in Los Angeles, Claremont and San Diego produced recruiting dividends, as VISTA staffers had no difficulty luring applicants for low-paying positions in programs that deal with homelessness, drug abuse, hunger and unemployment.

At the Peace Corps, the pendulum's swing back toward volunteerism has been fueled by enthusiasm over serving in former communist bloc nations. Over the next year, the Peace Corps plans to open 250 to 500 field positions in the Commonwealth of Independent States, formerly the Soviet Union.

In 1991, the 30-year-old Peace Corps organization waded through 13,735 applications to fill just 3,800 trainee positions. Three months into 1992, the Peace Corps already has 1,100 more applications than at this time last year and expects to surpass 1991's figure by at least 3,000.

From the perspective of some top federal administrators, the volunteer agencies' resurgence on campus is seen as a return to the 1960s style of idealism after the self-absorption of the Me Decade of the 1980s, when college graduates felt compelled to land high-paying jobs and quickly move up career ladders.

William Baldwin, a University of Southern California senior contemplating several volunteer options, said many students are "learning that there's more to being satisfied than making $50,000, $60,000 a year."

"The '80s showed us that those values may be satisfying in the short run," Baldwin said. "But eventually they go belly up. These programs have a lasting value that isn't going to disappear."

In contrast to the subsistence allowances received by VISTA and Peace Corps volunteers, Teach for America volunteers are paid normal starting salaries by local schools, ranging from $15,000 in rural Arkansas to $29,000 in Los Angeles.

For many volunteers, altruistic motivations override economic concerns.

Some even bypass lucrative private-sector alternatives, as did Jameson Hill, a 27-year-old Teach for America instructor in rural Louisiana. He passed up a job in international banking.

"College students are a lot more idealistic than the media give them credit for," said Teach for America founder Wendy Kopp, whose program recruits graduates who majored in fields other than education to spend two years teaching in needy school districts.

"This isn't a '60s thing for me—I'm not a neo-hippy," said USC senior Beth Lipton, a journalism major whose bleak job prospects have led her to consider joining VISTA. "I'm interested in doing something about literacy, but I'm also interested in finding a job. I know people with master's degrees who are driving taxis, so I'm trying to be flexible."

When he graduated from Northwestern University and fulfilled his Navy ROTC obligation, Marty Siewart did not anticipate that he would spend seven months unemployed, soberly pondering the real-world value of his college degree and military experience.

Discouraged and "just about to get panicky" over his job search, Siewart finally landed with a federal poverty-fighting program in Hollywood where, paradoxically, he tries to help others find employment.

"I've always been interested in social service, so this is a good opportunity to get a better feel for it," said Siewart, sitting in the small, cluttered office from which he finds temporary jobs for teen-age runaways and homeless youths. "Plus with the economy the way it is, I feel lucky to be working here—or anywhere."

Emblematic of a rise in volunteerism among college-age individuals that blends idealism with economic realities, Siewart recently began a one-year enlistment in VISTA, the Great Society–era federal agency dedicated to alleviating poverty.

Anita Fuchslocher, a Teach for America kindergarten teacher in Los Angeles, admits being relieved when she was accepted by the program and no longer had to worry about overcoming difficult economic conditions in New England, where she went to college and where her family lives.

"I saw so many friends having trouble finding good jobs that I was really scared," Fuchslocher said. "So I was happy when this came along."

3 Hourglass exercise: Arrange these facts in hourglass order, placing attribution where it is needed. (This story is taken from the *St. Louis Post-Dispatch*.) Attribute information to Capt. Ed Kemp of the Jefferson County Sheriff's Department, unless otherwise noted.

Who: Two bank couriers

What: Helped police capture four suspects in a robbery

When: Last night

Where: At the Boatman's Bank of Pevely, Mo.

How: One courier, Dennis Boushie, who lives near Festus, chased a suspect on foot. The other courier, Willie Moore of St. Louis, drove a bank van, chasing a getaway car.

Police have booked three people on suspicion of drug possession. The three, who were found in the getaway car, are being held in the jail at Pevely.

Backup information:

"This is beyond the call of duty. They acted more like police officers than private citizens or bank couriers," said Capt. Ed Kemp.

Boushie said he had asked the teller who was robbed if the robber had a weapon, and she said he did not. He said his pursuit of the robber had been "just common sense."

A man entered the bank shortly after it opened Tuesday morning and shouted, "Give me the money or else!" The teller gave the man an envelope containing the money, and the man ran out the front door.

Boushie chased the man on foot, and when the suspect jumped into a car, Boushie pointed the car out to Moore, who pursued it in a bank van. A few minutes later, Boushie got in a police patrol car and helped police track the getaway car.

The getaway car pulled off the highway and let out a man, who ran into the woods. Police arrested a man near Barnhart after a 10-minute search.

Police broadcast a description of the getaway car, which had continued north on I-55 carrying two men and a woman. Police spotted the car, stopped it and arrested three suspects.

Police said they had found several thousand dollars in the car. The female suspect had stuffed money down her pants, police said.

Police were seeking federal warrants for bank robbery.

4   List technique exercise: Write this story (based on a story from the United Press International wire service) using the list technique:

Who: Report of a study by the National Institute for Occupational Safety and Health

When: Report issued in today's *New England Journal of Medicine*

What: Findings that working at a video display terminal (VDT) does not increase the risk of miscarriage

Why: No significant difference in miscarriage rates between the two groups of women studied

How: Survey conducted among 2,430 telephone operators over a four-year period

Background and elaboration:

From Teresa Schnorr, government epidemiologist: "We looked at the question every which way and could find nothing. The answer is clear—there's nothing about the VDTs that causes spontaneous abortions."

The study included some of these details: Half of the women worked at terminals and half did not. Of the women in the study, 730 got pregnant during the study period, some more than once, for a total of 876 pregnancies. Over the four-year study period, there was no significant difference in miscarriage rates between the two groups (those who did and did not work at terminals). The results held true no matter how many hours a week the women sat at terminals and during the entire pregnancy.

From Karen Nussbaum, executive director of 9 to 5, National Association of Working Women, who was critical of the study: "We continue to get reports from VDT users having fertility problems."

"We are pleased with these findings," says David Legrande, health and safety director, Communications Workers of America.

5   Pyramid exercise: Write this story using pyramid form. Here are your notes, based on information from a story by the McClatchy News Service:

Who: Burglars who broke into a shoe warehouse twice in one week

What: They ransacked the place, causing about $5,000 in damage.

When: This week

Why: Because they were infuriated. Among the 50,000 shoes, no two pieces matched.

Background: Attribute to Georgia Hehr, a Sacramento nurse who founded One Shoe Crew, the owners of the shoe warehouse. One Shoe Crew is a non-profit group that supplies new footwear to amputees and people who have different size feet. Hehr founded the organization about five years ago. Her feet aren't the same size. She was forced to buy two pairs of shoes to get one that fit before she founded this organization.

"Apparently, when all (the burglars) found was one-sies, they got so mad they destroyed our desk equipment."

One Shoe Crew gets the shoes free from manufacturers. It distributes them to customers who pay only the postage, a one-time registration fee and, if they can afford it, a small handling charge.

6   Sections technique exercise: Find a long story or project in a newspaper, and organize it in section form. Mark where it could be divided into sections, and rewrite the kickers if needed.

COACHING

TIPS

Gather as many specific details as possible while you are reporting. Take notes of your observations as well as information from sources.

Use show-in-action techniques. Describe what people are doing.

Use vivid, action verbs.

For narrative writing, try to envision yourself at the scene. Gather details and chronology to reconstruct events as they occurred.

Think of your story as a plot with a beginning, middle and climax. Envision your sources as characters in a book; make your reader see, hear and care about them.

Storytelling Techniques

13

> The victim wasn't rich. She wasn't the daughter of anyone powerful. She was simply a 36-year-old woman trying to make a life for herself. Her name was Karen Gregory. The night she died, Karen became part of a numbing statistic. . . . It was what people sometimes casually refer to as "a little murder."
>
> Tom French, *St. Petersburg* (Fla.) *Times*

But it was more than that to Tom French. He was fascinated by Karen Gregory's case. He wrote a 10-part series about her murder and the man on trial for it. It was called "A Cry in the Night."

Something very unusual happened when the series began in 1988. Readers ran out to greet the newspaper delivery trucks each day to get the next chapter in the series. Why were they so eager to read these stories?

You decide. The previous passage was an introduction to the series. The first story began with this description of the trial of George Lewis, a firefighter who lived across the street from Karen Gregory and was charged with her murder.

> *We're supposed to be tellers of tales as well as purveyors of facts. When we don't live up to that responsibility, we don't get read.*
>
> Bill Blundell, *The Art and Craft of Feature Writing*

His lawyer called out his name. He stood up, put his hand on a Bible and swore to tell the truth and nothing but. He sat down in the witness box and looked toward the jurors so they could see his face and study it and decide for themselves what kind of man he was.

"Did you rape Karen Gregory?" asked his lawyer.

"No sir, I did not."

"Did you murder Karen Gregory?"

"No sir."

He heard a scream that night, he said. He heard it, and he went out to the street to look around.

He saw a man he did not know, standing over in Karen's yard. The man said to go away, to not tell anyone what he'd seen. He waited for the man to leave—watched him walk away into the darkness—and then he went up to Karen's house. There was broken glass on the front walk. He knocked on the front door. There was no answer. He found an open window. He called out to ask whether anyone needed help. There was still no answer. He looked through the window and saw someone lying on the floor. He decided he had to go in. He climbed inside, and

there was Karen. Blood was everywhere.

He was afraid. He ran to the bathroom and threw up. He knew no one would believe how he had ended up standing inside that house with her body. He had to get out of there. He was running toward the window to climb out when he saw something moving in the dark. He thought someone was jumping toward him. Then he realized he was looking at a mirror, and the only person moving was him. It was his own reflection that had startled him. It was George.

Tom French, *St. Petersburg Times*

The entire series was written like a mystery novel. But it was all true, based on interviews with more than 50 people and 6,000 pages of court documents. The writing style, called narrative writing, was a form of dramatic storytelling that reconstructs the events as though the reader were witnessing them as they happened. French later turned the series into a book called *Unanswered Cries,* published in 1991.

French said he never believed his series would be so popular. "The way the readers responded was so gratifying," he said.

French relied heavily on dialogue throughout the series, even from the dead woman. Although most of the dialogue and description are based on interviews and his own observations, Karen's dialogue was second-hand information, based on recollections about her.

"After I wrote it, I spent three weeks checking everything with all the participants," French said. "I read it to them word for word to make sure it was accurate."

Narrative storytelling requires very detailed reporting. The writing is equally difficult, especially if you have interviewed more than 50 people and used thousands of documents to gather the information.

French said he favors the narrative style. He tried it after reading a Latin American writer, Gabriel Garcia Marquez, who wrote "The Story of a Shipwrecked Sailor," a riveting story about a man who survived 10 days at sea without food and water. Marquez used compelling storytelling to reconstruct the sailor's experience.

Marquez originally wrote this story as a 14-part series for a Colombian newspaper, *El Espectador,* and later turned it into a book.

French also was influenced by literary journalists, a group of writers in the 1960s and 1970s who used the storytelling techniques of fiction for non-fiction newspaper and magazine stories. Influenced strongly by Truman Capote's non-fiction book *In Cold Blood,* these journalists—Joan Didion, John McPhee, Tracy Kidder, Tom Wolfe—immersed themselves in a subject and wrote their stories with characters, scene, dialogue and a plot. It was factual reporting written like fiction.

Storytelling

Today many editors beg for more storytelling; others frown on literary writing, especially in 15-inch stories. But the narrative writing style, which has been used extensively in magazines for years, is gaining popularity at many good newspapers, especially for in-depth stories.

Most journalists think storytelling techniques must be reserved for feature writing. But as you will see in this chapter, you can apply storytelling techniques to news about crime, courts and many other news stories. However, you need to use good judgment to decide when these techniques are applicable to your subject. The same criteria apply as in deciding whether to use soft or hard leads. In first-cycle stories, when the news is very serious and important—a disaster, a major tax increase, a significant development in a crime story—the hard-news approach is preferable. You also can use storytelling for only a part of the story, as in the hourglass structure.

Storytelling involves two basic kinds of writing:

Descriptive writing: Gives the reader a picture, preferably through concrete details. It describes characters, scenes or events.

Narrative writing: Tells the reader a story, preferably through the characters' actions, words and feelings. In a broad sense, the body of any story may be called the narrative. In a storytelling sense, however, narrative writing reconstructs the event and puts the reader at the scene. It lets the reader experience what happened. It uses dialogue, when possible, plus description and anecdotes. It has the basic structure of a plot, with a beginning, a middle and a climax. But in newspaper writing, the nut graph—why the reader should care—still must be high in the story.

These two types are not distinct. You often will use description when you write in narrative style.

Descriptive Techniques

If you want to make the reader see, you have to learn to see as a reporter. You have to practice the observation techniques you studied at the beginning of this book.

William Ruehlmann, author of *Stalking the Feature Story,* says writers must concentrate when they observe and then analyze what they observe. He gives this example: "Flies take off backwards. So in order to swat one, you must strike slightly behind him. An interesting detail, and certainly one a writer would be able to pick up on. Other people see flies; a writer sees how they move."

How do you convey your observations to the reader? Show people in action. Write specific detail with vivid nouns and verbs. Avoid vague adjectives. Norman Mailer, in a speech at the University of Iowa, gave this advice:

> The adjective is the author's opinion of what is going on, no more. If I write, "A strong man came into the room," that only means he is strong in relation to me. Unless I've established myself for the reader, I might be the only fellow in the bar who is impressed by the guy who just came in. It is better to say: "A man entered. He was holding a walking stick, and for some reason, he now broke it in two like a twig." Of course, this takes more time to narrate. So adjectives bring on quick tell-you-how-to-live writing. Advertising thrives on it. "A super-efficient, silent, sensuous, five-speed shift." Put 20 adjectives before a noun and no one will know you are describing a turd.

For example, what is a "fat" man? David Finkel leaves no doubt in his story about a circus performer (which is presented in full in Chapter 25). Not only does he tell you the "World's Biggest Man" is 891 pounds, he describes him specifically. And he uses another descriptive device: analogies, which are comparisons with something familiar to a reader.

Now: 891 and climbing. That's more than twice as much as Sears' best refrigerator-freezer—a 26-cubic-footer with automatic ice and water dispensers on side-by-side doors. That's almost as much as a Steinway grand piano.

He weighs himself on scrap yard scales and at roadside weigh stations. He travels mostly by car, but sometimes by plane—when two first-class seats are available. He can walk up to 30 yards without resting. He eats three meals a day.

Favorite breakfast: two eggs, coffee, toast with strawberry jam. Lunch: two ham sandwiches, one slice of ham each. Dinner: Whatever. Maybe an Italian-sausage sandwich from a carnival booth. Maybe a salad.

"In a 24-hour period, I average maybe 2½ to 3 pounds of food," he says. "When I was young, I used to eat a lot—eight-egg omelets, with onions. But that was it. No breads or anything. See, it's not the food; it's hormones. They found when they took the food away, the growing didn't stop."

David Finkel, *St. Petersburg Times*

"Description, like every element in either fiction or non-fiction, should advance the meaning of your story," says Bruce DeSilva, writing coach for *The Hartford* (Conn.) *Courant.* "It would be a good idea to describe the brown house in more detail only if those details are important. Description never should be there for decoration. It never should be there because you are showing off. And when you do describe, you should never use more words than you need to trigger that mental image readers already have in their minds."

One way to trigger that image is through analogies like those in the preceding story. Writers use two types of analogies: similes and metaphors. A simile is a comparison using *like* or *as,* although the words *like* and *as* may be implied rather than directly stated. Here's an example of a simile:

> As stories of marriages go, John and Betty's is more like a Mel Brooks comedy than an Ingmar Bergman drama.

A metaphor is a direct comparison, without *like* or *as.* It describes one thing in terms of another:

> *Manhunter* is a dark locomotive of a movie, dragging the audience with it.

You can also use metaphorical language as a modifier, as in this example:

> His pain burns search-beam bright in his blue eyes.

These examples of similes and metaphors were all from *The Oregonian,* where writing coach Jack Hart encourages the staff to use analogies. "Clever, witty or revealing figures of speech provide one of the basic pleasures of reading," he says in *Second Takes,* a coaching bulletin he writes for the staff. "An especially apt metaphor surprises and delights. It gives readers incentive to keep moving ahead, confident that more rewards wait in the next column of type."

You can also use analogies to make something clearer to a reader, just by describing something in terms the reader can understand. This technique is especially helpful when writing about technical information, as in environmental stories. For example, scientists often describe pollutants in terms of parts per billion. To help the reader visualize how much that is, make a comparison:

> The toxic chemical concentrated in the water amounted to five parts per billion. That's equivalent to a thimbleful of pesticide in an Olympic-size swimming pool.

In the following passage from John McPhee's book *Oranges,* the author describes the seven stages of processing concentrated orange juice. McPhee uses comparisons to help the reader visualize:

At the fifth stage, the juice is already thicker than the ultimate product that goes into the six-ounce can—and it has the consistency of cough syrup, with a biting aftertaste. . . .

After the seventh stage, the orange juice . . . is thick enough to chew, and its taste actually suggests apricot-flavored gum.

Too much description will clutter a story. Too little will leave the reader blank. How much is enough? First decide if the story even lends itself to description of the scene or person. In a hard-news story, when the person is just expressing an opinion, you don't need it. In a personality profile or story about a flood, earthquake, protest or other visual-type event, you do.

Beware of the weather report or time of day description: "It was a dark and stormy night." Just as with soft leads, don't lead with a weather scene unless it is relevant to the story. In this story about the Iditarod race through Alaska, the weather was relevant, because it was a cause of the character's problems:

Appropriate

A ground blizzard raged across the barren tundra high in the Alaska Range Tuesday night when Bobby Lee of Trapper Creek drove his dogs out from Puntilla Lake.

Ahead of him waited the 45 miles of trail over the pass and down through the Dalzell Gorge to Rohn.

Once before in an Iditarod Trail Sled Dog Race, Lee had been over this trail behind a dog team. He figured if he left in the wind he could gain a small advantage on the other mushers bunched with him at Rainly Pass Lodge.

It was not to be. Instead, Lee almost lost everything.

Craig Medred, *Anchorage* (Alaska) *Daily News*

In the next example, the story is about a reading program. Although the lead about the weather is backed up by a quote, the weather had nothing to do with the focus or the rest of the story.

Inappropriate

It was a beautiful springlike Sunday, and the heat on the first floor of the Kansas City Public Library Downtown was on full-blast. But that didn't stop about 400 people from crowding inside to read and hear their favorite selections from African-American authors.

The crowd, people of all ages and races, was there to take part in the national Read-In sponsored by the Black Caucus of the National Teachers of English.

"That is true commitment," said Mamie Isler, program director for Genesis School, which helped coordinate the event in Kansas City.

The second annual Kansas City Read-In opened with a performance by 30 students from the Genesis School choir and a word from Mayor Emanuel Cleaver.

The Kansas City (Mo.) *Star*

Physical descriptions   Use physical descriptions only when they are relevant to the content. They work well in profiles, in stories about crime, courts and disasters, and whenever they fit with the context. They don't work when they are tacked onto impersonal quotes.

Avoid stage directions, descriptions of people's gestures, facial expressions and physical characteristics inserted artificially as though you were directing a play. You don't need to describe what city commissioners are wearing at a meeting or how they gesture unless their clothing and movements enhance what they are saying and doing.

Appropriate

A Florida jury needed only 77 minutes to find that William Kennedy Smith was not guilty of raping a woman at his family's estate in March, bringing to a swift end the most highly publicized trial of its kind in recent times.

Smith first closed his eyes, then broke into a small smile when the verdict was read. And clearly jubilant, he bounded to his feet and embraced his main lawyer, Roy Black, in a clumsy bearhug.

Paul Richter, *Los Angeles Times*

Inappropriate

The study shows college students are becoming more conservative, the researcher said, blinking her blue eyes and clasping her carefully manicured hands.

The color of the researcher's eyes and her hand motions have nothing to do with her comments about the study.

Sexist/racist descriptions   When you decide to include descriptions of people, beware of sexism, racism or other biased writing. Writers often describe men with action verbs showing what they are doing and women with adjectives showing what they wear and how they look. One way to avoid bias is to ask yourself if you would use a similar description for both men and women or equal treatment for all racial and ethnic groups.

This example is from a profile of an African-American author:

Inappropriate

The daughter of West Indian immigrants, (Paule) Marshall grew up in Brooklyn listening to the stories her mother and her friends told her after working all day in the homes of white New Yorkers.

"That is where my preparation as a writer began," she recalls in a cultured voice that flows as slow as honey.

Atlanta Constitution

Would a story about a male author describe his voice in such terms? Some African-Americans might also claim the statement is somewhat racist, because it implies that most African-Americans don't have a cultured voice.

Or in this example, when have you read about a man who was "perky" and "adorable" in his running outfit?

Inappropriate

Even Chandra Smith, busy being adorable in her perky non-runner's running outfit, actually looked at the track. A minute later, she was jumping around and yelling, along with most of the other 41,600 people on the old wooden benches at Franklin Field.

The Philadelphia Inquirer

The story about the Penn Relay Carnival, a track meet in Philadelphia, also mentions a few men among those 41,600 people, including some volunteers who wear gray trousers and red caps. But they aren't adorable or perky.

You don't have to avoid describing people. You just need to consider relevance to the story and equal treatment for all people.

Cheryl Lavin, a feature writer, always uses description to let the reader see her subjects, from what they are wearing to how they sound. But her description relates to the story. Here is an excerpt from a profile about George Burns when he was 90:

Appropriate

From stage right walks a little old man, stooped over, wearing a tuxedo in a size that would fit a bar mitzvah boy. There's a neat little gray toupee on his suntanned head, shiny black shoes on his tiny feet, a perky red silk hanky in his breast pocket. His eyes are sparkling behind his round black-rimmed glasses; his ears are huge. He looks like an organ grinder's monkey.

When he gets to center stage—he's taking his time about it—he turns to the audience and says what they're all thinking:

"Look at that! And he walks, too!" Then he carefully flicks the ashes off his big, smelly El Producto, waits for the laugh, gets it, and rolls right on to the next bit. His timing, as ever, is impeccable.

"Usually a performer gets a standing ovation at the end of his act," he says, his head engulfed in a cloud of smoke. "I get mine at the beginning. You're afraid I won't make it."

Cheryl Lavin, *Chicago Tribune*

Chapter 19 will deal with racist and sexist writing in more detail.

Show-in-action technique One of the most effective ways to describe people or places is to show action. Cheryl Lavin combined physical description with show-in-action in the George Burns story. In this example, the show-in-action technique is used to describe the start of the worst circus fire in the city's history:

As always, the circus started with the clowns. Then came the animals—first a parade of them all—then the big cats alone, leaping through the air and snarling from their perches at the crack of a whip.

Next came the high-wire human pyramid act of the Flying Wallendas. At 2:40, five Wallendas were on a platform with their bicycles and balancing poles, high above the crowd, and thousands of eyes followed them as they got ready to balance on the high wire.

The 29-piece band was playing ballet music, the exit tune for the big cats still leaving the tent through 3-foot-high steel tubes, called chutes, connected to their cages. Suddenly bandmaster Merle Evans switched to the quick march of "Stars and Stripes Forever."

It was a signal to the circus performers that something was wrong. From his perch in front of the band, Evans had noticed something.

A few other people saw it— a horseshoe-shaped flame creeping up the side of the tent near the main entrance.

And then someone screamed that word.

FIRE!

The death toll was 168—124 females, 43 males and one whose body was so mutilated that the sex could not be determined. Thirty-nine of the dead were 5 to 9 years old; 17 were even younger.

Bill Ryan, *The Hartford* (Conn.) *Courant*

Lively verbs   News is action, says Jack Hart, *The Oregonian*'s writing coach. But writers often "squeeze the life out of an action-filled world," he says. "We write that thousands of bullet holes were in the hotel, instead of noting that the holes pocked the hotel. We report that a jumper died Monday when his parachute failed, instead of turning to action verbs such as plummeted or plunged or streamed," Hart says in one of his monthly newsletters to *The Oregonian's* staff.

Instead he recommends sentences filled with action verbs like these: "Miners strike. A bomb explodes, gutting a nightclub. An airplane plummets from the sky. Tanks rumble from city streets. A mob surges through the city square."

Mitch Albom, a sportswriter, knows the value of action verbs. Notice the ones he uses in this story about the day Detroit Tigers baseball player Cecil Fielder hit his 50th home run. Also notice the analogies.

He swung the bat and he heard that smack! and the ball screamed into the dark blue sky, higher, higher, until it threatened to bring a few stars down with it. His teammates knew; they leaped off the bench. The fans knew; they roared like animals. And finally, the man who all year refused to watch his home runs, the man who said this 50 thing was "no big deal"—finally even he couldn't help himself. He stopped halfway to first base and watched the ball bang into the facing of the upper deck in Yankee Stadium, waking up the ghosts of Maris and Ruth and Gehrig.

And then, for the first time in this miraculous season, Cecil Fielder jumped. He jumped like a man sprung from prison, he jumped like a kid on the last day of school, he jumped, all 250 pounds of Detroit Bambino, his arms over his head, his huge smile a beacon of celebration and relief.

The Big Five-O.

Mitch Albom, *Detroit Free Press*

Narrative Techniques

Narrative writing combines show-in-action description, dialogue, plot and reconstruction of an event as it occurred. It puts the reader on the scene as though he or she were witnessing it. This type of writing requires a bond of faith with the reader, because attribution is limited. You need to make it clear where you got the information, but you don't need to attribute repeatedly. You also can use an overview attribution for portions of the story and then attribute periodically, especially when you are quoting sources.

Before you can do narrative writing, you need to do thorough reporting. It takes a different kind of questioning to gather the information you will need to reconstruct a scene with dialogue and detail. Narrative writing is not fiction. You must stick to the facts even though the story may read like a novel. You need to ask questions like these: What were you thinking at the time? What were you feeling? What did you say? What were you wearing? What were you doing? You need to get details about colors, sounds, sights, smells, sizes, shapes, times, places.

If you were witnessing the event, you would see, hear, smell and feel—perhaps even taste—the experiences of your subject. Since you are reconstructing the event, you need to ask the questions that will evoke all those images.

Martha Miller did that when she interviewed a veteran who wanted a Purple Heart medal for his injuries from the Vietnam War. But she interviewed him 20 years after the war. She wanted him to reconstruct the experience. So she asked him what he was thinking, doing, saying, feeling and experiencing at the time. As you read the following excerpt from her story (another part appears later in the chapter), consider the questions you would ask to get the same information. In this portion, Pvt. Daniel R. Vickroy is setting a mine:

He ran wire from where the men were camped to the spot he was going to place the mine. Vickroy squatted and ran his hand along the wire to feel any kinks or knots. He set the mine down and adjusted it.

Kneeling on his right knee, he attached the blasting cap to the end of the wire. A blasting cap, a silver tube with two wires sticking out, explodes the mine.

He had to make sure he was far enough away from the mine's backblast. "Far enough" was 20 meters, a little more than the distance between a baseball pitcher and a catcher. Vickroy needed someone to tell him if he was in the ballpark.

Nobody was watching, and he couldn't yell because he would give away the other GIs' position. To be safe, he decided to move out another three yards.

The mine was set, and he unscrewed the ear to disengage it.

He took one last look back.

Vickroy's 6-foot, 180-pound body was hurled 15 feet into the night air. His glasses flew off and his eyes opened. All he could see were swirls of red, black and white.

"I knew it went off," Vickroy said. "I thought for a couple of seconds and I knew I was in for trouble because I was so close."

His first thought was survival. He remembered First Aid training. Keep your head above your heart. . . .

He looked down.

"I saw two white, chalky bones sticking out and no hand."

He heard voices through the ringing in his head. Someone yelled for a medic.

Vickroy's eyes were burning from the smoke and dirt raining on him. But he could see the whole right side of his body and it was smoldering.

His right leg was gone. . . .

The medic pulled off his white helmet and put his head on Vickroy's chest. He heard nothing.

The helicopter engine was at full throttle.

"Shut her down! He's dead!" the medic yelled to the pilots.

The engine slowed.

"Don't stop!" Vickroy thought to himself.

He had to let them know he was alive.

With all the strength he could gather, he slowly raised his left arm and made a fist out of his only hand.

The eyes under the white helmet saw it.

The medic shouted: "Let's go!"

Martha Miller, *Iowa City* (Iowa) *Press-Citizen*

Storytelling Structure

Up to this point in the book, even though you have had many story structures to choose from, you probably have been organizing your stories by focus and supporting topics or in chronological order. Even with a storytelling approach, you still need to get the focus first. A narrative story can then be arranged topically or chronologically, or it can follow a literary plot form—with a beginning, a middle and an ending called a "climax."

"Most news stories are endings without beginnings attached," says Jon Franklin, a Pulitzer Prize–winning writer and author of *Writing for Story*. Reporters miss the dramatic point of view when they concentrate only on the end result instead of on the actions leading up to the event. Franklin says stories should be built around a complication and a resolution. In the middle is the development, how the central character gets from the problem to the solution.

If you have a story that lends itself to this kind of plot, your focus would be the complication the main character has to overcome. The organization could be chronological, starting with the inception of the problem. The middle would be how the character wrestles with the problem, and the climax would be the resolution of the problem.

Or you can start in the middle of the action, as long as you explain to the reader why you are telling this story now (the "so what" factor). This approach is somewhat like using the time frame organization—starting with the present, going to the past, back to the present and on to the future. The technique of developing the story in sections, perhaps arranged by points of view, can also work in a narrative story. You can even use storytelling with a topical organization or any of the methods suggested in Chapter 12.

Regardless of the technique you choose, you should plan your order before you write.

Applications

On the following pages you will see how writers have used storytelling techniques in a variety of ways. As you read them, consider the basic techniques for storytelling:

• Use concrete details rather than vague adjectives.

• Use dialogue when possible and appropriate.

• Set a scene.

• Use action verbs.

• Observe or ask questions involving all your senses.

• Use show-in-action description.

• Tell a story like a plot, with a beginning, middle and climax. Get a chronology or sequence of events. You may want to use the chronology in all or part of your story. Even if you don't use chronological order, you need to understand the sequence.

• Follow Mark Twain's advice: "Don't say the old lady screamed—bring her on and let her scream."

Narrative Style for Crime News

Here is a short crime story that uses narrative storytelling for part of the story. The writer uses a build-on-a-quote lead and then organizes the story in pyramid form, with dialogue and storytelling.

WASHINGTON — Rep. Ben Nighthorse Campbell found out he's no longer an Olympic athlete. But a would-be-robber found out that the former judo champ still isn't a man to mess with.

Campbell, of Colorado, said he was returning to his Capitol Hill apartment from a grocery store Wednesday night when he was approached by a man with his hand in his jacket.

"Give me your money, I have a .45," said the man, according to Campbell.

"Let's see the gun," Campbell replied.

The assailant, who evidently had been bluffing, hit Campbell in the face.

The congressman, a member of the 1964 U.S. Olympic judo squad, hit back. A brief fight ensued and ended when the would-be robber ran. Campbell tried to give chase.

"I found out in one fell swoop I wasn't a 28-year-old judo champ anymore," said Campbell, who tore ligaments in his ankle and wound up on crutches. "I found out I'm a 58-year-old out-of-shape congressman."

But he took satisfaction from the outcome all the same. "He didn't get my peanut butter and jelly," cracked Campbell.

The Associated Press

Storytelling for a Court Case

This story uses the descriptive technique of analogy. The writer compares the court case to a television script. The nut graphs are the 11th and 12th paragraphs. Would you stop reading before you get there?

A strangled wife— and a tangled case grips a town

WILKES-BARRE (Pa.) — It could be a made-for-TV movie. A young dentist's wife is found twisted in bloody sheets at the foot of her bed, strangled. Her handsome, athletic husband calls for help from a phone in the kitchen downstairs. He says he was knocked out by an intruder.

The dentist is taken to a hospital with minor injuries.

Police investigate, but the clues don't add up. Then, the dentist's brother, who arrived at the house before police, dies mysteriously after missing an appointment with investigators.

The dentist becomes the prime—and only—suspect in the violent slaying of his wife. Word gets out that he had been having simultaneous affairs with two women, and had slept with one—his former dental assistant—the day before his wife's death.

No arrests are made, and the dentist and his young daughter move to Arlington, Va. One of his lovers joins them.

The unsolved killing grips the town—so strongly that it becomes a factor in a local election. The dentist calls one of the town's newspaper columnists and theorizes that his wife might have been killed by "druggies."

Three years after the slaying, the dentist returns to his home town—in handcuffs and shackles.

He is charged with the cold-blooded murder of his wife.

No, this isn't Fatal Vision 2. And despite similarities to that well-known story, in which a military doctor was convicted of killing his family after blaming a drug-crazed gang, the outcome of this drama is far from certain.

For this is a story still unfolding, day by day, before the watchful eyes of this Pennsylvania community.

Its cast of characters is real, starting with the victim, Elizabeth "Betty" Wolsteffer, who was strangled between 2:30 a.m. and 6:30 a.m. Aug. 30, 1986.

Last week, her husband, E. Glen Wolsteffer, 36, sat calmly and expressionless during a preliminary hearing as prosecutors laid out the circumstantial evidence that they hope will eventually convict him.

The hearing will continue next week, after a judge decides whether to compel two women, including Wolsteffer's live-in lover, to testify. A district justice will determine whether there is enough evidence for a trial.

The case is fraught with so much intrigue that it is easy to forget that there is no script—and that real lives lie in the balance.

Jodi Enda, *The Philadelphia Inquirer*

Narration and Description for a Tragedy

This follow-story, or sidebar, about a plane tragedy uses a combination descriptive and narrative approach. It reconstructs the experiences of passengers. The writer tells what they were doing, wearing, thinking, feeling and saying before the plane landed. It is not an appropriate approach for a first-day main story about a tragedy; that type of story should have a hard-news lead.

Laura Falci of Chicago was already asleep in seat 24A when United Airlines Flight 811 took off for New Zealand early Friday, her hair falling over her black double-breasted jacket, her white Reeboks on the floor. Like most airline passengers, she never paid much attention when the flight attendants went through all those instructions about how to adjust oxygen masks in an emergency.

Nearly at the back of the jetliner, Dr. Jack Kennedy, a

surgeon from Melbourne, Australia, casual in shorts with big red-and-white stripes, had found a couple of vacant seats to sleep.

And then the routine became extraordinary. There was a bang, a whoosh of air, and suddenly the cabin filled with flying debris and terror.

Ms. Falci gripped the hand of the Japanese man next to her and started to read the little plastic emergency card in the seat pocket. Dr. Kennedy looked out the window and saw fires from the two starboard engines and said to his sons in front of him, "I think this is it—you'd better say your prayers."

Nobody in the back yet knew that the nine business-class passengers near the front of the main passenger deck, and their seats, had been sucked out of the plane when the cargo door broke loose and a huge piece of the fuselage peeled away.

But 25 harrowing minutes later Capt. David M. Cronin, his co-pilot G. Al Slader, and the second officer, R. Mark Thomas, all based in Los Angeles, managed to bring their Boeing 747 back to Honolulu Airport for a safe landing on just the two left engines.

Robert Rheinhold, *The New York Times*

Descriptive Writing Example

This story is an example of descriptive writing with portions of narrative writing. David Silverman wrote it when he was an intern at the *Chicago Tribune* in 1988. At the end of the summer, the *Tribune* hired him—which Silverman attributes largely to this story.

The story is a follow-up feature about a child who was murdered. The parents were not granting interviews. Silverman used the sponsorship technique, asking the family's rabbi, whom Silverman knew, to intervene for him. The rabbi did. Then Silverman called the family, and they agreed to the interview. He convinced them that Nicky's story needed to be told.

The story reflects the reporting skills of observing and gathering detail. Even Nicky's parents couldn't remember his exact time of birth, but Silverman noticed it on a hospital record in a stack of materials the parents showed him. He wrote it in his notebook without knowing if he would need it. When he began to write his story, he discovered that the detail about the birth was exactly what he needed for the emotion he was trying to convey. (Remember to gather more information than you think you might need.)

Silverman also used the feature technique of weaving portions of the child's journal into the story to reveal Nicky's thoughts and to show the passage of time. He gathered anecdotes by asking the parents for specific memories of their child—a good technique when covering grief. After the story ran, Silverman received scores of complimentary letters and phone calls. But the one that meant the most, he said, was from Nicky's father, Joel Corwin.

Reporting techniques: observation, establishment of chronologies, sponsorship, narrative reconstruction of events, anecdotes

Writing techniques: weaving of time frames—past and present—with a journal, descriptive detail without adjectives, chronological storytelling in parts, narrative and anecdotal writing, use of contrast, pacing (mixing short and long sentences)

Nicky's story

By David Silverman
Chicago Tribune

Journal quote lead to introduce Nicky in his own words: establishes Nicky as focus of story

"Hi, I would like to tell you about myself. I'll start with my hobbies. I like sports a lot. My favorite one is baseball and then football. Oh, I forgot, my name is Nick. Nick Corwin, really. My initials are N.B.C., Nicholas Brent Corwin. My birthday is April 9th. I am 7 years old."

It was September 1987, the first week of school in Mrs. Amy Deuble's 2d grade class at the Hubbard Woods School, and all the students in Room 7 were writing about themselves on sheets of wide-lined paper.

Other key characters introduced through journal device (note use of italics)

"I have two brothers, one older, one younger. They are 5 and 10. My dad's name is Joel. His job is a lawyer. My mom's name is Linda. She takes care of us as her job. My favorite color is blue. My favorite letter is N. My favorite number is 3."

It was the first entry in a journal each student would keep throughout the year. On special occasions, they would write about how they felt, and Mrs. Deuble would take a picture of each of them, to be glued at the top of the page.

Descriptive detail with strong verb (advertised)

In September, Nicky Corwin had a suntan. He leaned toward the camera with his hands on his legs, just above his knees. A broad smile advertised the gap between his new front teeth.

Scene: journal used as transition from past to present

The small handwritten booklet now sits unfinished on a coffee table in the bright living room of Joel and Linda Corwin's Winnetka home. It is among a stack of stories, drawings and dreams they found in Nicky's small school desk, just a few feet from where he was murdered.

Descriptive detail based on observation

Photographs of him are everywhere in the whitewashed living room. On the piano against the wall. On the mantle above the fireplace. On the bookshelves. Linda and Joel sit close to each other on an overstuffed couch near the center of the room, surrounded by memories of their son and the horror of what happened at 10:25 a.m. on May 20.

Show-in-action technique

Foreshadowing and nut graph: reason for story

They remember it was the first day Nicky was allowed to ride his bicycle to school. He was late, but his older brother waited for him anyway.

"It's okay, Mom. I want to ride with Nicky," he shouted from the edge of the driveway.

After two weeks spent learning the rules of the road, Nicky had earned this privilege.

Narrative device: quote reconstruction based on recollection

If he passed the written bicycle safety test at school that day, he could ride with his brother until the end of the year.

Linda Corwin had watched as her two sons rode off.

Background leading up to murder: scene setting

"They had one and only one day to ride their bikes to school together," she said. "And that was it."

Quote establishes source for previous information

The nation knows what happened during Nicky Corwin's bicycle safety test that morning. Around 10:15, just as he began the test, a ragged, dark-haired woman wearing shorts entered the 2d grade classroom and sat down. She said nothing and soon left. She returned at 10:25 with two guns and opened fire.

Key background to set up story: narrative style based on fact; no attribution needed

Five children were wounded. Eight-year-old Nicholas Brent Corwin was killed. He was shot once in the heart.

Short sentences for drama

On a hazy Sunday morning almost two months later, the Corwin house is quiet. No more national magazine coverage or live

Contrast through description

television interviews. The flood of thousands of letters has slowed to a trickle. The new phone number is unlisted.

What remains are the stack of papers from school, the photographs and daily reminders of a boy whose name meant "giver of gifts."

"There is a void," Joel says. "It's like a picture, and there's a blank there. We'll always have the feeling that he's there, but he's not."

"We're just left with the grim reality," Linda said, continuing her husband's thought. "I've been experiencing a kind of sensory deprivation. I can't see him or touch him. It's very painful.

"Our world view has been permanently altered. All the rules were broken with this incident."

Transition through repetition of key word (rule)

The elementary rule in Winnetka used to be: Our children are safe—safe from the crime and violence the Corwins thought they left behind when they abandoned the city for Winnetka 11 years ago.

Transition to background of couple through time device (11 years ago)

They had met at Yale University and graduated as part of the first coeducational class there. They were married and went on to the University of Minnesota to earn advanced degrees: his in law, hers in public affairs. They moved to Chicago and began to climb. The urban lifestyle suited the new corporate lawyer and his wife, a city planner. But when Linda became pregnant, she willingly gave up her career, and the couple prepared for a change.

"I could have done a lot of things, but there wasn't anything I could have done that was more important," she said. "Anybody can be a lawyer or city planner, but there was one job no one else could do, and that was to be a mother to my own kids."

They sought refuge in the heart of the North Shore, where the homes were expensive and large, and the schools were the best. They chose a red brick and white stucco house on a street lined with close-cut lawns and 50-foot-tall oaks. It reminded Linda of her childhood home in Waterloo, Ia., which she remembers as being "a suburb without a city."

"We sought the peace of mind, the perceived peace of mind, that we thought we would have for our children—not having to worry about anything happening to them," Joel explained, shaking his head.

Quotes placed to back up concepts but not repeat them; each quote adds new information

The house was too big for the couple and their only child, a newborn son. But they were planning ahead. They were going to fill the rooms with a family.

Three years later, son No. 2 practically jumped into the world.

Joel had little time to spare when he rushed Linda to Highland Park Hospital on April 9, 1980. They arrived at 12:45 p.m. Nicky Corwin was born in the emergency room at 12:48.

"I got there just in the nick of time," Joel said, displaying a brief smile as he recounted the hospital dash. "That was part of the reason for his name. He was in a hurry to get into life."

Detail from birth certificate: sets up emotional quote

A third son followed three years later, and the family was complete. Joel and Linda Corwin had created the suburban dream. They had a Volvo station wagon in the driveway, a beautiful family and success.

But all the rules would be broken.

Pacing: short sentence for power

Laurie Wasserman Dann, a troubled 30-year-old with a history of bizarre behavior, shattered the Corwin's lives before ending her own during a brief but violent

Secondary nut graph: why read this story

rampage. Her story and those of the five children and the young man she wounded are well known. But somehow, Nicky Corwin was lost in the crush of publicity.

Aside from a brief statement the Corwins released the day of his death, and a funeral sermon two days later, the story of Nicky's short life was left to the memory of the neighbors, classmates and friends.

"A friend told us her daughter asked: 'Why are there so many pictures of the bad lady in the paper and hardly any pictures of Nicky?'" Linda said. "There was a little bit of that feeling on our part. But I guess bad guys always make the headlines."

Repetition of key word for transition (paper)

The papers the Corwins brought home from the Hubbard Woods School show life through Nicky's eyes. It's a collection of stories, drawings and journal entries that reveal a creative young boy who passionately loved sports and learning.

"If I could study anything I wanted, I would choose math," Nicky wrote to his teacher on one of the sheets.

"That's the cruel irony," Linda says. "Normally he wouldn't have been in that room at that time; he would have been in an older [kids'] class for math. But they had the bicycle test that day. That's why he was in that room."

Show-in-action technique plus observation

She picks up the journal Nicky kept and begins to leaf through it. It's loosely bound in green construction paper, the handwriting is large and neat, and the words are descriptive. After the first day of school, the next entry was added at Halloween.

Journal used as device to move through time

The picture shows Nicky and Linda in the classroom, mugging for the camera. The words tell of a party and candy.

The next page is from Thanksgiving, and a brightly colored turkey fills the page instead of the usual entry. In its giant feathers, Nicky wrote of the things he was most thankful for.

"Mom, Dad, little brother, older brother, house, bed, money, doctor, grandma, school, my friends, my life, and me."

In January, the assignment was to write about three important strengths.

"I'm kind of nice. I am smart. I have good athletic ability."

Linda Corwin laughs as she rereads the entry aloud.

"Only kind of nice?" she asks. Her eyes begin to glisten as she stares at the picture on the top of the page. Nicky was growing. He was taller, and his dark brown hair was longer. The teeth in the smile were bigger, but the gap remained.

The final entry came after the Spring Sing, a class performance in April in which Nicky had a speaking part between songs.

"I had a really good time. Afterward we went to Peter's for dinner and played Nintendo [video] games."

He looked grown up, dressed in a coat and tie, head cocked a little to the left. And there was the smile.

Nicky Corwin had just turned 8.

"He played soccer, hockey, tennis, baseball and football," Linda said. "He was very much a natural athlete. He had a natural grace about him. I think he learned early on that to be cocky wasn't going to get him anywhere. So he was very supportive of the other kids on his teams. He was very aware of the talents he had been blessed with."

Repetition of key word for transition (talents)

One of those talents happened to be climbing. Anything upright was fair game, especially the tallest trees. Acting the part of a monkey, he would climb to the top before calling his mother to see his accomplishment.

"I had to call the fire department because I was so petrified," she says, laughing outright. "He loved to climb high. He loved to scare us with his daredevil climbing feats."

Joel remembers the autumn football. Nicky teamed with his older brother, against his dad and younger brother, for backyard games that would last past dark. When the snows came, it moved to the living room. Linda played quarterback, sending Nicky deep to the fireplace while rock blared on the stereo.

Key word (fireplace)

The floor in front of the fireplace now is covered with baskets of condolence letters. Some have been answered. Others wait. Linda has promised herself she'll get to them all. The signatures are those of parents, strangers mostly, compelled to let the Corwins know they weren't alone in their anguish.

"I've gotten so many beautiful letters," Linda said. "It means a lot to us to know that so many other people care, and it means a lot to know that he touched so many people, even though he was only around for such a short time."

Pictures used as recurring theme to set up quotes and recollections

On the mantle above the baskets, a display of pictures depicts family trips to Arizona and Walt Disney World. Joel plucks a favorite from the bunch. Nicky, wearing a comically too-large cowboy hat, is tucked snugly under his father's

arm as they sit perched on the edge of the Grand Canyon.

"We were really on top of the world," he says, absorbed in the memory.

"He wanted to go to Maine," Linda says. "I don't know how he even knew about Maine, but he kept asking if we could go. One of these days I may be brave enough to get there."

Foreshadowing for ending

There's a knock at the door. One of their oldest son's friends appears in the hall, dressed in a Little League uniform, carrying a glove and bat. Linda and Joel remember there's a game in an hour, and they have to stop for juice boxes on the way.

Natural progression from past to present to future

"In the beginning, they asked, 'Why?'" Linda said. "They don't ask about it anymore. Partly because they know there really is no answer. Partly because I think they are trying to protect our feelings, too."

On the day of the funeral, Rabbi Robert Schriebman had the family write notes to Nicky, to be placed in the casket with him.

"Our youngest just wrote, 'I love you, Nicky,'" Joel said. "He understands what happened."

After the funeral, Joel took his sons back to the cemetery. Together they walked the grounds near Nicky's grave, looking at the other names. He wanted to make them understand.

"All the graves near his are of much older people," Joel said. "There's one nearby where the person was 88. And I told the boys that's how long a person should live—88, not 8."

Frustration. Anger. Fear. Grief. Linda and Joel Corwin are

left with these emotions, and a million more, every time they replay the events of May 20. All the activity has left them little time for each other, and the emotions.

"We've probably not done very well with that," Linda said. "One does not feel a whole lot like giving in this situation. I don't know, I don't feel I have a lot to give right now. I used to enjoy living life to the fullest. Now it's a struggle.

"I think a loss is a loss. If you lose a child through an illness or a car accident, it's a terrible loss and no less painful than this. But the horror of the way this happened is really too difficult for us to contemplate."

And what about the anger? Anger at a woman who can never stand trial for her crime. At a legal system that neglected, or couldn't act on, repeated calls to remove her from the streets before she lashed out.

"It goes beyond that," Joel says, almost in a whisper. "There aren't words to express that.

"But there are a couple of primary feelings. We miss hugging him . . . basking in his radiance. At the same time, there is a frustration that is difficult for me to deal with. He is missing everything life had to offer."

Even harder, perhaps, were the things that had to be done shortly after Nicky's death. There were necessary and painful things such as retrieving his bicycle from a deserted rack after all the other kids had gone home, cleaning out his desk and carefully removing his name tag so as not to rip it.

"There is no way to put closure on this kind of loss," Linda said. "All we can ever hope to do is come to terms with it. This is the kind of pain that will always be there. There may be some layers of protection over it, but it will always be there.

"Every day I see him smiling at me with a twinkle in his eye. That keeps me going." *Sets up mood for ending*

"Nicky would have wanted us to go on. He would have said, 'Don't fold,'" Joel says.

The Corwins have to go. The kids are shooting baskets in the driveway, and Little League waits for no parent. They are gracious and say they would love to talk about Nicky all day, but it is time to pile everyone into the station wagon. It is time to move on. *Ends on future note with simple sentence: intentional understatement for highly emotional story*

Narrative Writing Example

Martha Miller interviewed Dan Vickroy several times before she wrote this story. Each time he remembered more. She asked him to recall what he was thinking, feeling, saying and experiencing when he was injured, 25 years earlier.

Miller also reconstructed dialogue, based on Vickroy's recollections. The technique is acceptable but not preferable. If you can't confirm the dialogue with the original source, you can attribute it to the source who related it. If it is not controversial and you are sure it is accurate, you can reconstruct it as Miller has done.

After she finished all her interviews and filled several notebooks, Miller sat down to write the story. She was overwhelmed. She planned the story and organized it by different periods of Vickroy's life. Then she tried free-writing, just writing what she remembered to get it out of her head. After that she began refining the story, and before she revised her final draft, she read the story aloud.

This part of the story, the second section, contains almost no direct attribution. It is all based on Vickroy's recollections. Do you need attribution? Is the story believable?

Reporting techniques: establishing chronology, gathering detail, asking questions to get source to reconstruct specific events using all senses

Writing techniques: organized by section technique in time sequences; although most of the story takes place in the past, each section deals with a different part of the character's life. Primarily follows chronological order, with cliffhanger endings for each section. Other techniques: short sentences, pacing, dialogue, definitions, description, narration.

A soldier's story

By Martha Miller
Iowa City Press-Citizen

Descriptive beginning for section: sets scene Reconstructed dialogue

Two hands lifted the sheet that covered what was left of Dan Vickroy's body.

"You're one tough son of a bitch," the surgeon said from behind a green mask.

"I'm a Vickroy," Dan said. "Take me in and sew me up."

They did.

(Gene) Miller chop Narrative chronological storytelling through Vickroy

Vickroy regained consciousness. He figured he was in the base hospital at Cam Ranh Bay. He could see nothing through the bandages over his eyes, but he could hear the squeaks of rubber soles in the hallway and hushed conversations between doctors as they hurried from bed to bed. It sounded like a busy place.

He was scared, scared to death he was blind.

His ears wanted to believe what he heard, but his eyes would believe what they saw.

The nurses told him they were bandages and that he was strapped down. They told him he had been in bed for almost two weeks. And they told him he had a 104-degree temperature. He knew that. He couldn't stop shivering.

As he lay there, his memory returned. He knew the mine had exploded and that he was badly hurt. He remembered waking up twice in surgery. The last time, he felt a surge of pain. He saw a surgeon cutting off his leg with a bone saw.

The days and nights came and went. All the same. Dark.

This time, it was night. Someone shut off all the lights in his hospital room. The doctors were back. Slowly, they unraveled the gauze around his eyes.

Vickroy held his breath. He opened his eyes and saw a faint light. It burned, but this time it was a good sign. Doctors had worked through the night cleaning his eyes. What he saw made him want to put the bandages back on.

There were wire stitches in his stomach and his right hip. There were tubes in his nose and left arm. Instead of legs, he saw blood-

Clues of attribution without direct attribution (he remembered)

Scene

soaked gauze wrapped around two stumps.

The doctors told him what happened: His right leg was blown away by the explosion and his left leg was amputated in surgery; his right arm was amputated below the elbow; and he had lost part of his stomach. Being so close to the mine saved his life; the blast threw him up and out of the way.

His face was intact, saved by that last glance back to camp.

Vickroy took the news better than most.

Direct quote, no attribution; speaker is understood

"Psychologically, I was pretty positive."

He had no legs, but he did have a wife and new baby. He had married Sharon Kay in 1968 in Tulsa. She was 8½ months pregnant when he left for Vietnam. Danny Ray was born March 28, 1969.

Baby pictures were taped, one under the other, on the side of his bed so Vickroy could look at Danny Ray while laying on his back.

Those pictures and thoughts of heading back to the United States kept Vickroy's hopes up. But back home, his family wasn't so positive.

Short sentences and pacing

Dan's mother, Louise, was waiting tables in a Cedar Rapids restaurant when an Army officer handed her a telegram. She cried.

Louise had never wanted her youngest to join the service. She wouldn't sign his enlistment papers and couldn't see him off.

Vickroy had started to believe he could live without legs until the day a nurse read him a letter. It had arrived at Cam Ranh Bay several days earlier, but nobody wanted to read it to him.

It was from his wife. She wanted a divorce.

Punch ending to this section; short sentences

"She told me she didn't want half a man."

Activities

1 Write a descriptive paragraph about your roommate, professor or a classmate, showing the person in action.

2 Go to a busy place on campus or to the cafeteria and listen to people talking. Gather information about the scene. Then write a few paragraphs setting the scene and weaving in dialogue.

3 Study some objects on your campus. Write similes and metaphors to describe the objects.

4 Narrative writing exercise: Interview a classmate about any experience he or she has had, preferably a traumatic or emotional one. If your subject can't think of one, ask him or her to describe the morning routine from today or yesterday. Imagine that the nut graph is "And then (your subject) disappeared and hasn't been seen since."

You will need to ask specific questions, such as what was the person wearing, what color and kind of car was he or she driving (if a car is involved), what time of day did the events occur, what was he or she thinking, feeling, doing, saying. Get the person to reconstruct the event exactly as it happened by asking questions about sequence of events and details.

Then write the information in narrative style in a few paragraphs or a brief story.

5 Write a few descriptive or narrative paragraphs in the form of vignettes. Here are some suggested topics:

Valentine's Day memories of people on campus

Scenes from a hospital waiting room

A day in the life of . . . (a police officer, an AIDS counselor, an ambulance driver)

A day in court, particularly small claims court

6 Here is a suggestion from Tina Lesher, journalism professor at William Paterson College in New Jersey. This is an idea she borrowed from *The Journal-Bulletin,* Providence, R.I., which published a book by its writers called *How I Wrote the Story.* Lesher suggests doing the same, writing a page or two describing how you wrote your story. List problems you encountered in reporting and writing and techniques you used; explain how you thought about organizing your story.

7 **Narrative and descriptive writing exercise:** The following information is taken from a *Chicago Tribune* story by Paul Weingarten. This story lends itself to either a narrative or a descriptive lead. First write a descriptive lead, and then a narrative one, up to the nut graph. Then choose the lead you prefer and finish organizing the story.

The story is about a Holocaust memorial in Euless, Texas. The memorial features an exhibit called The Hiding Place, a high-tech exhibit that takes visitors into a boxcar that disgorges its "prisoners" into a simulated concentration camp. The camp is a large room decorated with tattered prison garments and a hangman's noose. There a graphic presentation, filled with special lighting and visual effects, tells the story of Corrie ten Boom, a Dutch woman who was banished to the Ravensbruck concentration camp for helping to hide hundreds of Jews in her home during World War II.

> Against a collage of photos of cadaverous concentration camp victims and naked bodies being fed into ovens comes the voices of Nazi guards who are joking about extracting gold fillings from the teeth of Jews.
>
> The exhibit is located at the Mike Evans Ministry, a fundamentalist Christian church in a town of 24,000 just outside of Fort Worth, Texas.
>
> Evans, 40, a born-again Christian evangelist whose mother was a Jew, says he created the exhibit "because this was the story of a Christian family that was willing to lay down their lives for the Jewish people, which in our opinion is a great way of combating anti-Semitism."
>
> During the war, the ten Booms constructed a false wall to create a 2½-foot-wide space behind a full-length bookshelf in Corrie ten Boom's third-floor bedroom.

In the end of the presentation, Corrie ten Boom, who died in 1983, explains why she risked her life for the Jews: "Because my savior and Lord is Jewish. I do it for his sake."

In the stark room cold and dim, a red Nazi flag hangs above a small wooden desk. A glaring portrait of Adolf Hitler adorns another wall.

"Achtung! Achtung!" a voice barks from loudspeakers. "All Jews must be identified. Step forward."

A grim-faced Nazi soldier emerges from the shadows and directs a group of wide-eyed eighth graders from the Brandon Street Christian Academy to step through a railing and stand behind a yellow line.

Suddenly, lights glare in their eyes. Each is handed a yellow cloth Star of David.

"According to our records, all who are in this room are Jews," the voice booms. "This yellow patch must be worn on your chest in plain sight at all times. No exceptions. No exceptions."

Immediately another door swings open, and the new "Jews" are herded down a hall amid a cacophony of angry voices and screams.

"All of you vermin move into the car," a voice snarls.

The students clamber into a wood-slatted railroad boxcar. The Nazi soldier shoves the laggards from behind, and the door clangs shut.

Inside, the boxcar begins to pitch as if in motion, and two lanterns clatter against the iron ceiling. There are voices in here, too.

"Mama, mama," a child calls.

"I wonder where we are going."

And then there is a woman's voice, which identifies itself as that of Corrie ten Boom. She is asked by another passenger if she is Jewish, and she says no.

"But why should you be taken with us? What crime have you committed?" the other passenger persists.

"For obeying God, for loving his chosen people . . . for hiding them in our home," ten Boom replies.

Later, the visitors crowd into a narrow "hiding place," listening to the muffled voices of Nazi troops searching the house. The real hiding place is now a museum in the ten Boom home and clock shop in Haarlem, Netherlands.

8 Storytelling exercise: Here is a storytelling exercise designed by Alan Richman, former writer and writing coach for *The Boston Globe* and now a writer for *GQ, (Gentleman's Quarterly).* Richman wrote this story when he was at *The Globe.* His assignment was to follow up on a news story with a feature. The news story is reprinted here; then you will get Richman's notes. Use those notes to write a feature in no more than 750 words—about 16 inches in a newspaper story. The point of the exercise is to see how many details and rich quotes you can fit in that amount of space. As you read

Richman's notes, consider how much detail he gathered. You will also have to decide if you should use anonymous sources.

An East Boston man confessed to stealing a car last Thursday and spending most of the $10,000 in cash he found in the glove compartment before he was caught on Saturday, police said.

Michael Yanelli, 22, of 569 Bennington St., East Boston, was arrested at 9:15 Saturday night and charged with stealing a 1979 Cadillac belonging to Rene Gignac of Laconia, N.H.

The car, which had been discovered missing at 11:45 a.m. Thursday, had been parked in front of 880 Saratoga St., East Boston. Police said that besides a briefcase, papers and wallet on the seat of the car, the glove compartment contained $30,000 in checks and $10,000 in cash.

Yanelli's arrest came after a police investigation and tips from neighborhood contacts. A police spokesman said Yanelli admitted to the theft in a deposition, and said he had spent most of the money he found. He turned over $2,682 in cash and $1,972 worth of plane tickets, the spokesman said.

Yanelli was charged with larceny over $100, and will be arraigned in East Boston District Court tomorrow morning, police said.

The Boston Globe

Three days after this story appears, an editor gets the idea that it should be followed up. Who is this guy? How did he manage to spend more than $7,000 in less than two days? How does he feel about his windfall?

You are assigned to write the follow-up story. All you know, in addition to what you read in the brief news story, is that Boston has the highest car theft rate in the United States and East Boston, one of the neighborhoods within the city, has the highest car theft rate in Boston. It's a lower-middle class, blue collar neighborhood. You go out to report your story. This is what you find out:

Yanelli lives on a tree-lined residential street not far from Wonderland, a greyhound race track. A church, St. Mary's Star of the Sea, is across the street from his home. In the same building, below his apartment, is Carlo's Cold Cut Centre, a tiny neighborhood grocery. The building he lives in is a little seedy, with a broken window, ugly asphalt shingle sidings, no names on the mail boxes.

You talk to a teen-age girl with deep lavender eye shadow. She is walking down the street. She won't give her name. She knows Yanelli, says he's a little slow. She says, "If I found $10,000, I wouldn't tell anyone. I'd get right out of the car."

You go to 880 Saratoga St., which is four blocks from his apartment. It's one address in a series of garden apartments called "Brandywine Village." You stop three elderly ladies walking down the street. They won't give their names, but they tell you that Gignac was helping his mother-in-law move and the money in the glove compartment was for a down payment on a new house or condominium for her.

"The daughter told me that," the first lady says.

"I wouldn't leave that money in a car," says the second. "I'd put it in my bloomers."

You go to the local police precinct, District Seven. They know Yanelli by reputation.

"He's a little addle-brained," one cop tells you.

The crime report is down at District 1, police headquarters. You call and find out that Yanelli is charged with larceny of a motor vehicle worth more than $9,000, stealing $10,060 in U.S. currency, stealing three credit cards and three checks. He pleaded not guilty and was sent to Charles Street Jail, the city jail. He did not post bail. His court attorney is Paul Luciano. You call him but he is out of town.

The detective investigating the case tells you, off the record, that Yanelli destroyed the checks, kept the cash and bought two first class airline tickets to Las Vegas for $1,800. He kept the money in a brown paper bag. He changed plates on the car. The tips came when he was seen flashing a lot of money around the neighborhood.

At the East District Court, people tell you that Yanelli is a big kid with a shaved head, a little slow.

You find it interesting that everyone you speak to tells you how dumb Yanelli was to keep the car. Everybody—even the policemen—says that he should have ditched the car as soon as he found the cash.

You try to call Rene Gignac in New Hampshire. He has an unlisted number.

The Charles Street Jail is run by the Suffolk County sheriff. You call and ask to speak to Yanelli. A public relations official for the sheriff's department says she will make the request. She says she will also advise Yanelli to talk to his lawyer before talking to you. You get lucky. Yanelli tries for more than a day, but his lawyer is still out of town. He says he'll talk to you. The following are your quotes from the interview:

You: What did you feel when you saw the money?

Him: My heart went 90 miles an hour.

You: Describe what the money looked like.

Him: It was about this big. (He makes a 4-inch space with his hands.) It was 100s, 50s, 10s. The glove compartment was open. There was a briefcase in the front seat with $60 in it.

You: Why did you steal the car in the first place?

Him: A joyride. Just to take the car. It's a habit with me. It ain't going to happen anymore.

You: What did you think after you got in the car and were riding around?

Him: This guy (Gignac) is so stupid. I got to talk to the guy. I've only been charged with larceny of a motor vehicle. I wasn't charged with stealing money. If I have to do any time, I want them to prove it. I have three previous larcenies of motor vehicles—all the cars had keys in them. One in Malden, one in East Boston, one in Winthrop. This is the fourth.

Him continued: I drove away and noticed the car was on empty, so I went for gas. I opened the briefcase. There was $60 in it. I put $20 in and got half a tank. I opened the glove compartment, looking for something to blow my nose. I threw out a white envelope. 20s and 50s and 100s piled out.

You: What did you spend it on?

Him: I was going to Vegas the next day.

Thursday afternoon I had the money. I bought a couple of things, a color television for my best friend because he was getting married. I went out and bought $600 worth of clothes, paid back a couple of debts. The two airline tickets to Vegas cost $1,972. I was going to go, but didn't. I was going to take a friend but he said he wanted to stay home for the 4th of July. My brother said to me, "Get rid of the car." Yeah, I know, I know. Why didn't I? I almost did. I even drove to Revere (a small city adjoining Boston) on Thursday to Cerretani's parking lot (a grocery store), wiped my fingerprints off the car. I was throwing the keys away. I hesitated. I said no. I needed a couple more things. I went to lunch. I took a cab home. I went to the dog track, lost a couple hundred. Thursday night I went to Jeveli's (a restaurant) in East Boston and ate. I went home. Friday morning a friend of mine picked up the briefcase. He gets rid of the briefcase. This guy (Gignac) is completely stupid—there's $60,000–$70,000 in money orders in the briefcase. The checkbook shows 80,000 bucks. I'm down on this guy. It's his fault. Friday morning I went back to get the car. A friend and I went to Suffolk Downs (a thoroughbred racing track in East Boston). I end up winning $1,500. I had the perfecta in the last race. (Note: You check the race results. In the 10th at Suffolk Downs, Fleet Concessioner, an 8-1 shot, finished first and Marshua's Romeo finished second. The perfecta paid $115 for a $2 bet.)

Him: I said to my friend, "I'll go get my mother and father a color TV. A Sears TV." My mother turned it back. She wouldn't take it. I spent $1,700 on a TV for a friend's mother and father, a Sony Trinitron. I gave the store $50 to have it delivered. Friday night another friend and I went out to the Kowloon (a glittery Polynesian restaurant). We were there from 8 until 11:30. We had four pu-pu platters. We ditched the car in Lynn (another city) and went home. They never would have found it, I hid it so good. On Saturday, Tommy and Jimmy, two cops who arrested me before, came to my house. They told me I might as well admit it. They're good cops. I gave them the rest of the money. I told them where the car was. (He thinks that Gignac saw him in the car and picked him out from a mug book.)

Him: I know all the guards. They like me. (He has been in Charles Street Jail before.) I got to learn my lesson sooner or later. I got to serve time so I don't do this anymore. And tell people to leave their cars locked up and don't leave $10,000 in the car where anybody can get it. He left his wallet in the car, too. This guy is a complete idiot. (He tells you he's 22, unemployed, living in East Boston practically his whole life, graduated from Boston Technical High School in 1978 and is well-liked around the neighborhood.

Him: I can't hold on to a job. I got a temper and a half.

You: Did you have a good time?

Him: Yeah. It was great. I love flashing 100s around. I spent it on true friends, though.

You: What else did you buy?

Him: Watch, clothes, ring, radio, 4 Beatles tapes. If I do time, I want to do it here (Charles Street Jail). I like it here.

He is dressed in a T-shirt, army fatigue pants and basketball shoes. He says he also bought four pairs of basketball shoes.

The editor tells you to write it in 750 words.

COACHING

Try TV talk: Explain your story to a friend in 20 seconds.

Write a highlights box: List the key points. Then turn them into a story containing no more than three paragraphs.

After you have written your story, correct it by removing every extraneous word. Remove all quotes that don't advance the story.

Check for unnecessary transitions. Ask yourself: Do the quotes naturally follow the previous thought without a transition?

Read the story aloud.

Use short sentences. Learn to love the period.

The Art of Brevity

14

The more you know, the less you may have to write about it. Newspapers and magazines are relying more and more on brief stories to entice readers who are in a rush. Public relations writers must usually sell their audience on an idea in less than a page of copy (see Chapter 15). And the broadcast media excel in delivering news in brief form (see Chapter 16).

A writer in this multimedia age should master a variety of writing styles, from in-depth stories to briefs, which are stories that range from one to three paragraphs. The tips for brevity in this chapter can apply to writers in all media.

It is often easier to write a long story than a short one. A brief story requires the writer to be selective. And that's hard to do when you have gathered a lot of information. But writing briefs can be a tool to help you find focus and organization for any story. If you coach yourself to gather the most important information in a few paragraphs for a brief, you can easily add to that core when you want a longer story.

At newspapers many briefs are written by copy editors who pare down wire stories for a column of these news nuggets. But reporters also need to know how to write briefs in place of full stories when the event doesn't warrant a complete story or space is tight.

Resist the temptation to tell everything you've learned; much of it doesn't matter.

Richard Aregood, editorial writer, *Philadelphia Daily News*

Briefs

A brief is an abbreviated story, from one sentence to a few paragraphs long. Briefs can serve as teasers to full stories inside the newspaper or as stand-alone summaries of news. Almost all newspapers use briefs and "summary teasers" in some part of the paper.

Newspaper briefs are similar to the briefs and teasers used by television. Notice the similarity between these print and broadcast briefs (ignore the peculiarities of broadcast style, such as writing out numbers).

Broadcast	**Newspaper**
New statistics indicate the number of reported cases of child abuse is increasing—and so is the number of children dying from that abuse. The National Committee for Prevention of Child Abuse says nearly two-point-seven million cases of abuse were reported last year—up six percent over 1991. And it says nearly 14-hundred children died of abuse in 1991—an increase of 10 percent.	Nearly 2.7 million cases of child abuse were reported last year, an increase of 6 percent over 1990. And an estimated 1,385 children died of abuse in 1991, a 10 percent increase, the National Committee for Prevention of Child Abuse says. Experts say a more violent society, harsh economic times and drug abuse are partly to blame.

Briefs give the main points and eliminate details. Here is the same story about child abuse in a more complete version, with reaction and detail. (Note that although the *Associated Press Stylebook* says to write out the word *percent, USA Today* uses the symbol.)

The number of deaths from child abuse increased 10% from 1990 to 1991, the National Committee for Prevention of Child Abuse said Thursday. Increases reflect hard times, says NCPCA senior analyst Karen McCurdy, who blames "the recession, poverty and stress that may cause parents to lash out," along with increasing substance abuse by parents.	The number of deaths rose from 1,253 to 1,383 as a result of physical abuse (64%) and neglect (36%). Seventy-nine percent of victims were under 5; 54% were 1 year or younger. The total number of child abuse reports rose about 6% to 2.7 million in 1991, McCurdy says. That's 42 reports (physical, sexual, emotional abuse and neglect) for every 1,000 children in the USA.

McCurdy says states' growing sophistication about tracking the numbers is partly responsible for the increase; she also cites greater public awareness of child abuse—and greater willingness to report it.
USA Today

Many full-length television news stories run less than 30 seconds, which would qualify them as newspaper briefs. Borrowing this concept of brevity from television, the *Boca Raton* (Fla.) *News* even labels its front-page column of briefs "30 Seconds" to tease readers to stories inside the newspaper.

The New York Times and *The Wall Street Journal* have been using briefs as summary teasers or as substitutes for full-length stories for years. However, briefs are gaining an even more crucial role at newspapers as they strive to serve readers on the run. "Most people on weekdays are incredibly starved for time," says Susan Miller, vice president of the editorial division of the Scripps Howard newspaper chain. "We've got to put in one place an overview of the news and one-sentence summaries that are so intelligently written that people will read them and say, 'Maybe I could learn a lot if I read that story. I don't have time now but I'm going to go back and read it later.' This is where journalism is moving and the reporter in the future will be expected from day one to be able to write a summary. Editors are going to take it for granted that you know how to do that."

How do you decide what is the most crucial information to state in a few sentences? One way is to verbalize the gist of the story as television anchors do. Consider it a teaser of news to come after a station break. If you had 10 seconds to tell your friend or editor what your story was about, what would you say? Chances are that you would state the most important information: what happened. And you might also include who, where and when. Those are some of the same ingredients of a summary lead for a hard-news story.

To help you determine the essence of the news, think of a brief as an extended summary lead. Most of the basic questions—who, what, when, where, why and how—still need to be answered. You just eliminate some of the background and explanatory backup that would go into a full news story.

Although some briefs have a teaser lead, most have hard leads, because soft leads take more space. They usually follow inverted pyramid format.

This brief is from *The Wall Street Journal's* front-page daily column called "What's News." Note how it answers some, but not all, of the five W's.

The Supreme Court agreed to review the principal legal strategy used by women's groups and abortion-rights groups to obtain court injunctions halting protests that block access to abortion facilities. The case involves an appeal by an anti-abortion group barred from blockading clinics in the Washington, D.C. area.

The Wall Street Journal

Who: Supreme Court
What: will review a case
Why: appeal by anti-abortion group

Now consider this brief, which substituted for a full story in the "Life" section of *USA Today:*

UNTOLD TWAIN TALE: Scholars poring over the recently discovered first half of Mark Twain's *Adventures of Huckleberry Finn* manuscript have found a lost passage about Jim's encounter with a cadaver. Twain deleted it, probably because it was too gruesome. The 2,000-word episode takes place after Huck escapes his father and flees to Jackson Island, where he meets Jim. While the two wait out a rainstorm, Jim describes his disastrous efforts at trying to warm up a cadaver for a medical student who was to dissect it. Publication of the new section is prohibited because a New York City foundation owns the rights to unpublished Twain material.

USA Today

Who: scholars
What: found a lost manuscript
When: recently
Why: passage was too gruesome

This brief answers the questions of who, what, when and why. After some elaboration, it even explains "so what" (the impact): Publication is prohibited. Most of the basic elements of the story are there. The reader gets the essence of what happened. And the newspaper saves space so it can include more stories.

The brief is also a tool for public relations writers. Although some press releases and media kits are very detailed, other releases can be as brief as this one from Crayola Products in Pennsylvania. Note that this is advocacy writing to promote a product, not to give a balanced story.

Children who enjoy drawing on more than just paper can now take their creativity to the streets—or at least the sidewalks, with new Crayola Sidewalk Chalk.

Three jumbo chalk sticks, ideal for use on sidewalks and driveways, are included. Jumbo sticks of chalk make it easy for young children to draw and write with. The large size also provides added strength, reducing breakage. Cleanup is easy. Sidewalk Chalk simply rinses away with water.

Crayola Sidewalk Chalk comes in three colors: blue, red and white. Available March 1, the suggested retail price is 70 cents.

Binney & Smith Inc.

Brights

When a story has a humorous or unusual angle, the brief may be written in a less serious tone with a punchy lead or ending, often in chronological order. This type of brief is called a "bright."

Writing briefs will help you write better hard-news leads. Writing brights will encourage you to try creative leads.

Unlike the hard-news approach, which immediately tells the reader what happened, brights can be written as mini-mysteries. The punchline is at the end. To write a bright, imagine that you are telling your friend a joke. Put in a dose of suspense, build up to the end, and deliver a punchline. The writing style works best with short sentences.

Caution: Use judgment before you try to treat a subject with humor. News stories about death or any crimes in which people are injured do not lend themselves to brights. At first you may think the following examples contradict that statement. But read on.

The Philadelphia Inquirer publishes brights on Page 3 in a daily column called "The Scene." It's a compilation of unusual news stories written in a storytelling manner. The following examples tend to be longer than three paragraphs, but they still qualify as brights.

A hairy rescue

British firefighters managed to rescue a couple and three children from a blazing house in Dudley, England.

But the family was quite concerned about a pet trapped in the inferno.

Firefighters rushed back in.

They found the pet and scooped it up with a soup ladle.

"Thank goodness it was a bit groggy from the smoke, and they were able to put it in a plastic ice-cream container," a fire brigade spokesman said.

"We understand it is now recovering."

The pet? A tarantula.

Tom Torok, *The Philadelphia Inquirer*

On death and taxes

When Marjorie Clapprood opened her W-2 form from the state of Massachusetts, she had to pinch herself.

The form said she was dead.

"Boy, when you're out, you're out," said Clapprood, a former state representative who lost her bid for lieutenant governor last year.

But she was by no means alone. State W-2 tax forms mailed recently listed all 199 members of last year's Legislature as dead.

Some residents of the financially troubled state suspected that all along.

But members of last year's Legislature are taking exception to their recent demise, which was caused by a clerical error.

Clapprood, for one, said she isn't about to let the IRS consider her dead.

"They owe me money, I think," she said.

Corrected forms are to be mailed to the resurrected shortly.

Tom Torok, *The Philadelphia Inquirer*

Sometimes the news is so unusual that you don't have to strain at all to make it offbeat. In this bright, the writer just presents the facts. But the facts are stranger than fiction.

Man ticketed for walking his lizard

FORT LAUDERDALE (Fla.) —Walking your dog along the beach here is illegal—and so is lounging with your lizard, Chris DeMango found out. Mortimer, DeMango's 20-pound purple-tongued monitor lizard, complete with matching pink doll sweater and leash, was out for exercise Monday. DeMango said a walk makes Mortimer more docile, but police said it makes him an illegal lizard—animals are banned on the beach. DeMango was ticketed, and his lizard law violation could cost him 60 days in jail and a $500 fine, said police spokesman Ott Cefkin. DeMango was not amused. "I would think that would be the most absurd thing, if I were to go to jail for this," he grumbled. "There's a war on (the Persian Gulf war), and they'll throw me in jail for walking my lizard on the beach."

St. Petersburg Times

How to Tighten Full-length Stories

When *USA Today* began publication in 1982, journalists throughout the country decried its brief, punchy writing style and nicknamed it "McPaper." Many journalists still object to the paper's format and style. But by the '90s its success was indisputable.

At first, the newspaper's major influence in the industry was graphic design. *USA Today* features colorful charts and illustrations on every section cover. Other newspapers have also emulated *USA Today's* concise writing style, characterized by many lists. Its guidelines for writers state: "Tell the story quickly and clearly. Save the reader time; don't waste words."

Editors at *USA Today* acknowledge that its style is not right for all newspapers: "Our readers are upscale, well-informed and looking for a supplement to—not a replacement for—their regular sources of news and information," the writers' guidelines state. "So our stories may contain less background on events, more emphasis on impact and what's new. Our paper has limited space; every word counts."

Long, in-depth stories still have a place in newspapers. If they are written well, readers will read them. But today almost all newspapers are using shorter stories. The average newspaper story used to be 25 inches; now it is more likely to be 10 or 12 inches. Briefs are even shorter, 1 to 3 inches.

Although the emphasis on tight writing is not new, in 1991 the American Society of Newspaper Editors started awarding a prize for it. Julie Sullivan, a writer at *The Spokesman-Review* (Spokane, Wash.), was the first recipient. Her tips and award-winning stories will appear in Chapter 25.

One of the best ways to tighten your writing is to revise your stories—the correcting step of the four-step coaching process. After you have written your first draft, remove all extra words or unnecessary quotes. Read the story aloud so you can hear if you have any extraneous words or cumbersome phrases.

USA Today Guidelines

"The true key to brevity is first to think," said J. Taylor Buckley Jr., senior editor of *USA Today*. "That's tough work."

Buckley said *USA Today* has a special audience. "Our readers aren't buying the paper for terrific transitions and clever phraseology," he said. "They're buying the paper for information. If they come away with a sense of understanding, they don't count on us to do more than select the facts carefully and present them in an unbiased and uncolored list. Much of what people require of a newspaper today is a list of information put in a way they can get it quickly."

Buckley likened newspaper reading to grocery shopping: "Why do they put all the jelly on the same shelf in the supermarket? So you can find it easily. And don't you get pissed off when the dietetic jelly is in another place?"

Almost all the spaces in *USA Today* are pre-ordained. Each page has a definite layout, which means that most stories don't exceed 12 inches, except for the cover story on each section. And those stories rarely exceed 32 inches.

USA Today writers are not only urged to think verbally; they must think visually. Reporters and editors must consider whether the story will need photos, illustrations, charts or lists. Information in the graphics does not need to be repeated in the story.

Some of the guidelines *USA Today* gives its writers are just common sense, for stories of any length. For example: "Think and talk [to editors] first, then do an outline or a list. Then start a draft. Then rewrite."

Another one of the paper's guidelines has been mentioned several times in this book: "Explain what it means; why I should care. Do it clearly, concisely and in exactly the way you'd explain it to your mother on the telephone."

Here are some other *USA Today* guidelines for writers:

Squeeze a fact on every line. Allow one idea per sentence.

Focus tightly. Think about what the real story is, and choose a slice of it. Emphasize what's new, what's coming and what it means to readers. Tell them the impact—how they can act on or use this information.

Make the story move. Make your point early. Use only the information that helps make that point.

Avoid the dash. It is long and overused. (*USA Today* tends to ignore this last point; dashes abound in the paper.)

Keep it tight. Propel the story with punctuation. Colons, semicolons and bullets can replace some words and help the reader move faster.

Use specific details rather than adjectives. Instead of writing "the ancient windmill," refer to "the 100-year-old windmill."

Don't overattribute. You don't need a "he said" after every sentence, although it should be clear where the information came from.

Use strong, lively verbs.

Use the present tense whenever possible. (Editors at many newspapers follow this rule for feature stories, not for basic news stories.)

Choose quotes that advance the story. Avoid quotes that merely illustrate the last point made. And don't paraphrase if you have a good quote. Be selective. Don't repeat. Put information first.

Avoid weak transitions. A well-organized story needs only a few transitions.

Use impact leads. Don't ignore the news just to be different, but avoid rehashing what readers already know. Think "forward spin." Instead of writing "A jet crashed Tuesday killing 534 people," write "Airline takeoff procedures might be overhauled after Tuesday's crash that killed 534 people."

Be careful. Aim for accuracy and fairness above all things.

Here are some examples of how the guidelines work in the newspaper.

Impact lead If you think a sexual partner with genital herpes won't infect you if he or she doesn't have sores, you're wrong.

Backup for lead That's confirmed in one of the first studies to follow couples in which just one partner started out infected.

Elaboration The study, in the Feb. 1 Annals of Internal Medicine, also confirms that men pass herpes to women more easily than women transmit it to men.

New fact in every paragraph Researchers from the universities of Washington and New Mexico followed 144 heterosexual couples for about a year. They were told to avoid sex when the infected partner had genital sores and record sexual activity and symptoms.

Abbreviated introduction Results:

List of results

- Transmission occurred in 14 couples—9.7%. Nine transmissions occurred when infected partners had no sores and no symptoms, such as itching, that precede an outbreak.
- 11 of 65 women at risk—16.9%—became infected.
- 3 of the 79 men at risk—3.8%—became infected.

Perspective Up to 500,000 people in the USA are diagnosed with genital herpes each year.

Condoms can greatly reduce, but not eliminate, risks.

Kim Painter, *USA Today*

Here is an example of how the writing style differs in *USA Today* (on the left) and *The Philadelphia Inquirer* (on the right). The major difference between the two versions of the same story? The *Inquirer* story contains more background and supporting facts.

USA Today

Suspected northern ozone hole 'frightening'

An ozone hole may be forming over populated areas of North America and Europe, scientists said Monday.

"Everybody should be alarmed about this," says Michael Kurylo of NASA.

The Philadelphia Inquirer

Northern ozone hole predicted

The news from the ozone front was grim yesterday.

The highest levels of ozone-destroying chemicals were found in the skies over Maine and eastern Canada last month, a team of scientists announced.

USA Today
(continued)

The Earth's ozone layer blocks the sun's cancer-causing ultraviolet light.

While a springtime hole forms over Antarctica annually, NASA has now found:

• Eastern Canada and Northern New England—with record levels of ozone-depleting chemicals overhead—seem the most vulnerable to ozone damage this winter.

• Airborne chemicals from last June's eruption of Mount Pinatubo in the Philippines have helped worsen damage to the ozone layer.

"It's frightening," says Liz Cook of Friends of the Earth.

Environmental scientists and government scientists say the findings justify a speedier plan for eliminating ozone-eating chlorofluorocarbons.

A current treaty ends most uses of CFCs by 2010.

"If the phenomenon ever occurs on a broader scale, it could be the final curtain call for life on the planet," says Karen Lohr of Greenpeace.

Paul Hoversten, *USA Today*

The Philadelphia Inquirer
(continued)

Alarmingly high levels of these same chemicals were also detected over London, Moscow, Berlin and other major cities in Europe and Asia.

And a hole in the ozone layer is virtually certain to form over the upper reaches of the Northern Hemisphere during the next decade.

It is possible that one will even form this winter, scientists predicted.

"None of the news is good," said James Anderson, a Harvard University chemist who is the project director of the $10 million expedition that has been studying the ozone layer over the Northern Hemisphere.

"People should be alarmed by these latest findings," said Michael Kurylo, manager of NASA's Upper Atmosphere Research Program. "We're seeing conditions primed for ozone destruction. The situation is far worse than we had thought."

Since the 1970s the planet's ozone has been thinning because of the release of man-made chemicals, such as chlorofluorocarbons (CFCs) and halons, into the atmosphere.

In 1985, a huge hole in the ozone layer was discovered over Antarctica, and each September it has formed again.

A hole over the Northern Hemisphere, home to most of the world's population, would be further evidence of destruction of the ozone layer—the gaseous shield 10 to 35 miles above the Earth. This layer blocks the destructive amounts of ultraviolet radiation from reaching the planet's surface.

The Philadelphia Inquirer (continued)

Scientists are concerned about the loss of ozone because increased ultraviolet rays could cause tens of millions of cases of skin cancer, cataracts and immune system diseases in the coming decades. The radiation has also been shown to damage crops such as soybeans and rice, harm trees, and disrupt tiny marine organisms that serve as food for many species of fish.

The new findings about the ozone layer reported yesterday were based upon research gathered by two specifically equipped aircraft that have been flying over the Arctic since last fall. They are also based on scientific instruments aboard the Upper Atmosphere Research Satellite, which was launched last September. The effort involves 120 scientists from six universities, NASA and two national laboratories.

Joe Waters, a scientist with Jet Propulsion Laboratory in Pasa-dena, Calif., said the satellite had shown levels of chlorine monoxide, a chemical closely associated with ozone destruction, at 1.2 parts per billion—60 times higher than normal—over major cities in northern Europe and Asia early last month.

"These readings are very scary," he said.

Levels of 0.3 parts per billion—about 15 times higher than normal—have been found over Philadelphia and other U.S. cities. . . .

But even if the production of these chemicals were halted today, their impact would continue for at least 100 years, Waters said. That is because they remain in the atmosphere for many decades.

"It will take at least a century before the hole in the ozone layer disappears," he said.

Jim Detjen, *The Philadelphia Inquirer*

As you can see, the *Philadelphia Inquirer* story is far more complete; 10 paragraphs on the types of chemicals causing ozone depletion were even left out. But it took up 20 inches compared to 5 inches for the *USA Today* story.

Tips From an Award-winning Writer

Richard Aregood doesn't waste words. He doesn't have space. He's an editorial writer for the *Philadelphia Daily News*. A good one. So good that he has won a Pulitzer Prize and the Distinguished Writing Award from the American Society of Newspaper Editors. How does he do it? He explains in this column he wrote for the ASNE publication *The Bulletin:*

Writing short is simple, but it ain't easy.

What it requires is a lot of hard work before the first finger hits the key, work that answers the classic questions of just what the hell we're trying to do here. The first step of that has to come from a writer who is willing to throw out his or her best sentence if it doesn't fit. The writer must focus everything on advancing the story, not in filling space.

A piece about a cesspool overflow need not include the entire history of solid waste on the planet, complete with graphics. All it needs to tell is the basic disgusting story.

Some things that help:

• Forget about all those dimwit professors who weighed blue books to determine grades and the editors who equate importance with length.

• Focus hard on the point of the story.

• Resist the temptation to tell everything you've learned; much of it doesn't matter.

• Pounce on every sentence and get rid of every word that doesn't clearly and simply say what needs to be said.

• Avoid the jargon sources use; translating it adds clarity and keeps you from getting woozy.

• Remember that you're writing for actual people.

• Let your mind wander through a story before the typing starts. I find it a lot easier in the end to write the best possible first draft because I'm one of those people who has to get it right the first time.

• Thinking a story through helps even more with the long ones, which have a tendency to grow like kudzu if there is no vision going in. Even then, advance thought can turn something that would have consumed 40 columns into merely 30.

None of this is easy. In fact, it's a lot easier simply to regurgitate everything and slap a lead on a 12-part meaningless series. The trouble is that no one will read the damn thing.

Finally, the hardest of all—convincing an editor that a really sparkling five paragraphs deserves good display.

That's all I have to say. I'm outta here.

Activities

1 Write a column of summary briefs as teasers to stories inside your campus or local newspaper.

2 Write three briefs to substitute for full stories in your local paper, or use any of the full stories in Chapter 12.

3 Find a newspaper story that lends itself to a bright, and write one.

4 Cover a news event on campus or in your city—such as a meeting, a press conference or some other breaking news story—and write it in the style of *USA Today*.

5 Find a story in your local newspaper or some other paper and rewrite it, using the guidelines of *USA Today* or Richard Aregood.

COACHING
TIPS

Study your audience. Find out if the editors you want to reach prefer hard-news or soft-news style, short or in-depth releases, and single releases or media kits.

Find your focus. Use the focus statement as a headline or guideline for your lead.

Consider graphics—charts, illustrations, photographs, diagrams—to make your package more appealing.

Write a facts sheet. Even if you don't include a separate fact sheet with your release or media kit, use it as a writing tool to make sure you have provided crucial facts about the organization in your story.

Always include the name and telephone number of a person to contact, the date information can be released, an address and the date the release was written.

Public Relations Writing 15

In 1985, just five years after she graduated from college, Evie Lazzarino stood in front of the Great Wall of China promoting a bunch of dolls called Cabbage Patch Kids. She was coordinating part of a world tour featuring children from America who went to seven foreign countries as "ambassadors" for the dolls, then among the most popular toys in the United States.

"The Chinese people had never seen a Cabbage Patch doll. It was fun to see people's first reaction to them," says Lazzarino, who was then working for a Los Angeles public relations agency that handled the Cabbage Patch Kids account. "My job was like an advance job for a politician. I went to China to set up a party, places we could visit, and I met with all the Western press such as bureaus of *The New York Times* and *Los Angeles Times*. I tried to get them to cover what we were doing. We did a photo shoot on the Great Wall and the photo moved worldwide."

The trip to China was one of the high points in a varied career that has been somewhat circular. After Lazzarino graduated from the University of Kansas with a journalism degree, she began working as a reporter and editor for her local newspaper. Now she works for the country's largest metropolitan newspaper, the *Los Angeles Times.* But she isn't a reporter or an editor. She is the manager of its community relations department. In this job she supervises many public relations programs the *Times* sponsors, such as a summer camp for underprivileged children, the newspaper's speakers bureau, its scholarship fund and other events in the community.

We are writing from the point of view of the corporation. We are not trying to tell everything. My job is to protect the interests of this company.

Charles W. Hucker, division vice president for public affairs and communications, Hallmark Cards, Inc.

277

Evie Lazzarino, community relations manager, Los Angeles Times

Courtesy of Evie Lazzarino

Lazzarino's experience reflects the wide range of jobs in the public relations field. In addition to working with the media, she has been responsible for developing products, writing speeches for corporate officials, coordinating trade shows and promoting plans for several major accounts, including Polaroid and Mercedes-Benz of North America.

Although Lazzarino has a newspaper background, other people featured in this chapter started directly in public relations work after college. Lazzarino's route from newspaper reporting to public relations was a series of opportunities that just presented themselves. As features editor for *The Lawrence* (Kan.) *Journal-World,* she often dealt with people at Hallmark Cards, Inc., in Kansas City. One day they offered her a job in public relations. "I hadn't really thought about going into public relations," she says. "But I found the transition delightful. It blended a growing interest I had in business with my interest in journalism."

That job led to one in Los Angeles with a public relations agency, which also handled some work for Hallmark and other clients, such as Cabbage Patch Kids. After three years with Quinn/Brein Inc., she became vice president in the Los Angeles office of The Rowland Company, the fifth largest public relations firm in the world. By 1990, when the *Los Angeles Times* had an opening for a public relations specialist, she took it because she wanted to work in public relations for one company instead of an agency.

Cabbage Patch doll at the Great Wall of China

Courtesy of Evie Lazzarino

"The advantage of working in-house is that you can focus on one client, which is your company," she says. "At an agency you will have several clients. That can be good or bad. I was just ready to focus on one client."

Whether you work for one client or an agency that serves many, in public relations you are serving several masters at once, Lazzarino says. If you are writing a press release, you are not only trying to please your client, you also have to please an editor at a newspaper, magazine or television station. So in a sense, you are working for several people.

She says her journalism background helped her understand the kind of writing the media wanted. "You have to write as professionally in public relations as if you were writing in a newspaper. Avoid hype and be realistic about what you are selling."

One of the major assets of her background was a respect for deadlines. "In journalism you know how important they are," she says.

Students going into public relations may think deadlines in public relations are not as strenuous as they are in newspapers. But you have many deadlines because you may have five or 10 clients you are trying to serve at one time, Lazzarino says. "People are paying a lot of money for your services," Lazzarino says. "When it's someone else's money, there's a real sense of risk that you could lose clients."

One of her main suggestions is to know your audience. "You have to know different styles. Some magazines may prefer something clever, but if you are pitching something to *The Wall Street Journal,* you should have a great news story. You have to study your market. Go out and meet editors and find out what they want."

Media Resistance

Sending press releases to the media doesn't guarantee that your material will be used. In 1991 a California marketing communications agency conducted an unscientific survey of 30 print and broadcast media organizations to find out how many of the press releases they received were actually read. Then the company sent out this press release about its findings:

Paper Waste Irresponsible

PR Agency Surveys Media, Adopts Green Policies

NEWPORT BEACH, CA—The public-relations division of InterCommunicationsInc, a marketing communications agency here, is making an effort to reduce the amount of paper it sends to newsrooms for clients and thus minimize the agency's impact upon the environment.

The company has changed its media relations policies and practices after reviewing the amount of paper it distributes to working journalists and conducting a telephone survey of Los Angeles-area newsrooms.

Survey Confirms Need

InterCom surveyed assignment editors June 3–14 to determine the impact of unsolicited public-relations material upon newsrooms' waste streams. A total of 30 newspapers, magazines, radio and television stations, and wire services were contacted.

Major findings: (1) the 30 newsrooms received an average of 122 press releases every day (from a minimum of 20 to a maximum of 600), (2) less than 10 percent of the press releases received were "actually read," (3) of those, assignment editors considered less than 20 percent "useful," (4) most assignment editors (27) indicated that press releases and other media materials printed on both sides of paper wouldn't hinder readability, (5) 28 assignment editors indicated that press kits contained "too much" paper, and (6) two thirds (20) subscribe to services such as BusinessWire and PR NewsWire and prefer to read company announcements via those rather than receive hard copy in the mail.

All assignment editors indicated a desire to reduce their individual newsroom's waste stream. . . .

# # #

The press release went on to explain that the company would counsel clients on what is newsworthy so the company could avoid "useless, newsless paper."

Although the point of the release was to promote the company's attitude toward environmental responsibility, here is what *The Wall Street Journal* printed from the press release in a brief for the "Odds and Ends" column:

InterCommunications, a California marketing communications agency, says fewer than 10% of the press releases that newsrooms receive are read. Of those, only one in five is considered "useful" by assignment editors, the agency's survey found.

The Wall Street Journal

The *Los Angeles Times* printed a similar blurb, ignoring any positive aspects of the company's actions.

Judy Brower, account supervisor in charge of media relations for InterCommunicationsInc., says the press release was sent by her former boss against her wishes. "I knew the media would be interested in it, partly in fun and partly in a serious manner. The public relations and journalism people are on two sides of a fence. I felt the results of the survey were negative toward an industry in which I've invested 10 years of my life." Little came of the release, except that the company began conserving paper within the office. Brower says editors and clients prefer releases printed on one side of the paper, despite the survey's findings.

Media's Needs

There is some validity to the survey's findings that many press releases are not read all the way through. But most editors at least skim the releases to find out if there is some newsworthy information. Community newspapers and local television stations rely heavily on news releases about events in their area. And a good public relations practitioner can be an invaluable source to a reporter.

Newsworthiness

Brower, whose company specializes in serving clients in real estate and shopping center development, says the test of newsworthiness is the same for a public relations release as it is for a newspaper, magazine or television station. The basic principles of timeliness, local interest and unusual nature apply. With magazines, especially trade magazines, information that imparts new knowledge or something that will help readers is especially helpful, she says. For example, one article that she placed in a real estate trade publication was geared to helping developers plan long-term strategy for economic growth in the commercial building market.

"If you are looking to place something in the media, take your subject and envision the headline the newspaper might print. Use that as an angle to force yourself to determine what is newsworthy about your information," Brower says.

She also stresses the importance of visuals—charts, graphs and photos. "Magazines and newspapers have become much more graphic," she says. "Although many of the larger newspapers prefer to use their own photographers, the weeklies and small community newspapers prefer something they can just grab."

Writing Ability

There is no substitute for good writing. "The more we can write the way journalists want the information to come out, the more chance it has of being published," Brower says. "You must have the basic skills for news writing." She has even implemented a writing test for people she wants to hire.

Although Brower works extensively with the media, she didn't learn her basic skills on a newspaper. She graduated from the University of California with a communications degree. She says the most valuable training she received was through internships at public relations firms while she was in college. "Even if you don't get paid for it, an internship is worth the experience," she says. She also strongly advises students to gain experience on the college newspaper.

Despite the similarities between public relations and newspaper writing, there is a major difference in approach, Brower says. Public relations practitioners are advocates for their clients.

Credibility

"Journalists sometimes claim p.r. people don't tell the truth," Brower says. "That isn't the case. I look at my clients as family. I prefer to think we always tell the truth, but just like comments about our family, we don't bring up negative qualities. If you are asked a negative question, you would probably try to soften the answer. But it is important to be honest. If the media find you are dishonest, you're done. They won't ever believe you again."

Honesty is stressed in the code of ethics for the Public Relations Society of America, cited in the chapter on ethics: "A member shall adhere to truth and accuracy and to generally accepted standards of good taste," the code states.

Charles W. Hucker is also concerned about the image that public relations practitioners have with the media. Hucker is division vice president in charge of public affairs and communication for Hallmark Cards, Inc., in Kansas City, Mo. He says he doesn't even like the term *public relations*. "In some respects it is a term lacking in credibility, so why use it?" Hucker says. "To me the term has too much connotation of flim-flam connected to it. The word I use is *communication*. We are in the communication business. If you look at the entire range of communications activity we are engaged in, only a relatively small share of that activity is really aimed at the media."

In addition to promoting Hallmark products in the media, the communication division has a separate department just for internal corporate communications, such as in-house publications for the employees and product development plans. Hallmark's communication division also sponsors many community functions to promote the image of the company, one of the largest in Kansas City.

Charles W. Hucker, division vice president for public affairs and communication, Hallmark Cards, Inc.

Courtesy of Charles W. Hucker

Point of View   Hucker prefers to think of corporate communications as writing from a point of view rather than advocacy journalism. "We are not trying to be investigative journalists within the confines of these walls," he says. "We are writing from the point of view of the corporation. We are not trying to tell everything. My job is to protect the interests of this company. That takes precedence over a reporter trying to get all the facts for his or her story."

Hucker says he struggled with that concept for a couple of years when he made the transition from his previous work as a reporter, magazine writer and editor. A graduate of the University of Missouri with a degree in political science, Hucker started work as a political reporter for a newspaper and later worked at *Congressional Quarterly Weekly Report* in Washington, D.C., as the political editor and managing editor. He wanted to return to Kansas City, and Hallmark offered the right opportunity in 1984. Now promoting the company's point of view comes naturally.

But he doesn't believe it should be blatant. "We avoid too much self-promotion," he says. "We get the Hallmark name into news releases but we don't load the release so heavily that it stinks when it lands on the desk of a newspaper."

Media Kits

Hallmark has an established association with holidays, natural times to promote cards and other Hallmark products. During Christmas time, the company can get 400 to 500 calls from the media about ideas for holiday stories. Hucker attributes some of the media's interest to what he calls "relationship building"—meeting editors, discovering their needs and maintaining contacts.

Although Hallmark sometimes sends out just a press release, more often it sends "media kits." Media kits are usually folders containing a variety of press releases, fact sheets about the company and its products, and samples of Hallmark cards. Hucker says he favors media kits because they leave more of an impression and tend to be kept around. "The objective is to plant enough seeds or hooks so an editor can go through the material and find an angle and develop the idea into a fuller story."

A media kit that Hallmark issued for Easter 1992 contained this overview letter:

Easter 1992

Dear Editor:

The latest in Easter card and gift-giving trends from Hallmark Cards is tucked inside. We hope you find this information helpful as you prepare your spring-time holiday stories.

Thanks for continuing to tell the stories about America's favorite celebrations. If you need additional information or product samples, please call.

The holiday experts at Hallmark and their phone numbers are listed on the enclosed news releases.

Happy Easter!

Your Friends at Hallmark Cards

The media kit also contained some sample Easter cards, a few press releases and a fact sheet geared primarily to newspaper and magazine feature stories.

In the following press release, notice how the writer weaves in the name of the company—and Crayola, which it also owns—throughout the story but avoids overdoing the promotional aspect. The names of people to contact and their phone numbers were listed at the top of the release, followed by the release date—crucial information to include in all press releases. Here is the text:

FOR IMMEDIATE RELEASE

Easter—A Time for Sharing Fun, Renewing Tradition

(Kansas City, Mo.)—Easter, the third largest greeting card-sending occasion, is also one of the nation's most popular family celebrations.

"Easter, like Christmas and Thanksgiving, has many traditions that families celebrate together," says Regi Early, administrator of Kaleidoscope—a Hallmark-sponsored children's art workshop—and a former art educator. "To help nurture family identity and closeness, today's young parents continue favorite traditions from their own childhood as well as starting new ones."

According to Hallmark research, the top three ways Americans celebrate Easter are getting together with family, attending church and exchanging greeting cards. This year, more than 170 million Easter cards are expected to be exchanged.

Other favorite activities include coloring and hunting for eggs, sharing Easter dinner and making the Easter basket.

Easter Baskets: A Fond Tradition

"Every Easter, my mother would fill Easter baskets with small gifts and hide them throughout the house," recalls Early. "My sister and I would search behind draperies and under chairs until we found the basket with our own name on it. If we found each other's basket, we weren't allowed to reveal its hiding place, and we always raced to see who could find their own basket first. When I became a mother, I continued the ritual by making baskets for my own kids."

For Easter 1992, Hallmark offers approximately 250 gifts and party items and nearly 1,500 greeting cards to help families nurture their own traditions.

Hallmarks' gift line includes an exclusive selection of Crayola® Bunny-theme items, including stuffed animals, basket stuffers, stickers, washable markers and coloring books. Other designs are featured on a variety of lapel pins, candy containers, porcelain banks and figurines, and gifts for infants, such as decorated bibs and nightlights.

"Traditions such as hiding Easter baskets, exchanging greeting cards or baking Easter cookies can help families establish a sense of family connection," says Early. "Such rituals can give a child a sense of feeling special, and in turn, contribute to a child's self-esteem."

Early suggests these activities to build family Easter traditions while promoting a child's individuality:

• Decorate and fill Easter baskets that reflect each child's interest. For example, if a child is an artist at heart, fill a basket with Crayola® markers or colored pencils as well as coloring posters, stickers, bunny-shaped note pads and a vinyl apron. To aid cleanup, include the Hallmark card that features a magic bunny sponge.

• Start traditions early. Even a baby can receive a basket filled with bibs, caps, nightlights and small stuffed toys.

• Let children create dyed eggs that reflect their individual tastes. One way to do this is to "half dye" eggs by dipping a portion of the egg in the dye and then letting the child decorate the white space with stickers or crayons.

• Create Easter cookies by using cookie cutters shaped as eggs, bunnies, carrots and crosses. Let each child decorate cookies with colored icing. At the Easter dinner, display the cookies by placing them in the center of the table on a tray surrounded by a picket-fence paper garland.

• Purchase plastic eggs with string loops attached and let the children decorate a small outside tree. This could be done several weeks before Easter. To add exuberance to this event, hide the eggs in the yard and let the children search for them. Once found, the children hang the eggs on the designated tree's branches.

• Make an Easter wreath. As the children receive cards from friends and relatives, attach the cards to a white grapevine to hang on the front door.

# # #

The fact sheet that accompanied the press release was more promotional, but it contained information that news writers might deem worthy of including in a general story about Easter traditions even without promoting the company. Again, the contacts and phone numbers were at the top of the release. Notice the list format and the subheadings. Here is the text:

Easter Card and Gift Fact Sheet—1992

Observance:
- Easter is observed on the Sunday following the first full moon after the vernal equinox, sometime between March 22 and April 25. This year, Easter is April 19.

Card-sending customs:
- Easter is the third largest card-sending occasion, with 170 million cards expected to be exchanged in 1992, according to Hallmark Cards research.
- More than 70 percent of all Easter cards are given to relatives.

Card design trends:
- Hallmark offers nearly 1,500 different Easter cards, the largest selection in the industry.
- New for 1992 is "Bunnies by Design," a selection of 12 cards with special features designed to create play value and make colorful, fun decorations. The cards have movable parts or added attachments and feature bunnies, of course. One "Bunnies by Design" card can be shaped to form a three-dimensional Easter basket, complete with artificial grass.
- In response to customer requests for traditional religious cards, Hallmark offers Easter cards with messages reflecting the important role spirituality plays in people's lives. Many of the religious cards include a Bible verse.
- Because cards reflect the times, the importance of traditional values is a recurring theme in Hallmark's 1992 Easter cards. One example is this message: "The Easter traditions we share year to year bring our hearts still closer when springtime is here. They're part of the joy that is ours all year through and why I'm so happy to share life with you."

Gift-giving trends:
- Most Easter gifts are purchased by mothers or grandmothers of children ages 12 and under. The items generally are purchased to be used as Easter basket stuffers.
- Hallmark research shows that parents are increasingly using Easter as a time to start family traditions. Popular family activities include decorating eggs, hunting for Easter baskets, attending church or decorating an outdoor tree and baking Easter cookies together.

• Hallmark offers about 250 gift and party items for 1992. Most gifts are under $5.

• Hallmark's Easter gift line includes: wicker baskets in an assortment of sizes and colors; soft, stuffed animals; activity products for children such as washable markers, stickers and coloring books; wind-up toys; lapel pins, barrettes, T-shirts and suspenders, candy containers, Easter gifts for infants, such as growth charts, decorated bibs and nightlights, gift wrap and partyware; and decorations, including paper garlands, windsocks and yard signs.

• New for 1992 are "Kids' Gifts With Loving Messages," an Easter gift selection designed to help adults express their feelings to children. The offering includes porcelain figurines, ceramic mugs, frames, plaques and banks that feature sentiments such as "Who loves you? Grandma and Grandpa do!" and "I thank my lucky stars for you!"

• In addition to Hallmark's regular line of Easter products, selected Hallmark Crown stores will be offering exclusive Easter items, such as Hallmark Keepsake Easter ornaments, Crayola® Bunny candy, and fresh cut flower bouquets. Hallmark Gold Crown stores are designated by Hallmark as outstanding and must be re-certified annually.

# # #

Writing Skills for Press Releases

With the exception of the difference in point of view, Hucker says there are more similarities between corporate communications and newspaper or broadcast writing than there are differences. He says he isn't impressed when job applicants tell him they are good with people. "When I hire people here, I want good writers," he says. To Hucker that means good technical skills. His preferences:

Good grammar

Subject and verb in natural order

Simple sentences, short paragraphs

Limited or no adjectives

"People don't want a lot of breathless prose; they want the ideas and facts," he says. He also wants writers to have good analytical skills, especially for corporate proposals. "We're paying a lot more attention to critical thinking, the ability to sort through a mass of stuff."

He likens writing a press release or proposal to organizing a hard-news story: "Figure out what is the most important point for the lead. Then organize it by key points explained and argued in such a way that the audience understands. Never forget who the audience is."

A Direct Approach

Mark O'Brien offers the same advice, but his writing style is more direct. As media communications representative for Binney & Smith, makers of Crayola products, he favors a brief approach. He targets newspaper editors as his first audience.

"You have to listen to the editors out there," O'Brien says. "They get a lot of material across their desks each day. If you have to read a page before you get to the meat of the subject, that's too much. Very few newspapers are going to print your story exactly. The release is just to pique their curiosity."

O'Brien, who began work in public relations for General Foods after graduating from the University of South Florida, says he studied what worked by comparing releases and newsletters that got published and those that didn't. Now his news releases rarely exceed two double-spaced, typewritten pages; most are just a few paragraphs on one page. (Double spacing is another requirement for press releases, because it is easier to read.) But he also includes fact sheets in a media kit with product samples, all enclosed in a folder with a bold graphic of smiling crayons or a cover similar to the familiar gold and green Crayola box of crayons.

And his releases get results. In one year *USA Today* printed six front-page stories based on his releases. Scores of newspapers throughout the country—including The Associated Press, with its national distribution—wrote stories based on the following release. O'Brien included these essential elements:

The company address

A contact (himself, in this case) with telephone number

The date of the release

When the release can be published (for immediate release, in this case)

O'Brien sent this release out a week earlier than the date on it so editors could publish it the day the news supposedly was announced. That's another quality of a good publicist. Editors want timely information. Unless special arrangements are made to hold the news, they usually will print it as soon as possible. As a result, "for immediate release" is a good way to write the release date.

On a day when the headlines on the front page of *USA Today* were "U.S. ships Haitian refugees home" and "Mortgage rates start climbing," tucked in the right-hand corner of the paper was the story based on O'Brien's release. The story was set on a pink background, called a "screen," with a picture of Crayola crayons. The picture was supplied by the company, and the quote was taken directly from the release. Compare the release and the story, which also included information (underlined) from fact sheets in the media kit and a phone call to the company. (Note that because Crayola is a trademark name, it should be capitalized in all news stories.)

Illustration from media kit

Courtesy of Binney & Smith Inc.

Press release

Binney & Smith, Inc.

1100 Church Lane

P.O. Box 431

Easton, Pennsylvania 18044-0431

(Company telephone number)

For Immediate Release

Contact: Mark J. O'Brien

Media Communications

Telephone number plus direct extension

Crayola Introduces New Crayons That Are Literally "Off the Wall"

Feb. 4, 1992, EASTON, Pa.—Parents can put away the scrub brushes and stain remover thanks to Binney & Smith. The maker of Crayola products has introduced a totally off-the-wall product—washable crayons.

Unlike the billions of crayons produced before them, Crayola washable crayons are made from a patented formula that washes from most surfaces, including walls and fabric.

"Washable crayons address our number one consumer complaint—getting crayon marks off different surfaces," says Mark O'Brien, Binney & Smith spokesperson. "Each year we receive thousands of calls and

Front-page story

Crayola cleans up kids' act

Parents can now offer junior artists a crayon that won't leave permanent impressions of childhood—on walls, draperies and floors.

Binney & Smith, maker of Crayola brand, is introducing a crayon made from a formula that can be cleaned with soap and water.

"Washable crayons address our number-one consumer complaint," says company official Mark O'Brien.

That's good news for parents: According to Binney & Smith, the USA's kids spend almost 6.3 billion hours a year with crayons in hand.

Unlike traditional crayons, washable ones aren't made of the waxy substance paraffin. The substitutes are water-soluble compounds found in cosmetics.

Grown men and women colored on walls coated with a variety of paints and wallpapers to test formulas.

"They are truly Mom-friendly," says Binney & Smith's Brad Drexler.

So your toddler's wayward works of art can be cleaned off

Press release (continued)

letters regarding crayon stains, mainly from parents of preschool children. With the introduction of washable crayons, parents can breathe a little easier when it comes to crayon mishaps."

The difference between traditional and washable crayons is in their formulas. Washable crayons contain special water soluble polymers found in many health and beauty aids. This allows them to be removed from most surfaces by simply using soap and water. Tests have shown washable crayon marks can even be removed from walls and fabric one to two months after being stained. However, crayon marks are easiest to remove if washed soon after they happen.

Crayola washable crayons are non-toxic and available in two sizes. The So Big size, for younger children, comes six to a box and has a suggested retail price of $2.99. Boxes of eight, large size washable crayons will sell for approximately $2.59.

# # #

Front-page story (continued)

most walls and other surfaces up to two months after they're made.

One rub: Washable crayons are being marketed for preschoolers only in Crayola's large and "So Big" sizes.

But they come in the same eight colors—red, green, orange, blue, black, brown and violet—as the first Crayolas in 1903.

USA Today

Unlike the Hallmark holiday feature releases, this one contained more hard news, one reason for its wide acceptance. But front page in the nation's largest newspaper? O'Brien says part of the release's success was due to the product, one that is "ingrained in our society as part of our culture." The other reason was some relief from depressing news, he says. "It's nice to put something on the front page that's not devastating."

Here's an excerpt from a 15-inch feature story based on the same release. It is based on more extensive interviews with O'Brien.

The folks at Crayola finally have seen the handwriting on the wall.

And they're going to wash it off.

Yes, the company that since 1903 has brought you rainbows inside a gold-and-green box is offering washable crayons—many years and paint jobs too late for thousands of American families but just right for what the company quite politely refers to as "crayon mishaps."

For years, says company spokesman Mark O'Brien, parents' No. 1 complaint has been that Crayola stains don't wash off walls or out of clothes. So, he says, Crayola scientists have been working in their Pennsylvania offices for those years—"night and day" for the past three—to develop a washable crayon that also meets Crayola's standards for vibrancy.

The Wichita (Kan.) *Eagle*

The Structure of Press Releases

Press releases differ very little from basic news stories. Some have a feature approach; others are organized the same as a hard-news story, with a summary lead. As with any news story, you need to get to the point quickly in a press release. If you have a soft lead, put the nut graph high in the release, preferably by the second or third paragraph.

Lead If you have a strong news angle, use a summary or impact lead. Get to the point quickly. If the story is geared to a feature section of the newspaper or a magazine, use any of the soft-lead techniques. But still get to the point quickly with a high nut graph.

Here's an example of a press release that is hard to read because the lead starts with too many phrases and is too long:

Offering 15-second transmission speed, an easy-to-read liquid crystal display, and a five page automatic document feeder, Sharp Electronics Corporation recently introduced two new low-end facsimile models which boast a number of features not usually found in comparable priced units. The UX-101 and UX-111 facsimiles have now joined Sharp's successful lineup of personal home office facsimiles.

Focus Write a sentence explaining the main point and the "so what" factor above your story. This could be your headline or your lead, just as in a news story.

The following example, also a hard-news approach, is much clearer than the first one. Note how the headline is the focus and the basis for the lead as well.

JC Penney to Study Site for Distribution Center

DALLAS, June 22—J.C. Penney Company, Inc. has acquired an option on a 150-acre site in Rockingham, County, Virginia, near Harrisonburg, and will study the feasibility of locating the company's seventh catalog distribution center there.

Backup   Rodney M. Birkins, president of JCPenney Catalog, says the company acquired the option on a portion of the Jordan farm, which is located at the northeast corner of Route 682 and I-81. He emphasized that the action was merely exploratory at this time.

The next example, from a greeting card company, is a four-page release that lacks a clear focus. It appears to be a history of the company, not the kind of news most editors are seeking. Also note the use of adjectives and the strong self-promotional tone.

American Greetings' 86-Year Growth Record
Attributed to Excellent Service Record

American Greetings Corporation continues the aggressive leadership drive today that is rooted in its founder, Jacob Sapirstein. His leadership and beliefs formed the company's philosophy in 1906: know your customer, develop the product to meet his need, never compromise on quality, and provide service before and after the sale.

Through careful planning and attention to these basics, the company has grown to its Fortune 500 status, with worldwide operations.

Sapirstein, known as J.S. to family, friends and employees, grew up with seven brothers and one sister in the small town of Grajeyvo, Poland. When he turned 20, in 1904, Russia was at war with Japan and Poland's young men were being drafted for the Czarist forces. . . .

After three more pages, an ending with a possible angle for news   Now, American Greetings is debuting "In Touch" personal expression cards, a revolutionary new concept for the industry. These cards will help people communicate their everyday feelings via nonoccasion cards.

Backup   Just as you would in a news story, you should back up the lead with a quote or supporting facts. Before you write, jot down the crucial information a reader needs—who, what, where, when, why and how. If you are promoting an event, make sure you have the date, time and location—or rain-date possibilities. Think of your list as an empowerment box. Use the basic role-playing technique: If you were buying the product, attending the event or seeking information about the company, what questions would you have? Answer them quickly.

Ending You often can end press releases with a fact or basic information about price or other sales information. Keep it simple; don't strain.

Revision Use the basic coaching method: conceive, collect, construct, correct. In the final step, strike out every superfluous word. If you had to limit your release to one page, what would you delete? Revise your release, checking for spelling and factual accuracy, and try to limit it to one or two pages.

Corporate Publications

When you are writing press releases for the media, use newspaper style. If you are writing a company magazine with news and features about people and events in the organization, newspaper style still applies. But when you are writing a memo or proposal to the company president or other corporate officials, you need to state your position in an analytical way.

That's where many business writers have difficulty, says Anne Baber, a writing coach who conducts seminars in corporations to improve communication techniques. She has also conducted seminars for the International Association of Business Communicators and has written books and many articles about career topics.

The key factor is to know the audience, she says. "There are some psychological problems people have when they write for folks up the ladder in management. One of my theories is that power warps communication. When people are writing for a boss, it's like a teenager talking to a parent. The parent says, 'Where are you going?' The teenager answers, 'Out.' The teen isn't saying everything he or she knows because of the power structure. In corporations, the power structure also affects communication. The writing becomes very formal, very passive. The writers don't want to put themselves forward as being initiators of action. They hide behind the third person. They write *the employee* rather than the word *you*."

Baber bases her theories on many years of experience in corporate communications. A former director of communications for United Telecom (now called Sprint), she heads her own consulting firm, Baber and Associates, in Kansas City, Mo.

Many of the coaching techniques she uses are similar to those described earlier in the book. But the outcome is different. "News writing operates on the idea that if you give the public enough information, they will inform themselves," she says. "We're not doing that in an organization. We want to create attitudes or actions. It's much more like advertising."

Here are Baber's tips for writing proposals and company plans:

Reporting steps

Make a list. Ask what the audience—in this case management—really wants to know. Then itemize all the points you can. (This is the same as brainstorming for a news story.)

Envision the result. Ask yourself, what kind of action is the reader expected to take as a result of this information?

Make a checklist of what and why. Write a sentence beginning "I want to tell you that . . . ," and then answer why. Then add this teaser to support the why factor: "This is necessary because . . ." (This teaser is similar to the focus—"so what"—sentence on top of your news stories.)

Writing the proposal

Draw a "mind spill." Get all the research together. Draw a circle in the center of a large piece of paper. Put the main topic in the center circle. Then draw circles, filling each circle with an idea. Take a colored pencil or highlighter, and mark the key components related to the main idea. Draw a line to connect one related idea to another so that all like information is grouped together. Then number the points, preferably in the order you will write them in the proposal. (This is the same technique as mapping for ideas or reporting.)

Organize the order. Write a topic sentence (the same as a focus sentence) that completes this thought: "I believe that . . ." For example, "I believe that we should market Mother's Day cards a different way." Then write the word *because* followed by point one, point two, point three—like the list technique. The most persuasive structure is three in parallel order.

Use inverted pyramid style. Put the strongest point of the proposal in the lead, and then plan your proposal with supporting points.

Put information in perspective. Ask yourself: What does the reader know already, and what is new? If this is one of a series of proposals, you may need just a summary sentence referring to past information the reader already knows. The reader is going to read this proposal quickly and will get irritated if he or she has to wade through previously known material.

Write a strong conclusion. Summarize, but do not repeat, your lead. If you have written a proposal about marketing Mother's Day cards and you have given the supporting points that answer why you should change the method, the ending could be a strong statement like "We should start marketing these new cards in six months." If that time frame is part of your proposal, you could just end with a statement telling why it is a good idea.

Check your verbs. After you have written your draft, go back and circle the verbs and see if they are strong, action words. If not, revise.

Press Release Checklist

Editors expect press releases to follow a fairly standard format:

• Include the name of a contact person, preferably two people, and phone numbers.

• Include a date when the release was written, and indicate "For immediate release" or another date for publication.

• Write a headline that states the focus of your release. Although not required, a headline is recommended because it lets the recipient see the focus immediately, just as in a newspaper story.

• Double- or triple-space the type.

• Try to limit the release to one or two pages.

• Write on one side of the paper. (This preference could change as environmental awareness increases.)

• Write *More* at the end of the page if the release continues; mark the end with the symbol # # # or the word *END*, set off by dashes.

Certain writing conventions are expected as well:

• Cover all the basics: who, what, when, where, why, how and so what.

• Use simple sentences, strong verbs, short sentences and short paragraphs. Try to limit a paragraph to four or five lines of type.

• Consider your audience, and write in the style most suited to that medium.

• Favor the inverted pyramid or a simple style that gets to the point quickly, even if you start with a creative lead.

• Use the list technique if you have several points to make, preferably in parallel construction.

• For a proposal, write a strong lead and support it with clear points. Again, consider the list technique for clarity.

• Consider whether a media kit would work better than a single release. If so, include one or several releases to provide different ideas, a fact sheet, graphics and perhaps a sample or other teaser.

Activities

1 Gather information from an organization for an event on your campus or in your city. Write a press release announcing the event.

2 Study a company in your community. Devise a media kit to promote some product or aspect of the company. This activity may require some coordination so many students do not bother the same firm. If a team of students or the whole class is studying a large company, divide the responsibilities and have students study different aspects of the company.

3   Do your own survey of the media. Find out what editors read and what newspapers, magazines, and radio or television stations in your area prefer in the way of press releases.

4   Sketch two story ideas from the Hallmark Easter card press release and fact sheet.

5   Here is some information from PUMA USA, a company based in Massachusetts. Write a press release geared to newspapers' business sections. Use your name and phone number as the contact. Give yourself the title director of public relations. Put this address on your release: PUMA USA, 492 Old Connecticut Path, Framingham, MA 01701. Use your phone number again as the company's phone number. Write a headline and text from the following material:

Who: Christopher H. Smith, company president and chief executive officer

What: Announced a new policy about sales. PUMA products will no longer be sold through discount merchants.

When: For immediate release

Where: At company headquarters

Why: The policy is an outgrowth of the company's recently announced termination of the so-called "White Box" special product and marketing program. In the future, PUMA will target trade customers including athletic footwear specialists, sporting goods stores, and national retailers of quality footwear and apparel.

Backup information: New policy states that the company will not sell to dealers or retailers whose regular business practices include the frequent and aggressive discounting and advertising of quality national brands of athletic footwear, apparel and accessories.

From Smith: "This is a serious promise by PUMA and it will result in a significant drop in current volume that we've got to scramble to make up. We want sporting goods dealers and athletic equipment retailers to know that once current shoes are out of the pipeline, they will not see PUMA shoes being sold at mass merchant discounters."

Facts about the company: PUMA USA designs, produces and markets high-quality performance athletic footwear, apparel and sporting goods in the United States through a national network of sporting goods stores, specialty shops and department stores.

6   Convert a news story from your newspaper into a press release.

COACHING

Use conversational, tell-a-friend style.

Use short sentences, one idea per sentence.

Use active voice.

Give attribution first—who said what before what was said.

Read your copy aloud.

Broadcast Writing

16

I
t's a slow news day at KSNT-TV, and John Rinkenbaugh is worried. He's the news director, in charge of all news operations at the station in Topeka, Kan. It's 9 a.m. and Rinkenbaugh is conducting the first news meeting of the day. Only three stories have been scheduled so far. A typical broadcast has a minimum of six stories, more often 10 to 12.

He looks in the planning file for this day. Not much going on. A community meeting about crime fighting is scheduled tonight. One reporter is working on a story about new management of the Expocentre, an entertainment and sports arena. Another is covering teachers' negotiations with the school board. And another reporter is checking out a few news tips.

Rinkenbaugh looks through the local newspaper. "We will not do any stories out of the paper as a given rule," he says. "We should beat the newspapers most of the time. I just look to see if there is a story we should do better."

But the newspaper offers little help today. "I don't start to panic until 1:30," he says. He'll need to know what will air on the 6 p.m. newscast by 2:15, when he conducts his next news meeting. "When you're desperate, you can pull off the network," he says.

The station is an affiliate of NBC. Not all of the 1,497 television stations in the United States are affiliated with a national network, but they are all ranked by market size. With 152,000 viewers, KSNT is ranked 141st out of 210 markets for television stations. It is one of three television stations in

In broadcast writing one of the most important decisions you have to make is not what you can put into your story but what you can leave out.

Leona Hood, news producer,

KUSA-TV, Denver

John Rinkenbaugh, news director, KSNT-TV, Channel 27 in Topeka, Kan.

Courtesy of Philip Meiring

Topeka, and it is the kind of station where reporters get their start. All but two of the 17 employees in the news department have less than two years of experience.

Rinkenbaugh has 14 years of experience in broadcast journalism. He started as a reporter in Kansas City. Then he worked in Minneapolis, Little Rock and Phoenix as a "producer," the person who writes the script that the newscaster, called an "anchor," reads.

At KSNT and many local television stations, two anchors share the newscast. Sometimes anchors rewrite their portions of the newscast to suit their own style. Reporters write their own stories and submit the copy to the producer, who incorporates it into the newscast. And at a small station like KSNT, reporters double as photographers and shoot the video for their stories or for another reporter.

Although print journalism is enhanced by photos and graphics, broadcast journalism depends on visuals. "A good TV reporter will let the pictures tell the story," Rinkenbaugh says. "You strive for more visual than verbal. A newspaper reporter can write a story without ever leaving the building. A TV reporter almost always has to be where it is happening."

The writing style also differs in some ways. Although the conversational, tell-a-friend style is suggested throughout this book for newspaper writing, it is essential for television. Clarity is crucial. A newspaper reader can reread a sentence or paragraph that may not be clear; a television viewer doesn't get a second chance to hear an unclear sentence.

Brevity is also more critical in television. The typical story a television reporter writes seldom runs longer than a minute and a half (written as *1:30* in broadcast copy). That includes the "sound

Reporter Mary Elbow setting up an interview with a source
Courtesy of Philip Meiring

bites," segments of the story showing the source in direct speech (called "actualities" in radio).

Here is the breakdown of a 30-minute newscast at KSNT:

- 10 minutes total for news
- 3:50 minutes (three minutes and 50 seconds) for weather
- 4:30 minutes for sports
- 1:20 total for introductions to the stories, called "lead-ins"—each running about 15 seconds
- 11 minutes of advertisements

At this point in the day, Rinkenbaugh can only count on stories to fill about five minutes of air time. A couple of reporters are working at their desks when reporter Rick Blum comes into the office. Two story ideas he was pursuing have fallen through. But he says he is pursuing a phone tip about a government red tape story. "I know I've got a story; I don't know how good it is," Blum says.

Reporter Janie Peterson says she's working on a story about neighbors' reaction to a recent police search in an apartment complex.

The day is getting better. Leigh Anne Stout, the assignment editor, checks the wire services—one from NBC and the other from The Associated Press. Nothing important to localize. But she's beginning to get a story budget together for the nightly newscast. She's also checking press releases and planning assignments for tonight's 10 p.m. newscast and for the next day. In addition, Stout is listening to the police scanner. If a major news story breaks, she will send the reporter and photographer closest to the scene. But on this day, nothing major happens.

Planning a Newscast

It's 2:15, time for the afternoon meeting to plan the 6 p.m. newscast. The two anchors and the producer have arrived; they'll stay through the 10 p.m. newscast. The assignment editor gives a rundown of the stories in the works. Rinkenbaugh and his staff discuss the stories and the order in which they will appear on the newscast.

Stories can be arranged in various order:

• By topics, blocking similar stories about crime, government, education and so on, starting with the most significant story (the most common order)

• By importance, from the most significant stories to the least

• By location, such as local, regional, state and national stories

• By some combination of these factors

In most cases, the producer will look for a theme that ties several of the stories together so that transitions between them are natural.

On this day, producer Tami Hale decides there is a topical theme: trouble. She uses a combination of significance and topical order. The lead story will be about new management at the Expocentre, a convention and sports center that has had financial troubles. Then she plans to run the story about trouble between teachers and the school district. With two months left before school starts, the contract impasse is important but not critical. She'll follow with two briefs about Kansas banks in trouble and the state's wheat crop in trouble because of too much rain.

News director John Rinkenbaugh conducting the afternoon news meeting
Courtesy of Philip Meiring

News director John Rinkenbaugh discussing a story with producer Tami Hale
Courtesy of Philip Meiring

After a commercial break, Hale plans to run two stories about crime, one local and the other regional. After a few more stories, she'll end the newscast with a kicker, a story on the light side that she calls a "feel good" story.

Next to each story on the budget, Hale marks the minutes and seconds it will take in the newscast, including the time for an introduction.

By 3:30 p.m. several of the reporters have returned to write and edit their stories.

Nancy Mandell is editing the tape of her story about the Expocentre. She views the tape for sound bites, the segments that show the source speaking. When she finds the quotes she wants, she writes down the number indicated on the tape counter where the source's quotes start and stop and marks how many seconds the sound bite takes. In her written script, called "copy," she'll write the first few words of the direct quote—preceded by the word *IN*— and the last few words—marked *OUT*—to let the producer, anchors and broadcast director know when the source will speak and when the reporter will resume narration.

Here is one of the sound bites from Mandell's story. At KSNT all copy is typed in capital letters, and sound bites are set off by lines. The left side gives instructions for the "director," who coordinates

*Reporter Janie Peterson
editing film while
compiling her story*
Courtesy of Philip Meiring

the technical operations; the right side is for the copy. (In this example, explanations of terms are in italics.)

SUPER *(superimpose name of source, which follows, on video):* JOSEPH BRIGLIA V.P. SALES/SPECTACOR MANAGEMENT GROUP	BITE: (:12) *(sound bite will take 12 seconds)* IN: 8:18 "ABOVE ALL I . . . *(first three words of quote, which are at 8:18 on tape counter)* OUT: 8:30 . . . IN THIS AREA" *(last three words of quote, located at 8:30 on tape counter)*

After Mandell chooses her sound bites, she combines them with her own recorded comments and records it all on another tape for the final version. She also writes a "lead-in," the introduction to her story that the anchor will read. The complete story with sound bites is called a "package."

Reporter Rick Blum returns with his government red tape story. He writes his copy first and then views the tape to choose sound bites. He took thorough notes of the quotes during the reporting process, so when he views the tape, he spots the strongest sound bites quickly. "I try to use less of me and more of the sources," he says. "The story has a lot more meaning when it comes from them."

It's 4 p.m. The reporters check in with producer Hale. She begins writing the newscast. She writes the script that the anchors will read and decides the order in which the reporters' packages will be aired.

For the 6 p.m. newscast Hale doesn't include much national news, because it will be covered by the network newscast that precedes this local one. But for the 10 p.m. show, she'll write briefs of national news for viewers who missed the network newscast. She pulls some wire stories and rewrites them. The news director does not permit "rip-and-read," or direct reading of wire copy.

Since this is a small station that does not have computers, Hale still types all her copy on special forms with six carbon duplicates. She types directions on the left side of the page and copy on the right. The pages are then fed into a TelePrompTer, a machine that projects the copy onto a video screen from which the anchors read. At stations that have computers, the copy can be sent directly via computer into the TelePrompTer. But even computerized stations still provide printouts of the newscast to the anchors, the director (who coordinates the technical production) and the producer.

At this station, all copy is typed in capital letters and double-spaced. Some news directors prefer to have the instructions typed in capital letters and the story copy typed in uppercase and lowercase letters.

About 30 minutes before the newscast, Hale gives her copy to the anchors. Art Navarro, one of the anchors, rewrites some of the copy to suit his own style. Today he has time. On a busy news day, he may not. "I try to write as much copy as possible. I want a very conversational style with simple sentences," he says.

It's almost air time. The anchors take their place behind a semicircular desk. The cameras are in place. In the control room, technicians are ready to coordinate the tapes from reporters with the anchors' lead-ins and stories. Hale has marked each page with a number to indicate the order of the newscast.

The red light goes on; the news program is on the air. Anchor Helen Neill reads from the script on the TelePrompTer, although both she and co-anchor Navarro have printed copies as well. Their cues and words are on the right side; the directions on the left are for the control room. Script directions for Navarro and Neill are marked with their first names. Here is the beginning of the script:

EXPOCENTRE MANAGER 6/30/92 6 PM

PKG Lead-in	**ART**	AFTER SIX MONTHS OF NEGO-TIATIONS, THE KANSAS EXPOCEN-TRE FINALLY HAS A NEW MANAGE-MENT.
		GOOD EVENING AND WEL-COME TO THE KSNT NEWS AT SIX.
	HELEN	SHAWNEE COUNTY COMMIS-SIONERS HAVE AGREED TO SIGN A

KSNT anchor Helen Neill
Photo courtesy of Philip Meiring

ART
	FIVE-YEAR CONTRACT WITH
	PHILADELPHIA-BASED SPECTACOR
	MANAGEMENT GROUP.
	KSNT'S NANCY MANDELL
	TELLS US THE NEW COMPANY
	HOPES TO PUT THE EXPOCENTRE
	UP IN LIGHTS.

Nancy Mandell's package follows this lead-in. The newscast continues with nine more stories and ends with a "feel good" feature story about a Big Brothers and Big Sisters program. Somehow the staff managed to come up with enough stories to fill both programs. News director John Rinkenbaugh has gone home. Maybe tomorrow will be a better news day.

Writing for Broadcast

When Leona Hood writes a newscast for her television station, she uses the "WIFM principle"—What's in It for Me. The *me,* in this case, is the viewer. Hood is news producer for KUSA-TV in Denver, an affiliate of the ABC network. She says you need to make people understand how the story affects them and why it is important.

"The big thing in broadcasting is that people only get one chance to hear what you say. If they miss something, they have so many other choices in these days of channel clickers," Hood says. "Every sentence has to contain something that interests them. Tell them something about this story that will make them care."

KUSA-TV is a large station, ranked 21st out of 210 in market size. But every viewer sees the broadcast as one person, Hood says. "Even though you are reaching hundreds of thousands of viewers, you try to talk to them on an individual level. These people are looking at you talking to them. The illusion you are trying to create, is 'Gee, did you hear what happened in your neighborhood today?' " The concept is the same as the tell-a-friend technique used throughout the book. Except that Hood uses tell-a-neighbor.

"When you write, think to yourself, 'How am I going to say this?' Think like you talk and then write like you think," Hood says. "That way you can imagine yourself telling someone a story. For every sentence you write, ask yourself: 'Would I say it this way to my neighbor?' "

One way to write conversationally is to write simple sentences. Keep the subject and verb close together, and avoid extra clauses and phrases. "That doesn't mean 'See Jane, See Dick, See Spot run,' " Hood says. "It means write so people can understand it the first go-'round. Don't make the viewer try to figure it out."

Making things simple for the viewer isn't so simple for the writer, however. You gather much more information than you can use. "In broadcast writing one of the most important decisions you can make is not what you can put into your story, but what you have to leave out," Hood says. "A lot of facts in a newspaper story are not important to a TV story. What you end up doing is just giving a nugget of the most important information."

For example, the names, ages and addresses that you would include in a newspaper story might bog down a TV story. In one KUSA story, suspects in a kidnapping case were caught because neighbors videotaped the kidnapping attempt. "We decided that in the context of the story, the names of the suspects were not important. The important information was that neighbors video-taped it. If you use the names of all the people involved, by the end of the 25 seconds for the story, you have completely lost the viewer."

To judge how much they can say in seconds or minutes, KUSA-TV writers get some help from a sophisticated computer system. The computer has a timer that converts the number of words into the length of time it would take an average reader to say them.

But it doesn't help writers coordinate their stories with the video sound bites. That's another skill that newspaper writers don't have to contend with. However, there are some similarities between using sound bites and using quotes in a print story. Broadcast writers must avoid repeating what the source will say in a sound bite. That's like avoiding a stutter quote in a print story—giving a transition that repeats the quote. "Parroting what the subject will say is a cardinal sin," Hood says. "You enhance the pictures, not narrate them. You don't want to be a play-by-play announcer."

However, you do want to repeat some information in the story. Unlike a newspaper or magazine reader, who may stop reading and resume later, a broadcast viewer has to be listening. But the phone may ring, the kids may cry, and the dog may bark, says Hood. So when you write for broadcast, you need to repeat some information—the location of the story or the name of a key person—if that is crucial to the story.

For example, suppose a plane crashes. You tell where in the beginning of the story. But perhaps the viewer wasn't paying attention. Then, as you start talking about the crash or showing the scene, the viewer perks up. So you need to repeat the information in a different way. If you said in the lead that the plane crashed in Denver, in the middle you could make a reference to Denver police. If location isn't important, but a person or situation is, refer to those facts again in a subtle but clear way. Repetition is particularly important in stories about tragedy, Hood says. "Never leave the viewer wondering where it happened."

Here are some other basic writing tips:

Write in active voice. For example:

Active   Teachers in the Topeka School District are declaring an impasse tonight.

Passive   An impasse was declared by teachers in the Topeka school district tonight.

Use present tense whenever possible to give the story a sense of immediacy. For example:

Present tense   Democratic leaders in Congress are vowing quick action to guarantee a woman's right to abortion.

Past tense   Democratic leaders in Congress have vowed quick action to guarantee a woman's right to abortion.

But don't strain to convert a sentence to present tense. Use the tense that fits the story naturally. In the next example (with verbs underlined), the present tense is awkward because it is mixed with the past tense:

72 people <u>go</u> to jail after an abortion protest in Milwaukee <u>turned</u> disorderly.

It's better to use the past tense (or present tense) consistently:

72 people <u>went</u> to jail after an abortion protest in Milwaukee <u>turned</u> disorderly.

Avoid long introductory clauses. Favor simple sentences with subject-verb-object order, instead of using complex sentences.

Subject-verb order   43-thousand General Motors workers will be returning to work. A nine-day strike at a G-M assembly plant in Ohio ended a few hours ago. Members of a United Auto Workers local in Lordstown, Ohio, overwhelmingly approved a new contract. The local plant produced parts for nine other G-M assembly plants.

Introductory clause   After a nine-day strike at a General Motors assembly plant in Lordstown, Ohio, that idled 43-thousand workers nationwide, members of a United Auto Workers local overwhelmingly approved a new contract a few hours ago. The Ohio plant produced parts for nine other G-M assembly plants.

Put a human face on the story whenever possible. Try to find someone personally affected by the issue. You can start with the specific, using a person first and then going to the nut graph:

Iris Duncan woke up one morning and said she thought someone had put waxed paper over her eyes.

   SOUND BITE: It was all fuzzy and cloudy and I couldn't see. I had no idea what was wrong.

   She went to her doctor that afternoon. She learned she had glaucoma. The disease strikes one of every 200-thousand people.

Starting with a general statement and going to a specific person is less effective:

Glaucoma strikes one of every 200-thousand people.

   Iris Duncan is one of them. She woke up one morning and said she thought someone had put waxed paper over her eyes.

Tell who said something before telling what was said. If the attribution is delayed until the end of the sentence, the statement may sound as if it is the reporter's opinion.

Say   Police say a 42-year-old woman whose body was found in a Kansas City motel early this morning may be the latest victim of a serial killer.

Do not say   A 42-year-old woman whose body was found in a Kansas City motel early this morning may be the latest victim of a serial killer, police say.

Use contractions with caution. Write them out. Let the anchors contract them if they want to. Avoid *can't*. It may sound too much like *can*.

Use action verbs. Avoid sentences starting with "There is." Those are wasted words with a weak verb.

Weak verb   There is a new type of brain surgery that can cure epilepsy, a disease suffered by two-and-a-half-million Americans.

Stronger verb (and two simple sentences)   A new type of brain surgery can cure epilepsy. The disease affects two-and-a-half-million Americans.

Omit needless words. Words like *that, which* and *who is* aren't always needed.

Wordy   Investigators from Houston, Texas, are on their way to Tuscaloosa at this hour to help in the search for two Alabama men who are wanted in a mass killing.

Tighter (with action verb)   Investigators from Houston, Texas, flew to Tuscaloosa this morning to help search for two Alabama men wanted in a mass killing.

Limit the use of numbers. They can be numbing, especially to the ear. Use percentages to give comparisons, when possible. If you must use numbers, round them off. Say "320-million dollars," not "320-million-122-thousand-three-hundred-44 dollars." The style for writing numbers is explained later in the chapter.

In general, remember to keep your writing short and simple. Follow this advice from KSNT news director John Rinkenbaugh: "The shorter the message, the greater the impact."

Broadcast Versus Newspaper Writing

A broadcast package ends up being quite different from a newspaper story on the same issue. The following example compares treatment of the Supreme Court ruling on an abortion case. The day of the court's decision, KSNT reporter Rick Blum localized the story for the evening newscast. The story appeared in the newspaper the next morning. In the broadcast version, note the dashes in place of commas to indicate pauses and the minimal use of punctuation. The explanations in italics are not part of the script.

ABORTION
6/29/92

PKG LEAD-IN   **HELEN**   THE SUPREME COURT HAS RULED MOST OF A RESTRICTIVE PENNSYLVANIA ABORTION LAW PASSES CONSTITUTIONAL MUSTER.
GOOD EVENING AND THANK YOU FOR JOINING US.

ART   THE PANEL STOPPED JUST SHORT TODAY—OF OVERTURNING

HELEN	ROE VERSUS WADE—THE 19-73 DECISION LEGALIZING ABORTION.
	KSNT'S RICK BLUM REPORTS TODAY'S RULING CARRIES STRONG IMPLICATIONS NATIONALLY—BUT MAY NOT HAVE MUCH OF AN EFFECT IN THE SUNFLOWER STATE.
TAKE PKG (start reporter package)	TODAY'S FIVE-FOUR SUPREME COURT DECISION COULD MAKE ABORTION TOUGHER TO GET AROUND THE NATION.
	YET LOCAL WOMEN'S ORGANI-ZATIONS SEE HOPE IN TODAY'S RULING.
SUPER (sometimes labeled CG for character generator, the machine that creates the super):	BITE: (:09)
SARAH WOOD-CLARK PRESIDENT CAP CITY NOW	IN: 28:04 "IT IS A SURPRISE . . . OUT: 28:13 . . . AS WE THOUGHT."
SUPER: RICK BLUM KSNT TOPEKA	BOTH SIDES IN THE ABORTION BATTLE AT THE CAPITOL SAY THE RULING WILL SUPPORT BOTH THE RECENTLY PASSED BILL AND THE REASONS THEY WORKED FOR IT.
SUPER: GOVERNOR JOAN FINNEY	BITE: (:10) IN: 32:01 "I BELIEVE THIS IS . . . OUT: 32:11 . . . LAST SPRING."
SUPER: REP. KATHLEEN SEBELIUS (D) TOPEKA	BITE: (:12) IN: 23:17 "I AM PLEASED . . . OUT: 23:29 . . . PARTNERS."
	THE PENNSYLVANIA LAW UP-HELD BY THE SUPREME COURT HAS SOME PROVISIONS JUST LIKE THE KANSAS LAW. THEY INCLUDE INFORMED CONSENT OF THE PATIENT, A WAITING PERIOD AND PARENTAL CONSENT FOR MINORS.

BUT PRO-LIFE GROUPS SAY SINCE
ROE VERSUS WADE WAS NOT
OVERTURNED, THE POLITICAL
RAMIFICATIONS ARE MINIMAL.

SUPER: CYNTHIA PATTON
KANSANS FOR LIFE

BITE: (:10)
IN: 9:31 "I THINK THESE . . .
OUT: 9:41 . . . GOING TO HAPPEN
NOW."

BUT EVEN THOUGH ABORTION
MAY NOT HAVE SO MUCH POLITI-
CAL FIREPOWER THIS
YEAR—BOTH SIDES MAY NOT
HAVE LONG TO WAIT.
    A DECISION ON WHETHER ROE
VERSUS WADE IS CONSTITU-
TIONAL COULD COME BY THIS
TIME NEXT YEAR.
    RICK BLUM, KSNT NEWS, TO-
PEKA *(standard out cue, SOC, or re-*
porter signing off with the name
of the station)

# # #

The next morning, the *Topeka* (Kan.) *Capital-Journal* published on the front page one national story on the ruling, with a graphic outlining the way the Supreme Court justices voted, and another story of local reaction. Four more stories covered past decisions on abortion, future legislative battles, and ways the ruling reflects the conservative and moderate views of Supreme Court justices. The newspaper stories would have taken about 30 minutes to read aloud, compared to Blum's package of 1:30 minutes. Compare Blum's lead-in with the beginning of The Associated Press version and of the *Capital-Journal* reaction story:

A divided Supreme Court ruled Monday that states can't ban abortions, upholding the core of its Roe vs. Wade decision. But the court said the states may raise new hurdles for women seeking to end their pregnancies.

    The court, by a 5-4 vote, said women have a constitutional right to abortion. But a separate 7-2

coalition of justices substantially weakened the right as defined by the 1973 landmark ruling.

    Dramatically concluding its 1992 term, the court upheld most provisions of a restrictive Pennsylvania abortion law.

    Crowds of abortion-rights advocates and foes filled the plaza of the Supreme Court building for the court's latest, but surely not its last, word on this most divisive and emotional of national issues.

The decision not to abandon Roe vs. Wade was written by three conservative justices—Sandra Day O'Connor, Anthony M. Kennedy and, in his first vote on abortion since he was appointed by President Bush, David H. Souter.

The other Bush appointee, Justice Clarence Thomas, was one of the four who voted to let states outlaw virtually all abortions.

The decision lets states, among other things, instruct women seeking abortions on the available alternatives, and to make them wait 24 hours after receiving such information.

The Associated Press

The story continues with more detail. Note the use of clauses and specifics in the newspaper version, compared to the short, clipped broadcast version.

Here is the local reaction story:

Gov. Joan Finney said Monday she knows of no facet of the state's new abortion law, which goes into effect Wednesday, that would be altered by a U.S. Supreme Court decision on a much stricter Pennsylvania law.

"I have some information on the decision, and from what I can tell now, there is apparently no effect on our law," Finney said.

Attorney General Bob Stephan, anti-abortion and prochoice activists, and several state lawmakers instrumental in passage of the Kansas law said it is apparently untouched by the high court decision.

The court upheld the basic premise of Roe vs. Wade but

created some new areas in which states can move to restrict access to abortion.

"This issue isn't over," Finney said. "I don't know what the Legislature will propose next year in terms of abortion legislation, but I have said and I'll stick to my promise that I will not initiate any abortion legislation myself."

Stephan said he will have to study the full opinion on the Pennsylvania case, but "from its highlights, I don't see any real changes, except for a section that is somewhat troubling about the reporting of abortions."

Martin Hawver, *Topeka Capital-Journal*

The story continues with reactions from pro-choice and anti-abortion advocates and Kansas legislators. As you can see, the writing styles differ considerably.

The Writing Process

The coaching process used for newspaper writing can apply to broadcast writing as well. And although television writing is stressed here, most of these tips also apply to radio writing:

1 Conceive: In addition to planning a story for its verbal content, you must consider its visual impact. Will your story contain sound bites from sources on camera, action at the scene or graphics to superimpose on the screen? Will the story contain a reporter "standup" (talking on camera)?

2 Collect: Just as with reporting for a print story, you need to gather more information than you can use. You don't need to describe a source or scene that will be shown on the screen, but you should gather other details about the scene of an accident, disaster or breaking news event. Make sure you get the correct spelling and titles of your sources so their names can be superimposed on the screen.

3 Construct: For broadcast writing, as in newspaper or magazine writing, you need to plan your story like a road map. But with only 30 to 90 seconds to tell the story, it isn't a long-distance trip. Selectivity is even more important in broadcast writing because you have so little time to tell the story. Start with a focus sentence to guide you. Jot down the most important idea you want to express. Then review your notes and select only a few other key points to include in an average 90-second story. As Hood suggests, consider what you can leave out. You can eliminate much of the detail you would write for a newspaper. Pictures and sound bites will take their place.

4 Correct: After you have written your story, edit it to remove unnecessary words, and then read it aloud.

Story Structure

Like a newspaper story, a broadcast story has a lead, a body, and an ending. In many respects, they are the same in both media. But the differences are important.

Lead Every story needs its own lead. Max Utsler, a broadcast journalism professor at the University of Kansas, said the No. 1 consideration for a lead is that it must fit the pictures the viewer sees. "Good television writing is not the craftsmanship of words; it is the presentation of the words and pictures fitting together," he said.

Once you have decided which pictures to use at the beginning of your package, you can decide whether the story needs a hard or soft lead. That decision will also depend on the content of your story. Feature stories may take softer leads; a breaking-news story calls for a very direct approach. In all cases, you must get to the nut graph—the main reason for the story—very quickly, generally by the second or third sentence.

Regardless of the type of lead, most of the basic news elements—who, what, when, where, why, how, so what—must be included in the story. But you can't include all of them in a simple, coherent sentence for the lead. So select the ones that are most important to your story.

In broadcast writing, the placement of points of emphasis for these elements often differs from print journalism. The most common elements to stress in a broadcast lead are where, when and who; why and how often take too long to explain in a simple sentence. Here are some ways to use these elements in hard-news leads:

Where: Because most radio and television stations reach such a broad audience, the location of a story is even more important in broadcast than in print. Newspapers can use datelines to indicate location. Broadcast reports can superimpose the name of the location on the screen, but you also need to say it in the story. If the story follows a series of other stories from different regions, you might start it this way:

> In Pawtucket, Rhode Island, police are looking into the suspicious death of a 15-month-old baby.

When: Almost all broadcast stories, except features, have a "today" element. Avoid using *a.m.* or *p.m.* If the specific time element is important, say something like "An earthquake struck Southern California at 7:15 this morning." In most cases, a general reference, such as "this morning" or "earlier today," is sufficient. Place your time element after the verb, which is more natural, conversational order:

Awkward At least five people today were arrested in an anti-abortion protest outside a Milwaukee clinic.

Preferred At least five people were arrested today in an anti-abortion protest outside a Milwaukee clinic.

Who: Identify a speaker by title before the name:

Say African National Congress leader Nelson Mandela said today his supporters would ignore any state-of-emergency conditions imposed by the South African government.

Do not say Nelson Mandela, leader of the African National Congress . . .

Avoid using unfamiliar names in a lead and too many names in a story. When you have video sound bites, you may not even need the name in the story. The person can be identified by a superimposed title under his or her image in the taped segment.

For a delayed identification, follow the same guidelines as for print journalism. Identify the person by an age, a location, an occupation or some other generic identifier. Then follow with the person's name:

One of two suspects in the fatal kidnapping of Exxon executive Sidney Reso (Ree-Soh) has pleaded guilty.

Irene Seale entered the plea to charges of extortion and conspiracy to commit extortion.

She appeared in court in Newark, New Jersey.

The Associated Press

Not all stories directly affect viewers' lives. But when possible, try to stress the impact within the first few sentences. Use an element that will make viewers care or understand why this story is important, unusual or of human interest. Don't be afraid to use the pronoun *you,* especially in consumer stories, to heighten impact. Instead of writing a story about a drought in California that will cause lettuce prices to increase, try this approach:

You're about to pay more for your salad. A drought in California is raising the price of lettuce.

When you can, "advance the lead"—that is, stress the next step—to gain immediacy.

Immediacy   Two people remain in serious condition following a car accident this afternoon.

No immediacy   Two people were injured in a car accident today.

The focus-on-a-person lead works as well in broadcast as in print, especially for a feature or a news story that the anchor introduces with a hard-news lead-in. Like the *Wall Street Journal* formula, this type of lead goes from the specific to the general. The person is one of many affected by the problem.

Judy and Joe Westbrook spent the morning cleaning up the furniture in their front yard. The Blue River had overflowed its banks and forced its way into their Independence home.

More than 25 families share their predicament. Late this afternoon all of those families were awaiting word about their flood insurance claims.

The mystery-teaser lead is another effective soft-lead technique, as long as you don't keep the viewer wondering what the story is about for too long. You must get to the point within the first few sentences.

In some ways it looks like an ordinary camp. It has hiking trails, a swimming pool and tennis courts.

But you don't have to worry about what clothes to wear. In fact, this is one of the few places where you'll feel out of place wearing clothes.

At this camp near Denver men and women of all ages frolic in the nude.

SOUND BITE: Nudism is about the only recreation that anybody can do whether they're rich or poor. We all share in the same satisfaction, so it's a very great equalizer.

Adapted from NBC News Channel

Body   As with all story structures, you first identify your focus. Then jot down the order of your supporting points—facts or quotes from sources in sound bites.

Limit transitions. One point should follow another one naturally. You have little time for wasted words or redundant transitions that parrot what the source will say in a sound bite. If you need transitions from the present to the past in your story, you can start the sentence with the time element—"yesterday" or "earlier today," for example.

One common transition device in broadcast news is the key-word technique, picking up on a word in the last sentence and repeating it in the next. It's also a useful technique for bridging thought from one story to the next in the newscast. In this example, the reporter uses the word *shoes* as a transition device for the next paragraph:

The Nike commercial touts Michael Jordan's basketball prowess. Spike Lee says it's gotta be the shoes.

But Mike and his buddies wouldn't even have to wear shoes to waltz to the Olympic gold.

Some of the story structures described in Chapter 12 can apply to broadcast writing as well as print. However, because of the need for simplicity and brevity, the structure of broadcast news stories should be guided more by conversational storytelling than by rigid form. Here are some ways of organizing broadcast stories:

Problem/solution: The most common structure starts with a statement of the problem, provides support in sound bites and facts, offers background, and discusses the solutions if any exist. It often ends with the next step in the action.

Statement of problem   Three-hundred Korean-American merchants demonstrated for the sixth straight day in Los Angeles. They're demanding they be reimbursed for their losses resulting from the L-A riots.

Background   The merchants held up signs and chanted outside L-A's City Hall. They're particularly upset about a rebuilding ordinance passed by the City Council. The law allows stores destroyed in the riots to skip the usual 75-day process to obtain a building permit. But the law does not apply to liquor stores and gun shops.

Future tag: next step   The merchants are also considering a hunger strike.

NBC News Channel

The next example starts with an impact lead, offering the solution to a problem that has been resolved. Then it provides support for the lead, followed by background.

Impact: solution to a problem   If you took your car to Sears for repairs in the past two years, you may get a re-fund.

Support for lead   The company agreed to settle charges that it cheated customers by doing shoddy or unnecessary car repair work.

An estimated 12-thousand-500 Missourians will be eligible to receive 50-dollar credit coupons for any Sears merchandise.

Background   The alleged problems took place between August of 1990 and January 31st of this year.

Time sequence: A story may lend itself to order by time. Since broadcast stories need immediacy, the time sequence is usually a reverse chronology that starts with the present action, goes to the past (background) and ends with a future element. Here is an example of reverse chronology:

Present   Animal-rights activists are protesting this morning outside the Pittsburgh hospital where doctors transplanted a liver from a baboon to save a man's life.

Past (background)   About 15 protesters carried signs and chanted at the entrance to the University of Pittsburgh Medical Center. One member of the Pittsburgh Animal Activists says they don't believe one species should be sacrificed for another.

Pickets are holding signs saying, "There are no lesser creatures" and "Animals are not expendable."

Future   Doctors say if their patient continues to recover for the next month or more, they'll do three more of the same transplants.

The Associated Press

Hourglass: This structure is a type of time sequence. However, you start with a hard-news summary lead and then rebuild the story chronologically:

Summary lead A toxic chemical spill near Superior, Wisconsin, forced hundreds of residents from two cities to flee their homes. At least two children received hospital treatment. A hospital official says more people will need treatment.

Beginning of chronology The problems began this morning when 13 freight cars derailed just outside Superior. One Burlington Northern car fell into the Nemadji (Neh-Ma'-Jee) River, spilling some of its cargo of benzene. Benzene is a flammable solvent, and its fumes can cause hallucinations, dizziness and coughing.

In Superior and neighboring Duluth, Minnesota, officials ordered the evacuation of hundreds of homes within a mile of the river. And the Coast Guard says it's placed a boom across Superior Bay to prevent the benzene from spreading.
The Associated Press

Circle: Envision your story as a circle. The main point is the lead. All supporting points should relate to the focus in the lead. Unlike an inverted pyramid, where points are placed in descending order of importance, in a circular construction, each part of the story is equally important. Your ending can refer back to a point in the lead, as in this example about a water problem in a Kansas community:

Lead If you live near Baldwin City, you may want to avoid drinking the water tonight.

Supporting points The Kansas Department of Health and Environment is warning folks in Water District No. 2 in Douglas County about the water. Officials found bacteria in the water which may be harmful.

SOUND BITE (from Greg Crawford, an official with the Kansas Department of Health and Environment): These are indicator bacteria which may indicate the presence of more serious bacteria. Bacteria can cause a number of gastro-intestinal problems. And we would like people to prevent those problems by boiling their water or using bottled water or perhaps treating their water with Clorox or other liquid bleach.

Crawford says bacteria come from dead animals. Until officials can clear up

Ending referring back to lead the problems, people in the area should take precautions.
KSNT-TV

Ending In broadcast writing, endings are called "tags" or "wrap-ups." Newspaper stories often end with a quote from a source, but in broadcast writing, the reporter has the last word in a package, followed by her or his name and the station identification. Often the only time the viewer sees the reporter is at the end of the story. However, many news directors now prefer using reporter standups within the story rather than at the end.

The most common endings:

Summary: A fact that reinforces the main idea without repeating previous points.

Future: The next step in some action.

Factual: A background statement or just another fact.

Consumer: Helpful items, such as where to call or go for additional information. If this information is important to the viewer, avoid giving it only one time. Warn the viewer that you will be repeating telephone numbers or locations later in the program.

Teasers and Lead-ins

A "teaser" is a few sentences to entice the viewer to stay tuned for the story that will come on the next newscast or after the commercial. (A teaser before a commercial is also called a "bump" or "bumper" at some stations.) A "lead-in" is the anchor's introduction to a story that a reporter will present.

Although teasers and lead-ins precede the story, they are written by the producer or anchor after the reporter turns in the story.

The concept behind all these promotional briefs is "Stay tuned, you'll want to hear this." Use the tell-a-friend technique, as though you were saying "Guess what?" or "You won't believe what happened." Write one to three brief sentences that are enticing enough to arouse curiosity.

Here is a teaser for a 10 p.m. newscast:

Coming up on the KSNT news at ten . . .

Diedra Davis will tell us about a group of city leaders coming together to fight crime in Topeka . . .

And . . .

You're never too young to learn the dangers of smoking . . .

We'll show you how one program is teaching pre-school children how to stay smoke-free . . .

These stories and more coming up on the KSNT news at ten.
KSNT-TV

A teaser before the commercial break can be preceded by such phrases as "Just ahead," "Still to come," "When we continue," "Stay tuned." Or you can end the bump with the statement "We'll have that story for you when we come back." Sometimes stations do a teaser and end with "But first . . ." Here are two examples of a teaser before a break:

A battle over the French abortion pill heads to the U.S. Supreme Court. Stay tuned.

Earthquake aftershocks rattle Southern California. We'll have the details on the damage and the cleanup when we come back.

Sometimes fragments can get the point across better than complete sentences. Teasers especially lend themselves to phrases without verbs:

In a moment . . . sex behind bars. A scandal brewing in Georgia.
CNN

Lead-ins immediately precede the story package by a reporter. They are written more like a lead to a story, but they should not repeat the reporter's lead. The lead-in gives the essence of the story, like a focus line, and ends with a statement that the reporter, usually cited by name, has more:

Many women exercise hard to get in shape. But a new study says too much exercise can often lead to serious health problems for women. Ileana Bravo tells us how some female college athletes could suffer from eating disorders as a result . . .
NBC News Channel

Here is how one NBC promo would vary depending on how it was used:

Teaser for next newscast Patients of a dentist who died recently are very concerned over the news that his death was due to AIDS. Phones are ringing off the hook at the local health department in Bowling Green concerning Dr. Donald Hewitt. We'll have that story and more for you on our 6 o'clock newscast.

Teaser before commercial Patients of a dentist who died recently are very concerned over the news that his death was due to AIDS. Phones are ringing off the hook at the local health department in Bowling Green concerning Dr. Donald Hewitt. We'll have that story when we come back.

Lead-in Patients of a dentist who died recently are very concerned over the news that his death was due to AIDS. Phones are ringing off the hook at the local health department in Bowling Green concerning Dr. Donald Hewitt. Reporter Mike O'Connell has more.

Just ahead you'll learn how to write a reporter package with directions for a newscast. But first . . .

Copy Preparation and Style

Broadcast copy differs considerably from newspaper copy. When writing copy to be read aloud, punctuation changes. Everything should be written so the anchors or reporters can read it easily. The less punctuation, the easier it is to read. Although many producers use points of ellipsis (three dots) to indicate pauses, broadcast professor Max Utsler says the comma, semicolon or dash is preferable. "Ellipses tend to lead to run-on sentences," he says. "If you want a short pause, use a comma; for a longer pause, use a dash. Even better, write short sentences and use periods."

Some of the rules for copy preparation differ from station to station. For example, although many stations use capital letters for both text and directions, others use lowercase and uppercase letters for story text or just for the sound bites. You will have to adapt to the news director's preferences.

Here are some general guidelines:

• Give the story a "slug" (a one- or two-word title), and write it at the top left-hand corner of each page. Follow it with the date and the name or initials of the writer. Put a slug on every page. If the same story continues for several pages, use that title. When the story changes, use a new slug for that story.

• Double- or triple-space all copy. Write on only one side of the page. However, single-space directions on the left side of the page.

• Number every page. If a story continues to another page, you may prefer to number it 1A, 1B, and so on until the next story, which would start with the number 2.

• Use a separate page for each story, including briefs or teasers. If a story continues on another page, write *More* in parentheses or set off by dashes at the bottom of the page. Mark the end of the story with a # # # symbol or *(End)* or *-30-*.

• Use capital letters for instructions to the director; type them on the left side of the page. For computer copy, you will need a two-column format.

• Type the story on the right side of the page in a column approximately 3 inches wide. Capital letters are preferred by many news directors and producers for this copy also, but not universally.

• Indent paragraphs.

• Do not split and hyphenate words at the end of a sentence. Let the anchor see the whole word.

• Use dashes for pauses.

• If you have a typo or need to change a word, cross out the mistake completely by typing X's over it or blacking it out with pencil. Write the correct word next to it. Do not cross out part of a word for a correction. That makes the copy difficult to read. Strive for clean copy.

• Set off sound bites with double lines above and below the bite.

Punctuation Avoid quotation marks. Generally, sound bites take the place of quotations. But if you want to quote someone, write out the word *quote* in this way: "She said . . . quote . . . this situation is impossible" or "and these are her exact words . . ." Don't bother with *unquote* or end marks. The reader's emphasis should make the end of the quote clear.

Limit punctuation to the comma, period, question mark and dash.

Numbers Write out the numbers one through nine; use numerals for numbers over 10. Write out *hundred, thousand, million, billion* and *trillion.* Round off numbers when possible.

Write numbers to be read, as follows:

"13-hundred, two-thousand, 14-thousand, one-million, 17-million." More complicated numbers would be written this way: "320-thousand," not "320,000"; "15-million-230-thousand," not "15,230,000."

For decimals, write out the word *point:* "It comes to 17-point-two-million dollars." Write out the word *dollars* also, instead of the symbol.

There are some exceptions. Addresses, telephone numbers and time of day are written in numerals, even if the figures are lower than 10: "She lives at 5 Westbrooke Avenue"; "The accident occurred at 10:30 this morning" (avoid *a.m.* and *p.m.*); "The telephone number to call for information is 5-5-5-1-2-3-4" (separate the numerals with dashes so they are easier to read).

Names and titles Spell difficult pronunciations of names and locations phonetically. Some anchors prefer only the phonetic spelling instead of the real name followed by the phonetic pronunciation. For example, KUSA producer Leona Hood's name would be pronounced *Lee-Ahna Hood,* and KSNT reporter Rick Blum's name would be written *Rick Bloom.*

Identify a person's title before the name: "Secretary of Labor Lynn Martin is pleased with the results of a crackdown on fraudulent coal dust testing," not "Lynn Martin, secretary of labor, is pleased with the results . . . ."

Using Broadcast Terms

Before you can write your own story or newscast, you need to understand some basic terms. Some of these have already been mentioned.

Anchor: Reads the news.

Backtiming: Exact time in the newscast that a segment will air. For example, a story that will air 12 minutes and 15 seconds into the newscast will be labeled 12:15. If the last segment in a 30-minute newscast is one minute, the backtiming will be 29, alerting the anchor that the segment must start at precisely that time or it will have to be cut.

Brief: Abbreviated news story, from 10 to 20 seconds.

Bump: "Stay-tuned" teaser before a commercial, to entice viewers to continue watching the broadcast for stories that will follow after the break.

Character generator: Computer-type machine that produces the letters, numbers or words superimposed on the screen to label a visual image, such as a person or place.

IN: Indicates the first few words of the source's quote to start a sound bite.

News director: Oversees all news operations at the station.

OUT: Indicates the last few words of the source's quote, ending the sound bite.

Package: Reporter's story that includes narration, visual images and interviews with sources.

Producer: Writes the copy that anchors read for the newscast.

Reader: Story the anchor reads without visuals or sound bites.

Rip-and-read: Copy from the wire services that is read exactly as it was written instead of being rewritten.

Seg time: Length of time for a news segment. Brief may be :10, or 10 seconds; reporter's package, including the lead-in by an anchor, may be 1:45.

SOC (standard out cue): Reporter's sign-off comments at the end of the story. For example, "This is Rick Blum for KSNT TOPEKA."

SOT (sound on tape): Similar to a sound bite; indicated in copy along with the amount of time the taped comments will take. For example, *SOT:15* means the comments on the tape will take 15 seconds.

Sound bite: Video segment showing the source speaking.

Super: Letters, numbers or words produced by the character generator and superimposed over visual images; often used to identify the person appearing on the tape. At some stations, the letters *CG*—for character generator—are used to indicate the super.

Teaser: Introduction to a story on the next newscast, to tease viewers to tune in.

TelePrompTer: Video terminal that displays the script for the anchor to read.

VO (voice over): Anchor's voice over video images. Words and images should coincide.

VOB (voice over bite): Anchor's voice over video images with a sound bite from a source.

Writing a Package

The example in this section is a reporter's package from KUSA-TV in Denver. The story is slugged *POW*—for "Person of the Week," a regular feature at the station. It focuses on a person who had a great impact in the community that week.

Note that the directions for the anchor and technical crew are on the left and the story text is on the right. The story text is in capital letters. The explanations in italics were not in the package.

This story is about a teen-ager who died trying to save his mother and sister. The shooting happened on a Monday; the package aired on Friday during the regular POW segment. It ran 2:35 minutes, which is longer than the normal 1:30 minutes.

KUSA writes out sound bites for close-captioned television so hearing-impaired people can see the words. Generally, you would just introduce the sound bites in copy with the first three words and last three words.

The story is labeled *G* because it comes in the G segment of this broadcast. At KUSA, segments A through C are for news, D for weather, F for sports and G for a special feature. The last story is H.

Ed is Ed Sardella, the anchor who is reading this package.

The word *BOX* indicates that a super with the name and picture of the person of the week, Kevin Woodson, will appear over Sardella's shoulder, even though the story does not mention Woodson's last name until the end.

This story was introduced by a teaser saying, "Coming up, we'll introduce you to our person of the week."

Note the style: double-space for copy, single-space for directions.

ED ON BOX

POW (graphic called box appears over Sardella's shoulder, containing name of Kevin Woodson and slug Person of the Week; anchor's introduction to story)

───────── G-1 ─────────

DOMESTIC VIOLENCE TOO OFTEN CHOOSES THE INNOCENT TO BE ITS VICTIM. TOO OFTEN, IT DESTROYS FAMILIES—THIS WEEK, IT TOOK ANOTHER.

A MOTHER IS DEAD. HER 15-YEAR-OLD SON DID WHAT HE COULD TO PROTECT HIS MOTHER AND HIS SISTER. BUT HE LOST HIS LIFE TOO.

HE IS OUR 9 NEWS PERSON OF THE WEEK.

TAKE PKG ─────────────

(start taped package)

(NAT—BEST FRIEND)

(FRIENDS ARRIVING)

(anchor reading all words in capital letters; **NAT** means natural sound, in this case of friends arriving at house; G-2 means next part of this segment)

───────**TAKE PKG**───────

───────── G-2 ─────────

SHOCK AND HORROR SHATTERED A QUIET MONDAY MORNING. FRIENDS WERE OVERWHELMED WITH GRIEF. TRACY STUART AND HER SON KEVIN WERE DEAD. POLICE SAY TRACY'S HUSBAND RAY STUART BROKE INTO THEIR HOME AND KILLED HER FIRST. KEVIN GRABBED A GUN AND TRIED TO STOP HIM; TRYING TO PROTECT HIS MOTHER AND SISTER. HE DIDN'T KNOW HIS MOTHER MIGHT ALREADY BE DEAD.

KEVIN SHOT HIS STEP-FATHER. BUT STUART FIRED BACK, AND KILLED KEVIN.

A TRAGIC LOSS OF LIFE.

FUNERAL TAPE #1

(file tape)

Teachers work and work and work and they find some students coming to leadership, and zap they're gone.

CG KAREN SCOTT

KEVIN'S TEACHER

5:13-5:18

(CG means character generator, to superimpose name under person speaking in sound bite; numbers are location of sound bite on tape; bite is 5 seconds long)
TAPE TOWN SHOTS
(anchor resumes reading)

Why do we have to lose young people of youth like this, this is what we need for our country, for our little town.

IN THIS LITTLE TOWN, KEVIN WAS A TYPICAL TEENAGER. HE LOVED SPORTS, ESPECIALLY BASKETBALL AND BASEBALL.

FUNERAL TAPE #2
CG SHAWN LOTTMAN
KEVIN'S BEST FRIEND

He was always playing first, and I was over at 3rd, and I threw at the ground in practice and hit him in the nose, and he's always been giving me heck about that all the time.

CG MIKE GRANDSTAFF
SCHOOL PRINCIPAL

Pretty solid athlete, he made a turn around from an average student to an honor roll student.

A lot of growth in the last couple of years from Kevin, he really tried to take care of his mom and sister.

BYERS SHOOTING #2
(anchor resumes over tape of shooting in Byers, Colo.)

HIS FRIENDS SAY HE NEVER LET ANYONE TEASE HIS SISTER TRISHIA. THEY STUCK TOGETHER. SHE CRIED OUT FOR HIM, WHEN THE SHOTS WERE FIRED MONDAY.

CG BARBARA ALEXANDER
VICTIM'S ASSISTANCE
COUNSELOR

Her brother was her protector. She felt like her brother was there for her. She has a feeling her brother may have saved her life.

FUNERAL TAPE #2
(anchor resumes over pictures of funeral tape)

BUT HE WAS UNABLE TO SAVE HIS OWN. AND WHILE FRIENDS MOURN HIS DEATH, THEY ALSO REMEMBER KEVIN THEIR FRIEND.

CG KEN LOTTMAN
KEVIN'S BASEBALL COACH

Always a person with a smile on his face, and always there for anybody.

The smile, and his energy, the leadership.

They will remember him as an athlete and friend. We'll still have tournament games and as of now, we'll go on with that, I think they will handle it, and play for Kevin—that's what they'll do.

BYERS TAPE
(FLOWERS IN FRONT OF HOUSE)
ED SINGLE

(anchor finishes package,
with camera on him)

THEY WILL REMEMBER KEVIN, A YOUNG MAN WHO HAD SO MUCH LIFE AHEAD. BUT RISKED IT ALL FOR HIS MOTHER AND SISTER. KEVIN WOODSON IS OUR 9 NEWS PERSON OF THE WEEK.

KEVIN'S SISTER, TRISHIA, IS 13. SHE IS GOING TO LIVE WITH HER AUNT IN LONGMONT. A FUND HAS BEEN SET UP FOR HER AT THE BYERS STATE BANK.

# # #

Activities

1 Write a broadcast brief, about 15 seconds, based on this information from an NBC News Channel story:

Who: A consumer group, the Florida Consumer's Federation

What: Filed a suit charging the Publix Grocery Store chain with discrimination

Why: Group claims that the grocery chain failed to put enough women, blacks and Hispanics in management jobs and that the company doesn't have enough stores in minority neighborhoods.

When: Today

Backup information: Publix management agrees with some of the complaints but says it is working to overcome them, according to Publix president Mark Hollis.

2 Write a broadcast package based on the following newspaper story. Write the quotes you want to use in sound bite form; estimate the time of the sound bites.

A 16-year-old boy, driving without a license, led Louisville police on a 13-minute chase yesterday afternoon, driving at up to 80 mph on streets in the Highlands sections where the sidewalks were crowded with pedestrians.

The pursuit ended at 5:05 p.m., when the boy—whose name police did not release because of his age—rammed his father's 1991 Honda Accord into the rear of Officer Bob Arnold's patrol car on Trevilian Way just east of Valley Vista.

No one was injured, and the police car suffered only a minor scrape on the rear bumper. The other car was damaged more.

Officer John Butts said the chase started near Cherokee Park when he tried to stop the boy for running over a stop sign, and the boy refused to pull over. Butts radioed for help and Arnold joined the chase.

"I was concerned, because he came close to hitting several pedestrians who were out walking because of the nice weather," Butts said last night.

"Anxiety sets in when a chase continues on for this amount of time," he added. "It's longer than any officer would prefer to be in a high-speed vehicle pursuit."

Butts said the boy forced several cars off the road during the chase, which came to an end when Arnold managed to get in front of the boy and slowed down.

He said the boy will be charged with numerous felonies and traffic violations; among the charges are wanton endangerment and resisting arrest. The boy was taken to the Jefferson County Youth Center.

Butts said he did not know why the boy refused to stop, but added, "He has no license, and he was not supposed to be driving his father's car."

The Louisville (Ky.) Courier-Journal

3 Design a newscast from your local newspaper. Choose 10 to 12 stories for your newscast. Decide which ones should be briefs and which should be longer packages. List the stories in the order you would present them: by topics, location, significance or a combination.

4 Cover an event on campus, and write it up as a broadcast package. Write your quotes as sound bites.

5 Write a teaser for the "Person in the News" story in this chapter.

6 Write lead-ins for the stories in this chapter in the "Body" section.

7 Choose three stories from your local newspaper and write teasers, leads and lead-ins for them.

FOUR

Understanding Media Issues

Accuracy and Libel

Ethics

Multicultural Sensitivity

COACHING

Seek documents to substantiate source's claims.

Check resumes and other materials from sources.

Seek other sources with alternate points of view.

Role-play: If you were the source or the source's attorney, what would you find libelous or objectionable in the story?

Accuracy and Libel **17**

M *iami Herald* reporter Paul Shannon thought the tip he received from a teacher would make a good story. A 10-year-old child in Fort Lauderdale, Fla., was dying from sickle-cell anemia. Her mother, a Bahamian citizen, wanted to be by her side when she died. But the mother's visa had expired, and U.S. immigration officials were trying to deport her.

Shannon began to check out the story. He visited the mother and her daughter at their apartment. The mother showed him documents, including a letter from a doctor confirming that the child had this incurable disease and a letter from a university clinic. The child talked about her blood transfusions and the trances during severe attacks of the disease when she would almost lose consciousness.

Shannon returned to the newsroom and called the doctor, who confirmed that the child had sickle-cell anemia. Then the doctor's beeper sounded and he had to hang up, but he promised to call back later.

Shannon checked with the child's school principal and a woman in the mother's prayer group. "It is a sad story," the woman said. Then he called some local medical experts.

If the trancelike seizures are coming often, her life expectancy is very short, one expert said.

Deadline was approaching. Shannon began drafting his lead:

There is no such thing as a minor mistake, not even just one or two little errors in a lengthy manuscript.

Steve Weinberg, former director, Investigative Reporters and Editors, Inc.

In the clinical jargon of doctors, 10-year-old Celestial Jones has a short life expectancy.

She will change in the matter of a few months from a giggling little girl to one bent over and bedridden like a very old woman. The trance-like seizures have already begun. As her immune system is slowly sapped, the infections will start, one after another. Then comes the crippling stroke.

Finally, unless the crisis mysteriously fades, Celestial will die. Her mother wants to be at her bedside.

Paul Shannon, *The IRE Journal*

He told his editors he would have the rest of the story in 15 minutes.

Shannon had talked to immigration officials. One promised to reopen the case so the mother could have a hearing.

Then the child's doctor returned his call. Shannon read his lead to the doctor to check its accuracy. "I don't believe that is correct," the doctor said. The disease was in remission, he said. It might not return until the child was in her forties. He added: The child fakes her trances; she has major psychological problems.

Shannon spiked the story. Three weeks later, the local competition ran a story with this lead:

Sometimes, when the pain becomes too much for her to bear, Celestial Jones loses consciousness.

Nowhere in the story was the doctor quoted. Apparently he could not be reached for comment.

Shannon, who recounted the experience in an article in *The IRE Journal*, a publication of the Investigative Reporters and Editors organization, said one of his editors had suggested writing a story about how the mother was trying to deceive immigration officials, but the idea was discarded.

How do you know when a story is inaccurate? You don't unless you check it out. It's easy to be fooled, especially when you're dealing with emotional stories. Make one more phone call. Check one more document. And when you can't reach someone for comment, try and try again.

Deadline pressure, especially for breaking news, may force you to run the story when some key source can't be reached for comment. You should say that in the story so the reader knows you tried. But one try isn't enough.

The Importance of Accuracy

Accuracy is paramount for a good journalist. Every mistake you make jeopardizes the newspaper's credibility with readers. Because of that credibility factor, newspapers throughout the country print corrections every day, many for the incorrect spelling of names. That's another reason why you should always double-check the names in your stories.

Imagine how you would feel if you were fined $25 every time you misspelled a name or wrote an inaccurate fact. That's the policy instituted in 1991 by the editor of *The Quill,* a magazine published by The Society of Professional Journalists, to stress the importance of accuracy to contributing writers.

You won't be fined at a newspaper, but you could be fired for inaccuracy. Inaccurate stories can lead to lawsuits.

Checking Information

ABC television reporter Mark Potter found out the hard way how important it is to check not only names but also information on resumes. He was reporting a story about a drug rehabilitation counselor in Detroit who said he was an All-American football player in college. Potter and his camera crew completed the interviewing and taping for the story. Then Potter returned to his home base in Miami and called the university to get some tape of the former football star in college. The university had never heard of the man. Potter killed the story. He said he could have kicked himself for not checking the man's resume before he and the camera crew went to Detroit.

Some sources falsify their resumes to make themselves look better; other sources use the media to serve their own purposes.

Reporters at *The Arizona Republic/Phoenix Gazette* found themselves subject to both situations in 1986. Darrow "Duke" Tully, the newspaper's publisher, had bragged for many years about his impressive record of service with the U.S. Air Force as a fighter pilot and as a lieutenant colonel in the reserves. He said he had been shot down during the Korean War in 1952, had flown 100 missions in Vietnam and had earned innumerable medals, including the Purple Heart and Vietnam Gallantry Cross. He was often photographed in his medal-studded Air Force uniform at various functions.

But the county attorney serving the Phoenix area had some doubts. The newspaper had been publishing a series of stories criticizing the attorney, Tom Collins, for his "free-spending" use of his government expense account. Collins claimed the newspaper was conducting a smear campaign. So he investigated the publisher's background.

On Dec. 26, 1986, Collins announced at a press conference that Tully had never served in the military. Tully, aware of the forthcoming revelations, had resigned as publisher shortly before the press conference. He later confessed that he had fabricated his military record nearly 30 years earlier to help him gain promotions, and over the years the lies just mushroomed. The medals and uniform that he wore so proudly were purchased in a San Francisco uniform shop.

Tully had his motives for lying; Collins had his motives for exposing the lies. To its chagrin, the newspaper got caught in the middle.

You don't have to suspect everyone of lying, including your own publisher. However, you should make an effort to check documents and seek balance in your stories. And you should realize that many sources, especially politicians, try to use the media to promote their own agendas.

Journalist Bill Moyers said in a speech shortly after he resigned as President Lyndon Johnson's press secretary: "Time and time again I am asked: Do presidents really lie? And press secretaries? I reply: Before there were presidents and press secretaries, there were Adam and Eve, and there is a little of each of them in all of us."

Moyers said that although government officials have a credibility problem, so do the media because of inaccuracy. "Nothing undermines the credibility of the press like sloppy reporting." In fact, most problems with inaccuracy result not from sources but from carelessness.

Showing Copy to Sources

Paul Shannon checked the accuracy of his information by reading the lead of his would-be story to the doctor. Should you show your story to sources or read it to them before you print it? Many of your sources will ask you to do that.

And many editors will say you shouldn't. They claim the risks are too great that sources will recant what they have told you or ask you to delete any information that puts them in a bad light.

Steve Weinberg, former director of Investigative Reporters and Editors and a leading authority on researching records, says it's time to change that traditional way of thinking. "I am convinced that my practice of pre-publication readbacks and manuscript submission has led to more accurate, fair and thorough newspaper pieces, magazine articles, and books," he wrote in *The Quill*.

While working on an unauthorized biography of industrialist Armand Hammer, Weinberg asked about 300 of his sources to check the accuracy of portions of the manuscript in which they were quoted or cited. As a result of his checks, he identified two errors in his 1,000-page manuscript. "There is no such thing as a minor mistake, not even just one or two little errors in a lengthy manuscript," he wrote.

Weinberg makes it clear that the source who is checking the story has the right only to check for accuracy, not to make any changes.

If you don't show the entire story to your source, it is considered acceptable—even wise—to check with a source any technical information you may not fully understand. You can read what you have written and, like Weinberg, ask the source to check its accuracy.

If you are sure your information is accurate and you don't want to read the information to sources before publication, you could try this suggestion from Bill Marimow, two-time winner of the Pulitzer Prize. Marimow, assistant to the publisher of *The Philadelphia Inquirer,* suggests calling a source the day after the story is published and asking if the story was accurate and fair. He claims that call will deepen the source's respect for you, and the source may even give you information for a follow-up story.

Several newspapers also check reporters' accuracy by contacting sources after the stories have been published. But that system usually antagonizes reporters.

Libel

The First Amendment to the U.S. Constitution provides the media with protection against censorship, and it is often referred to during the defense of libel suits:

> Congress shall make no law respecting an establishment of religion or prohibiting the free exercise thereof; or abridging the freedom of speech, or of the press; or the right of people peaceably to assemble, and to petition the Government for a redress of grievances.

"Libel" is publication of a falsity that causes injury to someone's reputation. Anyone can sue or threaten to sue for libel, claiming injury to his or her reputation. The real concern is whether the person has grounds enough to win.

"Libel is essentially a false and defamatory attack in written form on a person's reputation or character. Broadcast defamation is libel because there is usually a written script. Oral or spoken defamation is slander," according to Donald Gillmor and his co-authors in *Mass Communication Law: Cases and Comment.* The "script" is not limited to a news story, the authors explain; it can take the form of headlines, photos, cartoons, film, tape, records, signs, bumper stickers and advertisements.

The key factors for a writer to consider are whether you published untrue information that hurt the reputation of an identifiable person and whether you were either negligent or reckless in failing to check the information.

Are you publishing something you aren't sure is truthful?

Are you carelessly publishing something that is inaccurate?

Are you publishing something accusatory that you haven't checked out?

If your answer is yes to any of those questions, you could be in trouble for libel.

Times v. Sullivan

Those standards were the ones the U.S. Supreme Court applied in 1964 in a landmark libel case, New York Times Co. v. Sullivan, and the standards have been applied since then.

The *New York Times* case stemmed from an advertisement the newspaper accepted in 1960 from a group of people in the civil rights movement. The group was trying to raise money for the Committee to Defend Martin Luther King. The ad claimed that King had been arrested seven times and that his home had been bombed. It also claimed that black students who had staged a non-violent civil rights demonstration at Alabama State University had been the target of police brutality. The advertisement accused the Montgomery, Ala., police department of being armed with shotguns and using tear gas to subdue students.

Even though the police commissioner, L.B. Sullivan, had not been named in the advertisement, he sued for libel. He claimed that the ad contained factual errors concerning the police and damaged his reputation. He claimed that the police did not ring the college campus or padlock the college dining hall, as the ad had claimed.

Sullivan won in the lower courts and the Alabama Supreme Court. But the U.S. Supreme Court reversed the decision in its landmark ruling about "actual malice." Malice, in this context, does not mean intent to harm someone; it means that you published something knowing it was false or not bothering to check its truth or falsity. The justices said:

> The constitutional guarantees require, we think, a federal rule that prohibits a public official from recovering damages for defamatory falsehood relating to his official conduct unless he proves that the statement was made with "actual malice"—that is knowledge that it was false or with reckless disregard of whether it was false or not.

The court placed the burden of proving libel on the plaintiff, the person who is suing. The justices made this a constitutional issue, applying the First Amendment right of a free press to publish matters of public concern. In the ruling, Justice William Brennan wrote: "Thus we consider this case against the background of a profound national commitment to the principle that debate on public issues should be uninhibited, robust, and wide-open, and that it may well include vehement, caustic, and sometimes unpleasantly sharp attacks on government and public officials."

The original Times v. Sullivan ruling applied only to people who are public officials. It was later broadened to include "public figures." People may be considered public figures if their achievements or notoriety place them in the public eye or if they seek attention by voluntarily thrusting themselves into a public controversy. But if they are brought into the public spotlight involuntarily, they may not be public figures. A court usually will determine whether the person qualifies as a public figure.

Private Individuals

The issue of "public figures" was clarified in 1974 in another major case, Gertz v. Robert Welch. Chicago lawyer Elmer Gertz sued the John Birch Society, which had called him a communist in a magazine article. The court ruled that Gertz was not a public figure. He ultimately won his libel suit.

The case is significant because the Supreme Court ruled that private individuals do not have to show actual malice to collect damages; they only have to prove that the published information was false and that it was the result of "negligence" or carelessness by the publication. The rationale was that private individuals deserve more protection because they have less access to the media than public officials and do not voluntarily seek involvement in public debate.

However, the primary reason most newspapers get sued is for careless errors. Although newspapers get sued by people targeted in major investigative projects, the majority of libel suits stem from much less important stories. Incorrect captions, defamatory headlines, an inaccuracy in a police story or a feature can result in a libel suit.

Printed corrections don't prevent libel suits. They may assuage an angered source enough to forestall a lawsuit or they may be evidence of the newspaper's good faith, but corrections do not undo the harm of inaccurate published material. It's up to a jury to decide if you were negligent, careless or reckless in your disregard for the truth.

A printed correction by the *National Enquirer* didn't stop entertainer Carol Burnett from suing the tabloid in 1976 for insinuating that she was drunk. The article said that she had an argument with Henry Kissinger at a Washington restaurant and then "accidentally knocked a glass of wine over on one diner—and started giggling." Burnett denied the incident occurred, and even though the *Enquirer* apologized in a retraction, Burnett pressed her lawsuit. She was awarded a total of $1.6 million by a Los Angeles jury and ultimately settled for an undisclosed amount.

Even when you use the word *alleged,* meaning that the accusation is a charge without proof, you are on dangerous ground.

This word, although widely used by reporters in police cases, does not save you from libel. It is better to attribute the information to official sources or records.

If you don't name the person against whom the accusation is made, you still can be sued for libel. A person who can claim he or she was identified—either by enough information to describe the person physically or by position—could sue.

Nor does attribution save you. Say that a candidate for mayor tells you his or her opponent is a crook. You print the statement and attribute it to the candidate. The opponent could sue you and your newspaper. Just because you named the source of the statement, you are still responsible for it. And if it isn't true and you haven't documented it as true, you could be considered guilty of reckless disregard for the truth.

If you are going to print any accusations that could be defamatory, you should always check with the person being accused and ask for a response. Cross-checking may not save you from libel, but it at least gives you a chance to prove you were not reckless.

There are times when you can print accusatory or damaging information, especially when you are writing about crime. You have certain privileges as a member of the press, and so do some of the officials who deal with you.

Privilege

Privilege—in a legal sense—comes in two forms: absolute and qualified.

"Absolute privilege" means that public officials, including law enforcement officials, can make statements in the course of their official duties without fear of being sued for libel. This form of privilege extends to court proceedings, legislative proceedings, public and official meetings, and contents of public records.

As a member of the media, you have "qualified privilege." You may print defamatory statements made by people who are absolutely privileged as long as you are being fair and accurate and the information is from a public proceeding or public record. But if your report contains errors, you could lose that qualified protection.

If a city council member calls another member a crook during a public meeting, you may print the accusation. If the same city official makes the same comment to you during a telephone interview or after the meeting, you can't print it without risking libel. The key is that the defamatory statement must be made in an official capacity during an official proceeding. Or you may use, with attribution, something stated in court records.

Say that a police officer tells you something about a suspect. You may print that information if the officer is acting in an official capacity and if the information is documented in a public record, such as a police report or court files. However, you still should be careful about how you word accusations in crime stories. (More detail will follow in Chapter 23.) The police officer may say the man stabbed his wife, but you may not say the same thing without attribution. If the information is not stated in a public record, such as a police report or court record, it can be libelous. Generally, statements made outside of the court by police are not privileged, but some states may extend privilege to these comments.

Never call anyone a murderer unless he or she has been convicted of murder in court. Don't call suspects robbers or use any other accusatory term before they are convicted. Use terms such as "the suspect," "the man accused of murder," "the woman charged with the robbery."

Suppose a man has been murdered and you go to the neighborhood for reaction. A neighbor says the man's wife killed him. The neighbor isn't an official acting in an official capacity, and the wife hasn't been convicted. The neighbor's comments could be libelous, and you could be sued for printing them.

The best defense for a reporter is the "truth" defense, proving that what you wrote is true.

What you can do and what you ought to do may differ. You may have the right to print statements from court records or meetings, but if you think they could be untrue or unfair, should you print them? Those are the kinds of ethical decisions journalists must make, and they will be explained more fully in Chapter 18. Most editors advise: When in doubt, leave it out.

Fair Comment and Criticism

Suppose you are writing a review of a play, concert or book and your review is very negative. Can you be sued? Yes. You can always be sued. But you are protected under the right of fair comment.

Writers of editorials, analysis stories, reviews and other criticism may express opinions, but they may not state inaccurate facts. A factual error can be grounds for libel; an opinion is protected.

To qualify as fair comment, a comment must generally be on a matter of public interest, it must be based on facts known or believed to be true, and it may not be malicious, or made with reckless disregard for the truth. In this case also, truth is considered a good defense.

Invasion of Privacy

Issues of privacy involve ethical decisions, not matters of accuracy. However, with the proliferation of invasion of privacy lawsuits, a journalist should understand individuals' privacy rights as well as definitions of defamation.

A child drowns and a mother stands on the dock as her son's body is dragged from the river. She is hysterical. A photographer takes her picture without her consent. Has the photographer invaded her privacy? Perhaps, if the photographer was on private property. The photographer could be considered an intruder.

The courts have acknowledged four grounds for invasion of privacy lawsuits:

Physical or mental intrusion into a person's solitude. Eavesdropping, harassing someone and trespassing on private property can be considered intrusion. So can using a telephoto lens, listening behind doors and using any device to enhance what the unaided eye can see or the unaided ear can hear on private property.

Public disclosure of private facts. Publishing such facts as information about a person's sex life or medical history that the public considers offensive could be considered invasion of privacy, even if it's true. But if the facts are taken from the public record, such as court documents, they probably will be considered privileged.

Publicity that puts a person in a false light in the public eye. If a published story or picture gives the wrong impression and is embarrassing to the person, the possibility exists that the court will consider a "false light" verdict. For example, in one case a television station doing a story about teen-age pregnancy took pictures of a young woman walking down the street. The television station did not say she was pregnant, nor did the station identify her. However, she claimed the picture put her in a false light—indicating that she was a pregnant teen-ager—and she won her lawsuit against the station. False light is related to defamation, but the story or picture does not have to defame a person to be considered false light. It does have to portray the person inaccurately. Truth is a defense in these cases.

Use of a person's name or picture without his or her permission. This doctrine applies when the picture is used for commercial purposes, such as advertising or promotion.

The best guideline for reporters is to be careful. If you are accurate and fair, you can defend your actions. If you aren't sure whether something is libelous or invades privacy, check with an editor. In many cases, newspapers retain lawyers to review information that could be considered grounds for a lawsuit. You can't be expected to know all the legal angles; you can be expected to be careful.

Activities

1 For a week, check the corrections in *The New York Times,* your local newspaper or any other newspaper that prints daily corrections. Analyze the nature of the corrections: Are they for names, facts, photo captions or other errors?

2   Interview a classmate for biographical information as though you were writing a profile or an obituary. Ask questions that will elicit quotes, such as why the person chose this college or what memorable experiences the person has had in college or high school. Write a brief paragraph containing the factual material: date and place of birth, information about high school, college major, hobbies, other interests. After you have written it, ask your classmate to check its accuracy.

3   You are the editor of your campus newspaper. A female student at your university says that last semester a male professor asked her for sex in return for a good grade. She says she dropped the class and filed a complaint of sexual harassment a few months ago with the university's Office of Affirmative Action. She gives you the professor's name. However, the student insists that you not use her name. She says she doesn't think the university will do anything, so she wants the press to know about it.

The Office of Affirmative Action keeps all records confidential and will not confirm or deny the existence of the complaint, but the student has provided you with a copy. The professor refuses to speak to you, and officials in his department and in the university refuse to comment.

You publish news that a complaint has been filed, and you name the professor. In addition, you print the unnamed complainant's side of the story, including her sexually explicit version of the professor's comments to her, which are not in the complaint.

Discuss whether you should have printed the professor's name and the steps you would have taken before doing so. Discuss what information in the story, if any, could be considered libelous. Would the professor be considered a public or private figure?

Would the situation be any different if you substituted a politician for the professor? This time, you are the editor of your local newspaper. A U.S. senator has decided to seek re-election. Five women who worked for him several years ago say he sexually harassed and abused them while they were in his office. The women refuse to be named. Their allegations range from stories that he plied them with drugs and alcohol and then sexually abused them to accusations of rape. All the women are reputable, including a political lobbyist and a former secretary to the senator, but none have gone to the police. As a result, you have no record of formal complaints about their allegations. However, three years ago a formal complaint by a former employee charged him with sexual molestation, but the charges were dropped. Will you print these women's allegations and use his name? Does the senator have grounds for a libel lawsuit?

4   A candidate for city council in your community had a nervous breakdown 10 years ago. The candidate's opponent has slipped you a hospital document confirming this fact. Should you print the story? Why or why not? If you do, does the candidate have any grounds to sue you for invasion of privacy?

COACHING

Examine all your alternatives.

Consider all the parties who will be affected. Do you need other points of view?

Weigh the benefits and harms of your decision.

Justify why you are making this decision.

Ethics

18

I magine that you are a reporter for your local newspaper. A drunken driver almost kills a young girl in an accident in your town. You call the hospital for information about her condition, but officials will not release it except to family members. So you ask a fellow reporter to call the hospital and identify himself as the girl's uncle. He gets the information.

Would you do that? Is it ethical?

This was one of 30 cases presented to 819 journalists in a survey conducted by Ohio University journalism professor Ralph S. Izard for the Society of Professional Journalists. Eighty-two percent of the journalists who responded said they would not ask their colleague to lie to gain information.

If someone is going to be hurt by what gets printed or broadcast about them, then journalists need to provide a reason—a good reason—for going with it. 'That's my job,' doesn't cut it. Nor do appeals to First Amendment freedoms.

Deni Elliott, director, Ethics Institute, Dartmouth College

Ethical Dilemmas

Test yourself. Would you go along with the actions of journalists in these other cases presented in the survey? You can compare your answers with those of survey respondents, whose answers appear later in the chapter.

Agree Disagree Reporters investigating alleged racial discrimination by real estate agents were getting nowhere. They had interviewed officials of the local realtors' association and scores of realtors, all of whom denied that they steer black buyers away from houses for sale in white neighborhoods. The city editor sent two white reporters, posing as potential buyers, to see what houses several real estate firms showed them when they expressed interest in a new house of a certain size and price range. Then she sent two black reporters to the same firms with the same requests.

Agree Disagree Police informed a reporter of plans to make arrests for prostitution at a local park. They requested that the newspaper publish the names of the persons arrested. The paper normally does not publish the names of persons arrested on minor morals charges, but the city editor decided to use the list on this occasion.

Now consider these situations, all of them real ethical dilemmas faced by reporters and editors:

Yes No You have heard rumors that a politician has had extramarital affairs. You stake out his townhouse and confirm that he has spent the night with a woman who is not his wife. Will you write the story?

Yes No A woman has accused the nephew of a prominent U.S. senator of raping her. Your newspaper has had a policy of not printing the names of alleged rape victims. The paper also withholds names of suspects in criminal cases until they are formally charged with the crime. In this case, police have acknowledged that the nephew is a suspect, but he has not been charged yet. Will you print the name of the woman who claimed she was raped? Will you print the name of the senator's nephew?

Deception

The cases about the accident victim and about racial discrimination both deal with deception. Did you decide that it is all right to use deception to get a story? Is it OK in some cases but not in others?

In the case about the accident victim, 82 percent criticized the deception. But in the case involving racial discrimination, 95 percent of the journalists in the survey agreed that they would use deception.

In 1978, investigative reporters at the *Chicago Sun Times* decided that deception was the only way they would be able to prove that city officials, including building inspectors and some police officers, were soliciting bribes. So reporters and photographers, posing as bartenders and waiters, operated a bar called The Mirage. And they were able to provide firsthand evidence that city inspectors solicited bribes to allow them to operate. Although the series won several awards, the Pulitzer Prize board ruled that the reporting methods were unethical and rejected it for the media's highest award.

The case renewed debate about deception, and today this type of reporting is considered a last resort by many editors. Before using deception, ask yourself if there is any other way to get the story.

Sensitivity

In the case involving the prostitution sweep, about 70 percent of the respondents in the survey said they disapproved of printing the names of the people arrested.

This case may not seem to pose much of an ethical dilemma. But in 1977, acting at the request of police, *The Enterprise* in Brockton, Mass., published the names of prostitutes and "johns," the men arrested for soliciting the services of the prostitutes. A 47-year-old man committed suicide three days after his name had been published in connection with the prostitution arrests. In his suicide note, he did not mention the arrest. The editor of the paper said there was no connection between the suicide and the published report. But the case is often cited when editors weigh the dilemma of whether they are doing more harm than good by printing names of people charged with soliciting services of prostitutes.

In 1991, several newspapers decided they would do more good for the community by printing the names of arrested johns. Editors at the *Rockford* (Ill.) *Register Star, The Hartford* (Conn.) *Courant, The* (Trenton, N.J.) *Times* and *The Trentonian* (N.J.) all said publication of these names would serve as a deterrent to prostitution, which had become a major problem in their communities.

What do you do if a subject threatens to commit suicide? Reporters and editors often are faced with this decision when they are working on stories that will put people in a bad light. Do you withhold the story? "It doesn't have to be a choice between a story and life," says Deni Elliott, director of the Ethics Institute at

Dartmouth College. She suggests talking to sources who threaten suicide so they know you are concerned about their feelings. She also suggests holding a story until the source has time to seek help.

Invasion of Privacy

The consequences of publication may not be life-threatening, but they can be serious. There is much controversy these days over the publication of private information about people in (or formerly in) the public eye. Publicizing the names of crime victims is another controversial issue. Invasion of privacy is also a concern of photojournalists.

Public officials Would you print information about the sex life of a politician? When is the private life of a public figure relevant? When does it serve the public interest to publish such details?

Reporters and editors at *The Miami Herald* decided the private life of a politician was relevant in the summer of 1987. Former Sen. Gary Hart was seeking the Democratic nomination for the presidency. Rumors of Hart's infidelity to his wife had circulated for months, and during the campaign they called into question his character and credibility. When asked about the rumors, Hart challenged reporters to "follow me around. . . . They'd be very bored." Acting on a tip that Hart had a relationship with a Florida model, *Herald* reporters staked out his townhouse. They revealed that Hart spent the night with the woman, Donna Rice. Hart never admitted that the relationship with Rice was sexual. Nevertheless, he withdrew his candidacy the day before *The Washington Post* was set to reveal evidence about his involvement in another affair.

Four and a half years later, during Bill Clinton's campaign for the presidency, rumors of his infidelity surfaced as well. But the circumstances differed from the Hart coverage. The *Star,* a tabloid newspaper, broke the story. It printed allegations by former television reporter Gennifer Flowers that she had had a long-term affair with Clinton; the *Star* paid Flowers for her story. The mainstream press, which had not been able to verify the allegations, then picked up the story. Their justification was that it had become news, especially after Clinton appeared on the CBS "60 Minutes" show to respond to allegations. He admitted that he and his wife had had marital problems over the years but denied Flowers' claim of a 12-year affair with him. The American public didn't decry his behavior, the public blasted the press instead.

The ethical dilemma of when to publish information about the private lives of public officials surfaced in another political campaign in 1992. *The Seattle Times* published a story of eight unidentified women who had accused U.S. Sen. Brock Adams of sexual harassment and physical molestation. The senator dropped his re-election campaign the next day. In a sidebar to the story, editor Michael Fancher told readers he felt the story was in the public interest because it reflected on the senator's fitness for office.

Celebrities   A case that seemed to cause even more media backlash in 1992 was the disclosure that tennis star Arthur Ashe had AIDS. And it posed even greater ethical hand-wringing, because Ashe was not running for a public office and, unlike Magic Johnson, who had voluntarily announced he had the HIV virus, Ashe was no longer playing in the professional circuit.

Is the private life of a public figure always fair game for disclosure in the media? Ashe didn't think so. When *USA Today* received an anonymous tip that Ashe had acquired the disease from a blood transfusion many years earlier, a sportswriter from the newspaper interviewed Ashe to check it out. Ashe didn't confirm or deny anything. But he called the paper's managing editor for sports to find out the status of the story. The editor, Gene Policinski, said the newspaper would not print the story without confirmation from a credible, named source but that the paper would pursue it. Ashe still did not confirm the story. Instead, he called a press conference the next day and reluctantly told the world. He said he was sure some newspaper eventually would publish the story, and he wanted to be able to tell the story on his terms. Although he acknowledged that he was a public figure and that the story was newsworthy, he said he felt his privacy had been invaded. Public opinion polls seemed to agree. The day the story was published in *USA Today,* the newspaper received 481 phone calls, most from readers critical of the coverage, even though the newspaper published it only after Ashe announced he was going to have a press conference.

Policinski, in a sidebar to the press conference story, explained his reason for pursuing the story: "There was no question that this was a significant news story. A great U.S. athlete could be critically ill. If he had cancer or a heart attack—as he did in 1979—it was and is news."

Privacy issues like these are among the most difficult ethical dilemmas for the media. Is the story fair? Is it in the public interest to know? What harm or benefit will result? Those are questions reporters and editors often ask before they publish such stories. And rarely is there unanimous agreement on the decision.

DeWayne Wickham, *USA Today* columnist, disagreed with his newspaper's decision to pursue the Ashe story. Wickham, quoted in *The Quill* magazine, said:

> Journalism teeters on the edge of a very slippery slope when, by confronting Ashe with rumors of his infection and thus forcing him to go public or lie, it attempts to pass off voyeurism for news

judgment. . . . To say he is a public figure and thus fair game for such intrusive news coverage ignores the fact that even celebrity rape victims are afforded a cloak of anonymity by this and most other newspapers.

Rape victims Whether to name rape victims—regardless of celebrity status—is another continuing ethical debate in the media. Because of the stigma associated with rape, most newspapers withhold the names of people who claim they have been raped.

Geneva Overholser, editor of *The Des Moines* (Iowa) *Register,* wanted to eliminate the stigma. In 1989 she wrote a column saying the stigma of rape would be reduced if it were treated like any other crime and if the names of rape victims were used.

Nancy Ziegenmeyer was moved by the column. She had been raped. She agreed to tell her story to *Register* reporter Jane Schorer and to let the newspaper use her name in a series published in 1990. Schorer won the Pulitzer Prize in 1991 for that story (an excerpt will appear in Chapter 26). But she agonized over many ethical decisions in the process of writing the series.

Ziegenmeyer had divorced her husband. Although she was living with him, they had not remarried, and she asked Schorer to withhold that information from the story. Schorer did so reluctantly, after consultation with her editors. Schorer discreetly checked Ziegenmeyer's background, and many of her neighbors had unkind things to say about her infidelity and other behavior as a wife and mother. But Schorer decided the background wasn't relevant to the rape story, another ethical decision.

The story took an emotional toll on Schorer. Many times when she thought about the story, she would burst into tears.

After Schorer wrote it, she received calls from rape victims from all over the country who expressed gratitude that such a story had been told. A year later Schorer wrote in the *Washington Journalism Review* that the series wasn't the first in which a rape victim was named but perhaps marked a point where society first showed itself ready to listen to rape victims.

The Register still has a policy of printing the names of alleged and confirmed rape victims only with their permission. *The New York Times* didn't ask for permission before it decided to use the name of a woman who accused a nephew of Sen. Edward Kennedy of raping her. And the story raised a firestorm of controversy.

In addition to withholding names of alleged rape victims, the majority of newspapers, including *The Times,* usually withhold the names of suspects before they are formally charged with a crime. But newspapers throughout the country printed the name of William Kennedy Smith before he was charged with the crime, justifying their action by saying the prominence of his uncle warranted it.

The *Times* editors said they made the decision to name the woman in a profile about her because the woman had been named in a supermarket tabloid, *The Globe,* and on NBC television. Therefore, her name was already in the public domain. Media critics blasted *The Times* for weak justification. But naming rape accusers (the term *victim* implies that the suspected attacker is guilty) is gaining more favor at many newspapers.

The *Times* profile of the woman raised other objections as well. It included public records about her traffic tickets, her family history, her dating habits and the illegitimacy of her 3-year-old daughter.

The writer, Fox Butterfield, did not know the woman would be named. That decision was made by his editors without his input. However, in an interview in *FineLine,* a journalism ethics newsletter, he said he stood by the story because it was factually accurate.

Butterfield said the Palm Beach case raises an important ethical dilemma: What should reporters do if, while investigating the background of a rape victim, they find she has a less than impeccable record. He stresses that a woman's background is irrelevant to her being raped but cannot be ignored if you are writing a profile of her. He asks, "Should we suppress it because it is an unflattering portrait of a woman? Should we write profiles of women only if they fit the public perception of virtuous? Would we apply the same standard to men?"

Media critics would ask the same question. Why didn't *The Times* apply the same standard to men and publish a profile of William Kennedy Smith? Why publish a story about the accuser's background at all? Is it relevant?

Deni Elliott, discussing the issue in another *FineLine* column, wrote: "The road from reporting to publishing is paved with selected facts and cropped pictures. Editorial judgment creates news stories out of the mix; relevancy provides the framework by which journalists decide what stays in, what gets cut. . . . Would it be relevant that a man who said he was mugged or sexually assaulted had a child outside of marriage? Or that he had a string of traffic tickets?"

In addition to relevancy, journalists need to consider the harm that will result from their decisions. This is especially true when dealing with matters of privacy.

Ultimately William Kennedy Smith was judged not guilty, and after the trial his accuser, Patricia Bowman, revealed her identity in press conferences and television interviews.

Photo subjects   Many privacy issues involve photographs. Should a photographer take a picture of a grieving mother whose son has drowned, even if she doesn't want the picture taken? At what point is a photograph an invasion of privacy?

Another concern for photo editors is taste: what the reader needs to see versus what the reader wants to see. For example, should newspapers print pictures that depict gore and tragedy even if they would upset readers? In 1987, Pennsylvania state treasurer R. Bud Dwyer convened a press conference the day before he was scheduled to be sentenced for conviction of mail fraud, perjury and racketeering. At the end of the conference, he took a gun from his briefcase, put the barrel in his mouth and pulled the trigger, killing himself instantly. Stunned photographers for television stations and newspapers shot vivid pictures of the event.

Many television stations did not air the footage of him with blood gushing from his head. Several newspaper editors also decided that some of the photos were too graphic and would be too upsetting to readers. But other newspapers published a series of three photos, including a gory one of his head as the bullet pierced it. Readers in several locations protested loudly. The objections were so strong from *Miami Herald* readers that editors withdrew the offending photo from a later edition of the paper.

Such ethical dilemmas arise daily at newspapers and television stations. And editors agonize over the decisions. But how do they make those decisions, and how can you decide what is ethical?

Objectivity Versus Fairness

One of the main criteria journalists employ when reporting and writing a news story is fairness. Is the story accurate? Is it balanced? And, as many add, is it objective?

But can anything be really objective? No, says Clifford Christians, author of *Media Ethics:* "There is not a serious journalist who believes in objective truth anymore. . . . Textbooks all emphasize the facts are neutral. Texts don't say the means of reporting is not neutral." Your background, your genes, your sex and other factors affect the way you think, act and select information in the reporting and writing process, he says.

Louis Hodges, a media ethics expert at Washington and Lee University, puts the dilemma another way: "Do you swear to tell the truth, the whole truth and nothing but the truth? You can't do that. You only can give your perception of the truth."

Moral Reasoning

Instead of striving to be objective, journalists should strive to be fair. And that's where the ethical dilemmas arise. How do you determine what is fair?

The first step is to understand what is meant by "ethics." Louis Hodges defines it as a study of moral choices. "It is reasoned inquiry into the moral life. There are two questions to ask: What ought we as human beings to do to each other or avoid doing to each other? By what method or what criteria should we decide?"

Journalists use several methods to justify their decisions. In most ethical dilemmas, editors and reporters discuss the issue and the consequences of publication before making the decision. They consider how newsworthy the story is and if the public really needs this information.

The process of moral reasoning can be broken into three steps:

1 Define the dilemma. Consider all the problems the story or photograph will pose.

2 Examine all your alternatives. You can publish, not publish, wait for a while until you get more information before publishing, display the story or photo prominently or in a lesser position, or choose other options.

3 Justify your decision. Weigh the harms and the benefits of publication, or weigh such factors as relevance and importance of the story to the public.

The Poynter Institute Model

Bob Steele, associate director in charge of ethics at the Poynter Institute for Media Studies, suggests that journalists ask these questions before making decisions in ethical dilemmas:

Why am I concerned about this story, photo or graphic?

What is the news? What good would publication do?

Is the information complete and accurate, to the best of my knowledge?

Am I missing an important point of view?

What does my reader need to know?

How would I feel if the story or photo were about me or a member of my family?

What are the likely consequences of publication? What good or harm could result?

What are my alternatives?

Will I be able to clearly and honestly explain my decision to anyone who challenges it?

People using the same moral reasoning methods may emerge with different decisions. There is rarely one right decision. In the cases presented at the start of this chapter, you may have made a decision different from that of your classmate. But it is your reasoning process that matters.

Take the racial discrimination case, for example. If you use the Poynter Institute's questions to reach a decision, you might decide that deception was justified because the story would do more good than harm if the public learned about this issue. Another person might decide that deception causes more harm to the newspaper or television station's credibility and that another way should be used to get the story.

In the prostitution case, the editors decided that the benefit to the community of preventing prostitution was greater than the harm to the people whose names were printed after they were arrested. But you may prefer to wait until people are convicted before using their names or not use their names at all because you think more harm than good will result to individuals who may be innocent.

Philosophical Approaches

The harms-versus-benefits concept is one of several derived from philosophers. Their reasoning forms a framework for many moral decisions. Jay Black, a media ethics professor at the University of Alabama, and Dartmouth ethics director Deni Elliott apply the reasoning of philosophers this way:

John Stuart Mill: His philosophy is based on a principle known as "utilitarianism." Ethical decisions should seek the greatest amount of happiness or benefit to the greatest number of people while at the same time seeking to harm the least number of people. If Mill were editor, he would ask his staff to (1) list all persons likely to be affected; (2) decide the likely consequences of each option; (3) weigh the benefit or harm that would result, giving added weight to the major benefit or harm; and (4) choose the consequence that provides the most benefit to the largest number of people or the least harm to the smallest number of people.

Aristotle: If Aristotle were editor, he would tell his staff to act as "virtuous journalists," arguing that moral virtue lies somewhere between the extremes of excess and deficiency. In other words, he would seek a "golden mean," a middle ground between the two extremes.

John Rawls: He would ask his reporters to pull on a "veil of ignorance" as they grapple with ethical dilemmas—basically, to consider the points of view of all people involved. The steps would be to (1) make a list of all people who will be affected by the decisions, including readers, sources, co-workers, yourself; (2) put yourself behind a veil of ignorance, giving up your identity and assuming the identities of the other people affected by the decision; and (3) assume that a discussion takes place among the various players, with none of the participants knowing what their ultimate identities will turn out to be when the veils of ignorance are removed.

Although many journalists tend to rely on Mill's harms-versus-benefits approach, a single philosophical approach will not apply to every ethical dilemma. But you should ask the questions. You may not please your readers. You may not even please yourself. But you should at least believe that you have made the best decision you could under the circumstances at hand.

"If you don't act in accordance with moral rules, you are blameworthy," Elliott says. "If you act in accordance, you are not praiseworthy. No one congratulates you for not lying."

Codes of Ethics

In addition to making decisions about what to report and write and how to present stories, journalists must consider whether their behavior is ethical as they perform their professional duties.

Many newspapers have devised codes of ethics that govern the behavior of employees. These include policies about accepting gifts or free-lance assignments, as well as guidelines about conflicts of interest. Journalism societies, such as the Radio-Television News Directors' Association and the Public Relations Society of America, also have basic codes of ethics to guide members.

One industry standard that all journalists are expected to comply with is a prohibition against plagiarism—passing off the materials of another source as your own without giving any credit to the original source. If you are copying information from another publication, you must attribute the source (as mentioned in Chapters 1 and 6).

This prohibition against plagiarism is one of many declarations in a code of ethics adopted by The Society of Professional Journalists in 1926. The code, meant to serve as a guideline for the broadcast and print media, has been revised several times. Some of the guidelines in the code:

- Gifts, favors, free travel, special treatment or privileges can compromise the integrity of journalists and their employers. Nothing of value should be accepted.

- Journalists and their employers should conduct their personal lives in a manner that protects them from conflict of interest, real or apparent.

- There is no excuse for inaccuracies or lack of thoroughness.

- News reports should be free of opinion or bias and represent all sides of an issue (unless labeled analysis or editorial comment).
- The news media should not communicate unofficial charges affecting reputation or moral character without giving the accused a chance to reply.
- The news media must guard against invading a person's right to privacy.
- It is the duty of news media to make prompt and complete correction of their errors.

The code is an unofficial set of guidelines for news organizations to follow if they wish.

The code of ethics of the Public Relations Society of America adheres to the same basic principles of truth, accuracy and fairness. However, since public relations practitioners are advocates for clients, the code includes these principles specifically applying to the industry:

- A member shall deal fairly with clients or employers, . . . with fellow practitioners and with the general public.
- A member shall conduct his or her professional life in accord with the public interest.
- A member shall adhere to truth and accuracy and to generally accepted standards of good taste.
- A member shall not represent conflicting or competing interests without the express consent of those involved, given after a full disclosure of the facts; nor place himself or herself in a position where the member's interest is or may be in conflict with a duty to a client, or others, without full disclosure of such interests to all involved.
- A member shall safeguard the confidences of present and former clients.
- A member shall not engage in any practice that tends to corrupt the integrity of channels of communication or the processes of government.
- A member shall not intentionally communicate false or misleading information.
- A member shall be prepared to identify publicly the name of the client or employer on whose behalf any public communication is made.
- A member shall not make use of any individual or organization purporting to serve or represent an unannounced cause, or purporting to be independent or unbiased, but actually serving an undisclosed special or private interest of a member, client or employer.

- A member shall not intentionally injure the professional reputation of another practitioner. (If the member has evidence that another member has been guilty of unethical, illegal or unfair practices, the member shall present the information to the authorities of the Society for action.)

- A member called as a witness in a proceeding for the enforcement of this code shall be bound to appear, unless excused for sufficient reason by the judicial panel.

- A member, in performing services for a client or employer, shall not accept fees, commissions, or any other valuable consideration from anyone other than the client or employer in connection with those services without the express consent of the client or employer, given after a full disclosure of the facts.

- A member shall not guarantee the achievement of specified results beyond the member's direct control.

- A member shall, as soon as possible, sever relations with any organization or individual if such relationship requires conduct contrary to the articles of this code.

Other news organizations have their own policy statements and codes. Staff members who violate these policies at newspapers can be fired, and many have been. From 1984 to 1987, at least 48 newspaper staffers were fired for ethics violations, according to a survey conducted by the Society of Professional Journalists. Since then, several more have been dismissed. In some cases reporters have been fired for entering business relationships with a source or for using for personal gain information they get from sources.

The Philadelphia Inquirer has a comprehensive staff guide that prohibits conflicts of interest. It prohibits staff members from taking any advantage of their professional work for private use. "For example, it is improper for a staff member to write a letter of complaint to a merchant on *Inquirer* stationery," the guide says. Some other policies regarding ethical conduct at the *Inquirer:*

- **Relationships:** A staff member should not write about, photograph or make news judgments about any individual related by blood or marriage or with whom the staff member has a close personal, financial or romantic relationship.

- **Admissions:** Inquirer staff members do not accept, for themselves, their families and their guests, free entertainment offered on the basis of the staff member's positions with *The Inquirer.* These include tickets to sports events, movies, theatrical productions, circuses, concerts, recitals, museums, exhibits, ice shows and other events. For events in which free admission customarily is accorded to the working press, such as a press box at a sports event or a critic's ticket at the theater, a staff member may accept free admission only if he or she has been assigned to cover the event for *The Inquirer.* . . . The cost of meals and nightclub admissions or cover charges incurred in the course of professional duties shall be paid by *The Inquirer*. . . . When an institution refuses *The Inquirer's* request to pay for a staff member's meals or admission to a public event, *The Inquirer* will make an appropriate donation to charity and notify the institution that it has done so.

• **Gifts:** Staff members do not accept business-connected gifts, free rooms, sample merchandise, special reduced rates, funds provided by gaming establishments and race tracks, or any other low-pay or no-pay arrangement. Gifts of insignificant value—a calendar, pencil, key chain or similar item sent out routinely by a corporation, for instance—may be accepted if sending them back would be awkward. . . . When it is impractical to return a gift, the item is given to charity and the donor advised of the reason.

• **Free-lancing:** Staff members may undertake free-lance writing, photography or editing for publications that are not in competition with *The Inquirer* so long as the assignment does not conflict with activities planned by or under way for *The Inquirer*.

• **Advocacy:** Staff members should be careful not to offend or give wrong impressions to members of the public by blatantly espousing or expressing viewpoints on public issues. Such actions as wearing an antiwar button, publicly espousing a cause or festooning an *Inquirer* workspace with one side's placards during a campaign can create a perception, intended or not, of partiality. Particularly, staff members should refrain from signing petitions or otherwise identifying themselves with public issues.

As you can see, being a journalist involves more than getting the story. How you get it and how you behave on and off duty are part of the ethical responsibilities of journalists.

Activities

1 Apply moral reasoning, using the Poynter guidelines, to the following cases (or to other cases described in this chapter):

a An anonymous source tells you that a U.S. senator for your state has voted against many gay rights issues even though he is gay. You have heard other rumors that the senator is homosexual, but the senator has denied that the rumors are true. What will you do about this story?

b Would you have pursued the story about Arthur Ashe? If you had been able to confirm the report that he had AIDS, even if he had not admitted it, would you have printed the story?

c You have heard rumors that your local nursing home is abusing its clients. However, no complaints have been filed with state regulatory agencies or with the police. You have contacted some of the clients' family members, who say they are concerned but have no proof. Will you go undercover as a volunteer aide at the nursing home (no special training required) to investigate?

2   Choose any ethical dilemma you have faced in your life, especially in your journalism studies. Define the dilemma, and then apply any of the moral reasoning methods described in this chapter. Then consider how the decision you make now compares with the one you made before.

3   Devise a code of ethics for your campus newspaper.

COACHING

Seek sources from different racial and ethnic backgrounds for all kinds of stories, not just stories about minorities.

Ask your sources how they prefer to be addressed.

Ask yourself if you would write the same type of description for a man as for a woman, for a white source as for a person of color, for a disabled person or member of any other ethnic or special group.

Multicultural Sensitivity 19

D on't call him articulate. You might be tempted to do that if you meet Tim Gallimore. A lot of people who wrote letters of recommendation for him after he got his doctorate from Indiana University called him articulate. They meant well. But Gallimore says the term is really an insult.

Gallimore is an African-American. And he says when the term *articulate* is used to compliment him, it presumes that most African-Americans can't express themselves well. So in reality it is a slur.

Gallimore, an assistant professor of journalism at the University of Missouri, teaches multicultural sensitivity in his journalism courses.

In a study he conducted about the interpretation of mass media messages, he asked students to define a number of words, including *majority, ghetto* and *inner city*. He concluded that it is hard, if not impossible, to get people to agree on one meaning for a word. Gender, race, and geographical and ethnic background influence interpretation. Consider, for example, the word *majority*. "It is remarkable that women view themselves as minorities although they are a majority of the population in every society," he says. "This can be explained only through the connotation of majority as possession of power—the white male-dominated majority."

Other loaded words are *ghetto* and *inner city*, which Gallimore's students tended to define as an area with drugs, poverty, crime and gangs rather than as an urban geographical location. On television, when a news anchor says "inner-city youth," the phrase is almost always followed by descriptions

We need to be aware of how we communicate—of our built-in biases. Language is not a neutral thing.

Tim Gallimore, assistant professor, University of Missouri School of Journalism

and visuals of young blacks killing one another for crack or high-priced athletic shoes, Gallimore says. "Language is not a neutral thing," he says.

The Language of Multiculturalism

Tim Gallimore, assistant professor of journalism
Courtesy of Tim Gallimore

Language changes, too. *African-American* is the term now preferred by many blacks, but it is not accepted at all newspapers. *Chicano* is preferred by Mexican-Americans in some parts of the country, yet it is offensive to many older members of the group.

How can a journalist know the proper term to use? The University of Missouri's Multicultural Management Program tried to address that problem by producing a booklet, *Dictionary of Cautionary Words and Phrases*. It was highly controversial: Some journalists blasted it for "sanitizing the language," and others labeled it "hypersensitive newspeak."

Any terms that might be acceptable today could be out of vogue tomorrow. So instead of memorizing the popular term of the day, Gallimore suggests that reporters ask people of different ethnic or special interest groups how they prefer to be addressed. "The newspaper can demonstrate sensitivity with the words the person uses to define himself or herself," he says. "That gets the newspaper off the hook. If someone objects, you could say that is the person's term."

Jose D. McMurray, executive director of the National Association of Hispanic Journalists, also stresses dealing with people as individuals, especially before using labels. *"Hispanic* is a generic term created in Washington so bureaucrats can conglomerate an ethnic group," he says. "In California, second and third generation Hispanics prefer to be called *Latinos;* some second and third generation Mexican-Americans prefer *Chicano.* It is very much an individual decision. I'm Irish Basque. I prefer to be called Latino. But I'd rather be called Jose."

McMurray says it is also a misnomer to refer to Latinos as a minority in some areas of the country. "We are not a minority in El Paso, San Antonio or Los Angeles. *Ethnic* is a better term."

Minorities in the News

Journalism professor Gallimore recommends gathering a list of advocacy sources for different groups: by race, age, disability, gender and so on. If you choose a person from that group to check things out that might be insensitive or controversial, you have a better chance of being sensitive, he says. "We make most of our mistakes in the information gathering," Gallimore says. "No amount of expert wordsmanship can overcome faulty materials. Go to a variety of sources. Be more aware of different points of view. If the story involves some statement about a group, go to members of that group."

Mervin Aubespin, associate editor and director of staff development at *The* (Louisville, Ky.) *Courier-Journal,* says one way the media can become more sensitive to the needs of minorities is to hire more minorities. Although the employment of minorities in newsrooms nearly doubled from 1982 to 1992 (see Exhibit 19-1), there's still room for improvement. In the early nineties, less than 10 percent of the employees in the news department at newspapers were minorities, says Aubespin, and more than 50 percent of the newspapers in the United States had no minorities at all. Other sources show that in broadcast news organizations, minorities made up about 13 percent of the work force. The need for minority representation in the media work force and in media coverage is only going to increase. By the year 2010, 87 percent of the growth in the United States will be in minority communities, and the media must reflect the concerns of this significant population.

Aubespin says hiring minorities is only the first step; editors have to encourage minority reporters to express their diversity. One of the problems is that white editors "really want black faces that write like whites," he says.

A board member of the National Association of Black Journalists and recipient of numerous awards for his contributions to journalism, Aubespin says he doesn't believe there is a specific set

Exhibit 19.1

*Employment of minorities
in newsrooms*

Bob Laird/*USA Today*

USA SNAPSHOTS®

A look at statistics that shape your finances

Minorities at newspapers

More than 5,100 minorities work at U.S. daily newspapers, vs. 2,800 in 1982. Percentage of newsroom employees:

5.5%

9.4%

The News

Top 50 U.S. newspapers, **5B**

'82   '92

8%
6%
4%
2%
0

Source: American Society of Newspaper Editors   By Bob Laird, USA TODAY

of guidelines to give journalists sensitivity. "There is no formula, no one way to write about a minority group," he says. "The best guideline is to treat each person as an individual. We are as different as you are."

As for Hispanics, McMurray is also concerned about stereotypes. "I would like to say there is a stereotype of Latinos as hard working, family oriented, loyal people but I seldom see that," McMurray says. "Instead I get the sense there is this group of people—Lord knows where they come from—that are not trustworthy, that point guns."

However, McMurray says some gains are being made to portray ethnic sources in a positive light, especially by *USA Today*. "If they have five front-page pictures, two or three will be of people of color who are not involved in crime," he says. "We need to praise the positive changes and use them for inspiration." *USA Today* newspaper uses multicultural sources in as many stories as possible (as discussed in Chapter 6).

Multicultural sensitivity involves not only the sources you use but also the kinds of stories you choose. Innumerable studies have been conducted to show how women and minorities are portrayed in biased or stereotypical fashion. Minorities often are featured in stories about crime but excluded as sources in general stories about lifestyles, the economy and other stories where experts are cited. Conversely, women and minorities often are portrayed as unusual if they have operated a successful business or accomplished some of the same newsworthy feats as white males.

Adrienne Rivers, a journalism professor at the University of Kansas, conducted a study to determine if there was bias in the Kansas City, Mo., print and broadcast media. She found that news sources thought coverage was biased, showing African-Americans in a negative light or not at all. News managers and editors thought the coverage at their stations and newspapers was very fair.

Although bias was not pervasive, Rivers found many examples of insensitivity. In one case, two city councilmen had an argument at a meeting. The headline said two black councilmen argued. "What difference did race make in that case?" Rivers says. In another story, a writer reviewing a musical performance of a group from England mentioned that one of the band members was Chinese, yet the ethnicity of the other members was not mentioned. "Are Chinese people not supposed to live in England? What was the significance of that?" The stories about Clarence Thomas all stressed that he was a black Supreme Court nominee and, if approved, would be the second black justice (to replace Thurgood Marshall, the first black justice). "I think we would be remiss if we didn't acknowledge race somewhere in the story," Rivers says. "But every story didn't have to cite race as his middle initial."

Rivers says the most pervasive stereotype is the picture of the black suspect in handcuffs, often on the front page, whereas stories and pictures of white crime suspects often are played inside the paper. "I suggest a reality check," she says. "Ask yourself, if you are going to use a picture or a phrase, would you do the same for people of other categories?"

Rivers stresses the need for a variety of multicultural sources in all kinds of stories. She says reporters tend to go to the same ethnic sources over and over. "They anoint people as leaders of the community and get their voices. There may be other people of that race or ethnic origin with other points of view."

The Ethnic Beat

Murray Dubin understands the need to be sensitive to racial and ethnic groups. It's his job. A reporter for more than 25 years at *The Philadelphia Inquirer,* Dubin created a new beat in 1986: the ethnic and racial issues beat. "I decided that the only stories on racial and ethnic issues were stories about violence. It was clear to me in 1986 that the nation was changing in terms of its color and ethnicity. But we weren't doing stories about their lives and what was going on. It seemed to me that *The Inquirer* and newspapers in general were missing that story," he says.

Dubin now writes stories about Ethiopians, African-Americans, Puerto Ricans, Vietnamese and every other racial or ethnic group in Philadelphia. He doesn't speak their language. He hasn't had their background. He describes himself as "a white, Jewish boy from South Philadelphia." But he doesn't have any trouble getting people to talk to him.

"Sometimes I wish I were Korean or Cambodian or Latino and knew the language," he says. "But I do the best I can. You just have to be sensitive. I try very hard to be non-threatening. I try to explain to them that besides them doing me a favor by talking to me, it's possible I'm going to do them a favor. I'm going to help people understand them. I tell them, 'It can only make your life better if people know what you are going through.'"

And Dubin says he drops a lot of names. He has developed sources locally and nationally among every racial and ethnic group. He tries to introduce himself with the sponsorship technique, using the name of someone both he and the source know, or the matchmaker technique.

"When I first started the beat, I called people and said, 'Help me out. This is who I am and what I do.' People like to be asked questions about what they know and where they feel smart. They like to share information. I don't care whether you are a plumber or a Cambodian asked about a ritual. When I'm done, I ask, 'Is there anyone you know who is even smarter than you?' They laugh and give me two names. Now I have a list of hundreds of names of people around the country."

Dubin's stories don't come from press releases. Most of them come from what he calls "schmoozing," talking to people, having a cup of coffee or a meal with them, or just from observation. "There's a saying that if you drive to work and can't come up with an idea from what you see out of your car window, you ought to drive to work a different way," Dubin says. "The Cambodian Association doesn't send out press releases. You have to go out and look."

Dubin's stories range from a feature about an ethnic festival to a trend story about how Puerto Ricans in Philadelphia cope with divided loyalties to their new country and their homeland. Here's an excerpt from the series on Puerto Ricans, written by Dubin with two other reporters:

Angelo Navarro is hunched deep in a waiting room chair at Philadelphia International Airport, his eyes red and puffy.

In a few minutes, the skinny, freckled teen-ager will board a plane to go live in Puerto Rico—for the second time in six months.

A week ago he had smiled at the prospect. This morning he cried and pleaded with his parents to stay in Philadelphia.

On Navarro's final day at school, his teacher, Cynthia Alvarez, had tried to console him and then offered a prediction:

"I know I'm going to see you again."

She is probably right.

Angelo Navarro can catch an afternoon flight and reach Puerto Rico in time for supper. For him and thousands of Philadelphia Puerto Ricans, easy travel has stretched loyalties and the meaning of home.

Is home Puerto Rico, where he was born and where his grandmother still lives in the town of Caguas? Or is it the gritty Howard Street neighborhood in North Philadelphia where he grew up?

Unlike others who migrated here and cannot easily return to their homeland, Puerto Ricans shift between two cultures, two languages, two lives.

Doreen Carvajal, Murray Dubin and Denise-Marie Santiago, *The Philadelphia Inquirer*

Here is an unusual news story by Dubin:

It's official

They're American Indian, so they can get married

The Indian war is over.

The Indians and true love won; the bureaucrats lost.

On Thursday, Brenda Lynch and William Dimalanta, native American Indians who live in Kensington, were refused a marriage license.

Neither the clerks nor their supervisors in the Marriage License Bureau would permit them to write "Native American Indian" as their race on the application form.

"I don't know if Indian is a race. I'm not an anthropologist," said Thomas F. Gehret, attorney for the bureau in City Hall Room 413. "We don't put down Afro-American or Italian-American. Is Indian equal to Italian-American or is it closer to Caucasian?"

Gehret said the marriage bureau had never faced a problem like this.

"We don't want to prevent them from getting married," he said. "Have someone show us it's a race and we'll do it. Saying it doesn't make it a race. Show me something."

How about the U.S. Census, which lists "American Indian" as an acceptable answer to its question on race?

Or talk to Temple University anthropology professor Judith Goode.

"Native American is a racial designation," she said.

The state marriage license form is dated 1969. Under the designation of "Color or Race," it says: "White, Negro, Other, Specify."

So there appears to be room, intellectually at least, to have replies other than white or Negro. Gehret said acceptable answers in Room 413 are "white, black and brown."

How do the clerks designate race for Asian brides and grooms-to-be?

He said "yellow" was an acceptable answer.

After complaints from Lynch's employer, United American Indians of Delaware County, Gehret yesterday scheduled a meeting with Orphans Court Administrative Judge Edward Pawelec. Orphans Court oversees the bureau.

"The judge had done some research," Gehret said after the meeting. "Native American Indian" was a race, the judge said, and will now be an acceptable response to clerks and supervisors in the marriage bureau.

Shortly after the 11:30 a.m. meeting with the judge, Lynch and Dimalanta went into Room 413, sat on the molded plastic chairs, gazed at the red cupids and hearts and cuddly bears on the walls, and filled their forms anew.

No problems.

Lynch and Dimalanta are from North Carolina. She is a Haliwa-Saponi; he is from the Lumbee tribe.

"I'm relieved that we got the license and I'm happy we're going to get married, but everything is not all right," Lynch said.

"Things have to be changed. The applications should be changed. And those people's attitudes should be changed."

The wedding date is April 11.

Murray Dubin, *The Philadelphia Inquirer*

Dubin says that when dealing with ethnic groups, especially with people who are not accustomed to being interviewed by the media or whose language skills are different, face-to-face interviews are preferable. "I try to chat with people on their own territory," he says.

He also believes in cleaning up quotes when his sources don't speak English well. Or he limits the quotes in his stories. "If I'm not doing a story about language difficulties, I don't feel you should be faithful to the way they speak, because you don't want to embarrass them."

In spite of language and cultural differences, Dubin has not had much difficulty understanding people from other cultures or being sensitive to their needs. But one time, he confesses, he messed up. He was writing a story about the growing Ethiopian population in Philadelphia. His first source was the head of the Ethiopian Association. Then something else came up, and he dropped the story for a while. When he got back to it, he called other sources and searched for an academic source who had expertise about Ethiopia. The University of Pennsylvania recommended a white Italian professor who had that knowledge. Dubin used the professor's comments in the story along with many other sources. But by this time, he neglected to include the comments from his first source because he really didn't need that information anymore. When the story ran, the Ethiopian source was furious.

"He felt he had lost face in the community because he wasn't quoted," Dubin says. "He was angry that I had talked to a white man. I had no inkling that was going to happen. In retrospect, I should have understood that he would have looked bad and lost face. I could have found a way to include him in the story. I still would have used the white professor's comments. But I could have kicked myself for not being more sensitive."

However, Dubin says he tries to do a job few other reporters are doing at newspapers. It's a beat that he thinks is crucial for the future. "I think newspapers and the media in general ought to be devoting more energy to how people with brown skins and yellow skins and whatever color are changing the way America looks and America works and America plays and America eats," he says. "Sometimes it's just a little story about the way things are changing. If there's more bok choy in the market than there used to be, we ought to tell people that. I think we miss too many stories because no one wrote a press release. We ought to tell people what is going on."

Gender Differences

One of the ways America is changing involves women's roles. Women make up 52 percent of the population, but studies show they don't get nearly that much media coverage.

Two studies conducted for the Women, Men and Media Project at the University of California in 1989 examined gender in photos, bylines and story sources at 10 major metropolitan newspapers. One study revealed that women were represented in newspapers as follows:

27 percent of the bylines on front pages

24 percent of the photos (women were usually with their family)

11 percent of the people quoted

Another study conducted for the project showed that in broadcast news, women were the focus of interviews in news stories 13.7 percent of the time at ABC, 10.2 percent at CBS and 8.9 percent at NBC. As Exhibit 19-2 shows, the coverage of women in newsmagazines is also far less than proportionate to their numbers.

Like many other studies, the report from the Women, Men and Media Project blamed many of the problems for story sources and story selection on the male-dominated power structure in the media; in 1989 only 6 percent of the top media bosses were female. "The messages the American people receive pass through a male filter," the report said.

By the early '90s, the percentage of women in top management hadn't increased. But coverage of issues about women had— although not necessarily because of sensitivity. At newspapers, for example, female readership declined 26 percent in the mid-'80s.

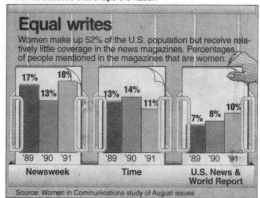

USA SNAPSHOTS®

A look at statistics that shape the nation

Equal writes

Women make up 52% of the U.S. population but receive relatively little coverage in the news magazines. Percentages of people mentioned in the magazines that are women:

Newsweek: '89 17%, '90 13%, '91 18%

Time: '89 13%, '90 14%, '91 11%

U.S. News & World Report: '89 7%, '90 8%, '91 10%

Source: Women in Communications study of August issues

By Marcy E. Mullins, USA TODAY

Exhibit 19.2

Coverage of women in newsmagazines

Marcy E. Mullins/*USA Today*

Studies showed that an increasing number of women were working, and they had little time to read newspapers. In focus groups with women, media executives discovered that women said they would read newspapers if there were more stories of interest to them, such as stories about education, women in business and women in general.

Many newspapers began focusing more on such stories. In the 1970s, partially because the feminist movement was stressing equal rights, newspaper sections devoted primarily to women's issues gave way to the more generic "lifestyles," sections. But by the '90s, women's sections began reappearing. The *Chicago Tribune,* for example, created a women's section called "Womanews." Television news also featured more stories about health, parenting, education, day care and other issues believed to be of interest to women.

A danger accompanies this well-meaning attention. The result can be an overemphasis on "gee whiz" stories that stress how amazing it is for a woman to succeed. The point is instead to focus on the newsworthiness of women's achievements.

Just as women are victims of stereotypes, so are men. Women are supposed to be emotional; men are supposed to be strong. More often the men featured in the news have no feelings at all. Women have an agenda of child support and social issues; men want to read about sports.

Nonsense, says Jack Kammer, a free-lance writer about gender issues. In an article in *Editor & Publisher,* he says it is a mistake to conclude that women have no interest in sports or business sections and that men have no interest in lifestyle sections. In fact, he says, one study showed that 84 percent of the men surveyed said family mattered most to them. Men also want a say about child care, sexual harassment and social issues.

The principles for coverage of gender are the same as they are for coverage of minorities. Make an effort to include female sources as experts, as well as males and multicultural sources, in general stories, not just stories geared to women. Seek diversity of opinion, but write about people as being all equal. When you write about a woman, don't include descriptive details about her appearance unless you would also include descriptive details about a man's appearance.

Consider the following story about Dolly Parton, for example. The writer says the focus of the story is Parton's new movie, a point the writer makes in the 18th paragraph. The writer also acknowledges that Parton (the writer doesn't call her anything but Dolly) has achieved great success—a $100 million fortune—from records, movies, TV shows and her Dollywood amusement park in Tennessee. Read the story and decide if the story, despite its tongue-in-cheek tone, is offensive:

NEW YORK—No way they're real, not *that* big.

Women would kill to have them. Men would kill to somehow get them off Dolly Parton and onto their wives. They are just so . . . so . . . what, titanic?

Ooooo, the way they sit right *up there,* so prominently, so, so, so openly.

And up close, they look different from each other. The one on the left is almost square. The other's got a kind of pear shape to it. No wonder two security guards, with guns and walkie-talkies, are right outside the fancy hotel room.

But it just seems far too crass to mention them, to come right out and ask: "Dolly, are those *real* diamond rings?"

And so you don't.

Instead, you just sit there and stare at this tiny little woman, talking and giggling, giggling and talking, just as she does with Johnny Carson or Phil Donahue.

You've got to hand it to her—she's no different right there on the couch than she is on the teevee. Just as bubbly, just as self-deprecating. And talk about *looks.*

No lie. She is sitting there in these spike-heeled, knee-high black leather boots, jeans that must've pinched her when she was 12. And for a top, she's got on some kind of black frilly, lacy thing. Whew. It's all topped off by a silver-gray leather jacket that's got Lawrence Taylor shoulder pads and surely cost about what Lee Iacocca has made in all his years with Chrysler.

Lord have mercy, why doesn't this woman just spontaneously combust?

Of course, it's a look that Dolly Parton, now 46, has cultivated for years.

"I *l-o-v-e* all this gaud," she squeals. "It's like a kid with paints and crayons. I think it has

to do with me growing up poor and wanting more. I lived in fairy tales with stories about kings and queens with their robes and diamonds. And that's what I always wanted to be."

Dolly giggles.

"I patterned myself after the trash in my home town. There was this woman, I swear." She giggles again, and leans in a bit to share a story.

"You know how every small town has a trollop or a tramp or a slut or whatever. Well, there was this woman when I was growing up. Every Saturday she'd walk the streets until somebody would pick her up. Men would be driving around, tooting the horn. She had long, blond hair that was peroxided. She wore bright red lipstick. She had long, bright-red fingernails, and tight skirts in these bright colors, and high heels.

"I thought, THAT IS HOW I WANT TO LOOK WHEN I

GROW UP. I didn't know she was the town tramp. I didn't even know what that meant. So, sure enough, when I grew up, I looked like trash. But I don't feel like trash."

The giggle.

Oh, this woman is fun. Of course, she's not here just to explain her lifetime fashion philosophy. She is here because she's got a new movie out: Straight Talk, which opened Friday.

In ST, Dolly—sorry, but it just doesn't feel right calling her Parton—plays Shirlee Kenyon, a small-town Arkansas dance instructor, thrice divorced and stuck in a nowhere relationship.

The Philadelphia Inquirer

Most sexism is not so blatant. And even if you think something is amusing, try to envision whether women, or men or minorities, might be offended by your sense of humor.

How can you avoid sexism and gender stereotypes? Here are some tips published in *The Gannetteer,* a magazine for employees of Gannett newspapers:

• Avoid using masculine pronouns such as he or his. Instead of "Everyone should eat his own biscuit," say, "everyone should eat a biscuit." (If you must use a pronoun, use his and her together.)

• Avoid words that, by definition, refer to one sex or the other but not both. Instead of governess, use tutor.

• Avoid words starting or ending with man. Instead of mailman, use mail carrier. Instead of fireman, use firefighter; police officer in place of policeman.

• Avoid stereotypes in illustrations and graphics. Not all quarterbacks are white. Not all basketball players are black. Not all single parents are women. Not all newspaper editors are men. Not all pro golfers are men.

• Avoid calling groups of people men, unless they are all male. A congressional group should be called lawmakers or members of Congress, not Congressmen.

• Avoid the stereotype of a mother. Don't say "chicken soup like your mother used to make." Maybe father made the soup once in a while. Avoid phrases like "old wives' tale," "tied to her apron strings" or "Dutch uncle."

• Avoid referring to women by their first names in stories. This is almost always patronizing, and not usually done to men.

• Avoid describing women with adjectives that dwell on sexual attributes. Ask yourself whether you would describe the walk of an IBM executive as "suggestive" if you were profiling a man, or would the walk just seem "confident." Ditto for "feisty." When is the last time you saw a man described as "feisty?"

• Be careful with "first" stories: the first woman to pick up the garbage for a living, fly into space or run for the school board. *(However, if it is a first, it may be worth mentioning, but it does not have to be the focus of the story.)*

• Avoid phrases that carry an element of surprise such as "smart and dedicated woman." Is it unusual that someone who is smart and dedicated is a woman, too?

• Beware of approaching any story with the subconscious idea that it is more of a man's story or a woman's. Almost always we quote women in stories about child care. Why not men? A lack of child care is just as big a problem to them—or should be.

Guidelines for Writing About Special Groups

During baseball's 1991 World Series between the Atlanta Braves and the Minnesota Twins, Native Americans protested the use of team names that they considered degrading to their heritage. They wanted the teams with names like Redskins, Braves and Indians to change their names, and they wanted the media to stop using the old names.

William Hilliard, editor of *The Oregonian,* took the request seriously. He instituted a policy requiring the newspaper staff to use the names of the cities (such as Atlanta played Cincinnati) in place of the names of the teams. Hilliard said many people didn't understand his decision (his mail was 60-40 against the policy). But until Native Americans raised the issue, he hadn't thought the names could be offensive. "I, too, am a product of a white male–dominated environment," he wrote in an article for the American Society of Newspaper Editors. And Hilliard is an African-American. He continued:

> Very few, if any, of my coworkers have any understanding of what I, and other persons of color, endure on an almost daily basis because of an indignity—a racial slur here, a slight there, even a show of surprise. . . . This is a color question, and whites in America have not had to deal with that one. Our society is multicultural and multiracial. If we are to make all Americans feel free and equal, then we must find innovative ways to solve problems associated with race.

Every group has some special needs and concerns about language. A man who uses a wheelchair probably doesn't consider himself handicapped (a derogatory term). He may, however, have a disability that requires him to use a wheelchair. A person who has AIDS is not a victim but rather an AIDS patient or a person living with AIDS. And not all people over age 65 are ready for the stereotypical rocking chair.

You cannot be expected to memorize dictionaries for each special interest group. However, if your beat is a specialty that frequently deals with aging, disabled people, AIDS or some other minority interest, you could call an umbrella organization and ask for guidelines. Most organizations have these printed.

Your first source, however, should be the people you interview. Ask them how they prefer to be addressed. Next, consult the *Associated Press Stylebook,* which includes guidelines under such listings as *handicapped* and *AIDS.* You'll minimize trouble by avoiding the use of adjectives to describe people.

People With Disabilities

Do not characterize someone as disabled unless that condition is crucial to the story. Avoid the word *handicapped,* unless the person uses it to describe himself or herself. If the disability is a factor, don't say "disabled people." Instead, use "people with disabilities." Avoid such terms as *crippled* and *deformed.*

Many euphemisms—such as "physically challenged," "partially sighted" and "physically inconvenienced"—have come into vogue. However, disability groups object to such euphemisms, because they are considered condescending, according to the Research and Training Center for Independent Living at the University of Kansas. The center, which offers guidelines for writing about people with disabilities, says euphemisms "reinforce the idea that disabilities cannot be dealt with up front." When in doubt, ask your sources how they prefer to be addressed.

Here are some more tips:

• When interviewing people with disabilities, do not speak louder unless the person has a hearing impairment. A common complaint of people who have disabilities unrelated to their hearing is that everyone treats them as though they were hearing impaired. Treat people with disabilities exactly as you would any other source.

• Avoid overcompensating by writing about people with disabilities as though they were superhuman. The hidden implication is that all people with disabilities are without talent and that your source is unusual. The same principle says to avoid calling an African-American articulate or qualified, implying that other African-Americans are not.

• Avoid writing about people with disabilities as though they don't have any fallibilities.

• Avoid using adjectives as nouns to describe disabled people in a group, such as "the deaf" or "the retarded." Say "people who are deaf" or "people with mental retardation." For people who are blind, "visually impaired" is a preferred term.

• For mental illness, avoid such terms as *crazy* and *demented*. *Psychotic* and *schizophrenic* should be used in context—and only if they are the proper medical terms. Preferred terms are "people with emotional disorders" or psychiatric illness, mental problems or mental disabilities.

Stories About Aging

If there were ever a group subject to "gee whiz" stories, it would have to be people over age 65. Most newspaper feature stories treat people in this age group as absolutely amazing just because they walk, run, dance or accomplish anything. People over 65 are usually described as spry, sometimes feisty, but always remarkable.

Consider this feature:

> This place hops.
>
> The food's tame, the dance steps slower than they used to be, the stiffest drink comes from the water fountain.
>
> Still the Gray Crowd jams the Armory Park Senior Citizens Center. Typically, 1,200 men and women gather daily for gossip, games, and yes—even to cast some plain old-fashioned goo-goo eyes.
>
> *The* (Tucson) *Arizona Daily Star*

Or the story will feature a twist—surprise, surprise, they're old!

> The teams, each with two rows of participants, face one another. As the blue balloon floats through the air, the two seemingly docile teams transform into aggressive competitors.
>
> You'd think they were teenagers. They were . . . perhaps 50 or more years ago.
>
> *Tulsa* (Okla.) *World*

Make age a factor, not the focus of a person's accomplishments. Readers can decide for themselves if the person's accomplishments are surprising because of the person's age. Especially avoid the astonishment factor: Isn't it amazing this person can accomplish such and such at this age?

At this point in American society, people over age 65 are often classified as older Americans entitled to certain privileges. The *Associated Press Stylebook* also uses age 65 as a delineator. Here are some general guidelines for dealing with people of this age:

• When writing about people over age 65, avoid such adjectives as *gray-haired* or other terms unless you would use the same type of description if the story were about a younger person with blond or brown hair.

• Avoid stereotypes. Don't introduce rocking chairs or similar stereotypical images if the people in the story aren't using them.

• Avoid "the graying population," "senior citizens" and other group designations unless you are writing a trend story. And then use such a term only if it is relevant, necessary and appropriate—for example, if a group uses the term in its own name, as in Gray Power.

• Avoid saying such things as "She doesn't consider herself old," unless she says it. Even though you are meaning to extend a compliment, by writing such denials you are introducing a stereotype.

You may not always use the right term, but if you have the right attitude and try to be sensitive to cultural differences, you are at least on your way to improving news coverage in a multicultural society.

AIDS Stories

Feb. 16, 1989, started out as a good day. Carolyn Warmbold was working on the final stages of her dissertation for her doctorate in English at the University of Texas, Austin.

At 1:40 that afternoon, her husband, Ted, called. He had the worst headache he had ever had. Nine days later he died at age 45.

The doctors attributed his death to cryptococcal meningitis. The *San Antonio Light,* the newspaper of which Ted Warmbold was editor, attributed it to AIDS.

"On Sunday (a week before Ted died), when the doctors told me of his meningitis, they did not tell me of his AIDS," Carolyn Warmbold says. "The managing editor of the newspaper told me. The paper was going to mention it in his obituary. My first reaction was to get a gun and shoot both Ted and myself because he would not survive the disease, and I would not survive the stigma."

The story of how Ted Warmbold died from an AIDS-related illness got into the newspaper. This is the story that didn't. It is the story of Carolyn Warmbold, an assistant professor of communication at Trinity University, San Antonio, and her crusade to make journalists sensitive to the needs of people living with AIDS.

At first she worried about why the newspaper insisted on printing the cause of her husband's death from an AIDS-related disease. "How could it help the community? My privacy would be invaded," she says. "I foresaw what the disclosure would mean. People would speculate that I, too, had AIDS. The announcement would make us unpeople—unemployable, uninsurable. I swore while he was dying that I would try to keep it out of the paper. But the newspaper editors said it was likely to be rumored anyway, and if they covered it up, how could they deal with others."

The *Light* announced it only locally. The note that went to The Associated Press didn't say AIDS, but the Texas AP revised it and included the term.

When her husband died, Carolyn Warmbold had resolved that he could not be just another AIDS statistic. She decided to give the eulogy at his funeral. "His death had to account for something."

For the first time Warmbold, a former reporter, was on both sides of the news. It was the last "gloriously free moment" she would experience in two years. She gave speeches and became an advocate for AIDS patients. But she suffered from the stigma.

"The doctors said I was free of the AIDS virus. But after my husband's death, the pest control man came for his regular visit and wore rubber gloves for the first time. He pointed a sprayer at me as though I were some giant cockroach. I was stuck with a scarlet letter *A* for *AIDS* on my breast."

Warmbold and her husband of 22 years had experienced sexual difficulties throughout their marriage. But it was only in the two years prior to his death that she suspected he was gay. However, the couple had not discussed her suspicions. She says during one period when they had separated, her husband was sexually promiscuous and could have contracted the disease at that time.

She admits it is hard for people to understand why she did not suspect her husband was gay long before his death. She dismisses such concern. She was busy getting her doctorate, he was busy running a newspaper, and they hadn't engaged in sex for years anyway.

Today Warmbold is committed to trying to make people sensitive to the needs of people living with AIDS (not dying with AIDS, she stresses). She says the media need to write more personal narratives about people with AIDS so they are not statistics and so the stigma of having AIDS ultimately will be reduced. "We must have stories with names," she says. "What is more effective than the Vietnam Memorial when you see all those names? That shows the numbers more than anything."

The writer's task Writing about AIDS is different from writing other stories, Carolyn Warmbold insists. The biggest problem is the public perception, she says. "The public views people with AIDS as innocent victims—those who get it by transfusions, wives who are infected—and guilty victims—the gays and drug users. The very acronym implies guilt—Acquired Immune Deficiency Syndrome, as something you go out and acquire like a car. But you need to persuade people that there is no such thing as a guilty or innocent victim. You are just dealing with people. Nobody asks to get AIDS. It happens."

Warmbold admits her attitude borders on advocacy journalism. But she says it is not possible to be objective about such stories. "It's not like covering city council. You are dealing with death. I don't think it's wrong to feel emotion."

Asking questions about death is difficult. But Warmbold says reporters shouldn't go into the story with a hopeless attitude. "People with AIDS are going to die, but at the same time the quality and quantity of their life depends on having a positive attitude," she says. "When you are interviewing, you want to keep that in mind. Most will talk about death. Take the cue from them. Most of them are going to accept the fact that their life is going to be short. Talk about it matter-of-factly." Warmbold suggests these kinds of questions: "Are you frightened by it? Do you think about the pain?"

Warmbold also suggests that before publication, reporters check parts of the story with the people who are affected. You don't have to read them the story, but check the facts and tell them what you are going to say. Make sure they are comfortable about using names. "You have to take the whole family into consideration," she says.

There is no formula for covering AIDS stories. Just be a compassionate human being, Warmbold says.

A Pulitzer Prize AIDS story   There was no formula to prepare Jacqui Banaszynski, a reporter at the *St. Paul* (Minn.) *Pioneer Press,* for the emotional toll that AIDS can take on the patients and on the reporter who writes about them. Her stories about the life and death of a Minnesota farmer and his partner won her the 1988 Pulitzer Prize for feature writing. She spent 15 months reporting how Dick Hanson and Bert Henningson lived and died with AIDS.

She became as close to them as a family member—actually, closer than some of their family members. When Henningson was dying, his family even asked her to help decide whether they should pull the plug (she refused).

The rules change for this kind of story, Banaszynski says. "You have to be empathetic. On the other hand, you have to be honest and true to the reader who may be hostile to the subject. You walk a fine line between not blaming and not whitewashing."

The idea for the series was to find an AIDS patient who was willing to be chronicled throughout the disease. She found Hanson. He was willing to talk about his disease, but he couldn't face the thought of dying.

"I'll never forget the day I had to confront him with the prospect of dying," Banaszynski says. "It was the hardest thing I've ever done as a journalist, knowing I was going to ask if I could watch him die. I said I want to do the whole story, that means to the end. But he was in denial (about death). He kept saying, 'I want you to do a story about life.' I told him, 'If you beat this, you'll be the first man to do this. But if you die—and everybody dies from AIDS—I want to be there at the end.' I was hoping he would say no.

"He got very quiet. And then he got very angry. I said I'm going to leave. I allowed him some time to think. He cried and realized he was dying. Then we made our pact to do the story."

For the next 15 months, she became attached to these two men. "You can steel yourself emotionally if it's just one story, but they became a beat for me."

The series appeared as three stories on different dates, the first chapter on June 21, 1987, when Hanson was still alive. He died on July 25, and the third chapter appeared two weeks later. When Henningson died a year later, she wrote an epilogue to the series that was not part of the Pulitzer package.

Banaszynski says there is no question that the story took an emotional toll on her. "I allowed myself a limited time to be emotional, never during the interviews." And then she forced herself into her role as journalist and wrote the stories.

Banaszynski says one of the reasons AIDS stories differ from other stories is the social stigma. "The disease is one story, the social context of the disease becomes another story. If you ignore the opportunity to deal with the societal revulsion, you miss the whole crux."

Readers don't want to read about AIDS or deal with it, she says. So she decided that the best approach was to portray these two men as two ordinary Minnesotans who had a commonality with readers. "If Joe and Suzy Reader could not relate to two gay pig farmers, they could relate to two men who plant impatiens, feed kittens and tend a vegetable garden, because that's what all Minnesotans do."

In her introduction, she stresses that this is a story about people living—as well as dying—with AIDS:

Death is no stranger to the heartland. It is as natural as the seasons, as inevitable as farm machinery breaking down and farmers' bodies giving out after too many years of too much work.

But when death comes in the guise of AIDS, it is a disturbingly unfamiliar visitor, one better known in the gay districts and drug houses of the big cities, one that shows no respect for the usual order of life in the country.

The visit has come to rural Glenwood, Minn.

Dick Hanson, a well-known liberal political activist who homesteads his family's century-old farm south of Glenwood, was diagnosed last summer with acquired immune deficiency syndrome. His partner of five years, Bert Henningson, carries the AIDS virus.

In the year that Hanson has been living—and dying—with AIDS, he has hosted some cruel companions: blinding headaches and failing vision, relentless nausea and deep fatigue, falling blood counts and worrisome coughs and sleepless, sweat-soaked nights.

He has watched as his strong body, toughened by 37 years on the farm, shrinks and stoops like that of an old man. He has weathered the family shame and community fear, the prejudice and whispered condemnations. He has read the reality in his partner's eyes, heard the death sentence from doctors and seen the hopelessness confirmed by the statistics.

But the statistics tell only half the story—the half about dying.

Statistics fail to tell much about the people they represent. About the people like Hanson—a farmer who has nourished life in the fields, a peace activist who has marched for a safer planet, an idealist and a gay activist who has campaigned for social justice, and now an AIDS patient who refuses to abandon his own future, however long it lasts.

The statistics say nothing of the joys of a carefully tended vegetable garden and new kittens under the shed, of tender teasing and magic hugs. Of flowers that bloom brighter and birds that sing sweeter and simple pleasures grown profound against the backdrop of a terminal illness. Of the powerful bond between two people who pledged for better or worse and meant it.

"Who is to judge the value of life, whether it's one day or one week or one year," Hanson said.

"I find the quality of life more important than the length of life."

Much has been written about the death that comes from AIDS, but little has been said about the living. Hanson and Henningson want to change that. They have opened their homes and their hearts to tell the whole story—beginning to end.

Jacqui Banaszynski, *St. Paul Pioneer Press*

Ground rules for sensitive questions   When you write about AIDS, you have to ask about dying and you have to ask about sex. How do you approach either of these sensitive questions?

"The only thing to do is to set it in context," Banaszynski says. "When I get to it, I ask as directly as I can: How many men did you sleep with? I don't warn them that this is a hard question. I set that up in the ground rules. I say, 'We're going to talk about a lot of personal things, and a lot may be embarrassing. You don't have to answer, but I'll try to get you to answer.' If you ask honestly and directly with no judgment in your voice so there is no shame involved, they will answer. If you are embarrassed, they will pick it up. I ask the question as matter-of-factly as I would about the weather."

Banaszynski says people are really very eager to tell their stories. "I think you can ask anybody any question if you are non-judgmental and a good listener. Nobody listens anymore."

She also used another interviewing technique in her many visits with Hanson and Henningson. "I did something I don't normally do," she says. "I reminded them of my mission. They got to like me so much. My job was to be responsible and remind them that I was there as a reporter. I broke rules and invented new ones. I said when the notebook was down they could talk freely. Nothing was fair game until the notebook was out. And then I would remind them again that it was now on the record."

When she wrote the stories, she also did something that is not general practice in journalism. "I called each person involved in the story and read them their quotes, and I told them the context. For example, in one case I said, 'I set you in the context of a fight with your family.' Then I told them, if you can convince me that I have erred or been insensitive, I'll consider changing it."

Only one person complained. She didn't take out any of his comments, but she added a sentence that appeased him.

She also took the newspaper to Hanson and Henningson the night before it hit the morning newspaper stands so they could see it first. "They couldn't change anything, but that's just courtesy. If they allow me to invade their privacy, I owe them that courtesy."

Banaszynski says the ground rules are different when you are writing about people who are not accustomed to dealing with the media. "I do a lot of real-people stories," she says. "These people don't know the rules. I have more responsibility to tell them what I'm going to be writing, the general thrust, and what I'm trying to do."

Sometimes in stories about AIDS, family members don't know about the diagnosis or are not willing to have the information made public. Banaszynski tells AIDS patients that she must use their name and picture. She gives them time to tell their family.

For her Pulitzer series, "AIDS in the Heartland," the family knew the stories would be public, but not all the members were cooperative. In fact, she got threats from some people who were upset that she was doing the story. The turmoil is part of doing the whole story, Banaszynski says, and she thinks the statements from family members may have been one of the most powerful parts of the series.

Here is an excerpt from the second chapter, where Banaszynski writes about a family quarrel she witnessed:

Tom Hanson is angry at Dick Hanson for making news of such a shameful disease, at his sister, Mary, for siding with Dick, at his brother Grant because "he's not man enough" to say that homosexuality is wrong, at a local minister for refusing to denounce homosexuality from the pulpit, at the media for exploiting his family.

"I feel Dickie is helping the public by talking about this," he said. "But he could have done it without bringing his name into it or his picture or the town. This is not fair what he's doing to the family. . . . It's not easy being single trying to go through this, having girls come up and say, 'His brother's gay and he has AIDS. Is he gay, too?' . . .

"He never stopped to think of the innocent people who would be suffering for his glory."

Jacqui Banaszynski, *St. Paul Pioneer Press*

Some things she heard that night with the family were so powerful, but so private, that Banaszynski worried about using them, even though they were said "on the record."

She uses this method to determine whether a revealing quote that could hurt someone is really necessary: First she writes it in the story. Then she takes it out and shows the story to several people at her newspaper. If they can get the meaning and emotion from the story without the sensitive quote, she leaves it out. If they aren't moved by what she is writing, then she considers that the quote might be necessary. She also uses ethical reasoning: Is it for the greater good? Will more people be helped by this information than harmed?

Terminology   The language of AIDS is changing, as it is for many special interest groups. The best advice is to ask the people you are covering how they preferred to be addressed.

People with AIDS do not like to be called "victims." They prefer to be called "AIDS patients" or "people *living* with AIDS."

The *Associated Press Stylebook* says the scientific name for the AIDS virus is the human immunodeficiency virus. People who test positive for it are referred to as HIV-positive. That doesn't mean they have AIDS; it means they are carrying the virus. To have AIDS means they have developed the symptoms of the disease and have been diagnosed with the disease, not merely with the virus.

Banaszynski isn't always willing to use the technical term, such as "HIV-positive," if it won't be readily understood by readers. She often writes about the "AIDS virus." Banaszynski says what she writes must pass "the Ethel test," in honor of her mother, Ethel. "My mother is very bright, but she lives in a small town and is not very worldly. She is the common reader. If I don't think Ethel will understand a term, I won't use it." But the terms you use will depend on your newspaper's policy.

Banaszynski predicts that it will get increasingly difficult to interest the public in AIDS stories. "The one thing you always have to remember about AIDS is that it has an overlay of homosexuality," she says. "It is a stigmatized disease that the public doesn't want to read about. You have to get past a big barrier of rejection.

"You have to focus on the common denominator. This could be your brother or neighbor or your doctor. AIDS serves as an extreme example of all the challenges in reporting more than other stories. You have got to find ways to have it connect to everyone's life."

Activities

1   Interview members of various ethnic and racial groups in your community or on your campus about their concerns and the kinds of stories they think newspapers are not writing about them. Devise 10 story ideas based on your interviews.

2   Write a trend story based on one of the story ideas you developed in activity 1.

3   Sexism, ageism and racism: Look for examples of language, description or other elements of stories that you think are sexist, racist or ageist.

4   Using highlighters of two different colors, read the news sections of your newspaper for a few days. Use one color to mark the female sources quoted and the other color for the male sources. Analyze the types of stories that feature women more than men and vice versa. Also try to determine if multicultural sources are used in the news stories.

FIVE

Applying the Techniques

COACHING

TIPS

Ask yourself: What made this person memorable?

Have you written this obituary well enough for it to be saved in someone's family Bible?

Check the accuracy of spellings and information. Also, make sure you call a funeral home or family member to confirm that the person really died.

Obituaries

20

He is known as "Dr. Death." Years ago, when he was an investigative reporter for the now-defunct *Philadelphia Bulletin,* he risked death; the Pagan motorcycle gang members he investigated threatened to firebomb his home. Now he writes about death. And he does it so well that he has won awards for a type of writing rarely honored. He's Jim Nicholson, whose obituaries for the *Philadelphia Daily News* are being used as models by newspapers around the country.

They read more like profiles. Nicholson says that's what they are—stories about the lives of people, not about their deaths. Like the obituary for Lawrence Pompie "Mr. Buddy" Ellis, a retired maintenance man who was a leader in his church:

> He came to be known affectionately among friends as "Dial-A-Prayer" for his unceasing availability to those who wanted him to pray with them. If he couldn't meet personally with someone, he would pray with them on the telephone, said his wife, Fannie, who shared 38 years with him. . . .
> At 5-foot-7 and 205 pounds, Ellis loved to eat. "He loved everything about a pig," said his wife, "and if he didn't watch out, he'd catch his grunt."

Jim Nicholson, *Philadelphia Daily News*

Remember that you are not writing about death. You are writing about life.

Jim "Dr. Death" Nicholson, obituary writer, *Philadelphia Daily News*

Jim Nicholson ("Dr. Death"), obituary writer for the Philadelphia Daily News

And there's Edward E. "Ace" Clark, who used to haul ice in Philadelphia with his favorite horse, Major:

> Ace could go into a house with ice, through the back door, across the alley and out of the front door of the house in the next street, and Major, who knew the route, would walk himself around the block and be there waiting on the next street.
>
> Jim Nicholson, *Philadelphia Daily News*

And Ella Hurst, a homemaker:

> She could cook, quiet babies, protect small children, pass down religion, boss people around, give advice, listen to problems, have patience, be tough or be soft, and had all the other attributes of an authentic grandmother. . . . She enjoyed reading magazines and watching soaps, especially "The Young and the Restless," which she liked to say was filled with love, sex and trash.
>
> Jim Nicholson, *Philadelphia Daily News*

Custodians, homemakers, sanitation workers—they don't have to be rich and famous to make Nicholson's list of special people for an obituary. To Nicholson, all people are special.

Nicholson makes them memorable by the questions he asks family members and friends. He wants to write character portraits, warts and all, he says. "Cleaning up someone's act after he or she has died does not serve the cause of the deceased or loved ones," Nicholson says. "A sanitized portrait is indistinguishable from any other. It is the irregularities that give us identity. A person described as being a strict parent, impatient with unprofessional conduct, becomes real people to the reader. The ultimate acclaim may be when a reader thinks, 'I wish I had known this man or woman.'"

Although Nicholson has won acclaim for investigative reporting, writing obituaries is more rewarding, he says. His investigative stories are saved in dusty library archives; his obituaries are saved in family Bibles. Nicholson's own file cabinets at the *Daily News* bulge with letters from grateful relatives of people he has profiled in obituaries. Most reporters don't consider obituaries their most important stories. But they are among the most well-read items in the paper, and their significance to relatives and friends of the deceased cannot be overstated.

The Importance of Facts

A misspelled name or a factual error is a major problem in any story; in an obituary they are disastrous. So you should check every fact, every name, every reference. And you should check with the funeral director and the family to make sure the person you are writing about is dead.

Someone from the *Detroit Free Press* didn't do that. And the death of Dr. Rogers Fair turned out to be greatly exaggerated, as Mark Twain would say. Fair, a Detroit physician, woke up one morning to read in the newspaper that he had died of cancer. The newspaper had received the obituary information by telephone from a woman who claimed she was Fair's aunt. And the reporter didn't call back to check with family members or a funeral home.

Fair, 40, claimed the "aunt" was a 21-year-old woman who was infatuated with him. She had wooed him with flowers and love notes, but when he rejected her and began dating another woman, he began receiving harassing telephone calls, bomb threats and vandalism to his home. "She is obviously an obsessed person," Fair told the *Free Press*. "She has stated that if she can't have me, nobody else can."

The follow-up story was an embarrassment to the paper:

The obituary for Dr. Rogers Fair in Tuesday's Free Press took a lot of people—especially Fair—by surprise.

"My beeper was just jumping off the hook," the 40-year-old physician said Tuesday. "My secretary called me. She was in tears. . . ."

The erroneous report of Fair's demise was the second phony obituary published by the Free Press in recent years. The first, in July 1985, prompted a revision of reporting practices, requiring all obituary information phoned in by friends and relatives to be confirmed either by a funeral home or law enforcement officials.

But Fair's obituary wasn't properly double-checked, and a woman identifying herself as Fair's aunt was able to hoodwink the Free Press with details of his death. . . .

Detroit Free Press

An obituary, by general definition, is just a notice of some-one's death, but in a newspaper it is defined as a news story about the person. Most newspapers have free or paid death notices—announcements from the family about the deceased. In addition, funeral directors and families call the newspaper to request an obituary. How do you decide who deserves one?

Almost all newspapers will publish an obituary about anyone prominent in the community. Some newspapers, especially those in large cities, have policies to determine who else should be profiled on the obituary page. Generally, reporters scan the paid death notices to look for interesting people, long-term residents or those active in community service.

Nicholson sometimes just picks a name at random or focuses on a person whose family calls him to request an obituary.

Then you make the phone calls—or double-check the validity of the ones you have received by calling a funeral home, checking the phone book and calling the family back or calling other relatives and friends. And, as in any other newspaper story, you check newspaper clips.

Calling people about death isn't easy. But it isn't as difficult as you might expect, especially for obituaries. Most families are grateful, because this is the last story—and more often the only story—printed about their loved ones. Usually someone in the family is prepared to deal with the media. And for many grieving people, talking about their loved one is cathartic. You're not going to be asking them how they feel that someone in the family died; you're asking them how that person lived and what was special about the loved one.

If the obituary is for a person who died under tragic circum-stances that might have and probably did result in a news story, you can call and ask if a family member or friend can give you information.

The easiest way to start is with the funeral director, if one has been selected. The funeral director should have the basic informa-tion and should be able to tell you which family members to call and their phone numbers.

Bare Essentials

Obituary writing follows some basic forms, even when you are writing a special profile. All obituaries, no matter how long or short, must contain the same crucial information:

Name: Use full name, middle initial and nickname if it was commonly used. Enclose the nickname in quotation marks.

Identification: Usually people are identified by occupation or community service. Always try to find something special to use following the name, such as "John Doe, a retired salesman" or "Jane Doe, a homemaker who was active in her church."

Age: In some cases, a family will request that you withhold the age. You should confer with an editor in deciding whether to honor this request.

Date and place of death: Use the day of the week if the death occurred that week, the date if it was more than a week prior to the obituary. State the name of a hospital, if applicable, or other location where the death occurred.

Cause of death: This fact is not required at all newspapers, especially if the cause of death was suicide or AIDS or when the family requests that the cause be withheld. This item has become especially controversial because of the stigma attached to AIDS deaths. Other newspapers require the cause of death, regardless of stigma or family wishes. So check your newspaper's policy before you gather the information. You may have to inform family members of the policy.

Address: Tell where the person lived when he or she died and previous areas of residence for any major length of time. Some newspapers use specific addresses; others just require the town. Generally, the smaller the newspaper, the more specific the address reference.

Background: Specify major accomplishments, organizations, educational background when relevant and any other highlights.

Survivors: Use the names of immediate family members (husband or wife, with her maiden name, children, brothers and sisters). Grandchildren are usually mentioned only by number: "He is survived by five grandchildren." New complications are arising these days because of changes in family relationships. Most newspapers still do not list unmarried partners as survivors or "bonded" partners (homosexual couples united in a marital ceremony), but that rule is changing. In the future, these relationships also may be part of obituaries.

Services: Specify the time, date and location.

Burial: Name the place, and provide memorial information when available.

Obituary writing follows a pattern. Most obituaries, except special feature stories, start with the person's name, identification, a statement that he or she died, and a cause of death. Follow with the age. Then add the other information. When the death occurred a week or more ago, it is customary to start with information about the service or a memorial if that has not yet been conducted.

Some style tips:

Terminology: A funeral is a service; don't be redundant and write "funeral services." They are not held; they are scheduled. Just write "Services will be Saturday" with the time and location.

Names of services: Mass is celebrated, said or sung. The word is capitalized when referring to the specific ceremony, such as Mass of Christian Burial, but in lowercase letters for a generic mass. Find out the exact wording you should use for the particular mass. Likewise, ask for the proper wording of a service for other denominations.

Courtesy titles: Although many newspapers have eliminated courtesy titles *(Mrs., Mr., Ms., Miss)* for news stories, several keep them for obituaries. Again, you must check your newspaper's policy.

Titles for religious leaders: Check the proper title for a rabbi, minister or priest. When writing about a priest, do not use *Father* or *Pastor* for the title. Use *the Rev.* (the reverend) followed by the priest's name: "the Rev. Vince Krische." For a rabbi, use *Rabbi* before the name on first reference: "Rabbi Jacob Katz." On second reference for clergy, including priests, use only the last name. But for second reference to high-ranking clergy, use "the cardinal," "the archbishop" and so on. Check the *Associated Press Stylebook* for specific religious titles.

Basic Obituary Examples

This example about the death of a local citizen follows all the basic guidelines; it also includes information about contributions:

Lucy Davis Burnett, a Dallas native and longtime civic leader, died of cancer Saturday at her home. She was 79.

Services for Mrs. Burnett will be at 2 p.m. Tuesday at Highland Park United Methodist Church.

A graduate of Woodrow Wilson High School in Dallas and Mary Baldwin College in Staunton, Va., Mrs. Burnett was active in numerous cultural and civic affairs.

She was past president of the Southern Methodist University Lecture Series, vice president of the Dallas Junior League and president of the Junior League Garden Club.

She was a founding member of the Dallas Slipper Club and also held memberships in the Dallas Woman's Club, the Dallas Arts Museum League, the women's division of United Way of Dallas and Highland Park United Methodist.

She is survived by her husband, F.W. Burnett of Dallas; a daughter, Lucy Chambers of Vancouver, British Columbia; a son, F.W. Burnett Jr. of Dallas; and six grandchildren.

Memorials may be made to Children's Medical Center of Dallas, the Dallas Chapter of the American Cancer Society or a charity of the donor's choice.

The Dallas Morning News

This obituary is an example of how to "advance" the story by starting with the services. Note the use of courtesy titles.

Services are scheduled Saturday for Hulda Kettler Stoner, who was believed to be the oldest living native Californian. She died Jan. 21 at the age of 109.

Mrs. Stoner, who lived in Santa Monica, was born Dec. 4, 1881, on her pioneer German immigrant family's ranch in the Wilmington area. The 240-acre ranch had been purchased from the holder of a Mexican land grant.

While visiting a cousin in 1906, Mrs. Stoner personally experienced the San Francisco earthquake.

Her granddaughter, Laurie Merryfield, said Mrs. Stoner often recalled other events in her long life—including arduous family vacation trips to Calabasas by horse and wagon, and the first automobile, radio and phonograph in Los Angeles County. She had been equally intrigued, the granddaughter said, with television coverage of the 1969 moon landing.

Mrs. Stoner, a former teacher who maintained an apartment until she was 103, attributed her longevity to a moderate lifestyle and good luck.

Survivors in addition to her granddaughter include a sister, Lucy Marshall of Newport Beach, a daughter, Eileen Abel of Santa Monica, two great-granddaughters and two great-great grandsons.

The memorial service will be at 11 a.m. in the First United Methodist Church, Santa Monica.

Los Angeles Times

This example advances the story by starting with the service. *The Oregonian* always prints the cause of death. Notice in this case that the person died of complications from AIDS, not from AIDS. That is the proper way of writing about death related to this disease. Also notice the use of courtesy titles. Many newspapers, including this one, pass along the family's requests of donations to a specific organization.

A memorial service for William Frank Peterson of South Carolina, a former resident of the Portland area, will be at 2 p.m. Friday in the Damascus home of his parents, Clinton and Nancy Peterson.

Mr. Peterson died Sunday in a Charleston, S.C. hospital of complications arising from AIDS. He was 32.

Born Feb. 24, 1960 in Corvallis, Mr. Peterson lived in a number of cities in Oregon. He was a graduate of Sam Barlow High School in Gresham and served in the U.S. Navy for three years. Mr. Peterson had owned a landscaping business in South Carolina for a number of years.

Survivors besides his parents include his sisters, Karen Southard of Damascus, Marsha Peterson-Tengwall of Hood River and Sonja of Portland; and his brothers, Dwight of Portland and Jerry of Chicago.

The family suggests remembrances be contributions to Cascade AIDS Project or to the Ronald McDonald House.

The Oregonian

Feature Obituaries

More extensive obituaries, written like feature personality profiles, are the specialty of Jim Nicholson. When you begin working on an obituary, he recommends starting with the funeral director. Then when you call the family, start with known facts that the source can remember easily.

"You may know facts about the services, but the object is to get the source talking," Nicholson says. "You might start with the professional background of the deceased—'Why did your father choose to become a tree surgeon?' The interview can progress as any feature profile interview would. The fact that the subject is dead is almost incidental, although how some people face death can be an important part of an obituary because it may reveal how they handled the previous 70 or 80 years of their life."

Nicholson also suggests asking for a photo. The family will probably be happy to furnish it, and it can add a great deal to your story.

Obituary Guidelines

A feature obituary, like any good story, needs quotes. Quote people the way they talk, Nicholson says, including fragmented sentences and slang expressions. Even though many editors permit writers to correct the grammar in quotes, Nicholson says the exact quotes give a better portrait of people.

He also believes someone's bad habits and criminal background, if there is any, should be part of an obituary. This view also is controversial; obituaries tend to be flattering portraits. But Nicholson says they should be true portraits. Many editors would disagree. And families are not likely to be happy with unflattering material. Generally, news editors weigh whether criminal background was a crucial part of the person's life and if the crime was highly publicized. If a person was arrested at one time for shoplifting or for another misdemeanor, most editors would recommend omitting such information. When you are faced with such decisions, it is wise to confer with an editor.

Less disputable is Nicholson's recommendation to include vivid details. Some of the items, such as the type of liquor a person drank or the jewelry he or she wore, may seem unimportant, but Nicholson says those are the details that make the obituary special. And he adds another type of question rarely considered in an obit: historical notes. "Sometimes in a few sentences or graphs, you can put the subject in his youth or childhood and thus place the reader in another era of the city or town's history," he says. "For example, 'Bob Smith was raised in the east end of town in the early 1920s, when Zeke Clayton's blacksmith barn was still standing only a few hundred yards from the Smith family's clapboard house. Years later, Bob would tell his grandchildren how he would wake up most mornings to the hard ping of a hammer bouncing against an anvil.' "

In addition to the basics previously listed, here are some less traditional items that Nicholson includes in his obituary information checklist:

Physical description (height, weight and build, hair color and style)

Dress (favorite type of clothes or item of clothing)

Occupation (how long, what previous jobs)

Speech (tone of voice, gestures, description of smile, method of eye contact, favorite expressions and sayings)

Temperament

Habits (favorite easy chair, places, preferences, mannerisms)

Scene indicators (for example, orange sofa with threadbare cushions)

Weather/lighting ("In warm weather she would sit on her porch in her favorite chair with an ever-present Pepsi")

Historical notes

Feature Obituary Examples

Here is an example of how detailed information translates into the kind of obituary that won Nicholson the 1987 Distinguished Writing Award from the American Society of Newspaper Editors. Notice how many of his guidelines he follows in this story:

Edward E. 'Ace' Clark, 85

Richmond ice & coal dealer

Edward E. "Ace" Clark, who hauled ice through Port Richmond by horse-drawn wagon and by truck for nearly 40 years, died Saturday. He was 85 and lived in Port Richmond.

Clark also had been active in church activities and local sports teams since the mid-1930s.

"Ace," who got his nickname as a kid from the gang that hung out at Tucker and Cedar streets, quit school in the sixth grade because life on his father's ice wagon seemed more interesting than books. He took over the business—Pastime Ice & Coal Co.—when he was 17.

His favorite among his horses, which he stabled at Seltzer Street below Somerset, was one named "Major." He could go into a house with ice, through the back door, across the alley and out the front door of the house in the next street, and Major, who knew the route, would walk himself around the block and be there waiting on the next street.

"We used to say that if us kids had of been horses, we'd have been the best-raised kids in the neighborhood because Dad knew more about horses than he did kids," said his son, Bob Clark, with a laugh.

Powerful arms and shoulders atop spindly legs, Ace Clark was a man of many friends who had a zest for life and would toss out the old icemen's line: "Every man has a wife, but an iceman has his pick."

Bob Clark said his father had keys to many of the homes; if someone wasn't home, he would bring in the ice, empty the refrigerator and then repack the food around the ice.

"Can you imagine someone doing that today for a quarter?" said Clark, adding that the only day's work he ever knew his father to miss was when he got loaded the night of VJ Day and couldn't get up the next morning.

In the winter, when the ice business dropped off by as much as 75 percent, Ace delivered coal.

Though he loved horses, getting a Ford truck in 1937 meant he didn't have to feed the horses on Sundays. And Sundays for Ace Clark were for the church.

He was a past president of St. Anne's Holy Name Society and the St. Anne's Men's Club. He also was one of the organizers and first president of the Icemen's Union in Philadelphia in 1933.

"We had the first telephone in the neighborhood," said his son. "I think it was a fringe he got for being president, to do union business. But I don't think he did much business on it."

Ace Clark loved sports. He was manager of St. Anne's softball team in the 1930s and '40s and the basketball team in the 1940s and '50s.

Normally an easy-going sort, Ace Clark turned rogue elephant when his team was on the court or field.

"People used to go to the games just to watch him," said Bob Clark. "He'd throw his cigar down and get over the referee's case. He always thought his team was getting short-changed."

By 1950, the ice delivery business itself was going the way of the iceman's horse a decade before, and Clark went to work for A&M Beer Distributors in Frankford. His son said he believes his father enjoyed that job even more than delivering ice, because he could pause for a "boilermaker"—a shot of whiskey chased by a glass of beer—to get him on his way.

After six years delivering beer, he went to work for Highway Express and was still loading and unloading trucks when he retired at age 68.

After retiring, he became involved with senior citizens' organizations.

His late wife was the former Agnes M. Bannon.

In addition to his son, Robert J., he is survived by two other sons, Edward A. and Francis X.; two daughters, Anna M. McMenamin and Agnes M. Conahan; 29 grandchildren; and 27 great-grandchildren.

Mass of Christian Burial will be celebrated at 10 a.m. tomorrow at St. Anne's Church, E. Lehigh Avenue and Memphis Street. Burial will be in Resurrection Cemetery, Hulmeville Road below Bristol Road, Cornwells Heights, Bucks County.

Friends may call from 7 to 9 tomorrow night at the Hubert M. McBride Funeral Home, 2357 E. Cumberland St.

Jim Nicholson, *Philadelphia Daily News*

For more prominent people, obituaries are like profiles. They can contain more reactions from other people and more quotes from the person when he or she was living. In cases of famous people who are ill or elderly, many newspapers write advance obituaries and keep them on file, because the research takes time.

When Theodor Seuss Geisel, "Dr. Seuss," died in 1991, many newspapers ran an obituary and separate reaction stories. Others wrapped the reaction in the obituary. Here's an obituary that began in the traditional form:

Theodor Seuss Geisel, "Dr. Seuss," perhaps the most popular children's author of all time, died at his home near San Diego Tuesday night. He was 87. . . .

The Philadelphia Inquirer

Here is a feature obituary for Dr. Seuss. The story begins with the writer's death, some basic information about his accomplishments and then a chronology of his life. It ends with information about survivors. No information was available about services, but if it had been, it would have been included at the end.

Theodor Seuss Geisel, alias Dr. Seuss, whose rhymed writing and fanciful drawings were loved worldwide and helped teach generations to read, died Tuesday night at his home in La Jolla.

Geisel's stepdaughter, Lea Dimond, told reporters the world-famous author died with his family around him. No other information was released regarding the cause of death, but Dimond said Geisel, 87, had been ill for several months.

In the 1950s and '60s, Geisel's books gave millions of children relief from the drab textbook adventures of Dick and Jane. His 48 children's books were translated into 18 languages and sold more than 100 million copies.

Geisel also drew most of the fanciful illustrations in his books, creating a menagerie of Whos, grinches, ziffs and zuffs, talking goldfish and loyal, sweet elephants. He was awarded a special Pulitzer Prize in 1984 for his contribution to children's literature.

Geisel's tales were filled with his own moral concerns, particularly for the environment and world peace. "The Lorax" warns against polluting the environment, while "The Butter Battle Book" tells of an arms race between creatures who disagree about whether it is better to eat bread with the butter side down or up.

When asked recently whether he had any final message, Geisel told a reporter from the San Diego Union: "Whenever things go a bit sour in a job I'm doing, I always tell myself, 'You can do better than this.' The best slogan I can think of to leave with the USA would be 'We can do this

and we've got to do better than this.'"

Geisel was born in Springfield, Mass., on March 2, 1903. His father was a brewer and superintendent of parks, which included the zoo, where Geisel said he started drawing animals.

He graduated from Dartmouth College in 1925, having drawn cartoons for the school humor magazine. He went to England to study literature at Oxford University, but dropped out, in part, after receiving encouragement in his artistic ambitions from another American student, Helen Palmer. She became his first wife a few years later.

Geisel spent a year in Paris, where he got to know Ernest Hemingway, James Joyce and other expatriate US writers. He returned to the United States in 1927, hoping to become a novelist.

He wrote humor for the magazines "Judge" and "Life," adopting his now-famous pen name, Dr. Seuss, as a spoof of scientific developments.

His first children's book was released in 1937, the same year as his first novel for adults. But the former, "... And to Think That I Saw It on Mulberry Street," which initially had been rejected by 27 publishers, became a smashing success. His career was off.

Among his most famous books are "The Cat in the Hat," "Green Eggs and Ham" and "Horton Hears a Who!" which was made into a popular TV special, as was "How the Grinch Stole Christmas!"

He moved to La Jolla soon after the end of World War II.

During the latter part of the war he served in the Army, helping director Frank Capra make training and documentary films. Two Geisel documentaries, "Hitler Lives?" and "Design for Death," co-written with his wife, won Academy Awards for their producers in 1946 and 1947.

After the war, Geisel's work continued to be translated to movies, with his cartoon short "Gerald McBoing Boing" winning an Oscar in 1951. He turned his attention to television in the 1950s, designing and producing cartoons, including the Peabody Award-winning "How the Grinch Stole Christmas!" and "Horton Hears a Who!"

Michael Watenpaugh, a former teacher and administrator in the Capistrano Unified School District, used to dress up as the Cat in the Hat each year to celebrate Dr. Seuss Day on Geisel's birthday. Reached at Hill Middle School in Novato, where he is now a principal, Watenpaugh said children understand Dr. Seuss' message.

"Kids get it and it's enjoyable to them," Watenpaugh said. "It was a real avenue for me to encourage kids to read, encourage kids to write. I consider his books to be children's literature."

Geisel did not have any children of his own. His first wife died in 1967. He later married Audrey Dimond, who has two daughters from a previous marriage. He also is survived by his niece, Peggy Owens, and her son, Theodore Owens, of Los Angeles.

Laura Bleiberg,
The Orange County (Calif.) *Register*

Activities

1 Gather information from news clips or magazines about a celebrity or otherwise prominent person in your community who is still alive. Write an obituary, and include comments the person has made and comments about the person.

2 Using the following facts, write a basic obituary. If you want to write a feature obituary, you may do library research to add to this information.

Facts: Jim Henson. Age 53. Died May 17, 1990 (but use yesterday as your time factor). Creator of the Muppets, puppets that became famous on the "Sesame Street" television program. Some famous creations: Kermit the Frog, Miss Piggy, Big Bird, the Cookie Monster. Considered one of the most famous puppeteers in the world. Entertained millions of children and their parents who watched "Sesame Street," the public television program now seen in more than 80 countries.

Circumstances of death: Died at New York Hospital 20 hours after entering with a bacterial infection, streptococcus pneumonia. He was given a high dose of antibiotics, but his kidneys and heart failed. He died at 1:21 a.m.

Residence: He lived in Manhattan. He also had homes in California, Connecticut and London.

Funeral plans: The family is planning a memorial service but has not yet announced details.

Background:

Born in Greenville, Miss. Grew up in Washington, D.C.

Was a theater arts major at the University of Maryland. First appeared on television with his own show, called "Sam and Friends," when he was a freshman in college. Married Jane Nebel in 1959, a woman he met in college and who helped him operate the puppets in his first television show.

In 1956 he built a hand puppet called Kermit. "I suppose that he's an alter ego," Henson once said. "But he's a little snarkier than I am—slightly wise. Kermit says things I hold myself back from saying."

In the 1960s, Henson began appearing with his puppets on "The Ed Sullivan Show."

In 1969, the creators of Children's Television Workshop began "Sesame Street," which featured Henson's puppets.

In 1976, he gained fame with his own show, "The Muppet Show," which featured Kermit and Miss Piggy. The show was seen in more than 100 countries by an estimated 235 million viewers.

When Henson died he was in the midst of concluding a deal with the Walt Disney Co. to sell Henson Associates, Inc., which owns the Muppets, for a price estimated at $100 million to $150 million.

Henson coined the name Muppet to describe a combination of marionette and foam-rubber hand puppet. The Muppets' heads are hand puppets, but other parts of their bodies may be controlled by strings and rods.

Survivors: Henson's wife and five children (whose names were not included in this obituary).

From Peggy Charren, founder of Action for Children's Television: "He could make you laugh while you were crying."

From Erwin Okun, spokesman for Walt Disney Co.: "I never met a kinder, gentler wonderful soul in the entertainment industry or anywhere."

From Joan Ganz Cooney, chief executive of Children's Television Workshop: "Jim was dedicated to children's education, and with all his commercial success, he never lost his idealism."

Prepared statement from officials of the Public Broadcasting Service: "His legacy is the lesson that one can both laugh and learn."

COACHING

TIPS

Do your homework. Check clips and other sources for background about the speaker or issue at a conference or meeting.

Listen for what the speaker doesn't discuss. Then ask questions to find the answers that the readers (or viewers) will want.

Ask yourself what the most interesting information was — whether it came during a speaker's prepared comments or afterward. Then lead with that information.

Try to get as many good direct quotes as possible. Favor full quotes over partial ones.

Use graphics as a writing tool. Write a highlights box — to accompany your story or to organize your story.

21

Speeches, Press Conferences and Meetings

obert Zausner writes for his readers, not for his sources. And sometimes he makes his sources mad. Like the time he wrote about Pennsylvania Gov. Robert Casey's press conference: "The news conference was missing one important element: news."

The governor complained.

"I'm not here to be a tape recorder," Zausner says. "The governor said essentially nothing in his news conference. He was just trying to get publicity. I made fun of him. I think it's in my purview to do that."

Zausner covers the Pennsylvania Legislature for *The Philadelphia Inquirer,* a beat that often produces stories considered boring but important. But not for Zausner: "I do things that I think are fun." Like the story (in Chapter 5) about how the state spent taxpayers' money on a machine to change light bulbs:

> How many state employees does it take to change a light bulb?
>   Only two.
>   But they also need a $9,447 machine to reach the socket, at least in part of the East Wing of the Capitol complex. . . .

Robert Zausner, *The Philadelphia Inquirer*

"I was just walking down the hall and they were changing the light bulbs," he says. "I was curious.

Most press officers at the

Pentagon wouldn't tell you

if your coat was on fire.

Don Campbell, director,

Paul Miller Fellowships,

The Freedom Forum

Robert Zausner, reporter,
The Philadelphia Inquirer

"I think you have to keep your eyes open on this kind of beat. Some of the stuff that happens around here is unbelievable. Every Monday I ride the elevator to the fourth floor of the Senate offices and just visit people. Usually by the time I hit the ground floor again, I've got something. I think you need to do the legwork to know what's really going on. If you write from a press release, you may have the story, but you won't have more than a surface understanding of something."

One of Zausner's elevator rides produced this story about the Senate Appropriations Committee:

In a debate over hiring five new Common Pleas Court judges for Philadelphia, Sen. Richard A. Tilghman protested because he said the cost was too high, especially since each judge would get to hire a maid.

"Well, everyone was aghast," recalled Tilghman (R., Montgomery) about members of the Senate Appropriations Committee when he passed on that tidbit of information during a meeting several weeks ago.

The senators were aware of the costs judges incur for office rentals, staff and automobiles. But maids?

When questioned, Tilghman said he had gotten the scoop from one of the top Common Pleas Court judges in Philadelphia, with whom he had spoken over the telephone about the estimated cost of judgeships.

"He told me it was a couple hundred thousand dollars per judge and they get maids," Tilghman said. "I wasn't the least bit surprised. I figured they get everything else."

But the case was one in which Tilghman might have been better advised to have had a face-to-face conversation with the judge. That way he could have, in the words of another Republican, read his lips.

"It may have been my hearing aid," Tilghman acknowledged later on, laughing at his own mistake. "I don't wear it on the phone. It whistles."

Upon further review, it turned out that what the judge evidently had told Tilghman was not that judges in Philadelphia get *maids*, but that they can hire *aides*.

Robert Zausner, *The Philadelphia Inquirer*

Behind the fun is a more serious goal. Zausner wants his readers to understand the way the government really works. "You have to make them read it," he says. "Spit it back in simple terms that people can understand. It's safer to use the bureaucrats' terminology. It's easy. It's lazy. Someone introduces a bill, you get three quotes and you have a story. But if you just regurgitate the stuff in the bureaucratic language, you lose everyone.

"In the past reporters used to tell the editor the story was important and they'd put it on Page One. But nobody would read it. You have to write the stories onto Page One."

One way of making stories readable and relevant is to focus on the people affected. Zausner says he doesn't always have time to talk to as many people as he would like. But when he does, the reader gets a story like this one about the impact of Gov. Robert Casey's order to fire 2,450 state employees:

For the last 20 years, Mark Holmes has worked for the state. He has enjoyed his $45,000-a-year job as a telecommunications expert and the other major benefit that came with government employment—security.

But now Holmes is wondering how he will support his wife and nine children, how he will keep his oldest in college. He is pondering food stamps. He thinks about the sudden predicament he finds himself in at the age of 43. And then, offering an apology, he starts to cry.

Holmes is one of the 2,450 people behind the numbers. He will be out of work by month's end under a dismissal plan being put into effect to reduce a deficit approaching $1 billion. The firings, ordered by Gov. Casey, are estimated to save $154 million this fiscal year.

Robert Zausner, *The Philadelphia Inquirer*

Zausner also believes in interpreting an issue for readers. Although some editors might criticize that approach as editorializing, Zausner says he thinks it is the reporter's responsibility. Consider this story with an impact lead about the Pennsylvania governor's proposed budget cuts:

It's not that Gov. Casey is a killjoy, but if he gets his way it will cost more in Pennsylvania to go to a state museum or enjoy a Sunday picnic. Even the price of driving around with a cutesy license plate will go up.

It will cost more to be born, and more to die.

For buried amid the big news of Casey's proposed budget, with its whopping business and cigarette taxes, is the governor's plan to raise an extra $80.1 million in new and increased fees for seemingly everything.

Boating and billboards, state museums and learners' permits, camping and coal mining would all be affected. Even state employees, who are already being hit with firings and pay cuts, would have to start paying $5 biweekly for their parking spots at the Capitol.

Casey officials made little noise about the proposed fee increases on Wednesday, when they presented the budget for fiscal 1992, which begins July 1.

Robert Zausner, *The Philadelphia Inquirer*

A reporter for 15 years, Zausner says he has "just been around long enough" to understand how government works. And he tries to make sure the reader does, too. "It's not only nice to interpret, it's your responsibility," Zausner says. "If a guy announces that he's introducing a bill, but he's only trying to score some political points and you know the bill is not going anywhere, you have to say that. If you write that story and you don't say what he really wants, you are doing people a disservice. You'd be better off not to write it. I don't think it's editorializing. I think it's serving the reader."

Media Manipulation

Sources who give speeches or conduct press conferences are often using the media to further their own causes. There's nothing wrong with that. It's a way of presenting news. But a responsible reporter should ask good questions after the speech or press conference and add points of view from opposing sources when possible.

For example, in the summer of 1991 Operation Rescue, an anti-abortion group, waged massive demonstrations to close an abortion clinic in Wichita, Kan. The sources from that group had a definite agenda; they clearly were trying to manipulate the press, says Steven A. Smith, managing editor of *The Wichita* (Kan.) *Eagle*. One of the leaders of Operation Rescue conducted a press conference during which he held up a fully developed fetus, which supposedly had been aborted at about seven or eight months. Smith says the situation posed a difficult ethical dilemma for the *Eagle* staff. The leader's actions were news. But there was no evidence that the fetus had been aborted at the Wichita clinic. The result: *The Eagle* published news about the protest and the leader's actions, including the statement that there was no proof the fetus came from the Wichita clinic. But the paper did not publish a picture of the fetus. Smith says he was convinced the situation was staged to manipulate the press. Television stations also refused to show the fetus.

Throughout the summer, protesters on both sides of the abortion issue came from around the nation to converge on Wichita, and 2,600 of them were arrested for violating city laws and defying court orders prohibiting them from blocking the abortion clinic. Both sides sought to manipulate the press. Smith says the newspaper tried so hard to give balanced coverage that some of the editors actually measured the number of inches of type given to the pro-choice and anti-abortion sources to make sure they had equal treatment.

The problems of manipulation were even greater for the three local television stations. Operation Rescue leaders staged their press conferences shortly before the 5 p.m. newscasts in hopes of receiving live coverage from television. News directors, concerned about issues of accuracy and fairness, limited the live coverage. They edited the tape to be shown at the end of the 5 p.m. newscasts or only on the 10 p.m. programs, so they could have more control and present balanced viewpoints.

Abortion is far from the only issue plagued by attempts to manipulate the press. One of the most blatant problems of media manipulation came during the Persian Gulf War in 1991. War coverage was carefully controlled by the military. Only selected "pools" of journalists were allowed to attend the briefings or travel to war zones with a military escort; they then shared their reports

with journalists outside the pool. But before they could release their reports, U.S. military officials in Saudi Arabia "reviewed" or censored stories, photos and videos.

Preparation

Most speeches and press conferences do not pose such severe problems. Still, reporters always need to do more than listen and repeat what they hear. They need to ask good questions after the event as well.

To ask good questions, however, it is important to prepare for the event. You need to find out all you can about the speaker and the issue. Be sure to check the clips.

With a prominent speaker, you can often get the text of the speech in advance. But be careful not to rely on it. The speaker may depart from the prepared text. However, you can still use the prepared text. Just say, "the speaker said in prepared remarks" or "in a written text." Reporters sometimes have to rely on the written version, especially if their deadlines come before the speech or press conference is over.

During the speech, try to get full quotes of the important points (especially if they vary from the written text), and jot down reactions of the speaker and the audience. Note when and if the speaker shows emotion and how the audience responds. Jot down follow-up questions to ask the speaker after the speech or press conference.

Stories About Speeches

Your story should always include some basic information:

Size of the audience

Location of the speech

Reason for the speech

Highlights of the speech

Reaction of the audience, especially at dramatic points during the speech

Although you need to include this basic information, don't clutter the top of your story with it—unless it is crucial to the event. Write the story just as you would any other good story.

You can lead with a hard-news approach emphasizing a main point the speaker made or a soft-news approach describing the person or using an anecdote from the speech. Just don't lead with a no-news approach: Someone made a speech. Tell the reader what the speaker said.

For example, here is the kind of lead to avoid; this one appeared on a story in a campus newspaper:

> Students from Gay and Lesbian Services spoke yesterday to a psychology class about their lives and experiences.

What did they say? It's better to focus on some interesting point they made.

Speakers usually don't make their strongest points first and follow in chronological order, so your story shouldn't be written in that order. Put the most emotional or newsworthy information first. Then back it up with quotes and supporting points.

Sometimes the most interesting information isn't what happens during the speech. It can be what happens after the speech or outside the place while the person is speaking, especially if there is a protest or other major reaction to the speech. Reaction can also be important to the story.

In most cases, the audience is a minor part of a speech story. But in the next example, the people who came to protest the speech were more newsworthy than the speech itself:

Five gay-rights activists were arrested Saturday after disrupting a speech by U.S. Rep. William Dannemeyer at a seminar on "The Preservation of the Heterosexual Ethic."

While the five were handcuffed with plastic restraints after entering Power Community Church, 1026 S. East St., to disrupt the seminar, about 100 other activists picketed on the sidewalk shouting "bigot" and "hatemonger."

Dannemeyer, R-Fullerton, who has announced his candidacy for the U.S. Senate in 1992, shrugged off the protest, saying, "I've reached the point in my political career that if I'm not picketed, I really haven't had a good day."

Before the interruption, Dannemeyer urged an audience of about 120 people to support laws requiring doctors to notify health officials of patients who test positive for AIDS. . . .

Scott Thomsen,
The Orange County (Calif.) *Register*

In the following speech story, the writer used a descriptive lead and included the audience's reaction in the first paragraph. However, if the audience's reaction is not a significant factor in the speech, you should put it lower in the story or eliminate it.

Descriptive lead (includes quote to highlight what speaker said and audience reaction)

Basic W's

Desmond Tutu stood behind the podium, arms outstretched, a picture of triumph. "We will be free, all of us!" he cried. The 3,000 audience members stood up and cheered. Some of them wept.

The archbishop of Cape Town and winner of the 1984 Nobel Peace Prize brought his message of freedom and equality for all South Africans to Chester County yesterday when he spoke at Lincoln University's 131st commencement.

Archbishop Tutu told the crowd and the 250 graduates at the predominantly black university that they will soon see an end to apartheid in South Africa.

"We know we are going to be free because our course is a just and noble course," said Archbishop Tutu, who was awarded an honorary doctorate of humane letters. "We seek not to dominate over anyone. We are seeking to be free, black and white together. We know that our freedom is not a gift

Size of audience, location

Speaker's quotes and news (note dramatic quality)

Description of speaker's manner

Background leading to next point

we go begging for, but an inalienable right."

An animated speaker who peppered his remarks with jokes, Archbishop Tutu said he was amazed and delighted by recent developments—the recent release of Nelson Mandela and other political prisoners, and the start of talks between the government and African National Congress officials on the eventual abolishment of apartheid and the redrafting of the South African constitution.

"Last September, police shot and killed people protesting. We could not walk on God's beaches because we are black. Police dogs could walk on those beaches, but we could not," Archbishop Tutu said.

"But now, we have this historic mind-boggling event—Mandela released and sitting across the table from the president of South Africa. Our dreams seem to be coming true."

In a brief news conference before the commencement, Archbishop Tutu told reporters that it was not time to lift the economic sanctions.

"The sanctions must remain in place until the process of eliminating apartheid is irreversible and taking place," he said. "Then we will call for their removal."

Archbishop Tutu said that he could not predict precisely when the system would change, but that he has no doubt that it will. But even after apartheid is officially dismantled, Archbishop Tutu said, it will take time before all South Africans are considered equal.

"The consequences of apartheid, of all the inequities, will take a while to correct. Things such as building schools for all people and providing housing for all people will take time," he said.

Larry Borksa, *The Philadelphia Inquirer*

Press conference before speech incorporated into story

Quote kicker

Here is an example of a feature approach to a controversial speech. This story, too, contains balance and background:

Leonard Jeffries holds up two pictures. One is actor Al Jolson, a white man in blackface. The other is a lynching. A black man has been hanged, his body burned.

"This is our history," says the professor from New York City. "This is what we cannot allow to happen again."

To some who listen to Jeffries' impassioned call for equality for African-Americans and the need to make American education inclusive of many peoples, he is a cultural hero.

But to others, who hear in his speeches vicious attacks on Jews and other groups, he is as racist as those he tars as bigots.

The controversial chairman of the Black Studies Department at City College of the City University of New York spoke Tuesday night to about 800 people at the University of South Florida. He said his message had been mangled by a "hysterical conspiracy" of Jewish leaders and "rich white men with property and power."

Jeffries says his message "is not anti-white, not anti-gay, not anti-Semitic, not anti-Jewish."

Rather, he said he is trying to reverse a systematic attempt by whites to enforce a stereotype of people of color that keeps them second-class citizens.

A "white supremacist" education that focuses on the contributions of whites and Europeans leaves young blacks and whites "ill-equipped to deal with the realities of the human experience," Jeffries said.

The controversy around the 55-year-old professor has increased since last summer when he gave a speech in Albany, N.Y., that led many people to label him a bigot and call for his resignation. Jeffries says that he receives death threats regularly and that universities across the country where he is invited to speak have been pressured to cancel his appearances.

But that didn't temper his words Tuesday, when he attacked the "Jewish moguls" in Hollywood who, he says, are responsible for generations of systemic stereotyping of blacks, like the Al Jolson character in his photograph.

On Tuesday, he talked of some of his most controversial statements, the ones that say European whites are "ice people," aggressive and individualistic, and African blacks "sun people," warm and communal.

Jeffries said that the geography of the Ice Age shaped Europeans, making them "aggressive and progressive" to survive. And life in the climate of Africa's sun shaped blacks, he said.

"The Europeans are very proud of their ice experience. So why are they raising hell about me?" Jeffries said.

Although protesters attended some of Jeffries' appearances, his speech at USF was unmarked by dissent and met with warm applause.

Jennifer Orsi, *St. Petersburg* (Fla.) *Times*

Stories About Press Conferences

Press conferences are like speeches, except that the questions reporters ask after a press conference may be more important than the prepared comments the speaker makes. The answers to those questions are an important part of the story—and sometimes are the story. Consider news reports after the U.S. president conducts a press conference. His prepared remarks often are less interesting than his answers to the press corps.

Stories about press conferences must include certain pieces of information:

Who conducted the press conference

Reason for the press conference

Highlights of the news, including responses to questions

Location, if relevant

Reaction from sources with similar and opposing points of view

One of the following stories includes information the reporter got by calling an official who wasn't at the press conference—but who might have an opposing view—for a reaction. The reporter also included related background and perspective. The other story concentrated only on the report presented at the press conference. It lacks perspective and balance from other points of view. See if you can tell which is which:

Version 1

The surgeon general said yesterday that alcohol is leading the nation's youth into emergency rooms and jails, and she cited statistics ranging from date rape to drownings to make her case.

It's part of a crusade that Surgeon General Antonia Novello has been on for months, and the alcohol industry was clearly irritated after her news conference.

Jeff Becker, a spokesman for the Beer Institute, said the industry has been trying to get Novello to discuss the issue quietly.

Novello cited figures to show the problems caused by young people abusing alcohol, including accidents, deaths, assaults, rapes, bad grades and dropping out of school.

She didn't offer much that was new; even the statistics that she released were drawn from reports already published in newspapers, magazines and medical journals during the past 10 years.

Among the statistics:

• About a third of the youths committing serious crimes consumed alcohol just before them.

• More than 70 percent of teen suicides involved frequent use of alcohol or drugs.

• Alcohol figures in more than half the rapes among college students.

• Nearly 40 percent of drownings and 75 percent of fatal accidents with all-terrain vehicles involved use of alcohol.

Just last month she called on the alcohol industry to change its advertising, which she said glam-

Version 2

Risky sexual behavior, crime, suicide and bad grades are overlooked repercussions of teen-age drinking, a government report out Monday says.

"Alcohol is not consumed in a void; there are consequences," says Surgeon General Antonia Novello.

Among those cited in *Youth and Alcohol: Dangerous and Deadly Consequences,* the report reviewing research:

• Sexual assault—55% of perpetrators, 53% of victims said they were under the influence during the assault. In a high school student survey, 40% of the boys and 18% of the girls said it was OK to force sex if a girl was drunk.

• Risky sex—One survey found half of 16- to 19-year-olds were more likely to have sex if they and their partner had been drinking. Also, 17% said they were less likely to use a condom when drinking.

• Suicide—70% of youths trying suicide were frequent drug and/or alcohol users.

• Grades—Among 1991 high school seniors, twice as many binge drinkers (five or more drinks in one sitting) had grades of "C" or lower.

Novello wants clearer warning labels, better enforcement of drinking laws, voluntary advertising reform and education. A teen rarely realizes, she says, that after he or she "takes a drink, then another, (that) finally the drink takes the teen-ager ... and according to these reports, where it

Version 1 (continued)

orized drinking and played down its risks by showing people climbing mountains, racing cars or steering boats.

Her attacks on alcohol and tobacco have not been warmly embraced by the White House. Presidential spokesman Marlin Fitzwater said last month that "we generally stay away from intrusion in marketplace decisions."

Richard L. Vernaci, The Associated Press

Version 2 (continued)

leads him or her is not a pretty sight."

Another report out Monday says a fourth of U.S. teens are at serious health risk from alcohol and drugs, sexually transmitted diseases, poor nutrition, depression and violence.

Fateful Choices, written by Fred M. Hechinger for the Carnegie Council on Adolescent Development, calls for more school-related health centers, federal gun control laws and health insurance for all teens.

Mike Snider, *USA Today*

The Associated Press version is the one enriched by reaction, background and perspective.

Stories About Meetings

The decisions that affect readers' daily lives—such as where they take their trash, get their water and send their children to school—are made by local government officials at meetings. Yet meeting stories often are written without explaining their real impact on the reader. They are the BBI stuff of newspapers—the boring but important stories.

Countless surveys conducted by newspapers and news organizations reveal that local news is near or at the top of the list of the kinds of stories readers want. They just don't read them all the way to the end. Sometimes they don't read past the lead, especially when the lead is dull.

The stories don't have to be boring. They may not be as compelling as a story about a murder trial. But they can be written with flair and with an emphasis on the meeting's significance to readers.

The reporter's role as watchdog is as important on the local government level as it is on the national level. Corruption can and does flourish in local government as much as in federal government. Many of the great investigative stories have started at meetings where reporters watched how local officials made their decisions.

All states have open-meeting laws requiring officials who have the authority to spend public funds to conduct their business in public. These boards may conduct executive sessions behind closed doors for certain discussions, such as personnel matters or collective bargaining, but all decisions must be made in a public meeting. Although open-meeting laws vary from state to state, most of them require public agencies to give advance notice—usually 48 hours—of their meetings and to conduct public hearings.

Understanding the System

To understand the potential for abuse in government, you must understand the system. The task is complicated because each community has variations in the way its government operates, from city officials to school boards.

Suppose you are covering a zoning board meeting. The board is discussing a zoning application from a developer for a major shopping center. If the board approves a zoning change, is that the final decision? Probably not. Most zoning boards are advisory and must submit their recommendations to a city or county board of officials for final approval. When you write the story, that is essential information to include.

Now suppose the zoning board chairman recommends approval. But you find out that the developer is his brother-in-law. That meeting story can lead to an investigative story.

If you are covering meetings of your university administration, find out who can make the decisions and which boards are advisory. Who can raise the tuition, school officials or a board of regents? Is the action taken at a meeting a recommendation or a ruling?

The structure of government varies greatly from one community to another. In one city a mayor may be elected and appoint a city manager. That mayor has strong authority to make decisions. In another city the council or commission may appoint the mayor, who has limited authority and can act only with approval of the board.

As with any story, do your homework. If you are going to cover a government agency, find out who the board members are and what authority they have.

Writing the Advance

Many times, knowing what is going to happen at a meeting is more important to readers than knowing what did happen. A story that tells readers what is being proposed can alert residents to make their concerns known before a measure is adopted by local officials. A pre-meeting story is called an "advance."

An advance is especially crucial if local officials are planning to conduct a public hearing about an issue. If the public doesn't know about it, how can the public be heard?

City and school boards usually publish an agenda in advance of their meetings. This agenda lists the items to be discussed, although new items can and will be presented.

When you receive an agenda, look through it for items that might be of special interest to readers. Call board members and ask for comments or ask them to pick out the items they expect to be most interesting or controversial. If the issue has been in the news previously, check clips and call other interested parties.

The point of your advance is to inform readers about items that they may want to discuss during the public comment part of a meeting or just to let readers know what their officials are proposing.

Here are some examples of leads from meeting advances. After the lead, each reporter interviewed people involved on both sides of the issue:

For the first time in its 107-year history, Temple University may require all undergraduates to take a course related to race and racism.

The proposal, which grew out of black students' demonstrations at Temple in spring 1990, is to be debated by the school's faculty senate on Friday.

Among the faculty, however, the proposal has already sparked intense discussion. The debate mirrors that of other campuses—including Stanford, Wisconsin, Michigan and Berkeley—where courses related to race are required.

Huntly Collins, *The Philadelphia Inquirer*

BELLEVUE (Wash.)—With one step, the Bellevue School District could begin a child-care program unrivaled throughout the nation.

Parents could bring infants to school with their older elementary-age children and pick them all up after work. Toddlers could begin school at 3. Schools could tend mildly ill children and provide child care for handicapped children.

A debate on whether to take that step has spread with fervor in the schools and the community since early last month. It will resume when board members meet Tuesday.

Mary Elizabeth Cronin, *The Seattle Times*

Covering the Meeting

Arrive early. Find out the names of board members (usually they have nameplates), and find out who is in charge.

Check items on the agenda, and get any background that you need.

Check the consent agenda, a list of items on the agenda that the board will approve without discussion. They may include bids for approval or other points the board may have discussed in work sessions. A "gem" of a story may be buried in the consent agenda.

One reporter wondered why the school board had approved $30,000 in "token losses." That's a lot of money to be considered "token" losses. She discovered that they were losses of bus tokens that the school board sold to students who had to ride public buses because there were no school buses in the city. Why $30,000 in losses? The school district had no system of monitoring the sales, and the money had been stolen at several schools. By school officials! The board didn't want to discuss this item publicly, so it was buried in the consent agenda. But the reporter wanted to discuss it. In a front-page story.

Don't remain glued to a seat at a press table. When members of the audience give public comments, get their names and more comments. Many times they will leave immediately after their testimony. Follow them out of the meeting. You can catch up with the action inside later. Or sit in the audience. Sometimes the comments of people attending the meeting are more interesting than the ones the board members make.

Stay until the end, unless your deadline prohibits it. The most important issue could emerge at the end of a meeting when the board asks for new business or public comments. Or something dramatic could happen. The mayor could resign. Violence could erupt. You never can tell, especially if you're not there.

Writing the Story

First, how not to write it. Do not say the city council met and discussed something. Tell what they discussed or enacted. This is the kind of lead to avoid:

> The 41st Annual Environmental Engineering Conference met yesterday at the Kansas Union to discuss solutions to environmental problems.
>
> Representatives of the Kansas Department of Health and Environment, the Environmental Protection Agency and other organizations spoke to about 180 people who attended the conference.

So what did they say? This lead reveals nothing.

Some meetings are long. They can be boring. Avoid telling the reader how much you suffered listening to board members drone on and accomplish nothing in a long meeting. The reader doesn't care how much you suffer. The reader wants the news. If the length of the debate is crucial to the story, you should include it. But if the meetings are usually long and the time element is not a major factor related to the focus, don't mention it.

Here are some points to include in your story:

Type of meeting and location: But if the city council or school board meets all the time in the same building, don't mention the location.

The vote on any major issue: For instance, say "in a 4-1 vote . . ." If the issue is particularly controversial, say who voted against it—or for it, if an affirmative vote was more controversial. If the measure was approved unanimously, say so. Don't give the vote for every minor item, however.

The next step: If a major issue or ordinance cannot be adopted until a public hearing is conducted, tell readers when a hearing is scheduled or what the next step is before the action is final.

Impact on readers: Explain how the decision will affect them.

Quotes: But use only quotes that are dramatic, interesting or crucial to the story.

Background of the issues: What do readers need to know to understand what has happened?

To write the story, select one key issue for the focus. If the board approved several other measures, add them at the end: "In other business." If several important actions occurred, consider breaking another key issue into a separate story, if possible. If not, try a lead mentioning both items, or put the second key point in the second paragraph and give supporting background later, after you have developed the first point. For example: "City commissioners yesterday approved plans for the city's first shopping mall but rejected plans for a new public golf course." Then proceed with the discussion about the shopping mall.

Consider advancing the story with a second-day lead. This kind of advance tells readers the next step or how the story will affect them. In most newspapers, this type of lead is becoming more popular because it makes the news more timely. However, it is optional, and a first-day lead may be acceptable.

Although many meeting stories are written with summary leads, especially if the news is significant, they do not have to follow that form. If you think a softer lead is appropriate for the type of news that occurred, you can use it.

Here are some more writing tips:

• Use the tell-a-friend technique to make the story readable. This technique is especially helpful with stories about meetings.

• Remember the kiss-off technique if you have three or more sources: Block comments from a single speaker in one place and don't use the source again. However, the mayor or another well-known official may be used as a source intermittently.

A few matters of style:

• *Board* is a collective noun and therefore takes a singular verb: The board discussed the issue at *its* meeting, not *their* meeting. If this approach seems awkward in your story, say that the board *members* said *their* next meeting would be Tuesday.

• Capitalize *city council, city commission* and *school board* when they are part of a proper name—such as the Rockville City Commission—and when the reference is to a specific commission in your town—the City Commission. If you are referring to a city commission in any city, use lowercase letters.

• Capitalize the titles of board members or other officials when they come before the name, as in *Mayor John Corrupt.* If the title follows the name—*John Corrupt, the mayor*—use lowercase letters.

• For votes, use *3-1,* not *3 to 1.*

Stories about meetings can take a hard, soft or advance-impact approach. Whichever one you use, make the story relevant to readers. Here's how:

Basic hard-news meeting story

LAGUNA BEACH (Calif.) —Despite neighbors' objections, a North Laguna Beach couple were given permission Tuesday to adorn their home with a 17-foot-high outdoor sculpture of 30 water heaters and two house trailers.

Summary lead: what happened

The City Council, after viewing a scale model of the artwork, voted 3-1 to endorse the sculpture. It will climb around a pine tree in the back courtyard of Arnold and Marie Forde's home.

Vote

Mayor Neil Fitzpatrick dissented, saying the sculpture infringed on neighbors' views. Councilwoman Martha Collison was absent.

Dissenting vote

"It's a victory for the freedom of expression," said Los Angeles artist Nancy Rubins, who will craft the sculpture. "It would have been a sad day if a community that sees itself as supporting the arts struck down an artwork in a private yard."

Reaction

The sculpture had been the focus of an intense neighborhood battle.

Impact: so what

Residents who live near the Fordes have called the sculpture junk and complained that the artwork would block their view and spoil the neighborhood character.

David DeLo, who lives across Cliff Drive from the Fordes, said he was considering challenging the council's action in court.

"If the council wants to place a piece of junk in a residential neighborhood, that's their prerogative, but this council has been overturned before," he said.

To appease neighbors, the council approved the sculpture on the condition that the Fordes place it as low as possible in the yard and landscape the area with another tree and a hedge. The additional plants should hide the sculpture from neighbors, officials said.

The $5,000 sculpture will take a week to build. Rubins said she did not know when it will be finished.

Harrison Fletcher, *The Orange County Register*

More reaction
Next step

Backup: conditions of council action

Future kicker

Meeting stories may also be written with a creative lead—if the news lends itself to a soft approach. Here are some examples of creative leads:

Conversational style

Life used to be so simple.

Whenever families were discussed, the couple was assumed to consist of one male and one female: one mom, one pop.

The City Council's Public Safety Committee entered the 1990s Tuesday night. Members noted that couples now come in three configurations: male-female, male-male and female-female.

"Let's face reality. You can't get around homosexuality," said Alderman Eugene Thompson. "If we said, 'two adults,' that should cover everything."

The matter came before the committee as it approved the sale of family passes for the use of the swimming pool in Garfield Park. To play it safe, "family" was defined as any two adults and up to four dependents.

Kevin Cullen, (Danville, Ill.) *Commercial-News*

Anecdotal approach

The bottle on his front door with a note offering free testing of the water used by Dennis Schwartz in his Tecumseh home near Topeka was too good to resist.

So Schwartz returned a water sample.

And the company that offered the testing returned the verdict that his water was unfit to drink.

Schwartz, who manages Shawnee County Rural Water District No. 8 and routinely tests the water from his system to make sure it meets federal standards, was not pleased. Nor was he pleased when a company representative tried to sell him more than $2,000 in treatment equipment to solve his water problems.

"The people who are selling these things have very little knowledge, if any, of water treatment," Schwartz said.

He told his story Tuesday to explain a staff recommendation to the policy committee of the Kansas Water Authority that steps be taken in the 1992 version of the Kansas Water Plan to deal with the unrestricted business of home water treatment devices.

Authority members are at Salina's Ramada Inn for two days. Their meeting ends today with a 10:30 a.m. session.

Schwartz, who heads the policy committee, said he had received numerous complaints about such devices from customers of rural water districts.

Linda Mowery-Denning,
The Salina (Kan.) *Journal*

The next example demonstrates how to advance the story:

A little spray paint would go a long way—about 1,000 hours long—for those who scrawl graffiti on walls and fences in Chicago, under an ordinance amendment before City Council.

Impact lead

Vandals who take a few seconds to paint their "tags" and then are caught could be forced to scrub off their unsightly work—and someone else's, as well.

With no debate and little discussion, the Police and Fire Committee Tuesday unanimously approved the ordinance change, which would increase the maximum number of mandatory hours of community service work for vandalism convictions from the current 120 hours to 1,000 hours.

"I think this is a step in the right direction," said Ald. William Beavers (7th), the committee chairman, who said he would ask the full City Council to approve the change at Wednesday's meeting. . . .

Next step

Robert Davis, *Chicago Tribune*

Activities
1 **Speech:** You are writing a story on deadline, a story about Clarence Thomas' testimony during confirmation hearings for his appointment to the Supreme Court. At this point your story cannot be fully balanced, because Thomas' testimony precedes the comments by Anita Hill.

You may have strong feelings for or against Clarence Thomas after you read this material, as did millions of Americans who watched his testimony on television. Part of the challenge of this assignment is to make sure you keep your bias out of the story. However, you may include any material from the following background information.

Before you begin writing your story, write a highlights box or identify quotes that you would use as pull quotes to graphically enhance your story.

Background:

On Oct. 16, 1991, Clarence Thomas was confirmed as the 106th justice to the Supreme Court. His approval by the Senate came after five days of controversial, often explosive testimony in what may be considered the stormiest confirmation hearings conducted by the Senate Judiciary Committee for a Supreme Court nominee. The committee was exploring allegations by University of Oklahoma law professor Anita Hill. She claimed Thomas had sexually harassed her when she worked for him in 1981 at the Department of Education and a year later, at the Equal Employment Opportunities Commission, when Thomas became chairman.

Thomas was nominated for the Supreme Court post on July 1, 1991, by President George Bush, to replace retiring Justice Thurgood Marshall. Thomas, then a U.S. Court of Appeals judge, was 43 at the time. Marshall was the first black justice; Thomas is the second in U.S. history.

The first set of confirmation hearings took place Sept. 10 to 20. Hill's allegations originally were made to the FBI. The committee reopened hearings on Oct. 11 only after Hill's allegations were reported by National Public Radio reporter Nina Totenberg and *Newsday* reporter Timothy Phelps. Although the reporters were both accused by the Senate of illegally receiving FBI confidential material, they refused to reveal their sources.

Below is Thomas's statement to the Judiciary Committee on Oct. 11, when the committee resumed hearings on the sexual harassment charges. Thomas made this opening statement prior to Hill's testimony that day. In her testimony, Hill gave graphic detail of her allegations against Thomas, which he denied again later in the day. She claimed he had talked about pornographic materials and repeatedly asked her for dates. After her testimony, Thomas added more emotional denials. For purposes of this assignment, some of Thomas' responses later in the day are included.

Here are excerpts from the statement Thomas made on Oct. 12; it was televised nationally. Write the story as though you were covering the hearings, and use today or yesterday for your time element.

Mr. Chairman, Sen. Thurmond, members of the committee. As excruciatingly difficult as the last two weeks have been, I welcome the opportunity to clear my name today.

The first I learned of the allegations by Professor Anita Hill was on Sept. 25, 1991, when the FBI came to my home to investigate her allegations. When informed by the FBI agent of the nature of the allegations and the person making them, I was shocked, surprised, hurt and enormously saddened. I have not been the same since that day.

For almost a decade, my responsibilities included enforcing the rights of victims of sexual harassment. As a boss, as a friend and as a human being, I was proud that I had never had such an allegation leveled against me, even as I sought to promote women and minorities into nontraditional jobs.

In addition, several of my friends who are women have confided in me about the horror of harassment on the job or elsewhere. I thought I really understood the anguish, the fears, the doubts, the seriousness of the matter. But since Sept. 25th, I have suffered immensely as these very serious charges were leveled against me. I have been racking my brains and eating my insides out trying to think of what I could have said or done to Anita Hill to lead her to allege that I was interested in her in more than a professional way and that I talked with her about pornographic or X-rated films.

Contrary to some press reports, I categorically denied all of the allegations and denied that I ever attempted to date Anita Hill when first interviewed by the FBI. I strongly reaffirm that denial.

Throughout the time that Anita Hill worked with me I treated her as I treated my other special assistants. I tried to treat them all cordially, professionally and respectfully, and I tried to support them in their endeavors and be interested in and supportive of their success. I had no reason or basis to believe my relationship with Anita Hill was anything but this way until the FBI visited me a little more than two weeks ago.

I find it particularly troubling that she never raised any hint that she was uncomfortable with me. She did not raise or mention it when considering moving with me to EEOC from the Department of Education, and she'd never raised it with me when she left EEOC and was moving on in her life. And to my fullest knowledge, she did not speak to any other women working with or around me who would feel comfortable enough to raise it with me.

During my tenure in the executive branch as a manager, as a policy maker and as a person, I have adamantly condemned sex harassment. I cannot imagine anything that I said or did to Anita Hill that could have been mistaken for sexual harassment.

But with that said, if there is anything that I have said that has been misconstrued by Anita Hill or anyone else to be sexual harassment, then I can say that I am so very sorry and I wish I had known. If I did know, I would have stopped immediately, and I would not, as I've done over the past two weeks, have to tear away at myself, trying to think of what I could possibly have done.

As if the confidential allegations themselves were not enough, this apparently calculated public disclosure has caused me, my family and my friends enormous pain and great harm. I have never in my life felt such hurt, such pain, such agony. My family and I have been done a grave and irreparable injustice.

When I stood next to the president in Kennebunkport being nominated to the Supreme Court of the United States, that was a high honor; but as I sit here before you 103 days later, that honor has been crushed.

I have complied with the rules. I responded to a document request that produced over 30,000 pages of documents, and I have testified for five full days under oath. I have endured this ordeal for 103 days. Reporters sneaking into my garage to examine books I read. Reporters and interest groups swarming over divorce papers looking for dirt. Unnamed people starting preposterous and damaging rumors. Calls all over the country specifically requesting dirt.

This is not American; this is Kafkaesque. It has got to stop. It must stop for the benefit of future nominees and our country. Enough is enough.

I'm not going to allow myself to be further humiliated in order to be confirmed. I will not allow this committee or anyone else to probe into my private life. This is not what America is all about.

To ask me to do that would be to ask me to go beyond fundamental fairness.

I am proud of my life, proud of what I have done and what I have accomplished, proud of my family, and this process, this process is trying to destroy it all. No job is worth what I have been through, no job. No horror in my life has been so debilitating. Confirm me if you want. Don't confirm me if you are so led, but let this process end.

I never asked to be nominated. It was an honor. Little did I know the price, but it is too high.

I enjoy and appreciate my current position, and I am comfortable with the prospect of returning to my work as a judge on the U.S. Court of Appeals for the D.C. Circuit.

Instead of understanding and appreciating the great honor bestowed upon me, I find myself here today defending my name, my integrity, because somehow select portions of confidential documents dealing with this matter were leaked to the public.

I am a victim of this process. My name has been harmed. There is nothing this committee, this body or this country can do to give me my good name back. Nothing.

I will not provide the rope for my own lynching or for further humiliation. I am not going to engage in discussions, nor will I submit to roving questions of what goes on in the most intimate parts of my private life or the sanctity of my bedroom.

This is not an opportunity to talk about difficult matters privately or in a closed environment. This is a circus. It's a national disgrace. And from my standpoint as a black American, as far as I'm concerned, it is a high-tech lynching for uppity blacks who in any way deign to think for themselves, to do for themselves, to have different ideas, and it is a message that unless you kowtow to an old order, this is what will happen to you. You will be lynched, destroyed, caricatured by a committee of the U.S. Senate rather than hung from a tree.

2 **Press conference:** Write a story based on excerpts from the following press conference as though you were covering it; use today or yesterday for your time frame. When you write the story, include material from both the prepared remarks and the questions and answers. You may use any material from the facts boxes or the background. You also should consider the graphics and facts boxes you would include.

Background:

Earvin "Magic" Johnson Jr., a basketball superstar who played for the Los Angeles Lakers, stunned the nation in 1991 when he announced that he was retiring from the game because he had contracted the AIDS virus, meaning he had tested positive for AIDS (Acquired Immune Deficiency Syndrome). The 32-year-old player ended his 12-year career with the National Basketball Association in a press conference at the Forum in Inglewood, Calif., the Lakers' home court (see Exhibit 21-1). Johnson, who is 6 feet 9 inches tall, was drafted by the National Basketball Association in 1979 after playing basketball for two years at Michigan State University in his original home town of East Lansing, Mich.

He announced his retirement in November 1991. He had been married a few months earlier, on Sept. 14, to Earletha "Cookie" Kelly, who was seven weeks pregnant at the time of his press conference. He said his wife did not have the AIDS virus.

RENO GAZETTE-JOURNAL

35¢

FRIDAY, NOVEMBER 8, 1991

SPORTS SHOCKER
Basketball loses its Magic

PERSONAL VIEW

Johnson shared delight for life

Sports Editor Jamie Turner has covered Earvin Johnson since "Magic" was a high school star in Michigan.

By Jamie Turner
GAZETTE-JOURNAL

Until today, I believed the days of Lou Gehrig and John Kennedy had passed into American mythology. Not the men, particularly, but the country they represented.

A country that believed in heroes. A country that picked out a man or woman and imbued him or her with stature and dignity grown from a national faith in their essential decency.

The Iron Horse. "I consider myself the luckiest man on the face of the earth." Utter strength against impossible odds.

Camelot. "Ask not what your country can do for you, but what you can do for your country." Profiles in Courage.

And then a man whom I have watched from his teens stepped up to a national audience Thursday and smiled before a personal abyss. In 10 minutes, Earvin Johnson confronted a deadly ailment and a national stigma as professionally as he would have a National Basketball Association championship series.

See **MAGIC** on page **8A**

"It can happen to anybody — even me, Magic Johnson."
Revealing he has AIDS virus on Thursday

■ **Earvin Johnson retires:** Lakers star has AIDS virus
■ **Cause:** Uncertain
■ **Outlook:** 'I'm going to go on'; NBA champ promotes safe sex
■ **Reaction:** Fans, players sad

Complete report, 1,2E

■ **In Reno:** News strikes high school, UNR basketball players and bettors at sports books like a thunderbolt.

■ **How do you feel:** Call the Gazette-Journal TalkLine, 324-0025, ext. 3267.

■ **Telling kids:** Be sympathetic, non-judgmental, experts advise.

■ **Praise from ex-coach:** Pat Riley shaken.

HIV AND AIDS
KNOWING THE DIFFERENCE

■ **HIV:** The virus that causes AIDS.
■ **AIDS:** A result of HIV infection. The AIDS virus attacks the immune system so a person can no longer fight off other infections, which become fatal.
■ **How AIDS is spread:** AIDS is caused by a virus that spreads through sex (vaginal, oral or anal) and blood-to-blood contact (such as sharing needles or syringes with someone infected with the virus). HIV cannot spread by ordinary social contact.
Source: American Red Cross HIV-AIDS Instructor's Manual.

Exhibit 21-1

Basketball star Magic Johnson at a press conference, announcing that he has the AIDS virus

The Reno Gazette-Journal

Here is a career highlights box that appeared in *The Orange County Register:*

• Holds the NBA career assist record at 9,921.

• Named the NBA's Most Valuable Player in 1987.

• Led the Lakers to championships in 1980, 1982, 1985, 1987 and 1988. The Lakers also made the league finals in 1983, 1984, 1989 and 1991.

• Selected MVP of the regular season and the NBA finals in 1987. One of only four players so honored.

• Raised more than $9 million for the United Negro College Fund and other charities.

The *Reno* (Nev.) *Gazette-Journal* added this information box on its front page:

HIV and AIDS

Knowing the difference

- **HIV:** The virus that causes AIDS.
- **AIDS:** A result of HIV infection. The AIDS virus attacks the immune system so a person can no longer fight other infections, which become fatal.
- **How AIDS is spread:** AIDS is caused by a virus that spreads through sex (vaginal, oral or anal) and blood-to-blood contact (such as sharing needles or syringes with someone infected with the virus.) HIV cannot spread by ordinary social contact.

Here are excerpts from the press conference (from The Associated Press). The wording is exactly as Johnson expressed it.

First of all, let me say good after—good late afternoon. Because of the HIV virus I have attained, I will have to announce my retirement from the Lakers today.

I want to make clear, first of all, that I do not have the AIDS disease, because I know a lot of you want to know that, but the HIV virus.

My wife is fine, she's negative, so no problem with her.

I plan on going on, living for a long time, bugging you guys like I always have. So you'll see me around. I plan on being with the Lakers and the league—hopefully David (Stern) will have me for a while—and going on with my life. I guess now I get to enjoy some of the other sides of living—that because of the season and the long practices and so on.

I just want to say that I'm going to miss playing. And I will now become a spokesman for the HIV virus because I want people, young people, to realize they can practice safe sex. And, you know, sometimes you're a little naive about it and you think it could never happen to you. You only thought it could happen to, you know, other people and so on and on. And it has happened.

But I'm going to deal with it and my life will go on. And I will be here enjoying the Laker games and all the other NBA games around the country. So life is going to go on for me, and I'm going to be a happy man.

Now, medical questions that you have, you have to direct them to Dr. (Michael) Mellman and he can answer all those questions

for you. Anything concerning the Lakers and so on, we have Jerry West (Lakers general manager) here, I'm sure—of course, the league, we have our commissioner, who I want to thank. I want to thank everybody up here, as well as my teammates because they've been behind me all the way.

I want to thank Kareem (Abdul Jabbar) for coming out here. Man, cool, cool. We stood side by side and won a lot of battles. Larry Drew, another good friend of mine who I played with. But the commissioner, David Stern, has been great in support of me and I will go on and hopefully work with the league and help in any way that I can.

I want to thank also Jerry West for all he's done. Dr. (Robert) Kerlan, Dr. Mellman who— he will tell you who my other doctors are that will help me through this—as well as, like I said, my father in a sense, Dr. Jerry Buss for, you know, just drafting me and me being here.

Now, of course, I will miss the battles and the wars and I will miss you guys. But life goes on.

Now any other questions medical-wise you can ask, like I said, Dr. Mellman. Anything with the Lakers, Jerry West. Or anything with the league. I'll take a few questions about myself and my plans.

Stop here and write a list of questions; then compare your questions with the excerpts from the question/answer period following Magic Johnson's press conference (also from The Associated Press):

Q: Can you please describe for us, this has been your life, Michigan State, the Lakers. Emotionally for you right now, knowing this part of your life is over, how do you feel, how do you deal with mortality?

Johnson: Well, I think mortality is—I always wanted to be, after it was over, just live a normal life anyway. And now my life will change, no question about it, but I think I'll still be a part of the game—with working with the Lakers, working with the league—and as I do that then I'm hopefully still on a team. Basketball will still be a part of my life. I told (Michael) Cooper and Kareem, both of them a while ago, that I'll be calling them to play them one-on-one. And we'll have some fun that way. I just won't be a part of the Lakers.

Q: Can you give us a special message for your biggest fans, the kids?

A: Well, no question—for the kids, that's why I am going to be a spokesman for this HIV virus, because I want them to understand that safe sex is the way to go. I think sometimes we think, well, only gay people can get it, only—it's not going to happen to me. And here I am saying that it can happen to anybody. Even

me, Magic Johnson, it could happen to.

So yes, I will be going out, telling them. I'll be speaking around the country about this.

Q: When did you know?

A: Well, Wednesday, so that's yesterday.

Q: How did you get HIV? How did you acquire the virus?

A: We'll get into that medically through the doctors, OK.

Q: How do you feel right now?

A: I feel really good. I feel great. A part of my life is gone. But my wife is healthy, that's great. And we're going to go on.

Q: Magic, when did you take the test?

A: Well, I took the test only because of a life insurance policy. And that's what happened. And they kind of thought something was wrong. They didn't know quite what it was, so they—that's why we've been going through all these tests and then, finally yesterday.

Q: What will be people's response regarding your statement on AIDS?

A: Well, I think that everybody will be more careful. That's

what I want to preach—and for everybody to understand that they just have to be more careful.

Q: Do you have something to say to your fans?

A: Well, I'm going to miss them. I'm going to miss them. I'm going to miss coming in at 5 o'clock. I'm going to miss saying hello to the security people when I first get there. Then the ushers. Then I get to see most of you about 6 o'clock. Oh, man. "Magic, what about this? What about that? What about the team?" I'll miss that. I'll miss the battles and the wars. But most of all, what I'll miss is the camaraderie that I had with the guys, being one of the fellows.

Q: This is such a tough illness to deal with. Are you scared right now?

A: No. No. You know, what you have to do—it's another challenge, another chapter in my life. It's like being—your back is against the wall. And I think that you just have to come out swinging. And I'm swinging. You know the only thing I can do is have a bright side. If I slip, then it might be over. If I'm down and out—you know, I can't be like that. I never have been, that's why I'm telling you now, today, you know that's why I'm here right now. And that's why I'm going to be a spokesman for the virus, because I want other players to be tested. . . . Just the everyday person, the same thing. Also practice safe sex. The whole thing.

But I am going to go on. I'm going to beat it. And I'm going to have fun, OK? So thank you again, and I'll see you soon.

Questions for others:

Q: What, exactly, has happened to Johnson and how does it affect his life?

Dr. Michael Mellman: Earvin Johnson has been infected with the HIV virus. He does not have AIDS. The HIV virus is something that over years can and does impair an individual's immune system, which is what we all have to defend against other illnesses. So there's no immediate effect on his life other than we have advised him to avoid those activities which can further impair his immune system, which is playing professional basketball.

Q: What is the prognosis for a complete recovery?

A: . . . Some people last a decade or longer before they get ill, some people get ill very quickly. We have Earvin at one point in time in a very healthy state. There is no way to give you a prognosis that is accurate at this point other than to say that he is healthy now, we expect him to remain healthy and we expect to have him around for a long time.

Q: What type of medication is available for AIDS?

Dr. Esther Hayes: In treatment of HIV disease, the medications that we have are very important in prolonging life and making quality of life better at the stage when someone is HIV positive. Dr. Mellman is his physician, but we—so I don't know whether he will be taking any medication immediately. But I can say for someone who is HIV positive like Mr. Johnson, there are a lot of options for treatment and help to prolong life.

Q: Dr. Mellman, has Magic authorized you to discuss how he contracted the AIDS disease?

A: No. The answer is that I don't believe we know at this point specifically.

Q: Could you speculate on the impact that a player coming forward like Magic Johnson who is saying he has HIV could have on public perception of the disease?

A (Mellman): I think what we have witnessed today is a courageous act by a very special man. He is not compelled by any legal, um, legal descriptions or legal requirements to disclose what he has disclosed today. He is not a person who is invisible. And because of his presence, because of his potential impact on society with a situation that is not only serious, but for which we are all at risk, I think that he should not only be commended, but held as a modern-day hero. And I hope that we in our activities, and the impact that it has on us, reflect that. This is a very, very special person and a very, very special admission.

3 Cover a speech or press conference on your campus or in your community.

4 Cover a meeting of your local city or county commission, school board, or student government on campus.

COACHING

TIPS

Write an impact, "so what" sentence on top of your story.

Try impact leads; your impact sentence could be a lead.

The more complex the information, the simpler your sentences should be.

Avoid jargon.

Write for your readers, not your sources.

Use quotes that advance the story, not the egos of the bureaucrats.

Think about graphics before you write your story. Use boxes and charts for numbers and concepts in a proposal and empowerment boxes for information to help the reader.

Bureaucratic Stories

22

I t was after midnight on June 17, 1972. Five men, wearing dark business suits and rubber surgical gloves, broke into an office in a posh apartment/hotel complex in Washington, D.C. An alert security guard, Frank Wills, spotted a piece of tape on the lock of a stairwell door and called police. At 2:30 a.m., the five men were arrested. Police seized lock picks, pen-size tear gas guns, two 35-millimeter cameras and bugging devices.

The burglary at the Democratic National Committee headquarters in the Watergate complex occurred a month before the convention where Sen. George McGovern would be selected as the Democratic candidate for the presidency in 1972. It was only a small piece of a plot to spy on the Democrats that had begun almost three years earlier with the Republican administration.

It was also the starting point of an investigation by *Washington Post* reporters Bob Woodward and Carl Bernstein, who relied heavily on anonymous sources, particularly on one nicknamed "Deep Throat." Despite their stories tracing illegal campaign activities to the president's top aides, in November 1972 Richard Nixon was re-elected president.

Within the next year, however, *The Washington Post*—and other newspapers—published stories revealing a major cover-up of political intrigue and espionage that led directly to the president.

On Aug. 9, 1974, Richard Milhous Nixon, the 37th president of the United States, resigned.

We can uncover the most serious breaches of public trust, but unless our findings are written with clarity and focus—and presented in a format that readers can easily understand and use—the impact will be lessened or lost.

Bob Ritter, editor,

Gannett News Service

Since then, scores of books and articles about Watergate have been published, some questioning the motives of *The Post* and wondering whether its role in exposing the scandal was as significant as journalists have claimed. Nevertheless, *The Washington Post* was one of the only newspapers to vigorously pursue the story in its early stages.

Carl Bernstein, in a speech five years after Watergate, said the reporting he and Woodward did on Watergate was "the kind you first learn when you get into this business, or even that you learn in journalism school." He said they just knocked on a lot of doors. "We started from the bottom. We talked to secretaries, clerks, chauffeurs, administrative assistants, and gradually worked our way up. Our methodology was not extraordinary in the least."

He said that too often reporters merely report officials' pronouncements without checking thoroughly to find the truth. "The job of the reporter is not to be some kind of recording secretary," he said. "As a reporter, I think the best advice I ever heard from a politician about how to cover the news came from John Mitchell (former U.S. attorney general), at the beginning of the Nixon Administration," Bernstein said. "He was meeting with a group of reporters and he said, 'Watch what we do, and not what we say.' I suggest that if we had done that (before Watergate), maybe there would have been no Watergate, and maybe the events of the Nixon Administration might have been much different. We need to make a commitment to get back to the basics in everything we cover and follow John Mitchell's advice."

Writing With Impact

As a source, John Mitchell wasn't reputable, but his advice is, especially for reporters covering government. And local government is a basic starting beat for beginning reporters. Although much of your information may come from meetings and press conferences, you should follow Carl Bernstein's advice and go beyond reporting only what officials tell you. You should learn how government operates and how it affects readers, not just the officials you cover. Many of the tips for starting a beat mentioned in Chapter 6 can apply to government coverage.

Here are some other tips for covering bureaucracies:

Human interest: Make government relevant to readers by finding people who are affected by the actions of government agencies.

Bulletin boards: They contain job offerings and other announcements that could result in stories.

Memos and letters to and from city officials: Check with the city clerk or secretaries for access to files about any issue involving public funds. Most of these—except for personnel and labor matters—are public record.

Planning commission: This agency can be a source of stories, not only about future plans but also about the past. Some great stories can result from plans gone awry.

Consultants: Check who gets consulting contracts and fees, and investigate previous studies on the same subject. Sometimes government agencies hire consultants to write studies on subjects that have already been studied frequently.

Zoning meetings: They can be full of human interest. People care about what is going up or down in their neighborhood.

Legal notices: Check them for bids and other notices. Government must advertise for any major purchases. Check with disgruntled bidders for major contracts. Many good stories lurk behind these seemingly boring subjects.

Audits: Read them carefully. They can reveal misuse of public funds.

Union leaders: Cultivate heads of unions in school districts and cities as sources. They know what is going on behind the scenes.

Non-officials: Talk to the people who do the work. In school districts, get into the schools and write about what teachers and students are doing. In cities, talk to people on the job. Spend some time learning about what they do, how they do it and whether they do it. Many good stories can result from finding out how little people work in government.

The system: Learn how it works. Are officials in your town following the laws? If you don't know how government is supposed to operate, you won't be able to find out if it is working properly.

Records: Check expense accounts, purchasing vouchers and other records pertaining to issues or officials you are covering.

Writing Tips

Presuming you have found good stories, how can you make them readable? Many newspapers started cutting back on government coverage in the early 1990s because editors thought readers didn't want to read it. However, surveys repeatedly show that readers are interested in local news. It's not the news that's boring, it's the way it is written. Here are some tips for brightening bureaucratic stories:

Use graphics as a writing tool. Before you write your story, think not about what you can put in it; think about what you can pull out of it. Use highlights boxes, facts boxes and charts to break out key concepts of a proposal or budget. Then you don't need to clutter the story with the same information. Consider empowerment boxes: information that tells readers what the story means to them and what they can do. These boxes should contain information about where they can call for help, more information or other facts that would be useful to the reader. Once you have decided what can be displayed visually, you can present the remaining information verbally. Here's an empowerment box from the *Reno Gazette-Journal* that accompanied a story about overdue parking tickets. The city adopted late fees that would add $30 to tickets not paid within a month.

TO PAY

• Pay at the city clerk's cashier office, using cash, check or Visa or Mastercard.

TO PROTEST

• Make an appointment. The hearing officer is setting aside time in Room 204 at City Hall. Call 334-2293.

• Hearing times are: From 5–8 p.m. on Nov. 4 and Nov. 6; 1–4 p.m. on Nov. 8; 5–8 p.m. on Nov. 13 and Nov. 14.

Use short, simple sentences. The more complex the information, the simpler and shorter the sentences should be:

Complex

The City Commission last night approved a resolution to authorize the city staff to apply for funding through the systems enhancement program of the state Department of Transportation for a $3.6 million project for the expansion of U.S. Highway 77 from two to four lanes for 2.2 miles between Interstate 70 and Kansas Highway 18.

Simpler

The City Commission last night agreed to apply for $3.6 million from the state Department of Transportation to expand a portion of U.S. Highway 77 from two to four lanes.

The project would widen the highway for 2.2 miles between Interstate 70 and Kansas Highway 18.

Keep the subject and verb close together. Long clauses and phrases before the verb make it hard for the reader to remember what the subject is—who said or did what:

Complex

A man wanted by Seattle and Tukwila police for questioning in the disappearance of his girlfriend, a housekeeper for a wealthy Seattle family, and for the burglary of $130,000 in goods from the family's Madison Park home has been arrested in Knoxville, Tenn.

Simpler

A man wanted by Seattle and Tukwila police for questioning in the disappearance of his girlfriend and a Madison Park burglary has been arrested in Knoxville, Tenn.

Tell the reader later what the man's girlfriend did and how much he stole.

Vary the pace. Avoid writing huge blocks of complicated concepts and sentences filled with clauses and phrases. In the following story about problems with air traffic control, the first paragraph is cumbersome. The next one is even more dense—that is, if the reader gets that far. For simplicity and clarity, the long sentences could be broken into sentences of varying lengths.

For thousands of travelers who fly in and out of the three major New York airports every day, the air traffic control system is a vital but unknown reality—heavily reliant on technology and on controllers who say they are underpaid and overworked, and it is a system burdened with 1.74 million flights last year, a volume undreamed of a generation ago.

Despite personnel shortages, wobbly morale, budget problems and modernization delays—and the recent crash of a Colombian jetliner approaching Kennedy International Airport—the almost unanimous view of government and airline officials, controllers and other experts is that the region's air traffic control system is essentially safe.

The New York Times

Focus on a person to explain impact. The way an issue affects one person makes it clear to many. That's the concept of *The Wall Street Journal's* formula, and it can be used effectively in government stories. Lead with an anecdote about a person, then go from the specific to the general. It's the "one of many" technique.

Linda Green paid $42,000 in 1982 for a house on a half-acre lot in Fontana, banking on the equity that would build over the years.

But if Fontana's new general plan is approved, Green is fearful her property may be worth no more than the day she bought it.

The proposed plan would change the zoning on her half-acre so no additional homes could be built on it, making the site less attractive to buyers.

Green is not alone in her fears. She was among several landowners complaining Monday that the revised general plan—a blueprint for Fontana's growth—will put their properties in less profitable zoning areas.

"I bought my land as an investment. If they zone it down, I will lose my money, and I worked hard to put my money into it," Green told the planning commission during the first public hearing on the new 20-year plan.

More than 130 people attended the hearing. . . .

Tony Saavedra,
The (San Bernardino, Calif.) *Sun*

How can you write about a monthly statistical report so readers can understand the impact? Use the focus-on-a-person approach with a twist. Instead of just reporting the statistics, this reporter decided to see how meaningful the unemployment statistics were to people:

Statistically speaking, last month was Nate Payne's best chance in 16 years to get a job.

Payne is a resident of Pennsylvania, where the unemployment rate in March dropped to a 16-year low of 3.9 percent—so low that, according to economists, practically the only people out of work are those who have quit their jobs to look for something better.

But statistics didn't do a thing for Payne, 29. He was laid off last month from his job as a heavy-equipment operator for a paving contractor and hasn't worked since.

He spent yesterday morning, the first workday after the release of the startlingly low unemployment figures, waiting for an interview with a job service counselor in the Pennsylvania Employment Service office at Broad and Master Streets.

He had plenty of company. At least 50 other men and women had come to the office by 10 a.m. to apply for unemployment compensation, to confirm that they had not found jobs and were still eligible for unemployment payments or to see whether any jobs were available that met their requirements.

Payne's assessment: "It's really grim this time."

Andrea Knox, *The Philadelphia Inquirer*

Use an impact lead or explain impact in the story. Tell how the reader will be affected by a bureaucratic action or proposal.

A $10,000 car would cost $25 more in taxes, a $40 power saw an extra dime and a $4 six-pack of imported beer a penny extra in Rockford if Alderman Ernst Shafer, R-3rd, gets his way.

Shafer wants Rockford to join the push in Springfield for a 0.25 percent increase in the sales tax. Locally the sales tax would rise from 6.25 to 6.5 percent under the proposal.

Brian Leaf, *Rockford* (Ill.) *Register Star*

Impact is especially helpful in budget stories. Interpret what the figures will mean to the reader. Here's the kind of budget lead to avoid:

The Rockville Housing Authority approved a revised operating budget for the year ending Dec. 31, 1990 at its monthly meeting Friday at the Community Center, 1250 Park Place.

It says nothing and is cluttered with unimportant information about the location of the meeting. Here is a better alternative:

Pinellas School Superintendent Howard Hinesley has proposed a list of budget cuts for the next school year that will mean fewer textbooks, fewer teachers and fewer administrators if School Board members approve them next Wednesday.

Patty Curtin Jones, *St. Petersburg* (Fla.) *Times*

Define jargon and technical terms. You should do this in any story but especially in environmental, medical, business and science stories. In the following story about acid rain, the writer defines *pH scale* and uses analogies to clarify jargon:

A spot inventory of Jeanne Johns' freezer shows the usual stuff. Ice cream. Frozen peas. TV dinners. Acid rain.

Acid rain? You bet.

Johns, who lives in Haslett, is one of four Michigan volunteers in the Citizen Acid Rain Monitoring Network. The network has more than 300 stations nationwide to monitor acid rain. . . .

She measures the acidity on a pH scale ranging from 0 to 14, with 0 being the most acidic. The scale increases tenfold, meaning a 4.0 reading is 10 times more acidic than 5.0.

Normal precipitation is usually about 5.6. A reading of 5 or under indicates human-generated acids in the rain. A pH of 5.0 is equal to the acid content in cola. Frogs die if placed in water with a pH of 4.0. Battery acid is 1.5.

Kevin O'Hanlon, *Lansing* (Mich.) *State Journal*

Use analogies to clarify concepts. Comparisons can make technical information clear to readers. Compare the statistic or term with a concept readers will visualize or easily understand. In this example of an analogy, the writer compares the concept behind the federal deficit to the kind of credit most readers would understand:

Picture a family hooked on credit cards living beyond its means.

New clothes? Charge it. More medicine? Charge it. A night on the town? Charge it.

Pretty soon the situation is out of hand. The parents have to borrow money just to pay the monthly interest. The balance owed on their credit cards keeps rising, faster and faster.

Some restraint is attempted, but results are mixed. The parents can't stop whipping out the plastic.

That is the situation of the federal government as it closes the borrow-and-spend decade of the 1980s.

It took two centuries for the government's debt to reach $1 trillion, but only four years—from 1982 to 1986—for it to balloon to $2 trillion.

Now the Treasury Department says the government cannot operate past Nov. 8 if Congress does not raise the limit on the government's debt to nearly $3 trillion. That's $3,000,000,000,000.

Charles Green, *The Philadelphia Inquirer*

This is an analogy from a story about pollution in Alabama's rivers:

> Each minute, about 30 million gallons of Alabama river water, or the equivalent of what it would take to fill 60 Olympic-sized swimming pools, flush into Mobile Bay, washing over oyster beds in the northern part of the bay closed to harvesting.
>
> Dan Morse, *The* (Montgomery) *Alabama Journal*

Use conversational style. Write the story as though you were having a conversation with a friend.

Bureaucratic version

> After a discussion at last night's City Council meeting with several property owners on North Addison Street that opposed the annexation of their land, Mayor Ed Weinman cast the vote needed to gain a majority in favor of an ordinance approving the third annexation since June. It involves about 56 acres around a trailer park.

Conversational version

> Despite objections from the property owners, City Council last night voted to annex 56 acres of land around a trailer park.

Here is how one reporter used the conversational style in the lead of a bureaucratic story:

> How'd you like an airport for a neighbor? Or maybe a landfill or an incinerator?
>
> Probably about as much as government officials like trying to find a site for these things.
>
> But what if you could negotiate noise insulation for your airport-area home? Or an agreement requiring the incinerator to douse its fires if it didn't burn hot enough to eliminate most pollutants?
>
> Those alternatives were offered Wednesday to a roomful of Twin Cities area public officials frustrated by their protracted and often doomed efforts to make people accept controversial facilities they don't want.
>
> In an area where officials are looking for places for new landfills, a new airport, light-rail transit routes and other public works projects, the Metropolitan Council sponsored yesterday's conference in an effort to see if there's a better way.
>
> There is, they were told by a specialist in how to make the risks of such facilities more acceptable to their neighbors.
>
> Steve Brandt, *Star Tribune* (Minneapolis)

Avoid numbing numbers. You need to use numbers, but you don't need all of them. And you don't need to put very many of them in the lead. Avoid writing many numbers in the same paragraph or the same block. They're hard to read.

Lists can help when you need to use a lot of numbers. Or spread them out and intersperse interpretation, as in this lead:

A survey by the American Bar Association has found an "astonishing rise" in reported alcohol consumption by lawyers—with 13 percent of them admitting to having six more drinks a day.

That compares with less than one-half of 1 percent of lawyers who said they drank that much in the last survey, in 1984.

Women lawyers reported even greater dissatisfaction and alcohol consumption than men. Twenty percent of the women lawyers surveyed reported having six more drinks per day, compared with 11 percent of the men.

The findings link the apparent rise in drinking by lawyers to greater dissatisfaction and stress among them.

The Associated Press

Another way to deal with numbers is to interpret them, as in this lead:

As real estate disasters go, 1990 wasn't all that bad in Orange County.

Yes, the county saw its first year-to-year decline in average sale price since 1983. And, yes, the home-price malaise was seen in virtually every type of neighborhood, from ritzy beach cities to supposedly "priced-to-move" markets of north and central Orange County.

But now that the final numbers are in, the 1990 price downturn has proved to be less a financial debacle than it was nerve-wracking.

Perhaps the biggest statistic for the 1990 housing market was this tiny number: 1.2 percent.

That's how far the average single-family home price fell in Orange County from 1989 to 1990, according to a survey of neighborhood home prices by TRW Marketing Services in Anaheim.

The real drop? About $3,000 for an average-price house, which at the end of 1990 was priced at $248,167.

Andre Mouchard, *The Orange County* (Calif.) *Register*

Storytelling Techniques

Even bureaucratic stories can lend themselves to storytelling. In this example, the writer uses an anecdotal-narrative approach to a story about statistics:

In the early morning of Jan. 25, a woman left a friend's Northwest Portland house and began walking home. As she neared Northwest Flanders Street and 21st Avenue about 3:30 a.m., a man grabbed her arm, forced her to the ground and threatened her with a handgun. Then he raped her.

She was one of 32 persons who told Portland police they were raped in the first four weeks of January. Police have not yet tallied the reports from the last five days of the month. But even so, the count already exceeds the 20 rapes that were reported for January 1990. In Oregon, rape is defined as forcible sexual intercourse.

That increase bears out a trend that rape victim advocates and law enforcement officials began seeing last year: The number of reported sexual assaults in Portland is on a slight rise. Police statistics show 427 rapes in 1990, compared with 412 in 1989, or a 4 percent increase, said Steve Beedle, a public safety analyst for Portland police.

Diane Dulken, *The Oregonian*

The following storytelling techniques apply well to bureaucratic stories:

Use lists. Use them in the middle or at the end of the story, especially to explain key points of an issue. Lists are particularly helpful in stories with numbers or explanations of proposals.

Avoid the city-dump syndrome. Be selective. Use only quotes and facts that you need. Don't dump your notebook into the story.

Use the kiss-off technique. If you have more than three speakers, block the comments from each one and then do not use the sources again, unless you re-introduce them. The reader can't remember all the officials by second reference only.

Budget Stories

Budget stories can be the most complicated and boring bureaucratic stories of all. Yet they are very important. Readers want to know how the government spends money—their money. Many of the clues Woodward and Bernstein followed in the Watergate story were based on the finances of the Committee to Re-elect the President, which was illegally using campaign contributions for spying operations.

First you need to understand the budget process of the agency you cover. Then you need to make it relevant to readers.

Budget planning starts several months before the budget is approved. Learn how to interpret the proposed budget by asking a financial officer of the city, school or agency to explain it to you before the budget is released. If he or she can't brief you on this year's proposal, use last year's budget to learn the system. In most cases, officials will be willing to cooperate, because they want you to present the facts accurately.

The Kansas House of Representatives, where state budgets are hammered out.

Courtesy of Philip Meiring

Basically, budgets have two sections:

Revenues: The income, usually derived from taxes—primarily property taxes, in municipalities. But there also are sales taxes, income taxes and fees. Look for clues about how the revenue will be raised. Will property taxes increase? If you are covering a university budget, will tuition be increased? Find out how the revenue will affect your readers.

Expenditures: Where most of the money will be spent. Will some departments be increasing expenses more than others, such as police or fire departments. If so, why? Will salaries be increased or more people be hired? How do the expenditures for this year compare with those of the past few years?

Generally, budgets include figures from the previous year or past few years. Look for major increases and decreases in revenues and expenditures.

Before a government agency can adopt a budget, it must conduct public hearings, where the public can comment about the budget. If the budget proposal is at the hearing stage, be sure to include the dates of the hearings in your story. Taxpayers often want to attend to protest cutbacks or request money for programs they support.

Budget and Tax Terms

You won't be able to understand or explain budgets unless you know what these terms mean:

Assessments and property taxes: Common in municipal budgets, where taxes are based on real estate. Homeowners pay taxes based on an assessment, or estimated value, of their property. This value is determined by a city property appraiser based on a number of factors: size of the property, number of bedrooms, construction, and so on. For example, suppose you decide to buy a condominium or a house selling for $80,000. That is its "market value," the price it sells for on the market. Some communities base their tax on the full market value, but most use only a percentage of the total value. The property is given an "assessed value," a value for tax purposes. If your community bases its tax on half the market value, your house would be assessed for $40,000. Your annual property taxes equal some percentage of the assessed value.

Capital budget: Money used to pay for major improvements, such as the construction of highways or new buildings. Capital is often raised by selling bonds, and people who buy the bonds receive interest. The government then uses the money and repays the bonds, plus interest, over a period of years in what is called "debt service." The process is much like buying a house: The bank lends you money; you live in the house and repay the loan plus interest on a long-term basis, often over 30 years.

Deficit: When government spends more money than it receives. Most municipalities and states require a balanced budget: The expenses must be the same as the income. The difference between the expenditures and the income is the deficit, or debt.

Fiscal year: Year in which budgeted funds will be spent. In government, the budget term often starts on July 1 and goes to June 30, instead of the calendar year beginning in January. So if you use fiscal year, give the dates: "in this fiscal year, which starts July 1." Or if you are writing about when the money will run out: "in this fiscal year, which ends June 30."

Mill: Unit equal to $1 for every $1,000 that a house is assessed (or0.1 cent for each $1 of assessed valuation). Local school and city taxes are based on mills. Explain the impact of these taxes clearly. If the school tax rate is 25 mills, your story should say, "The tax rate is 25 mills, which equals $25 for every $1,000 of assessed property valuation." Or you could insert a definition: "A mill equals $1 for every $1,000 of assessed value on a property." Then give an example: "Under this tax rate, a homeowner whose property is valued at $40,000 (multiplied by 0.025) would pay $1,000 in school taxes." Try to avoid using the term *mills;* just say the tax rate will be $25 for every $1,000 of assessed property value. Follow with a specific example so residents can figure out how much their tax will be.

Operating budget: Money used to provide services (police, fire, garbage removal and so on) and to pay for the operation of government. Most of the money for this budget comes from taxes.

Other taxes: Wage tax, income tax and sales tax. Cities and states often charge these additional taxes. Check when you write your budget stories to determine whether they will be increased or decreased. If they will stay the same, say so.

Reappraisal: State or local decision to re-evaluate properties in the community, usually to increase their values. This action almost always generates good stories because it affects people dramatically. For example, Kansas had not reappraised properties for 20 years. When the state decided to do it, property values soared and a tax revolt resulted. People who had been paying $200 in taxes on their homes suddenly were paying $1,000. A similar situation occurred in Atlanta:

A groundswell of protest over the mass reappraisal of Atlanta and Fulton County property is threatening to become a wholesale tax revolt.

Thousands of homeowners have turned out at meetings throughout the city and county to express displeasure with their new assessments, in some cases more than double last year's.

At the South Fulton County Annex, more than one thousand people gathered Monday to talk about fighting the assessments.

"My assessment went up 190

percent and I'll gladly sell my home to the county for what they think it's worth," said Mitch Skandalakis, a leader of the Task Force for Good Government, as the crowd roared.

Mark Sherman, *Atlanta Constitution*

Writing Techniques

Impact is crucial in budget stories. So are graphics. A chart or list of key numbers can make a story more presentable. Also get reactions from city officials, residents at public hearings or the people most affected by budget cuts. If you are writing about university budgets, get reactions from administrators, students, professors and the officials whose departments will be affected most.

Here are some key points to include in a budget story, not necessarily in this order:

• Total amount of the budget (rounded off when possible: $44.6 million instead of $44,552,379; most budgets are supposed to be balanced, so the figure applies to both revenues and expenditures)

• Amount of increase or decrease

• Tax or tuition levy, or how funds will be raised (impact on reader, comparison to current tax)

• Major expenditures (major increases and decreases in department funds)

• Consequences (impact on the government or agency—cuts in personnel, services, and so on)

• Historical comparisons (how budget compares to previous year and past few years)

• Reactions from officials and people affected by increases or decreases

• Definitions and explanations of technical terms

Here is an example of the kind of budget story you should avoid writing. It is flooded with statistics but doesn't clarify how the budget will affect the reader.

The recommended 1991 Rockville city budget would require a 2.56-mill property tax increase.

City Manager Joan Weinman recommended to Rockville City Commission a budget of $55,672,309, which would require a local levy of 42.59 mills. Last year's budget of $50,322,409 required a levy of 42.03 mills.

A mill is $1 of tax for every $1,000 of assessed property valuation.

Weinman is recommending a 3 percent across-the-board salary increase for city employees. She is also recommending an addition of five police officers to the public safety department.

Here is the lead on another budget story, but this one explains the impact on homeowners:

HACKENSACK (N.J.)—A $39.2 million budget that offers residents their first property-tax break in 20 years has been adopted by the City Council.

The budget, which includes $4 million in new state aid, was approved by a 4-1 vote following a public hearing Monday. No residents commented.

Despite a 6 percent increase in spending, the boost in state aid means that total property taxes for the owner of a home assessed at $180,000, the borough average, will drop $54 a year.

Tom Topousis, *The* (Hackensack, N.J.) *Record*

The next story was a sidebar, but it contains the kind of information that should be included in a story about a city budget—the effect on residents:

Mayor Goode said last night that under his budget plan one of two things was certain—death or taxes. He said city residents needed to pay new and increased taxes to avert the fiscal demise of the city.

Goode proposed raising an additional $142 million for next year's budget by increasing the wage, net-profits and property taxes and by adding a 1 percent city sales tax to the state's 6 percent sales tax.

The Goode administration estimated that for someone earning $25,000 a year, the wage tax increases—to 5.36 percent—would add $100 to his or her current tax payment of $1,240.

The real estate tax increase of 2 mills, from the current 37.45 mills of assessed value, would add $32 to the current tax bill of $1,322 paid by the owner of a home with a market value of $50,000.

Dianne E. Reed, the executive director of the local chapter of the Pennsylvania Economy League, estimated that the average citizen would pay $80 more a year if the local sales tax were approved.

Matthew Purdy, *The Philadelphia Inquirer*

Don't forget that budgets affect people. So when you are writing advances and reaction stories, you can use feature techniques. Here is an example of an anecdotal-narrative approach to an advance on the city budget:

It was 8:05 on a Monday in August, Rosemary Farnon remembers, when her husband, Tony, called the police to report that their rowhouse in the Juniata Park section had been ransacked.

Amid a shambles of overturned furniture, scattered papers and food taken from the fridge, the Farnons nervously and angrily waited nearly five hours before an officer appeared. He explained apologetically that the local police district had no cops to spare.

Theirs is one story, from one neighborhood, but it typifies what is happening across Philadelphia:

Taxes are up and services are down—and residents are unhappy about it.

So Rosemary Farnon and hundreds of thousands of taxpayers will be listening closely Thursday when Mayor Goode proposes the budget for the coming fiscal year, which begins July 1.

Dan Myers and Idris M. Diaz, *The Philadelphia Inquirer*

University budget stories can use the same techniques. Here is a first-day budget story stressing the impact on students and reaction. Comparative statistics were given in graphic form (see Exhibit 22-1).

LONG BEACH (Calif.)—Despite an outcry from students, California State University on Wednesday increased academic fees 20 percent, to $936 a year.

Fees at all 20 campuses could climb even higher if the state budget crisis, which has left CSU with a $402.5 million shortfall, worsens this spring, Chancellor Ellis E. McCune warned the Board of Trustees.

Students will not only pay more in the fall, they will get less. They will have fewer professors to teach them, a smaller array of courses from which to choose, and bigger classes to attend.

Meeting at Cal State Long Beach, the trustees reduced the budget from $2.1 million to $1.65 million and called for:

• Eliminating 420 faculty positions and leaving vacant an additional 330.

• Not replacing 229 professors when they go on sabbatical.

• Reducing other staff by 856 positions.

"None of these is a happy solution," McCune said.

Steven Silberman, *The Orange County Register*

The next story is a budget advance, also with emphasis on the impact. This story, too, was accompanied by charts comparing tuition at California universities with those of comparable size elsewhere.

California public universities, once acclaimed for providing one of the finest and cheapest educations in the nation, soon are likely to rank among the most expensive state systems to attend.

In the coming weeks, officials of the University of California and California State University systems are expected to increase fees as much as 60 percent to ease a deepening fiscal crisis that some fear will force a turning away from the state's historic commitment to excellence and accessibility.

"The danger with continually increasing fees is that we're going to cease being as democratic or egalitarian as we have traditionally been," said Neil Smelser, a sociology professor at the University of California, Berkeley.

Gov. Pete Wilson is asking CSU and UC to do their jobs with about 8 percent less spending power. In one year, the university would suffer a budget blow equivalent to what they have absorbed in all the years since Proposition 13 started to tighten government spending in 1978, said San Jose State University President Gail Fullerton.

Tom Philp and Miranda Ewell,
San Jose (Calif.) *Mercury News*

Student fee comparison

Tuition and miscellaneous costs for a resident undergraduate at California State University and comparable public universities, 1990-91

Total

Rutgers, NJ	**$3,281**
Virginia Polytechnic Inst.	**2,840**
Cleveland State U.	**2,397**
U. of Maryland, Baltimore	**2,390**
Illinois State U.	**2,272**
U. of Wisconsin, Milwaukee	**2,258**
Georgia State U.	**1,812**
Arizona State U.	**1,640**
SUNY, Albany	**1,485**
U. of Colorado, Denver	**1,458**
U. of Nevada, Reno	**1,380**
N. Carolina State U.	**1,109**
CSU	**911**

20% increase

Sources: California State University and California Postsecondary Education Commission

CSU academic fees

Annual fee for full-time undergraduates who are state residents. Individual campuses might add some charges.

Source: California State University

'79-'80 $144
'80-'81 $160
'81-'82 $252
'82-'83 $430
'83-'84 $612
'84-'85 $573
'85-'86 $573
'86-'87 $573
'87-'88 $630
'88-'89 $684
'89-'90 $708
'90-'91 $780
'91-'92 $936

Exhibit 22-1

Graphics accompanying a story on a university's budget

The Orange County Register

A sidebar showed the impact on one university:

Imagine San Jose State University closing the entire School of Engineering, Silicon Valley's largest producer of high tech talent—and still needing to cut millions more just to balance its budget.

That is the severity of the looming financial crisis facing San Jose State.

The university's strategy to cut an estimated $14 million from the 1991–'92 budget, however, won't hurt an engineering professor any more than it will a football coach. Instead, every corner of campus will share the pain under a plan that is intentionally high on equity—and thus low on controversy.

Gail Fullerton, who became San Jose State's 21st president a month after voters enacted the tax-slashing Proposition 13 in 1978, has complained of one tight budget after another during her 13-year tenure. But this time, the magnitude of the financial crisis is something new.

"I feel like the shepherd who has cried wolf," Fullerton told the Academic Senate this week. "This is a budget year like no other."

Tom Philp, *San Jose Mercury News*

Activities

1 Read any bureaucratic story from your local newspaper, and determine what information could be taken out of the story and used graphically (if it is not already in graphic form). Then write an empowerment box (what to do, where to go for help or information) and/or a highlights box.

2 Using your local or campus newspaper, find a poorly written story about bureaucracy. Rewrite it using the techniques suggested in this chapter.

3 Get a copy of your town or city's budget, and write a budget story based on it.

4 Invent your own town. Break into groups in your class, and have each group head a different department your town would need. Design a budget for your town and a way of raising revenue. Then come together, share your information, and write a budget story.

5 Plan a budget for an organization you belong to, or discuss the budget with the treasurer of the group. Then write a story about it.

COACHING

TIPS

Use graphic reporting skills. Gather enough detail and specifics so you could draw a diagram or write a chronology of the crime as though you were designing a graphic.

Role-play: Ask yourself what you would want to know if you were affected by this crime.

Use the tell-a-friend technique.

Avoid the jargon of police or other legal authorities. If you don't understand a term, chances are the reader may not know it either.

Always include the background of the case, no matter how many days a police story or trial continues. Never take it for granted that the reader has read previous stories.

Be careful. Double-check your accuracy, and make sure you don't convict someone of a crime before a judge or jury does.

Crime and Punishment 23

T he police beat, which often includes the fire department, is considered an entry-level job. Most reporters move on to other beats after a few years of covering crime stories. Edna Buchanan did not. She covered the police beat at *The Miami Herald* for more than 20 years before resigning to write books. But while she was at *The Herald,* she turned police reporting into an art form. The most famous police reporter in the United States, Buchanan won the Pulitzer Prize for a collection of her stories in 1986.

A soft-spoken woman, she writes with a strong punch. One Pulitzer Prize juror said, "She writes drop-dead sentences for drop-dead victims. She is never dull." Consider:

> There was music and sunlight as the paddle wheeler Dixie Bell churned north on Indian Creek Thursday. The water shimmered and the wind was brisk. And then the passengers noticed that the people in the next boat were dead.

Buchanan is most famous for the lead she wrote on a story about a man who shoved his way to the front of a line at a fried chicken restaurant. The counter clerk told the man to go to the end of the line and wait his turn. He did. But when he reached the head of the line again, the restaurant had run out of fried chicken. He battered the clerk fiercely, and he was shot fatally by a guard in the restaurant. Her lead: "Gary Robinson died hungry."

I have never understood young reporters who considered covering the cops the least desirable beat. The police beat is all about people, what makes them tick, what makes them become heroes or homicidal maniacs. It has it all: greed, sex, violence, comedy and tragedy.

Edna Buchanan, former police reporter, *The Miami Herald*

"In truth, Edna Buchanan doesn't write about cops. She writes about people," *Herald* editors wrote in the Pulitzer entry. Buchanan is the first to admit that: "You learn more about people on the police beat than any other beat," she said in a speech at a convention of investigative reporters.

She said she has reported more than 5,000 violent deaths. How does she keep from getting upset by them and burned out on the job? "The thing that keeps you going is that you realize you can make things better. You may be affected like everyone else by a terrible tragedy, but you're in a position to do something about it. That's the real joy of this job. We can be catalysts for change. We can bring about justice. Sometimes we are all the victim has got. Police stories do make a difference.

"You've got to be accurate and fair and very, very careful, particularly in crime reporting. A news story mentioning somebody's name can ruin their lives or come back to haunt them 25 years later. It is there in black and white on file. It's like a police record; you never outlive it. You can do terrible damage. So you knock on one more door, ask one more question, make one last phone call. It could be the one that counts."

As noted in Chapter 8, when Buchanan made those phone calls and someone hung up on her, she just redialed the number and said, "We were cut off." The second time, she might have gotten a relative or someone else who was willing to talk, or the first person might have changed his or her mind. But she didn't try a third time; that would be harassment, she said.

Crime Stories

Buchanan gathered her information from interviews and records. And then she wove them into stories with leads that hooked the reader. She said that crime reporters need to talk to witnesses and get color, background, ages and details—what people were wearing, doing and saying when they became crime victims or suspects. In other words, crime reporters need access.

Access   If you have the police beat, you should make a habit of checking the daily police log, also called the "blotter," to see the listing of all crimes recorded by police for that day. The log will list the names of the victims and suspects and the nature of the crimes. This is public record and should be available to the press and anyone else. However, the supporting documents—the actual police reports filed by the officer at the scene—may not be available. Laws limiting access to these reports vary from state to state. Restrictions apply especially to records for cases under investigation, but if you develop good sources in the police department, you may gain access.

The arrest record, usually filed under the suspect's name, should contain the suspect's name and address, date and place of birth, sex, race, occupation, place of arrest, type of crime, a brief description of the incident, and names of witnesses. Of special importance to a reporter, the name of the arresting officer will be at the bottom of the report. For a major crime story, you will want to talk to the officer who was at the scene. However, police can withhold information about crimes that are under investigation.

To previous criminal records   If you are a good reporter, you will want to find out if a suspect has a previous criminal record for related charges. If you are lucky, you will be able to do that. But not necessarily from the police. Again, many states restrict access to previous criminal records.

However, if someone has been convicted of a crime, that court record is public and should be available to you in the court jurisdiction where he or she was convicted. If the person was charged with a crime and found not guilty or charges were dropped, that record also is public. You need to look up the court file (and get the case file number) under that person's name.

Depending on how the records are filed in your city, you probably will need the year of the court case, too. Filing systems vary in every municipality, so ask the court clerk for help. The court file should contain all pertinent information, including names of the lawyers involved, description of the crime and all motions filed in the case. Most important, it will tell what happened—the disposition of the case—including specific terms of the sentence or probation or dismissal.

In some cases, a person convicted of a minor crime can have his or her record erased—"expunged"—after a number of years with permission of the court. In other cases, a judge may permit certain records to be sealed, meaning that they will be withheld from the public and only available to law enforcement officers.

To university records   Many universities withhold names on crime records because of a federal law. The Buckley Amendment to the Family Educational Rights and Privacy Act prohibits government agencies from releasing any personal data about students and employees in institutions that receive federal funding. Universities have claimed that if they release such crime records, they could lose federal funding.

In 1991, a federal judge in Missouri ruled that Southwest Missouri State University must release names and records of crimes at that school after Traci Bauer, editor of the campus newspaper, sued for access. That ruling did not apply to all universities. But in 1992, a new federal law exempted campus records from the restrictions of the Buckley Amendment. Although the new law makes access to police records easier at many universities, it doesn't guarantee access. Universities are still not compelled to release information on crime records, but they will no longer risk losing federal funds if they do release the names.

To records of juvenile offenders   All states have laws restricting the release of records that identify juvenile offenders, people under age 18. The names are withheld by all branches of the juvenile justice system, including the social services system, but a judge can authorize their release. If a juvenile is being tried as an adult—a decision that is made by a judge—or if the juvenile's name is mentioned in open court, the name can be used. This sometimes happens when the crime is particularly heinous or the juvenile has an extensive criminal record.

Most newspapers and broadcast stations have policies to withhold the names of juveniles, but that is more of an ethical decision than a legal one. The media may use the name if they receive it by legitimate means.

To the crime scene   Police have the right to protect the crime scene and limit access to the press. If it is public property, reporters and photographers can get as close as police will allow. If the crime scene is on private property, access is at the discretion of the police or the owners of the property. Generally, police will allow some access as long as the media do not interfere with the investigation of evidence at the crime scene.

Use of Names

Many newspapers withhold the names of suspects in crime stories until they have been charged formally with the crime. Being arrested means only that someone has been stopped for questioning in a crime. The person becomes an official suspect after charges are filed in a court, usually at a hearing called an "arraignment." (The process will be explained in the section about courts.)

Some newspapers also withhold the names of crime victims to protect their privacy. A growing controversy at newspapers and television stations is whether to withhold the names of complainants in rape cases. Again, the policy varies, but most of the media do not publish the names.

When names are used in crime stories, always get the full name, including the middle initial, and double-check the spelling. Do not rely on police reports; many names on reports are spelled incorrectly. Check the names in telephone directories whenever possible. If a discrepancy occurs between the name in the phone book and the one the officer gave you, call the officer again or go with the information from police.

Using full names with initials helps reduce confusion and inaccuracies; there could be a dozen John Smiths in the community. John T. Smith is more specific, especially when followed by age and address.

Wording of Accusations

Remember that all people are innocent until they are proved guilty in court or until they plead guilty. When a suspect is arrested, the person is not officially charged with anything. A person can be arrested after an officer gets a warrant or on suspicion of a crime. But the police cannot charge anyone with a crime; a member of the district attorney's office must file the charge officially with the court. (More about that later.) As a result, you must be careful with wording so you don't convict a person erroneously. Most media wait until the person has been charged with the crime, except in sensational cases when the arrest is important news.

If you are writing about an arrest before the official charge, do not say, "Sallie R. Smith was arrested for robbing the bank" (that implies guilt). Do say, "Sallie R. Smith was arrested in connection with the bank robbery." If you are writing about the suspect after charges have been filed, say, "Sallie R. Smith was charged with bank robbery" or "Sally R. Smith was arrested on a charge of bank robbery."

Also be careful before you call anyone a crime victim. If a person was killed or visibly injured during a crime, it is probably clear that the person is a crime victim. In other cases, the suspect has to be proved guilty before you can say the other person is a victim. You can say "the *alleged* victim" or, if applicable, you can call the other person the accuser—for example, "The accuser in the rape trial was . . ."

Use the official charges when possible. If they are very awkward, and they often are, don't use them in the lead. Put them in the backup to the story. For example, one man who was accused of robbing a jewelry store was also accused of carrying a gun. But police didn't charge him with possession of a gun. They charged him with possession of an instrument of crime. And there are varying degrees in the charges, such as first-degree murder, which should be cited. But don't cite the other qualifications, such as Class E felony (a category for the crime), unless you are going to explain what they mean and why the reader must know. If categories are used at all, it is for explanation of the penalties, such as "The crime is a Class E felony, which carries a penalty of . . ." It is still preferable to explain the penalty without the category, which is meaningless to readers.

The word *alleged* is dangerous, so avoid it whenever possible. It means to declare or assert without proof. If you allege carelessly, you can be sued. Do not say, "Smith allegedly robbed the bank." You, the writer, are then the source of the allegation—and a good candidate for a libel suit. You can say, however, "Police accused Sallie R. Smith of robbing the bank" or "Police said Smith robbed the bank." If you must use *alleged,* say, "Police alleged that Smith robbed the bank." "Police accused Smith of allegedly robbing the bank" is redundant and awkward. Besides, police rarely allege; they accuse. An accusation is OK if it comes from police (and they are citing charges on record), not if it comes from you. Other permissible uses include "The bank was allegedly robbed" or "the alleged robbery," although such uses are not preferable.

Here's an example of the proper use of *alleged:* When William Kennedy Smith, the nephew of Sen. Edward Kennedy, was accused of rape at the Kennedy mansion in Palm Beach in 1991, newspapers properly wrote "The alleged rape at the Kennedy compound." Unless and until a court rules that the suspect is guilty, there is no proof that a rape actually occurred. So in this type of case, "alleged rape" is accurate. You also could use "the reported rape at the Kennedy compound." A jury later found Smith not guilty. The statement "the rape at the Kennedy compound" would have been inaccurate as well as libelous.

Also be careful when using the word *accused.* Follow the *Associated Press Stylebook* guidelines: A person is accused *of,* not *with,* a crime. In addition, you should not say, "accused bank robber Sallie R. Smith" (this convicts her). Instead, say, "Sallie R. Smith, accused of the bank robbery."

Attribution

Follow the guidelines for attribution explained in Chapter 3. In crime stories, make sure you attribute all accusatory information and much of the information you received secondhand (not by direct observation). Factual information does not need attribution. The location of a crime, for example, usually is factual. If someone has been charged with a crime, you can state that as a fact.

To reduce the use of attribution after every sentence, you can use an overview attribution for part of your story, especially when you are recounting what happened: "Police described the incident this way."

Newspaper Clips

The first thing you should do before you write your story is check newspaper clips in your library. They may make a big difference in your story.

In one case at *The Hartford* (Conn.) *Courant,* a man was arrested on a charge of rape. Small story for a big paper. But the reporter checked clips and discovered that the man had been arrested previously on rape charges and was free on bail when he was charged with this other rape—a much bigger story. Three months later, a different reporter was making police checks. A man had been accused of rape. The reporter checked the clips. It was the same man charged with a third rape, which occurred when he was free on bail still awaiting trial in the first rape case—a very big story. And this story led to a major front-page follow-up story on the system in Connecticut that allows rape suspects to be released on bail, no matter how many times they have been arrested and charged with that type of crime. (Bail is the amount of money, set by a judge, that the suspect has to deposit with the court to be released from jail pending a hearing or trial. If the suspect flees, the bail money goes to the court.)

One caution: Clips on file in your newspaper library or computer data base may not be up to date. They may contain stories of someone's arrest but not the disposition of the case. Always check to see if charges were dropped or if the person is still waiting trial or was convicted.

Guidelines for Reporting Crime Stories

In any story you will seek good quotes and answers to the five W's. Here are the basic questions to ask and the basic information to include in crime stories:

Victims: Get full names, ages, addresses and occupations, if available (use if relevant).

Suspects: Get full names, ages and addresses, if available; if not, get a description. Guidelines about whether to include race or ethnic background are changing. Check your newspaper's style. A general rule is to avoid mentioning race or ethnicity unless it is crucial to the story or to a description of a suspect.

Cause of fatalities or injuries: Also describe the injuries, where injured people have been taken and their current condition (check with hospitals.) In stories involving property, specify the causes and extent of damage.

Location of incident: Don't forget to gather specific information for a graphic.

Time of incident: Be as specific as possible.

What happened: Make sure you understand the sequence of events; always ask about any unusual circumstances.

Arrests and charges filed: If people have been arrested, find out where they are being held, when they will be arraigned (a hearing for formal charges) or when the next court procedure will be. If they have already been arraigned, find out the amount of bail.

Eyewitness accounts: Comments from neighbors may also be relevant. Be careful about using accusations against named individuals. When in doubt, leave them out.

In addition to gathering the basic information, you may want to try some of these other reporting techniques:

Role-play. Imagine that it is your car in the accident, your home that was burglarized or burned in a fire, your friend or relative injured in a crime. What information would you want to know if you were personally affected by the story?

Play detective. What information would you want to gather to solve the crime?

Gather graphics. What information would you need to diagram the car accident, draw the crime scene or a locator map, write a highlights box or a chronology of events, or design a chart or graphic depicting how and where the crime occurred? Ask questions to gain the information you will have to convey to the artist who will draw the graphics for your story.

Use the telephone. Often you will gather information for crime stories over the telephone. Usually you will get the information from a dispatcher or public information officer who was not at the scene and is just reading a report to you. Make sure you ask police officials to repeat any information you did not hear clearly. Also ask the police officer releasing the information to give you her or his full name and rank. Police often identify themselves only by title and last name, such as Sgt. Jones. Ask the officer to spell the names of all people involved; you can spell them back to double-check the accuracy.

Stories About Specific Types of Crimes

For a major crime story on a first-day cycle, the preferred approach is a hard-news one. For follow-up stories and sidebars, consider some of the storytelling techniques.

Motor vehicle accidents   Vehicle accident stories usually are hard-news stories, unless there is an unusual angle. Make sure you have this information:

Speed, destination, and directions of vehicles and exact locations at time of accident

Use of required equipment, such as seat belts and bicycle or motorcycle helmets, by victims

Weather-related information, if relevant

Rescue attempts or acts of heroism

It is customary to lead the story with fatalities and injuries. This example is very basic, structured in inverted pyramid form:

Summary lead: delayed identification, fatality and cause	A Santa Ana boy was killed when a van rear-ended the car he was riding in while it was stopped at a turn signal, police said. The van's driver was booked for vehicular manslaughter.
Identification	Robert Taylor, 10, died at UCI Medical Center in Orange.
When, where, other injured people	The 3:17 p.m. accident at First and Bristol streets in Santa Ana also critically injured the boy's mother, Griselda Taylor, 29, and his sister, Lynelle, 8. An 8-year-old boy in the car sustained minor injuries, police said. His name and relation to the Taylors were not released.
What happened Who was involved	Taylor was waiting on the eastbound side of First, in the left-turn

lane, at a red light when a van driven by Don Currie Edwards, 49, struck the back of her car, police said. The impact pushed her car into the intersection, and it was then struck by a westbound car driven by Phillipe Hernandez, 18.

Taylor sustained a broken neck. She was in guarded condition at Western Medical Center in Santa Ana, hospital officials said. Lynelle sustained critical head injuries, police said. *Condition of injured people; hospital sources*

Edwards was treated for minor injuries and arrested, police said. Hernandez was not injured.

The Orange County (Calif.) *Register*

Burglaries and robberies A burglary involves entry of a building with intent to commit any type of crime; robbery involves stealing with violence or a threat against people. If you are away and a person enters your home and steals your compact disc player, that's a burglary. If you are asleep upstairs and the person is downstairs stealing the player, that's still a burglary. But if the person threatens you with force, that's a robbery. A burglary always involves a place and *can* involve violence against a person; a robbery *must* involve violence or threats against a person.

For both burglaries and robberies, ask the basics. Then add:

What was taken and the value of the goods

Types of weapons used (in robberies)

How entry was made

Similar circumstances (frequency of crime in that location, overlooked valuables or any other odd conditions)

In burglary and robbery stories, mention in the lead any injuries or deaths. Keep the tone serious when the story involves death or serious injuries. In other cases, use your judgment and lead with any unusual angles. If there are none, stress what was taken or how the burglars entered the building, if that is the most interesting factor.

Whether you write a hard or soft lead depends on how serious the crime was, if it is a first-cycle story and whether you have enough interesting information to warrant a soft approach.

Here's a hard-news version of a burglary story:

COUNCIL BLUFFS, Ia. (AP)— A first issue of "Iron Man" was among 44 rare comic books stolen from a Council Bluffs store.

The books, some valued at $200 to $225 each, dated back to the 1950s and '60s.

Other books stolen from Kanesville Kollectibles included a 1964 first issue of "Daredevil," 17 issues of "Spider Man," four is- sues of "The Incredible Hulk," "Mystery in Space," "Tales of Suspense," "Captain Marvel" and "Thor."

Police reports said rare comic books valued at $2,950, about 300 used rock 'n' roll compact discs valued at $2,200 and $50 in cash were taken from the business.

The Associated Press

In this burglary story, the tone is lighter and a soft lead is used, because of the subject matter:

Someone took Burger King's "Have It Your Way" slogan too literally this week and stole a three-foot-wide Whopper ham- burger display costume from a van parked in northeast Salem.

Shannon Sappingfield, a mar- keting representative for local Burger Kings, said the missing burger was made of sponge.

The Whopper was in a van parked at Boss Enterprise, 408-A Lancaster Drive NE. The com- pany owns nine local Burger Kings.

When Sappingfield came to work about 6 a.m. Tuesday, she saw that the van's window had been broken. The cardboard box containing the Whopper costume was missing; two other boxes con- taining a milk shake costume and a french fry costume were un- touched.

"I'm not convinced they real- ized what they had until they were away from the site and opened the box," she said.

She estimated that the costume was worth about $500. But to get another one, the company would also have to buy another milk shake and french fry costume, which cost $500 each.

Salem, Ore., *Statesman-Journal*

This is a basic hard-news robbery story with a description of the suspects:

Two armed, masked men robbed a Huntington Beach restaurant late Tuesday, escaping with $2,000 in cash.

Police Lt. John Foster said the holdup occurred shortly before 11 p.m. at Jeremiah's, 8901 Warner Ave.

He said two men armed with shotguns and wearing stockings over their heads entered through the kitchen door, forced cooks into the main area of the restaurant, then made employees and patrons lie on the floor.

The robbers took the cash from a floor safe and fled, Foster said.

The men were described as Caucasian, wearing dark clothing. One was 6-foot-1 to 6-foot-3 with a thin build and dark, curly hair. The second was 5-foot-8, about 170 pounds with a medium to stocky build.

Detectives believe the same shotgun-wielding men robbed a Pizza Hut at 17342 Beach Blvd. about 9:40 p.m. Monday. The bandits took an undisclosed amount of cash and sped away in a small blue car, possibly a Toyota or Nissan.

The Orange County Register

In this robbery story, note the focus on the unusual angle:

A robbery was committed Tuesday with a can of deodorant spray, Des Moines police said.

James Vogel was at his insurance office at 3432 Forest Ave. when a masked man entered and displayed the deodorant spray. Police said the intruder attempted to spray Vogel and a struggle followed.

Vogel's glasses were broken, cutting his face, and the bandit grabbed Vogel's wallet, which contained about $20 cash and other items, and fled.

The Des Moines (Iowa) Register

This robbery story lends itself to a storytelling approach because no one was injured and the circumstances were unusual. The writer used a build-on-quote lead. Note that because the suspects are juveniles, their names are not used.

DES MOINES, Wash.—Police are calling it the "Two Stooges Robbery."

After robbing a Seafirst Bank branch in this Seattle suburb, police say, two teen-agers found that their beat-up getaway car had a dead battery.

When they got out to check under the hood, they locked their keys and the loot in the car.

Fleeing on foot, they ran straight to the car driven by a police detective dispatched to the crime scene.

"This was a bungled job from start to finish," Des Moines police Sgt. Mitch Barker said. "All we needed was Curly. We had Larry and Moe."

The 17-year-olds, one from Seattle and the other from Sumner, southeast of Tacoma, were in custody Friday at a juvenile detention center.

When the boys entered the bank, they handed a note to a teller that read, "Fast cash or die," court documents say.

Then, as the teen-agers turned to leave, the teller called them back and handed them additional money—including marked bills —which they took, according to court documents.

The Associated Press

Here is how the hourglass form can be used to eliminate some of the attribution in a crime story. The story on the left does not use the hourglass structure, but the one on the right does. Attributions are highlighted with underlining (note the overview attribution in the right-hand story).

Without hourglass structure	**With hourglass structure**
A robber took money from a clerk at Tom's Amoco, 3827 Topeka Blvd., early Sunday but had a change of heart, returned most of the cash and apologized before fleeing, <u>police said.</u>	A robber took money from a clerk at Tom's Amoco, 3827 Topeka Blvd., early Sunday but had a change of heart, returned most of the cash and apologized before fleeing, <u>police said.</u>
The man showed no weapon but held what appeared to be a handgun beneath his sweater, <u>said Detective Sgt. Greg Halford.</u>	The man showed no weapon but held what appeared to be a handgun beneath his sweater, said Detective Sgt. Greg Halford.
<u>Halford said</u> a 19-year-old male clerk was counting money inside the business about 4 a.m. when he saw the robber walk across Topeka Boulevard toward the service station.	<u>Halford described the incident as follows:</u>
<u>The clerk told police</u> he tried to get the money out of sight before the man came into the service station, but was unable.	A 19-year-old male clerk was counting money inside the business about 4 a.m. when he saw the robber walk across Topeka Boulevard toward the service station.
The robber gave the clerk five nickels and asked for a quarter, <u>Halford said,</u> then announced the robbery as the clerk was getting the quarter.	The clerk tried to get the money out of sight before the man came into the service station, but was unable.
The clerk asked the man if he was sure he wanted to go through with the robbery. The clerk then told him that three security guards from a nearby motel often come into the service station, <u>Halford said.</u>	The robber gave the clerk five nickels and asked for a quarter, then announced the robbery as the clerk was getting the quarter.
At that point, the nervous-looking robber went behind the counter and grabbed the money out of the clerk's hands, <u>the detective said.</u> Some of the money dropped onto the floor, so the robber picked it up, <u>Halford said.</u>	The clerk asked the man if he was sure he wanted to go through with the robbery. The clerk then told him that three security guards from a nearby motel often come into the service station.
The robber started to leave, <u>Halford said,</u> then came back, apologized, returned almost all of the money, said he needed only a small amount of cash and left with a small amount. . . .	At that point, the nervous-looking robber went behind the counter and grabbed the money out of the clerk's hands. Some of the money dropped onto the floor, so the robber picked it up.
	The robber started to leave, then came back, apologized, returned almost all of the money, said he needed only a small amount of cash and left with a small amount. . . .

Topeka (Kan.) *Capital-Journal*

Homicides   *Homicide* is the legal term for killing. *Murder* is the term for premeditated homicide. *Manslaughter* is homicide without premeditation. A person can be arrested on charges of murder, but he or she is not a murderer until convicted of the crime. Do not call someone a murderer until then. Also, don't say someone was murdered unless authorities have established that the victim was murdered—in a premeditated act of killing—or until a court determines that. Say the person was slain or killed. Some additional information to gather:

Weapon used (specific description, such as .38-caliber revolver)

Clues and motives (from police)

Specific wounds

Official cause of death (from coroner or police)

Circumstances of suspect's arrest (result of tip or investigation, perhaps at the scene)

Lots of details, from relatives, neighbors, friends, officials, eyewitnesses and your own observations at the crime scene

For many first-cycle stories about death, you may choose to use a hard-news approach. You should get the news about the death in the lead. But if there is a more compelling angle, you could put it in the second or third paragraph. Again, you must use judgment in deciding whether the story lends itself to a hard-news or a storytelling approach.

This is a hard-news approach to a homicide story:

A 32-year-old man was charged Tuesday with killing his former girlfriend when she wouldn't leave the back porch of his home.

Lester Paul Stephens of 3357 N. 2nd St. was charged with first-degree intentional homicide while armed in connection with the death of Ruby L. Hardison, 42. Hardison was shot in the head Saturday.

According to the criminal complaint, Stephens told police that he and Hardison recently had ended their relationship. But Hardison came to Stephens' home Saturday and began knocking and banging on the door and front window.

Stephens told police he got upset about the noise, and went to the back door to tell her to leave him alone. Then he went back inside and got a .32-caliber semi-automatic pistol and walked back to the porch, the complaint says.

Stephens told Hardison to get off the porch and go home, then fired one shot in the air to scare her away.

The complaint says that he then put the pistol to the right side of her head, and after they continued to argue, the gun discharged.

Stephens, who faces life plus five years in prison if convicted, was being held on $50,000 cash bail. A preliminary hearing was scheduled for April 30.

The Milwaukee Journal

Here is an excerpt from a homicide story written in a storytelling style. This story includes reporting done according to most of the guidelines: interviews with neighbors, description based on observation, information from the police report and from officials. Remember that if you can't get to the scene, you can use your cross-directory to find neighbors to contact by telephone.

Soft lead

MELBOURNE (Fla.)–June Anne Sharabati had planned every aspect of her children's lives, from their tasteful clothes to their exposure to classical music.

She missed only one detail: She forgot to plan a bullet for herself.

Backup for previous statement

The woman charged in the slaying of her two children Thursday night told deputies she would have committed suicide but she ran out of ammunition.

Basic news (five W's)

When deputies were called to her home at 2410 Washington Ave., they found Stephen Faulker, 14, dead on the floor of his bedroom. The Central Junior High School student had been shot in his stomach and head with a .38-caliber revolver.

Type of weapon

Two-year-old Aisha Sharabati was in her mother's bedroom dying from similar wounds.

Possible motive (note attribution)

Sharabati, who divorced Aisha's father in 1989, told deputies that Stephen had been a discipline problem, but she gave no explanation for her daughter's death, said Brevard County sheriff's spokeswoman Joan Heller.

Stephen's father died about nine years ago. Sharabati's former husband, Mohamad, lives in Canada and is en route to Melbourne, deputies said.

The first sign of the shootings came to light shortly before midnight Thursday with Sharabati's frantic calls to police and neighbors.

John Marrell said he was sleeping when the phone rang.

The call was from Sharabati, his 32-year-old neighbor. He had known her for 11 years and had helped her from time to time.

Narrative based on interview with neighbor

"She said, 'Didn't you hear the shots?' and I asked, 'What shots?' " Marrell said.

Dialogue

"And then she said, 'You need to get over here and get these kids. They've suffered enough.' "

Marrell said he grabbed a gun and a flashlight, thinking maybe a prowler was threatening the single parent and her children.

Instead, Sharabati met him at her screen door and told him she had "killed the kids."

Marrell said he ran home and called police, not knowing they had already been called.

When deputies arrived at the house, Sharabati met them unarmed on the doorstep and said, "Kill me. Kill me," Heller said. Sharabati was taken into custody, and deputies went in to find the bodies.

Information from officials

In the investigation report, Deputy Scott Nyquist said the suspect shot her son "in a fit of rage."

Police report

On Friday, many neighbors in the middle class neighborhood were struggling to understand how a seemingly "ideal mother" could have committed the slayings.

Reaction from neighbors

"She was the kind of mother who would attend parent-teacher

Occupation of neighbor (relevant to statement)

conferences," said Frances Edwards, a retired high school guidance counselor who lives across the street from Sharabati. "She often said her children were her life. I sure didn't see this coming."

Observations

Sharabati's light blue, one-story home—like most in the wooded, spacious subdivision—was well maintained. In the back yard, three lawn chairs were lined up alongside Aisha's child-sized chair.

Edwards said Sharabati wanted only the best for her children.

"She bought them Mozart records to listen to and dressed them beautifully," she said. . . .

"We are in deep shock—very, very deep shock," said Helen Faulker, Sharabati's mother.

Sharabati is being held in the Brevard County jail, where she is scheduled to make her first court appearance at 9 a.m. today.

Backup for lead

Reaction from relatives

Where suspect is, next step in court process

Laurin Sellers and Lynne Bumpus-Hooper, *The Orlando* (Fla.) *Sentinel*

Fires Although fire stories may not be crime stories, unless arson or other criminal behavior was involved, police reporters often are responsible for fire stories. These are the important elements:

Time fire started, time fire companies responded, time fire was brought under control

Number of fire companies responding, number of trucks at scene

Evacuations, if any, and where people were taken

Injuries and fatalities (make sure you ask if any fire officials were injured)

Cause (ask if arson is suspected—intentional setting of fire), how and where fire started

Who discovered the fire, extent of damage, insurance coverage

Description of building

Presence and condition of smoke detectors or sprinkler system (especially in a public building or apartment building, if city requires them)

Fire inspection record, fire code violations (usually for a follow-up story, especially in public buildings)

When fatalities or injuries occur in a fire, they should be mentioned in your lead, preferably a hard-news lead. If no one is injured or if heroic rescue attempts are involved, a soft lead may be appropriate. Follow-up stories and sidebars provide many opportunities for storytelling techniques.

This example follows all the guidelines for reporting fires—including questions about smoke detectors:

Summary lead: focus on death and rescue efforts

Two young brothers were killed in a South Side fire early Friday, despite the efforts of neighbors who broke through the windows to try to reach the victims.

Backup

Corey and Keither Schaeffer, 10 and 11 years old, were killed in a blaze in the three-story building at 551 E. 38th Place. Four children were in critical condition.

Mention of smoke detectors

Fire Department spokesman David McKoy said there were no smoke detectors in the home, which is part of the Chicago Housing Authority's Ida B. Wells complex.

Cause (note attribution)

Detective Charles Gardner of the Police Department's bomb and arson unit said the fire was ignited by the "careless use of smoking materials." He said it started in an overstuffed chair on the building's second floor and swept upstairs.

Interview with neighbor for dramatic quotes

"I heard the little girl screaming and looked out the back door and saw smoke," said Tamra Jackson, 24, who lives next door. "The neighborhood got together and got the kids out, but we couldn't get two of them. There were a lot of people and they got bats and stuff, breaking the windows, trying to get the babies."

Some of the neighbors who helped rescue the children were treated for minor smoke inhalation, said McKoy.

Others injured and their condition

The mother of the boys, Debra Schaeffer, and her boyfriend, Bobbie Stewart, were injured when they jumped from the burning building. They were treated and released from Michael Reese Hospital, a spokesman said.

Two more of Schaeffer's children—Wilbur, 6, and Wanake, 14—were listed in critical condition late Friday at Cook County Hospital, suffering from burns and smoke inhalation.

Two other children burned in the fire also were in critical condition Friday. Lisa Dotson, 2, was at Cook County Hospital, and Calvin Dotson, 3, was at Loyola University Medical Center.

Linnet Myers, *Chicago Tribune*

Court Stories

Writing about a crime is only the first step. The next step takes place in court. To cover courts, you need a basic understanding of the process and the terminology that is used. A complete understanding would require a three-year course called law school. But you can learn most of what you need to know about the courts as you do your reporting. Whenever you hear a term you don't understand, seek a definition. And don't use legal terms in your stories unless you explain them. In fact, avoid them as much as possible. Go by this guideline: If you don't understand something, chances are the reader won't either. It's up to you to make the story clear.

Court cases are full of drama. They are the stuff of television series and movies. Yet many times newspaper stories about them are dull. Even if you use a hard-news approach to report a conviction or testimony, you can still use storytelling techniques of dialogue, description and narrative writing for portions of the story so the reader can experience the human drama that filled the courtroom.

Some basic guidelines for writing court stories:

• Get reactions, facial expressions, and gestures of the defendant and the accusers, attorneys, relatives and other people affected by the case, especially in trial stories and verdict stories.

• Use descriptive detail and color—lively quotes, dramatic testimony and dialogue.

• Translate all jargon, and avoid legal terminology.

• State exact charges in the story.

• Give the background of the crime, no matter how many stories have been published about this case.

• Include the name of the court where the trial or hearing is being held.

• Get comments from defendants, prosecutors, defense attorneys, relatives and plaintiffs (the people who brought suit or filed charges) and jurors in all verdict stories.

• In verdict stories, include how long the jury deliberated. Also include how many jurors were on the case; not all cases have 12-member juries, the most common number. In some cases, the amount of time the jury deliberated may be a major factor. In the trial of ousted Panamanian dictator Manuel Noriega, for example, the jury deliberated for five days before reaching a verdict of guilty on eight drug and racketeering charges. In all cases, however, the length of deliberations is part of the story, as in this case:

A Floyd Superior Court jury found David Gentry guilty of murder yesterday for ending his mother's life last May 3, despite his contention that he acted out of compassion when he smothered her with a pillow.

During the weeklong trial, the defense characterized Gentry as a dutiful son who merely complied with what he believed were his ailing mother's wishes when he helped her commit suicide.

But prosecutors said Gentry, 26, acted out of more than compassion, particularly because he stood to inherit more than $108,000 from her estate.

After deliberating more than 7½ hours yesterday, the jury apparently agreed that Gentry, who sat motionless and expressionless as the verdict was read, "knowingly" killed his mother and was therefore guilty of murder.

David Cazares,
The (Louisville, Ky.) *Courier-Journal*

• Write the next step—the next court appearance or, in verdict stories, plans for an appeal if the defendant is found guilty.

Before you can write vivid court stories, you must understand some basics about the judicial system. Court procedures vary from state to state and even in counties within states. You need to find out how the system works in the area where you are working.

If you know how the system works, you can write stories about how it doesn't work. That's what reporters H.G. Bissinger, Daniel R. Biddle and Fredric N. Tulsky did in 1987. And they won the Pulitzer Prize for it. Here's how their story began:

Behind the scenes, Common Pleas Court Judge George J. Ivins privately agrees to take a case from a defense lawyer who is a longtime friend—and then sentences the lawyer's client, convicted of killing a young nurse in a car crash, to probation.

In another courtroom, on another day, Municipal Court Judge Joseph P. McCabe reduces bail for a murder defendant—without legal authority and without informing the prosecutor.

In yet another courtroom, Common Pleas Court Judge Lisa A. Richette sentences a convicted killer to prison—and then, after the victim's gratified family has left the scene, changes the sentence to probation.

In a fourth courtroom, Municipal Court Judge Arthur S. Kafrissen gets up from the bench at 10:45 a.m. and walks out for the day, leaving behind baffled witnesses, police officers and lawyers.

Day by day, this is the Philadelphia court system, where many judges and lawyers freely admit that, all too often, what is delivered is anything but justice.

H.G. Bissinger, Daniel R. Biddle and Fredric N. Tulsky, *The Philadelphia Inquirer*

You may not win a Pulitzer Prize for your court stories, but you can make them readable if you understand some basic information about the system.

Criminal and Civil Cases

Court procedures fall into two categories: criminal and civil cases. Criminal cases are violations of any laws regulating crime. If you are arrested on suspicion of drunken driving, you could be charged in a criminal case. Civil cases involve lawsuits between two parties. If your landlord says you have not paid the rent or you have damaged your apartment, he or she can bring a civil lawsuit against you. Divorces, malpractice, libel, contract disputes and other actions not involving criminal law are civil cases.

For example, the case mentioned in Chapter 6 about protection of anonymous sources was a civil suit. Dan Cohen, the publicist who sued the *Star Tribune* (Minneapolis) and the *St. Paul Pioneer Press* for breaking a promise to withhold his name from the story, filed a civil suit charging the newspapers with fraudulent misrepresentation and breach of contract. After an eight-year battle that went to the U.S. Supreme Court, he ultimately received $200,000 in damages for breach of contract.

Federal Courts and State Courts

The court system functions on two levels: a federal level and a state level. Federal courts have jurisdiction over cases involving matters related to the U.S. Constitution (such as civil rights), federal tax and antitrust matters, and any other federal laws. Federal courts also hear cases between people from different states. The federal court system:

U.S. District Court: This is the lowest level of the federal judicial system, where most cases involving federal issues are first heard.

U.S. Court of Appeals: There are 12 of these courts for geographical areas, plus the U.S. Court of Appeals for the D.C. (District of Columbia) Circuit. It is the intermediary court, where cases from the federal district courts are appealed.

U.S. Supreme Court: This is the highest court in the nation. Cases may be appealed to this court, but the justices do not have to rule on all the cases.

Most states also have three levels of courts: a trial court, an appeals court and a state supreme court for appeals of the last resort on the state level. Cases from the state's highest court may be appealed to the U.S. Supreme Court if there is a federal angle, such as a constitutional matter—a First Amendment issue, for example—or a civil rights violation.

The names of the state courts can be confusing. In one state a superior court may be a trial-level court, whereas in others it may be an appellate court.

There also are municipal courts, where violations of local laws, such as traffic laws, or city ordinances may be heard.

In addition, within the state system there are juvenile courts (for cases involving people under age 18) and probate courts, where disputes involving wills and estates are heard.

When you write your court story, find out the proper name of the court—whether it is called a district court, a circuit court or a common pleas court—and write that in the story.

Criminal Court Process

Crimes are classified as misdemeanors or felonies. *Misdemeanors* are considered minor offenses that carry a potential penalty of up to a year in jail and/or a fine. *Felonies* are more serious crimes punishable by more than a year in jail.

Criminal procedures differ from state to state, but there are some general processes in the court system that you should understand:

1 Arrest: The person is stopped by police for suspicion of having committed a crime and is taken to the police station for questioning or further action. Police are required to read a person his or her rights—to remain silent (if the person does not want to discuss the issue before a court procedure) and to retain an attorney. These are called the Miranda warnings, based on a court case by that name. A person also can be arrested if someone has filed a complaint with police and the police find enough probable cause to believe the complaint is true. At this point the police can notify the person of the charge that will be filed—basically, why he or she is being arrested—but the charge is not official yet. If someone is wanted for a crime, police also can seek a warrant for someone's arrest, a legal document provided by a judge that gives police the right to arrest a suspect.

2 Booking: The suspect is taken to a booking desk in the police station, where he or she is fingerprinted and photographed. Information about the person—age, address, physical description and so on—is then recorded in a police book, the log. At this point the person may be held in jail or released until formal charges are issued.

3 Charges: The arresting police officer confers with a member of the district attorney's office, who decides if a charge should be filed with the court against the suspect. It is important for the reporter to find out if the person has been charged officially with the crime, because many newspapers don't publish news of an arrest until charges have been filed. Many states have standard bail fees for common or misdemeanor crimes, and the person may be able to post a bail bond at this time and be released without a hearing.

4 Arraignment: Usually within 24 to 48 hours, a suspect will have a first hearing. At this point the charges against him or her are read in court. In some places, at this time the suspect can enter a plea of guilty, not guilty or no contest—not admitting guilt but not contesting the charge either. If the suspect pleads guilty, the sentence can be issued at this point, and the matter can be settled—or the judge may delay sentencing for another hearing. Misdemeanor cases often are settled at this level. In other jurisdictions, the arraignment may be held just to formally read the charges; the plea comes at a later hearing. If the person pleads not guilty, he or she has the right to a trial, and the judge can set bail at this time. At the hearing, the judge will determine bail. If the person fails to show up for the next court appearance, the total amount of bail is forfeited to the court. When the person has no previous record, the judge may release the suspect on his own recognizance (recognition) without any bail.

5 Preliminary hearing: In felony cases only, a judge weighs the facts presented by a prosecutor from the district attorney's office and by the defense attorney at a special hearing. Then the judge decides whether there is enough evidence (probable cause) to hold the person for trial. If not, the person is released, and charges are dropped.

6 Grand jury: In certain cases, particularly those involving political crimes or major drug cases and those in federal courts, a grand jury will be convened to investigate the circumstances of the case and determine if there is enough evidence—enough probable cause—that the crime has been committed. Like a trial jury, the grand jury is a group of citizens, from 12 to 33 members, chosen to serve on the case. They listen to testimony from prosecutors and witnesses. Unlike the trial jury, however, the grand jury does not rule on guilt or innocence. It only recommends to a judge whether there is enough evidence to take the case to a trial. If there is, the grand jury hands up (because the judge sits on a higher bench than the jury) an indictment, also called a "true bill." The defendant then enters a plea at another hearing. If the case goes to trial, another jury will be impaneled to serve at the trial.

Grand jury proceedings are secret; the jurors are sworn not to reveal deliberations to the media or anyone else (in most states). However, many reporters with good sources can find out the essence of what happened. After deliberations, if and when the grand jury issues a report, that is usually public record.

7 Pre-trial hearings and motions: Before the trial, attorneys usually file a number of motions (formal requests to the court) seeking to have the case dropped, to have the trial moved to another location (called a change of venue) or to have evidence suppressed. The judge has to rule on each motion.

8 Trial: If the case goes to trial, a jury is selected and the case is heard. In some cases, particularly civil cases, a judge may decide the case without a jury.

For a not-guilty verdict, the *Associated Press Stylebook* says use the word *innocent* in the story. That rule is a holdover from the days of lead type to guard against the word *not* inadvertently being dropped. Many newspapers no longer adhere to this style rule. Unanimous verdicts are required in criminal trials in most states. If the jury can't agree on a guilty or not-guilty verdict, it is called a "hung jury," and a mistrial is declared. The defendant is then technically not guilty.

If the defendant is judged guilty, you may then call him or her a murderer, rapist, or whatever accusatory term fits the crime involved. But do not use accusatory terms in stories before a guilty verdict.

9 Sentencing: After the trial, if the person is found guilty, there will be another hearing. The judge will then decide on a sentence. Sometimes the judge issues the sentence immediately after the verdict.

At any time during the criminal court process, the suspect may change his or her not-guilty plea to a guilty one and eliminate the need for a trial. To avoid a trial, lawyers often will engage in a process called plea bargaining. The defense lawyer and prosecutor will agree on a lesser charge in exchange for a guilty or no-contest plea. The defendant then forgoes a trial and gets sentenced to a lesser penalty.

10 Appeal: A person convicted of a crime can appeal the decision to a higher court. It is logical to ask in all court trials with convictions whether an appeal is planned. The information should be included in the story.

Exhibit 23-1 outlines court procedures for both criminal and civil cases.

Civil Court Process

A civil case starts with a suit filed by a person or a company. Anyone can file a lawsuit for a fee. After filing, the lawyers for both sides file various motions with the court. If the case is not settled between the two parties at a pretrial hearing, a court hearing date is set. Civil cases may be argued in front of a judge or before a jury if one is requested. Civil suits can drag through the courts for many years. If the case goes to trial, the process is the same as for criminal trials.

Most civil cases never even get to the trial stage. At any point after motions have been filed, the judge may dismiss the case or may grant a request for a summary judgment, a ruling on the case when both parties agree to forgo a trial.

Terms Used in Court Reporting

You should become familiar with these terms so you can better understand and explain court proceedings:

Acquittal: Finding by a court or jury that a person accused of a crime is not guilty.

Adjudicate: To make a final determination or judgment by the court.

Affidavit: Sworn statement of facts.

Appeal: Plea to ask a higher court to review a judgment, verdict or order of a lower court.

Appellant: Person who files an appeal.

Arraignment: Court hearing in which a defendant in a criminal case is formally charged with the crime and given a chance to enter a plea of guilty, not guilty or no contest (nolo contendere). At this time bail usually is set.

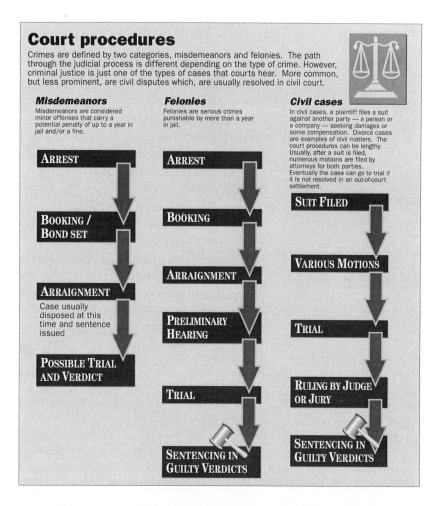

Court procedures

Crimes are defined by two categories, misdemeanors and felonies. The path through the judicial process is different depending on the type of crime. However, criminal justice is just one of the types of cases that courts hear. More common, but less prominent, are civil disputes which, are usually resolved in civil court.

Misdemeanors

Misdemeanors are considered minor offenses that carry a potential penalty of up to a year in jail and/or a fine.

ARREST

BOOKING / BOND SET

ARRAIGNMENT

Case usually disposed at this time and sentence issued

POSSIBLE TRIAL AND VERDICT

Felonies

Felonies are serious crimes punishable by more than a year in jail.

ARREST

BOOKING

ARRAIGNMENT

PRELIMINARY HEARING

TRIAL

SENTENCING IN GUILTY VERDICTS

Civil cases

In civil cases, a plaintiff files a suit against another party — a person or a company — seeking damages or some compensation. Divorce cases are examples of civil matters. The court procedures can be lengthy. Usually, after a suit is filed, numerous motions are filed by attorneys for both parties. Eventually the case can go to trial if it is not resolved in an out-of-court settlement.

SUIT FILED

VARIOUS MOTIONS

TRIAL

RULING BY JUDGE OR JURY

SENTENCING IN GUILTY VERDICTS

Exhibit 23-1

Process of criminal and civil cases

Courtesy of Bill Skeet

Bail: Amount of money set by the court that the defendant must guarantee to pay if he or she does not show up for a court trial. If the defendant can't raise the money through a bail bondsman or personal sources, he or she stays in jail.

Bond: Written promise to pay bail money on the conditions stated. The bond for bail is usually 10 percent of the total amount of bail set. The term is often used interchangeably with *bail.* Very often a person will borrow money from a bondsman. Then if the person flees, the bondsman loses the money.

Brief: Legal document filed with the court by a lawyer, stating the facts of the case and arguments citing how laws apply to this case.

Change of venue: Procedure to seek a change of location of the trial, usually when defense attorneys contend the defendant can't get a fair trial in the current location because of too much pre-trial publicity.

Charge: Official allegation of criminal wrongdoing.

Civil suit: Lawsuit to determine rights, duties, claims for damages, ownership or other settlements in non-criminal matters.

Complaint: Formal affidavit in which one person accuses another of violating the law.

Condemnation: Civil action to acquire ownership of property for public use. When a municipality wants to build a road or sidewalk, the government will condemn the property to gain right of way.

Contempt: Action that disregards the order or authority of the court. A lawyer who screams obscenities at the judge probably will be found in contempt of court.

Defendant: In a civil case, the person being sued. In a criminal case, the person charged with breaking the law.

Deposition: Written statement of testimony from a witness under oath.

Discovery: Pre-trial examination of a person (including depositions), documents or other items to find evidence that may be used in the trial.

Dismissal: Order to drop the case.

Docket: List of cases pending before the court. A trial docket is a list of cases pending trial.

Extradition: Procedure to move a person accused of a crime from the state where he or she is residing to the state where the crime occurred and where the trial will be conducted.

Felony: Major crime punishable by a sentence of a year or more. Crimes such as robbery, homicide and kidnapping are felonies; lesser crimes such as shoplifting are misdemeanors. Legally, a felony is defined as a crime punishable by death or imprisonment in a state prison.

Grand jury: Group of citizens selected by the court to investigate whether there is enough evidence or probable cause that a crime occurred and that the person should be charged, or indicted.

Hung jury: Jury that cannot reach a unanimous verdict, a requirement in most criminal trials.

Indictment: Recommendation by the grand jury that there is enough probable cause to charge a person or group of people with the crime under investigation. The grand jury hands up an indictment to the judge (because the judge sits on a platform higher than the jury); the judge hands down rulings. It's preferable to use the word *issued.*

Injunction: Order by the court instructing a person, group or company to stop the action that was occurring, such as picketing. For example, an injunction can order a group to stop marching outside an abortion clinic.

Innocent: Term used for a not-guilty verdict, according to Associated Press style. It is used as a safeguard so the word *not* will not be dropped accidentally from a story. But this usage is old-fashioned. *Not guilty* is the preferable wording.

Misdemeanor: Crime less serious than a felony; crime punishable by less than one year in jail and/or fines.

Mistrial: Trial that is set aside or declared invalid because of some mistake in proceedings or, in a criminal trial, because the jury cannot reach a unanimous verdict.

Motion: Request for the court to make a ruling or finding.

Nolo contendere: Latin for "I will not contest it" (no contest). This plea has the same effect as a guilty plea, but it is not an admission of guilt. It means the person will not fight the charge. If you agree to pay a fine for a traffic ticket but do not agree that you were speeding, you are pleading no contest. This type of plea is used as a form of bargaining to get the defendant a reduced charge in exchange for his or her agreement not to protest and to eliminate the need for a trial. Use the English *no contest* in a story, and explain briefly that it is not an admission of guilt.

Plaintiff: Person who sues in a civil case. The defendant is the one being sued.

Plea: Defendant's response to a charge, admitting that he or she is guilty, not guilty or not willing to contest the charge.

Plea bargain: Agreement between the prosecutor and the defendant (or defense attorney) to accept a lesser charge and a lesser sentence in return for a guilty or no-contest plea. Plea bargaining is used extensively as a way to eliminate court trials. Once the defendant pleads guilty or no contest, there is no need for a trial. However, a plea bargain must be approved by the court.

Probable cause: Determination that there is enough evidence to prosecute a criminal case. Police officials also need probable cause—enough reason to believe a crime is being committed—when they seek a search warrant or any other warrant for a person's arrest.

Probation: Condition in which the person is released from serving a jail sentence if he or she meets certain terms, such as serving in the community, entering drug treatment or accepting whatever restrictions the judge decides.

Recognizance: Literally, "recognition." A person may be released from jail based on his or her own recognizance—meaning the recognition of a previously good reputation. This ruling is essentially the judge's way of saying that, because of the person's reputation, he or she is not considered a high risk for skipping the next court hearing or trial.

Subpoena: Court order commanding a person to appear in court or to release documents to the court.

Summary judgment: Procedure in a civil suit asking the court to give final judgment on the grounds that there are no further questions and no need for a trial.

Summons: Document notifying a defendant that a lawsuit or complaint has been filed against him or her.

Suspended sentence: Court order stating that the punishment of the defendant will be suspended if certain conditions are met. A person who receives probation gets a suspended sentence.

Temporary injunction: Court order to stop an action, such as a protest, for a specific amount of time until a court hearing and ruling whether the action should be enjoined, or stopped permanently.

Tort: Civil case involving damages, pain, suffering or other allegations of wrongdoing.

True bill: Indictment issued by a grand jury.

Verdict: Decision by a jury about guilt or innocence.

Warrant: Court order directing law enforcement officials to arrest a person. A search warrant gives officials authority to search a premise.

Court Story Examples

A court case is a continuing saga. From the time a person is arrested until the case is resolved, whether in a trial or a settlement, you will write many stories about it. But never assume the reader is familiar with the case, no matter how sensational it may be. Always include the background.

Whether you take a soft or hard approach, make sure your nut graph explains who is being accused of what, and place it high in the story.

If information is part of a court record, you may use it as fact—but it still may not be true. It's up to a judge or jury to decide whether the claims in court documents and trials are true. So you need to attribute your information, although not necessarily in the lead.

Unlike other stories, many court stories do not appear balanced. On any given day, one side in the case may present its arguments, so you won't always have a story that seems fair to both parties. The testimony will be biased; you should not be.

Some reminders:

Explain charges and background.

Describe defendants and witnesses.

Specify the court where the proceeding takes place.

Tell a good story.

When the verdict is issued in a major trial that has garnered interest locally or nationally, a hard-news story is appropriate. A soft lead also may work, but make sure you put the verdict very high in the story. The following story is an example of a basic hard-news approach to a case that gained national attention in 1991. In this case, the judge sentenced the defendant immediately instead of at a separate hearing.

Summary lead: verdict, delayed identification	EXETER, N.H.—A high school instructor was convicted yesterday and sentenced to life in prison without parole after a sensational trial on charges that she manipulated her student-lover into murdering her husband.	"You know how I feel about that," Linda Wojas said when asked if she thought her daughter had gotten a fair trial. Wojas wore a yellow ribbon every day, symbolizing her belief that her daughter was a hostage of the judicial system.	*Descriptive detail*
Defendant's reaction, charges, name of court	Pamela Smart, 23, stood motionless as the Superior Court jury foreman pronounced her guilty of murder-conspiracy and being an accomplice to murder.	"I feel terribly bad for the Wojas family," Judith Smart said. "I can imagine how I would feel and I feel very, very bad for them."	*Reaction quotes*
Relative's reactions	The victim's mother, Judith Smart, cried out as each verdict was read, and said afterward, "She got what she deserved."	The jury, which heard three weeks of testimony, deliberated 12 hours over three days before returning its verdict. Smart also was convicted of witness-tampering for encouraging her student-intern to lie to police.	*Jury information: time deliberated and length of trial* *Other charges*
	Judith and William Smart then left the court for the cemetery where their son is buried.		
	"We're going to tell Gregg," William Smart said. "We're going to tell him that, by God, she did do it."	Rockingham County Superior Court Judge Douglas Gray immediately announced the mandatory life sentence for the accomplice-to-murder charge. An appeal is expected.	*Identification of court and judge, sentencing, expected appeal*
Brief background	Gregg Smart, a 24-year-old insurance agent, was murdered May 1 last year, six days before his first wedding anniversary.	Smart was the school district media coordinator when she met William Flynn, now 17, as one of his instructors in a self-awareness program at Winnacunnet High	*Background and highlights of trial*
More reactions	Pamela Smart's parents, John and Linda Wojas, were stone-faced as they left the courthouse.		

School in Hampton in late 1989.

Prosecutors said the former high school cheerleader and college honor student tantalized and seduced Flynn, then 15 and a virgin, and then threatened to end their affair unless he murdered her husband. Smart testified that she broke off the affair just before the murder.

Prosecutors said Smart feared losing everything in a divorce, including her dog and furniture.

Fate of others involved (note plea bargain)

The defense called Flynn and two confessed accomplices "thrill-killers" who shot Smart on their own, then framed his widow to avoid life prison terms. In plea bargains, they face minimum sentences ranging from 18 to 28 years.

Color details

The Boston Herald, which dubbed Smart the "Ice Princess," invited readers to call in their verdicts on a 900 number. They voted guilty, 543 to 101.

More highlights of trial

The most damaging evidence against Smart were four secretly recorded conversations she had with Cecelia Pierce, 16, her student-intern and confidante. The profanity-laden tapes, made after the murder, show that Smart urged Pierce to lie to police, that she feared being jailed herself, and that she had known her husband would be murdered.

Key testimony

Flynn, sobbing as he testified on March 12, admitted pulling the trigger on a .38-cal. pistol he held to Gregg Smart's head.

He and Patrick Randall, 17, testified that they entered the Smarts' condominium through a basement door that Pamela Smart had left unlocked for them and waited for Smart to arrive home. They also said they forced him to his knees as he begged for mercy.

Shortly before the verdict, John Wojas said people were misjudging his daughter.

Reaction quote kicker

"She's not a cold little woman like they're trying to describe her," he said. "She doesn't show a lot of outright emotion. She never has."

The Associated Press

Here is an excerpt from a story about testimony in a continuing trial. The writer weaves feature techniques of dialogue with a hard-news approach to convey the drama of this trial. Note that she includes descriptions of the courtroom and the defendant.

NEW LONDON, Conn.—Richard Crafts took the witness stand Thursday in the most dramatic moment of his 12-week murder trial, and calmly denied killing his wife and using a chain saw and wood chipper to dispose of her body.

"And do you know whether Helle Crafts is alive or not?" defense attorney J. Daniel Sagarin asked his client.

"I certainly hope she is," Richard Crafts replied. "I believe she is."

Crafts testified in a courtroom so crowded with more than 65 spectators and reporters that a sheriff stood at the door turning away late-comers. Despite the crowd, the courtroom was silent except for the exchanges between Sagarin and Crafts.

The 50-year-old airline pilot—who prosecutors say killed his wife by unknown means, cut up her body with a chain saw, and disposed of it with a wood chipper—testified with a voice and manner that was so calm it bordered at times on nonchalance. . . .

Helle Crafts was last seen Nov. 18, 1986. Richard Crafts testified she left their Newtown home in the early morning of Nov. 19, 1986, and her last words were, "I'm leaving now."

"She was all right the last time I saw her, the morning of Nov. 19, 1986," Crafts testified.

Lynne Tuohy, *The Hartford* (Conn.) *Courant*

Stories about upcoming court trials lend themselves to story-telling techniques. If the story is important enough to "advance" the trial, it probably has a good story behind it. A narrative writing technique was used to advance this trial in a story that uses almost no direct attribution, except for quotes. The story is based on court records and previous admissions by the defendant. If the defendant had not admitted the crime, this story would be too accusatory.

MIAMI—He was a distraught man that day, a man who sang lullabies and wept. With one hand, he held a gun. With the other, he stroked the smooth face of his daughter, a 3-year-old existing in limbo between life and death.

An hour before, he had given her what he thought was a fatal dose of Valium. But here she was still breathing, her tiny chest rising and falling rhythmically, if ever so slightly.

She was in a crib at Miami Children's Hospital, lying on her back. She had been there for eight months, since the day she nearly suffocated. He leaned over the crib railing and looked at her eyes. They were open. They stared ahead, mirrored no emotions, saw nothing. It was the same for her other senses. The damage to her brain was total and irreversible, and because of it, she couldn't hear his weeping, and she couldn't feel his last touch goodbye before he aimed the gun at her heart.

He shot her twice. He dropped the gun. He prayed that her suffering was over. He fell into a nurse's arms, cried and said he wanted to die. He said, "Maybe I should get the electric chair to make things even. I killed my daughter. I shot her twice. But I'm glad she's gone to heaven."

On Tuesday morning in a Miami courtroom, almost five months after the death of his daughter, Joy, Charles Griffith is scheduled to go on trial for murder. The defense, says Griffith's attorney, Mark Krasnow, will be mercy. "It was an act of love," Krasnow says, "not an act of malice. . . ."

David Finkel, *St. Petersburg* (Fla.) *Times*

The next example is a story about a lawsuit in a civil case that has not yet come to trial. When you cover a story about a suit that has been filed, always try to contact the people involved or at least their lawyers, whose names are listed in the suit. If you wade through all the legal writing, lawsuits can be very entertaining.

What has no arms or legs and wiggles in the night?

According to Gladys Diehl and her husband, John Brehm, it's their Sealy Posturpedic mattress.

In a lawsuit filed yesterday in Bucks County Court, Diehl and Brehm contend that they endured many nights of fitful slumber because an uninvited guest shared their bed—a 26-inch snake living inside the mattress.

"There was a lot of wiggling going on," said Stephen A. Shelly, the attorney representing the Quakertown couple.

Diehl and Brehm are seeking more than $20,000 from Sealy

Mattress Co., the manufacturer, and Hess's department store, which sold the mattress. They say the incident traumatized them and caused sleep disorders.

According to the suit, the couple bought a mattress on May 13, 1988, from Hess's in Richland Township, Bucks County. Soon after, they began to notice an unfamiliar movement in their bed, which they "suspected could be a living creature."

In July, they exchanged the mattress at Hess's for another Sealy, hoping for a better night's sleep. They didn't get one. The replacement mattress also slithered and shimmied, according to the couple.

After four months of suspicious bumps in the night, Diehl and Brehm took the second mattress to Laboratory Testing Inc. in Dublin for examination. Inside, workers found a dead 26-inch ribbon snake. The species is not poisonous.

The suit contends that both the manufacturer and the department store breached their warranties. . . . No date has been set for a hearing on the case.

John P. Martin, *The Philadelphia Inquirer*

Most court stories are serious, but some have a humorous angle. Here is a light-hearted story in a conversational style that tries to involve the reader. It is an example of how a plea bargain works—or in this case, how it didn't work out very well. This story is written in pyramid form with the clincher at the end; unfortunately, the headline gives the twist away.

Man gambles on plea, loses

He admits guilt, then is acquitted

You're the defendant. You make the call:

You're Marvin E. Johnson, 40, convicted three times of drug possession. You're facing a minimum 15 years in prison without parole if convicted of being a felon in possession of a handgun.

On Wednesday, the jury at your federal trial in Kansas City deliberates three hours without reaching a verdict. On Thursday, the jury deliberates three more hours and announces it is hopelessly deadlocked. A hung jury and a new trial loom on the horizon.

The prosecutor, Assistant U.S. Attorney Rob Larsen, offers a deal. If you plead guilty, he'll reduce the government's sentencing request to a range of 15 to 22 months.

While you ponder that deal, the jury buzzes. It has a verdict.

Do you:

A) Sign the plea agreement and serve at least 15 months in prison? Or

B) Roll the dice with the jury's verdict? If it's guilty, you get at least 15 years; if it's not guilty, you walk away.

On Thursday afternoon, Marvin E. Johnson signed the plea agreement.

Five minutes later, the jury found him not guilty.

"I'm sure glad I struck that plea agreement," Larsen said.

"I can't win for losing," said Johnson's defense lawyer, John P. O'Connor.

Tom Jackman, *The Kansas City Star*

Activities

1 **Accident story:** Read an accident story from your newspaper, and see if it is clear enough for you to draw a diagram of what happened.

2 Visit your campus or local police department, and write a story based on a police record.

3 **Crime story:** Although the police report in Exhibit 23-2 is labeled "Standard Offense Report," it is not. Each state has its own form; however, this one is similar to many. Most of the report is self-explanatory, with some exceptions. For instance, most information is in codes so the state bureau of investigation may insert the information into a computer data base. *ORI* stands for the organization where the report originated, followed by the number for that police department. The case number is important for

Exhibit 23-2

Police report

Standard Offense Report Page 1

| 101. NAME OF AGENCY | 102. ORI | 103. CASE NO. |
| Ourtown, Allstate Police Dept. | 0230100 | 92-123456 |

| 104. 1. DISPATCHED 2. CITIZEN 3. ON VIEW | 105. DATE REPORTED 05-29-92 | 106. TIME REPORTED 22:56 | 107. TIME ARRIVED 23:01 | 108. TIME CLEARED 23:59 | 109. DATE OF OFFENSE 05-26-92/05-29-92 | 110. TIME OCCURRED 0:700/22:30 |

111. OFFENSE—LIST MOST SERIOUS FIRST	112. STATUTES	113. LOCAL CODE	114. TYPE OF PREMISE:
A. Burglary	A. 21-3701		1. STREET 9. RESTAURANT
B. Theft	B. 21-3715		2. SINGLE RESIDENCE 10. STORAGE/WAREHOUSE
C.	C.		3. MULTIPLE RESIDENCE 11. TAVERN/BAR/LIQUOR
			4. COMMERCIAL 12. VEHICLE
			5. GAS STATION 13. BANK
			6. CONVENIENCE STORE 14. OPEN AREA (PARK, FIELD, ETC.)
			7. PHARMACY/DOCTOR OFFICE 15. OTHER
			8. PUBLIC/COMMUNITY BLDG.

| 115. LOCATION OF OFFENSE | 116. REPORT AREA |
| 2345 Felony Lane | 124 |

TYPE (INSERT NUMBER): 2

CODES: V = VICTIM B = BUSINESS W = WITNESS P = PARENT DC = DISCOVERED CRIME RP = REPORTING PARTY

| 117. NAME—LAST, FIRST, MIDDLE | 118. CODE | 119. RESIDENCE ADDRESS—PHONE |
| Doe, John | DC/RP | 2337 Felony Lane, Ourtown, Allstate |

| 120. RACE W | 121. SEX M | 122. AGE 25 | 123. DATE OF BIRTH 2/10/67 | 124. HT. 5 11 | 125. WT. 170 | 126. HAIR Bro | 127. EYES Bro | 128. OCCUPATION | 129. BUSINESS ADDRESS—PHONE |

| 130. NAME—LAST, FIRST, MIDDLE | 131. CODE | 132. RESIDENCE ADDRESS—PHONE |
| Smith, Jon J. | V | 2345 Felony Lane, Ourtown, Allstate 555-4321 |

| 133. RACE W | 134. SEX M | 135. AGE 30 | 136. DATE OF BIRTH 3/10/62 | 137. HT. 6 00 | 138. WT. 195 | 139. HAIR Blo | 140. EYES Blu | 141. OCCUPATION | 142. BUSINESS ADDRESS—PHONE |

| 143. NAME—LAST, FIRST, MIDDLE | 144. CODE | 145. RESIDENCE ADDRESS—PHONE |
| | | |

| 146. RACE | 147. SEX | 148. AGE | 149. DATE OF BIRTH | 150. HT. | 151. WT. | 152. HAIR | 153. EYES | 154. OCCUPATION | 155. BUSINESS ADDRESS—PHONE |

| 156. DID VICTIM(S) RECEIVE MEDICAL ATTENTION? | 157. ADDITIONAL INFORMATION (LOCAL USE ONLY) |
| Vic. #1 _____ Vic. #2 n/a Vic. #3 _____ | |

158. DESCRIBE BRIEFLY HOW OFFENSE WAS COMMITTED.

Person(s) unknown forced entry to the residence and removed items.

PROPERTY STATUS: S-STOLEN RA-RECOVERED FOR YOUR AGENCY RO-RECOVERED FOR OTHER AGENCY F-FOUND

159. STATUS	160. QTY.	161. DESCRIPTION OF PROPERTY	162. CODE	163. MODEL-SERIAL-OWNER APPLIED NO.	164. VALUE	165. NCIC
S	1	Zenith VCR	0618	SNL-528VF3	400.00	
S	1	Smith & Wesson .38 cal. rev.	0702	E 92356	150.00	
S	1	Social Security check	0121	unk.	----	
S	1	Cockatoo (bird)	1002	N/A	1,500.00	

| 166. PROPERTY DAMAGE | 167. TOTAL VALUE PROPERTY STOLEN |
| 100 | 2050.00 |

| 168. REPORTING OFFICER Off. John Law | 169. DATE 05-29-92 | 170. TYPED BY j1 | 171. DATE 05-29-92 | 172. REVIEWED BY | 173. DATE | 174. COPIES TO: __ DET. __ JUVENILE __ KBI __ OTHER __ SO/PD __ CO. ATTY. __ KHP |

1-85 Page ____ of ____ KBI/BR 1

reporters; if you want to follow the case through the court system, you need this number, which stays the same for all actions in the case. Time is computed as military time, from one to 24 hours. Where the stolen property is listed, codes are used to signify the type of property. A complete code sheet is usually on the back of the police report.

You acquired the police report earlier today, along with an attached narrative:

> At 22:56 the office was contacted by Mr. James Doe, next-door neighbor of the victim. He was watching Smith's house while Smith was away. Doe checked the door to Smith's residence at 0:700 before he went to work. When he returned home at 22:30, he again checked Smith's residence and noticed that someone had pried the deadbolt lock on the front door. I was dispatched to the residence. I searched premises but did not find any suspects. When Mr. Smith returned home, he advised that items missing were VCR, Smith-Wesson gun and cockatoo, who answers to the name of Homer. Owner described bird as white and 10 years old. He said the bird could say his name and had limited vocabulary of "damn," "rotten" and a few curse words.

You called the police to ask more about the theft of the bird, since that was unusual. The police told you that the bird was valuable and that was probably the reason it was stolen. They told you there is no rash of bird burglars, although there had been some thefts of stolen birds several months ago. But this bird theft does not appear to be related to those, because other items were taken, the police said. The police are still investigating.

Now write the story.

4 Court story analysis: Find a court story that you think is well written and one you think is poorly written. Clip them and attach them to your critique. Write a brief (half-page to one-page) analysis about the following aspects of each story:

Lead: Is it a soft or hard-news lead? What grabs you about the lead and makes you want to read further? Why does the technique in the lead work for you?

Organization: Is the story easy to follow? How is it organized—chronologically, by themes, inverted pyramid, a combination? What techniques has the writer used that make the story readable?

Court terminology: How has the writer handled the information about the charges?

Background: How and where has the writer included background?

Quotes and color: How and where were there good quotes? What were they about—reaction to charges, a verdict or testimony?

Ending: Is there an abrupt ending, a quote kicker or other type of ending? Has the writer taken care to make the ending good?

5 Visit your local courthouse. If you have a specific case in mind, ask for the court record. If not, check on any recent court case. Write a story based on the record, stressing the latest court action.

6 Court hearing: If possible, go to your local courthouse and cover a hearing or a case in municipal court. You might cover small-claims court, in which people represent themselves in civil cases where they are seeking damages. If you can attend an interesting trial in your community, write a story based on that day's testimony.

COACHING

Gather as much detail as possible for graphics and for your story.

Seek human interest stories and anecdotes.

Get information to reconstruct a chronology of events.

Use descriptive and narrative techniques for sidebars.

Double-check all information; initial reports and statistics will change quickly.

Use role-playing reporting techniques: If you were a relative of someone in a tragedy, what would you want and need to know?

Envision highlights boxes and empowerment boxes when you are reporting, so you get crucial information.

Disasters and Tragedy 24

It was close to 9 p.m. on Sunday, Aug. 16, 1987. The telephone rang on the city desk. A caller said a plane had crashed at Detroit Metropolitan Airport. Reporter Jim Tittsworth, who had received the call, dialed the sheriff's department. "It's a passenger plane," he whispered, covering the mouthpiece. "A big one." Fifteen minutes earlier, Northwest Flight 255 had crashed to the ground, killing 156 people.

Only two reporters were in the office at the time. How does a newsroom mobilize and cover such a major disaster? Nolan Finley, day city editor of *The Detroit News,* explained how in an account he wrote for the newspaper, from which these excerpts are taken:

Death is always and under all circumstances a tragedy, for if it is not, then it means that life itself has become one.

Theodore Roosevelt

Dividing the city-desk-staff home directory, we began dialing numbers. On the other side of the room, the copy and photo desks were doing the same. Those who lived closest to the airport were called first and sent to the scene. Others were told to come to the office to make phone calls and handle rewrite.

Deadline for the first edition was in 90 minutes. At that point we knew we had a plane crash, but not much more. The wire services had moved only a brief piece, and television reports were sketchy. Our reporters and photographers en route to the airport and hospitals had not yet called in. Telephone calls being placed by reporters inside the office had turned up little to put in the newspaper. We had no guarantee that photographs would arrive in time for that first edition.

Reporter Ric Bohy, rewrite man for the main story, sat in the middle of the room, two phones to his ears, typing notes into a computer terminal. Reporters at other desks took notes from others at the scene, tearing off printouts and rushing them to Bohy.

Bohy divided the notes with Scott Martelle, who was writing a color piece based on eyewitness accounts. Those two stories anchored the main package. Both arrived just on deadline and would be updated a half-dozen times before the night ended.

Picture Editors Joan Rosen and Greg Anderson coordinated assignments and film deliveries from several locations. In the graphics department, Assistant Managing Editor George Rorick and artist Jeff Goertzen worked intently on Macintosh computers, drawing a base graphic from information supplied by reporters and photographers. They built a graphic that included a detailed map of the airport and crash site and a diagram of the plane that crashed, the MD-80. . . .

The news and copy desk laid out, copy edited and assembled the pieces of the package and pushed them to the printing plant in minutes. Each edition would require those copy editors to rework the pages—and assemble new ones.

During the hour before the second-edition deadline, we would push the paper up another page, add stories from Fred Girard about a little girl, the lone survivor, being pulled from the wreckage and how emergency crews responded to the crash; photographs and a story explaining the history of the MD-80 aircraft. In addition, all the original stories would be rewritten and expanded.

The two hours between the second and third editions allowed us time to plan. . . . We had sent reporters and photographers to the crash site, airport terminals and—still not sure about the number of survivors—to all area hospitals. Now we had to decide where else to go, what else to do.

Reporters were sent to Saginaw, where the flight originated, and to Phoenix—the final destination of Flight 255. Meanwhile, photo editors had arranged to receive pictures from Phoenix, where people were gathering at the airport to meet relatives and friends they'd expected to arrive on Flight 255.

The upcoming editions added a more detailed story about the crash's lone survivor, Cecelia Cichan; a piece on how the crash would be investigated; vignettes from witnesses and rescue workers; a report on how the victims would be identified; and other stories and photographs.

From phone calls and wire reports, we came up with a partial list of the dead and included a story profiling some of them in later editions.

By Monday afternoon, the reporting emphasis had shifted to explaining the cause of the crash, and identifying the dead. Reporters and editors were divided into teams: One team to pursue the cause of the crash, one to identify and write about the dead.

Despite our determination to be on top of the investigation, the human side of the crash was neither forgotten nor downplayed. The horror of 156 people dying in the flaming wreckage of an airplane, and the loved ones they left behind, became the focus of our coverage of the human element in the story.

On Friday, 156 profiles were repackaged in the second special section of the week. It was the first time a complete list of the dead was published.

All elements of coverage later came together in a comprehensive Sunday package. . . . The human toll of the tragedy, how insurance companies would put a price tag on the human loss, . . . the impact of deregulation on the airline industry, . . . the factors that may have caused the crash.

Nolan Finley, *The Detroit News*

Disasters take their toll on the people who experience them and on the people who cover them. But they are some of the most memorable stories a reporter may write.

When you cover a disaster, inevitably you will cover tragedy. If you are at the scene of a disaster, you might prefer to pitch in and help. But consider that your role in getting the news is crucial. People are anxious to know what happened to their loved ones and to people they might know. You are performing a service— a difficult but necessary one.

To cover disasters, you need all the reporting and writing skills you have studied—hard news, soft news, narrative reconstruction, descriptive details, and most of all, human interest stories. You also need to gather information for graphics. In this chapter, you will learn how to ask those difficult questions involving grief. You will also read examples of how reporters covered such stories.

If the story is about a major disaster, chances are you will be part of a team reporting and writing several stories. They include the hard-news accounts of what happened as well as many human interest sidebars about the effects on people in the area. Other sidebars could focus on history—other crashes or major storms.

The techniques of reporting and writing these stories are the same as for any other story. But there are some differences in how you gather the information.

Reporting Techniques

Before you venture out of the newsroom, you should find out a few facts and go prepared. Many major metropolitan newspapers have plans for covering disasters. In Fort Lauderdale, Fla., for example, the *Sun-Sentinel* has a detailed plan for coverage of disasters, particularly hurricanes. The plan spells out the responsibilities of each editor; assignments for reporters (hospitals, areas of the city, agencies); and telephone numbers of police, fire and rescue agencies, hospitals, utilities, and other places crucial to disaster coverage.

Cities also have major disaster plans, and police and fire departments frequently conduct drills to test them. If you have a municipal beat, find out if the government has such a plan and get a copy of it. If a disaster occurs, a good follow-up story is to check whether the plan was effective.

In the event of a disaster, you should follow these basic procedures before leaving your office or home:

• Check a map to see what routes lead to the scene. Are there alternative routes in case major arteries are blocked?

• Find out if temporary headquarters have been established for officials and media.

• Take plenty of change to make telephone calls to the newsroom to keep editors informed. If you are calling in your story on deadline, remember that information changes momentarily.

• Take proper clothing, if necessary: boots, rain gear, a change of clothes (in cases of flood coverage) and emergency rations— food and beverage if you think you'll be stuck somewhere for an extended period, flashlight, and so on. You could be reporting for a long time in an area without utilities. It's a good idea to have this emergency kit of supplies in your car at all times.

• Make sure you have a full tank of gas for your vehicle.

• Take plenty of notebooks and pens.

When you are covering the breaking news of a plane crash or earthquake or you are in the middle of a major storm, the sources of information are disorganized and unreliable. The news changes momentarily. The death toll often changes radically within the first few hours. Chaos reigns. You get the best information you can from eyewitnesses and officials at the scene. And then you check back repeatedly.

How do you know what to ask? Checklists follow. But you can't take a checklist to a disaster. What you need is the role-playing, "what if" technique of reporting. What if I were in this person's place? What if I were waiting to find out about a relative? What would I want to know?

For example: What if it were spring or winter break and you were expecting friends or relatives to visit you? Suddenly you hear over the radio that a plane has crashed at the international airport closest to you. What do you want to know? Make a list. Chances are that the information you want to know is the kind of information any reader would want to know. What airline, what plane, how many people died, who died, who survived, what caused the crash, how did it happen, where did it crash? Those questions will produce information for your lead and the top of your story. Then you gather detail.

Think statistics. You need specifics: numbers of people killed and injured or evacuated. Think human interest. How did people cope? How did they survive? What are their losses? What are their tragedies? Three hundred people could die in a plane crash, but the human interest stories of a few people make that crash vivid and poignant for the reader.

Think about narrative storytelling techniques for sidebars. How would you reconstruct the incident—what was the chronology? Try to gather information about the sequence of events if the story involves such disasters as explosions, plane crashes and other events that are not acts of nature. However, even with tornadoes, earthquakes, floods and hurricanes, it helps to get the sequence of events—specific times that events occurred, the minutes that it took for destruction.

Graphics

Almost all disaster stories are accompanied by graphics—maps, illustrations, charts—to help the reader visualize where, when and how (see Exhibit 24-1). But only a few newspapers have graphics reporters. The job of supplying information to the graphic designer or artists falls to the news reporter.

You need to gather details. Get information about exact locations: streets and measurements in yards or feet of where the accident, explosion or plane crash occurred. Try to get a map from

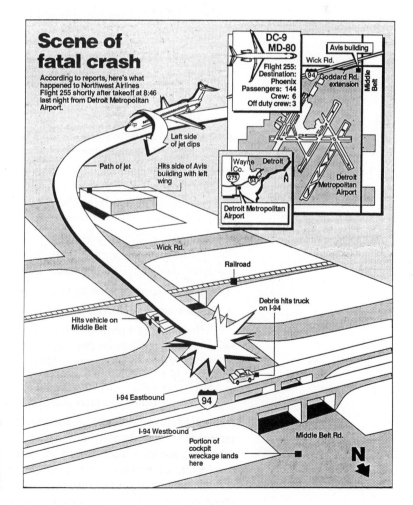

Exhibit 24-1

Graphic accompanying a story about a plane crash

Courtesy of Jeff Dionise and
Jeff Goertzen, *The Detroit News*

a local gas station or convenience store. Consider whether the incident lends itself to a graphic using the time of the accident. Get a chronology in minutes or hours.

In the process of gathering all the information you will need to describe the scene to a person who will draw it, you will be gathering some details you can use in your story. And, of course, the observation skills you develop will help with all the descriptive writing you do to make the reader see and care.

Disaster Checklist

Here is a checklist of basic information to collect for disaster coverage:

• Number of dead and injured

• Identification of victims

• Total number of people affected or in danger

• Cause of disaster

• Time and location of disaster

• Details about the disaster scene

• Eyewitness accounts

• Survivors: numbers; interviews

• Property loss: homes, commercial buildings, land, public utilities; estimated cost of damages

• Rescue and relief operations: evacuation (number of people and exact area involved); acts of heroism; unusual equipment used or unique rescue unit operations; number of official personnel and volunteers

• Warnings: health department, public utility commission, police and highway departments; roads closed, areas cordoned off, health measures such as drinking water sanctions

• National Guard involvement

• Human interest stories: impact of disaster on individuals

• Shelters and temporary headquarters: where people were taken, whether they have been evacuated; relief agencies such as the Red Cross or others in the community

• Hospitals

• Looting or other criminal activity; arrests

• Investigations: Status. All commercial plane crashes are investigated by the Federal Aviation Administration and the National Transportation Safety Board. If the disaster is caused by an explosion or human error, also check if local, state or federal authorities are investigating.

• Insurance, federal and state aid: In major disasters, a governor may declare the area a disaster area, meaning it could qualify for federal aid. For sidebars and follow-up stories, you could ask whether people will be insured or be eligible for government loans. Consider consumer stories about how people can get help.

• Lawsuits: Check for follow-up stories.

• History: previous problems, similar disasters

• Perspective: severity of this disaster compared to others

• Road closings

• Utilities: electricity, water and other services that may be interrupted; status of repair operations

• Weather: conditions at the time; the forecast, if the disaster was weather-related

The sources for this information include the governor's office, state and local police, the National Guard, hospitals, churches, the Red Cross, eyewitnesses, survivors, the weather service (for a weather-related disaster), the health department, utility companies, and the highway department.

Airplane Crash Checklist

Almost all of the information listed in the disaster checklist also applies to an airplane crash. One of your first concerns should be the number of dead or injured people. Initially you will get only estimates, and most likely they will be wrong. But you need some accounting of the death and injury toll.

Although an actual cause may not be known for months, ask anyway, because you need some idea.

You should also seek the names, ages and home towns of victims and survivors. In major plane crashes, the list of passengers and their status usually is not released for a day or more, until the relatives have been notified. The names and status of the pilots and crew members may be available sooner.

In addition to accounts from eyewitnesses, reactions from relatives or people at the airport, and other human interest stories, here is some information to include in plane crash stories:

• Airline and flight number

• Type of plane and manufacturer; number of engines, for small plane

• Origin and destination of the plane; takeoff time and expected landing time

- Altitude of plane at the time of trouble
- Weather and flying conditions
- Last words of pilot (not available until investigators get the recording)
- Police, fire and rescue units at the scene (numbers, time of response)
- Fire and other destruction in the area as a result of the crash
- Numbers of crashes that year, in that state, previous crashes for that airline, and so on
- Perspective: how this crash ranks in severity (worst crash in a decade, for example)
- Information from the flight recorder (when it has been recovered)
- Last contact and last comments from the tower (air controllers)
- Official inquiry (Federal Aviation Administration, National Transportation Safety Board)

The sources for this information include airline representatives; airport officials; police, fire and rescue officials; air traffic controllers; National Transportation Safety Board and Federal Aviation Administration officials; hospitals; the coroner; relatives; and witnesses and survivors.

Interviews With Grief-stricken People

The plane has crashed. You have the list of people who died. Your editor wants you to call the families of crash victims to get biographical data and reactions. What do you do? Quit your job? Cry? Get sick? Many reporters feel like doing all three. But there are sensitive ways to cover grief. And it's difficult, if not impossible, to avoid dealing with such situations if you are going to be a newspaper or magazine reporter. So here are some suggestions about how you can cover such stories.

Jacqui Banaszynski, a reporter for the *St. Paul* (Minn.) *Pioneer Press,* also has covered numerous stories involving grief, so many that she claims she has the grief beat. She won the Pulitzer Prize in 1988 for her coverage of the story of a man who was dying of AIDS (discussed in Chapter 19). When she is reporting about tragedy, she often tells the people she interviews that if at the end of the interview they don't like the way she has conducted herself, she will offer them her notebook and won't write anything. So far, no one has ever taken her up on her offer.

How can you ask questions about grief? Try this classroom exercise: In groups of three or four, list all the fears and anxieties you have about interviewing people who are grieving. Then discuss some reporting techniques you can use to deal with each of these concerns. After compiling your concerns and solutions, discuss them with the class as a whole.

Here are some concerns students usually express during this activity:

What if the person hangs up on me? You could try the Edna Buchanan technique of calling back and suggesting you were disconnected. Or you could just forget that interview and try calling someone else. Another suggestion is to call a neighbor and ask if he or she knows someone in the house who might talk to you. Or call the house and ask if anyone could talk to you about the situation. You don't have to ask for the person who is in the greatest pain.

If you are on the scene and the person does not want to talk to you, you might give him or her your card (or a note with your name and phone number) and ask if you could talk at another time.

What questions do I ask? Don't ask, "How do you feel about your son's death?" Obviously, the person feels terrible. You might instead ask specific questions about what the person was like, biographical questions. What was the person planning, or where was he or she going when the accident happened? Then you could ask for memories about the person.

What is the first thing I should say? Introduce yourself and state your purpose. You might also express your condolences.

What if I start to cry? You can be empathetic and even a little teary. Try not to weep. But be sincere. Do not fake your emotions.

What if the person I'm interviewing starts to cry? Stop interviewing and ask if you can get the person a glass of water or a tissue, or just be quiet for a while. You might also ask if the person would prefer you to come back another time, depending on the severity of the situation.

What if I say something insensitive without knowing it? Apologize.

Why do I have to interview people in times of grief? Because these types of stories make a news event more significant and real to readers. Because people relate to other people, not to vague generalities. And remember, for some people, talking about their pain is a form of catharsis. For others, grief is a very private matter. So some people will talk to you and others won't. Respect their needs. You won't get every story, especially if reporters from other newspapers and television stations already have talked to them. But the ones you do talk to can be wonderful.

Sidebars

Sidebars are not synonymous with soft news. Many sidebars are human interest stories, but they also can be hard-news stories or informational self-help stories. A sidebar is basically a story that gives the reader some new information or more information than the mainbar can provide. The mainbar in a disaster story is comprehensive; each sidebar should be very narrowly focused on one topic. The mainbar can allude to information that is in the sidebar, such as a quote from an eyewitness, but the sidebar should not be repetitious. A mainbar without emotional quotes from people would be boring. However, an entire sidebar about the people who have been quoted extensively in the mainbar is too repetitious.

Here are some ideas for sidebars and questions you can ask to determine whether you need them:

Helpfulness: If I were the reader, what information would I find helpful? For example, if a disaster affects utilities, as in a flood, should you have a sidebar on how to cope without electricity or fresh water? Or if it affects roads, consider a story about alternate routes. Or a story about how to get government aid.

Human interest: Is there a human interest story that the reader might find compelling? Does someone have a story that is unusual?

Perspective: Would the reader find it interesting to know the history of other disasters of this type?

The location: Is there a color piece that is compelling about the scene or a location affected by the disaster, such as a story about the hospital scene or the shelters where evacuated people were taken?

Other angles: Is there enough information worth telling about a specific angle of the story, such as the rescue efforts, the efforts of investigators or previous problems with that type of aircraft?

Analysis: If your community has been working on a disaster plan, is there a need for an analysis piece about how rescue or government workers coordinated the disaster operations?

In most cases, especially in human interest sidebars, you can use all the feature techniques of descriptive and narrative writing that you have studied. You should try to make the story vivid and compelling.

A sidebar still stands alone as a story, so you need to insert a reference to the main news—a brief line about the disaster or crash—especially if you have only one sidebar. If you have a huge package of several sidebars, you don't need to rehash the news statement in each one. You need to coordinate with the editor just how much of the main news needs to be in your story.

The Detroit News package on the plane crash included several sidebars: human interest stories, eyewitnesses, a chart of the worst commercial air disasters, and stories about the plane and the airline.

This is an excerpt from one of the sidebars about grieving relatives. Notice from the quotes that the reporters did not ask, "How do you feel?" The quotes and backup information contain specific memories and details about the people who died.

Grief cuts wide swath

*Relatives draw close
as horror sinks in*

**By Jon Pepper and
Rachel Reynolds**

The names of the dead trickled out slowly.

Among them was a professional basketball player. A weight lifter. A high school cheerleader and a successful businessman. A nursery school teacher from St. Clair Shores.

There were boyfriends and girlfriends, granddaughters and grandsons, husbands and wives.

None of the dead were positively identified by this morning. The few names that trickled out came from friends and relatives.

Kurt Dobronski, 28, vice-president of a Scottsdale, Ariz., construction firm and a former star football player at Dearborn Edsel Ford High and Central Michigan University, had come home to Dearborn for the wedding of a friend and found his 10-day visit "the best vacation he ever had," said brother Karl Dobronski.

"Things were going great for him," Karl Dobronski said. "This is a shock."

Things were also going well for Nick Vanos, a 7-foot-2 center for the Phoenix Suns basketball team. After playing only sparingly in his first two years in the National Basketball Association, Vanos was expected to start for the Suns this fall. He had come to Detroit to visit a girlfriend and boarded Flight 255 for his return to Arizona, team officials said.

"Nick Vanos was a young man who was just beginning to come into his own as a professional athlete and was about to take a giant step," said Suns general manager Jerry Coangelo. "It was very sad because he gave everything he had with his abilities. . . ."

Bill Horton of Phoenix lost his wife, Cindy, 37, who had been visiting her parents in Wisconsin. She had flown to Detroit to catch a flight to Phoenix. At midnight Sunday, he tried to calm his two stepchildren, aged 11 and 7. "They're hysterical," Horton said, sobbing. "How do you explain something like this to them?"

The Detroit News

Airplane Crashes

Whenever possible, try to get a death and injured toll in the lead. You can deal with the uncertain death toll by hedging with terms like "feared dead" and "at least . . . are believed dead." You don't have to make corrections when the death toll changes. You could state that the death toll has risen—or is lower than originally estimated—if there is a major difference.

**Development
of a Story**

The following examples of leads show how the plane crash story developed through different editions of *The Detroit News*. Note how the numbers of the dead change, even within hours. In the first story, no specific death toll was available. News of possible survivors was added for the second edition.

First edition (about 11 p.m.)

146 feared dead in Metro crash

A Northwest Airlines passenger jet with 146 aboard crashed at about 8:45 p.m. Sunday shortly after takeoff en route to Phoenix from Detroit Metropolitan Airport.

Witnesses said the airborne plane burst into flames before coming down at the intersection of Middle Belt and Wick. Several cars were hit on the ground and at least two motorists were killed.

Northwest Flight 255 was carrying 141 passengers and five crew members when it departed from Metro runway 3-center at 8:46 p.m.

Two people also died when the truck in which they were riding was struck by the plane's wreckage.

Another unidentified man, apparently not a passenger, was injured and found wandering down I-94 from the crash scene.

Ric Bohy and Mike Martindale, *The Detroit News*

Second edition (an hour later)

148 feared dead in Metro crash

A Northwest Airlines jet with 147 people aboard crashed just after takeoff Sunday night at Detroit Metropolitan Airport.

Witnesses said the airborne plane burst into flames before coming down at the intersection of Middle Belt and Wick Roads. Several cars were hit on the ground, and two people died when the truck in which they were riding was struck by the plane's wreckage.

Northwest Flight 255 was carrying 141 passengers and six crew members when it departed from Metro runway 3-center at 8:46 p.m., en route to Phoenix.

Early reports indicated that a 4-year-old girl may have been the only surviving passenger of the downed plane.

Ric Bohy and Mike Martindale, *The Detroit News*

By the third edition, information about the 4-year-old girl had been moved up to the second paragraph. The death toll had risen by the time of the fourth edition, and more details were available.

Third edition (two hours later)

147 feared dead in Metro crash

A Northwest Airlines jet with at least 147 people aboard crashed shortly after takeoff Sunday night at Detroit Metropolitan Airport.

A 4-year-old girl, found in the wreckage under the body of a

Fourth edition (first afternoon edition)

154 die at Metro in airliner crash

A Northwest Airlines jet with 153 people aboard crashed just after takeoff Sunday night at Detroit Metropolitan Airport, killing at least 152 aboard and two people on the ground.

Third edition (continued)

woman assumed to be her mother, is thought to be the only surviving passenger.

Witnesses said the airborne passenger liner, Northwest Flight 255, burst into flames before coming down at the intersection of Middle Belt and Wick roads. The flaming debris scattered hundreds of feet north of the crash site to and beyond I-94.

Flight 255 was carrying at least 141 passengers and six crew members when it departed from Metro runway 3-center at 8:46 p.m. bound for Phoenix.

Two people, yet unidentified, died when the truck in which they were riding was struck by the plane's wreckage. Another unidentified man, apparently not a passenger, was injured and found wandering on I-94 from the crash scene. He was taken immediately to Heritage Hospital, Taylor, and later was airlifted to University Hospital Burn Center in Ann Arbor, where he was listed in critical condition.

Ric Bohy and Mike Martindale, *The Detroit News*

Fourth edition (continued)

Investigators Monday struggled to piece together what happened in the worst accident in the airport's 32-year history.

A 4-year-old girl, found in the wreckage under the body of a woman assumed to be her mother, may be the only surviving passenger. However, another report said the child may have been a passenger in a car struck by the plane's debris.

Witnesses said the airborne passenger liner, Northwest Flight 255, burst into flames before coming down at the intersection of Middle Belt and Wick roads. The flaming debris scattered hundreds of feet north of the crash site, into and beyond I-94.

Within minutes of the crash, looters were seen sifting through the wreckage. Early this morning, authorities said six suspected looters had been arrested.

For several hours after the crash, Northwest spokesmen said the plane carried a total of 147 people. But the figure grew when it was determined that two infants—flying without tickets and seated on the laps of their parents—were among the 144 passengers. Six working crew members and three off-duty airline employees also were aboard.

Airline officials refused to identify those aboard Flight 255, pending notification of family members.

Ric Bohy and Mike Martindale, *The Detroit News*

Follow-up Stories

All major disasters require follow-up stories for many days. The second-day story should attempt to explain the cause, if that was not clear the first day. If the cause still isn't clear, you can lead with what officials are investigating. If there isn't any new information, you can describe cleanup attempts at the scene. The death toll should remain in the lead, especially if it has changed from earlier reports, or should be in the first few paragraphs.

In follow-up stories, you still need to mention what happened—when and where the plane crashed. In successive stories, that information can go a little bit lower. But it should still be high in the story on the second day.

Here is the second-day lead on the mainbar about the plane crash:

Loose and broken parts caused the breakdown since mid-1985 of four jet engines like those on Northwest Flight 255, which crashed Sunday at Detroit Metropolitan Airport.

At least 154 people were killed after witnesses saw an explosion in or near the aircraft's left engine. However, the head of a National Transportation Safety Board team investigating the crash said other witnesses saw no such fire and "very preliminary" findings are that there was no failure or fire in the left engine.

Documents describing the engine failures, known to the Federal Aviation Administration (FAA) and the National Transportation Safety Board (NTSB) since April, were obtained in Washington Monday.

A U.S. Department of Transportation source claimed Monday that a serious fuel leak problem with the jet was reported by crew members less than two weeks ago. FAA officials refused to confirm such a report.

In Romulus, workers began the soul-bruising task of collecting human remains from the crash site for identification by pathologists, friends and relatives.

Ric Bohy, Fred Girard, Mike Martindale and Joel Smith, *The Detroit News*

In addition to the mainbar, the paper carried numerous sidebars: human interest stories, eyewitness accounts, a chart of the worst commercial air disasters, victim stories, and stories about the plane and the airline.

Here is a story about another plane crash, more complete in its initial details. But this wire service story lacks detail and color that a reporter might gain from observation of the scene; eyewitness accounts were published in a sidebar. The main story also lacks comments from survivors and relatives. However, the story is a good example of how to organize a lot of material. Most of the elements in the airplane disaster checklist are included.

20 die in
La Guardia crash

The Associated Press

Lead: airline,
number of people
aboard, where
crashed, when,
death toll,
destination,
flight number

NEW YORK—A USAir jet carrying 51 people crashed in a snowstorm Sunday while trying to take off from La Guardia Airport and skidded part way into the frigid waters of Flushing Bay. Authorities said at least 20 people were killed.

Witnesses said USAir Flight 405, bound for Cleveland, left the ground, then fell back and exploded before sliding into the water.

Eyewitness account, color quote

"It looked like the sun coming up," witness Manny Dias told WNBC-TV. "The sky lit up. It was just about to take off. It just exploded."

Backup for lead: death toll, survivors, missing

Sgt. John Murphy of the Port Authority said 20 people were dead, 27 were known to have survived and four others were still missing.

Elaboration

Divers said they found passengers, and the plane's pilot, strapped upside down in their seats in the submerged part of the wreckage.

Status of airport, diversion of flights

The airport was closed after the accident, which occurred about 9:30 p.m. Incoming flights were diverted to nearby John F. Kennedy International Airport.

Elaboration

Twenty-one people climbed out of the plane in the water and to the Delta shuttle terminal, Port Authority police said.

Neither the airline nor the Federal Aviation Administration had any immediate explanation for what caused the plane to crash during takeoff or whether the bad weather was a factor. The National Transportation Safety Board sent investigators to the scene.

Suspected cause

Port Authority police said the plane veered left at the end of the runway and hit a snow-covered barricade just before the water.

Detail

The nose, wing and engine snapped off while the rest of the plane was in the water with its top sheared off.

At Cleveland's Hopkins International Airport, friends and relatives of passengers aboard the plane were in seclusion.

Relatives, friends: secluded (no reaction possible yet)

USAir spokeswoman Lynn McCloud in Arlington, Va., said 51 people were on the jet, including 47 passengers, two pilots and two flight attendants. The airline said the flight originated in Jacksonville, Fla., and five passengers were booked all the way through to Cleveland.

Airline official's comments substantiating earlier facts

Origination point

McCloud, the USAir spokesman, said the temperature was 31 degrees, wind about 15 mph, and the runway was wet with patches of snow. She said visibility was three-quarters of a mile.

Weather

The aircraft was a 6-year-old Fokker-28 4000 commuter jet, McCloud said.

FAA spokesman Fred Farrar described the plane as a "relatively small two-engine jet with both engines on the rear of the fuselage."

Detail about plane

It was the second time in three years a plane has skidded off a runway at La Guardia. Both were USAir flights.

Perspective: other crashes

Natural Disasters

All disaster stories should include the same basic information: death toll, survivors, eyewitness accounts, human interest quotes from survivors, and details of the scene and of recovery efforts. For natural disasters, add information about the natural forces at work, such as weather conditions and forecasts. If you are covering floods,

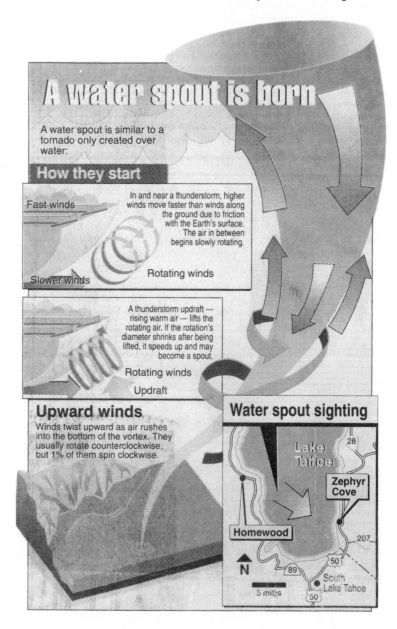

Exhibit 24-2

*Graphic explaining
a natural disaster*

Courtesy of Paul Horn and
Dave Hardman, *Reno Gazette-Journal*

find out how high the river crested—if that was a factor—or the height of water in feet. If winds were a cause of the destruction, get the specific miles per hour of the wind velocity. In the case of an earthquake, find out the magnitude and the location of the epicenter. Explain in simple terms how the natural phenomenon occurred. A graphic may be better than words (see Exhibit 24-2).

Tornadoes, earthquakes, hurricanes and floods all cause extensive damage and leave people homeless. Find out where people are finding shelter and what is being done to help them. Insurance is also a big factor in natural disasters. Also include consumer information, such as areas readers should avoid and the names of impassable streets, or how people can cope. Utilities are often affected, so make sure you check about the safety of drinking water, food supplies and electricity.

Many of these consumer elements may be in sidebars. But when you write the first-day story, the format is similar to that of a plane crash or any other disaster. Give the basic facts and a death or injury toll in the lead.

> FERNDALE, Calif.—A powerful earthquake rocked California's remote North Coast on Saturday, knocking brick facades off buildings, sparking fires that destroyed several businesses and two post offices, and sending at least 35 people to hospitals with cuts, broken bones and chest pains.
>
> *Los Angeles Times*

You can take a softer approach in follow-up stories. In the following story about a major flood, the soft lead is accompanied by specifics about the flood, the costs and the sources. The newspaper also published sidebars about the Red Cross, how to clean up after floods, the disaster's impact on businesses and human interest stories.

Lora Morgan sat outside her basement apartment among her furniture and clothing, which were drying in the afternoon sun.

The last heavy rain of the weekend had changed her and her husband's plans early Sunday morning about moving out of their Coralville apartment in August.

They moved out for good Sunday—thanks to 10 inches of filthy brown water that sloshed inside the walls of their home.

"The first thing you do is look at the unreplaceable things," Morgan said. Her piano was sitting in several inches of water.

"It's kind of ironic—two months before we move out anyway," she said.

Not everyone is moving out. Many area residents awoke this morning to the smell of musty basements, the squish of waterlogged carpets and the impending cleanup—all left by three heavy rains Saturday and early Sunday. Others are moving back to their silt-filled homes after spending two nights with friends or in area motels.

Many people went in search of equipment to clean out their homes.

"It's a nightmare," Lloyd

Baumgartner said this morning. He is the owner of Aero Rental in Iowa City.

"We've been up since Saturday trying to help people." The store's supply of pumps, shop vacuums, fans and de-humidifiers is rented out.

No flood-related injuries were reported in Johnson County. But the property and crop damage could be in the millions of dollars. Johnson County was one of seven Iowa counties declared disaster areas Saturday by Gov. Terry Branstad. The state damage estimate was $21 million.

Iowa City Pollution Control said 3.25 inches of rain fell Saturday in the area, and 1.65 inches fell Sunday for a total of 4.9 inches.

It chased Tiffin and Coralville residents from their homes, filled businesses, stranded cars, turned streets into rivers and washed out roads and bridges throughout the county.

Highway 6 was closed through Coralville until 1 p.m. Sunday. A two-mile section of Interstate 80 between Interstate 380 and Highway 965 also was closed as Clear Creek overflowed its banks.

Mark Siebert and Marge Gasnick, *Iowa City* (Iowa) *Press-Citizen*

Personal Tragedy

In the beginning, hordes of reporters descended on the tiny town of Buckner, Mo., to cover the tragedy of three brothers who died in an icy pond. It was a personal tragedy of national magnitude.

Tad Bartimus, an award-winning writer for The Associated Press, was not among the initial reporters. Bartimus called the family several weeks later and said she wanted to do a story because she didn't think the real story about the boys had ever been told. To her surprise, the family consented. But Bartimus said it was a very painful story to write.

She said her reporting style for tragedy is to treat the family as though it were her own. "I can get anyone to tell me anything. And I can empathize with people. Those are my top two strengths."

But why do the media love to do stories about personal tragedies? The media are often criticized for their coverage of grieving families. A grief counselor in Bartimus' story expresses the reason well: "The human spirit is resilient beyond belief, and that is the hope here," said Ms. Howard. "At a time like this you can get swamped by the grinding pain of it. But out of that pain comes some of the most substantial character and human elegance to be found on Earth. You learn how people can rise up and care for one another."

And that is a theme of this story. Readers want to read about how people cope with tragedy.

Bartimus didn't ask the parents insensitive questions about how they felt. When parents lose their three children, the answer is obvious. Instead she focused on how the community reacted and the parents' memories of their children.

As a reporter, you undoubtedly will have to cover a personal tragedy at some point—probably many times—in your career. Many of those stories will focus on the community and how people cope with a tragedy that happens to their neighbors or members of their immediate family. Bartimus' story can serve as a model for questions to ask and approaches to take. It is similar to the personal tragedy story written by David Silverman (in Chapter 13) about the parents whose child was killed when a woman went on a shooting rampage in an elementary school in suburban Chicago. His approach focused more on the parents, three months after the tragedy.

As you read Bartimus' story, note the sources she used and the way she structured the story. Like Silverman, she also used a circular ending that returned to the beginning of the story for concept but focused on the future.

Band of brothers

Tad Bartimus
Associated Press

"We few, we happy few, we band of brothers . . ."
William Shakespeare, *Henry V*

BUCKNER, Mo.—There is so little left.

A red cardboard valentine with torn paper lace, which proclaims, "I love you Mom." A carefully penned Thanksgiving essay in which the writer says he's grateful for his family "to have someone to love me." A child's "Life Story" book with extra pages left blank for future adventures.

Chad Eugene Gragg, 12, Aaron Wayne Gragg, 11, and Stephen Douglas Gragg, 8, died together at dusk on the cold afternoon of Feb. 4.

It was Aaron's 11th birthday. Despite admonishments from a teacher and a chum who rode home with him on the bus, he chose to celebrate it by sliding on the frozen surface of a farmer's pond.

The ice broke. Aaron fell into the frigid water. His big brother Chad, doing what his parents had always taught him to do, attempted to save him. He, too, fell in. Stevie, strong for his age, also tried to be his brothers' keeper. His body plunged through the thin crust.

A horrified neighbor boy ran for help. Frantic firemen pulled the brothers from the pond within 30 minutes. They weren't breathing and had no pulse. Two helicopters and an ambulance rushed them to three separate hospitals.

Thus began the agonizing pilgrimage of Charles and Mary Gragg, two ordinary people who now stagger in the footsteps of Job.

Meanwhile, word of the tragedy spread like woodsmoke over this western Missouri town of 2,800. The event would change forever Buckner's image of itself.

As doctors at St. Mary's Hospital in nearby Blue Springs told the parents their son Chad was dead, teachers and friends arrived to surround the stunned couple in a protective cocoon.

Hoping against hope, the Graggs next went to St. Luke's Hospital in Kansas City, only to be told Aaron, too, was gone.

By the time they reached Children's Mercy Hospital the Graggs were at the heart of a caravan of grief. They found Stephen on a life support system. At 10 p.m., he passed away.

In the space and time it took for the sun to set and the moon to rise, three healthy, happy, handsome little boys vanished from the lives of all who knew them.

They left behind bits of homework and smiling celluloid images, a puppy named Scooter who looks for them everywhere, empty school desks, classmates who struggle to remember their last words, teachers who wish they'd known them better.

They left behind the townspeople of Buckner, who were galvanized by the loss to dig deep within their hearts and pockets to bury the children with dignity, and continue to mourn them with honest tears.

They left behind their mother and their father, but Mary and

Charles Gragg, both 41, are no longer parents. The sounds of laughter, of life, are gone from their empty house. The only noise comes from the television set. The door to the boys' bedroom is closed.

The unbearable must now be borne.

"In our age, children aren't eligible to die because our expectations have been set up that children can survive anything," said Kathryn Howard, a grief counselor with Comprehensive Mental Health Services in nearby Independence, Mo.

"All the time we read about children who fall into freezing water and survive. Why not Aaron, or Chad, or at least Stevie? They couldn't be saved because the water wasn't deep enough or cold enough. But because of modern medical miracles, we are conditioned to believe it is outrageous that they died."

Ms. Howard, whose nonprofit agency has contracts with both the local school district and fire department, had headed grief and death counseling in Buckner since the drownings. She also helped the Graggs plan their children's funeral.

"The human spirit is resilient beyond belief, and that is the hope here," said Ms. Howard. "At a time like this you can get swamped by the grinding pain of it. But out of that pain comes some of the most substantial character and human elegance to be found on Earth. You learn how people can rise up and care for one another.

"This is now a community that speaks with one voice. That

phenomena is rare—too often we are too big and fragmented a society for this to happen. But if you listen to Buckner today, what you hear is, 'We care. This matters to us. They were our children, too.'"

The Graggs had no close relatives living nearby. Acting out of instinct and compassion, Buckner Elementary School Principal Richard Thompson stepped into the abyss.

"The school in a sense became their family," said Thompson. "Working with me, Kathryn Howard, and Jerry Brown, the funeral director, Charlie and Mary decided to have the funeral in the junior high gymnasium. The parents wanted the teachers to speak, and to be pallbearers.

"This became a chance for the community to fulfill what a community is all about. Before the accident happened you could have counted on one hand the number of people who knew Charlie and Mary Gragg. Now everyone knows them and wants to help them."

The Parent-Teacher Association mobilized to take food to the Gragg home for the next two weeks. Secretly thanking God it wasn't their own kids, mothers reached into closets and brought forth suits and ties for the boys to wear to their graves.

Funds were established to accept donations to offset medical and funeral expenses. The local bank, the savings and loan and a florist donated flower sprays for the coffins.

"It is so hard to take it in," said James B. Jones, president of the First State Bank of Missouri, where nearly $20,000 was sent in

the first two weeks after the accident.

Pondering the event's anguishing mathematics, Jones wondered, "If people had only one child and lost it, isn't that just as terrible as having three and losing them all? I don't know, I simply don't know, it's just so hard to make yourself think about it."

Mortician Brown tried not to think about his own boys, aged 7 and 8, as he plotted the funeral like a general planning a battle.

"We went into this with no idea there'd be any money to pay for it. I was estimating a minimum of $2,500 each. I went to my vault manufacturer and coffin supplier and explained the situation. They were willing to share the burden, no matter what happened," said Brown, whose family has served as Buckner's only morticians for three generations.

Brown decided on three identical coffins, three identical hearses. He reserved three side-by-side plots on a gently sloping hillside in the town cemetery.

From the graves you can look out over the walnut and oak trees, past the dormant farm pastures, and down toward the creek where an angry crawdad once bit Aaron's big toe, where Chad caught a two-pound lunker of a catfish, where Stevie loved to hunt for frogs.

Those are the same hills and hollows Brown scampered over as a child. He, too, remembers sliding across frozen ponds with his buddies.

Brown steeled himself not to think about any of those memories, or the event that brought him into the Graggs' circle, "because it is so overwhelming, so awesome, that it stops you in your tracks." He'd think later. First, he had a big job to do.

When he'd finished embalming and dressing the dead children in their new clothes, he tucked each boy's favorite toy into the silk-lined caskets.

As Brown ministered to the dead, Thompson and Ms. Howard, along with every clergyman in town, local teachers and reinforcements from other schools, consoled the living.

"The day after it happened we conducted emotional triage in the halls, the library, the cafeteria, and the classrooms," said Ms. Howard. "We had kids crying with counselors in corners everywhere you looked. Part of being young is learning how to deal with your pain. The kids were shown they could support one another and that they wouldn't be alone."

Teachers read "The Taste of Blackberries" to all fourth and fifth graders. The book relates the tale of a boy who loses his best friend. Younger children heard "The 10th Good Thing About Barney," a story of a little boy whose cat dies.

Thompson sent letters home with every student, detailing the day's upheaval and warning parents their children "might have tears or depression but that is expected and is normal in the grief process. . . ." Attached were four pages of guidelines for dealing with the situation.

"That day we just put a Band-Aid on it; we flew by the seat of our pants," recalled Thompson. "We decided to leave the Gragg boys' desks empty to stress the

finality of death, to show some physical remains. We talked about the details. We tried to cope with the onslaught of the media but refused to let reporters talk to teachers or students. And we braced for the funeral."

Thompson is described by faculty, city fathers, and the Graggs as the glue that held everything together through that long weekend.

Besides organizing the school's response to the tragedy, Thompson set up the junior high gymnasium for the funeral, helped teachers prepare their farewell remarks, acceded to any family wishes, and comforted students who attended the open coffin visitation and closed casket funeral.

"It was tough trying to make an appropriate setting for a funeral out of a basketball court, but we did it," said Thompson.

He had a carpenter build a wooden schoolhouse which was then covered with flowers and presented by the students of Buckner. Thompson also gave the parents a brass school bell engraved with the boys' names. The gift usually is reserved for retiring teachers.

"We consider that your boys have retired to a heavenly school," Thompson told the Graggs.

More than 600 mourners heard fourth-grade teacher Jeanne Young describe the Gragg children as "three adventuresome, energetic little boys . . . each of us has a special place in our heart, locked and guarded—it's the place just for Chad and Stephen and Aaron."

Symbols of each boy's inter-

ests rested atop the blue-gray caskets: art materials for Aaron, a soccer ball for Stephen, a basketball for Chad.

Finally, the three brothers were laid to rest in the winter's hard ground.

Mortician Brown left town for a convention in Florida, allowing himself to cry most of the way.

Mental health counselor Kathryn Howard began planning a series of forums on death and dying for the Buckner community.

Principal Thompson fielded calls from People magazine and tried to get his school back to some semblance of normalcy.

"The tragedy will long be remembered in this community," said Thompson, pausing to wipe tears from his eyes and catch his breath over the big lump in his throat. "They were rambunctious country boys who were one for all and all for one.

"Two of the boys willingly gave up their lives for the other. That is the only thing that makes it comprehensible."

Mary and Charlie Gragg's relatives have gone home and neighbors visit less now. Gragg has resumed the commute to his metal treating company in Kansas City. His wife has returned to shift work for a janitorial contractor at the nearby Lake City Army Ammunition Plant.

The Graggs believe they'll stay in the neighborhood where dogs run free and kids' boundaries are defined by a stop sign on a country road.

They speak of their sons in the present tense.

Looking at a small pile of photographs, Mary Gragg remembers each of her sons as a sturdy blue-eyed, blond-haired baby.

"They were so good. They slept through the night every night.

"Aaron is my artist, my loner, he loves his dinosaurs. Chad is his daddy made over, my helper, everybody's helper, such a good student. He loves school, he never misses, and he loves riding his bicycle. Stevie's a little slow, a shy kid. Stevie loves Alf . . ."

Charlie Gragg takes up the sentence.

"You'll never see kids that alike, that close. If one goes out the front door the other two are right behind. . . . I wasn't surprised they all died trying to pull each other out of that pond.

"I always told them, 'No matter what happens, you help your brothers.' I told them that more than once. I told Chad he was responsible. He was in charge. He went to help Aaron, and Stevie followed."

Is there anything anyone can do for the Graggs? They say there is nothing. They are baffled

that there might be an answer to such a question.

Soon it will be spring, time to go fishin' again, and frog huntin', and crawdad catchin'. That's when the children of Buckner Elementary School will plant three new trees in the memory of Aaron, Chad, and Stevie.

By then, the ice will be gone from the ponds.

Activities

1   Write a feature about the emergency response units in your community.

2   Make a list of questions you would ask and sources you would contact if a plane crashed in your community.

3   Plan a package of stories for a flood, tornado, earthquake or other natural disaster that might occur in your region.

4   **First-day airplane crash story:** Now it's your turn to cover a disaster— a major plane crash at the international airport closest to your city. This is an exercise designed to help you learn how to organize massive amounts of information into one coherent story. Since it is not possible to simulate this reporting experience, you'll have to do some brainstorming. List the sources you would contact. List the information you think would be crucial to get for a main story. List the sidebars you would need for a large package.

For this assignment, you may consider yourself an Associated Press reporter if you want to write the story as the information is presented. If you want to make it more local—and more of a reporting lesson—substitute local sources, your nearest metropolitan airport and local hospitals for those named in the story.

Much of the information for this story is based on the actual crash of Delta Flight 191 at Dallas International Airport on Aug. 2, 1985. Some of the information is based on reports from the former *Dallas Times Herald* and *Sunshine* magazine of the *Sun-Sentinel* newspaper in Fort Lauderdale, Fla. Other parts are fictional.

You should check the chart at the end of the notes to include any perspective you think is necessary. Also, you may find conflicting information, as you would at the scene of any major disaster. You will have to decide how to handle it.

Before you begin reading this assignment and writing it, consider the writing process. In a story of this nature, you should use the FORK technique:

Focus: You have your focus—the news about the plane crash—for the mainbar.

Order: After you read all the information, you should jot down an order before you begin writing.

Repetition of key words: Consider key words as a tool to get you from one thought to another.

Kiss off: The kiss-off technique is most useful here. You will have many sources, far too many for the reader to remember. So use each one and then kiss her or him off. If you need to use a source again, re-introduce the person.

This is a deadline writing assignment. Limit yourself to about one hour writing time if possible—no more than 90 minutes.

Now, imagine that you are a reporter for the morning paper. It is 3 p.m. You hear on the police radio that ambulances are racing to the Kansas City (Mo.) International Airport and that the Kansas City fire department is also responding to a call for help. A plane has crashed. You call the city police department and find out that a major commercial airliner has crashed, but you can't get anything more at this time.

You call the airport public information department and learn that the plane was a Delta Airlines jetliner from Dallas–Fort Worth International Airport that was due to land in Missouri at 2:30 p.m. The spokeswoman, P.R. Informer, tells you the plane crashed at 2:55 p.m. and is in flames, but she can tell you nothing more at this time.

Your city editor sends you to the airport to get the main story and another reporter to get quotes from people at the terminal for a color sidebar. A third reporter is on standby in the city room waiting to hear from you to determine the extent of the crash and to make phone calls to get additional information for your story. This reporter will get background from clips and call hospitals. Your deadline for the first edition is 9 p.m. You will have to update for later editions until midnight.

It is raining hard. Lightning slices through the sky frequently as you drive to the airport. You arrive at the airport and head for the Delta Airlines terminal in the C concourse. You race to the runway where the plane has crashed and see the charred pieces of metal strewn over the edge of the runway. The tail section is intact; it has broken away from the rest of the plane and is resting on a stretch of grass, about 150 feet from the edge of the runway. The area is already cordoned off. The scene is chaotic. Scores of airport fire trucks and fire apparatus from all fire companies in the city and county, as well as ambulances, are at the scene. Firefighters are still spraying foam on the smoldering wreckage. The entire area is a sea of foam, as though the runway had been blanketed by a heavy snowstorm. Rescue workers are carrying bodies on stretchers. People are screaming.

It appears as though the nose of the plane exploded on contact with the ground, just at the edge of the runway. Wreckage is strewn over about 500 feet. Body parts, suitcases, pieces of clothing and mangled shreds of metal litter the ground.

You get to a roped-off area and talk to a man who seems to be in charge. He is the airport fire marshal, John L. Smoke. He has no specific figures, but he says it appears that more than 100 people are dead. The plane exploded as it hit the edge of the runway on its approach for a landing, he says. He says it seems that about 25 people who were in the rear of the plane survived, but he has no official count. Smoke says the airport authorities are taking care of the survivors who were not injured, but he is not specific about where they were taken. As he talks to you, injured passengers on stretchers moan and wail as they are loaded into ambulances. You are not allowed to get near them. Bodies draped in yellow plastic are still at the site. You count at least 20, but there is so much confusion you can't get an accurate count or even a good estimate.

You have been on the scene about 30 minutes, and by now the flames are out, helped by pouring rain.

The tail section is so covered with foam that you cannot make out any details. A dozen fire engines surround the plane.

You head back to the terminal to talk to airport authorities. On your way back, you corner an ambulance driver, Samuel L. Savior. He tells you this is the worst experience he has ever had. "It isn't the injuries that strike me," he says. "I have never seen so much terror in people's eyes. It's horrifying."

In the airport, you get to P.R. Informer, information director for the airport. She is conducting a news conference in a few minutes. At the news conference, she says it was a Delta Airlines L-1011, Flight 313 from Dallas International Airport. The plane was made by Lockheed Aircraft. She says many of the passengers originated at Kennedy International Airport in New York and changed planes in Dallas for the final destination to Kansas City. She says the three-engine plane was carrying 275 passengers and a crew of six flight attendants (plus the pilot and two co-pilots).

At this point it appears that at least 200 people are dead, including the pilot and two co-pilots. She says there are 25 survivors and she does not know the fate of others who are not accounted for yet. She says a passenger list will not be released to the press until all the families of the passengers have been contacted—which could take at least a full day and perhaps longer. Airport and Delta Airlines personnel will work around the clock, she says.

In answer to your questions, Informer says the dead are being held in an airport hangar until they can be identified. The injured are being taken to area hospitals. Most of them are being taken to the University of Kansas Medical Center, St. Luke's Hospital and Liberty Hospital.

"This is a terrible tragedy," Informer says. "We are doing everything we can to notify relatives as quickly as we can. This is the worst thing that has ever happened in this state. It was a freak accident. We flew 2 million passengers in and out of this airport last year and our safety record was perfect. The only thing we can ascertain at this time is that the weather may have been a factor."

"If the weather was so bad, why wasn't the airport closed?" you ask.

"We safely land and depart planes all the time in thunderstorms, and this one did not seem prohibitive to air traffic," Informer says. "We have just completed a $65 million airport expansion project, and our airport is one of the safest in the country."

She tells you the airport is closed to all traffic at this time and will remain closed until all rescue operations are completed. You check later and find out that the airport reopened five hours later but the northeast concourse will remain closed indefinitely. It will be at least three days and maybe a week before officials from the Federal Aviation Administration and the National Transportation Safety Board have investigated and the wreckage is removed.

About 50 firefighters and eight units responded.

A Delta Airlines spokesman, I.M. Devastated, says the plane had six flight attendants and three crew members. He says the pilot was Captain Ted Connors, the co-pilot was Rudy Price, and Nick Nassick was the flight engineer. All three crew members are confirmed dead. He says Connors was from Fort Worth and was 57. He had been with the airline for 30 years and was one of its most experienced pilots. He was due to retire in three years. Price was 42 and had been with the airline for 14 years. He was from Lithonia, Ga. Nassick was 43. He was from Atlanta. He had been with the airline for nine years. Devastated says it appears that the only survivors were in the rear of the plane. He says he does not know the fate of the flight attendants. He is not releasing their names until he is sure their relatives have been notified. "The airline is doing everything possible," he says.

Devastated says Delta Airlines has 35 L-1011s. He says this was a 125-ton jumbo jet with a capacity of 300 passengers and 11 crew members. "This is a terrible tragedy, and our company will do everything we can to give support to the loved ones of those who perished and those who were injured," he says.

Investigators from the National Transportation Safety Board arrive on the scene shortly before 6 p.m. They say they are looking for the black box that records the pilot's communications. Retired Coast Guard Adm. Patrick Bursely, a member of the NTSB team, says he has no official cause of the crash, but weather factors such as wind shears are suspected because of the violent thunderstorms that struck Kansas City shortly before the plane crashed.

Wind shears, which are sudden and violent changes in wind direction, were responsible for several other plane crashes, including the crash of a Pan American World Airways 727 jetliner that crashed after takeoff from Kenner, La., in 1982, killing 153 people.

You head for the Delta Airlines counter. Hundreds of people are jamming the area. Many are canceling flights. Others are waiting gloomily until the airport reopens. Some are sitting on their luggage; others are lounging on the carpet. Others are in the airport bar. You see no sign of survivors or relatives. Airport personnel have taken them into a private room and will not allow the press to talk to them. At this point you meet up with Sarah Sidekick, the reporter who was assigned to get color. She says she was able to get some quotes from survivors and relatives before airline personnel got to them.

It is now 6:30 p.m. You call the city desk, and the editor tells you to come back and start writing. You are the main writer on the story. (In reality, someone inside the newsroom probably would be assigned to be the main writer, and you would stay at the scene.) You will take some of the color quotes from Sarah Sidekick and notes from other reporters who have done hospital checks, background and telephone interviews with officials.

Sidekick is writing a color sidebar with more reactions, but you need some quotes from her for your story.

Here is the information gathered by the other reporters:

Weather report: Severe thunderstorms started in the Kansas City area about 2 p.m. Winds in some parts of the city were as high as 65 mph. Trees were knocked down, and severe flooding occurred in some areas. The storm lasted for about two hours and then blew toward the west.

From survivor Milton I. Goldberg, 65, from New York: He was on his way to visit his daughter, Millie Muffin, 35, of 3600 Westbrooke, Lawrence (a city 30 miles west of Kansas City). "It was terrifying. Everyone was screaming and shouting. They were diving out of their seats and pushing. Some were getting trampled on. One of the flight attendants grabbed me and threw me out the emergency door. I'm lucky to be alive.

"I heard this earsplitting crackle. I think it was lightning. I was sitting in the back of the plane. I looked out the window and saw the wing crack. The next thing I heard was a deafening explosion. From that point on, all I heard was screaming. The cabin began to fill with smoke. There was mass panic." He began to sob and couldn't continue.

From Martha Mayhem, 59, of 2300 Harvard Road, Lawrence: She was waiting at the Delta Airlines gate where the passengers were supposed to come in when she heard the news of the crash. "I was waiting for my fiance. He was my childhood sweetheart. I waited for him all these years. I never married, but he did. Then we met in New York a year ago. He was widowed. We fell in love all over again. We were planning to get married this week. I can't believe that he isn't walking through that door. He told me he would take the first seat on the plane so he could get off fastest and never keep me waiting again. I don't think anyone in front of the plane survived. I feel like my life is over, too." Her fiance's name was Joseph Heartfelt.

From Joseph I. Frightened, 35, of Kansas City, Mo.: He was at the Delta Airlines ticket counter canceling his travel plans to fly to San Francisco. "Too many plane crashes. I just don't feel safe on a plane anymore."

From Enid R. Intrepid, 25, a University of Kansas graduate student in journalism: She was waiting for a flight to Seattle to visit her parents. "It was a terrible tragedy, but the law of averages is on the side of safety. I'm going ahead with my plans. Hundreds of people die in traffic accidents, but you still get in a car. You can't let these things frighten you. This was a freak accident. The storm is over and the sun is shining. I just know I'll be safe when I fly."

From Sam Adams, 23, a computer technician from Kansas City, Mo.: He was driving past the airport on his way home. "I saw this big orange flash in the sky. I wondered if that was the sun coming out after the storm. It was so bright. Then I saw the horrible flames and smoke and heard what happened on the radio."

From a spokesman at St. Luke's Hospital: "We've been told to expect 30 victims. We can't handle any more. All personnel have been called in, and our emergency room is full. We can't release any names at this time."

From a spokesman at the Kansas University Medical Center: "We have five of the survivors in our intensive-care burn unit. Fortunately we have the best facility in the state, and we're doing all we can. We are expecting more injured people momentarily."

From Mayor Emanuel Cleaver of Kansas City: "Our hearts go out to the loved ones of those who died and were injured. It's a miracle that anyone survived. The state will lend all resources possible to investigators in this terrible tragedy.

"This is the worst tragedy imaginable. The city will provide hotel facilities for all the relatives, and we will do everything possible to assist in funeral arrangements for the victims. It appears as though our emergency disaster plan has been effective, but the city will do a thorough evaluation when the appropriate time comes. Right now every available rescue operator is working, and we are doing everything possible to cope with this disaster."

Your newspaper will run a separate chart on previous airplane crashes. You should use this information in your story for perspective:

Major U.S. air disasters in a 10-year period

March 22, 1992: USAir Fokker F-28 crashed at La Guardia Airport during snowstorm; 51 aboard, 20 killed.

Aug. 1, 1988: Delta Airlines Boeing 727 crashed and burned on takeoff at Dallas–Fort Worth International Airport; 104 on board, 13 killed.

Nov. 15, 1987: Continental Airlines DC-9 crashed on takeoff at Denver; 28 killed.

Aug. 16, 1987: Northwest Airlines MD 80 crashed on takeoff at Detroit; 156 killed.

Aug. 31, 1986: Aeromexico DC-9 hit small plane over Los Angeles suburb; 82 killed.

June 18, 1986: De Havilland Twin Otter plane and Bell 206 helicopter collided over Grand Canyon; 25 killed.

Sept. 6, 1985: Midwest Express Airlines DC-9 crashed after takeoff at Milwaukee; 31 killed.

Aug. 2, 1985: Delta Air Lines Lockheed L-1011 crashed at Dallas–Fort Worth; 133 killed.

Jan. 21, 1985: Chartered Galaxy prop-jet crashed after takeoff at Reno, Nev.; 68 killed.

July 9, 1982: Pan Am Boeing 727 crashed after takeoff at Kenner, La.; 153 killed.

Jan. 13, 1982: Air Florida Boeing 737 crashed after takeoff at Washington, D.C.; 78 killed.

5   Plane crash follow story: On the day after the crash, you are to write a second-day mainbar only. Again, this is a deadline assignment. You have about an hour. Use whatever human interest material you need for the mainbar.

By the second day, many of the facts have changed, including the number of dead and injured. You have received a passenger list, so you now have the names of those who died and those who survived. You are contacting relatives for some of your information (there will be separate sidebars on them) and officials of the airline, the airport, the National Transportation Safety Board, hospitals and so on.

The names of the dead from the passenger list the airline has released will be published separately, but you have used that list to gather information. You can't possibly put all of the names in the mainbar. Not all the dead have been identified. You have contacted some relatives, and you will be at the airport to meet others who are arriving on two flights. Delta Airlines has flown in the relatives free of charge. One plane, Flight 222, is coming from Dallas; another, Flight 333, is arriving at 10 a.m. from New York.

Rescue workers worked through the night to clear the last of the bodies from the plane and the area. The wreckage of the plane is still on the edge of the runway. Investigators from the NTSB are still combing the wreckage. Although concourse C remains closed, the airport is open and planes are taking off on schedule at other concourses.

Delta Airlines spokesman I.M. Devastated says the death toll was higher than originally expected. The total death toll at this point is 234, with 50 survivors. Devastated says it is possible that some infants who were not on the passenger list might also have died, raising the death toll, but he is not certain at this time.

Included in the death toll are the pilot and two co-pilots and five of the six flight attendants. Also, five people who originally survived have died overnight in area hospitals. All but five of the survivors are in the hospital. The five others were released last night.

Most of the injured have broken bones, and 15 of them have severe burns. The burn victims are at the University of Kansas Medical Center. The others are at Liberty Hospital and St. Luke's Hospital.

The following information comes from other reporters, but you may use it in your mainbar:

From Elsa M. Nurse, spokeswoman for KU Medical Center: She said she has never seen such extensive burns in all her 33 years at the hospital. "It's a wonder they survived at all," she said. "All the burn victims are in shock."

From St. Luke's Hospital: Every doctor and nurse has worked double shifts. The emergency room is filled with at least 40 area residents who are donating blood. "It's the least I can do," said Steve Marcus, 19, a KU sophomore. "We were lucky. My brother, Bob, was on that plane, and he survived. He's here with a broken leg, a broken collar bone and a concussion, but at least he's alive." Marcus and his brother live at 2330 New Hampshire St. in Lawrence, Kan. Bob is 21, a senior majoring in journalism at KU. Bob is one of three survivors from Lawrence. Forty-five of the people who died also were from Lawrence.

From survivor Annie Grace Lucky, 47, a Dallas resident: She had flown to Missouri to visit a friend in Kansas City. She was one of the five released from the hospital. She was at the airport arranging with authorities to provide her limousine transportation to Dallas. This was her first plane trip. "I had always had a fear of flying," Lucky said. "I figured at my age, it was time to get over it. Now I'm afraid I'll never get over it. I'll never fly again. I expect this airline to get me home on the ground."

From survivor John Microchip, Bigstate Computers in Dallas: Dallas is corporate headquarters for his firm. He is a computer salesman who came to Kansas City for a business conference. He is in St. Luke's with a broken leg, a broken neck, several ruptured vertebrae and a broken arm. He said he saw the thunderclouds around the jet as it circled the airport, but he wasn't concerned at first. When the passengers behind him cried out in alarm at the turbulence, he said he told them, "Don't worry about it. It's just a typical thunderstorm. We're going to be safe."

Then he added: "Suddenly it felt as though somebody stepped on us. The plane kind of rocked, and people began screaming and yelling. Nobody was expecting it. I saw the ground coming up. Then we hit. The plane bounced once. Then it bounced again. I opened my eyes, and there I was dangling 30 feet above the grass, still strapped into my seat belt. I thought that I had either arrived in heaven or on earth. Then I unbuckled my seat belt and fell to the ground."

From Janet Sorrow of Dallas: She lost her whole family. She arrived from Dallas on the morning flight. She was sobbing as she was escorted by airline personnel to the Delta Airlines hospitality suite where officials were waiting for her. Airline officials tried to stop reporters from talking to her, but she said before she went in that her husband, Bob, and her three children—Janet, 2, Robert Jr., 3, and Amy, 6—were coming to Kansas City to start a new life. Bob was a carpenter, and there wasn't any work in Dallas because of the oil recession. He finally got a job in Kansas City after nine months of unemployment in Texas.

"We were so happy at getting a new chance. I stayed behind and planned to join them in a few weeks because I had to handle the final details of selling our house. Now I have no home, no husband, no family. I wish I had died with them."

From Jennifer Agony, 25, wife of crash victim James L. Agony, both from Dallas: She said her husband was taking a long weekend to visit friends in Kansas City. "Two months ago he got bumped from another Delta Airlines flight and was given a free ticket for another round trip. They told him he could fly anywhere, anytime he wanted to. He made the wrong choice," she said, sobbing.

From NTSB investigators: They said they are not sure yet, but they blame the crash on weather conditions. The winds were between 60 and 65 mph at the time the plane crashed, and lightning was in the area. Retired Coast Guard Adm. Patrick Bursely, the lead NTSB investigator, said it appears the plane might have hit a microburst, an upward air current surrounding a center of downward winds. It's known as wind shear, and it will force a plane to plummet, he explained. It's a dangerous weather phenomenon.

Bursely seemed very upset. He said there is a question whether the pilot had received the most up-to-date weather forecast before he attempted his landing. Bursely said the black box has been recovered. He said: "There is indication of a weather forecast being delivered to controllers some 10 minutes before the accident, and that was not passed along to the pilot. It appears that both controllers involved and the pilots involved in this accident were not concerned about the immediate weather conditions."

He said controllers were advised about 45 minutes before the crash that cumulonimbus clouds had formed east of the airport. Such clouds are often associated with thunderstorms that contain violent wind shears. The latest weather forecast the pilot received before the crash was an hour old, he said. He added that he is basing all that information from the recording in the black box, which was recovered last night.

The National Weather Service reported that at the time the plane was making its final approach, a huge thunderstorm was 5,000 feet above the airport and was unleashing winds and lightning. The storm arose over the airport area only about 30 minutes before the plane crashed. Bursely said the pilot never got that information. The plane was in a landing pattern at 2,000 to 3,000 feet at that time.

From Dr. Richard C. Froede, Kansas City Medical Examiner: He is in charge of death certificates for all the victims. He said that determining the identity of all the dead could take days. He said so far about 215 of the dead have been identified, but he is waiting for dental records to confirm the identification of the others. "There are fragments of bodies that have been recovered. This was a gruesome crash. We may get to the point where some bodies may never be identified. I'm amazed anyone survived."

COACHING

TIPS

Use observation to record descriptive details about the person and to show the source in action.

Do background research to find unusual questions the subject will enjoy discussing.

Try to find a unifying theme that you can weave through your story, a dominant or recurring concept about the person's life.

Write an order for your story; think about organizing it by topics or time frames (present, past, back to present and future).

Use the GOAL method to frame your questions.

Profiles

25

There's always something

interesting about everybody.

Nobody has lived a totally

uneventful life.

Alan Richman, writer,

GQ (Gentlemen's Quarterly)

Alan Richman walked into Bo Jackson's hotel room and got lucky. Bo Jackson was watching the soap opera "All My Children" on television. "I had a friend who wrote that episode of the soap opera, so I said, 'You want to know what's going to happen tomorrow on this show, I can tell you.' I called my friend and asked her what was going to happen. Bo loved this," Richman says. "Right away he thinks, 'This guy is not going to be as boring as the next guy.' "

Bo knows journalists. They always ask the same questions. The celebrated athlete, who for a time played both football and baseball, is reluctant to answer them.

Alan Richman knows athletes and celebrities. He interviews them all the time for profiles in GQ *(Gentlemen's Quarterly)*. He always asks something they haven't been asked before. It's a key to a successful celebrity profile.

With Boris Becker, that unique question came from a newspaper clipping about plans to list Becker in an encyclopedia. Richman handed him the clip and asked, "Why should you be in the 1991 World Book?" Becker was intrigued. He came back to the question six times during the interview. He speculated: Was it because he had done so much so young, that he was so well known, that he had won his first Wimbledon title at age 17?

"You've got to nail them with a question they like," Richman says. "They are so bored. I always ask myself, 'What question can I ask this guy that he'll enjoy answering.' It takes thinking."

*Alan Richman,
magazine writer*

Courtesy of Alan Richman

That's good advice for any profile interview, whether for a magazine, a newspaper or a broadcast. Do your homework. Read clips about the person, and ask the subject's friends for anecdotes so you get ideas for interesting questions. But most important, whether it is a profile of a celebrity or just a person in your community, find a focus for the story. Decide why the person is newsworthy—the "so what" factor. What makes the person special enough to read about?

If you can master the skills of interviewing famous people, the less renowned people are easy. The basic techniques are similar.

"Everybody's got one good story to tell," Richman says. "If you talk to them long enough, you'll find it. Nobody has lived a totally uneventful life."

To find that story, Richman uses what he calls the "Columbo school of interviewing": "I sort of hang around looking harmless. I try to be as unthreatening as possible. Then I use a weave-and-jab style of questioning. You can't be afraid to be a little bit rude," he says. "If the point of the interview is that they were a bigamist, I'll say: 'We all want to have two wives; tell me how you got away with it.' If it's a profile of a man growing award-winning roses, I'll say: 'I can't believe someone would spend 15 years to grow a decent rose.' "

Writing Profiles

Richman has been writing about famous people for more than 20 years, first as a sportswriter for the defunct *Philadelphia Bulletin,* later as a sports columnist for *The Montreal Star,* which also folded. He also was a columnist and writing coach for *The Boston Globe* and a metropolitan reporter for *The New York Times.* Prior to his current job at *GQ,* he wrote profiles for *People* magazine.

"*People* was the hardest place to write for," Richman says. "They demand an incredible amount of information in a short amount of space. They want ages, parents and an extensive family history in every story."

Sometimes those background questions can be boring. So Richman just puts his subjects on notice. He tells them: " 'It's that time now; I've got to ask these questions.' Basically they think I have some secret, that I'm going to ask them, 'Tell me about when you were 11 years old and you slept with a goat.' Then I tell them, 'I've got to go over your life.' They're relieved. I don't mess around and pretend it's going to be fun. It's more like, do me a favor. I don't trust press releases or clips. I always ask the background stuff. You never know what you are going to get."

Like these comments from Bo Jackson:

"I used to steal pocket change from my mother," he says. "I learned about sex from peeping in windows. I stole bicycles. I'd take them home, strip everything off the frame, throw the frame in the fire to burn the paint off, spray-paint the bike and ride it down the street. I was best known in the community for throwing rocks. I hit somebody every day with a rock. I was bad, the bully of the neighborhood. I beat up kids. I beat up girls. I beat the hell out of girls. I didn't care. I thought girls were just one of the guys."

He grew up in Bessemer, Alabama, just south of Birmingham, the son of Florence Bond and A.D. Adams, who never married. (His mother's maiden name was Jackson, her first husband was named Jackson, her second Bond.) The eighth of ten children, Bo was named Vincent after Vince Edwards, the actor then appearing in the popular television series "Ben Casey." As a child, says Bo, "I had tons of nicknames—my mother always called me 'sweetie'; sometimes 'knucklehead.'" The one that stuck came because he was such an ornery kid that friends compared him to a boar, or bo, hog.

That's a natural transition to Bo's mother (in Alabama) and her background, the *People* magazine technique Richman still uses in his current job:

Florence Bond sits in a small living room overstuffed with trophies, smiles fondly and talks about the child she "had to whip more than any of the others," the one she tried to educate with this basic message: "If you don't change your ways, you're going to be in jail or hell, sure as I'm sitting here."

Today, from her living room, she looks out onto Bo Jackson Avenue, shakes her head and wonders how that child of hers who liked stealing as much as he liked his stuffed animals could have turned out so well. The city fathers were not overly altruistic when they offered this narrow, soft-shouldered country lane in tribute to her son. At the speed Bo travels, approximately 100 yards every 9.5 seconds, he could traverse the length of it, dead end to dead end, in less than half a minute. The neighborhood is of mixed affluence, the houses ranging from practically middle-class to practically condemned. There are a few too many abandoned cars to classify it as suburbia. Bo wants his mother to move to a better place. She tells him, "I'm going to stay on this corner until God moves me."

Bo and his mother battled every day of his childhood. They're still at it today. He wants her to stop working at the motel where she cleans rooms. She tells him, "Look, honey, my working brought you up to where you are now. I'm proud of my job. All I've done is work."

Sometimes it seems Bo loves his mother more than anybody, even his wife.

"He better love his wife more," Florence warns.

His wife, who has a master's degree in counseling psychology from Auburn, says he couldn't possibly have been as bad a kid as he says he was or he wouldn't have grown into such a responsible man.

Alan Richman, *GQ*

Transitions

Richman's stories are virtually seamless. He weaves in background where it fits naturally. And he doesn't always put it in one block. It goes where it flows. One thought leads to another. Richman hates artificial transitions. The repetition-of-keyword technique is used all the time in *Sports Illustrated* and other magazines and newspapers—and it works, Richman admits. But he doesn't like it. "I want the story to conversationally slip from one paragraph to another. It should have a natural storytelling rhythm."

In a long profile—Richman's average is 6,000 words—that's not always possible. No problem. When it doesn't flow, he just puts in a break. "Eventually a train of thought has to drop," he says. "Someone once said, 'Nobody ever wrote a concert in one movement.' A break is good for the reader."

Theme

All Richman's profiles have a theme that binds the story. The nut graph is the "so what" reason you are doing the profile, but the theme is a unifying angle that weaves through the story, such as a recurrent image or concept, and ties the story together.

"I think the nut graph is even more important to the writer than the reader. You need to know what you are writing about," he says.

In the Bo Jackson profile, the theme is what makes this highly publicized but little-known athlete tick. The nut graph focuses on the fact that he is the only athlete to play both professional football and baseball, the "so what" factor. That point is made in the first paragraph and later in the story in this sentence: "No professional athlete in memory has succeeded at playing both football, a sport of speed and power, and baseball, a sport of timing and coordination." That's the reason for the story printed in 1990, before Jackson was injured and gave up football. Here is the lead; notice that the soap opera also made it into the lead:

Bo is in bed this weekday afternoon, the blankets pulled so high over his head only two wary eyes peep out. Outside his Oakland-airport hotel room, frenzied kids roam the hallways keening for autographs, quote-starved writers probe for the secret of his two-sports life, a telethon bank of ladies in the lobby phone for a few minutes alone with the best body ever to play any game. When you're Bo Jackson, the inhuman highlight machine—star of Nike ads, baseball's All-Star Game and Sunday-afternoon NFL scoring clips—pulling the covers over your head seems a sensible way to hide.

The eyes would be closed except the soaps are on, a lineup of people lying and stealing and screwing around, which is the stuff of nostalgia for Bo, inasmuch as he gave all that up years ago when he decided to make something of himself. "Nothing else to do until the game starts but sit in the hotel watching soaps," he says.

Alan Richman, *GQ*

"I always go in with a preconceived idea for a theme," Richman says. "I hope something better will click for a theme during the interview. But if you don't go in with an idea of what you can talk about, you are doomed."

When he interviewed Arnold Schwarzenegger, Richman stuck with his preconceived idea. Richman, who also is a restaurant reviewer and wine critic for *GQ*, enjoys eating. At 5 feet 10 inches and 180 pounds, he isn't nearly as out of shape as he portrays himself. But his paunchy self-image worked for him as a theme: "Schwarzenegger the sleek, who seems to have inherited the earth, pummels one of the meek, who has inherited the girth." The focus or nut graph, the reason for the profile, is in the second paragraph.

(Note that this is a magazine story, where first-person references are acceptable. In newspapers the *I* is not used in news stories, only in columns and a few first-person stories or occasionally in features written in magazine style.)

The elevator wasn't working, but I met the challenge. I climbed to the second floor, caught my breath on the landing, then went inside to confront Arnold Schwarzenegger.

On January 22, Schwarzenegger was named chairman of the President's Council on Physical Fitness, directed by George Bush to "raise the consciousness of all Americans on the importance of good health through physical fitness." On January 23, I traveled to the World Gym in Venice, California, where Arnold trains, to present myself as a man with a consciousness (and a chest) badly in need of raising. I told Arnold I was there to represent the typical American man.

"It couldn't be that bad," Arnold said.

Arnold is in his forties. I am in my forties. Arnold was wearing multicolored polka-dot Bermuda shorts. I was wearing elastic-waistband sweatpants. Arnold is a five-time Mr. Universe and a seven-time Mr. Olympia. I am not. There are other differences between us, pretty much all of them favorable to Arnold. I wanted him to see firsthand that chairmanship of the President's Council was not going to be a Sunday afternoon pitching horseshoes on the White House lawn. I stood before him, a symbol of all that he was duty-bound to improve.

"I resign," Arnold said.

I suggested he begin his reign as America's health czar by exercising with me. I wanted to learn the secrets that had transformed him from skinny Austrian schoolboy into the best body ever built.

"You want to exercise with me?" Arnold asked, grimacing. "You're crazy. I'm not on a mission of killing people."

Alan Richman, *GQ*

The theme doesn't always work that well. "I go into all interviews with a notion of what I could write if all else fails." Everything did when he met Robert De Niro, another celebrity who, like Bo Jackson, hates to be interviewed. Richman was going to meet De Niro at a bar to see if the star would agree to an interview. He hadn't planned to do the interview at that time. He never got a second chance. This scenario from the *GQ* story—an exchange between De Niro and Richman—should convince you to be prepared from the minute you talk to a source:

He startles me by asking what my first five questions would be if we did an interview.

Does he mean any five, fire away? To ask anything at all of De Niro is surely a hyperventilating moment in celebrity journalism. My breath shortens. The genie has popped from the bottle and granted me five wishes. No, you fool, he doesn't mean that. This is a test. I have to come up with five questions he'll like. I'm not prepared. . . .

"A-hummina, hummina, hummina," I say.

He interrupts. He says two questions will be enough.

I haven't said a coherent word yet and I've blown 60 percent of this interview. Later, I'm told that I should have asked him about Brando. He loved Brando in "The Freshman," wants to do character roles like that, ones in which he doesn't have to carry the film.

I don't think of that. I choke and ask the obvious. I ask him why he's agreed to consider an interview if he hates them so much.

Alan Richman, *GQ*

De Niro gives a strained response. Richman is ready for question No. 2. He never gets to ask it. De Niro says he has to leave. He does. And Richman is stuck without a story.

So he calls De Niro's friends and associates. "After the interview failed, I went back and called all those people to figure how to make the story work," Richman says. "I asked them, what question can you ask that he (De Niro) would answer. Everybody told me something about De Niro you couldn't ask." Those comments about De Niro were probably more insightful than the actor would have been about himself.

And that was the theme of the profile: how to interview a celebrity who doesn't like to be interviewed.

The Writing Process

Richman returns from an interview and types all his notes into the computer; he doesn't use a tape recorder. "Then I immediately start writing. I try to write a first draft as fast as I can. It's fun because I know it won't make sense. By the time I finish, if the theme hasn't already emerged, I know it should. Then I write many drafts. I revise and revise and revise. Usually the second draft is the hardest for me, because that's the one that has to make sense.

"I'm not an outliner. I always know where I am going to end before I start. If I know that, I can get there. If I have a lead, a nut graph and an ending, I can write a 100,000-word story, and I know it's going to be okay."

In the revision process, Richman works on word choice. "If your language is not bright and interesting, people will get bored," Richman says.

His suggestion: "Tell a good story and look for something to make the reader smile"—perhaps an ending like this one from the Bo Jackson profile:

I ask him how he would have treated me if, as kids, I had wandered into his neighborhood. He looks me up and down, dismissing the thought of resistance.

"I'd probably have walked up to you and asked you for your money," Bo says.

If I didn't have any?

"I'd beat you up."

Okay, so maybe I did have some.

"If you had any, I'd take it, then beat you up so you wouldn't tell your mother."

Me, run crying to my mother? I guess it's true what they say in those Nike ads.

Bo knows.

Alan Richman, *GQ*

So does Alan Richman.

The GOAL Method

The GOAL method (goals, obstacles, achievements, logistics), which was discussed in Chapter 8, can also work for you in profiles. To help find your focus or theme, consider the obstacles the person faced. These are often more interesting than the achievements. The achievements could be your nut graph—why you are writing the story—but the obstacles could be your theme—how you are presenting the story.

The GOAL method also works in the interviewing process. Some questions: What were the person's goals? What are the next goals? (These can work for an ending or even a lead and focus.) What obstacles did the person face in the past, and what new ones loom? What pleasure or pain have the achievements brought? What logistics—the background—led to the current condition? Don't stick to any particular order when asking these questions. Use a conversational interviewing approach.

Basic Elements of Profiles

Celebrities are considered worthy of profiles because they have accomplished something more special than the average citizen has. But many profiles, especially in newspapers, focus on people in the community who have done something noteworthy but do not have celebrity status. Still, whether it is a famous, infamous or relatively unknown person in the community, you need a newsworthy angle—why you are writing about the person.

Then you need a focus. Say that someone has won an award. That's a reason for the story, but it won't carry a whole story. The focus could be developed around either of these questions: Why did the person win? What motivated that person to achieve? Or your story might have a coping focus: How did the person cope with success, failure or serious problems?

Coping is the subject of this campus-newspaper profile of a University of Florida nursing student who was stabbed a year earlier:

When Stacy LaRocca looks at a calendar today, she won't see that it's just Tuesday, April 10, 1990. Instead, her mind will flash back to Monday, April 10, 1989—the day 13-year-old David Rowe plunged a pocketknife with a three-inch blade into her body 17 times and almost killed her.

Much has changed since that day, both for Rowe and LaRocca. Rowe, now 14, has been convicted as an adult by a jury for attempted first-degree murder, and he awaits sentencing.

For LaRocca, a 21-year-old UF nursing student from Miami, much more has changed since the attack—physically and emotionally.

After undergoing five major operations the day of the attack to save her life, having other people feed and bathe her the following summer because she was too weak to do it herself, and testifying on the stand at Rowe's trial, LaRocca said she now has a different perspective on life.

"I think it's made me a lot stronger," she said in a recent interview. "I'm not afraid to stand up and speak out about something I feel needs to be said. It's certainly given me a different perspective on life. There are a lot of things I just don't take for granted anymore."

Duane P. Marsteller, *Florida Alligator*

Once you have determined why you are writing about the person, determine the scope. Will you write a whole-life profile, revealing the person's background from childhood to the present, or a partial-life profile, focusing only on the person's life as it relates to a current problem or news issue? If you are writing about people who are representative of a problem or issue, you will probably choose the partial-life profile. The previous example was a partial-life profile about the student's life as it related to the stabbing. If you are writing about a person who has received an award, you may opt for either type of profile.

Walter Dawson, metro editor of *The Commercial Appeal* in Memphis, Tenn., says that regardless of who the profile is about, "the heart and soul of a profile is making sure the reader understands the twists and turns and intricacies of human life." Dawson directs his staff to consider the following universal elements:

Patterns: Some lives build to a climax, such as a law school student who becomes a judge.

Decisive moments or turning points: Patterns are important, but most lives take turns along the way. Take the law school student; maybe she wanted to be a great defense lawyer but became a prosecutor instead. Or maybe your subject was an accountant who became head of a river-rafting company.

Future: Every profile subject has a future, and you need to explore the question. Ask your subject what could lie ahead, and let the person speculate, particularly about career goals. Ask the impertinent question: If this career doesn't work out, what could you do?

Some other basic elements to include in profiles:

Age and physical description: Use these facts when and where relevant to the topic you are discussing. Make the details work for you. In this example from a profile of Willie Darden, a convicted killer who spent 11 years on Death Row in a Florida prison, the writer weaves in the age and physical description by relating them to the pressures of waiting for death:

Darden maintains a normalcy, a serenity, that is surreal. His forehead is not cleaved by worry lines. His hair has not gone gray. He lifts his shackled hands and displays unbitten fingernails. "Calmness is a nice thing to have in times of stress," he says.

He gives his age as 62, but prison records say he is 52. He looks 42. It's as if the man has not only cheated the executioner, but time itself.

Or maybe time just stops when there is no future.

"Prison does tend to sustain one's youth," Darden says with an ironic grin. "You're not doing anything that you would normally do on the outside—such as working hard every day. You've got no family problems. The wear and tear, so to speak, is on the inside."

Richard Leiby, *Sunshine* (Sunday magazine, *Sun-Sentinel*, Fort Lauderdale, Fla.)

Conversely, in this profile of racing car driver Janet Guthrie, the detail about her age is relevant, but her physical characteristics are not relevant in this section of the profile. Typical of many profiles about women and people of color, it emphasizes the "first" factor, which is legitimate but tiresome. Strive to emphasize the person's achievement, not just the fact of being the first of her or his gender or race to earn the distinction.

> It was 1977, the year the 39-year-old Guthrie made history as the first woman ever to compete in the Indy 500 race. So remarkable was her feat that her driving suit and helmet are in the Smithsonian Institution.
>   Janet Guthrie's reputation and fame don't ride on one barrier-breaking race. In person, the former race driver is slender, tall and soft-spoken, with a dry ironic wit. On the race track, she was what all the statistics prove: a top racer.
>
> Catherine Reeve, *Chicago Tribune*

Background: Describe the family, education and key experiences that led to the person's current success or failure. Before the interview, check clips and obtain a resume if one is available so you can check the background. When you write the story, insert the background where it fits naturally. In many profiles, the background is just plopped high in the story, as if to tell the reader, OK, now we launch into the past. When you plan your order, decide where the background is most relevant.

Other points of view: Seek comments from friends, family, colleagues and other people affected by the person at work, such as students for a profile about a professor or employees for a profile about a manager.

Graphics

Use graphics as a way to visualize your story in both the planning and writing stages. Outlining your profile by planning a facts (highlights) box can help you determine what topics to include in your story.

If the background is boring, break it out of your story. You can put key dates and such information as birthplace, education, career moves or similar items in a box. But if that information is an interesting and crucial part of your story, leave it in the body of the profile. You also can use a box to add information that doesn't fit well into your story but might be of interest, such as hobbies, favorite books, favorite saying, major goal. The major goal should also be mentioned in your story, but it works well in a facts box.

Several newspapers and magazines use graphic devices to substitute for written profiles; others use highlights boxes to enhance profiles. For example, *The Kansas City* (Mo.) *Star* Sunday magazine profiles celebrities with blurbs following these headings:

Vital statistics (occupation, birthday, birthplace, current home, marital status, and so on)

My fantasy is

If I could change one thing about myself, it would be

The best times of my life

Behind my back my friends say

These words best describe me

Newsday (New York) regularly profiles a person in a neighborhood with a graphic approach instead of a story. Some of the topics in the graphic are job, biography (birthplace, education, previous jobs), residence, major accomplishment, current focus and major concern.

If you mention topics in a graphic, you don't have to repeat them in the story. And even if you don't present your profile in graphic form, you can use this concept to help organize the major topics.

Finding Profile Sources

When Mary Bishop wrote a profile of Billy Graham, she knew more about the evangelist's life than he did. She discovered that his mother walked a quarter-mile to pick beans the day before he was born, a fact he didn't know. For an in-depth profile, start in the cradle, if not in the womb, says Bishop, a reporter for the *Roanoke* (Va.) *Times & World-News*.

She uses records and human sources for her profiles. And she recommends that you think of yourself as an "amateur shrink." Put yourself in the subject's shoes. Check family photos, family background, classmates and teachers from the subject's school days—elementary school through college—old yearbooks, friends, relatives, neighbors and acquaintances.

In this profile about serial killer Jeffrey Dahmer (who was later convicted of killing 15 men), a picture in a high school yearbook provided the theme: his conflicting personality traits to seek attention and to hide his abnormal behavior.

On page 98 of Jeffrey L. Dahmer's Ohio high-school yearbook is a photograph of 45 honor society students lined up shoulder to shoulder; their hair well combed, their smiles confident.

One senior three rows from the top has no smile, no eyes, no face at all: his image was blacked out with a marking pen, reduced to a silhouette by an annoyed student editor before the yearbook went to the printer.

That silhouette was Mr. Dahmer in the spring of 1978, a couple of months before he says he killed his first person, with a barbell, 13 years before he confessed to one of the most horrific strings of slayings in modern times.

With grades that ranged from A's to D's, Mr. Dahmer fell far short of honor society standards, but he sneaked into the photo session as if he belonged. No one said a word until long after the flashbulb had popped and the shutter had clicked.

In all the years he cried out for attention, it was one of the few times he got caught. By then he had taught himself to live behind a mask of normalcy that hid his confused, often contradictory emotions. It was a mask no one pulled down until one night last month, when a man in handcuffs dashed out of Mr. Dahmer's bizarrely cluttered apartment in a tough Milwaukee neighborhood, called the police

and stammered that Mr. Dahmer had been trying to kill him.

The authorities say that at least 17 other men did not get away: that Mr. Dahmer drugged their drinks, strangled them, cut up their bodies with an electric buzz saw; that he discarded bones he did not want in a 57-gallon drum he had bought for just that purpose; that he lined up three skulls on a shelf in his apartment, but only after spraying them with gray paint, to fool people into thinking that they were plastic models, the kind an aspiring artist or a medical intern might study. . . .

The facts—a home where parents went through a bitter divorce; a brother he long believed was the favorite in the family; a mother who he told police had had a nervous breakdown; his own lack of close friends—stop short of explaining why he did what he says he did. But the increasingly gruesome details that have emerged about Mr. Dahmer have all led back to one basic question: who is this man?

James Barron and Mary B.W. Tabor,
The New York Times

Most journalists interview the subject's friends, relatives and acquaintances before the scheduled interview. But Alan Richman, the writer for *GQ*, takes an unorthodox approach to other sources. He interviews them after he interviews the celebrity. "One of my rules is never call up friends or acquaintances of stars and ask what they think of the person, because they will always lie," Richman says. "If you were doing a profile of Hitler, most journalists would call up Goebbels and Himmler and they would say, 'What a guy!' Instead, ask them for facts or anecdotes."

Richman's point is well-taken. When you interview your sources, ask for specific details and anecdotes about your subject. General impressions yield only quotes with vague adjectives. On the other hand, anecdotes enliven the profile and help the reader understand the person's character.

To get anecdotes, however, don't ask people what was the most memorable moment or a similarly unfocused question. Give the person clues. Put the question in a time frame: When she was in college, what signs did you see that she would pursue this career?

When using description, try to elaborate with an anecdote, as in this example about the late publishing tycoon, Robert Maxwell:

In the 1950s, his reputation for tying up hotel switchboards and making unappeasable demands on the staff made him unwelcome in some of New York's best hotels. On one occasion, unable to reserve a room at the hotel of his choice, he ended up at the Winslow Hotel on Madison Avenue, which he promptly denounced as a "flea-pit." To make his point, he released 1,000 fleas in the hotel elevator shaft.

Alessandra Stanley, *The New York Times*

Organizing the Profile

There is no one way to organize a profile, other than having a lead, a body and an ending. Just make sure you have a focus.

Descriptive show-in-action leads, anecdotes, contrast leads and scene-setting leads work particularly well in profiles. As with any lead, those in profiles need good backup in the story.

The body of the story can be organized in many ways:

Supporting themes: Block each concept, use all relevant material, and then kiss off that theme and go on to the next.

Time frames: Start with the present, go to the past, go back to the present, and end with the future.

Chronology: Look for a place in the story where chronological order might be useful, but don't write the entire profile in chronological order. A chronology might be most helpful for the background. It also might work if you are writing the profile in narrative style. In some cases, however, the story might lend itself to chronological order if a situation unfolds in that sequence. Just make sure your nut graph tells readers why you are writing about this person now.

Point/counterpoint: If the subject lends itself to pro-and-con treatment, you might consider this method. It can be helpful in profiles of politicians. You can include reaction quotes from other people after each controversial point is made. However, you still should use the kiss-off technique if you use this method.

Sections: Splitting the story into separate parts may work if the profile is very complex. For example, if you are doing an in-depth profile of a politician or crime victim or crime suspect, you might organize it in sections, either by time frames of the person's life, issues or different points of view.

Several types of endings work well with profiles. A quote kicker can be used to summarize a source's feelings about the subject or to summarize the subject's accomplishments. Or, with a circular ending, you can return to the lead for an idea and end on a similar note. An ending with a future theme tells what lies ahead for the person. Or try a simple factual sentence that conveys emotional impact.

Putting It All Together

The examples in this section demonstrate a variety of techniques suggested in this chapter. Although they differ in subject, organization and style, they all have a clear focus. That is the one indispensable element of a compelling profile.

Past, Present and Future

Here is a profile organized in sections. The three sections basically feature the present, past and future, although they are not so clearly delineated.

She is the finest of New Orleans' finest

From a gritty past to the city's best detective

By Matthew Purdy
The Philadelphia Inquirer

Descriptive lead to create contrasts with past and present

NEW ORLEANS—The white frame house on Barrone Street is small and gated, just as it was when Jacklean Davis was a shy, serious-eyed little girl in a world of grownup horrors.

Here, 12 blocks from the muddy-brown Mississippi River, Davis was raised by a prostitute, raped by a sailor, sexually molested by an uncle and pregnant at age 16.

By then, folks in the neighborhood were whispering that Davis was headed for the same hard life as the aunt who had reared her: selling herself to strangers. In a sense they were right—but in an entirely different way.

Nut graph

Now 34, Jackie Davis cruises the city in a police car—not just any cop but the most successful detective in New Orleans, this humid capital of good times and jazz that also happens to be one of the deadliest cities in the South, with 346 murders last year.

Backup for nut graph (comment from colleague)

"She was the best I ever saw at solving a murder case," said David Morales, her boss during her five-year stint in the homicide unit. "There was nobody close to her in the history of the homicide division."

More backup for nut graph

Davis solved 88 of her 90 murder cases—a record better than any other detective and all the

more impressive for the first black woman to join an elite corps of mostly white men who prodded her to fail.

Specifics: anecdotes

They destroyed her case reports, told tipsters she didn't work there, placed feces in her desk drawer, posted her mistakes on the bulletin board, and decorated her mailbox with a cartoon of a mop and bucket titled "black power."

Davis reacted by putting in longer hours. In solitary moments, exhausted, she would bow her head and sob.

"Every case that I got, I was looked at under a microscope: 'Well, what is she going to do now?'" Davis recalls matter-of-factly. "My biggest accomplishment, I consider, is not cracking under the pressure."

More backup for the "so what" factor

At a time when politicians have taken to bashing the poor for dragging on society, Davis stands out as a stunning example of someone who has succeeded precisely because of her harsh past. She is now the city's most celebrated officer—and the subject of a screenplay that has caught the eye of Whoopi Goldberg. . . .

In a life full of ironies and incongruities, Davis posed as a hooker, arresting so many men in the raucous French Quarter that 20 backup officers were assigned to her and her partner. But Davis' arrest rate so riled those in the tourist trade that her superiors had her wired to prove she wasn't entrapping men. Even so, business interest prevailed, and Davis was yanked off the street.

But not before she had nailed 300 johns.

"Having lived with a prostitute all my life, there are certain things you do, certain things you say," says Davis, chuckling over her record.

.

Christina Davis, 17, is a prep school senior with a B average who hopes to study engineering next year at Xavier University. It's Wednesday night in the blond-brick ranch home where she and her mother live with Gigi and Snoopy, their two dogs. Christina Davis is alone.

Her mother, like most officers in New Orleans, earns such a modest wage—$225 a week in take-home pay—that she has to work late-night security details for extra cash, stretching her workweek to 60 hours or more.

"I'm proud of her, but she had to sacrifice time with me and a lot of things we could have done together," Christina Davis says wistfully.

Losing days—and really, years—with her daughter is Jacklean Davis' greatest regret, she says one evening as she steers her unmarked Chevy through the bombed-out Desire housing project.

Her career started here 11 years ago, when she was the only woman street cop in the rough-and-ready urban squad, which worked the projects. . . .

A short woman with a stocky look about her, crimped hair combed into a tight ponytail, Davis always made it a point to later return to murder scenes in street clothes. It helped, she says, that she doesn't look like a cop: being a woman, looking young, using slang.

As she rolls through the broken streets, Davis says she worries about the good people in the projects who get ground down by the force of crime and neglect.

She could have been one of them.

Davis lost her father in a car accident when she was 3. Her bereaved mother squandered the insurance and had to give her children to an aunt.

As it turned out, Davis' grand-aunt was a prostitute who bedded down with sailors. But she was a protective, strong-willed woman with a heart of gold, Davis said.

Davis' aunt was married to a merchant marine. When he was home, little Jacklean lived in stifled terror. He was sexually molesting her. Her aunt didn't know until Jacklean was 14 and her uncle was dying of cancer.

Trauma set in again when Davis was raped at 12 by a sailor who visited her aunt. By 16, she was pregnant and people in her working-class black neighborhood were whispering that she had picked up her aunt's habits.

Davis' aunt died when she was 17, about the time she was about to give birth to Christina. But she still managed to graduate from high school, faltering when it came to college. A better life seemed always out of reach, she thought as she worked clearing tables at ritzy restaurants and driving a bus.

It all hit bottom one winter when Davis found herself homeless for a two-week stretch, huddled in her parked car with Christina, danger lurking all around.

"I knew this was it," she says. "There was no one else. I was on my own."

.

The idea to become a cop came to Jacklean Davis when she dated a rookie in the department. Problem was, when she took the exam, she flunked it—again and again and again.

It took Davis five tries to pass the test—and two to overcome her fear of guns and make it through the police academy. It was 1981 before she got her first job at the urban squad. . . .

Comment from colleague

"She puts her heart into everything," said Wayne Farve, an old partner. "I've seen her at shootings where she'll kneel down in the blood right next to them and ask them who did it and where she can get more information."

Anecdote

Back in the old neighborhood, Davis got out of her car one night, in front of her home, eight blocks from where she grew up.

"Sssssss," a man hissed, pointing a gun.

Davis froze. Here she was, holding two bags of groceries, her own gun in her handbag, in the car. She screamed, slowly stepping away, as he closed in.

Unable to reach her gun, Davis screamed louder—and the man fled.

Davis dumped her groceries, grabbed her gun and opened fire as she chased him. Then suddenly, he turned and fired back, hitting her in the leg.

As she recovered in a hospital, she took heart. No longer a frightened child, Jacklean Davis had fought back this time and won. A few months later, police caught the man. He had raped 14 women. Davis testified against him, helping to lock him away in Louisiana's dreaded Angola prison.

Return to present

All told, it may be the stuff of movies, Davis concedes. An agent is negotiating for her, and the latest news is that Goldberg is reading the screenplay of her life.

Quote kicker on future note

"I don't even like to think about it," she says, admitting superstition. "I don't want to put a mojo on me."

A Different Point of View

You are sent to the circus to interview the world's fattest man. How can you ask questions that might be insensitive? If you're David Finkel, you don't. You let the audience ask the questions. And then you write a profile, not only of the fat man, but of the audience as well. And you make the reader laugh, cry and feel ashamed for thinking of those questions.

In this unusual portrait, Finkel shows himself to be a master of tone—creating the mood of the piece. Note how the tone changes just before the nut graph, where Finkel tells you this is a profile of the "World's Biggest Man." Note also that Finkel uses very few adjectives.

But the piece is most unusual because Finkel masters a difficult technique of switching the point of view. First he lets you view the fat man as the audience does, through the second-person *(you)* point of view. At the same time you are viewing how the audience acts. Then he switches to the anonymous, third-person reporting role and lets the fat man describe himself.

This profile is a masterpiece for its use of the show-in-action technique and specific detail. Finkel is now a magazine writer at *The Washington Post*.

'Fat Albert' carves out an 891-pound niche

By David Finkel
St. Petersburg (Fla.) *Times*

COCOA (Fla.)—Behold the fat man. Go ahead. Everybody does. He doesn't mind, honestly. That's how he makes his living. Walk right up to him. Stand there and look. Stand there and stare. Gape at the layers of fat, the astonishing girth, the incredible bulk. Imagine him in a bathtub. Or better yet, on a bike. Or better yet, on one of those flimsy antique chairs. Boom! If you're lucky, maybe he'll lift his shirt. If you're real lucky, maybe he'll rub his belly. Don't be shy. Ask him a question.

"What's your name?"

"T.J. Albert Jackson. Better known as Fat Albert."

"How old are you?"

"Forty-three."

"How much do you weigh?"

"Eight hundred and ninety-one pounds."

"Gawd! How many meals you eat a day?"

"Three."

"What—three cows?"

Go ahead. Laugh. He won't mind. He'll even laugh with you, slapping his hand on his knee and chuckling so hard that his belly's shaking. You'll have to excuse him, though, if his eyes seem to cloud over, but truthfully, he's heard your joke before. About a thousand times before.

He knows the rule: you pay your dollar, you get a show. So go ahead. Ask one more question, the one that's on your mind.

"What's wrong with you?"

"Hormones," he says. "Pituitary gland. I was born with a birth defect."

Ah, the carnival life. T.J. Albert Jackson knows it well. Billed as "The World's Biggest Man," he's been doing this for 17 years now, ever since a promoter offered to make him the featured attraction in a show called "The Horrors of Drug Abuse." All he'd have to do, the promoter promised, was sit there with a snake around his neck, acting as if he was unable to speak, while the promoter intoned dramatically to the hushed and sickened audience, "Due to his delicate condition, we prefer that you not converse with him."

He turned that one down. But he did agree to a second suggestion that he simply sit there, looking big. And here he is, 17 years later.

"Hey, hey, hey," he rumbles, in imitation of the Fat Albert character created by Bill Cosby. "Hey, hey, hey."

This week, he's in Cocoa at the Brevard County Fair. Last week, it was Louisiana. He left there in the rain and drove straight through with his wife Carrie ("You're married!?!" people marvel) in his '71 Cadillac, the one with 73,000 miles on it and the heavy-duty shocks and the special front seat. Next week he hopes to be home on his 2½-acre spread in east Tampa, where he lives in a mobile home. "Double-wide," he says before you can ask.

It'll feel good to get home, he says. The season has been a long one, business has been down, a summer-long drive across Canada was brutal. Cocoa, though, should be an easy time. He's got a good spot near the heart of the midway, down the row from Fat Boy's Bar-B-Q, next to Flossie's Famous Funnel Cakes.

He arrived early in the day. With his wife at his side, he drove across the grass and mud, stopping directly in front of a narrow set of metal stairs leading to his booth. He got out of the car and stood up, no easy task. He made the torturous climb up the stairs, hoisting his stomach high enough to ride along the top of the hand rails. He sat, whooomph. And he was in business.

Outside, the curious began to gather. Carrie, seven months pregnant ("She's having a baby? His baby!?!") flipped a couple of switches. On came some lights illuminating a sign that says, "World's Biggest Man." On came a recorded announcement that would play over and over through an outside loudspeaker, repeating itself every 45 seconds, 90 times an hour, all night long. "Your attention! For the very first time at your fair, the world's biggest man! Recorded in Guinness' World Book of Records, Fat Albert weighs 891 pounds, is 6-foot 5-inches tall and has a 116-inch waistline. Unbelievable size! Unbelievable man! At his present rate of growth, doctors predict that he will soon weigh over one thousand pounds. He's here, he's real, and he's alive. For an unbelievable sight of a lifetime, you must see Fat Albert...."

Sitting in his seat, spread over a flattened couch cushion, Fat Albert does in fact seem enormous. He holds up a shoe, the

Pro-sports model by a company called King-Size. "Size 20 EEE," he says. He points to his shirt. "Size 96." He points to his pants. "I made them myself."

As if by rote, the fat facts come rolling forth.

Birth weight: 22 pounds.

Birth method: C-section.

Weight at age 5: 236 pounds.

At age 10: 337 pounds.

At 20: 800 pounds.

Now: 891 and climbing. That's more than twice as much as Sear's best refrigerator-freezer—a 26-cubic-footer with automatic ice and water dispensers on side-by-side doors. That's almost as much as a Steinway grand piano.

He weighs himself on scrap yard scales and at roadside weigh stations. He travels mostly by car, but sometimes by plane—when two first-class seats are available. He can walk up to 30 yards without resting. He eats three meals a day.

Favorite breakfast: two eggs, coffee, toast with strawberry jam. Lunch: two ham sandwiches, one slice of ham each. Dinner: Whatever. Maybe an Italian-sausage sandwich from a carnival booth. Maybe a salad.

"In a 24-hour period, I average maybe 2½ to 3 pounds of food," he says. "When I was young, I used to eat a lot—eight-egg omelets, with onions. But that was it. No breads or anything. See, it's not the food; it's hormones. They found when they took the food away, the growing didn't stop."

Most searing childhood memory: "I went to a carnival once, saw the big man and said, 'How can you do that?' I said,

'No way I'd ever let people gawk at me.' But things have a way of turning around. Now, here I am."

He was born in Mississippi. He says they wouldn't let him in school as a 5-year-old because he was too big. When he was 6, he moved to Philadelphia. When he was 14, he went with his father to England. Two years later, he was back in the United States, a 16-year-old weighing 600 pounds with no job prospects in sight.

He tried to wash cars. He tried to sell vacuum cleaners. He ran a little restaurant out of his house. He married, had four children, and got divorced. He became Fat Albert and began touring the country. He remembers the first day. "It made me feel like a king. Here I am, sitting in a chair, people are paying to see me. They're asking me the same questions they asked on the street, but now they're paying. I thought, 'My God, if only I had thought of this five or 10 years ago.' "

One day in 1979, he was in Baton Rouge when a 17-year-old girl came in, looked at him and said, "Are you Fat Albert?" It was Carrie.

He said, "Well, I'm not Pinocchio."

She said, "You don't have to get smart with me."

"It's just one of those 'true love' stories," he says now, thinking back to that moment. "She wasn't afraid of me."

They talked almost until the carnival closed. They exchanged phone numbers. She called him about 2 a.m., and they talked until dawn. That afternoon, she showed up with pork chops, rice

and gravy. She showed up the next day, and the next, and two weeks later, when the carnival left town, she was there for the ride, squeezed in beside him.

That was six years ago. Since then, she's learned a few things about people.

"They say, 'That's your husband?' I say, 'Yeah.' They say, 'Nah, that can't be your husband. He's just paying you to say that. That ain't true.' I say, 'It is.' They say, 'How do you handle this? Doesn't he squish you? What's the matter with you! You can't do no better than that?' I say, 'I don't care what people think of me. It's what I think of myself.' "

"My gentle giant," she calls him. Or "Fats."

"I like it when she calls me Fats," he says. "I like the way she says it."

They go everywhere together. While he sits, she sweeps up or takes tickets. On the road, he waits in the car while she makes sure their hotel room has a sturdy bed. Every night, she is there beside him, and when a customer gets overly abusive, she is there to defend him.

"When they call him a big, fat slob," she says proudly, "I say, 'You get away from here. He's not a slob.' "

Sometimes, she starts out after them. Fat Albert sees trouble coming and calls out to her to come back. "Carrie," he says, "it's okay."

She comes back.

He sits in silence. She leans on the railing and watches the people go past. On a busy night, it's a river out there. They come by holding food and stuffed animals. Some of them are drunk, some of them are on drugs. They stop and read the sign and are serenaded with the taped announcement: Over eight hundred and ninety-one pounds of living flesh. You must see him to believe him. . . .

They try to peek inside. "Hey Fatso," they yell. Or, "You big wobbly body." Or, "Fatty, fatty, two-by-four, couldn't fit in the kitchen door."

They pay their dollar and come in. They look at him. They shake their heads. They poke him. They gape in silence.

"Don't just stand there," he says. "Do something."

They do. They ask questions.

"You eat all the time?"

"Only when I'm hungry," he says.

"How do you ever get up?"

"I stand up."

"You're fat like a whale."

"You're skinny like a stick."

"How'd you get so fat?"

"Hormones."

"Why don't you go on a diet?"

"Everybody comes in here and says, 'Why don't you go on a diet?' They say, 'I got a brother-in-law who lost 150 pounds. I got a sister who weighed 300 pounds and now she's down to 179.' Do you realize how big I am? This is a disorder."

"You don't mind being this big?"

"I have no choice. If I had a choice, I wouldn't be this big."

"Isn't Florida too hot for you?"

"No, it's good for me to sweat. I only sweat from my brow. I don't sweat from my ankles or anything."

"You do this for a living?"

"Yes."

"You own a tux?"

"Yes."

"Do you eat a lot?"

"No."

"You got a girlfriend?"

"No, I got a wife. She's right there."

"You get any?"

"Yes."

"I'm sorry. I don't believe you weigh 800 pounds. I've seen people who weigh 400 pounds, and you don't look a pound more than them."

"Thank you."

"It's pillows, right?"

"It's pillows? Is this pillows?" He lifts up his shirt and shows there are no pillows. His chest hangs to his stomach. His stomach swells out like a great globe and hangs to his knees. "It's all me," he says.

The shirt comes down. The people leave. They walk down the steps, look back and say, "He's disgusting."

"I know what they say," Fat Albert says. "It's all right. You can call me a fat hog or a pig or a slob all day long. That won't hurt my feelings. I would be a pig if I let them bother me. I'm not a pig. I don't have to defend myself."

It has been this way for 17 years, he says, and it's not going to change.

In Louisiana, they call him "the human blimp."

In the Caribbean, "They're willing to give me $500 to stand up and take my pants off."

And on opening night in Cocoa, this: "Apparently, you're totally satisfied. You're not just satisfied, you're happy." The tone of the question is vehement, accusatory.

"Oh, I am happy," comes Fat Albert's sincere answer. "I'm overjoyed because God put me on this earth."

On it goes, all night long. It gets dark. The crowd thins. Flossie's Funnel Cakes prepares to close early. Then it rains, and the bugs come out, including dozens of mosquitoes that invade Fat Albert's booth.

What a meal they must see, huh?

But before the first one can begin feasting, The World's Biggest Man springs into action. He reaches to his left and rummages among the different bottles he keeps there. No, not the Listerine. No, not the Ban, or the eyedrops or the Vaseline. No, not the rubbing alcohol. Ah, there it is. The Raid Yard Guard.

He picks up the can and sprays. He sprays and sprays. He sprays until all the mosquitoes drop.

He has sprayed too much, though. The air is so thick with Yard Guard that it becomes impossible to breathe. Carrie, close to choking, heads outside toward the lights of the midway and inhales.

Fat Albert, of course, stays put.

Snapshot Profiles

Julie Sullivan doesn't waste words. She writes snapshot profiles that let the reader see, hear and care about the character—quickly. Her skill earned her the Best Newspaper Writing Award from the American Society of Newspaper Editors in 1991 for a new category—short news writing. The award was based on profiles she wrote for *The Spokesman-Review* (Spokane, Wash.). They average eight inches, less than 400 words. But she reveals a lifetime in her profiles.

Her method: short sentences, few adjectives, few quotes, many details.

She began writing at a weekly newspaper in Alaska after she graduated from the University of Montana in 1985. "I started out leaning toward brevity," she said. "My first editor in Alaska would always tell me, every time you finish a story, go back over it. Figure out what words are extraneous. What can you leave out?"

She takes voluminous notes but discards about half of them. "I write everything down. I don't trust my memory," she says. That includes her observations. A cracked cement step. An automobile battery under the sink. Cockroaches scurrying across the kitchen table. A toothless smile.

Julie Sullivan, reporter

Courtesy of *The Spokesman-Review,*
Spokane, WA

How does she know which details to include in her stories? "I write what I remember without looking at my notes. What details stand out. Like Joe Peak's teeth were so significant and personal. The contrast struck me. His place was so neat that I couldn't figure out how somebody who paid so much attention to his surroundings wouldn't take the same care personally. Then I found out how he lost his teeth."

She is equally selective about the limited quotes she includes. "I really think readers glaze over quotes," she says. "I do few quotes because I think most people are pretty plain-spoken and simple. You don't need to use it just because it's in quotes."

Her tips for writing briefly: "Trust your instincts about what is important, what struck you during the interview. The rest is chaff. I generally bounce my lead and the most important details off my co-workers, and I can gauge from their reactions if I'm on the right track." That's the basic tell-it-to-a-friend technique.

She also stresses observation. "Pay attention to details, from the right spelling of names to finding out the date of people's birthdays."

On leads and kickers: "I tend to think readers read the beginning and the end. Never discount the lead you were throwing out. It could be a great kicker."

On structure: "You try to make a point with every paragraph."

On brevity: "Short has its place, but it won't replace more in-depth pieces; that's what a newspaper does best. I hope to continue to do both."

The two profiles that follow were part of a series about the problems of low-income residents in a deteriorating Spokane apartment building, the Merlin.

The second example about Orval Aldrich contains a racist term. "I thought about it and then realized it was too rich a detail to delete," Sullivan said. "The racism made me uncomfortable. How sad for someone to carry that around, especially since the only person who cared about him was a black woman. But in profiles, it's real easy to make people two-dimensional—the good guys and the bad guys. I tried not to succumb to that. I went in without a lot of preconceived ideas about the people in this series. They emerged as humans."

See if you agree. Notice the details—not just a watch, but a Seiko; not just a car but a 1977 Ford. And notice the strong factual kickers. As you read these profiles, consider what information came from observations and what came from questions. And then decide how you could say it all in as few words.

It took twice as many words to describe Sullivan's style as she used in these stories.

Donald 'Joe' Peak

Joe Peak's smile has no teeth.

His dentures were stolen at the Norman Hotel, the last place he lived in downtown Spokane before moving to the Merlin two years ago.

Gumming food and fighting diabetes have shrunk the 54-year-old man's frame by 80 pounds. He is thin and weak and his mouth is sore.

But that doesn't stop him from frying hamburgers and onions for a friend at midnight or keeping an extra bed made up permanently in his two-room place.

"I try to make a little nest here for myself," he says.

Chock-full of furniture and cups from the 32-ounce Cokes he relishes for 53 cents apiece, Peaks' second floor apartment is almost cozy.

A good rug covers holes in the kitchen floor, clean-looking blankets cover a clean-looking bed. Dishes are stacked neatly in the kitchen sink.

But cockroaches still scurry across his kitchen table.

"I live with them," he says with a shrug. "I can't afford the insecticides, pesticides, germicides. I don't have the money."

With a $500 per month welfare check and a $175 rent payment, Peak follows a proper diet when he can afford it. He shops at nearby convenience stores where he knows prices are higher but the distance is right. He has adapted to the noisy nightlife in the hallways and sleeps when he is too exhausted to hear it.

Part Seminole Indian, Chinese and black, the Florida native moved to Spokane 20 years ago to be near relatives in Olympia. He quit school at 13 to help earn the family income and worked a string of blue-collar jobs. Along the way, someone started calling him Joe.

His voice is lyrical, his vocabulary huge, but Peaks' experience with whites is long and bitter.

When conditions at the Merlin began worsening three months ago, junkies and gray mice the size of baby rats moved in next door. He hated to see it, but he isn't worried about being homeless.

He's worried about his diabetes. He's frightened by blood in his stool and sores on his gums. He wonders whether the white-staffed hospitals on the hill above him will treat a poor black man with no teeth.

Julie Sullivan, *The Spokesman-Review*

Orval Aldrich

They call him the Jockey.

At 82, he is bent from too many spills from a saddle and too many ex-wives to name. But it's the stress of his home that is breaking Orval Aldrich.

He moved into the Merlin 12 years ago to be close to his friends, who shared a passion for horse racing, cards and "chewing the bull."

There was ample parking for his 1977 Ford. A dozen residents shared meals and long summer evenings together in the place they knew was rundown, but still livable.

"We had a pretty good bunch in here," he says.

Now Aldrich's friends have moved to quieter, safer apartment buildings. The friendly faces have been replaced by ones he doesn't recognize or trust.

And the Ford's battery is under the sink in his room so thieves won't steal it.

Born in Liverpool, England, Aldrich worked as a jockey and construction boilermaker in jobs that took him from the Space Needle in Seattle to refineries in eastern Montana.

He'll tell you he had six wives and show you pictures of two children, six grandkids and one great-grandchild, a pale blond beauty whose photo hangs in Room 8.

His gray room also has a stained sink on one wall and a gas stove on another surrounded by wisps of ash. Roach bombs must be set off every week.

The electricity is sometimes shut off for hours, and there are interruptions in water service. Rent has risen from $50 to $100 since 1985.

The black residents bother

him. He is afraid of them and calls them "niggers," though the woman who reminds him to take his medicine and calms him is black.

Lately, Aldrich's eyesight has begun failing. It takes two trembling hands to bring a small glass of beer to his lips. His family in Montana would like him to move, but he makes his own decisions, thank you.

The day the drug addict stole his watch and stuck a needle in her arm at his kitchen table, Aldrich sat stiffly on the crusty blankets of his bed.

"I'll get it back, you watch and see," he fumed later.

He did. The $50 Seiko was returned without explanation Thursday morning.

That night, they stole his food stamps.

Julie Sullivan, *The Spokesman-Review*

Campus Vignettes

Here are some examples of vignettes written by journalism students who were following Julie Sullivan's style. The assignment was to find people behind the scenes on the campus of the University of Kansas. Students were instructed to write profiles filled with revealing details in fewer than 500 words—about one to one and a half double-spaced typewritten pages. They were also told to stress show-in-action techniques. The frame was the university at work.

Journalism school librarian

Yvonne Martinez has carefully picked out her wardrobe.

Dressed in a navy blue skirt patterned with white boxes and a white blouse with the same pattern in blue, she had come prepared for another day of work at the School of Journalism library.

However, her outfit would not be complete without her size 6½ sneakers.

The 4-foot-11 librarian does not wear them simply because they help maintain a quiet atmosphere. That is just one of the added benefits.

She wears them because she is constantly on the move.

Whether it's searching for a student's request for the last two

years' worth of *Folio* magazine or sorting through the seemingly endless stack of newspapers the library receives daily, she rarely has time to sit down.

Recent cuts in the library's budget and staff have increased Martinez's work load. The sneakers are crucial.

"I'd rather be comfortable than in pain," she said.

Her duties have grown during

the two years she has been working behind the counter. But now her duties include repairing the copy machine.

It is the only copy machine the library can afford on its budget, Martinez said. Overuse causes it to break down at least once a day.

As she returns to the counter, she immediately is greeted by a professor who says the machine is out of ink. She reaches under the counter and pulls out a bottle of black ink.

As she pours, the bottle slips and ink covers her hands. More students who need to be helped arrive at the counter.

Martinez stands by the machine staring at her hands as if she were auditioning for the part of Lady Macbeth. She sighs and runs off to the restroom. She quickly returns to the counter and apologizes to the students.

After all, she is the only librarian on duty.

Ranjit Arab, *The University Daily Kansan*

Bus driver

The sounds of a screaming Mick Jagger shake the windows of the bus.

A basket of Jolly Rancher's candies sits on the dashboard. And the driver in the blue and white Rolling Stones baseball cap is smiling.

This is Hank's bus—slap him a high five on the way off, please.

Hank Jones, who is in the middle of his fifth year as a (University of Kansas) bus driver, likes doing something extra for his passengers.

"Why shouldn't I," he says. "A little extra effort can go a long way."

One passenger remembers Hank stopping his bus on Jayhawk Boulevard last Valentine's Day just to give her a candy heart. She's been a regular ever since.

Hank began driving those green and white buses when he needed some extra money and he enjoyed it so much, he stayed with it.

The students are the best part of the job, but Hank is not without his complaints.

"They're not too quick sometimes," he says. "But they're good kids, most of them."

He tries to keep it interesting—he never plays the same tape twice in one day on his portable Sony stereo.

"I'm always partial to the Stones," he says, cracking open his pack of Marlboro cigarettes. "But I'll play requests, too."

Hank plans to keep driving for KU as long as he still enjoys it—or until he finds a wife. At 34, he hasn't found the right woman yet.

But he's in no hurry.

"Who knows?" he says. "Maybe someone will get on my bus."

Kathy Hill

Flag raiser

Virginia Boyd is afraid of heights.

However, she does part of her job on top of Fraser Hall, one of the highest points on campus at the University of Kansas.

Boyd, an employee of the University's housekeeping staff, raises the flags on Fraser Hall each morning at 7 o'clock, where they fly nine stories above the ground.

After taking the elevator to the seventh floor, she climbs two flights of stairs before ascending two more 16-stair spiral staircases where the flag turrets are located. Climbing to the roof of the building is no easy task for her 51-year-old legs, she says.

"Kinda spooky, isn't it?" she says, wrinkling her freckled nose and gripping rickety wooden staircase railings covered with bird droppings.

She peers through the gratings over the vents in Fraser's turret and points to a trap door in the roof of the building.

"I used to peek out of there, just to see what it was like," she says.

Wind swirls around the tiny turret and Boyd looks up at the flagpole that sticks through the opening at the top.

"If the cord is whipping against that pole, it's too windy to put the flags up," she says.

She gently fingers the limp American flag attached to the cord at the bottom of the pole.

"As soon as it goes through that hole, it just gets sucked up," she says.

Boyd has only been on flag duty in Fraser Hall for about three weeks; she previously worked in the Art and Design building for two years.

She's thankful that she's only had to put the flags up three or four times since she has been working in Fraser.

"My knees just can't take this," she says, "so one of those young guys is going to take over."

Michelle Betts

Activities

1 Write a profile about a newsworthy person on your campus or in your community.

2 Write a short profile about someone on your campus, using Julie Sullivan's style. Plan it as a vignette, considering it part of a package or a larger subject so it has a frame of reference.

3 Plan a celebrity profile of someone you would like to interview. If you enjoy sports, plan a profile of an athlete on your campus. Use Alan Richman's tips and plan an interesting question you would use to begin the interview, as well as a preliminary theme you might pursue.

4 Coach a classmate on writing a profile. Ask your classmate some of the basic coaching questions: What's it about? What is the focus? Do you have a theme? Were there any patterns, any turning points? What anecdotes do you remember as most interesting? What is the point—why should the reader care? What order are you considering? As the writer discusses the profile, you as the coach can ask questions that occur to you.

COACHING

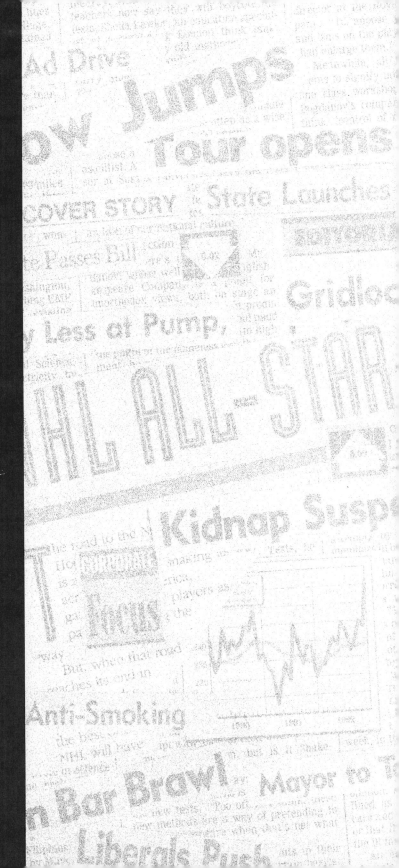

TIPS

Identify your focus; it is crucial in a feature story, which could have many different angles.

Look for a theme to unify the story, especially in sports stories and general features.

Try writing the first draft without looking at your notes. The most memorable details and information should emerge. Then plug in quotes and specifics.

Translate jargon.

When writing for specialty beats, gear stories to the average reader, not to sources who understand the field.

Features and Specialty Stories

26

Mary Ann Lickteig is strolling from one booth to another at the Iowa State Fair. A pitchman is hawking a Robo-Cut slicing machine. Space-age plastic, he bellows. Lickteig laughs. Great angle for a story, she thinks.

Backstage at the pageant to choose the state fair queen, 77 girls are primping and practicing to compete for the crown. Lickteig decides that will be a good angle for another story.

Now it is midnight. The fairgoers have gone home. Lickteig has not. In the center of the midway, a Catholic priest is baptizing four children. Lickteig listens. She can hear pool balls cracking in the background, where carnival workers may be playing.

The next day, *Des Moines* (Iowa) *Register* readers will hear them, too, when Lickteig writes about the baptism and describes the empty paths in the midway—quiet "except for the hum of a giant generator and the occasional crack of pool balls." Or when she describes these sights and smells in this excerpt from a story advancing the fair:

> The day before the fair opened to the public, hot dogs spit as they turned on roasters; tattooed midway workers smeared with grease hauled pieces of steel out of the back of trucks and turned them into carnival rides; brand new pig feeders stood waiting to be admired under a sign that pronounced them non-rusting, non-caking and non-corrosive.
>
> Odors emanating from the horse barn indicated the 1990 exhibits had arrived.
>
> Mary Ann Lickteig, *The Des Moines Register*

The difference between journalism and literature is that journalism is unreadable and literature is not read.

Oscar Wilde

Lickteig, a feature writer for *The Register,* finds the extraordinary in ordinary stories, from state fairs to a local hypnotist who received a national award:

You will read this story.

You will hang on its every word, and you will not get sleepy.

As you proceed, you will learn about hypnosis and a Clive hypnotherapist whose work has led her to the International Hypnosis Hall of Fame.

You are ready to begin. Shari Patton is sitting on the couch in her home telling you that she first went for hypnosis "like a doubting Thomas." She was a student at the University of Minnesota when a friend was going to be hypnotized and wanted Patton to come along. Listen, now to what she has to say:

"My friend had said, 'Go with me.' And I had said no, and after several requests begging me, I said 'All right. I'll go.' And I went to stop smoking, not believing that it would work, but very much wanting to stop smoking, and I was so amazed and delighted that it worked for me that I went back and started using hypnosis for weight control and lost 90 pounds."

That's how she got started.

Mary Ann Lickteig, *The Des Moines Register*

These are the kinds of stories that you probably will do when you get started at a newspaper. Even with more than five years of experience, Lickteig says she still loves writing features about the state fair and other routine kinds of stories. Because of her skill in finding special angles, she is also writing a column as a roving reporter focusing on offbeat tales about people and places in the Des Moines area.

The key to good feature writing, Lickteig says, is gathering good details and then selecting the ones that will work in your story. "You want people to be able to see your story," she says. "Choose the details that stick out in your mind, the ones you remember when you run back to the office and tell somebody what you've found."

Lickteig always looks for a good angle or theme for her features. Just as in profiles, the focus is the reason for the story, which should be stated in a nut graph, but the theme is a literary device of an angle or unifying approach.

The tone of a story can also be used as a theme, Lickteig says. For example, the focus or nut graph of the story about the hypnotherapist was that she had been inducted into the International Hypnosis Hall of Fame—the reason for the story. But the unifying theme was the stylistic tone of writing, as though the reader were being hypnotized.

"You hope the theme will present itself," Lickteig says. "Usually, if you see something that fascinates you, it probably will fascinate the readers."

That's one way to find the theme—or just an idea for a story, she says. "I don't think about covering the whole Iowa State Fair. You need to break it down—show the fair through one family, one idea, one theme."

Feature Stories

That is also a good way to define a feature. By dictionary definition, *to feature* means "to give special prominence to"—in other words, to focus on one aspect of an issue and give that special attention.

One example is the winner of the 1991 Pulitzer Prize for feature writing, a story by Sheryl James. Her newspaper wanted to explore why newborn babies were being abandoned. But James did not write a story telling readers everything they needed to know about the subject. Her approach was stated in the introduction to the series:

An alarming number of newborns are being abandoned in the Tampa Bay area. Some have died, discarded in Dumpsters. Others have been wrapped in towels and left for someone to find. Why is this happening? In this four-day series of articles, we focus on one mother who abandoned her baby. As this case shows, there are no clear-cut explanations, there are only observations, theories and, very often, regret.

Sheryl James, *St. Petersburg* (Fla.) *Times*

That is only one approach to a feature. The newspaper also might have written a story about the broader issue and used a different angle.

The Wall Street Journal publishes a feature almost every day about a broad issue, such as the hazards of farming (see Chapter 12). The features often follow a formula approach, leading with an anecdote or description about one person who exemplifies the broader issue. The key is that the feature must have a nut graph to explain the focus.

Features are sometimes defined as stories that have timeless qualities, meaning that unlike news stories, they are not pegged to immediate events. However, that is a misleading definition. Many features are stories geared to news events or are sidebars that focus on an aspect of breaking news.

Features generally treat one of four topics (the "P-principle"): people, places, programs, problems. They can also be classified by type:

News feature: Feature-style writing can be used to tell stories focusing on people affected by a news event, advance stories about a court trial, reaction stories to a news event or stories about a new program or service.

Consumer feature: Many feature stories tell how people can cope with a problem or give helpful information about products and issues. Some program stories fit this category, and so do many stories in the features section of the newspaper—often called the lifestyle section. Stories about parenting, health, entertainment and trends in lifestyles can be considered in a broad category of news you can use.

Profile: Features are often about people in the news, people of interest in the community, celebrities or people with unusual accomplishments—good and bad (as in profiles about criminal suspects).

Issue feature: Many stories about problems in the community—such as child abuse, drunken driving, pollution and other topics of concern—may be written as feature stories.

Slice-of-life feature: Features about a place, a community or some way of life within a community give a mood or sense of the place.

Organization

If you have mastered the techniques introduced in Chapters 12 and 13, you already have learned how to write features. However, features can be more difficult to organize than hard-news stories, because the order can be so flexible.

As with other kinds of stories, first you need to find your focus. Then, when you map out the order for your story, you need to consider the topics and supporting points. You have many options for organizing them, singly or in combination: time sequence, point of view, partial or total chronological order.

William Blundell, who has spent years writing features about issues and profiles for *The Wall Street Journal,* suggests in his book *The Art and Craft of Feature Writing* that features should be organized around "The Laws of Progressive Reader Involvement":

Stage One: Tease me, you devil. [Give the reader a reason to continue reading.]

Stage Two: Tell me what you're up to. [What is the story really about?]

Stage Three: Oh yeah? Prove what you said. [Include the evidence to support your theme.]

Stage Four: Help me remember it. [Make it clear and forceful, and give it a memorable ending.]

Blundell also says features should include the following elements, but not necessarily in this order:

Focus: What is the central theme?

Lead and nut graph: What is the point of the story? (Often it is introduced anecdotally or descriptively.)

History: How did the problem develop?

Scope: How widespread is the development?

Reasons: Why is this problem or conflict happening now?

Impacts: Who is affected and how?

Moves and countermoves: Who is acting to promote or oppose the development, and what are they doing?

Future: What could happen as a result of the situation and developments?

Blundell's organization is not always so rigid as suggested by the list. If the material lends itself to narrative storytelling, it can be told in chronological order or natural story development order. Blundell also suggests blocking material from any one source in one place in the story, especially if the story has many sources—which is basically the kiss-off technique.

Storytelling Techniques

Many of the storytelling techniques you have studied can be used in feature stories. Although they do not have the directness of the hard-news approach, the focus and the impact are still clear.

Descriptive Good feature writers rely heavily on description through detail and the show-in-action technique, as does the writer of this story. It first appeared in the campus newspaper of California State University, Long Beach. It won first place in the William Randolph Hearst Foundation contest for college journalism.

TIJUANA, Mexico—Shivering in the mud under a 2-foot high chaparral, Jose carefully lifts his head into the cold night mist to monitor the movements of the U.S. Border Patrol.

On a ridge above a small ravine, patrol trucks scurry back and forth while a helicopter above provides the only light, turning spots of the nighttime terrain into day.

In the distance, guard dogs growl, bark and yelp.

At one point a patrol truck speeds toward Jose and his group of six Mexican farm laborers. Squatting in the brush, they quickly slide flat into the mud like reptiles seeking shelter.

Within seconds the helicopter hovers above them as its search light passes nearby, then at once directly over them. All their faces are turned downward to avoid detection by the brightness of the light that illuminates every detail of the soil, roots and insects that lie inches under them.

Soon, the truck and helicopter make a slow retreat. Jose and his group, safe for the moment, will remain motionless in that same muddy spot for the next three hours as the mist turns to rain and then rain turns back to mist.

To those who have never passed this way before, the sights and sounds are of another world. But to the expert scouts called "coyotes," this alien land between Mexico and the United States is home.

Every weekday evening, approximately 2,000 people attempt to illegally cross the border from Mexico to the United States. On weekends the numbers can climb to between 5,000 and 10,000, said Victor Clark, director of the Binational Center for Human Rights in Tijuana, Mexico.

Nut graph

Brett C. Sporich, *Daily Forty Niner*

Anecdotal   Feature writers also rely on the use of anecdotes in leads and the middle of their stories. This feature story, about a support group, uses the anecdotal approach with a shock-teaser/then-and-now contrast lead:

Kay Cyr was deeply disappointed when she came back to life.

Floating above her two-story apartment building, staring at the lifeless body—her lifeless body—lying in the snow, she felt at peace for the first time. A brilliant pulsating light surrounded her. She remembers warmth and love.

Then a presence entered her; it ordered her to return to her body, told her it was her job to stay alive.

She argued. She fought. She didn't want to return.

Suddenly she found herself being transported to the hospital, her mother at her side. The doctor marveled that she was still alive.

She was 7.

Today, 47 years later, her death remains the most profound experience of her life.

"I died immediately," Cyr said recently, recalling with clarity the 1943 sledding accident in which she slammed head-first into a concrete bench. "I came out of my body and was up above floating and could see myself in a snow suit attached to the bench. I don't know how long I was up there.

"A great big arc of light came over me. It told me the body was mine to take care of, to grow and change and stay in that body. When I came back I was in a rage. When I looked around me I didn't like anything I saw. I didn't see why I had to be here. I liked it better where I was."

Cyr does not really know where she was. But her reaction to returning, as she had learned by working with others who have had near-death experiences, is not unusual. A member of the Delaware Valley chapter of the International Association of Near Death Studies, she earlier this month began a support group for people who have had NDEs, as they call them.

Nut graph

Ralph Vigoda, *The Philadelphia Inquirer*

Narrative   If the story is compelling, you could use the narrative style, reconstructing the events as though the reader were witnessing the action. It is a very effective technique for feature stories. Here are excerpts from the beginning of a story for which the writer won a Pulitzer Prize in 1990:

She would have to allow extra driving time because of the fog.

A heavy gray veil had enveloped Grinnell overnight, and Nancy Ziegenmeyer—always methodical, always in control—decided to leave home early for her 7:30 a.m. appointment at Grand View College in Des Moines.

It was Nov. 19, 1988, a day Ziegenmeyer had awaited eagerly, because she knew that whatever happened during those morning hours in Des Moines would determine her future. If she passed the state real-estate licensing exam that Saturday morning, she would begin a new career. If she failed the test, she would continue the child-care service she provided in her home.

At 6 a.m. Ziegenmeyer unlocked the door of her 1988 Pontiac Grand Am and tossed her long denim jacket in the back seat. The weather was mild for mid-November, and her Gloria Vanderbilt denim jumper, red turtleneck sweater and red wool tights would keep her warm enough without a coat.

The fog lifted as Ziegenmeyer drove west on Interstate Highway 80 and she made good time after all. The digital clock on the dashboard read 7:05 as she pulled into a parking lot near Grand View's Science Building. She had 25 minutes to sit in the car and review her notes before test time.

Suddenly the driver's door opened. She turned to see a man, probably in his late 20s, wearing a navy pin-striped suit. He smelled of alcohol.

"Move over," the man ordered, grabbing her neck. She instinctively reached up to scratch him, but he was stronger than she was. He pushed a white dish towel into her face and shoved her into the front passenger seat, reclining it to a nearly horizontal position. Then he took her denim jacket from the back seat and covered her head.

He wasn't going to hurt her, the man said; he wanted money. She reached toward the console for the only cash she had with her—$3 or $4—and gave it to him. He slid the driver's seat back to make room for his long legs, started the car and drove out of the parking lot.

"Is this guy going to kill me?" Ziegenmeyer wondered. "Is he going to rape me? Does he just want my money? Does he want my car?" She thought about her three children—ages 4, 5, and 7—and realized she might never see them again.

Jane Schorer, *The Des Moines Register*

Tone and Mood

Many features lend themselves to a special mood or tone. News stories usually have an objective tone. But if you are trying to portray a feeling about a place or situation, you should use examples and words that convey sadness, joy, irony or some other appropriate mood. You don't need to tell the reader the mood of the place was festive or mournful. You can show it by the images you select for your story.

Another more unusual way of creating tone is by your writing style. In Lickteig's story about the hypnotherapist, she creates a light-hearted tone throughout the story by writing it as though the reader were undergoing hypnosis.

Saul Pett, who wrote the following example, used vivid detail to convey the nation's sad mood after the assassination of President John F. Kennedy on Nov. 22, 1963. He wrote this unusual feature emulating Biblical style, which contributes to the reverent tone of the story. It is a story that breaks rules: The sentences are long, the writer uses the first-person *we,* and there is no attempt at objectivity. Yet it is one of the great features of the 20th century. This is descriptive writing through details, but the story contains no traditional-style quotes. Here is an excerpt describing the four days after Kennedy was shot:

And the word went out from that time and place and cut the heart of a nation. In streets and offices and homes and stores, in lunchrooms and showrooms and schoolrooms and board rooms, on highways and prairies and beaches and mountaintops, in endless places crowded and sparse, near and far, white and black, Republican and Democrat, management and labor, the word went out and cut the heart of a nation.

And husbands called wives and wives called friends and teachers told students and motorists stopped to listen on car radios and stranger told stranger. Oh, no! we cried from hearts stopped by shock, from minds fighting the word, but the word came roaring back, true, true, true, and disbelief dissolved in tears.

Incredibly, in a time of great numbers, in a time of repeated reminders that millions would die in a nuclear war, in a time when experts feared we were being numbed by numbers and immunized against tragedy, the death of a single man crowded into our souls and flooded our hearts and filled all the paths of our lives.

A great shadow fell on the land and the farmer summoned to the house did not find the will to return to the field, nor the secretary to the typewriter, nor the machinist to the lathe.

There was a great slowing down and a great stopping and the big bronze gong sounded as a man shouted the market is closed and the New York Stock Exchange stopped, just stopped. The Boston Symphony Orchestra stopped a Handel concerto and started a Beethoven funeral march and the Canadian House of Commons stopped and a dramatic play in Berlin stopped and the United Nations in New York stopped and Congress and courts and schools and race tracks stopped, just stopped. And football games were canceled and theaters were closed and in Dallas a nightclub called the Carousel was closed by a mourner named Jack Ruby.

In Washington, along Pennsylvania Avenue, they had waited all that Friday night outside the iron picket fence, their eyes scarcely leaving the lovely old house. Early in the morning the guards had kept them moving and so they walked slowly down the street, eyes right, and at the corner they turned and came back on the street side of the sidewalk, eyes left. They looked like a strange silent group of mournful pickets demonstrating love, not protest.

In the chill darkness before dawn they were still there, now motionless, standing, staring across the broad lawn and through the bare elms at the house, at the softly lighted windows in the family quarters, at the black crepe lately hung over the door under the north portico.

They saw the blinking red lights of the police cars up Pennsylvania Avenue and they knew this was the moment. The president was coming home. No sirens, no police whistles, no barking of orders that usually accompanied his return. At 4:22 a.m., Saturday, Nov. 23, 1963, there seemed to be no sound on the street or in the land.

The gray Navy ambulance and the six black cars behind it paused at the northwest gate and turned in. And along the fence, men removed their hats and teen-agers removed their hands from the pockets of their jeans and women tightened their fingers around the pickets of the fence. Tears stained their faces, their young and their old faces, their white and their black faces.

At the gate the procession was met by a squad of Marines and led in along the gracefully curving drive between the elms. In days to come there would be larger and more majestic processions, but none so slow, none so geared to the rhythm of tears, as the cadence of the Marines this Saturday morning. In two straight lines, glistening bayoneted rifles held across their chests at port arms, they marched oh so slowly up the drive and all that could be heard was the sound of their shoes sliding on the macadam.

Under the portico, under the handsome hanging lantern, they stopped and divided and lined up with the soldiers and sailors and airmen on the sides of the steps, at the stiffest, straightest attention of their lives. Jacqueline Kennedy emerged first from the ambulance, still wearing the same pink suit stained through eternity the afternoon before.

With her husband's brother, the attorney general of the United States, with his other brother, the youngest member of the United States Senate, with his sisters and his friends and aides whom he had led to this house, this far and now no farther, Jacqueline Kennedy waited in motionless silence while the flag-covered casket was removed from the ambulance. Then she and they turned in behind it and walked up the steps and through the glass doors and into the lobby and down the long corridor lined with stiff, silent men in uniform and finally came to a stop in the East Room.

There the casket was laid gently onto the black catafalque that held Mr. Lincoln on another dark incredible night almost 100 years ago. There, the kneeling priests began praying as they and others would through the long day and night by the flickering light of the candles which silhouetted the honor guard riveted to the floor.

It was now 10 o'clock in the morning of a Saturday and Jacqueline Kennedy, still sleepless, returned to the silent East Room. She kissed her husband for the last time and the casket was sealed. A few moments later, she returned with her children and spoke to them quietly, trying to tell them something of the fact and the meaning of death. A fact and a meaning for which millions groped that day.

Saul Pett, The Associated Press

Specialty Beats

The subject of a story may change, but the techniques of writing it stay the same. Whether it is about sports, medicine, education, business or religion, writers use either hard-news explanatory style or feature style with descriptive, anecdotal or narrative techniques. The challenge for writers on specialized subjects is to make them clear and define the jargon, so the average reader can understand the story.

Medical and Environmental Writing

Jonathan Bor, a medical writer for *The* (Baltimore) *Sun,* says he covered crime, courts, politics and education before writing medical stories. "I learned how to convert the blather of educators, bureaucrats and cops into plain English before tackling doctor-speak," he says in an article in *Coaches' Corner,* a publication devoted to techniques of coaching writers. "And I learned to look first for stories about real people. I believe the hallmark of good medical writing is clear, colorful prose that takes the lay reader inside a world whose inhabitants—doctors, scientists and insurers—speak a secret language."

Good medical writing, in many ways, is simply good reporting and writing, Bor says. "It is thoroughly researched. It is written cleanly, and when possible, with a human touch. Bad medical writing, among other things, is written for insiders."

Here is an excerpt from a story Bor wrote about a heart transplant operation. With this story he won a Best Newspaper Writing Award for deadline writing from the American Society of Newspaper Editors. He witnessed the operation and wrote the story on deadline after going without sleep for 48 hours. He used the basic techniques of descriptive writing: show in action and details. Note how clearly he explains a complex procedure.

A healthy 17-year-old heart pumped the gift of life through 34-year-old Bruce Murray Friday, following a four-hour transplant operation that doctors said went without a hitch. . . .

The team—consisting of a surgeon, a physician's assistant and a nurse—removed the donor's heart at about 1:30 p.m. They placed it inside a plastic bag filled with an iced-saline solution, and they laced that bag inside three outer bags. The package was placed inside a blue beer cooler that bore the stamp "Transplant."

By the time their jet landed at Teterboro at 3 a.m., Murray was in the operating room where he was being prepped for surgery. Anesthesia put the patient into a deep sleep. A respirator breathed air into Murray's lungs via a tube inserted in his throat. Doctors cut a slit the length of Murray's chest. As many as a dozen doctors, nurses and technical assistants hovered over the patient, passing instruments, attending to heart monitors and swabbing the patient's bleeding chest.

Meanwhile, a state police escort ensured swift passage from Teterboro, over the George Washington Bridge and to the hospital for the vehicle carrying the transplant team and beer cooler. Within 10 minutes after landing, the transplant team was rushing the beer cooler through the hospital emergency room and up an elevator 18 floors.

By the time the heart arrived in the operating room, Murray's chest was wide open. Doctors had used a power saw to cut through his sternum, and a clamp-like retractor spread his chest apart. Murray's diseased heart, about half-again larger than normal, was fluttering inside the exposed chest cavity.

Surgeons swiftly turned the task of pumping blood over to the heart-lung machine. Their hands moving with quick deliberation, surgeons inserted tubes inside the heart's major blood vessels and severed the vessels from the heart.

The tangle of tubes carried the blood to a cylinder that supplied it with oxygen. From there, the blood traveled to a large console, which performs the job of the heart. Three spinning disks pumped the blood through the clear, plastic tubes back to the patient's body.

In one careful, spectacular moment, the surgical team made the exchange.

At 4:33 a.m., doctors lifted the diseased heart—milky but purple—out of Murray's chest cavity and handed it to attendants. They, in turn, placed it in the steel bowl. On a platform at the foot of the operating table, the spent heart rested for the duration. . . .

The beer cooler was opened, and the donor heart was placed inside the patient's chest. The new heart, about as large as a relaxed fist, was attached to the blood vessels.

It jerked and fluttered and became Bruce Murray's.

Jonathan Bor, *The* (Syracuse, N.Y.) *Post-Standard*

Bor offers these tips for medical writers:

• Challenge the source to speak to laymen. If that fails, allow the scientist to speak his language, but constantly challenge him with your version of the facts—"Are you saying that . . . ?"

• Never forget to ask your source the cosmic questions. What does the new treatment mean for the AIDS sufferer? Will this prolong life for days, months or more? Will the patient live longer but just as miserably, or what? Does a new medical finding represent an incremental advance or a true "breakthrough" that will change the lives of many people?

• Don't forget to give your story a sense of true proportion. If health inspectors have closed down an inner-city nursing home because of rodent infestation, it doesn't hurt to say that inspectors observed mice chewing on patients' feeding tubes and lapping the IV fluids that oozed out. If it's that bad, say it and say it vividly. Reporters need to say, however, whether the horror was an isolated finding or a condition observed throughout the nursing home.

• Anecdotes can be wonderful or tedious. At best, they bring to life the suffering of the afflicted, the benefits of new treatments or the breadth and social costs of an epidemic. At their worst, they turn a story into a tear-jerking soap opera worthy of a tacky TV-movie.

When do anecdotes work? Perhaps they work when they vividly show the human side—the joy and suffering—of an issue. They also show the practical dimensions of a problem better than some doctor or bureaucrat spouting generalities.

- Metaphors can be nice, but they also can trivialize. I don't like stories that describe antibodies as little foot-soldiers engaged in hand-to-hand combat with disease-carrying bugs. I have seen this. Lacking something less trivial, I'd state the obvious: antibodies are substances produced by the body to fight infection.

These suggestions can be applied to stories from other specialty beats as well. All beats have a jargon, whether they be court, sports or business beats. The writer's task is to make that information clear to people who are unfamiliar with the subject.

Business Writing

The Wall Street Journal, a newspaper devoted to business writing, is famous for its features. They just happen to be about business, financial and social trends. But the newspaper's style of writing has been emulated by newspapers all over the country for all types of stories.

In the early 1950s, *The Wall Street Journal* issued a memo to its writers about how features for the newspaper should be written. Many of the style guidelines in that memo are still applied today at this newspaper and at many others that have adopted the *Wall Street Journal* formula. The suggestions in this memo are basic techniques that could apply to features about any subject, not just business stories.

> Our aim is to do very complete, very thorough research-type stories—but to avoid the obvious danger in such work of becoming dull and dry. To achieve maximum readability, we try to carry the reader along with a liberal sprinkling of color, examples and other illustrative gadgets. We try to keep our stories factually

Gina Henderson, assistant business editor of The Kansas City *(Mo.)* Star, *where the* Wall Street Journal *formula is applied to business stories as well as other types of stories*

Courtesy of Brian Crites,
The Kansas City Star

complete and correct enough to interest the banker, economist or other authority on the subject—yet always bearing in mind that it must be intriguing enough and simple enough to appeal to our average reader, who might be a retailer in Des Moines, a gas station owner in Dallas, a grain merchant in Oklahoma City or someone else with no familiarity with our subject.

The guidelines in this memo were specifically targeted to the Page One feature stories the newspaper publishes daily about trends and issues. With the current emphasis at newspapers to make stories more relevant to readers, these guidelines are as applicable to stories for today and the future as they were in the 1950s.

Here are some more suggestions from the memo (the italicized words are those the newspaper underlined for emphasis):

• These page one "leaders," as we call them, are interpretive stories. They most often report *trends*—what they mean and what they portend.

• The stories generally have one theme or point. This is usually put into a one- or two-paragraph nutshell summary high up in the story. Then the rest of the piece is made to hang together by harking back to this central theme. The story should be *clearly organized* or compartmentalized along the central thread of this theme—it should not meander around without a perceptible organization.

• We want to tell the story in terms of the *specific,* not in generalized or vague terms. One way we do this is to pack the story with lots of *detail.* For example, it isn't enough to make a general statement that there was inflation in X country until 1950 and then prices began to level off. We would want this nailed down with the official price index figures (specifying wholesale or retail, of course) showing the rise to 1950 and then the more recent leveling off. It would also be desirable—besides these concrete figures on the overall situation—to illustrate the trend with the prices of a few typical goods—such as shirts or soap—in 1946, 1950 and now, for example.

Another way we reduce the general situation to the specific is to give lots of colorful examples, anecdotes or small case histories to *illustrate* the overall situation we are describing.

We also lean heavily on illustrative *quotes*—attributable if possible though not necessarily so. The quotes need not be from government officials only; it could be from businessmen, shop-keepers, men-in-the-street, anyone who can shed some *color* on the situation or who can illustrate the general in specific, *individual terms.*

• Be sure to include all *background* the reader might need. We can assume no prior knowledge by our readers of the subject or of financial lingo. We try to spell out all situations *with super-*

simplicity and clarity—from how France's inflation has been brought about over the years to the recent economic history of Australia and what led up to its present economic situation. Please explain everything in clear-cut fashion.

• We try to achieve very tight writing—short, punchy sentences and all essential information on the subject conveyed *concisely*.

• At the same time, these leaders aim at being pretty *thorough* studies of the particular subject or trend. This means the inclusion of all detail and background and interpretation mentioned above. It also means we take pains to make sure the story contains the answers to every question that the story and its statements are likely to raise in the reader's mind. We can't use a story that raises questions it does not answer, so please re-check copy for this possible pitfall—and again, be sure all points are fully and *clearly explained,* and solidly *nailed down with fact.*

Here is how that memo translates into stories currently being published by the newspaper. This lead is from a trend story used as a leader on July 1, 1991.

ATLANTA—Ollie Smith's third graders are willing.

"The number is 2,427," says Mrs. Smith, a teacher at Cleveland Avenue Elementary School here. An eager volunteer, one of 17 blacks in a class of 18, walks to the blackboard beneath the U.S. flag in a scene familiar to anyone—until the chalk moves.

Instead of the numeral 2, the girl draws two lotus flowers, followed by four coiled ropes, two oxen yokes and seven vertical strokes.

"Very good, Jeannette," says Mrs. Smith, praising a perfect rendition of 2,427 in ancient Egyptian hieroglyphics. "You can take your seat."

Mrs. Smith's arithmetic lesson is part of a new Africa-centered curriculum that is fast spreading in urban schools. Atlanta, Baltimore, Detroit, Indianapolis, Portland, Ore., and Washington, D.C., are in various stages of similar course-content changes that stress, to a high degree, the history and culture of black people.

Gary Putka, *The Wall Street Journal*

Here is an example of how the *Wall Street Journal* formula can be applied to another type of specialty story—a religion story:

When Cliff and Rozan Mueller tell their Lutheran friends in western Kansas that they attend church on Saturday, they get some funny looks.

"They say, 'Are you sure this is a Lutheran church?' " Rozan Mueller said.

The Muellers' Trinity Lutheran Church in Mission is one of an increasing number of Protestant churches across the country to make Saturday a day of worship.

In the last decade an estimated 8 to 10 percent of all Protestant churches—adapting to changing lifestyles—have begun offering services to attract people who cannot or do not attend services on Sunday.

Some churches with limited space have added the Saturday service to accommodate growing congregations.

Such services have been a staple at many Catholic churches for more than 20 years. And now a few Protestant churches in the Kansas City area, mainly in suburban areas, are doing so.

Laurie J. Scott, *The Kansas City* (Mo.) *Star*

Sports reporter Mike Lopresti filing a story from a game site
Courtesy of *The Gannetteer,* Gannett Co. Inc.

Sportswriting

Sportswriters have always had to rely on feature techniques of descriptive and interpretive writing, even more than other writers at a newspaper. Their readers may have seen the game, but they still want to read about it. Others who haven't seen the game want to know what happened. So sportswriters face the challenge of providing readers something more than the basic facts.

Unlike most news stories, where reporters rely on information from sources, sportswriters covering a game are witnessing the action firsthand. They have the responsibility for interpreting what they saw through interviews with coaches and players and their own analysis. They need to stress angles: why and how the game was won or lost or what the strategy was. How was this game different from or similar to others?

But sports stories are not limited to game coverage. The range of topics on sports pages—profiles, trend stories and general sports features—is as broad as in any other section of the paper.

Years ago, sportswriters could rely on knowing their craft and writing primarily about games and the athletes. Today they need to be as well-versed in court reporting and other fields as the reporters who cover the news, because many stories involve athletes in legal contract disputes and court cases about drugs, violence and other criminal charges.

Today sportswriters also face more difficult challenges, says former sportswriter Alan Richman, whose techniques of interviewing celebrities and athletes are described in Chapter 25. The celebrity status and huge salaries of sports figures make it difficult

*The game itself,
no longer the sole focus
of sportswriters*

Courtesy of Philip Meiring,
The University Daily Kansan

to get good interviews, Richman contends. "In the old days an athlete would stay in the city for his career so it behooved him to have good press," Richman says. "They didn't have agents. These days it's more complex. Economically the press is useless to a player. Athletes are celebrities now. They are more isolated.

"Also the amount of press around complicates the issue. Locker rooms today are insane. Members of the press are falling over each other. They're like starving kids running after an ice cream truck in locker rooms. The players just want to get out of there. There's no chance to get any good story."

Still, today's sportswriters are getting good stories. Some of the best writing in the newspaper—as well as some of the worst—can be found on the sports pages.

Karen Brown, an associate at the Poynter Institute for Media Studies, says all writers, especially those facing tight deadlines, could take some tips from sportswriters. In the book she edited, *Best Newspaper Writing 1991,* she offers this advice:

- First, writers must see the same old story in different ways. . . . The characters and events in sports stories aren't necessarily more interesting than those in news stories. But in sports, more attention is paid to the people and the action. Personalities, motives and mannerisms are fleshed out to add color and meaning to stories.

- A second message from sportswriters is to keep your eyes on the story. "You can't look away when you're covering a sports story," said Merlissa Lawrence, a sportswriter for *The Pittsburgh Press.* "In that one moment something dramatic could happen."

- A third strategy is to write background information ahead of time and plan for likely eventualities. . . . It is a method commonly used by journalists covering major sports events on deadline.

- A fourth message is to give some thought to the best format for telling the story. Some games are worth only a box score. So are some meetings. Some stories require a brief; others need a long story or several textual and graphic elements.

- Finally, sportswriters write in ways that draw readers into stories. Often the readers know the score and have seen the event. The task for the writer then is to elucidate, analyze, amplify and soothe the reader with the pleasure of the words that recapture the event.

Many of the writing techniques sportswriters use to accomplish those tasks are the same ones you have studied for other basic news, feature and specialty stories. The major difference is that sportswriters must stress interpretation, how and why, more than in basic news stories. Good sportswriters try to do that by setting a tone and developing their stories with a theme.

In this example, notice how the writer weaves the story around a theme of surrender, incorporates statistics and puts the coach's comments in perspective:

CHESTNUT HILL, Mass.— Villanova surrendered last night.

Rollie Massimino didn't have to wave a white flag. Putting in walkons and sitting down starters with nearly 13 minutes left against Boston College served the same purpose.

The defeat was stunning in its totality. The Eagles, only a year ago a hapless 1-15 in the Big East, pounded Villanova, 82-46, at Conte Forum. Winning meant Boston College (14-7 overall, 6-6 in the Big East) took over sole possession of seventh place in the conference from Villanova (8-13, 5-7).

Afterward, Massimino was almost eerily calm. Of the Wildcats'

14 percent shooting in the first half, he said: "I think we've climbed into a little bit of an offensive rut." But when you make 16 of 61 shots, as Villanova did, it might seem the rut is more like a chasm.

The Villanova coach even found something about his team to praise. "I thought, when it was 11-2, we defended extremely well to keep it 11-3 six straight possessions," he said.

That's what this season has come to. Proudly proclaiming the times when the bad score doesn't get worse.

Diane Pucin, *The Philadelphia Inquirer*

Here are some of the basic facts to include in game stories:

Who played, where (stadium and city), when

Score (placed high in the story)

Major plays and players

Turning points

Injuries

Important statistics (conference standing, records for season)

Weather, if it had an effect on the game

Crowd count, if relevant (fully packed stadium or sparse attendance)

Outcome of previous games between these two teams, if relevant

Comments from coaches and players to explain the how and why of the game

Notice how many of the important elements are high in the next story—theme, names of teams, score, location of game, crowd size, conference records, analysis, perspective and "injury" (the flu) to the key player. Notice, too, the circular ending: a return to the flu theme.

Rolando Blackman had the flu and was home Friday night. At least he had an excuse.

Most of the other Mavericks were no-shows in a 97-91 defeat to the expansion-like New Jersey Nets before a crowd of 16,121 at Reunion Arena.

The flu wasn't the only bug to hit the Mavericks (6-8). They suffered from turnovers, bad defense and poor rebounding in losing to a team that had dropped 11 of its last 12 games, and had won only one road game before Friday.

Doug Smith almost provided the cure with the best game of his rookie season, a 14-point, eight-rebound effort. But after leading the rally from a 14-point deficit, he gave way with five minutes left for veteran Rodney McCray.

"I could not put Doug out on the floor because he doesn't know what we're doing, and we have six or seven late-game plays that we run," said coach Richie Adubato. "So we went with the guys we think will perform under pressure."

On this night, they didn't deliver. Playing without Blackman, their leading scorer and only true go-to player for clutch baskets, the Mavericks conked out on offense. In the final 3:29, they scored on only two of five possessions. . . .

The Mavericks shooting was poor, also. Some of that can be attributed to Blackman's absence. Besides leading the team with a 21.8-point scoring average, he is their only regular making at least 50 percent of his shots from the field.

Blackman's bug is just one the Mavericks have to find the cure for. Fast.

Mitch Lawrence, *The Dallas Morning News*

Note in the following example how the sportswriter combines analysis with many of the basics and with descriptive techniques:

NEW YORK—Maybe Jimmy Connors doesn't remember how old he really is. Maybe he thinks each new, heroic feat will add another chapter to an already legendary career. Maybe he just likes playing tennis so much he simply can't stop.

How else can one explain his come-from-behind, five-set victory over Patrick McEnroe in the first round of the U.S. Open early this morning? And how many more Connors-McEnroe classics can the boisterous New York fans endure before they simply keel over in exhaustion?

There was something so improbable—and so predictable—about this one. Six days short of his 39th birthday, and now ranked No. 174, Connors fought back from two sets down and 3-0 in the third to defeat the younger brother of his one-time nemesis in a 4-hour, 20-minute epic that induced a joyous riot at Louis Armstrong Stadium. The final score: 4-6, 6-7 (4-7), 6-4, 6-2, 6-4.

"I hate to lose more than I like to win," Connors said, "and I think that's one reason why I stay in there and grind it out time after time."

When the 1991 edition of the Connors-McEnroe ended at 1:36 a.m., 4,000 fans who braved 51 games erupted in cacophonous cheers. They whistled. They chanted "Jim-my." They waved shirts. They pumped their fists.

Then they stood in awe and, with arms extended over their heads, bowed down.

Alison Muscatine, *The Washington Post*

Sportswriters must exert extra effort to avoid cliches and jargon, both of which abound in sports stories. Even though they often appeal to an audience that is knowledgeable about the sport, the stories should be written for a general audience, just as *The Wall Street Journal* advises its business writers to write for readers who have no special knowledge of the business world. In fact, the next example follows the Wall Street Journal formula. In this story, which won a Hearst college journalism award, the writer uses a descriptive

*Sports from a
different perspective*
Courtesy of Philip Meiring

approach. He focuses on a person to lead to the nut graph in this trend story about African-American coaches:

Northwestern assistant basketball coach Tim Carter's share of Welsh-Ryan Arena is more of a stopping place than an office. Only the essentials—desk, chairs, bulletin board, calendar and a few notes—are there. A picture of his family serves as the only decoration.

His stint at NU, the fifth coaching job of his career, is just another stop on his way to what he hopes will someday be the big office: a head coaching position at a Division I school.

"There's no question that I want to be a head coach," Carter says. "If you don't have aspirations of being a head coach, you're wasting your time."

But if you are an African-American like Carter, the odds are not in your favor.

Of the 290 NCAA Division I head basketball coaches, only 50 are African-Americans, 18 of them at historically black colleges. The number is disproportionate, considering the fact that 56 percent of college basketball players are black.

Joshua A. Adande, *The Daily Northwestern*

In the following sports story, all of the feature techniques discussed in this chapter come into play. The writer develops a theme: the circus of people who surrounded Muhammad Ali in his heyday as the world's boxing champion and what happened when the greatest show on earth ended and Ali developed Parkinson's disease. The story is broken into sections, each from the point of view of a different person—his doctor, his "facilitator" (a man who took care of getting Ali what he wanted), his cook, his masseur, his bodyguard, his manager and his trainer. It starts with a portrait of Ali. The writer uses imagery and the color black to set the mood and tone of sadness. Notice the symbolism of the paintings of Ali, now streaked with pigeon dung. The writer also skillfully uses pacing—slow movement to show Ali's brain deterioration. It is a story filled with descriptive writing and concrete images to make the reader see and care. Because this is a magazine piece, the writer uses the first-person *I* in parts, a technique used by sports columnists as well but not used in other newspaper sports features. This is the first section, focusing on Ali:

Around Muhammad Ali, all was decay. Mildewed tongues of insulation poked through gaps in the ceiling; flaking cankers pocked the painted walls. On the floor lay rotting scraps of carpet.

He was cloaked in black. Black street shoes, black socks, black pants, black short-sleeved shirt. He threw a punch, and in the small town's abandoned boxing gym, the rusting chain between the heavy bag and the ceiling rocked and creaked.

Slowly, at first, his feet began to dance around the bag. His left hand flicked a pair of jabs, and then a right cross and a left hook, too, recalled the ritual of the butterfly and bee. The dance quickened. Black sunglasses flew from his pocket as he gathered speed, shirttail flapped free, black heavy bag rocked and creaked. Black street shoes scuffed faster and faster across the black moldering tiles: Yeah, Lawd, champ can still float, champ can still sting! He whirled, jabbed, feinted, let his feet fly into a shuffle. "How's that for a sick man?" he shouted.

He did it for a second three-minute round, then a third. "Time!" I shouted at the end of each one as the second hand swept past the 12 on the wristwatch he had handed to me. And then, gradually, his shoulders began to slump, his hands to drop. The tap and thud of leather soles and leather gloves began to miss a quarter-beat . . . half-beat . . . whole. Ali stopped and sucked air. The dance was over.

He undid the gloves, tucked in the black shirt, reached reflexively for the black comb. On stiff legs he walked toward the door. Outside, under the sun, the afternoon stopped. Every movement he made now was infinitely patient and slow. Feeling . . . in . . . his . . . pocket . . . for . . . his . . . key. . . . Slipping . . . it . . . into . . . the . . . car . . . lock. . . . Bending . . . and . . . sliding . . . behind . . . the . . . wheel. . . . Turning . . . on . . . the . . . ignition . . . and . . . shift-

ing . . . into . . . gear. . . . Three months had passed, he said, since he had last taken the medicine the doctor told him to take four times a day.

One hand lightly touched the bottom of the wheel as he drove; his clouded eyes narrowed to a squint. His head tilted back, and the warm sunlight trickled down his puffy cheeks. Ahead, trees smudged against sky and farmland; the glinting asphalt dipped and curved, a black ribbon of molasses.

He entered the long driveway of his farm, parked and left the car. He led me into a barn. On the floor, leaning against the walls, were paintings and photographs of him in his prime, eyes keen, arms thrust up in triumph, surrounded by the cluster of people he took around the world with him.

He looked closer and noticed it. Across his face in every picture, streaks of bird dung. He glanced up toward the pigeons in the rafters. No malice, no emo-

tion at all flickered in his eyes. Silently, one by one, he turned the pictures to the wall. Outside, he stood motionless and moved his eyes across his farm. He spoke from his throat, without moving his lips. I had to ask him to repeat it. "I had the world," he said, "and it wasn't nothin'." He paused and pointed. "Look now. . . ."

Black blobs of cows slumbering in the pasture, trees swishing slowly, as if under water rather than sky. Merry-go-rounds, sliding boards and swings near the house, but no giggles, no squeals, no children.

"What happened to the circus?" I asked.

He was staring at the slowly swishing trees, listening to the breeze sift leaves and make a lulling sound like water running over the rocks of a distant stream. He didn't seem to hear.

And I said again, "What happened to the circus?"

Gary Smith, *Sports Illustrated*

Activities

1 Write a feature about a program in your school or community.

2 Write a mood piece about a place in your area. For example, go to a bar, a hospital emergency room, a shopping mall or major gathering place on your campus. Observe and listen to people. Then write a descriptive mood piece, including dialogue if possible.

3 Write a narrative story reconstructing a traumatic incident in the life of a friend.

4 Using the *Wall Street Journal* formula, write a business feature about a trend in your community. For example, is business in your downtown area suffering or improving? Are stores closing or opening? Is there a new business catering to students or other people in your community?

5 Choose a specialty subject of your choice—medicine, education, religion, sports, environment—and write a feature about a topic or program in this category.

SIX

Job
Hunting

Media Jobs and Internships

COACHING

Call the employer and find out the person to whom you should send your application. Make sure you have the correct name, title and sex of the person. Ask how to spell the person's first and last name.

Limit your cover letter to one page.

Proofread your application carefully to eliminate spelling and typographical errors.

Make a follow-up telephone call a few weeks after you send your application.

Media Jobs and Internships

27

Michael Strong wasn't a traditional journalism school graduate. He was 42 when he earned his degree at the University of Kansas, and he had a varied background prior to entering journalism school. But when he applied for a newspaper job, his original cover letter gave no clue that he was any different from the thousands of other journalism school graduates. It began: "I am graduating in May . . ."

He got few responses from editors. So he rewrote it, and this time his cover letter revealed a little more about him: "How many reporters do you know who have experience meeting people when they are nude? That isn't exactly traditional training for a reporter, but I'm not a traditional candidate for a reporting job."

Strong had been a massage therapist for a Kansas City athletic club, as well as a photographer, computer operator and astronomic surveyor for the U.S. Air Force. Every editor who received the revised cover letter responded; several called him for an interview and subsequently offered him a job.

Your cover letter, too, should reveal something special about you. It's the first impression editors get of you. You may be a straight-A student with a fabulous personality and wonderful reporting skills, but if you can't sell yourself, you are just another applicant from a journalism school. Whether you are applying for a job in print or broadcast journalism or in public relations, most of the advice that follows applies.

A job on a newspaper is a special thing. Every day you take something that you found out about, and you put it down and in a matter of hours it becomes a product. Not just a product like a can or something. It is a personal product that people, a lot of people, take the time to sit down and read.

Jimmy Breslin, columnist

Job Application Skills

Paul Salsini is appalled by the letters he receives from applicants to *The Milwaukee Journal,* where he is the staff development director and writing coach. One applicant misspelled *Milwaukee* throughout her application. Another said, "I've always wanted to work at the *Minneapolis Star.*"

"Good for her," Salsini said. "Why should I care?"

One of the worst mistakes applicants make is that they fail to change the text in their word processors when they are sending out hordes of applications, Salsini said.

"I can't stress enough how important it is for the applicant to write a cover letter that is both clear and interesting and tells me this person is a good reporter and writer," he said. "If they're just saying they want a job, that doesn't excite me. I want that letter to entice me into their clips and resume. The cover letter is the only original thing they send."

Salsini prefers cover letters with catchy leads that reveal something special about the applicant. Here's one he liked: "When I was 10 years old, I wanted to be a detective. When I was 12, I wanted to be a child psychologist, and when I was 13, I wanted to be a news reporter. That was the career choice that stuck. Ten years later I'm still basically a nosy kid who enjoys the challenge of storytelling." Some editors prefer a hard-news lead on a cover letter. Salsini said that whether it's a straight lead or feature, it should be a good lead to a personal account of the applicant.

Salsini also stressed that applicants should attach some explanation to their clips of how they wrote the story. "If they would just write a couple of sentences to explain whether this was their story idea and why the story was important, it would help to put the clip in context. It helps an editor understand the story. That doesn't take a lot of work and it is so important. I rarely get that in an application, but when I do, it's what I read first."

Internships and experience on campus newspapers are important. Editors want evidence of how you report and write or what you can do as a copy editor. They want clips of stories you have written or edited. However, clips are edited, so they aren't always indicative of the person's writing, Salsini said.

What editors want is evidence that you write and think clearly. And you can demonstrate that you do in your cover letter.

Here are some tips for applying for a media job or internship:

Where to apply: Check *Editor & Publisher Yearbook* for the names of newspapers where you'd like to work. For public relations, magazine and broadcast jobs, check directories listing agencies and publications in those fields. Follow the same basic instructions as for

Newspaper newsroom

Courtesy of *The Gannetteer,*
Gannett Co. Inc.

newspapers. Get the exact name of the organization, its address and its circulation. Your chances for that first job are often better at a small newspaper or organization than a large one. However, some large newspapers have small bureaus and will consider reporters without previous experience. In public relations, however, you may have a better chance getting a job at a large corporation.

Who to contact: At most newspapers, you should apply to the managing editor, not the editor or publisher, unless the paper is very small and the editor or publisher is the only person in charge. For other types of organizations, check to find out who reviews the applications. Make sure you get the spelling of the person's name, the title and the gender. Some female editors and personnel directors have male-sounding names; some men's names are ambiguous, too. Do not assume that anyone listed in *Editor & Publisher Yearbook* or any other industry directory is still in that position. People switch jobs faster than the yearbook can publish their names. Your first step as a reporter or copy editor is to check the facts. Accuracy counts. Inaccuracy in addressing your application usually means you will not be considered.

Cover letter: Try to limit the cover letter to one page. Always address it to a specific person, never *Dear Sir* or *Dear Madam.* Write a good lead that tells something about you, but don't make it too flowery. Follow with a nut graph—your reason for writing. Write a few more paragraphs briefly explaining your experience, if any, and your major assets—why anyone should want to hire you. Then wrap it up with a brief paragraph thanking the editor for his or her attention. Your cover letter is the employer's first impression of you. Make it clear, interesting and simple.

Resume: Make sure your resume is free of typos and spelling errors. Give two or three references, and include phone numbers where they can be reached. Do not say "References available on request." Do everything you can to help the employer. By withholding references, you force the employer to spend more time checking on you. You may have your resume printed on heavyweight paper and designed in an attractive way. But for most print and broadcast journalism employers, a printed resume is not essential. A neatly typed, simple resume will suffice. Something fancier may be more advantageous for public relations positions, because that is a promotional field. Your resume may reflect your ability to package promotional material. However, most employers really just want the facts in an easy-to-read form.

Clips or videotape: Include five or six clips (or videotape for broadcast journalists, although clips help in this area as well). Choose clips with good leads. Editors rarely read past a bad lead. Try to include a variety: features and hard news, short and long. Short is better, unless you have a major project. If you have some good enterprise stories, those you developed through your own ideas, include them. And as Salsini suggests, attach a paragraph explaining how you got the story, why it was important or any difficulty you might have had in getting interviews. Say something about each clip to explain why you think it is representative of your work or why you enjoyed doing it.

Follow-up phone call: A week or two after you have sent your letter, call the organization to ask if your resume was received and if you could come for an interview. Find out when the editor you are calling is on deadline or in meetings, and try to avoid these times.

Research for the interview: If you are granted an interview, make sure you get a few copies of the publication in advance and read them thoroughly. Check the library. Or call the circulation department of the newspaper or magazine and get them to send you a few copies. For a public relations job, try to get a media kit about the company. A little money and time invested before your interview may pay off in a paycheck. Also do some research about the community. Find out if it has large ethnic groups. If you have special language skills that would be useful in this community, you can stress them in your letter and interview.

Follow-up phone call and thank-you note: After you have had an interview, wait a few weeks and then call to let the editor know you are aggressive and interested in the job. But don't be a pest. Even if you are not interested in the job, send a note thanking the editor for the interview. That's just basic courtesy. And if you are interested in the job, the thank-you note lets the editor know something else about you: You're thoughtful.

Cover Letters

Make your first impression on the editor a good one. Use proper business letter form, and keep it brief—no more than one page. Editors are busy people. Double-check and triple-check your spelling. Make sure all the names and titles are correct. A misspelled name, typo or other mechanical error can disqualify you for consideration.

Be straightforward; not cute, not boring. Avoid starting with "I am graduating in May." So are about 17,000 other journalism majors. Instead, start with why you are applying to this organization or something about yourself that makes you worth noticing. But get to the point quickly, why you are applying. Specify whether you are seeking an internship or full-time job. Explain why you are eager to work for this particular organization in the middle of your letter. Even though you are including a resume, mention its high points. Make special note of any unusual skills you may have, such as fluency in a second language. If someone at the organization has encouraged you to apply, mention this person's name. The adage "It's not what you know but who you know" has some validity.

Here is some additional advice from editors, excerpted from an article that Judith Clabes, editor of *The Kentucky Post* in Covington, wrote for *The Quill:*

> I'm editor of a medium-sized daily, and being deluged with letters to the editor comes with the territory.
>
> Believe me, by the time I've shuffled through the "Dear Stupid" letters to the editor, the "Dear Employee" memos from corporate, and the really important "Dear Resident" mail that somehow pours into the office, I'm in no frame of mind for a job-seeker's "Dear Mr. Clabes" letter.
>
> "Dear Mr. Judith Clabes" really ticks me off.
>
> Now, this may seem quirky, but we editors are entitled to an eccentricity or two.

Idiosyncrasies aside, we editors do seem to agree on the issue of introductory letters from job-seekers. We prefer:

- Straightforward, one-page letters,
- Simple resumes and
- Well-selected clips (yes, college newspaper clips are fine).

In the end, the clips speak loudest. But the introductory letter may determine whether a busy editor will even bother to listen.

"It's more important that the letter is not a turn-off than it's a turn-on," says Mike Phillips, editor of *The Sun-Tattler* in Hollywood, Florida. The following will automatically turn off an editor:

- Grammatical errors
- Typographical errors
- Misspelling the name of the newspaper
- Misspelling the name of the editor
- Form letters
- Incorrect titles, including courtesy titles
- Cutesy letters
- Bad writing, including poor sentence structure
- Phony sales pitches
- Lengthy, self-centered letters

"I'm impressed by the letter coming from someone who's got him or herself figured out, who knows personal strengths and weaknesses and has a flair for writing," says Phillips.

Typos are killers. "I can't remember bothering to interview an applicant whose letter contained typos or grammatical errors," says editor Dee W. Bryant of *The Leaf-Chronicle* in Clarksville, Tennessee. "If a person is that careless with letters, it raises the question about carelessness as a staffer."

Bryant's pet peeve, however, is the automatic—and mindless—"Mr." greeting. "If an applicant is seriously interested, he or she should have taken the time to find out. It irritates me that people make the invalid assumption that editors are men."

Bob Stiff, editor of *The Democrat* in Tallahassee, wants some evidence that the writer is familiar with the paper and the area. He prefers a follow-up phone call from the applicant, requesting a short interview.

Though we editors have our own pet peeves as well as hiring strategies, we shudder over the cute stuff, the gimmicks, the over-zealous attempts at creativity.

Angus McEachran, editor of *The Pittsburgh Press,* has compiled more than his share of to-the-editor eccentricities. . . . His attention was momentarily captured when he opened a letter and a stick fell out. The letter said:

"Dear Sir:

"Inside the envelope along with this letter I have sent you just what you don't need in filling editor slots at *The Pittsburgh*

Press—dead wood. "Tired of dead wood? Give me a call. My phone number is . . ."

That letter writer's phone did not ring with McEachran's call.

What will work is a simple, professional approach. Throw away fuchsia paper and the gimmicks. Invest time in investigating the newspaper. Write a simple, well-crafted (and proofread) one-page letter that demonstrates your interest in journalism generally and in that particular newspaper specifically. Include a brief resume and five or six well-selected clips.

Here are a few examples that brought students success. The first is an example of a cover letter from one student who was seeking an internship at a magazine. Note how the student leads with something special about herself.

Rachel G. Thompson
Home address
Date

Timothy Drew, Managing Editor of *Home*
Hachette Magazines, Inc.
1633 Broadway
New York, N.Y. 10019

Dear Mr. Drew:

I have always been an editor at heart.

In the sixth grade I drove my best friend away by editing letters she sent me. I read the letters for content, then went back over them with a red pen to correct any grammatical, contextual or spelling errors I found. I then sent the marked-up letter back to her, expecting her to respond "Thank you for pointing that out to me." Never once did I hear those words.

Although I gave up editing peer correspondence long ago, I still enjoy searching for a better word, finding a glitch in a photo and coming up with a great headline for a story. It was this curious enjoyment of editing that pointed me in the direction of journalism, which I am now studying at the University of ———— .

Please grant me an interview for a summer internship. I believe that my strong command of the English language, my working knowledge of the history of art and architecture, and my avid interest in interior design and home remodeling may be useful in the process of publishing *Home* magazine, which is my favorite magazine to read and secretly edit.

Although I do not have much experience, I believe that my ambition and enthusiasm to publish a flawless article, print a perfect photo and create the most captivating headline for a story will compensate.

Sincerely yours,

Rachel G. Thompson

This next letter, from a student requesting a copyediting position, also has a personalized lead. Although she uses a cliche, the student focused on the trait most people notice about her, and she turned it into an asset. It was also helpful for her to explain in an unobtrusive way that she is a minority student, because newspapers are seeking to increase the number of minorities on staff.

Tiffany Hurt
Home address
Date

Chris Cobbler, Assistant Managing Editor
The Coloradoan
P.O. Box 1577
Fort Collins, Colorado 80522

Dear Mr. Cobbler:

Good things definitely do come in small packages. Even though I only look 10 because I am 4-feet 7½ inches, I am actually twice that age, with the responsibilities and leadership roles of an ambitious college student.

Currently a manager trainer at McDonald's fast-food restaurant, I work with the public daily and oversee several crew people.

On campus I am a member of the editorial board for the campus newspaper. I also report and write stories for the arts and entertainment section occasionally. In addition, I am the chairperson and editor of the newsletter for the Black Student Union at the University of ———. The newsletter is published every month. I assign stories, lay out pages, edit copy and oversee the newsletter staff. I also have been the reporting secretary for a gospel group, the Inspirational Gospel Voices, since 1990.

As you can see, I enjoy working with people and working in leadership positions.

Please consider me for a copyediting or reporting position. I am majoring in journalism at the University of ——— and expect to get my bachelor of science degree in December 1993.

I am eager to work for a small newspaper such as *The Coloradoan* because I might get the chance to edit or report a greater variety of news stories than a larger paper would permit. Please grant me an interview so I may prove to you that I am a worthy candidate for an entry-level reporting or copyediting position.

Sincerely,

Tiffany Hurt

And this one is from a student seeking a reporting position at a newspaper. He got the internship.

Ranjit Arab
Home address
Date

Steven A. Smith, Managing Editor
The Wichita Eagle
825 E. Douglas Ave.
Wichita, Kansas 67201

Dear Mr. Smith:

The Wichita Eagle is under my bed.

Ever since I was 10 years old, I have been saving copies of *The Wichita Eagle*. It all started when you published the "Extra" edition announcing Ronald Reagan's inauguration, along with the freeing of the American hostages after their 444th day of captivity in Iran. I remember that particular morning as if it were yesterday.

As I sat at the breakfast table, dreading the thought of another day of fourth grade, I reached for the paper. My parents had always encouraged me to read the news, although I mainly read the comic and sports sections. This particular newspaper, however, would change my life.

The sight of the words "Extra! Extra!" both baffled and intrigued me. Suddenly, I realized there was more to a newspaper than "Ziggy" and box scores. I knew that this was history in the making. Unlike the news from television, this was a piece of history I could save forever. I had realized the power of printed words. From that day on, I made it a practice to save any paper that I felt contained a historical significance. My collection grew quickly.

In retrospect, I can honestly conclude that it was that specific newspaper that turned me on to journalism, which I am now studying at the University of ————. Whenever I begin to lose sight of my goal of becoming a journalist, I simply pull out the stack of musty yellow papers from under my bed, and everything seems to fall into place again.

Please grant me an interview for a summer internship. Although I may not have much experience, I know that I share the desire and passion for news that I have found consistently in your newspaper. *The Wichita Eagle* has taught me so much in the past. I know that there is much more I can learn by working for your newspaper.

Sincerely yours,

Ranjit Arab

Resumes

The cover letter should be accompanied by a resume, preferably limited to one page. The resume should list your education, work experience and references (see Exhibit 27-1). Before you list anyone as a reference, make sure you ask the person for her or his permission. Also list any special skills and awards you have or activities and organizations in which you have participated.

Interviews

The interview is your chance to explain how much you want to work for the employer and why you would be a good choice. It is also your chance to find out more about the employer and to assess whether you would really like to work there.

Here are some tips:

Dress conservatively. Women should wear a suit or dress, stockings, and dress shoes (nice flats or heels). Men should wear a suit or sport jacket and tie. No jeans and no sneakers!

Be prompt. Be on time for your interview. You may arrive 15 minutes early, but don't get there too early. Never be late. That's equivalent to missing a deadline. And that's equivalent to saying you are not fit for the job.

Be prepared. Be informed about the publication, organization or station. Read copies of the publication, particularly the most recently published ones. Public relations applicants should try to gather research about the company and the types of promotions the firm does. Memorize the names of key editors in advance.

Understand the costs. Some organizations will pay for your transportation and hotel. If not, be prepared to pay for them yourself. Small newspapers and other organizations may not have the budget for your travel costs. You have to decide if the cost is worthwhile to you. If the organization is out of state, it's fair to ask if your transportation and lodging costs will be reimbursed.

Concentrate. When you are introduced to people, try to remember their names, especially those of key editors such as the city editor or the sports editor if you are applying for a sports job. Homework helps.

Be enthusiastic. Your enthusiasm is your best asset, especially if you don't have experience. Show that you're interested in the job. Smile and enjoy the interview just as if you were doing an interview for a story. If you don't really want to work for the firm, don't waste everyone's time.

Your Name

Permanent Address   **Present Address**
(if home address differs from your
address during the semester)

Street   Street
Town, State, zip code   Town, State, zip code
Home phone (include area code)   Phone number (include area code)

Position
Desired   Reporting internship for summer of 1993

Available   May 17, 1993

Education   1990 to present: University of _____; Major: Journalism, news-
                     editorial sequence. Degree expected: B.S. in journalism, May 1994. Other
                     concentration: political science. G.P.A.: 3.80

                     1986-90: All City High School, State

Experience   (List any full-time or part-time jobs, particularly any related to your field, in order
                     starting from the most recent. You may add a line or two explaining your job
                     duties.)

January-May, 1993 Reporter, The Daily Campus newspaper; covered university administration

July-August, 1992 Reporting internship with City Newspaper; covered general news for city desk
                     and features

May-August 1991   Waitress, Starving Students, City, State

May-August 1990   Ditch digger, Municipal Works Department, City, State

Special Skills   (Omit this category if you have none.)
and Awards
                     Scripps Howard Scholarship for College Jounalism
                     Bilingual in Spanish and English
                     Skilled in operating computer programs: Quark, Pagemaker, WordPerfect

Activities   (List only important activities and organizations to which you belong, especially
                     those that show leadership or skills related to the job you are seeking; this
                     category may be omitted.)

References   (List only two or three who have given you permission to list them; these may
                     be listed on separate page if you run out of room. List their titles, addresses and
                     telephone numbers.)
                     John G. Reference,   Fred Favorable, Director
                     Associate Professor   Municipal Works Department
                     School of Journalism   City, State, zip code
                     University of ————   Phone number (very important)
                     City, State, zip code
                     Phone number (very important)

Exhibit 27-1

Format for resume

Be polite. Thank the editor or key person for granting you an interview, and thank the person at the end of it as well.

Be pleasant. Even if you are frightened, smile and be responsive.

Be yourself. Do not try so hard to make a good impression that you are insincere. Be honest about what you can and cannot do and what you want to learn. Never try to give a false impression of yourself.

Ask questions. The questions you ask are as important as the ones you answer. They show your curiosity and your concern about the job—qualities of a good reporter, editor or publicist.

Editors have their favorite questions, so it is hard to prepare for the interview. However, almost all of them will ask why you want to work for their organization and why you want to be a journalist. Try to be creative but sincere. "I've always wanted to write" is such a boring answer. Here are some other questions that are popular with newspaper editors (similar questions are often asked in other fields):

Why do you want to work for this organization? The answers are up to you: because you grew up in the area, want to remain in the area, are familiar with the community and so on. It's best to specify something you like about the paper if you are familiar with it. Or you could say you are seeking a variety of experiences, particularly if it's a small newspaper or television station, where reporters tend to do all types of stories. If it's a large organization, you could say you're attracted by the prestige of the paper or the chance to learn from very experienced journalists. If you are so eager that you will work anywhere, it's OK to say so. Just be honest.

Why did you want to become a journalist? Because it's more interesting than selling used cars, because you seek adventure, because you love the language, whatever. Here is your chance to give your real reason. It could be that someone influenced you or that you just like the type of work.

What are your goals as a journalist? You could say, "To get your job some day" or "To work here until *The New York Times* begs me to come there." If your goal is to be a foreign correspondent, at this point you might consider joining the Navy. Small papers don't have much use for foreign bureaus. Again, be sincere.

What books, magazines and newspapers do you read? Editors love this question. It tells them something about you.

What other interests do you have? This is another favorite question.

What can you do for this newspaper (organization), or why should I hire you? Don't say you can turn the paper around or make it wonderful. But do say something about the types of stories you would like to do, or say that you would be willing to do all types of stories. Don't be arrogant.

What do you think of this newspaper? Be cautious with this one. Don't say it's terrible and you can save it. Point out something good first. Then you might point out some weakness or area that you think could be improved. Perhaps you think it could use more human approaches to stories or more hard news. If you've read it, you have a right to your opinion. Just be diplomatic.

What was your favorite story that you wrote, and why did you like it? This is another question that gives insight into you—as well as your professional interests.

How would you cover this issue? The editor might give you an example of a topic that is of concern in that community. You'll have to think and do the best you can to come up with some interesting approaches.

What questions do you have? This question is very important. Here's where you get your chance to ask about the company, the workload, perhaps what the editors want or expect from reporters and copy editors. You could ask about a probationary period. You could also ask about salary, benefits and other compensation; generally, however, that shouldn't be your first question.

At the end of the interview, don't forget to thank the interviewer for his or her time and interest.

Activities

1 Depending on your field of interest, interview three newspaper editors, television news directors, magazine editors or public relations employers about the qualities they seek in job candidates and the kinds of applications they want.

2 Write a few descriptive paragraphs about yourself in the third person (*she* or *he*). This exercise will give you a clue to what makes you special, and it may help you find a lead for your cover letter.

3 Write a cover letter and a resume for a job or internship you would be interested in getting.

Style Guide

The Associated Press Stylebook and Libel Manual is an essential tool for all media writers. It is filled with valuable guidelines for punctuation, spelling and word use and with tips for clear writing. Although many newspapers have their own guidelines, the *Associated Press Stylebook* is widely accepted. It is also used for public relations writing. However, many of the guidelines for magazines and broadcast writing differ from those for newspaper and public relations releases. Basic style tips for broadcast writers are included in Chapter 16.

This style guide is in no way a substitute for the *Associated Press Stylebook*. However, for quick reference the following material, which is based on the *Associated Press Stylebook,* may be helpful.

A

abbreviations Avoid acronyms the reader would not easily recognize. Do not follow an organization's full name with the acronym in parentheses. If the acronym would not be clear on second reference, don't use it. See **months, state names.**

academic degrees Avoid abbreviations when possible. Preferred: *John Jones, who has a doctorate in psychology.* Use an apostrophe in *bachelor's degree* and *master's degree.* Use *Ph.D.,* for doctorate, and other abbreviations—such as *M.S.* and *B.A.*—only when needed after a name. Don't use both *Ph.D.* and *Dr.* to identify someone. Wrong: *Dr. Sam Jones, Ph.D.* Right: *Dr. Sam Jones, a chemist.*

academic titles Capitalize and spell out formal titles—such as *professor, chancellor* and *chairman*—when they precede a name: *Chancellor Gene Budig.* Use a lowercase letter after a name—*Gene Budig, chancellor, spoke yesterday*—and when used elsewhere without a name. Use a lowercase letter for modifiers before a title: *history Professor William Tuttle.*

addresses Use the abbreviations *Ave., Blvd.* and *St.* only with a numbered address: *1600 Pennsylvania Ave.* Spell out these words when they are part of a street name without a number: *Pennsylvania Avenue.* Do not use abbreviations for *Road, Drive, Terrace* or other words.

Use figures for street numbers: *6 University Drive.*

Spell out and capitalize *First* through *Ninth* when they are used as street names; use figures with two letters for *10th* and above: *7 Fifth Ave., 100 21st St.*

ages Always use figures: *He is 9 years old* or *The boy, 9, is missing.* When age is used as an adjective, as in *a 9-year-old boy,* use hyphens.

AIDS Acceptable in all references for Acquired Immune Deficiency Syndrome, a virus that weakens the immune system. The scientific name for the virus that causes AIDS is the human immunodeficiency virus, or HIV. People who test positive for the virus, who are said to be HIV-positive, do not have AIDS; they have the AIDS virus. People do not have AIDS until they develop several serious symptoms of the disease. When writing about the death of people who have AIDS, say they died from AIDS-related illnesses, not from AIDS. The actual cause of death is not AIDS; it is the illnesses that result from the weakened immune system.

allege Use this word with great care, and avoid it when possible. It does not spare you from a libel suit. Use it when you need to make it clear that the unproved action is not being treated as a fact: *the alleged rape.* Specify the exact charge and the source—police or court records—somewhere in the story. Avoid redundancy. Wrong: *Police* *accused her of allegedly stealing the bicycle.* Right: *Police accused her of stealing the bicycle.*

a.m., p.m. Use lowercase letters with periods. Avoid redundancy: *10 a.m. this morning.*

B

Bible Capitalize when referring to the Old Testament or New Testament. Capitalize related terms: *Gospels, Scriptures, Holy Scriptures.* Lowercase *biblical* in all uses. Lowercase *bible* as a non-religious term: *Her textbook was her bible.*

brand names Capitalize them. *She drank a Coke.*

brunet, brunette Use *brunet* as a noun for males and as an adjective for both sexes. Use *brunette* as a noun for females.

bus, buses These are transportation vehicles. *Busses* means kisses.

C

Capital, capitol *Capital* is the city where a seat of government is located. Do not capitalize. *Capitol* is the building for the seat of government in Washington or in the states: *The legislators met in the capitol; The capital of Connecticut is Hartford; The capitol in Hartford looks like a white fairy-tale castle with a gold dome.*

Catholic Use *Roman Catholic Church* in the first reference. Second or more references may be the *Catholic Church* or *Catholicism*—capitalized when referring to the religion.

cents Spell out the word *cents,* and use lowercase. Use numerals for amounts less than a dollar: *5 cents.* Use the *$* sign and a decimal system for larger amounts: *$1.05.*

city council, city commission Capitalize when part of a proper name: *the Hartford City Council* or *the Lawrence City Commission.* Retain the capitalization if the reference is to a specific council but the context does not require the city name: *The City Council passed an ordinance.* Use lowercase when the term is used in a generic sense, not referring to a specific body: *Every city in our state has a city council.*

city hall Capitalize if it refers to a specific city hall, with or without the name: *Hartford City Hall.* Lowercase when used in a generic sense: *You can find records in any city hall.*

Congress, congressional Capitalize *U.S. Congress* and *Congress* when referring to the U.S. Senate and House of Representatives. Lowercase *congressional* unless it is part of a proper name: *the Congressional Record.*

Constitution, constitutional	Capitalize references to the U.S. Constitution with or without the modifier *U.S.* Capitalize when referring to constitutions of other nations or states when using the name of the nation or state: *the Massachusetts Constitution.* Lowercase when not using the name of a state or in general references: *the state constitution, the organization's constitution.* Lowercase *constitutional* in all uses.
county, counties	Capitalize the word when it is part of a proper name: *Broward County.* Lowercase it in general references—*the county agency*—and when it is not used as a title—*the county of Broward*—and when it is part of a plural—*Broward and Westchester counties.* Capitalize *county* if it is part of a board's or agency's name: *the County Commission.*
courtesy titles	On first reference, do not use the courtesy titles *Miss, Mr., Mrs.,* or *Ms.* For second references, eliminate courtesy titles in most cases, unless your newspaper prefers to use them for all or for specific stories, such as obituaries. Use *Elma Smith* for the first reference, *Mrs. Smith* for the second reference in these selected cases. When courtesy titles are used for women, ask if they prefer *Miss, Ms.* or *Mrs.* When writing about a couple, on second reference you can use *Mr. and Mrs. Smith* or eliminate the courtesy titles and use their full names: *John and Betty Smith.*
court names	Capitalize the full proper names of courts at all levels. Retain capitalization if *U.S.* is dropped: *U.S. Supreme Court* or *Supreme Court, 2nd District Court, 8th U.S. Circuit Court of Appeals.*

D

datelines	Datelines should contain a city name all in capital letters, followed in most cases by the name of the state in uppercase and lowercase letters: *KANSAS CITY, Mo.* Major cities that are clearly identified with their states do not need to be followed by the state name. Some examples are *ATLANTA, PHILADELPHIA, NEW YORK, SAN FRANCISCO, SEATTLE, DALLAS.* Check your stylebook for a full list.
days of the week	Capitalize *Monday, Tuesday* and so on. Do not abbreviate except in tabular form.
dimensions	Use figures, and spell out *inches, feet, yards* and so on to indicate depth, height, length and width. Hyphenate adjectival forms before nouns: *He is 5 feet 6 inches tall; the 5-foot-6-inch man, the 5-foot man; The basketball team signed a 7-footer; The car is 17 feet long, 6 feet wide and 5 feet high.*

directions and regions Lowercase *north, south, east* and *west* when they indicate directions: *Go south for three miles, then turn east.* Capitalize when they indicate regions: *He lived in the South for three years before he moved to the Midwest.*

dollars Use the dollar sign, *$,* with a figure in all cases except casual references, usually only for a dollar: *He paid $3 for the book. Please give me a dollar.* For amounts of more than $1 million, use the word *million* or *billion.* For amounts less than $1 million, use numerals only: *$2,000,* not *$2 thousand.*

E

essential and non-essential clauses and phrases An essential clause cannot be eliminated without changing the meaning of the sentence. It should not be set off by commas: *Students who do not study their stylebook should not blame their professors for taking points off their papers.* The clause is essential; only students who do not study their stylebook are affected. If the clause is used in a non-essential way, it should be set off by commas: *Students, who do not study their stylebook, should not blame their professors for taking points off their papers.* This sentence means that all students should not blame their professors, whether they use the stylebook or not.

Use *who* to introduce a clause or phrase referring to a human being. Use *that* for essential clauses and phrases, *which* for non-essential ones.

everyone, every one *Everyone* is a pronoun that takes a singular verb: *Everyone has his book. Every one* means each item: *Every one of these papers is good.*

F

federal Use a capital letter when the word is part of a title: *the Federal Trade Commission.* Use lowercase when it is an adjective: *the federal court.*

fractions Spell out amounts less than one, using hyphens between the words: *two-thirds.* When using fractions with a whole number, write the whole number, a space and then the fraction: *2 1/2.*

G

governmental bodies Capitalize the full proper name of governmental agencies, and retain capitalization if referring to a specific body; lowercase when using in a general sense: *the Boston City Council, the City Council* (when referring to the Boston City Council); *the city councils decide how to spend the money.*

H

handicapped, disabled, impaired Do not describe people as disabled or handicapped unless the description is crucial to a story. If it is, ask the people how they prefer to be described. See Chapter 19.

holidays Capitalize them: *New Year's Eve, Easter, Hanukkah, Memorial Day.*

I

initials Use periods and no space when a person uses initials instead of a first name: *I.F. Stone.*

it's, its Learn the difference. *It's* is a contraction meaning *it is. Its* is a possessive pronoun: *The dog lost its collar.*

J

judge Capitalize before a name when it is part of the person's title: *U.S. District Judge John Jones.* Do not use *Judge* to precede the name on second reference; use only the last name: *Jones.* Do not capitalize when used without the name: *The judge issued a ruling.*

judgment Spell this word correctly without an *e*—not *judgement.*

K

kidnap, kidnapped, kidnapping Double the *p.*

L

legislative titles For congressmen and congresswomen, *U.S. Rep.* and *Rep.* are the preferred first-reference forms: *U.S. Rep. John Jones.* Capitalize when used before a name. On second reference, the word *congressman* or *congresswoman,* in lowercase, may be used when the name of the person is not used.

legislature Capitalize the names of specific bodies: *the Kansas Legislature,* or *the Legislature* when referring to the specific Kansas body. Lowercase when used in a general sense: *The legislature of each state must approve the amendment.* Lowercase when used as plural: *The Kansas and Missouri legislatures approved the amendment.*

M

media The plural for news organizations such as broadcast, print and magazines is *media;* use it with a plural verb: *The news media are upset about the ruling.*

military titles Capitalize a formal title on first reference; use the last name only, without the title, on second reference. You may abbreviate titles:

Sgt. Maj. John Jones, Lt. Col. James Comolli. See the AP Stylebook for a complete list of abbreviations.

million, billion Use either word with figures: *$1 million, $13 billion, $1.3 billion, 2 million people.* In casual reference, you may use *I'd like to make a million dollars.*

months Capitalize the names of months. When used with a specific date, abbreviate only *Jan., Feb., Aug., Sept., Oct., Nov., Dec.* For example: *Jan. 12, 1993, was the coldest day on record.* Spell out the name of a month when used without a specific date: *January 1992 was the warmest month on record.* Spell out other months: *July 4 is a holiday.*

N

nationalities and races Capitalize names of nationalities and races: *Arab, Asian, African-American, Caucasian.* Lowercase *black, white, red.*

none It means no single one and takes a singular verb: *None of the council members was willing to approve the measure.* Use a plural verb only if the sense is no two or no amount: *None of the taxes have been paid.*

numerals Spell out numbers that start a sentence: *Twenty-one people attended the event.* Spell out the numbers one through nine; use figures for 10 and above.

O

OK Use *OK,* not *okay.*

P

people, persons Use *person* when speaking of an individual, *people* when referring to persons in all plural uses: *Hundreds of people attended the lecture.*

percentages Use figures, and spell out the word *percent: Taxes will increase 1 percent.*

police department Capitalize the term when used with the formal title or when referring to a specific department: *The Los Angeles Police Department has a new chief. He will reorganize the Police Department.* Lowercase the term when it stands alone and when it's used in a general sense: *You can get the form at a police department.*

political parties Capitalize the name of the party and the word *party* if it is part of the title: *the Republican Party, the Democratic Party.* Capitalize *Republican, Democratic, Liberal* and *Socialist* when they refer to individuals who are members of a specific political party. Lowercase these words when used to signify a way of thinking: *He is democratic in his views.*

politicians	When identifying a representative or a senator, use the party affiliation and the abbreviation for the state: *Sen. Bob Dole, R-Kan.*
possessives	For plural nouns indicating possession, add only an apostrophe: *the boys' club.* For singular possessive nouns, add an apostrophe and an s: *The boy's book was lost.*
principal, principle	*Principal* is a noun and adjective meaning someone or something in authority or first in rank: *She is the school principal and the principal player on the team. Principle* is a noun that means a fundamental truth or motivating force: *They fought for the principle of self-determination.*

R

race	Specify only when pertinent in a story. Capitalize specific races; lowercase *black, white, red, mulatto* and so on. See **nationalities and races.**
religious titles	The first reference to a clergyman or clergywoman should include a capitalized title before the person's name. In many cases, *the Rev.* is the designation that is appropriate. For example, use *the Rev.* before a priest's name, not *Father: The Rev. Vince Krishe is the priest at St. Lawrence Roman Catholic Church.* On second reference, just use the last name: *Krishe.* If a person is known only by a religious name, repeat the title on second reference: *Pope Paul.* Use the word *Rabbi* before the name for first reference; use only the last name for second reference. For nuns, use *Sister* or *Mother* before the name in all references if the nun uses only a religious name: *Sister Agnes.*

S

sheriff	Capitalize when used as a formal title before a name; use only the last name on second reference: *Sheriff Bob Jones resigned Tuesday.* Lowercase when used after the name: *Bob Jones, sheriff of Rockville, resigned Tuesday.*
state names	Spell out state names when they stand alone; abbreviate when they are used in conjunction with the name of a city, town or village or with a dateline. Do not abbreviate the following state names: *Alaska, Hawaii, Idaho, Iowa, Maine, Ohio, Texas, Utah.* The abbreviations for the other states are as follows (note that many differ from postal abbreviations): *Ala., Ariz., Ark., Calif., Colo., Conn., Del., Fla., Ga., Ill., Ind., Kan., Ky., La., Md., Mass., Mich., Minn., Miss., Mo., Mont., Neb., Nev., N.H., N.J., N.M., N.Y., N.C., N.D., Okla., Ore., Pa., R.I., S.C., S.D., Tenn., Vt., Va., Wash., W.Va., Wis., Wyo.*
subjunctive mood	Use the subjunctive mood of a verb to convey wishes. Use the verb *were,* not *was,* to follow the singular pronoun used in a subjunctive sense: *if I were a rich woman, if it were possible.*

T

that, which, who, whom	Use *who* and *whom* when referring to people and to animals with a name. Use *that* and *which* when referring to inanimate objects and to animals without a name: *He is the man who has the book; She is the woman to whom I spoke yesterday; Fluffy is the dog who was lost; Get the record that the police filed.*
time	Use *a.m.* and *p.m.* with the specific time: *9:30 a.m., 10 p.m.*—not *10:00 p.m.* Use the day of the week in stories referring to any of the seven days before or after the current date, not *yesterday* or *tomorrow.*
titles	Capitalize when used before the person's name as part of the official title: *She confirmed that Sheriff John Jones made the arrest.* Lowercase when used to identify the person after his or her name or when used without the person's name: *John Jones, the sheriff, made the arrest; The sheriff made the arrest.*
trademarks	Capitalize brand names: *Coke, Kleenex.* Use lowercase for generic terms: *a cola drink, a tissue.*

V

verbs	Don't split infinitives—*to be* verbs: *She was ordered to leave immediately,* not *She was ordered to immediately leave.*
vice	Use two words with no hyphen: *vice chairman, vice principal.*
vote tabulations	Use figures for totals separated by a hyphen: *The House voted 230-205.* Spell out votes below 10 in other phrases: *The City Council needed a two-thirds majority.*

W

weather	Spell out the word *degree: The temperature was 75 degrees.*

Y

yesterday	Use the day of the week instead of *yesterday.*
youth	The term is applicable to boys and girls from ages 13 to 17; use *man* or *woman* for people 18 and older.

Credits

Introduction

Eugene Roberts anecdote, *Washington Journalism Review* (now called *American Journalism Review*), February 1985, pp. 11–12. Reprinted with permission.

Edna Buchanan excerpts from *The Corpse Had a Familiar Face*, Random House, New York, 1987, p. 265.

"Desperate days at the Merlin," *The Spokesman-Review*, Feb. 25, 1990. Reprinted with permission.

Part One

Opening photo: Bill Snead/*The Washington Post*

Chapter 1

Chapter quote: *Coaching Writers: Editors and Reporters Working Together*, St. Martin's Press, New York, 1992, p. 173.

"Watkins detects fevers via the ear," *The University Daily Kansan*, Sept. 27, 1991. Reprinted with permission.

"Papers a lesson in criminology," *St. Petersburg* (Fla.) *Times*, Oct. 26, 1991. Reprinted with permission.

"Nevada regents OK raises," *Reno* (Nev.) *Gazette-Journal*, Oct. 4, 1991. Reprinted with permission.

Empowerment box: "Nursing home complaints surge," *Reno Gazette-Journal*, Oct. 24, 1991. Reprinted with permission.

Pull quote about Earvin "Magic" Johnson: *The Washington Post*, Nov. 8, 1991. ©1991 *The Washington Post*. Reprinted with permission.

Exhibit 1–1: "Students default on Uncle Sam," June 3–5, 1992. Copyright 1992, *USA Today*. Reprinted with permission.

Activity based on: "Penn fraternities curb alcohol," *The Philadelphia Inquirer*, Sept. 19, 1990. Used with permission.

Activity based on: "Lefties live shorter lives, new study says," *The* (San Bernardino, Calif.) *Sun*, April 4, 1991. Used with permission.

Activity based on: "KU students' health at risk," *The University Daily Kansan*, Nov. 18, 1991. Used with permission.

Chapter 2

Chapter quote: Burl Osborne, *The Next Newspapers*, American Society of Newspaper Editors, April 1988, p. 6.

Quotes from *New Directions for News*,

Reaching Tomorrow's Readers Roundtables, pp. 31, 211, 346, School of Journalism, University of Missouri, 1989. Reprinted with permission.

Exhibit 2–1: *Boca Raton News*. Reprinted with permission.

Exhibit 2–2: News 2000 pyramid and photo of *Stockton Record*; *The Gannetteer*, Gannett Co. Inc. Reprinted with permission.

Eyes on the News, by Pegie Stark and Mario Garcia, The Poynter Institute for Media Studies, 1990.

"Water Shock," and Exhibit 2–3, "Water Cost Increase," *Reno Gazette-Journal*, Aug. 17, 1991. Reprinted with permission.

Comments from Geneva Overholser, editor of the *Des Moines Register*: "Newspapers as Wimps," *Editor & Publisher*, Feb. 1, 1992. Reprinted with permission.

Comments from Bill Kovach, curator of Nieman Foundation, "Stop tinkering and resume the mission," *Editor & Publisher*, Feb. 1, 1992. Reprinted with permission.

"Shawnee Heights ducks as funnels twist through," *Topeka Capital-Journal*, March 2, 1991. Reprinted with permission.

"Damage catches residents by surprise," *Topeka Capital-Journal*, March 2, 1991. Reprinted with permission.

"Homelessness Spreads to the Countryside, Straining Resources," Reprinted by permission of *The Wall Street Journal*, March 5, 1991, Dow Jones & Company, Inc. All rights reserved worldwide.

"26 hurt as school bus crashes head-on," Louisville *Courier-Journal*, March 19, 1992. Reprinted with permission.

"71-year-old gets 8 years in drug case," *The Oregonian*, Dec. 4, 1990. Reprinted with permission.

"Michael Jackson sorry," *Orange County Register*, Nov. 16, 1991. Reprinted with permission.

"Couple spends $6,000 looking for lost cat . . . ," *Rocky Mountain News*, Feb. 21, 1992. Reprinted with permission.

"Protesters gather to save schools," *Chicago Tribune*, May 22, 1991. Reprinted with permission.

"Speaking up about sexual harassment," The Associated Press, Oct. 10, 1991. Reprinted with permission.

Chapter 3

"Basic costs at Stanford hit $21,262," *San Francisco Chronicle*, Feb. 14, 1991.

"Family sues in corpse mix-up," *St. Petersburg Times*, Jan. 10, 1991. Reprinted with permission.

"Salmon spawn a new crisis," *Los Angeles Times*, Nov. 15, 1990. Reprinted with permission.

"Tyson is found guilty of rape," *The Philadelphia Inquirer*, Feb. 11, 1992. Reprinted with permission.

"Amnesia victim recalls abduction," The Associated Press, Dec. 21, 1990. Reprinted with permission.

"Drunken driver, after six attempts to serve his 30 days, sues sheriff," Knight Ridder Tribune News, Dec. 14, 1990. Reprinted with permission.

"New seat-belt law simple to enforce," *The Oregonian*, Dec. 2, 1990. Reprinted with permission.

"Bush plans college grants to middle class," Feb. 5, 1991. Copyright 1991, *USA Today*. Reprinted with permission.

"Teen stabbed in school fight," *St. Petersburg Times*, Dec. 21, 1990. Reprinted with permission.

"Students concern for society rises," Jan. 28, 1991. Copyright 1991, *USA Today*. Reprinted with permission.

"Man prowls dorms," *Iowa City Press-Citizen*, Sept. 22, 1990. Reprinted with permission.

"Thousands gather on Capitol steps for animal rights," The Associated Press, June 11, 1990. Reprinted with permission.

"Throw the book at them," The Associated Press, Sept. 4, 1990. Reprinted with permission.

"It's the water," Knight Ridder Tribune News, Jan 3, 1991. Reprinted with permission.

"Police hear of campus cults," The Associated Press, July 23, 1991. Reprinted with permission.

Quote from sunbathing story, *St. Petersburg Times*, Jan. 11, 1991. Reprinted with permission.

"In Spitak, survivors comb ruins of devastated town," *The Washington Post*, Dec. 15, 1988. © 1988 *The Washington Post*. Reprinted with permission.

"A mom's anguish for wounded son . . . ,"

The Seattle Times, Jan. 1, 1991. Reprinted with permission.

"Woman has second thoughts after her pursuit of burglar," *The Wichita Eagle*, June 21, 1991. Reprinted with permission.

"President starts process to seek second term," The Associated Press, Oct. 11, 1991. Reprinted with permission.

Transportation story excerpt, The Associated Press, Oct. 11, 1991. Reprinted with permission.

Excerpts from "Court Opinion Holding Fabricated Quotes Can Be Libelous," *The New York Times*, June 21, 1991. Copyright © 1991 by The New York Times Company. Reprinted with permission.

"39 students injured in 3-bus wreck," *The Atlanta Constitution*, Feb. 23, 1991. Reprinted with permission.

"Reactions to medicine affect 20% of seniors," Feb. 19,1991. Copyright 1991, *USA Today*. Reprinted with permission.

"Gulf war stirs memories of another side of King," *The Washington Post*, Jan 21, 1991. © 1991 *The Washington Post*. Reprinted with permission.

"Apartment blaze blamed on toddler," *The Wichita Eagle*, June 21, 1991. Reprinted with permission.

Activity based on "ISU won't officially recognize heterosexuals club, cites bias," *The Des Moines Register*. Used with permission.

Punctuation activity based on: "Science at work in average mug of beer," The Associated Press, Oct. 20, 1991. Used with permission.

Chapter 4

"Hunting dog can't find home," *The Des Moines Register*. Reprinted with permission.

"KU starting survey on sexual violence," *Lawrence Journal-World*, April 9, 1991. Reprinted with permission.

Press release about survey on sexual violence, University of Kansas Office of University Relations. Reprinted with permission.

Part Two

Opening photo: © Brian Palmer/Impact Visuals

Chapter 5

"Reno woman arrested in killing of boyfriend," *Reno Gazette-Journal*, Aug. 13, 1989. Reprinted with permission.

"In Spitak survivors comb ruins of devastated town," *The Washington Post*, Dec. 15, 1988. © 1988 *The Washington Post*. Reprinted with permission.

"Cold, noise permeate Laclede County Jail," *The News-Leader*, Springfield, Mo. 1990. Reprinted with permission.

"Iowans get ready, The state fair will be-

gin today," *The Des Moines Register*, Aug. 15, 1990. Reprinted with permission.

"Finding a friend in the mainstream," *The Des Moines Register*, April 26, 1987. Reprinted with permission.

"3 killed, more than 100 hurt as rush-hour subway derails," *The Philadelphia Inquirer*, March 8, 1990. Reprinted with permission.

"Planes collide at LAX," *Los Angeles Times*, Feb. 2, 1991. Reprinted with permission.

"In Capitol, a bulb change carries a high price indeed," *The Philadelphia Inquirer*, June 8, 1990. Reprinted with permission.

"Explosion levels home; five are hurt," *St. Petersburg Times*, Feb.1, 1991. Reprinted with permission.

Chapter 6

Scott Thurm, speech at conference of Investigative Reporters and Editors, Philadelphia, 1989. Used with permission of IRE.

Exhibits: *USA Today* library, *The Gannetteer*, Gannett Co., Inc. Used with permission.

David Shaw series, "Minorities and the Press," quote cited from "Negative news and Little Else," *Los Angeles Times*, Dec. 11, 1990. Reprinted with permission.

"Deadly Meat," and Exhibit 6–1, from series "Failing the Grade," *Kansas City Star*, Dec. 8–14, 1991. Reprinted with permission.

Records search, Bonnie Short. Reprinted with permission.

Excerpt from series "Grand Canyon, Deadly Skies," *Tucson Citizen*, Oct. 18, 1990. Reprinted with permission.

FOIA letter, Society of Professional Journalists, 1988–89 report. Reprinted with permission.

Chapter 7

Clark, Gerald, *Capote: A Biography*, Simon and Schuster, New York, 1988, p. 322.

Ruas, Charles, *Conversations with American Writers*, McGraw-Hill Book Co., New York, 1984, p. 52.

Chapter 8

Quote from Diana Griego Erwin, *Best Newspaper Writing 1990*, The Poynter Institute for Media Studies, St. Petersburg, Fla., 1990, p. 105. Reprinted with permission.

"For women on Death Row, an agonizing wait," Fort Lauderdale, Fla. *Sun-Sentinel*, Dec. 16, 1991. Reprinted with permission.

Bill Marimow comments made at conference of Investigative Reporters and Editors, Minneapolis, 1988.

"Mianus Legacy: Pain and Anger," *The

Hartford Courant, June 28, 1984. Reprinted with permission.

Part Three

Opening photo: © Eric Bouvet/Gamma-Liaison

Chapter 9

Peanuts cartoon, © 1969 United Feature Syndicate, Inc. Reprinted with permission.

Comments by Laura Sessions Stepp made at conference of Investigative Reporters and Editors, Minneapolis, 1988.

Comments by Steve Lovelady made at conference of Investigative Reporters and Editors, Minneapolis, 1988.

Dave Barry, "Childhood is a breeze compared to stress of moving," Reprinted with permission of Dave Barry.

Lansing Community College story, *Lansing State Journal*, 1989. Reprinted with permission.

Excerpt from *The Elements of Style*, William Strunk and E.B. White, Macmillan Publishing Co., Inc., New York, p. 23.

Excerpt from *On Writing Well*, William Zinsser, Harper & Row Publishers, New York, pp. 7, 14.

"A murder story," *St. Petersburg Times*, May 26, 1985. Reprinted with permission.

"Bigamist's family stunned," *San Jose Mercury News*, Oct. 11, 1991. Reprinted with permission.

FORK exercise, "Blind dates are back, romance experts say," *The New York Times*, Jan. 20, 1988. Copyright © 1991 by The New York Times Company. Reprinted with permission.

FORK exercise based on "The freshman food fight," *The Philadelphia Inquirer*, Sept. 16, 1991. Reprinted with permission.

Chapter 10

Edna Buchanan quote from speech made at conference of Investigative Reporters and Editors, Minneapolis, 1988.

Donald Murray, *Writing for Your Readers*, The Globe Pequot Press, Chester, Conn. 1983, p. 44.

"BBs strike stepfather after domestic violence," *St. Petersburg Times*, Nov. 18, 1991. Reprinted with permission.

"It's the water . . . ," Knight Ridder Tribune News, Jan. 3, 1991. Reprinted with permission.

"Jell-O Journalism," *Washington Journalism Review* (now called *American Journalism Review*), April 1982. Reprinted with permission.

"Phone companies tired of waiting for 'Caller ID,'" *The Orange County Register*, March 29, 1991. Reprinted with permission.

"Ordinance would outlaw reproduction of pets," *The New York Times*, Oct. 31,

1990. Copyright © 1990 by The New York Times Company. Reprinted with permission.

"Pet sterilization becomes law in San Mateo County," *Los Angeles Times,* Dec. 19, 1990. Reprinted with permission.

"MU fraternity punished for hazing," The Associated Press, March 6, 1991. Reprinted with permission.

"Justices won't reprieve men-only campus club," *The Washington Post,* Jan 23, 1991. © 1991 *The Washington Post.* Reprinted with permission.

"Brown expels student for using racial epithets," *The New York Times,* Feb. 12, 1991. Copyright © 1991 by The New York Times Company. Reprinted with permission.

"Tucked above a rudder: 2 men and cocaine," *The New York Times,* Jan. 29, 1991. Copyright © 1991 by The New York Times Company. Reprinted with permission.

"2 killed, 1 injured when boat flips in rough weather," *The Orlando Sentinel,* March 11, 1991. Reprinted with permission.

"Sunscreen ingredient may promote cancer," The Associated Press, March 22, 1991. Reprinted with permission.

"Students still in critical condition," The Associated Press, March 23, 1992. Reprinted with permission.

"Book thief gets 7 years of probation," *The Philadelphia Inquirer,* Feb. 1, 1991. Reprinted with permission.

"Man who confronts gunman is shot to death," *St. Petersburg Times,* March 12, 1992. Reprinted with permission.

"2 charged with theft of parking coins," Minneapolis *Star-Tribune,* March 8, 1991. Reprinted with permission.

"Man watching TV critically wounded," *Chicago Tribune,* June 11, 1991. Reprinted with permission.

"Con-man sentenced," *N.Y. Newsday,* Feb. 1, 1991.

"Woman seeks new trial in shooting of ISU prof," *The Des Moines Register,* March 26, 1991. Reprinted with permission.

"North County man, 88, killed in blaze started by smoking," *St. Louis Post-Dispatch,* March 12, 1991. Reprinted with permission.

"College student arrested after making 'megabomb,' " The Associated Press, December 1991. Reprinted with permission.

"Toddler's death tied to beating," *St. Petersburg Times,* Feb. 14, 1991. Reprinted with permission.

"Paroled killer held in kidnap, rape of 2 girls," *St. Paul Pioneer Press,* March 7, 1991. Reprinted with permission.

Clarence Thomas quote: Knight Ridder

Tribune News, Oct. 13, 1991. Reprinted with permission.

"S.J. gunman left 'little signs' before killings," *San Jose Mercury News,* March 10, 1991. Reprinted with permission.

"Sex discrimination persists, according to a U.N. study," *The New York Times,* June 16, 1991. Copyright © 1991 by The New York Times Company. Reprinted with permission.

"Penn imposes penalties on scientist," *The Philadelphia Inquirer,* Feb. 14, 1991. Reprinted with permission.

" 'Smelly politics' charged in pay dispute," *The Des Moines Register,* March 12, 1991. Reprinted with permission.

"U.S. reports sharp drop in casual drug use," *The Philadelphia Inquirer,* Dec. 20, 1991. Reprinted with permission.

"Women's incomes lagging," *The Washington Post,* April 27, 1990. Reprinted with permission.

"Rhode Island state business closes for a day," The Associated Press, March 9, 1991. Reprinted with permission.

"Open up crime reports, judge says," *The Kansas City Star,* March 14, 1991. Reprinted with permission.

"Doctor seeks vending machine ban," *Reno Gazette-Journal,* Aug. 19, 1991. Reprinted with permission.

"Neighbors squealing over pigs," *The Philadelphia Inquirer,* April 12, 1991. Reprinted with permission.

"Ex-lover must pay in video case," *The Philadelphia Inquirer,* April 23, 1991. Reprinted with permission.

"In Santa Barbara drought, it's not easy being green," *Los Angeles Times,* May 8, 1990. Reprinted with permission.

"Convenience clerk's terror put behind bars," *St. Petersburg Times,* March 12, 1991. Reprinted with permission.

"Home reaches out to teen moms," *The Orange County Register,* March 12, 1991. Reprinted with permission.

"Kansas bills many parents for foster care," *The Kansas City Star,* June 30, 1991. Reprinted with permission.

"Seminole man not real doctor, detectives say," *The Orlando Sentinel,* Dec. 9, 1990. Reprinted with permission.

"Colo. poison-gas site now a wildlife haven," *The Philadelphia Inquirer,* Dec. 18, 1990. Reprinted with permission.

"1964 case gets fresh interest," *St. Petersburg Times,* Feb. 7, 1991. Reprinted with permission.

Public library story, *The Philadelphia Inquirer,* 1990. Reprinted with permission.

"Cops hear it all, so he dummies up," The Associated Press, Feb. 20, 1991. Reprinted with permission.

"They know all about you," *St. Petersburg Times,* Jan. 6, 1991. Reprinted with permission.

"Lottery triangle," *Los Angeles Times,*

June 9, 1988. Reprinted with permission.

"Survivors tell of riding out the storm," *The Philadelphia Inquirer,* April 29, 1991. Reprinted with permission.

"U.S. colleges try to confront problem of campus drinking," The Associated Press, Jan. 4, 1991. Reprinted with permission.

"True love story," *St. Paul Pioneer Press,* Feb. 14, 1991. Reprinted with permission.

"L. Merion wants to ban cigarettes," *The Philadelphia Inquirer,* Feb. 1, 1991. Reprinted with permission.

"Postcards from sculptor carry messages via a piece of the rock," *Los Angeles Times,* Nov. 12, 1990. Reprinted with permission.

"The good and bad from city hall," *N.Y. Newsday,* Jan 28, 1991.

"10-year-old saves choking classmate," *The Orlando Sentinel,* Feb. 12, 1991. Reprinted with permission.

"5 children die, 30 hurt during gunman's rampage," *The Stockton* (Calif.) *Record,* 1989.

"Crack: Drug tightens grip on Niagara County," *Niagara Gazette,* 1989.

"Michener wraps up season in the sun," *St. Petersburg Times,* Feb. 2, 1991. Reprinted with permission.

"It may be back to class for professors," *St. Petersburg Times,* April 8, 1991. Reprinted with permission.

"The wild and woolly farm show," *The Philadelphia Inquirer,* Jan. 6, 1991. Reprinted with permission.

"Costly special classes serve many with minimal needs," *The New York Times,* April 30, 1991. Copyright © 1991 by The New York Times Company. Reprinted with permission.

"Officer fights earth crimes," *St. Petersburg Times,* Sept. 5, 1990. Reprinted with permission.

"Going after gators is in her blood," *St. Petersburg Times,* Sept. 3, 1990. Reprinted with permission.

Activity based on "Members of GLSOK address psychology class," *The University Daily Kansan.* Used with permission.

Activity based on "Students shy of sciences," *Rocky Mountain News,* March 3, 1992. Used with permission.

Activity based on "Police dog sniffs out suspect in house burglary," *The Topeka Capital-Journal,* June 21, 1992. Used with permission.

Chapter 11

"Temple racism course wins support," *The Philadelphia Inquirer,* Sept. 12, 1991.

"Anatomy of a road, Part 1," *The Tampa Tribune,* Dec. 5, 1988.

"We didn't get to love them," *St. Petersburg Times,* May 29, 1990. Reprinted with permission.

Copyright 1991, *USA Today*. Reprinted with permission.

Crayola brief, Binney & Smith Inc., Reprinted with permission.

"A hairy rescue," *The Philadelphia Inquirer*, Oct. 12, 1990. Reprinted with permission.

"On death and taxes," *The Philadelphia Inquirer*, Jan. 31, 1991. Reprinted with permission.

"Man ticketed for walking his lizard," *St. Petersburg Times*, Feb. 6, 1991. Reprinted with permission.

"Herpes spreads without sores or symptoms," Feb. 3, 1992. Copyright 1992, *USA Today*. Reprinted with permission.

"Suspected northern ozone hole 'frightening,' " Feb. 4, 1992. Copyright 1992, *USA Today*. Reprinted with permission.

"Northern ozone hole predicted," *The Philadelphia Inquirer*, Feb. 4, 1992. Reprinted with permission.

USA Today writing guidelines, courtesy of J. Taylor Buckley Jr., senior editor, *USA Today*.

"It takes a lot of thinking to write short," column by Richard Aregood, *The Bulletin*, publication of American Society of Newspaper Editors, January–February 1990. Reprinted with permission of Richard Aregood.

Chapter 15

"Paper Waste 'Irresponsible' " press release, InterCommunicationsInc., 1991. Reprinted with permission.

InterCommunications brief, *Wall Street Journal* brief, "Odds and Ends," Aug. 1, 1991. Reprinted with permission, *The Wall Street Journal*, Dow Jones & Company, Inc. All rights reserved worldwide.

Hallmark press releases, March 1992, Hallmark Cards Inc. Reprinted with permission.

"Crayola Introduces Crayons That Are Literally Off The Wall," press release, Feb. 4, 1992, Binney & Smith Inc. Reprinted with permission.

"Crayola cleans up kids' act," Feb. 3, 1992. Copyright 1992, *USA Today*. Reprinted with permission.

"Crayola introduces a washable product," *The Wichita Eagle*, Feb. 13, 1992. Reprinted with permission.

"JC Penney To Study Site for Distribution Center," press release, June 22, 1989, J.C. Penney Inc. Reprinted with permission.

"American Greetings 86-year Growth Record," press release, American Greetings. Reprinted with permission.

Chapter 16

Expocentre script excerpts, KSNT-TV, Topeka. Reprinted with permission.

Abortion ruling script excerpts, KSNT-TV, Topeka. Reprinted with permission.

Abortion ruling story, The Associated Press, June 30, 1992. Reprinted with permission.

"New Kansas law expected to stand," *The Topeka Capital Journal*, June 30, 1992. Reprinted with permission.

Exxon kidnapping story, The Associated Press broadcast wire, June 30, 1992. Reprinted with permission.

Nude camp excerpt, June 23, 1992, NBC News Channel wire. Reprinted with permission.

Korean merchants protest excerpt, June 23, 1992, NBC News Channel wire. Reprinted with permission.

Animal rights protest excerpt, The Associated Press broadcast wire, June 30, 1992. Reprinted with permission.

Toxic chemical spill excerpt, The Associated Press broadcast wire, June 30, 1992. Reprinted with permission.

Baldwin City water problems, September 1992, KSNT-TV, Topeka. Reprinted with permission.

Crime fighting teaser, June 30, 1992, KSNT-TV, Topeka. Reprinted with permission.

Exercise excerpt, June 23, 1992, NBC News Channel wire. Reprinted with permission.

Dentist's death teaser, June 23, 1992, NBC News Channel wire. Reprinted with permission.

Person of the Week script, July 13, 1992, KUSA-TV, Denver. Reprinted with permission.

"16-year-old boy with no license takes police on Highlands chase," *The Louisville Courier-Journal*, Feb. 23, 1992. Reprinted with permission.

Part Four

Opening photo: George Tames/N.Y. Times

Chapter 17

"The case of the dying child," *IRE Journal*, Fall 1986. Reprinted with permission.

"So what's wrong with pre-publication review?" *Quill*, May 1990. Reprinted with permission of the Society of Professional Journalists.

Comments by Bill Marimow made at convention of Investigative Reporters and Editors, Minneapolis, 1988.

Libel definition, from *Mass Communications Law: Cases and Comment*, by Donald Gillmor, Jerome A. Barron, Todd F. Simon and Herbert A. Terry; West Publishing Co., St. Paul, 1990, p. 172.

Chapter 18

Survey by Ralph Izard for the Society of Professional Journalists, 1984–85 Ethics Report. Reprinted with permission.

"Should Ashe have been exposed?" *Quill*,

June 1992. Reprinted with permission of the Society of Professional Journalists.

Jane Schorer's account of the *The Des Moines Register* rape story: "The Story Behind a Landmark," *Washington Journalism Review*, June 1991. Used with permission.

"What the media all missed," Fox Butterfield, *FineLine*, July/August 1991.

Deni Elliott's comments on William Kennedy Smith coverage: "When public should remain private," *FineLine*, June 1991.

Code of ethics, Society of Professional Journalists. Reprinted with permission.

Code of ethics, Public Relations Society of America. Reprinted with permission.

Excerpts from staff policy guide, *The Philadelphia Inquirer*. Reprinted with permission.

Chapter 19

Exhibit 19–1, "Minorities at newspapers," April 8, 1992, Copyright 1992, *USA Today*. Reprinted with permission.

"Torn by the tug of two lands," *The Philadelphia Inquirer*, May 7, 1990. Reprinted with permission.

"It's official: They're American Indian, so they can get married," *The Philadephia Inquirer*, March 23, 1991. Reprinted with permission.

Exhibit 19–2, "Equal writes," April 25, 1992. Copyright 1992, *USA Today*. Reprinted with permission.

Kammer, Jack, "She said. She said." *Editor & Publisher*, May 4, 1991, p. 120.

"Dress-up Dolly," *The Philadelphia Inquirer*, April 5, 1992. Reprinted with permission.

"How to avoid sexism, stereotypes in writing," *The Gannetteer*, Gannett Co., Inc., June 1989. Reprinted with permission.

William Hilliard's comments from "Newsroom Diversity," *The Bulletin*, publication of the American Society of Newspaper Editors, May/June 1992. Reprinted with permission from William Hilliard.

Excerpts from "AIDS in the Heartland," *St. Paul Pioneer Press*, June 21, 1987, and July 12, 1987. Reprinted with permission.

Part Five

Opening photo: UPI/Bettmann Newsphotos

Chapter 20

Obituary of Lawrence Pompie "Mr. Buddy" Ellis, *Philadelphia Daily News*, Dec. 18, 1986. Reprinted with permission.

Obituary of Edward E. "Ace" Clark, *Philadelphia Daily News*, March 19, 1986. Reprinted with permission.

Obituary of Ella Hurst, *Philadelphia Daily News*, July 22, 1988. Reprinted with permission.

Chapter 21

Chapter 22

Chapter 23

March 7, 1991. Reprinted with permission.

"Disorder in the court," *The Philadelphia Inquirer,* Jan 26, 1986. Reprinted with permission.

"N.H. Prosecutors get Smart," The Associated Press, March 23, 1991. Reprinted with permission.

"Crafts denies he killed wife," *The Hartford Courant,* June 17, 1988. Reprinted with permission.

"Joy Griffiths' killing: Act of love or murder?" *St. Petersburg Times,* Nov. 17, 1985. Reprinted with permission.

"A snake in a mattress twists its way into court," *The Philadelphia Inquirer,* April 4, 1991. Reprinted with permission.

"Man gambles on plea, loses," *The Kansas City Star.* Reprinted with permission.

Chapter 24

Excerpts from "The crash of flight 255" and Exhibit 24–1, *The Detroit News,* special report, Aug. 17–23, 1987. Reprinted with permission.

"20 die in La Guardia crash," The Associated Press, March 23, 1992. Reprinted with permission.

"Grief cuts wide swath," *The Detroit News,* special report, Aug. 17–23, 1987. Reprinted with permission.

Exhibit 24–2, water spout, Aug. 16, 1991, *Reno Gazette-Journal.* Reprinted with permission.

"6.9 quake rocks N. California coast," *Los Angeles Times,* April 26, 1992. Reprinted with permission.

"Wet and wild," *Iowa City Press-Citizen,* June 18, 1990. Reprinted with permission.

"Band of brothers," The Associated Press, February 1988. Reprinted with permission.

Plane crash exercise based in part on material from The Fort Lauderdale *Sun-Sentinel,* Used with permission.

Chapter 25

"Only Bo knows Bo," *GQ,* March 1990. Courtesy GQ. Copyright 1990, 1992 by The Conde Nast Publications Inc. Reprinted with permission.

"Arnold meets the Girly man." This article was originally published in *GQ,* May 1990. Copyright Alan Richman. Reprinted with his permission.

"You talkin' to Me?" *GQ,* January 1991. Courtesy GQ. Copyright 1990, 1992 by The Conde Nast Publications Inc. Reprinted with permission.

"Reflections: A year after her stabbing, Stacy LaRocca's painful memories re-

main," *Florida Alligator,* February 1991. Reprinted with permission.

"A time to die," *Sunshine* magazine, Fort Lauderdale *Sun-Sentinel,* July 28, 1985. Reprinted with permission.

"Life on the edge," *Chicago Tribune,* May 24, 1992. Reprinted with permission.

"Clues in the life of an accused mass killer," *The New York Times,* Aug. 4, 1991. Copyright © 1991 by The New York Times Company. Reprinted with permission.

Robert Maxwell anecdote, *The New York Times,* March 17, 1991. Copyright © 1991 by The New York Times Company. Reprinted with permission.

"She is the finest of New Orleans' finest," *The Philadelphia Inquirer,* Feb. 3, 1992. Reprinted with permission.

" 'Fat Albert' carves out an 891-pound niche," *St. Petersburg Times,* Nov. 10, 1985. Reprinted with permission.

Vignette profiles from "Desperate Days at the Merlin," *The Spokesman Review,* Feb. 25, 1990. Reprinted with permission.

Journalism school librarian vignette, *The University Daily Kansan,* Nov. 19, 1991. Reprinted with permission.

Vignette of bus driver, unpublished. Used with permission of Kathy Hill.

Vignette of flag raiser, unpublished. Used with permission of Michelle Betts.

Chapter 26

"Now's the time for State Fair," *The Des Moines Register,* Aug. 15, 1990. Reprinted with permission.

"Clive woman's spell of success," *The Des Moines Register,* March 13, 1991. Reprinted with permission.

"A gift abandoned," *St. Petersburg Times,* April 14, 1991. Reprinted with permission.

William Blundell organization tips, *The Art and Craft of Feature Writing,* New American Library, New York, copyright 1988 by William Blundell, pp. 98, 99.

"New life begins with help of coyotes," *Daily Forty Niner* (Calif. State University, Long Beach), 1991. Reprinted with permission.

"Their bond: They came back from near death," *The Philadelphia Inquirer,* Oct. 20, 1990. Reprinted with permission.

"It couldn't happen to me: One woman's story," *The Des Moines Register,* Feb. 25, 1990. Reprinted with permission.

"Nov. 22, 1963: A day when time stopped," The Associated Press. Reprinted with permission.

Jonathan Bor's guidelines, *Coaches' Corner,* September 1989. Reprinted with permission.

"It fluttered and became Bruce Murray's heart," *The* (Syracuse, N.Y.) *Post-Standard,* May 12, 1984. Reprinted with permission.

"Curricula of color," *The Wall Street Journal,* July 1, 1991. Reprinted by permission of *The Wall Street Journal,* Dow Jones & Company, Inc. All rights reserved worldwide.

"Churches changing times to change with the times," *The Kansas City Star,* Sept. 21, 1991. Reprinted with permission.

Karen F. Brown sportswriting tips, *Best Newspaper Writing 1991,* Poynter Institute for Media Studies, St. Petersburg, 1991, pp. 253–57. Reprinted with permission.

"Nova loses big to Boston College," *The Philadelphia Inquirer,* Feb. 16, 1992. Reprinted with permission.

"Mavericks bugged by loss to Nets," *Dallas Morning News,* Nov. 30, 1991. Reprinted with permission.

"Connors show goes beyond prime time," *The Washington Post,* Aug. 29, 1991. Reprinted with permission.

"Manning the sidelines," *The Daily Northwestern* (Northwestern University), 1991. Reprinted with permission.

Gary Smith, "Ali and his entourage," *Sports Illustrated,* April 25, 1988. Copyright © 1988, Time Inc. All rights reserved. Reprinted courtesy of *Sports Illustrated.*

Sportswriter photo, courtesy of *The Gannetteer,* Gannett Co., Inc.

Part Six

Opening photo: Cmdr. David R. Scott, "On the moon," 1971/NASA-Johnson Space Center

Chapter 27

"Cutesy cover letters are like bricks," *Quill,* October 1988. Reprinted with permission of Judith Clabes.

Cover letter by Rachel G. Thompson. Reprinted with permission.

Cover letter by Tiffany Hurt. Reprinted with permission.

Cover letter by Ranjit Arab. Reprinted with permission.

Newspaper newsroom photo, courtesy of *The Gannetteer,* Gannett Co., Inc.

Appendix

Style guide from *The Associated Press.* Reprinted with permission.

Index